REAL WOMEN HAVE CURVES & OTHER PLAYS

BY JOSEFINA LÓPEZ

WPR BOOKS: LATINO INSIGHTS

CARLSBAD, CA

WPR BOOKS: Latino Insights
3445 Catalina Dr., Carlsbad, CA 92010-2856
www.WPRbooks.com   760-434-1223   kirk@whisler.com

TABLE OF CONTENTS

Introduction

A Woman Of Her Word(s): Josefina López

Josefina López was born in Mexico in 1969. At the tender age of five she was brought to this country illegally settling with her family in Boyle Heights, East of Los Angeles. She started grammar school the following year and thus began the process of "Chicani-zation" in the school system and in this society. From her first day in school, López knew that although her parents had green cards, she was undocumented and therefore lived in constant fear of being deported. But she used her vivid imagination to get her through, living a kind of shadow existence for several years until she became a Temporary Resident through the Amnesty Program in 1987. The threat of deportation would inform several of her plays, becoming a kind of leitmotif in the lives of her characters. According to López, she "became a Chicana" at the age of twenty, ostensibly when she no longer feared deportation.

López first started writing plays in the fifth grade. However, her major influences were the televised version of the Teatro Campesino's La gran carpa de los Rasquachis, retitled "El corrido," and the live production of Luis Valdez's "I Don't Have to Show You No Stinking Badges". She had seen "El corrido" when she was in the 9th grade. "El corrido" was taped in part as a stage performance and López could see the possibilities in the live, staged version. Watching the program, the impressionable and imaginative author felt liberated from the constrictions of realism:

"I thought, wow, I didn't know that theatre could be this way. . .that's how I think. . . .that's what I loved about it, that one moment you're in Mexico and the next [you're in the US]. . . .transitions and transformation--

4

that's how I think; that it could be an epic, adventuresome. . .it doesn't have to stay in one place."

While attending the Los Angeles County High School for the Arts López saw I Don't Have to Show You No Stinking Badges, written and directed by Luis Valdez at the Los Angeles Theater Center in 1986. Yet, while Valdez's play was an inspiration to the young playwright, it also inspired her emerging feminism. As she searched Luis Valdez's works for a monologue to perform, López discovered that Valdez's female characters "were very flat--all mothers and girlfriends." It is important to remember that López was studying acting in high school with the intention of becoming an actress. Like many female actors who become playwrights, López decided to create her own vehicles to perform. If the male-dominated, sexist Chicano Theater Movement was not going to satisfy López's desire to act, she would take matters into her own hands. This volume is a testament to her commitment to create theatre that is relevant for all audiences, especially women.

ROMAN CATHOLIC NIGHTMARES: SIMPLY MARIA, OR THE AMERICAN DREAM

López participated in the Los Angeles Theater Center's Young Playwrights Lab from 1985 to 1988, gaining valuable experience, writing and watching all of the plays she could. Her playwriting career was initiated when Simply Maria, or the American Dream was produced as part of the California Young Playwright's Project in San Diego, California, in 1988. This play clearly demonstrates influences of the highly theatrical early Valdezian, Teatro Campesino style in which time and place are irrelevant as the characters traverse international borders by simply crossing the stage. In López's vision the actors transform into any number of characters and allegories in this coming-of-age play centered on the young (autobiographical) Maria. López dramatizes Maria's parent's courtship and elopement in Mexico, her birth, their crossing to the U.S. and her dreams of becoming a writer in a comically exaggerated critique of Machismo, the Church and Mexican patriarchy.

Simply Maria is not a "simple" play and should not be dismissed as such. As she will continue to do in her later plays, López is deconstructing traditional expectations, laying the blame for attitudes of what a "good Mexican girl should be" squarely on the patriarchal teachings of the Roman Catholic Church. She creatively and caustically indicts the Institution through her hilarious, yet poignant portrayal of the Church and its priests. After the Priest officiates at Maria's parents' marriage, three women, who

have been portraying statues of the saints in the church (allegories), come to life and transform into "three angelic girls" who chant a litany of what a Mexican girl can and cannot do. They recite that a Mexican girl must be: "Nice, forgiving, considerate, obedient, gentle, hard-working, gracious." She must like: "Dolls, kitchens, houses, caring for children, cooking, laundry and dishes." She must not: "Be independent, enjoy sex, but must endure it as your duty to your husband, and bear his children." Her goal must be to reproduce and her only purpose in life is to serve three men: "Your father, your husband and your son." By having the Three Marys transform into angelic girls, the playwright locates these ideas firmly in the name of the Church.

Later in the play Maria dreams about her own "White Wedding." This time the priest lists the duties of a good Mexican wife. He asks if she will: "...love, cherish, serve, cook for, clean for, sacrifice for, have his children, keep his house, love him even if he beats you, commits adultery, gets drunk, rapes you lawfully, denies you your identity, money, love his family, serve his family and in return ask for nothing?" After Maria agrees to the (exaggerated) marriage vows the priest puts a collar and leash on her and tells the groom "You may pet the bride." This caricature of the priest and parody of a Catholic wedding ceremony becomes an indictment of the Church itself, for the author makes it clear that the priest does not speak in isolation. López does not release the Church from its complicity; she refuses to show any transformations in Church doctrine or in the priest's traditional interpretation of marriage. In the end, Maria is triumphant, liberating herself from her father's and the Church's literal and symbolic clenches. Like the Teatro Campesino's early actos, Simply Maria is a modern morality play. However, in this play the teachings of the Church are subverted rather than promoted and the playwright incites her female audiences to challenge the patriarchy.

This simple, yet complex play, directed by a Mexican actor and director, Luis Torner, launched the young playwright on a trajectory that only she could have imagined. In 1989 this play was produced for the San Diego public broadcasting station, KPBS, also directed by Mr. Torner and won an Emmy for Children's Broadcasting. Shortly after the San Diego production, López participated in Maria Irene Fornes' now-legendary Hispanic Playwright's-in-Residence Laboratory in New York City in 1988, another life-changing experience.

THE CHICANA BODY:
REAL WOMEN HAVE CURVES

In 1989, López participated in the Teatro de la Esperanza's Isadora Aguirre Latino Playwriting Lab in San Francisco, California, taught by noted Mexican playwright, the late Emilio Carballido. With Carballido's guidance she began to write Real Women Have Curves and in 1990 the Teatro de la Esperanza produced the world premiere of that play. That production, directed by Hector Correa, was an instant success, particularly with female audiences. Real Women Have Curves became the most produced play written by a Chicana or Chicano for several years. The play has been produced by Latino and non-Latino companies--mainstream and community-based--from California to Florida, from Seattle to New York City. When the play was adapted for the screen, Lopez's reputation as an important theatrical voice was secured.

Like Simply Maria, Real Women Have Curves is also autobiographical, centering on the character of Ana, a young Chicana who is working in her sister Estela's small sewing factory in East Los Angeles. The play takes place over a period of five days during which the women work to finish an order of dresses. The dramatic action is pushed forward by the women's desire to save the financially strapped business, despite various setbacks, and the situation is given comic life by the conversations between the women about life, love, husbands, boyfriends or would-be suitors, and, of course, their bodies. The women finish the order on time, Estela decides to open her own boutique and in the process the women discover and empower themselves as women and creators.

In Virginia McFerran's words, the women discover "that traditional reality and its norms for women are actually completely unrealistic." This is a play about expectations--what society, especially Mechicano culture--expects of its women and how women might negate those expectations on a path towards liberation from the patriarchy. In the epilogue, Ana addresses the audience directly for the first time and concludes the play with a call for women's unity. She then relates how she did, indeed, attend NYU and when she came back her sister had opened her own boutique.

As the title suggests, Real Women Have Curves debates and exposes issues of the female body, especially "fat," "large," "plump" or "voluptuous" bodies, depending upon the gaze of the beholder. Based on her actual experiences, both with her body weight and working in her sister's sewing factory, López places her character at the center of the story as narrator and unhappy teenager who would rather be at NYU studying writing. In her analysis, Maria Teresa Marrero conflates the two prevalent issues in this play, body weight and immigrant status: "The fat body, like the immigrant,

requires fundamental alteration in order to 'fit,' to be assimilated into the dominant, circulating norms (be they aesthetic or cultural)." Marrero widens the topography of her discussion to include all Latinas struggling to survive in low paying jobs in this country. "To be a woman, undocumented and overweight places these characters as a target in the very center of a three-pronged U.S. cultural bias" Marrero reminds us (Marrero, "Real Women," p. 67). In other words, "three strikes and you're out."

A FATHER RETURNS FROM HELL: FOOD FOR THE DEAD

While in Fornes' workshop López wrote the first draft of her best-known play to date, Real Women Have Curves. She then enrolled in the undergraduate program at New York University's Tisch School of the Arts for one year. Whereas the Fornes workshop was a very positive experience for the young playwright, NYU was not as satisfying. Several years later, she wrote: "At that time I felt very alienated. I was the only Latina in my writing class and I felt like no one understood where I was coming from. I was experiencing so much cultural shock that I wanted to write something that celebrated my culture." Roused by her feelings of alienation, López mined creativity out of adversity and began to write a one-act comedy titled Food for the Dead. But she had to come back to California to see Chicanas and Chicanos interpreting her characters.

In the fall of 1989 López entered the undergraduate theatre program at the University of California at San Diego, eager to take advantage of the graduate actors and directors in the newly established graduate program in Hispanic-American theatre." Laura Esparza directed an early draft of Food for the Dead in the fall of 1989 with Latina and Latino graduate and undergraduate actors. Although this play is important for its treatment of a gay Chicano character, the play's real focus is on the liberation of a Mexican mother. Further, the use of devils, Hell and damnation, locate this play in the Spanish religious folk tradition as another modern morality play, complete with Lucifer and a Hells' Mouth spewing fire and smoke.

The action of Food for the Dead takes place on Halloween, the night Candela is concluding her nine-year mourning period for her husband, Rubén. Her grown children come home for this special event and we learn about each of the characters through their interaction at the dinner table. Candela is finally letting go of Rubén's macho grip. "I am going to say good-bye to Rubén and hello to the new me" she tells her children. Candela has only one more house payment, she is taking night school classes and she has even acquired her own credit card. Candela's children, a quartet of "twenty-something" Chicanos, represent an interesting and provocative spectrum of middle-class Chicana/o identities. The oldest son, José, is married, macho and homophobic. Rosario, the oldest daughter is a Beverly Hills attorney looking for a sperm donor. Her youngest daughter, Gloria, is a student at UCLA and wants to move into a commune with her Anglo boyfriend, Siddhartha. And the youngest son, Jesús, is a gay artist. But the most interesting and the most developed of the characters is really Candela. Here is a Mexican mother, liberating herself from the traditional and stereotypical role expected of her.

López is once again critical of Mexican patriarchal values, taking full advantage of her arsenal of creative and humorous devices to ridicule machismo. When Jesús reveals the fact that he is gay, an outraged Rubén returns from the dead and we discover that he is a larger-than-life parody of the Macho husband and father, interested in himself and his appetites alone. All Rubén wants to do before he "Beats the maricón" (fag) out of his son, is eat. When Candela asks him, "Didn't they feed you in hell?" he responds, "Yes, but in hell all the Mexican restaurants are full." Rubén's excessive behavior and the fact that he went to Hell tell us that he was not a good man. Indeed, it is revealed that this homophobe died while having sex with his male cousin.

When the Devil arrives, disguised as an Avon Lady, "she" demonstrates a new make up called "Lucifermagic," guaranteed to "cover up black eyes, scars, scratches, cuts on the face....Women in East L.A. are placing large orders," inferring that Rubén was abusive. Rubén is indicted by the author with the Devil's litany of physical abuses. Indeed, by telling us that "Lucifermagic" is "selling like hotcakes" in East Los Angeles, López implicates an entire community. When Rubén is dragged back "down" to Hell, in the fire and smoke, the moment recalls the very roots of Spanish religious folk theatre. A "miracle" has happened and once the man is gone, the family can go on with their lives, free of his machismo and homophobia, redeemed from society's censure.

COMIC MONOLOGUES GIVE LATINAS A VOICE: CONFESSIONS OF WOMEN FROM EAST L.A.

For her next play, Confessions of Women From East L.A., our playwright moves from plays to monologues. The world premiere of this play was directed by William Virchis for Teatro Máscara Mágica in San Diego, California in 1996 and later produced by the Teatro Campesino in San Juan Bautista. "Confessions" is an ensemble piece for four versatile actresses, giving each woman opportunities to explore a variety of

characters. Although the play locates these Latinas in East L.A., they could be in any city in this country with a population of Latinas and Latinos. The play opens with a motivational speaker, Victoria Marquez-Bernstein, Ph.D., ostensibly speaking to a group of Latina high school students but including the entire audience. This character and her message were originally inspired by Bettina R. Flores's self-help guide titled, Chiquita's Cocoon: A Cinderella Complex (1990) . And although Dr. Marquez-Bernstein's character sometimes parodies self-help gurus, her message, like Ms. Flores', is mostly sincere. Because the character speaks directly to the audience from the very beginning of the piece, the audience is not only included, but implicated. In the previous plays in this volume the fourth wall separates the audience from the characters, inferring their participation; in this play audience members are included, even to the point of active participation.

As different characters come forward to "confess," the other three actresses portray either audience members (e.g. high school girls) listening attentively, or assume male roles, such as a priest. As each monologue discloses "confessions" of various sorts, the listener(s) remain silent witnesses. The themes vary but are all promoting equality and opportunity for Latinas and by extension, all women. But the men in the audience will have to be careful not to assume the characters are talking about them— unless they fit the profiles: macho, sexist, abuser, narcissist, and etc. "There's a macho inside each and every one of you Latinos," the play is telling the men and hopefully, we males can learn from the truth being told to power. Most importantly, the monologues give voice to the too-often voiceless women of any barrio, USA.

López's writing and acting careers extend to television as well. In 1993 she was a staff writer for Fox's Living Single comedy series and in 1994 she was a writer, performer and segment producer for Culture Clash, also for Fox Television. In the fall of 1998 López entered the graduate program in screenwriting in the School of Theatre, Film and Television of the University of California at Los Angeles. In 2000 López achieved her ultimate goal of founding a theatre, CASA 0101, so named for the digital revolution happening in the U.S. and her beloved Boyle Heights. Many plays, performances, workshops and other empowering events have been held at CASA 0101. Originally located in a storefront, the company will move-into a newly-remodeled 99-seat theatre and performing arts center in 2011. López is also involved in film and television production, empowering other Latinas as well as Latinos to produce their own narratives. While for some, this would be a "miracle," for López it will be the logical outcome of her ambition, talent and tenacity.

REINSCRIBING THE CONQUEST: UNCONQUERED SPIRITS

In 1994-95 López's historical drama, Unconquered Spirits received its world premiere, produced by the Theatre Department of California State University, Northridge, directed by Prof. Ana Marie Garcia. Unconquered Spirits is López's homage to La Llorona as well as to the Mechicana pecan shellers who went on strike in San Antonio, Texas in 1938. In her play López combines myth with history, taking her audience back and forth through time and place, from the early twentieth century to the sixteenth century and back. Always, La Llorona is a presence and a character. In this epic historico-mythico play the playwright attempts to draw parallels between the present and past conditions of women in Mexico and in the U.S. She is also intent on redeeming La Llorona and all women from their marginalized and demonized positions.

López serves two histories in this play. She reminds her audience of the abuses of the Colonial Church and she also brings an important event in twentieth-century Mechicana (read: women's) labor struggles to light. With La Llorona as symbol of all oppressed Mechicanas, Unconquered Spirits gives women a voice and a reason. While most tales of La Llorona simply tell of this (anonymous) "evil woman who killed her children," few of the story tellers inform their listeners of who she was and why she did what she did. In many versions, La Llorona is conflated with La Malinche, Cortés's mistress and alleged "traitor of the Mexican people". But in the words of Aida Hurtado, "...most recently Chicana feminists have reinterpreted La Malinche's role in the conquest of Mexico from traitor to that of a brilliant woman whose ability to learn different languages was unsurpassed by any of her contemporaries". Just as many Chicana writers and critics are revisiting the Malinche myth, López, too, redeems her, and thus all women, in her version of the Malinche/Llorona myth. But the playwright does not redeem the Church for its role in the colonization, suppression and genocide of the Américas.

Sincerely,

Jorge A. Huerta, Ph.D.

BIBLIOGRAPHY FOR HUERTA'S INTRO

Green, Judith. "She's at that stage," San Jose Mercury News, 12 November 1989, Arts and Books, p. 5.

Maria Teresa Marrero, "Real Women Have Curves: The Articulation of Fat as a Cultural/Feminist Issue," Ollantay, I (January 1993):61-70.

McFerran, Virginia Derus. "Chicana voices in American drama: Silviana Wood, Estela Portillo-Trambley, Cherríe Moraga, Milcha Sanchez-Scott, Josefina López," PhD dissertation, University of Minnesota, 1991 (Ann Arbor, 1991).

DEDICATIONS

This book is dedicated to my wonderful and supportive husband Emmanuel who is the biggest supporter of my dreams.

I also dedicate this book to my manager Marilyn Atlas, my "Fairy Godmother" who has been fighting for my dreams to become real on the big and small screen – for being a visionary and getting the big picture.

This book is especially dedicated to all the wonderful people at CASA 0101 like Hector Rodriguez, Gaby Lopez de Denis, Eddie Padilla, Corky Dominguez, Miriam Peniche, Ramona Gonzales, Selene Santiago, Luke Lizalde, Luz Vasquez, Emma Nava, Mark Kraus, Elizabeth Otero, and all the rest of the CASA Familia who has helped make a dream come true by creating a cultural center in my barrio. Thank you for your energy and generosity to my community!

This book is also dedicated to all the women and men who have acted in my plays – thank you for breathing life into my characters.

Thank you Jorge Huerta for believing in me and not letting me give up on my writing.

Acknowledgements

Special thanks to: God, Catalina and Rosendo López, Keisuke Fukuda, Bill Virchis, Lupe Ontiveros, Irene Fornes, Emilio Carballido, Susana Tubert, Toni Curiel, Jorge Huerta, Jon Mercedes III, Luis Valdez, Sara Valdovinos, Angelica López, Esther López, Teresa Marrero, Carmen Roman, INTAR, LATC, El Teatro De La Esperanza, University of California San Diego Theater Dept., The Guadalupe Cultural Arts Center, El Teatro Bilingue de Houston, The Seattle Group Theater, Asolo Center for the Performing Arts, Victory Gardens Theater, Dallas Theater Center, The San Diego Repertory Theater, Borderlands Theater, Repertorio Español, and Spelman College and the many other theaters and High Schools which produced my play.

California State University, Northridge, the Deparment of Theatre School of The Arts, Jon Mercedes III, Bill Virchis, Catalina Maynard, Choral Thuet, Pola Allen, Kaddiz Gonzalez, Felipe Salazar, my mother Catalina, the lady who sells corn on the cob on the corner of First and St. Louis Street, K-mart, Dr. Maria Viramontes De Marin, Gronk, and Joseph Julian Gonzalez.

El Teatro Campesino, Amy Gonzalez, Phillip Esparza, the cast, UCSD's Teatro De Las Americas, Laura Esparza, East L.A. College Theater Department, Teatro Vision.

Anamarie Garcia for courageously taking on the challenge of bringing my vision to the theater, my father Rosendo López, Felipe Salazar, Keisuke Fukuda, Florentino Manzano, Philip Handler, John Furman, Winslow Rogers, Rosa Escalante, MEChA.

SPECIAL DEDICATIONS

REAL WOMEN HAVE CURVES is dedicated to the women on whom these characters are loosely based, my mother Catalina Perales and my sister Esther López, S. Orbach, the author of Fat is a Feminist Issue, and to all the undocumented and now documented garment workers of Los Angeles.

SIMPLY MARIA OR THE AMERICAN DREAM is dedicated to Luis Valdez, who showed me that theater belonged to all people, to my mother Catalina who taught me how to tell stories, and to my father Rosendo who gave me the courage to dream.

CONFESSIONS OF WOMEN FROM EAST L.A. is dedicated to the Mexican woman who sells corn on the cob on the corner of First Street and St. Louis in Boyle Heights, Dr. Maria Viramontes De Marin, my mother the telenovela addict, Jon Mercedes III, William Alejandro Virchis, Catalina Maynard, and Keisuke Fukuda.

FOOD FOR THE DEAD is dedicated to my father Rosendo Z. López, my little brother Fernando, Guillermo Reyes, Eduardo Machado, Jorge Huerta, Luis Valdez, and Phillip Esparza

UNCONQUERED SPIRITS is dedicated to La Llorona and all the "crying women" throughout history; to my mother Catalina; Emma Tenayuca for her courage beyond her years; Cal State, Northridge Chicano Studies Professor Rudolfo Acuña; author Rudolfo Anaya, historian Jose López, and to the unconquered spirit of the Chicana/Chicano.

REAL WOMEN HAVE CURVES

PLAYWRIGHT'S NOTES

When I was very young my best friend and I were walking to the corner store. My parents had warned me not to tell anyone I didn't have "papers" and to be careful walking the streets. On the way to the store we saw "la migra" (INS/immigration/Border Patrol). I quickly turned to my friend and tried to "act white." I spoke in English and talked about Jordache jeans and Barbie dolls hoping no one would suspect us. When I finally got my legal residence card, I remembered this incident knowing that I would never have to hide and be afraid again. I also laughed at my naivete and fear because what I had thought was la migra was only the L.A. Police Meter Maid.

In 1987 the Simpson-Rodino Amnesty Law, designed to stop the influx of undocumented people entering the country, granted thousands of undocumented people living in the U.S. since 1982 legal residency. This was an opportunity of a lifetime. However, thousands, not trusting the government, hesitated to apply, fearing this was a scheme to deport them. They, like me, couldn't believe that after hiding and being persecuted for so long they were finally going to have the freedom to live and work in this country.

I got my residence card soon after I graduated from high school and was then able to apply to college. I had been accepted to New York University, but I had to wait a year to be eligible for financial aid. During this year I worked at McDonald's, but I hated it. Then, desperate for a new job, I asked my sister to let me work at her tiny sewing factory. I worked there for five months and my experiences at the factory served as inspiration for REAL WOMEN HAVE CURVES. At the factory there were a few Latina women,

all older than me. They liked working for my sister because she wasn't stingy. We spent so much time together working, sweating and laughing, that we bonded. I remember feeling blessed that I was a woman because male bonding could never compare with what happens when women work together. We had something special and I wanted to show the world.

In the U.S. undocumented people are referred to as "illegal aliens" which conjures up in our minds the image of extraterrestrial beings who are not human, who do not bleed when they're cut, who do not cry when they feel pain, who do not have fears, dreams and hopes…Undocumented people have been used as scapegoats for so many of the problems in the U.S., from drugs and violence, to the economy. I hope that someday this country recognizes the very important contributions of undocumented people and remembers that they too came to this country in search of a better life.

Josefina López
Los Angeles
March, 1992

REAL WOMEN HAVE CURVES

ACT ONE

SETTING

A tiny sewing factory in East Los Angeles.

TIME: The first week of September 1987.

CHARACTERS

ANA   18, plump and pretty, sister of Estela, daughter of Carmen. She is a recent high school graduate and a young feminist

ESTELA   24, plump, plain-looking, owner of the "Garcia Sewing Factory"

CARMEN   48, a short, large woman, mother of Ana and Estela. She has a talent for storytelling

PANCHA   32, a huge woman who is very mellow in her ways, but quick with her tongue

ROSALI   29, only a bit plump in comparison to the rest of the women. She is sweet and easygoing

SCENE ONE: MONDAY MORNING, SEPTEMBER 7, 1987, ABOUT 7:00 A.M.

AT RISE: The stage becomes visible. The clock on the wall shows it is 6:59 a.m. Keys are heard outside the door. The door opens. ANA and CARMEN enter. ANA drags herself in, goes directly to the electricity box and switches it on. Automatically all the machines "hummmm" loudly. The lights turn on at different times. The radio also blasts on with a song in Spanish. CARMEN quickly turns off the radio. She puts her lunch on the table. ANA slumps on a machine. CARMEN then gets a broom and uses it to get a mousetrap from underneath the table. She prays that today will be the day she caught the mouse. She sees the mousetrap empty and is very disappointed.

CARMEN. ¡Pinche rata! I'll get you. *(CARMEN returns the broom. She takes two dollars from her purse, approaches ANA and presents them to her.)* Ten. Go to the bakery.

ANA. No. I want to go back to sleep!

CARMEN. ¡Huevona! If we don't help your sister who else is going to? She already works all hours of the night trying to finish the dresses. Por fin she's doing something productive with her life.

ANA. I know I'm trying to be supportive, **ayy**! I don't want to go to the bakery. I don't want any bread.

CARMEN. That's good, at least you won't get fatter.

ANA. ¡Amá!

CARMEN. I only tell you for your own good. Bueno, I'll go get the bread myself, but you better not get any when I bring it. *(CARMEN walks to the door.)* Ana, don't forget to close the doors. This street is full of winos and drug addicts. And don't you open the door to any strangers!

ANA. Yeah, yeah, I know! I'm not a kid. *(ANA locks both doors with a key. She goes toward the toilet and turns on the water in the sink. ANA splashes water on her face to awaken. She sticks her hand behind the toilet seat and gets out a notebook and a pen. Spotlight on ANA. She sits and writes the following:)* Monday, September 7, 1987…I don't want to be here! I only come because my mother practically drags me out of bed and into the car and into the factory. She pounds on the…No…(Scratches "pounds.") She knocks on…No…(She scratches "knocks.") She pounds on the garage wall, and since I think it's an earthquake, I run out. Then she catches me and I become her prisoner…Is it selfish of me not to want to wake up every morning at 6:30 a.m., Saturdays included, to come work here for 67 dollars a week? Oh, but such is the life of a Chicana in the garment industry. Cheap

labor…I've been trying to hint to my sister for a raise, but she says I don't work fast enough for her to pay me minimum wage…The weeks get longer and I can't believe I've ended up here. I just graduated from high school…Most of my friends are in college…It's as if I'm going backwards. I'm doing the work that mostly illegal aliens do…*(Scratches "illegal aliens.")* No, "undocumented workers"…or else it sounds like these people come from Mars…Soon I will have my "Temporary Residence Card," then after two years, my green card…I'm happy to finally be legal, but I thought things would be different…What I really want to do is write…

CARMEN *(off, interrupting)*. Ana, open the door! *(CARMEN pounds on the door outside. ANA quickly puts her writing away and goes to open the door.)* Hurry up! There's a wino following me! *(ANA gets the keys and unlocks both doors.)* Hurry! He's been following me from the bakery.

(ANA opens the first door. CARMEN is behind the bar door and is impatiently waiting for ANA to open it. ANA opens the door. CARMEN hurries in nervously. ANA quickly shuts the doors. ANA looks out the window.)

ANA. Amá, that's not a wino, it's an "Alelullah"!

CARMEN. But he was following me!

ANA. I know, those witnesses don't give up. *(CARMEN puts the bag of bread on the table. She fills a small pot with water and puts it on the little hot plate to boil the water for coffee.)*

CARMEN. Pos yo ya no veo. I can't see a thing. *(CARMEN goes to her purse and takes out her glasses. She puts them on. She looks out the window and sees no one.)* I should retire and be an abuelita by now, taking care of grandchildren…I don't know why I work, I have arthritis in my hands, I'm losing my sight from all this sewing, and this arm, I can hardly move it anymore…*(ANA does not pay attention as usual.)*

ANA *(unsympathetically)*. Yeah, Amá.

CARMEN. I wonder where's Estela. She should have been here by now.

ANA. I thought she left the house early.

(PANCHA appears behind the bar door.)

PANCHA. Buenos días, Doña Carmen. Can you open the door?

CARMEN. Buenos días, Pancha. ¿Cómo está?

PANCHA. Not too bad.

CARMEN. Que bien. I brought my mole today for all of us.

PANCHA. You're so generous, Doña Carmen.

CARMEN. It was in the 'frigerator' for three days, and I thought it was turning green, so I brought it. Why let it go to waste?

PANCHA. Is it still good?

CARMEN. Of course, I make great mole.

(ROSALI appears behind the bar door.)

ROSALI. Doña Carmen, the door.

CARMEN. It's open, Rosalí. Buenos días. How are you?

ROSALI (entering). Okay, like always, Doña Carmen.

CARMEN. I brought my mole for all of us.

ROSALI. Did you? Ayy, gracias, but remember I'm on a diet.

CARMEN. Just try a small taco, no te va hacer daño. Try it.

ROSALI. I'm sure it's delicious, but I'm this close to being a size seven.

CARMEN. Sí. You're looking thinner now. How are you doing it?

ROSALI. I'm on a secret diet…It's from the Orient.

CARMEN. A-ha…It's true, those Japanese women are always skinny. Pues, give me your secret, Rosalí. Maybe this way I can lose this ball of fat! (She squeezes her stomach.) No mas mira que paresco. You can't even see my waist anymore. But you know what it really is? It's just water. After having so many babies I just stopped getting rid of the water. It's as if I'm clogged. (ROSALI and ANA laugh.)

ROSALI. Sí, Doña Carmen.

ANA. Yeah, sure, Amá!

CARMEN. ¿Y tu? Why do you laugh? You're getting there yourself. When I was your age I wasn't as fat as you. And look at your chichis.

ANA. ¡Amá!

CARMEN (grabs ANA's breasts as if weighing them). They must weigh five pounds each.

ANA. Amá, don't touch me like that!

ROSALI. Where's Estela?

CARMEN. We don't know. Ana, I think you better call home now and check

if she's there.

ROSALI. Because her torment is outside washing his car.

ALL. He is?

(From under a large blanket on the floor ESTELA jumps out. The WOMEN are startled and scream, but they quickly join her as she runs to the window to spy on her Tormento.)

ESTELA. ¡Ayy que buenote! He's so cute.

ANA. Don't exaggerate.

ESTELA. ¡Mi Tormento! ¡O mi Tormento!

CARMEN. We thought you left home early.

ESTELA. No, I worked so late last night I decided to sleep here.

CARMEN. Then why didn't you tell us when—

ESTELA. I heard you come in, but I wanted to listen in on your chisme about me, Amá.

CARMEN. Me? I don't gossip!

ESTELA. Sure, Amá…I'm going to the store. *(ESTELA runs to the mirror.)*

PANCHA. I don't know why you bother, all he cares about is his car.

CARMEN. Vénganse, I think the water is ready. *(The WOMEN gather around the table for coffee. PANCHA and CARMEN grab bread. ESTELA goes to the bathroom and brushes her hair, puts on lipstick, then she puts on a girdle under her skirt, which she has great trouble getting on, but she is determined. She grabs a deodorant stick and applies it. She also gets a bottle of perfume and sprays it accordingly.)*

ESTELA. Aquí por si me abraza. *(She sprays her wrist.)*

ANA *(mocks ESTELA in front of the WOMEN)*. Here in case he hugs me.

ESTELA. Aquí por si me besa. *(She sprays her neck.)*

ANA. Here in case he kisses me.

ESTELA. Y aquí por si se pasa. *(She sprays under her skirt.)*

ANA. And here in case he…you know what. *(The WOMEN are by the door and windows looking out. ESTELA comes out of the bathroom.)*

ROSALI. He's gone.

CARMEN. Sí, ya se fue.

ESTELA. No! Are you sure? *(ESTELA goes toward the door, before she reaches it CARMEN shuts the door.)*

CARMEN *(scared).* ¡Dios mio! *(CARMEN quickly takes a drink of her coffee and can hardly breathe afterwards.)*

ESTELA. ¿Qué? ¿Amá, qué pasa?

CARMEN. I saw a van!

ROSALI. What van?

CARMEN. ¡La migra! *(All the WOMEN scatter and hide waiting to be discovered. Then after a few seconds PANCHA makes a realization.)*

PANCHA. Pero, why are we hiding? We're all legal now.

CARMEN. ¡Ayy, de veras! I forget! All those years of being an illegal, I still can't get used to it.

PANCHA. Me too! *(She picks up a piece of bread.)* I think I just lost my appetite.

ROSALI. I'm not scared of it! I used to work in factories and whenever they did a raid, I'd always sneak out through the bathroom window, y ya.

ANA. Last night I heard on the news that la migra patrol is planning to raid a lot of places.

PANCHA. They're going to get mean trying to enforce that Amnesty law.

ANA. Thank God, I'm legal. I will never have to lie on applications anymore, except maybe about my weight...

ROSALI. ¿Saben qué? Yesterday I got my first credit card.

CARMEN. ¿Pos cómo le hiciste? How?

ROSALI. I lied on the application and I got an Americana Express.

ANA. And now you have two green cards and you never leave home without them. *(ANA laughs her head off, but none of the WOMEN get the joke. ANA slowly shuts up.)*

PANCHA. Doña Carmen, let those men in their van come! Who cares? We're all legal now! *(PANCHA goes to the door and opens it all the way. They all smile in relief and pride, then ESTELA, who has been stuffing her face, finally speaks up.)*

ESTELA. I'm not. *(PANCHA slams the door shut.)*

EVERYONE. You're not?!!!

ANA. But you went with me to get the fingerprints and the medical examination.

ESTELA. I didn't send them in.

ROSALI. But you qualify.

ESTELA. I have a criminal record.

EVERYONE. No!

ESTELA. So I won't apply until I clear it.

CARMEN. Estela, what did you do?

PANCHA. ¿Qué hiciste?

ESTELA. Well, actually, I did two things.

CARMEN. Two?! ¿Y por qué no me habias dicho? Why is the mother always the last one to know?

ESTELA. Because one is very embarrassing—

CARMEN. ¡Aver dime, condenada! What have you done?

ESTELA. I was arrested for illegal possession of—

ROSALI. Marijuana?!

PANCHA. A gun?!

ESTELA. A lobster.

EVERYONE. No!

ESTELA. Out of season!

CARMEN. ¡Mentirosa!

WOMEN. You're kidding!

ESTELA. A-ha! I'm not lying! I almost got handcuffed and taken to jail. Trying to "abduct" a lobster is taken very seriously in Santa Monica Beach. They wanted me to appear in court and I never did.

PANCHA. That's not a serious crime; ¿de qué te apuras? Why worry?

CARMEN *(not amused)*. That was the first crime? You mentioned two.

ESTELA. I'm being sued for not keeping up with my payments on the machines.

ANA. Y los eight thousand dollars you got from your accident settlement weren't enough?

CARMEN. But I thought that everything was paid for.

ESTELA. I used most of it for a down-payment, but I still needed a new steam iron, the over-lock…I thought I could make the monthly payments if everything went as planned.

CARMEN. ¿Pos qué paso?

PANCHA. What happened?

ESTELA. You know that we never finish on time. So the Glitz company doesn't pay me until we do.

ROSALI. Pero the orders are too big. We need at least two more seamstresses.

ESTELA. Pues sí. But the money they pay me is not enough to hire any more help. So because we get behind, they don't pay, I can't pay you, and I can't pay those pigs that sold me those machines.

CARMEN. Ayyy, Estela, how much do you owe?

ESTELA. Two thousand dollars…

CARMEN. ¡Hora si que estamos bien jodidas! *(The WOMEN sigh hopelessly.)*

ESTELA. …I tried. I sent some money and explained the situation to them two weeks ago, but I got a letter from their lawyer. They're taking me to court…

PANCHA. So you had money two weeks ago? Hey, hey, you told us you couldn't pay us because you didn't have any money. You had money! Here we are bien pobres, I can't even pay for the bus sometimes, and you care more about your machines than us.

ESTELA. They're going to take everything!

ROSALI. ¡¿Qué?!

ESTELA. They're going to reposess everything if I don't pay them. And if I appear in court they'll find out that I don't have any papers.

ANA. Then why don't you apply for Amnesty?

ESTELA. Because I won't get it if they find out about my lawsuit.

ANA. You don't know that. Estela, you should talk to this lawyer I know…

ESTELA. Ana, you know I can't afford a lawyer!

CARMEN. Ayy, Estela, ¡ya ni la friegas! *(ESTELA fights the urge to cry.)*

ROSALI. If I had money I'd lend it to you.

PANCHA *(aside)*. I wouldn't.

ROSALI *(kindly)*. But I don't have any money because you haven't paid me.

ESTELA. Miren, the Glitz company has promised to pay me for the last two weeks and this week if we get the order in by Friday.

ANA. How much of the order is left?

ESTELA. About 100 dresses.

PANCHA. N'ombre. By this Friday? What do they think we are? Machines?

ESTELA. But they're not that difficult! Amá, you're so fast. This would be a cinch for you. All you have to do are the blusas on the dresses. Rosalí, the over-lock work is simple. It's a lot, but you're the best at it. And, Pancha, all you have to do is sew the skirts. The skirts are the easiest to sew. Now, Ana, with you doing all the ironing, we'll get it done by Friday. You see if we do little by little at what we do best…¡Andenle! We can do it. ¿Verá que sí, Ana?

ANA *(uncertain)*. Sure we can.

ESTELA. ¿Vera que sí, Amá?

CARMEN. Pos we can try.

ROSALI. Estela, we can do it. *(ESTELA looks to PANCHA. PANCHA remains quiet. CARMEN breaks their stare.)*

CARMEN. Wouldn't it be funny if the migra came and instead of taking the employees like they usually do, they take the patrona. *(The WOMEN laugh at the thought.)*

ESTELA. Don't laugh! It could happen. *(The WOMEN become silent.)*

CARMEN. Ayy, Estela, I'm just kidding. I'm just trying to make you feel better. *(Beat.)*

ROSALI. Bueno, let's try to be serious…I'll do the zippers.

ESTELA. Yes, por favor. And, Pancha, please do the hems on the skirts.

PANCHA. The machine is not working.

ESTELA. Not again! *(ESTELA goes to the machine. She fusses around with it trying to make it work. With confidence.)* There. It should be ready. Try it. *(PANCHA sits down on a chair and tries the machine. She steps on the pedal and the machine makes an awful noise. Then it shoots off electric sparks and explodes. PANCHA quickly gets away from the machine. The WOMEN hide under the machines.)*

WOMEN. ¡Ay, ay, ay!

ESTELA. Augghh! All this equipment is junk! *(ESTELA throws a thread spool at the machine and it explodes again.)* I was so stupid to buy this factory! *(ESTELA fights the urge to cry in frustration. The WOMEN stare at her helplessly.)*

CARMEN. Pos no nos queda otra. Pancha, can you do the hems by hand?

PANCHA. Bueno, I guess I have to.

ESTELA. Gracias…Ana, turn on the iron, I'm going to need you to do the ironing all this week…Tell me when the iron gets hot and I'll show you what you have to do.

CARMEN. I'll help Rosalí with the zippers.

ESTELA. No…I need you to do the blusas on size 7/8.

CARMEN. Didn't I already do them?

ESTELA. No.

CARMEN. I guess it was size 13/14 then.

ESTELA. You couldn't have, because there is no size 13/14 for this dress style, Amá.

CARMEN. No?…Hoye did you get any more pink thread from the Glitz?

ESTELA. Oh, no. I forgot…Go ahead and use the over-lock machine. That is already set up with thread.

ANA. What does the over-lock do?

ROSALI. It's what keeps the material from coming apart. *(ROSALI shows ANA.)*

CARMEN. Why don't you give me the pink thread from the over-lock machine, then when you get the thread you can set it up again?

ESTELA. No. I don't know how to set it up on that new machine.

CARMEN. Rosalí can do that later. She knows how to do it; qué no, Rosalí?

ROSALI. Sí, Doña Carmen.

ESTELA. Why don't you just do what I'm asking you to do?

CARMEN. Estela, no seas terca. I know what I'm telling you.

ESTELA. So do I. I want to do things differently. I want us to work like an assembly line.

CARMEN. Leave that to the big factories. I've been working long enough to know—

ESTELA. I haven't been working long enough, but I'm intelligent enough to—

CARMEN. Estela, my way is better!

ESTELA. Why do you think your way is better? All my life your way has been better. Maybe that's why my life is so screwed up!

CARMEN. ¡Desgraciada! I'm only doing it to help you!

ESTELA. Because you know I won't be getting married any time soon so you want to make sure I'm doing something productive with my life so I can support myself. I don't need your help! *(Beat.)*

CARMEN. Where did all that come from? I thought we were arguing about the thread.

ESTELA. You know what I mean. You know I'm right!

CARMEN. All right. If you want me to do the over-lock work I'll do it…I have to remember I work for you now.

ESTELA. Amá, don't give me that!

CARMEN. What?

ESTELA. Guilt!

CARMEN. Well, it's true! It's not usual that a mother works for her daughter. So I have to stop being your mother and just be a regular employee that you can boss around and tell what to do.

ESTELA. ¡Ayy, Amá, parele! You are my mother, but sometimes you get out of line. How can I tell Rosalí and Pancha to stop gossiping when it's you who initiates the chisme? You're a bad example!

CARMEN. Ay, sí. Blame me! ¡Echame la culpa! You gossip too when it's convenient.

ESTELA. Look, Amá, I don't want to argue with you anymore. I'm frustrated enough by the thought that I might get deported, at the sight of that machine, and at the thought that I am the biggest fool for buying all this junk. So I don't need my mother to make my life any worse! *(Beat.)*

CARMEN. So what are we going to do about the thread?

ESTELA. ¡Oiiiii! And we're back to the same thing! *(She goes to the over-lock machine and angrily tears a thread spool from the machine and throws it at CARMEN.)* Here! ¡Tenga! *(The thread spool misses CARMEN by a hair.)*

CARMEN *(dramatically)*. ¡Pegame, pegame! Go ahead! Hit me! God's gonna punish you for enojona!

ANA. Estela, the iron is ready.

ESTELA. Amá, give me a finished dress from the box.

CARMEN. Where are they?

ESTELA. Right next to you by the pile.

CARMEN. Qué size?

ESTELA. For the mannequin.

CARMEN. What size is it?

ROSALI. It's a size seven, Doña Carmen.

CARMEN *(sarcastically)*. Thank you, Rosali. *(CARMEN digs into the box and gets a dress. She gives it to ESTELA who begins to iron the dress carefully.)*

ESTELA *(to ANA)*. Pay close attention to how I'm ironing this dress. Always, always use the steam. And don't burn the tul, por favor. On the skirt just a couple of strokes to make it look decent. It's real easy, just don't burn the tul, okay?

ANA. Okay.

ESTELA. Check the water, and when it gets low...Tell me so I can send you to buy some more water for it.

ANA. Why do you have to buy the water?

ESTELA. Because regular water is too dirty, it needs distilled water for clean steam. *(ESTELA finishes ironing the dress. She shakes it a bit then puts it on the mannequin. All the WOMEN stare at the dress.)*

ROSALI. Que bonito. How I would like to wear a dress like that.

PANCHA. But first you have to turn into a stick to wear something like that.

ROSALI. Yeah, but they're worth it.

ANA. How much do they pay us for making these dresses?

ROSALI. Estela, we get thirteen dollars for these, no?

ANA. Oh, yeah? How much do they sell them for at the stores?

ESTELA. They tell me they sell them at Bloomingdale's for about two hundred dollars.

WOMEN. ¡¡¿Qué?!!

ANA. Dang!! *(Lights fade.)*

SCENE TWO: A FEW HOURS LATER, ABOUT 11:30 A.M.

AT RISE: Lights come on. The WOMEN are busy working. The "Cucaracha" is played on the horn by the lunch mobile outside announcing its arrival.

ANA. Okay, there's the lonchera. Anybody want anything for lunch?

CARMEN. The lonchera is here already?

ESTELA. Ana, just hurry back.

ROSALI. Can you get me something to drink? How much are those tomato juices?

ANA. A V-8?

ROSALI. Sí, eso.

ANA. I think they're 80 cents. You want anything else?

ROSALI. No, no, I'm not hungry.

ESTELA. Ana, lend me a dollar.

ANA. What do you think I am? A bank? This is the third time. One can only go so far on 67 dollars a week.

ESTELA. Ana, if you are not happy here go back to working at McDonald's.

ANA. I would...(*CARMEN stares at ANA.*)...But...You still want to borrow the dollar?

ESTELA. Are you going to charge me interest?

ANA. Of course. What do you want me to buy you?

ESTELA. A burrito de chicharrón.

ANA. Pancha, do you want anything?

PANCHA. Sí. Bring me four tacos.

CARMEN. Pancha, aren't you going to want some of my mole?

PANCHA. Ana, bring me three tacos, no más. *(PANCHA gives ANA money.)*

ESTELA. Ana, if you have money left, could you buy some distilled water at the corner store?

ANA. Anything else, boss? *(ANA leaves to buy the food. CARMEN waits until ESTELA shuts the door.)*

CARMEN. Bueno, if we are already going to hell for being a bunch of chismosas, there's no use in hiding it any longer. *(CARMEN digs into a pile of dresses and takes out a book. She shows it to PANCHA and ROSALI. CARMEN whispers.)* ¡Miren! *(ROSALI quickly sees the illustrations on the front cover and is shocked.)*

ROSALI. Doña Carmen!

CARMEN. I was cleaning the garage and I found a whole pile of dirty books. I think they belong to my oldest son.

PANCHA. What's the book called?

ROSALI *(reading title)*. Two Hundred Sexual Positions Illustrated.

PANCHA. I didn't know there were so many. *(ROSALI and PANCHA gather around CARMEN to look at the book. ESTELA has not noticed them. Instead she notices a letter being dropped in the mail slot. ESTELA reads the letter.)*

ROSALI *(shocked)*. Ay, Dios, how can these women do this?

PANCHA. They're probably gymnasts.

CARMEN. The photographer must have used a special lens on this picture.

PANCHA. Which picture?

CARMEN. The one on page 69.

ROSALI. I didn't know people could do that.

PANCHA. ¡Híjole! Imagine if you had married this man, and you had never

seen him until your wedding night.

CARMEN. ¡N'ombre, ni lo mande dios! How it hurt with a regular one.

PANCHA. Mire, Doña Carmen. This woman looks like you, but that doesn't stop her.

CARMEN. Ahh. She's so big. No le da verguenza.

ROSALI. I didn't know they had large women in porno books.

PANCHA. I guess some men enjoy watching big women.

ESTELA *(sees them looking at the book)*. What are you looking at? You're suppose to be working! The food has not gotten here yet.

PANCHA. Estela, come look. It's a dirty book.

ESTELA. Why are you looking at that?

CARMEN. Estela, no mas ven a ver. *(ESTELA hesitates, but is curious and gives in. She sees the pictures of the large women and is shocked.)*

ESTELA. People this fat shouldn't be having sex! Ichhh!

ROSALI. Look, Estela, there's a guy in here that looks like your "Tormento."

ESTELA. Where?!! *(ROSALI shows her, then suddenly the door is kicked open.)* Aughhhhhh!!!!!

(ANA enters with her hands full of food.)

PANCHA. Estela, calm down.

ESTELA. I thought it was la migra!

ANA. Sorry! I kicked the door open because my hands are full…

ESTELA. From now on these doors are to remain closed and locked at all times, okay? If you go outside, you knock on the door like this…*(She knocks in code rhythm.)*…so we know it's just one of us. Don't ever kick the door again.

ANA. Isn't that going a bit to extremes?

PANCHA. Vamos a estar como gallinas enjauladas.

ESTELA. No. We just have to be careful.

ROSALI. So how do you do the knock?

ESTELA *(exemplifies)*. Knock once. Pause. Then knock twice. Then repeat.

ANA. Well, if it makes you feel better…

ESTELA. Yes, it would.

ANA. All right. Here's the food. *(ANA places the food on the table.)*

ESTELA. Did you remember the water?

ANA. Yeah, I brought the water! *(ANA gives the bottle of water to ESTELA and distributes the food. To the WOMEN:)* What were you doing?

ALL *(hiding the book).* Nothin'.

ANA. What are you hiding?

ALL. Nothin'. *(Pause.)*

PANCHA. We don't want to pervert you.

ANA. You don't want to pervert me more than I've already perverted you?

ROSALI. It's a dirty book.

ANA. Let me see it.

CARMEN. No! You're too young to be looking at these things.

ANA. Fine. You've seen them once, you've seen it all.

PANCHA. Ana!

CARMEN. ¿Qué? Repeat what you just said. Don't tell me you've been "messing around."

ANA. No. It's just that I probably know more than most of you and you're thinking that you can pervert me. Stuuuuupiiid!!

CARMEN. And how is it that you know so much if you haven't done it?

ANA. …I read a lot.

PANCHA. But not because you read a lot means you know what's what.

ANA. Go ahead. Ask me anything you always wanted to know about sex but were afraid to ask. I'll tell you. *(All the WOMEN are tempted.)*

ROSALI. How do you masturbate…? *(PANCHA, CARMEN, and ESTELA stare at ROSALI in shock.)*

ANA. What?

CARMEN. ¡Híjole! If your Apá were to hear you…¡Híjole!

ANA. I wouldn't be talking like this in front of my father.

CARMEN. Can you believe her? Girls nowadays think they know so much that's why they end up panzonas.

ANA. No. They end up pregnant because they don't use contraceptives.

PANCHA. Are you sure all you do is read a lot?

CARMEN. Your husband's not going to like you knowing so much.

PANCHA. A girl shouldn't know so much.

ANA. I'm not a girl, I'm a woman.

PANCHA. Uuy, uy, la Miss Know-it-all.

CARMEN. In my day, a girl became a woman when she lost her virginity.

ANA. That was then. I read somewhere that calling someone a "girl" is just as bad as when white men used to call black men—

CARMEN *(starts to laugh uncontrollably)*. I…I…remember…

ESTELA. Amá, it's 12:20, no more stories. If we gossip people are gonna hear everything outside and even if we close the doors they'll know it's a sewing factory because only women talking chisme can sound like chickens cackling.

CARMEN. But it's what I know how to do best, my reason for living.

ESTELA. I'm begging you. *(CARMEN remains quiet for a few seconds then she begins to laugh uncontrollably again.)*

PANCHA. Why are you laughing? *(CARMEN continues laughing, unable to speak.)*

ANA. ¿Amá, qué le píco? *(The laughter is contagious.)*

CARMEN. I just got a back flash of when I lost my virginity.

ANA. That bad, huh?

CARMEN. The night I eloped with your father on the bike…

ESTELA. Bueno, if the migra deports me we know whose fault it is. Amá, no work, no money, no factory! Is that clear enough?!

CARMEN. Pero, don't get upset. Estela, it's lunch time.

PANCHA. Pues sí.

ESTELA. It gets me so annoyed to hear her talk and talk… And with all the work we have! Just promise me that you'll finish, all right? I'll stop bothering you if you can do that.

WOMEN *(look to each other)*. Pues bueno. We promise.

ESTELA. If not you'll go to hell?!

WOMEN *(look to each other again and think about it)*. Pues bueno.

CARMEN. Sí, sí, sí, we'll go to hell. Can I continue? Okay, pues after riding on his bike for so long, I had to pee so bad! So we stopped in the mountains somewhere. I ran behind a tree, squatted, and just peed. That night, after we got settled, I didn't know what was going to happen. After we did it, I started itching and scratching down there 'til my cuchupeta got so red. I thought something was wrong, but I asked him and he said it was suppose to hurt and bleed. Then I found out it wasn't him. I had peed on poison ivy. And how it hurt! *(The WOMEN laugh sympathetically and slowly gather around the table to eat.)* Panchita, try some of my mole.

PANCHA *(looking at mole)*. But, Doña Carmen, it's green.

CARMEN. It's green mole…Ana, you didn't try some mole. It's real good.

ANA. No way! It looks like…yukkkk!

CARMEN. Aver, Rosalí, come try some. There's plenty.

ROSALI. Thank you, pero, I'm not hungry.

CARMEN. But you haven't eaten anything.

ROSALI. I drink eight glasses of water a day and I don't feel hungry. Water gets rid of the fat.

CARMEN. Ana, you should be drinking eight waters.

ANA. And you should too…Oh no, you get clogged.

ESTELA. Amá, just be very careful with the mole. I don't want any of the dresses getting stained. *(PANCHA scoops some mole with a piece of tortilla. She eats the scoop.)*

CARMEN. You like it, Pancha?

PANCHA *(lying)*. Yeah, it's real good, Doña Carmen… *(ROSALI carefully strays away from the table and drinks her V-8. ROSALI swallows a pill. She goes to the window and peeks out through the curtain. She spots el Tormento outside.)*

ROSALI. ¡Míralo! There's Andrés! Estela, come to the window! Your

Tormento is outside! *(PANCHA, CARMEN, and ANA run to the window, beating ESTELA.)*

ESTELA. No, don't go to the window! Get away from the window!

ANA. No one can see us!

ESTELA. Get down! Make some room for me!

CARMEN. I don't see what you could possibly see in him.

ESTELA. He's cute and he likes me.

CARMEN. He doesn't even have good nalgas. They're this small. *(She exemplifies with her hands.)*

ANA. Amá, why are you so preoccupied with the size of a man's butt?

ROSALI. That's not what counts.

CARMEN. Because your father doesn't have any. *(ESTELA goes to the door and opens it. She fixes herself a bit and stands in front of the door.)*

PANCHA. Estela, I thought you said that door was going to remain closed.

ROSALI. Estela, get away from the door, because if the van passes they'll just see the nopal on your forehead and take you away.

ESTELA. But he wants to talk to me. He sent me a letter. *(ESTELA leaves, closing the door. CARMEN and PANCHA are still eating their tacos. They stick to the window like flies.)*

CARMEN. What could he be telling her? She's laughing her head off.

ROSALI. ¡Miren cómo coquetea! What a flirt. You never suspected she had it in her.

PANCHA. She's worse than Ana.

ANA. What's that suppose to mean? *(CARMEN holds her taco carelessly and the mole spills out onto some dresses.)*

PANCHA. ¡Mire, Doña Carmen! You're spilling the mole!

ANA. Amá, Estela is going to kill you!

CARMEN. ¡Ayy, no! *(CARMEN quickly puts the taco on the table. She grabs a cloth and tries to clean the dresses.)*

PANCHA. ¡Aguas! Here she comes!

CARMEN. What am I going to do?

ANA (*runs to the door and locks it*). Quick, Amá. Hide the dresses! We'll clean them later.

CARMEN. ¿Dónde los escondo?

ROSALI. Anywhere! (*ESTELA tries to open the door. While the women run around hysterically trying to find the best place to hide the dresses.*)

ESTELA. Let me in.

ANA. Who is it?

ESTELA. You know who it is!

ANA. I don't know who. (*She gestures to the women to hurry.*) You think we should open the door? What if it's la migra?

ESTELA. Ana, open the door! (*She pounds on the door.*)

ANA. How do we know it's you?

(*ESTELA finally knocks the secret code and ANA lets her in.*)

ESTELA. When the cat is away the mice come out to play. What were you doing?

WOMEN. Nothing!

CARMEN. Ahora sí. Show us the letter first, and tell us what you talked about.

ESTELA. It's private.

ROSALI. Come on, Estela, no te hagas de rogar, you know you want to show it to us.

ESTELA. ¡Que metiches! This letter is for me. He only intended for me to read it…All right, I'll read it out loud. (*The WOMEN pull out their chairs and get comfortable. ESTELA clears her throat and reads the letter dramatically.*) "Dear Estela…" (*The WOMEN get excited after the first "Dear."*) "Dear Estela…How I dig you. Let me count the waves."

ROSALI. Ahhh, it's a poem.

ESTELA. "Wave one: 'cause you look real nice when you pass by me and say, `Hi.' Wave two: 'cause you seem real smart. Wave three: 'cause your eyes are like fresas. And your lips are like mangos, juicy and delicious, listos para chupar."

PANCHA. Maybe he works at the supermarket in the fruit section.

ESTELA *(continues).* "So how about it? You wanna go cruising down Whittier Boulevard, see a movie, or anything else you wanna do?" I told him I liked the letter a lot. So we're going to the movies tonight.

ROSALI. To the movies? It sounds serious. But be careful with those wandering hands.

ESTELA. He's not that kind of guy.

CARMEN. So what are you going to wear? Don't go dressing up like a scarecrow now.

ESTELA. I don't dress like that.

CARMEN. That's why you scare them away.

ESTELA. Como es, Amá. He likes me for me. Didn't you hear? He said I'm intelligent. He doesn't care how I dress.

CARMEN. Estela, let me make you a dress, horitita te lo coso.

ESTELA. No. I can dress myself. And anyway, what are we doing sitting around. Lunch is over. Let's get to work. ¡A trabajar! *(Lights fade out.)*

SCENE THREE: A FEW HOURS LATER, ABOUT 3:45 P.M.

AT RISE: Lights fade in. The WOMEN are busy working in their designated working areas. PANCHA is by the racks attaching strings to hang the dresses.

ANA. Estela, there are no more dresses to iron. What else should I do?

ESTELA. Ah…Pancha, can you show Ana what you are doing? *(ANA goes to the racks. ROSALI turns on the radio.)*

PANCHA *(showing ANA).* Así hazlo. This way. *(ANA quickly understands what she has to do and begins her work. The phone rings. ESTELA picks it up. On the radio we hear the following:)*

RADIO *(voice-over).* It's 3:45 and another hot, beautiful day in L.A. This is KLOVE—Radio Amor…Now back to our talk show, "Esperanza."

ESPERANZA *(voice-over).* For those of you who just joined us today we are discussing abusive spouses. We have our last caller on the line. Caller, are you there?

CALLER *(voice-over).* Hi. I'm not going to give you my name because my husband listens to this station. I wanted to know what I can do to…Well, I want to know how I can talk to my husband when he gets angry.

ESPERANZA *(voice-over)*. How long has he been abusive?

CALLER *(voice-over)*. Ah…Well, he wasn't like this when we got married…
He was always sweet. So I don't know what has happened to him. He tells
me if I did whatever he asked he wouldn't have to hit me. But I do what he
says and it's still not good enough. Last time he hit me because…

PANCHA *(switches the dial on the radio)*. Isn't there anything else?

CARMEN. Pobre mujer, I'm lucky mi viejo doesn't hit me.

ANA. Lucky? Why lucky? It should be expected that he doesn't. That woman
should leave her husband. Women have the right to say "no."

PANCHA. You think it's that easy?

ANA. No, she's probably dependent on him financially, or the church tells
her to endure, or she's doing it for the children.

PANCHA. You're so young. Did it ever occur to you that maybe she loves
him?

ANA. I'm sure she does. But we can't allow ourselves to be abused anymore.
We have to assert ourselves. We have to realize that we have rights! We have
the right to control our bodies. The right to exercise our sexuality. And the
right to take control of our destiny. But it all begins when we start saying…
(ANA quickly climbs on top of a sewing machine to continue preaching.)…¡Ya
basta! No more! We should learn how to say no! Come on, Amá, say it! Say
it!

CARMEN. What?

ANA. Say it! "No!"

CARMEN. Okay, I won't.

ANA. Amá, say "No!"

CARMEN *(as in she won't)*. No.

ANA. Good! Rosalí, say it.

ROSALI *(casually)*. ¿Pues por qué no? No.

ANA. Pancha, say it. No! *(PANCHA stares at ANA, she won't say it.)*

ESTELA. Ya, ya, Norma Rae, get off and get back to work!

PANCHA. Why don't you run for office? Tan pequeña and she thinks and
acts like she knows everything.

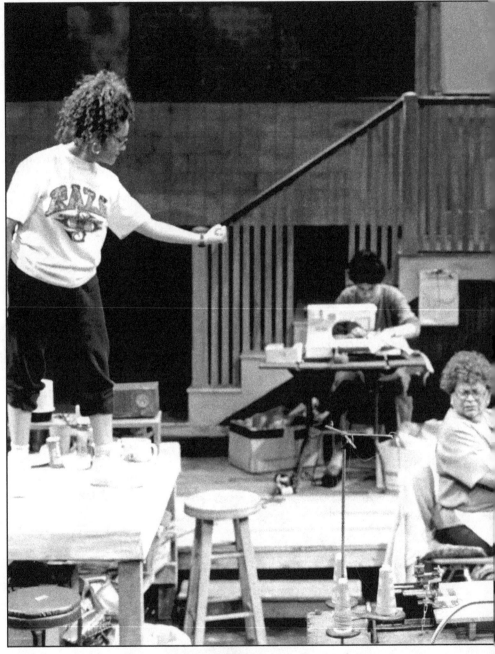

Ana (on the left and played by Josefina López) tries to get the women to say "NO". Lupe Ontiverso (center and facing the camera), who played Carmen in the San Diego Rep Production, gives Ana a hard time.

Photo by Ken Jacques, SD Rep

ANA. I don't know everything, but I know a lot. I read a lot. But it just amazes me to hear you talk the way you do. A women's liberation movement happened 20 years ago, and you act like it hasn't even happened.

PANCHA. Mira, all those gringas shouting about liberation hasn't done a thing for me…And if you were married you would realize it. Bueno, and if you know so much how come you're not in college?

ANA. Because I don't have the money. I have to wait a year to be eligible for financial aid.

PANCHA. I always thought that if you were smart enough a college would give you a scholarship. Maybe you should read some more and get one so you don't have to be here making 67 dollars a week and hearing us talk the way we do. *(A car honking is heard outside.)*

CARMEN. Ya llegó mi viejo. Ana, get ready. ¡Vámonos!

ANA. No, Amá, you go. I'll take the bus…I want to finish this last pile.

CARMEN. You do? Ah, I know why you want to stay, metiche. Bueno. Adiós.

WOMEN. Adiós. *(CARMEN leaves. PANCHA collects her belongings. A car honking is heard outside.)*

PANCHA. I'm leaving too.

ROSALI. Pancha, do you want a ride?

PANCHA. Sí, sí. *(They get ready to leave.)*

ROSALI. Adiós, Estela. Good luck on your date with your Tormento. Well, not too good. I hope you won't need to go to confession tomorrow. *(ROSALI and ESTELA giggle.)* Hasta mañana. *(They leave. Soon after ESTELA hangs up the phone.)*

ANA. So who was that?

ESTELA. María…She called to wish me a happy birthday.

ANA. Isn't it this Friday?

ESTELA. Yes, but she couldn't wait to tell me that she's getting married in three months. She wants me to make her wedding dress. *(They continue working.)* Ana, before el Tormento gets here you have to leave.

ANA. Why?

ESTELA. Because I don't want you writing about it. I know what you do in the bathroom.

ANA. Come on, Estela, where else can I write? I come here and all it is, is "work, work, work" from you and Amá. I go home and then she still wants me to help her cook, and clean…

ESTELA. So what are you writing?

ANA. I'm keeping a journal so when I become "rich and famous" I can write my autobiography.

ESTELA. Ana, who do you think you are? "Rich and famous."

ANA. I'm not going to be stuck here forever.

ESTELA. And I am?

ANA. No…I didn't say that. Amá y Apá, always said that you wouldn't do anything with your life, but you're proving them wrong. It takes a lot of guts and courage to do what you're doing. And even if you're in a mess, you have your own business, at 24! I'm very proud of you.

ESTELA (a little embarrassed). All right, Ana, you can stay.

ANA. So when is el Tormento picking you up?

ESTELA. In a few minutes. I won't even have a chance to freshen up. (ESTELA goes to the sink and washes her face. She stares at herself in the mirror.) Ana, do you have any makeup?

ANA. Not with me.

ESTELA (continues to stare at herself with an excited face). I don't have anything to wear! (ESTELA runs to look for clothes to wear. ANA goes to the bathroom and sits on the toilet and begins to write. Spotlight on ANA.)

ANA. Another day and we're in deep…trouble…I keep having arguments with Pancha, and even though she doesn't like me, I feel sort of sorry for her. I wish I could tell her what to do, but she won't listen to me. Like the rest of the women, she won't take me seriously. They make fun of me…So why do I stay?…It's true. I stay. Because no matter how much my mother could try and force me to come, I could decide not to come back. But I do…Why? (Fade out.)

(Lights come on. ESTELA is holding the pink dress. She looks to the bathroom to see if ANA is watching. She then holds the dress to her body as if wearing it. She dances slowly with it, imagining herself dancing with el Tormento. Lights slowly fade.)

SCENE FOUR: THE FOLLOWING DAY, ABOUT 7:10 A.M.

AT RISE: Lights come on after a brief pause. On the calendar it is Tuesday, September 8, 1987. On the clock it is 7:10 a.m. Before the lights are fully on, ESTELA's crying is heard. The WOMEN are gathered around her.

ANA. So what happened?!

ESTELA. He...He...

PANCHA. What did he do?

ESTELA. He...He...

ROSALI & ANA. What?!!

ESTELA. I don't want to talk about it! *(She pulls herself together.)* Let's forget about it and get started on the work... Amá, you said you were going to the bakery.

CARMEN. Ah, sí, sí.

ESTELA. Rosalí, how are you doing with the zippers?

ROSALI. I'm halfway done.

ESTELA. Ana, turn on the iron. There are a lot more dresses that need ironing. Pancha, are you almost done with the skirts for size 3/4?

PANCHA. No. I just started that lot a few minutes before I left yesterday.

CARMEN. Does anybody want anything from the bakery?

ESTELA. I want a juice...Ana, could you...? *(ESTELA decides to look in her purse instead. She takes out all of her pennies and gives them to CARMEN.)*

CARMEN. Estela, you can tell me. What could he have possibly done to get you this upset?

ESTELA. You're so stubborn, Amá! I said nothing happened. I'm just over-reacting.

CARMEN. Just remember, I'm your mother. If you can't trust your mother, who can you trust? *(The WOMEN agree with CARMEN, but ESTELA does not give in. CARMEN leaves. Quickly after, before ANA has a chance to lock the door, CARMEN runs back in and leans on the door to close it with her body. She is breathing heavily.)* It's out there again! Like a vulture!

PANCHA. What?

ALL. ¡La migra! *(They gasp. They all close the curtains and bolt the doors.)*

46

ROSALI. Was it going by slow or was it going by fast?

CARMEN. It was going slow like it was going to turn at the corner and circle around the block and come back!

ANA. You don't know that for sure!

CARMEN. Estela, it just occurred to me. Why don't you go home and work in the garage on our old sewing machine?

ESTELA. I could do that. But I can't. I don't trust you.

ROSALI. We'll work. Just go! ¡Rápido!

ESTELA. And you'll work?

ALL. Yes!!

ESTELA. What should I take with me to work on?

ROSALI. Just go! I'll get my Jaime to take you the work. Go!

ESTELA. Okay! *(ESTELA begins to leave. She opens the door.)* He's out there! *(ESTELA runs to the bathroom.)*

ANA. Who? The man in the van?

PANCHA. No. ¡El Tormento!

ROSALI. Estela, come out of there! Go before they come. ¡Por favor!

CARMEN. Estela, get out of there right now! ¡No seas mensa! Men are not worth crying over. And they're certainly not worth you getting deported. *(CARMEN waits for ESTELA to come out.)* Vas a verlo. ¡Entonces a la fuerza! *(CARMEN pulls on the curtain and tries to drag ESTELA out. ESTELA wraps herself with the curtain and CARMEN is unable to get her out.)*

ESTELA. No! Leave me alone! I'm not coming out!

ANA. Estela, who's that gringa he's kissing? *(The curtain flies open and ESTELA races to the door.)*

ESTELA. Who?!! Where?!!

ANA. I lied. Now go home! *(ANA pushes ESTELA out the door and locks it. Beat.)*

ROSALI *(looking out of the window)*. I don't think they're coming.

PANCHA. Are you sure you saw it, Doña Carmen?

ANA. They would have been here by now. ¿Qué no?

CARMEN. I guess so…I don't understand. *(They sigh in relief.)*

ESTELA *(offstage, knocking on the door).* Ana, let me in.

(ESTELA knocks on the door and ANA finally lets her in.)

ESTELA. I'm going to stay.

CARMEN. All right. *(ESTELA closes the door, locks it. The WOMEN begin working; machines roar.)*

ANA. Shit! I wish we had a fan here. *(ANA turns on the radio.)*

ESTELA. I don't want the dresses getting dirty with the dust. *(Lights fade.)*

SCENE FIVE: LATER THE SAME DAY. LATE AFTERNOON

AT RISE: Lights come on. The WOMEN are busy working. ANA goes to the bathroom. She sits on the toilet and starts writing in her journal. Spotlight on ANA.

ANA. It feels just as bad as when I was doing the fries at McDonald's. Pouring frozen sticks of potatoes into boiling lard and the steam hitting my face for $3.35 an hour…This place stinks! I hate going to the store and having to climb over the winos, and ignore the catcalls of the sexist dope addicts and the smell of urine and marijuana on the street, and…I went to the store today and I saw an old friend. She's pregnant, again. She says she's happy and she doesn't care if she's on welfare. When she was still in high school she told me she knew I was going to do something with my life. I don't want her to know I work here.

(Lights come back on. The WOMEN shift in their chairs, uncomfortable with the heat in their buttocks. ROSALI fans herself and notices that CARMEN has an odd facial expression.)

ROSALI. Doña Carmen, why do you have that strange look on your face?

CARMEN. I reached over to get the next dress and I felt something moving inside. I think I'm pregnant.

PANCHA. Don't say that, Doña Carmen, or I'll lose faith in God. You're almost 50 and already have eight children, I'm barely 32 and can't have any.

CARMEN. Isn't that odd, I'm suppose to be an abuelita by now. Pero no puede ser, it can't be.

ESTELA. Amá, don't tell me you still have sex? At your age and in your physical condition?

ANA. Cállense, I heard something on the news about a raid. *(The WOMEN listen to the radio.)*

RADIO *(voice-over)*. KNXW News all the time…The time now is 2:35 p.m. Twenty illegal aliens were captured today at the Goodnight pillow factory…

PANCHA. That's only a few blocks away!

RADIO *(voice-over)*. The INS was given a tip by anonymous sources yesterday of the factory's illegal hiring of aliens. The owner was fined up to 2,000 dollars per alien… *(PANCHA, CARMEN, and ROSALI do the sign of the holy cross.)*

CARMEN. Estela, why don't you call the Glitz company and ask them, no, demand that they pay you for the past order of dresses. Even if they were late, they still have to pay us. You have to get the money. *(The radio is still on.)*

ESTELA. I don't want to be too pushy. They're the only company that has been willing to give us a contract.

CARMEN. Then do it for Pancha and Rosalí. You haven't paid them and las pobrecitas can't even buy groceries.

ROSALI *(lying)*. I'm all right, don't worry about me.

ANA. Well, I'm not. Estela, just call. *(ESTELA thinks about it, then she decides to do it.)*

ESTELA. Here I go. *(ANA turns off the radio. ESTELA dials the number on the phone and waits.)*

PANCHA. ¿Saben qué? My neighbor who works at the Del Monte canning factory is missing. I have a feeling they deported her. I'm so scared that I'll be waiting for the bus one day and they'll take me.

CARMEN. But you're legal.

PANCHA *(realizing)*. Ayy, I keep forgetting.

ESTELA. Hello…Can I speak to Mrs. Glitz?….Hello, this is Estela. Estela Garcia…No, but we're almost finished…I know we agreed that you would pay me for the last two weeks this Friday, but I was wondering, maybe, if it isn't too much trouble, if I could get an advance check… today…I know…I know…You're right, Mrs. Glitz…Ah… But my workers…I know, but I've got a lawyer working on that…I'll get it to you by next week…No, I mean it this time. Next week…Okay, Mrs. Glitz…I'm sorry…Yes, I'll see you on Friday. *(ESTELA hangs up. Her face expresses worry and fear.)*

CARMEN. ¿Qué te dijo la vieja?

PANCHA. What did she tell you?

ESTELA. She asked about my proof of employment papers again. Then she warned me that if la migra shuts us down, she won't pay us for all the work we've done.

CARMEN. ¡Mendiga vieja!

ANA. Do you think she would really do that? (CARMEN and ESTELA talk among themselves.)

ESTELA. Amá, why is this happening to me? I'm going to get deported, aren't I, Amá?

CARMEN. Mira, supposing you do get deported, we'll get a coyote to smuggle you back in. Somehow we'll find the money.

ESTELA. But I would have let you and everybody down. I'll lose everything that I've worked for, the factory, and my self-respect. And I don't know if I can start again.

CARMEN. Estela, your Apá was thrown back to Mexico four times, but he kept coming back. If you did it once, you can do it again.

ESTELA. I hope so. (ESTELA pulls herself together and continues working. She picks up a bundle of sewn skirts and looks at them. She discovers that they have been sewn wrong.) Pancha, do you realize you sewed all of the size 3/4 skirts backwards?

PANCHA. I did? No, I didn't!

ESTELA. Look! This is the outside of the material and this is the inside. Have you been doing all the lots this way?

PANCHA. I think so.

ESTELA. ¡Ay, no! More repairs! Pancha, please do them again.

PANCHA. No! It's so hot. I don't even feel like working. How do you expect us to work with this heat?

ESTELA. Pancha, I'll help you take them apart.

ANA. Couldn't you open the door?

ESTELA. No!

PANCHA. I can't work like this.

ESTELA. We're going to have to. *(PANCHA grabs the skirt and begins to take them apart. ESTELA is looking at another lot and discovers the stained dresses that CARMEN hid.)* ¡Amá! What did I tell you about the mole?! *(ESTELA shoves a dress in CARMEN's face.)*

CARMEN. The stains are not so obvious. I was going to clean them, I swear. I didn't want you to see them and get worried.

ESTELA. It's going to be hell trying to take the stains out! *(ESTELA catches ANA accidently burning the tul.)* Not so close! You're burning the tul! Pay close attention to your work or don't do it. Have you been burning it on the other dresses too?! *(ESTELA quickly looks at the dresses on the racks and those that ANA has finished ironing.)*

ANA. I thought if I did it this way it would be okay and save us time. I can't stand the heat and the steam.

ESTELA. Can't any of you do anything right? Do I have to do everything myself so that these dresses get finished? *(PANCHA gets busy pulling on the two pieces of material on the skirt instead of cutting the sewn thread one stitch at a time.)* Pancha, don't pull on them or you'll tear them. I said I was going to help you do the repairs.

PANCHA. I want to get out of here and go home.

ESTELA. You have to finish this work.

PANCHA. Not in this heat!

ANA. Estela, please open the door!

ESTELA. For the last time, I won't!

PANCHA. Then I'll open it. *(PANCHA walks determinedly towards the door. ESTELA stands in her way.)* We're all burning in here. I'm getting dizzy.

ESTELA. I'm sorry it's so hot, but the van may be out there and I don't want them to see anything.

PANCHA. It's so selfish of you to keep the door closed when we are all burning!

ESTELA. I'm burning too!

PANCHA. But you're the one with the criminal record! It's not fair that we are all paying for your fault. We are all legal now!

ESTELA. Then go! Open the door, then leave.

PANCHA. All right! I'll leave, but with my work. *(PANCHA grabs the skirts,*

begins pulling on them, tearing the material.) Let's see what else I've done. *(PANCHA continues tearing. ESTELA tries to stop her by holding PANCHA's hands. PANCHA and ESTELA begin to get physical, almost ready to strike each other. ROSALI quickly steps between them to prevent them from hitting each other.)*

CARMEN. Estela, ¡párale!

ROSALI. ¡Basta! ¡No se peleén! *(ROSALI faints and falls to the floor. ESTELA and PANCHA stop fighting.)*

CARMEN. Rosalí!

ANA. Rosalí, are you all right?

CARMEN. What could be wrong with her?

PANCHA. It's this pinche heat! It's your fault, Estela. Here you have us all locked up! See what happened?!

ESTELA *(shakes ROSALI, who does not respond).* Rosalí, please wake up!

PANCHA. Let's take her to the hospital!

CARMEN. ¡¿Pero que locura?! The hospital is three blocks away. We can't carry her, la migra is going to see us.

PANCHA. Ayy si, ¿entonces qué quiere? You want her to die?

CARMEN. She's not going to die!

PANCHA. And how do you know?

CARMEN. Don't exaggerate! *(While PANCHA and CARMEN argue, ANA thinks quickly of what to do. She searches around the bathroom for something. She finds ESTELA's perfume and grabs some tissue. ANA uses it to wake up ROSALI. ROSALI becomes conscious and PANCHA and CARMEN finally stop arguing.)*

ROSALI. Ah…

PANCHA. Rosalí, you want to go to the hospital?

ROSALI. ¿Qué páso?

CARMEN. M'ija, you fainted.

ANA. Are you okay?

ROSALI. Sí…Sí…I'm okay.

PANCHA. I'm gonna take you home.

ROSALI. I'll just rest a little...I'll feel better...

PANCHA. You can't continue working like this. I'll take you home. It's no bother, because I'm going home myself. *(CARMEN gets a glass of water and an aspirin.)*

CARMEN. Pobrecita, here, drink this.

ESTELA. Rosalí, I'm sorry.

PANCHA *(helps ROSALI up)*. Where's your bag? *(ROSALI points to it. PANCHA gets the bag.)* Let's go. *(PANCHA leaves with ROSALI without hesitation or saying good-bye. ESTELA fights the urge to cry.)*

ESTELA *(to herself)*. I'm sorry, Rosalí.

CARMEN. Don't blame yourself. Something like this was going to happen.

ANA. Isn't Rosalí the only one who knows how to set up the over-lock machine? *(ANA and CARMEN look at each other worried. ESTELA has an expression of hopelessness. Lights slowly fade out.)*

END OF ACT ONE

REAL WOMEN HAVE CURVES

ACT TWO

SCENE ONE: WEDNESDAY, SEPTEMBER 9TH, ABOUT 8:15 A.M.

AT RISE: CARMEN and ESTELA are the only ones present, working silently. On the clock it is 8:15 a.m. On the calendar it is Wednesday, September 9, 1987.

CARMEN. I don't think Pancha's coming back.

ESTELA. She's only an hour late. Maybe she went to visit Rosalí at her house.

CARMEN. Pancha is never late. *(Footsteps are heard outside. Then the code knock is heard. ESTELA smiles and goes to open the doors.)*

ESTELA. See, Amá! I knew she would come. *(ESTELA rushes to open the door. ANA is at the door.)* Oh, it's just you.

(ANA quickly comes in carrying a brown paper bag with detergent which she puts on the table.)

ANA. ¡Miren! Come look out the window. There's this strange homeless person outside. *(They go look.)*

CARMEN. What's so strange about him?

ANA. I don't recognize him.

ESTELA. So?

ANA. I think he's just disguised. He doesn't look desperate enough.

CARMEN. I've never seen him before.

ANA. I think he's a spy?

ESTELA. A spy?

ANA. Look! There's Pancha!

ESTELA. God! Thank you! She's come back!

CARMEN. But look, he's talking to her and she's pointing this way! (They drop to the floor. A few seconds later they go back to looking.) I wonder what he's asking her?

ESTELA. I wonder what she's telling him?

ANA. ¡Aguas! Here she comes.

(They scatter. ANA takes out the stain remover from the bag. CARMEN goes back to sewing. The code knock is heard and ESTELA opens the door. PANCHA comes in.)

ESTELA. Pancha, what did the bum ask you?

PANCHA. The bum? Ooo. He asked me where your Tormento lives.

ANA. I guess he wasn't a spy after all.

PANCHA. ¡N'ombre! He's just another one of his vago friends.

CARMEN. ¡Bola de viejos cochinos! No good drug addicts!

ESTELA. Ya! Stop talking about him!

CARMEN. Are you defending him? After what he did?

ANA (aside). Amá, Estela finally told you?

CARMEN. No. I'm trying to get it out of her.

ESTELA. Forget it! I'll never tell you what happened on the date.

ANA. Okay, Estela. Be like that. I'll never tell you anything either. (ESTELA doesn't budge. ANA and CARMEN give up.)

CARMEN. Panchita, we were afraid you wouldn't come back.

PANCHA. Why?

CARMEN. Well, after what happened yesterday.

PANCHA. I have to come to work even if I don't want to…I went to visit Rosalí this morning.

ANA. How is she doing?

PANCHA. She's doing better.

ESTELA. Is there any chance of her coming back this week?

PANCHA. No se. She looks pale. This heat will be bad for her. I'm surprised I didn't faint myself.

ESTELA. Maybe I will get a fan.

PANCHA. Estela, what do you want me to work on?

ESTELA. I don't know how we are going to manage without her. Pancha, please finish the zippers that Rosalí was working on.

CARMEN. Estela, give me the manual for the over-lock machine. I'm going to try and set it up myself.

ESTELA. Alli esta en el cajon. We'll just have to go on without her. Ana, did you get the stain remover?

ANA. It's on the table. How many dresses need washing?

ESTELA. Twelve. I should put my mother to wash them, but since she'll be busy with the over-lock I guess I'll do them.

ANA. How many dresses have we finished?

ESTELA. They're on the racks. And there are a couple in that box that just need ironing.

ANA (looking at the racks). That's all?

ESTELA. I found ten dresses with the tul burnt in them. Those were almost finished, but now the tul has to be replaced.

ANA. I guess I'll do that.

ESTELA. Amá, can you stay late today?

CARMEN. Pues sí.

ESTELA. Ana, will you stay late too?

ANA. Stay late?…Sure. (ANA irons a dress carefully and slowly. ESTELA observes ANA for a few seconds.)

ESTELA. Ana, can you iron faster? Just make them look decent. *(ANA frowns at her suggestion and looks to PANCHA who is attaching hanging strings on the dresses next to her.)*

ANA *(to PANCHA)*. It's not that I don't iron fast enough, it's that whenever I finish ironing a dress I stop for a minute to really look at it. I never realized just how much work, puro lomo, as my mother would say, went into making it. Then I imagine the dress at Bloomingdale's and I see a tall and skinny woman looking at it. She instantly gets it and with no second thoughts she says "charge it!" She doesn't think of the life of the dress before the rack, of the labor put into it. I shake the dress a little and try to forget it's not for me. I place a plastic bag over it then I put it on the rack and push it away. It happens to me with every dress.

PANCHA. What an imagination. So what are you gonna study when you go to college next year? Where are you going?

ANA. To New York University. I'm going to study writing.

CARMEN. Así es que you better be quiet, don't tell her any chisme or one day you're gonna read about it.

PANCHA. And you think you'll make it?

ANA. I think so.

PANCHA. Pos, I do think you're a bit loquita, but if that's what you need. I think you'll make it.

ANA. Gracias, Pancha. *(PANCHA smiles at ANA seeing her differently for the first time. Meanwhile, CARMEN is frustrated with the over-lock machine.)*

CARMEN. ¡Ayy no! ¡No puedo! I try and I try and I can't! ¡Esta cochinada no sirve!

ESTELA. But what can we do? Who else could do it? Can you do it, Pancha?

PANCHA. I don't know anything about those new machines.

ESTELA. Amá, give me the manual. *(ESTELA grabs the manual and begins to work on the machine. Talking to the machine:)* Please, maquinita. If you behave I'll put on you all the oil you want. Maquinita, if you love me, help me.

CARMEN *(touching her stomach)*. Ana, come here, quick. Feel my stomach. *(ANA puts her hand over CARMEN's stomach.)* Can you feel the baby kicking?

ANA. No...Amá, are you sure you're pregnant?

CARMEN. I think so. Aver, Pancha, tell me if you feel anything.

PANCHA. I'm busy, Doña Carmen.

CARMEN. Just come quick, Panchita. Ana doesn't believe me. *(PANCHA gets up from her chair and goes over to CARMEN. She places her hand on CARMEN's stomach.)*

PANCHA. I don't feel anything. I think the heat is getting to you too.

CARMEN. ¿Cómo puede ser? I can feel it! *(PANCHA nods her head and walks away fanning herself. She heads to the bathroom.)*

ANA. How many months should you be pregnant by now? I haven't noticed you getting any bigger.

CARMEN. I don't know. I've always been fat. I haven't noticed either.

ANA. Have you the symptoms?

CARMEN. Not all of them, but I've been pregnant enough times to know.

ANA. Are you going to keep it?

CARMEN. What do you mean?

ANA. You don't have to have it.

CARMEN. Ana, I don't want to talk about this.

(Spotlight on PANCHA. PANCHA stands on the toilet in front of the small window. She opens the window and bathes her face with the breeze. PANCHA begins to cry.)

PANCHA. Que bonito viento. Wind, that's what I am. *(Touching her stomach.)* Empty, like an old rag...*(Praying.)* Diosito, why don't you make me a real woman? If I can't have children, why did you make me a woman? *(PANCHA wipes her tears.)*

(Lights come on.)

ESTELA *(talking to the machine)*. Maquinita, I'm going to set you up even if it's the last thing I do in this country. *(She holds the manual and follows directions.)* All right. Five threads. They all start from their spools onto the holes, then straight down, into the loops. Then they turn, go in between more loops underneath, then they all go into their needles. Then the electricity comes on...*(She turns on the machine.)*...I insert a piece of material, step on the pedal and...Ta-da! A chain of interwoven threads! I did it!

CARMEN. You fixed it? ¿Pero cómo?

ESTELA. I persisted and I did it!

CARMEN. ¡Mira que inteligente!

ANA. That's great, Estela! Now we don't have to worry about it anymore. (*They hear footsteps outside. They instantly freeze and become silent. They look to each other then CARMEN, ANA, and PANCHA quickly go to their purses. Someone is heard outside, then letters are slipped in through the mail slot. The WOMEN relax.*) Just the mailman...

(*The WOMEN suddenly realize that it probably means bad news for ESTELA. ESTELA picks up an envelope and reads it. No one asks what it says out of respect for her, but they all know it's another letter from the lawyer. ESTELA opens it and is about to read it when they hear footsteps outside. They grab their "Temporary Employment" cards from their purses. ESTELA hides behind CARMEN. Then the code knock is heard. The WOMEN rush to the door. ESTELA opens the door and ROSALI is behind the bar door.*)

EVERYONE. What are you doing here?!

ESTELA. Aren't you suppose to be resting?

ROSALI. I was in bed and I kept imagining Estela getting deported. So I had to come back. I know how badly you must need the over-lock machine.

ESTELA. I fixed it!

ROSALI (*disappointed*). You did? Well, where are the zippers so I can get started now?

PANCHA. I finished all the zippers.

ROSALI. You did?

ESTELA. Rosalí, I'd rather you go back and get well.

ROSALI. No, Estela, I'm fine. I can help.

ESTELA. It's not worth it if we're fighting and getting sick because of this heat.

ROSALI. It wasn't just the heat...I hadn't eaten and that's why I fainted. I didn't want you to think it was your fault.

PANCHA. But why do you need to lose weight? 'Tas flaca. (*ROSALI smiles, but doesn't believe PANCHA.*)

CARMEN. Have you eaten already, you still look pale?

ROSALI. No, I'm not hungry, Doña Carmen.

CARMEN. But that's what you have been saying and look what happened. Come on, eat something.

ROSALI. I am not hungry.

ANA. Rosalí, you can't see yourself the way we see you and that's why you think you're fat.

CARMEN. Rosalí, you need to eat something.

ROSALI. I'm not hungry!

CARMEN. You need to eat something! (*ROSALI looks at each of them and finally reveals the truth.*)

ROSALI. I'm not hungry because I've been living on diet pills.

CARMEN. So that's the secret diet? Ayy, Rosalí, don't you know those cochinadas are no good?

ANA. They're real bad for you because I read they're addictive.

ROSALI. I know. When I fainted I saw my body lying there, I thought I was going to die. I couldn't feel my body. And I just kept seeing Estela being deported. Estela, I want to come back to work. This is more important to me than being a size seven.

ESTELA (*embraces ROSALI*). Gracias…Can you work late?

ROSALI. Claro.

ESTELA. And you too, Pancha?

PANCHA. Pos bueno.

CARMEN. Entonces todas a trabajar! (*The WOMEN go to their sewing stations. ESTELA takes out her notebook and dictates the work.*)

ESTELA. Amá, let Rosalí do the over-lock work, she's faster. I want you to do lots size two through six. Pancha, you do lots size seven through twelve. Ana, you know what to do. (*ESTELA takes control and the WOMEN are determined to finish. The machines roar like race cars taking off. Lights slowly fade.*)

SCENE TWO: THURSDAY, SEPTEMBER 10TH, ABOUT 2:00 A.M.

AT RISE: Lights come on. It is 2:00 a.m., and street sounds are heard outside.

ROSALI looks around and then stares at her stomach.

ROSALI. Did you hear that?

ANA. No, what?

ROSALI. A stomach growling. Whose stomach was it?

ESTELA. I don't know, but I'm hungry.

ANA. Me too. Amá, is there any rice left?

ROSALI. Did you hear it again?

PANCHA. Rosalí, it's your panza.

ROSALI. Yeah, it's me! I haven't heard my stomach growling in so long.

ESTELA. What's there to eat?

CARMEN. I might have something in my purse. Why don't we make something?

PANCHA. All this noise is driving me crazy. I'm going deaf. *(PANCHA turns on the radio. CARMEN gets up, looks around the table then in the refrigerator. All the WOMEN search in their purses for food.)*

CARMEN. Aaaa, I found something. Tortillas and…the mole!

ALL. Not the mole!

PANCHA. I've got something. *(PANCHA takes out a large amount of food from her purse. The WOMEN are surprised with every item she takes out: a box of fried chicken, a hamburger, a bag of chips, a bag of cookies, and a Diet Coke.)* I'm on a diet!

CARMEN *(aside)*. Se ve. *(On the radio a "cumbia" has just finished. Then a DISC JOCKEY with a very mellow voice comes on the air.)*

DISC JOCKEY *(voice-over)*. It's 2:25 a.m. on an early Thursday morning… I'm falling asleep here to pay my bills. And if you're listening now, you probably are too. So this is for you night owls! The ones that do the night shifts no one wants to do! *(The song "Tequila" blasts on the radio. The WOMEN are so sleepy, they jump around to the music trying to awaken. They eat and shake at the same time. Lights slowly fade.)*

SCENE THREE: SAME DAY, ABOUT 2:00 P.M.

AT RISE: Lights come on. It is Thursday, September 10, 1987. On the clock

it is 2 p.m. The WOMEN are wearing the same clothes as the day before. As usual, it is extremely hot.

CARMEN *(smelling her armpits)*. Phueeehh! ¡Fuchi! I stink. Aquí huele a pura cuchupeta y pedo. Phuehhh! Who farted?

ESTELA. Amá, it's probably you who did it. Like they say, the one who smells it first is the one who has it underneath her skirt.

ANA. ¡Que calor! It feels like we're in hell!

PANCHA. How many more dresses to finish, Estela?

ESTELA. Fifteen.

ROSALI. Only fifteen?!

CARMEN. Dios mio, ya mero acabamos.

ESTELA *(counting dresses on rack)*. 184, 185, 186. No, we only need 14!

ANA. What a relief! We're almost finished. *(ANA decides to take off her blouse, leaving on her sweaty bra.)*

CARMEN *(shocked at ANA's actions)*. Ana, what are you doing?!

ANA. All this steam has me sweating like a pig.

CARMEN. We're sweating too, but we don't go taking our clothes off!

ANA. So why don't you? We're all women. We all have the same.

CARMEN. Not really. You have bigger chichis.

ANA. And you have a bigger panza!

CARMEN. That's because I'm pregnant!

ESTELA. You mean we're definitely going to have another baby brat to take care of?

ANA. Amá, do you really want to have it?

PANCHA. Doña Carmen, give it to me if you don't want it.

CARMEN. I can't just get rid of it, either way…But I don't want to have it.

PANCHA. But you're lucky, Doña Carmen.

CARMEN. No. It seems all I do is have children. One after another. I'm tired of this! I can't have this baby. I'll die. Last time I was pregnant the doctor said I almost didn't make it.

ANA. Amá, I didn't know that happened.

CARMEN. Every time your Apá touches me, the next day I'm pregnant. When he would leave me in Mexico to go to el norte, he would leave me pregnant so no man would look at me and desire me. I was very beautiful.

ANA. You still are, Amá.

CARMEN. I was always scared of him. And I let myself get fat after you were born hoping he would be disgusted by me and not touch me anymore.

ANA. Why didn't you just say "No"?

CARMEN. Because, M'ija, I was never taught how to say no.

PANCHA (comes forward and confesses). It's easy, Doña Carmen. You tell him "No!" and you get out from the bed.

ANA (realizing what PANCHA is saying). Pancha?

PANCHA. And then you take the blanket. (ANA embraces PANCHA as the WOMEN laugh.)

ANA (to the WOMEN). Aren't you hot in those clothes? I feel sticky. I'm going to take off my pants. (ANA takes off her pants. She is left wearing her bra and panties.)

CARMEN. Ana, aren't you embarrassed?

ANA. Why? You already think I'm fat.

CARMEN. You know, Ana, you're not bad looking. If you lost 20 pounds you would be very beautiful.

ANA. Story of my life…Go ahead. Pick on me.

CARMEN. Why don't you lose weight? Last time you lost weight you were so thin and beatifuller.

ANA. I like myself. Why should I?

PANCHA. Doña Carmen, Ana is very pretty. She looks good the way she is.

ANA. Thank you, Pancha.

CARMEN. It's because she's young. At this age young girls should try to make themselves as attractive as possible.

ANA. Why? Why not always? You're overweight too.

CARMEN. But I'm already married.

ANA. Is that it? Make myself attractive so that I can catch a man?

ESTELA *(sarcastically)*. Ana, listen to them, learn now, "or you'll end up like Estela."

ANA. Amá, I do want to lose weight. But part of me doesn't because my weight says to everyone, "Fuck you!"

CARMEN. ¡Ave Maria Purissima!

ANA. It says, "How dare you try to define me and tell me what I have to be and look like!" So I keep it on. I don't want to be a sex object.

ESTELA. Me neither.

CARMEN. ¡Otra!

ROSALI. What's wrong with being a sex object? What's wrong with wanting to be thin and sexy?

ESTELA. Because I want to be taken seriously, to be considered a person… You know with Andrés, on our date…

CARMEN. ¡Aver cuentanos! What happened on that infamous date?

ESTELA. On our date I got all fixed up…Then he showed up with jeans and a t-shirt and he smelled like he had been drinking…He wanted to take me to the drive-in and when I asked, "Why the drive-in?" He said because there he could kiss me and give me what I wanted…He said, "I don't care if you're fat. I like you even better; more to grab." That got me so angry! I thought he was interested in me because he was impressed that I owned this factory, my "intelligence," that I…"I'm smart"…When am I going to meet that man who will see the real me?

CARMEN. So that's what happened.

ROSALI. Pues if he has a brother, tell him about me. I think I'm going to die a virgin.

ANA. You're still a virgin?! Dang!

PANCHA. ¿Pero tu Jaime? Nothing?

ROSALI. Nothing. I've felt fat ever since I can remember and I didn't want anybody to touch me until I got thin.

ANA. Is that why you were starving yourself?

ROSALI. That's part of it.

ESTELA. Rosalí, you're not fat.

ROSALI. Of course I am. Look at my nalgas…And my hips! Paresen de elefante.

ANA. No they don't!

ROSALI. I look like a cow.

CARMEN. You look like a cow? Where does that leave us?

PANCHA. Rosalí, you're so skinny in comparison to all of us.

ROSALI. No I'm not. Here, look at my fat hips. (ROSALI pulls down her pants and shows them her hips.)

ESTELA. That's nothing. ¡Mira! (ESTELA pulls down her pants and shows ROSALI her hips.)

CARMEN (to ROSALI). At least you have a waist! (CARMEN pulls down her skirt and shows ROSALI her stomach.)

PANCHA. ¡Uuuu! That's nothing, Doña Carmen! (PANCHA raises her skirt and shows them her stomach.)

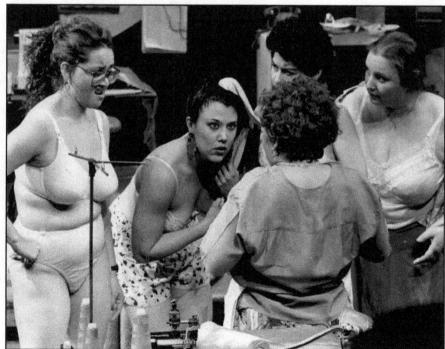

Photo by Ken Jacques, SD Rep

The women compare their stretch marks and are amazed by Carmen's (Lupe Ontiveros with her back to the camera) caesarian scar. Josefina López, on the left, plays Ana in the San Diego Rep Production.

ROSALI. But you don't understand. I've got all these stretch marks on my arms…(*ROSALI opens her blouse and shows them the stretch marks close to her breasts.*)

ESTELA. They're small. I have stretch marks that run from my hips to my knees. (*ESTELA takes off her pants to show them.*)

CARMEN. Stretch marks?! Stretch marks!! You want to see stretch marks? (*CARMEN lifts her blouse and exposes her stretch marks and scars.*) Stretch marks!!! (*ANA sits back as she watches the WOMEN slowly undressing. They continue to compare body parts ad libbing. Finally they are all in their underwear and they stop to notice CARMEN's stretch marks.*)

ANA. Amá, what's that scar you have on your stomach?

CARMEN. This one? That was Estela.

ANA. It's such a big scar.

CARMEN. Estela was a big baby.

ESTELA. I gave you the most trouble, didn't I?

CARMEN. A-ha. But that's okay. I've heard Elizabeth Potaylor has one just like it.

PANCHA (*suddenly realizing*). Look how we are? What if somebody came in and saw us like this?

CARMEN (*fanning her breasts*). Pero que bien se siente. It feels so good to be rid of these clothes and let it all hang out.

ANA. Pues sí. Nobody is watching us. Who cares how we look.

ESTELA. So this is how we look without clothes?

CARMEN. Just as fat and beautiful…(*They all hug in a semi- circle laughing triumphantly.*)

ANA. We can finally relax.

ESTELA. We're not finished yet.

ROSALI. Estela, all we need are 14 dresses.

PANCHA. Those we can finish tomorrow for sure.

CARMEN. So what are we going to do to celebrate?

ESTELA. To celebrate what? Finishing on time for the first time?

PANCHA. No. All of us, most of us, finally being legal.

CARMEN. It's true. And once you get the card you can do anything you want. Tengo fe…Estela, I've been thinking… You know what we could do? We could copy the patterns for these dresses, make the dresses ourselves, and have a fashion show. Maybe we could model them ourselves. *(The WOMEN laugh at the thought.)*

ANA. No, that's a great idea! Why don't we make them in larger sizes too?

PANCHA. Está loquita, but sometimes she makes sense. We could probably sell more if we made them in larger sizes.

ROSALI. You know what we could also do? Jaime could sell them in the flea market. If they sell, little by little we could grow…

ESTELA *(jumping in)*. And from there, if we make a lot of money, more money than what we're making now, maybe we can rent a place downtown on Broadway and start a boutique!!

ANA. But we'll need a name.

ROSALI. Well, why not just Estela Garcia?

ANA. I was thinking of something more French.

CARMEN. No. A French name would make it sound chafas. No, Estela Garcia sounds fine.

PANCHA. Estela, maybe you could go to school and study fashion design and design our dresses.

ESTELA. Yeah. I could do that. *(They all stop to imagine the possibilities.)*

CARMEN. So what are we doing to celebrate?

ESTELA. First let's finish, then we can talk about celebrating. *(They go back to work. CARMEN takes off her glasses as she fans her face.)*

CARMEN. Que calor. I'll be glad when all of this is over.

ANA. Estela, can we please open the door?

PANCHA. Open the door? ¿Pa qué? So people that pass by can see us like this?

ROSALI. But it's so hot!

ANA. I don't think they're coming. Besides we're almost finished. *(The WOMEN look to ESTELA for a decision.)*

ESTELA. Okay…Amá, open the door. *(CARMEN goes to open the door. She turns back to ESTELA as if to make sure. CARMEN opens the door and fans*

herself with it. Beat. CARMEN holds the door wide open and walks outside. The WOMEN can't believe their eyes. A few seconds later CARMEN runs back in screaming.)

CARMEN. Estela! It's out there! ¡La Migra! They're coming!! *(CARMEN shuts the door. All the WOMEN immediately get dressed.)*

ESTELA. No! It's not fair! We were almost finished!! *(The WOMEN dig into their purses for their cards. ESTELA can only cry in desperation. She cannot find her clothes and has to head for the door in her slip. ROSALI and ANA peek through the curtains and quickly make a realization.)*

ROSALI. Doña Carmen, that's not la migra!

ANA. It's the police!

CARMEN. The police? *(She peeks through the curtain.)* ¡¿Cómo?!

ANA. That's the guy I thought was a spy. He's an undercover cop!

ROSALI. Like in the movies.

ANA. It's a drug bust!

ESTELA. Where?

ROSALI. I think it's el Tormento's house. *(ESTELA moves for the door.)*

ANA. ¡Sí, el Tormento! They're taking him away. *(ESTELA and ANA jump up in excitement.)*

CARMEN. That's what he deserves! *(The police are heard driving away.)*

PANCHA. That's good they're taking him away in the van. ¡Bola de viejos cochinos! *(The WOMEN laugh together. Then ANA stops laughing.)*

ANA. Amá, was that the same van you saw Monday?

CARMEN *(nodding her head hesitantly)*. I think so.

ANA. On Tuesday?

CARMEN. I think so.

ANA. On Wednesday?

CARMEN *(sheepishly)*. Pos sí. *(She puts on her glasses.)*

ANA. Amá, that wasn't la migra. Everyone knows the vans are green!

CARMEN. I didn't.

ESTELA. How could you not know?

CARMEN. Pos no se; all those years of being undocumented I always imagined they were black.

PANCHA & ROSALI. Ayy, Doña Carmen!!!

CARMEN. Phueehhh! Tanto pedo y para nada.

ESTELA. Thank God! ¡Que susto!

CARMEN. It's time to retire! *(They laugh in relief then they become silent.)*

ANA. Well, it's over…for now. *(Beat.)*

ESTELA. If you want to take the rest of the day off…We'll finish tomorrow.

PANCHA. We can go?

ESTELA. Yes. I know how tired you must be. Go ahead. I'll stay and continue working.

ROSALI. I can't wait to go home and take a shower.

CARMEN. Si, porfavor, bañate…Tomorrow, I'm going to make a fresh batch of mole.

PANCHA *(scared for her life)*. Doña Carmen, why don't you make some rice? *(ANA, PANCHA, and ROSALI immediately run out.)*

CARMEN *(muttering to them)*. Ingrates! *(To ESTELA.)* Are you sure you won't need us anymore?

ESTELA. No. Now go! Before I change my mind. Don't you want to go outside? *(They gather their bags and quickly leave. ESTELA is left alone. Lights fade a little. She turns on the radio to a mellow jazz station. She goes around doing a final clean up, turning off lights and machines. She stops, recalling the five of them in their underwear, fantasizing about their own boutique. She grins to herself. She whispers.)* Large sizes? *(ESTELA shakes her head, dismissing the idea, but then stops and runs to a pile of stocked material. She eagerly searches and finds a roll of red fabric. ESTELA excitedly runs to a station and begins taking her measurements. As the lights slowly fade, we see ESTELA measuring herself with pride and pleasure, half laughing to herself, half defiantly…about to design and make her first dress. Lights slowly fade to black.)*

SCENE FOUR: FRIDAY, SEPTEMBER 11TH, ABOUT 2:25 P.M.

AT RISE: Lights come on. There are no more dresses on the racks. It is Friday, on the clock it is 2:25 p.m. ANA and PANCHA are busy blowing up balloons.

69

ROSALI is cleaning up. There is a birthday cake with a large candle of the number "25." A large sign reads: "Happy Birthday Estela." Footsteps are heard outside. ANA runs to turn off the electricity, the WOMEN hide…The door opens.

WOMEN. Surprise!!!!! *(ROSALI takes a picture. CARMEN stands motionless holding a pot.)*

ANA. Amá, we thought you were…

ROSALI. Doña Carmen, what's wrong?

CARMEN. I just got back from the doctor.

PANCHA. What did she tell you?

ANA. ¿Amá?

CARMEN. She says I'm not pregnant.

ANA. Then why are you sad?

CARMEN. She says, "it's only menopause." When you reach menopause it's over. You're no longer a woman. Se te seca allí abajo.

ANA. Amá, you are a real woman.

CARMEN. What I should be is a grandmother by now, but the way you and Estela are going, I won't be one for a long time…¿Y Estela?

ROSALI. She hasn't returned from delivering the dresses. She should be coming soon.

CARMEN. Here. *(Gives ROSALI the pot.)* I made rice.

(They hear footsteps outside. ANA turns off the lights. The door opens.)

WOMEN. Surprise!!! *(ROSALI takes another picture. Lights come on. ESTELA stands shocked in her new dress.)*

ESTELA. You remembered?

ROSALI *(gives ESTELA a gift)*. Happy twenty-fifth birthday, you old maid!

CARMEN *(referring to her dress)*. Estela, did you make it? Que bonita te ves, very nice. You see you're not ugly, you just didn't know how to dress.

ESTELA *(hugs ROSALI)*. I brought a gift for all of you. *(ESTELA goes outside and brings in a large fan.)*

PANCHA. Now the boss treats us pretty good.

ESTELA. Because now I have money.

CARMEN. Did Mrs. Glitz finally pay you?

ESTELA. Yes, she paid me, but she kept threatening me… I've written out all the checks. (*ESTELA pulls out the checks from her bag. She distributes them, the first check going to PANCHA.*)

PANCHA (*looking at her check*). This is the biggest check I've ever gotten. (*ESTELA gives ROSALI her check.*)

ROSALI. Too bad I've already spent it on the Americana Express.

CARMEN. ¡Válgame! I didn't realize how much money you owed me.

ANA (*looks at her check, disappointed*). Estela, come here. (*ANA and ESTELA talk among themselves.*) Estela, how come I only get this much?

ESTELA. I took out for taxes.

ANA. Taxes? But you're not reporting…

CARMEN. How much do you have left?

ESTELA. About six hundred. I'll send the lawyer some more money today. Maybe they won't take me to court.

PANCHA. But if they deport you and take everything, we won't be able to work towards the boutique.

ROSALI. We're also going to have to look for another job. (*The WOMEN stare at the floor.*)

ANA. Back to McDonald's. (*Beat.*)

PANCHA. Estela, I know my husband isn't going to like it, but here. (*PANCHA extends her check to ESTELA.*) Take it. Pay me back when you can.

ESTELA. Pancha, are you sure?

PANCHA. No, pero, take it before I change my mind.

ESTELA. Muchas gracias…(*They try hugging, but they find it difficult, it's awkward. To herself*). Let's see. How much more do I need? (*CARMEN stares at her check for a few more seconds and slowly says good-bye to it.*)

CARMEN. Ten, ten. Take mine too. What kind of mother would I be if I didn't give it back?

ESTELA (*hugs CARMEN*). ¡Que buena es!

CARMEN. You see, ¿No que no te quiero? It's because I love you that I make your life so miserable.

ESTELA. Don't love me so much. *(ROSALI thinks about it too.)*

ROSALI. I guess the Americana Express can wait…Here is my check too. *(ESTELA hugs ROSALI. Now they all look to ANA. ANA holds her check tightly.)*

ANA. No, not me…I'm going to buy a typewriter…I can't. *(The WOMEN don't say anything, but continue staring at ANA.)* I really need this typewriter. I have this essay I have to type up for a contest…All right…Take half of it. *(ESTELA semi-hugs ANA.)*

ESTELA. Excuse me for just a minute. I have to make a phone call. *(ESTELA picks up the phone and dials.)* Hello…May I speak to Mrs. Glitz? This is Estela Garcia. I'm just calling to thank you for keeping your word and finally paying us today. I also wanted to tell you that you are a mean, wicked, bitter, unsympathetic, greedy, rude, awful…

ANA. Capitalist!

ESTELA. Capitalist!…No! We quit…Yeah, well I'll see you in hell. *(The WOMEN are shocked, incredulous of her actions.)*

CARMEN. ¡Maldita! What have you done?

PANCHA. You got us fired, didn't you?

ESTELA. No, we quit. *(ESTELA laughs excitedly.)*…Don't worry about the work. I got us a contract with Señor Vasquez!

EVERYONE. Señor Vasquez!!!

CARMEN. How did you convince him?

ESTELA. I just told him that we are the most hardworking women he could ever ask for. I know, I lied, but I got it.

EVERYONE. ¡Ayy! *(All the WOMEN embrace excitedly. ROSALI brings out the birthday cake. They sing "Happy Birthday" not realizing that ROSALI is holding the cake backwards and it reads 52 instead of 25. They stop halfway through and turn it.)*

ESTELA. Fifty two?! *(They continue singing.)*

ROSALI. Ana, light up the candle so I can take a picture… *(ANA lights up the candle.)* Okay, Estela, blow out the candle. *(ESTELA stops to make a wish then blows it out. ROSALI takes a picture of her.)*

ANA. What did you wish for?

ESTELA. Maybe when you get back from New York you'll see. *(ANA and PANCHA give their gift to ESTELA.)*

ROSALI. Ana, here, take a picture of us to remember this week…*(ROSALI gives ANA the camera. The WOMEN gather for the photo.)*

ANA. Okay! Ready?…One…two…three! *(The WOMEN suddenly hold up their "Temporary Residence Cards.")*

WOMEN. Green!!! *(The WOMEN freeze in a pool of light. ANA steps out and turns to the audience. The WOMEN exit backstage. Spotlight on ANA.)*

ANA. I always took their work for granted, to be simple and unimportant. I was not proud to be working there at the beginning. I was only glad to know that because I was educated, I wasn't going to end up like them. I was going to be better than them. And I wanted to show them how much smarter and liberated I was. I was going to teach them about the women's liberation movement, about sexual liberation and all the things a so-called educated American woman knows. But in their subtle ways they taught me about resistance. About a battle no one was fighting for them except themselves. About the loneliness of being women in a country that looks down on us for being mothers and submissive wives. With their work that seems simple and unimportant, they are fighting…Perhaps the greatest thing I learned from them is that women are powerful, especially when working together…As for me, well, I settled for a secondhand typewriter and I wrote an essay on my experience and I was awarded a fellowship. So I went to New York and was a starving writer for some time before I went to New York University. When I came back the plans for making the boutique were no longer a dream, but a reality. *(ANA picks up a beautiful designer jacket and puts it on.)* Because I now wear original designs from Estela Garcia's boutique, "Real Women Have Curves."

(The lights come on and all the WOMEN enter the door wearing new evening gowns and accessories designed by ESTELA. The WOMEN parade down the theater aisles voguing in a fashion-show style. They take their bows, continue voguing, and slowly exit. Lights slowly fade out.)

The End

REAL WOMEN HAVE CURVES

GLOSSARY SPANISH

A trabajar - To work it is

Abraza(r) - to hug

Abuelita - grandmother, granny

Adios - good-bye

Aguas - look out

Ahora si - okay, now

Alli esta en el cajon - It's there in the drawer

Amá - mama

¡Andenle! - Come on!

Apá - papa

Aqui huele a pura cuchupeta y a pedo - It smells like pussy and fart

Así es que - therefore/so

Asi hazlo - Do it this way

¡Ave Maria Purissima! - Oh holy Mary of God!

Aver - Let's see, to have

Aver cuentanos - Come on tell us

¡Aver dime, condenada! - Damn you, tell me!

¡Ayy! - Ahh!, Oh!

¡Ayy que buenote! - He's so fine

bañate - take a shower

Barrio - neighborhood

Basta - enough

Besa(r) - to kiss

Blusas - blouses

Bola de viejos cochinos - bunch of dirty old men

Bueno - well, good

Buenos dias - good morning

Callense - be quiet

Chafas - tacky

Chicharron - pork rinds

Chichis - boobs, titties

Chisme - to gossip

Chismosa - gossip monger

Claro - of course

Cochinadas - junk

Como es - see how you are

¿Cómo estas? - How are you?

¿Como puede ser? - How can it be?

Corazón - heart

Coyote - someone who brings people across the border illegally for a price

Cumbia - Latin music from the Caribbean

¿de qué te apuras? - Why worry?

Desgraciada - ungrateful

Dios mio, ya mero acabamos - Oh,

God, we're almost finished.

Diosito - God

Doña - a term of respect, literally meaning "old mother"; usually applied to the oldest woman present

¿Dónde los escondo? - Where shall I hide them?

¡Echame la culpa! - Blame me!

El Tormento - the heartthrob, or "crush"; or tormentor

Enojona - grouch

Entonces a la fuerza - then by force

¿Entonces que quiere? - Then what do you want?

¡Entonces todas a trabajar! - Then to work it is!

¡Esa perra! - That bitch!

Eso - that

¡Esta cochinada no sirve! - This piece of junk doesn't work!

Está loquita - she's a little crazy

Estamos jodidas - We are screwed

Fresas - strawberries, snooty upper class people in Mexico

Gringa - Anglo-Saxon woman

Hasta mañana - until tomorrow

Hijole - short for son of a bitch

¡Hora si que estamos bien jodidas! - Now we're really messed up!

Horita te lo coso - I'll sew it for you right now

Hoye - listen

Huevona - lazy, good for nothing

La migra - US Immigration and Naturalization Service officials, border patrol

Las pobrecitas - the poor women

Listos para chupar - delicious enough to suck

Lonchera - the lunch mobile

Loquita - a little crazy

Maldita - goddamned woman

Maquinita - little sewing machine

¡Mendiga vieja! - Damn witch!

¡Mentirosa! - Liars!

Metiche - nosy

Mi viejo - my husband, my old man

M'ija - my daughter

Mira(r) - to look, Look!

Mira que inteligente - look how smart

Mira que paresco - see what I look like

¡Miren! - Look!

¡Miren cómo coquetea! - Look how she flirts!

Mole - a sauce made of chocolate and chili

Nada - nothing

Nalgas - buttocks

Ni lo mande dios - god forbid

No le da verguenza - she's not ashamed

No mas mira que paresco - Just look what I look like

No mas ven a ver - Just come take a look

¡No puedo! - I can't

No que no te quiero - And you say I don't love you

No se - I don't know

¡No se peleen! - don't fight

No seas mensa - don't be dumb

No seas terca - don't be stubborn

No te hagas de rogar - don't make us beg

No te va hacer daño - It won't do you any harm

N'ombre - no way

Nopal - cactus

¡Otra! - Another one!

¿Pa que? - For what?

Panza - stomach, belly

Panzonas - pregnant

Parele - stop it

Paresen de elefante - they look like they belong on an elephant

Patrona - boss

Pegame - hit me

Pero - but

¿Pero cómo? - But how?

Pero no puede ser - but it can't be

Pero que bien se siente - but it feels so good

Pero que loqura - what insanity

Pero tu - but you

Pinche - damn

¡Pinche rata! - Damn rat!

Pobre - poor

Pobre mujer - poor woman

Pobrecita - poor baby

Por favor - please

Por fin - finally

¿Pos cómo le hiciste? - Well, how did you do it?

Pos no nos queda otra - Well, we have no choice

Pos no se - Well, I don't know

¿Pos qué paso? - Well, what happened?

Pos yo ya no veo - I can't see a thing

Pues - Well

Pues por que no - well why not

Puro lomo - all back

Que bonita, te ves - How pretty you look

Que bonito - how pretty

Que bonito viento - what beautiful wind

¡Que buena es! - How good you are!

¡Que calor! - It's so hot!

¿Qué hiciste? - What did you do?

¿Que le pico? - What bit you?

Que locura - What madness

Que metiches - how nosey

¿Qué páso? - What happened?

¡Que susto! - What scare!

¿Que te dijo la vieja? - What did the old hag tell you?

Rapido - quickly

¿Saben qué? - You know what?

"Se prohibe chismear!" - "Gossiping is Prohibited!"

Se te seca alli abajo - it gets dried down there

Se ve - It shows

Señor - mister, Mr., Sir

Sí, ya se fue - Yes, he's already left.

Tambien - also

Tan pequeña - so young

Tanto pedo y para nada - all this fuss/worrying and for nothing

'Tas flaca - You're skinny

Ten - Take it

Tengo fe - I have faith

Tulle – "tul", a synthetic material

used for petty coats

Vago - loser, lazy, good for nothing

Valgame - oh my

Vamonos - let's go

Vamos a estar como gallinas enjauladas - we're going to be like caged chickens

Vas a verlo - you'll see

Venganse - Come you all

¿Verá que sí? - Isn't it true?

Y los... - And the...

¿Y por qué no me habias dicho? - Why hadn't you told me?

¿Y tu? - And you?

Ya basta - enough already

Ya llego mi viejo - my husband is here

¡Ya ni la friegas! - You blew it

REAL
WOMEN
HAVE
CURVES®

Simply Maria

★ ★ ★ ★ ★ ★ ★ OR THE ★ ★ ★ ★ ★ ★ ★

AMERICAN DREAM

written by JOSEFINA LOPEZ

SIMPLY MARIA OR THE AMERICAN DREAM

PLAYWRIGHT'S NOTES

I had thought about committing suicide, but I knew I wanted to live. I just wanted so badly to get my parents' attention and for them to understand me. So I wrote a play! I wrote SIMPLY MARIA OR THE AMERICAN DREAM when I was 17.

I wrote this play because I had to. I was so angry at my father for his machismo and all of his affairs. I was so angry at my mother for allowing my father to disrespect her and for being so dependent on him. I wanted to go to college because I knew that would be the only way I could become economically independent and self-sufficient. However, because I was undocumented at that time I couldn't get financial aid and my parents didn't have any money to give me or lend me. They would just tell me it was going to be a waste of time anyway and I should just get married. It is painful to think about this period in my life because I was hurting, I was confused, and I was mad as hell.

Very early on in my life I learned to channel my anger into something positive. I remember wanting to scream back at my father when he was yelling about house chores not being done. I couldn't yell back at him and disrespect him but my throat hurt as I held back the scream. I quickly grabbed a pen and stabbed the paper with my words. I wrote viciously with rage and said all the things that were in my gut and heart that I couldn't say out loud. The next day I read the piece of paper and was very impressed

with what I had written. Writing became a tool of empowerment.

I was a junior in high school and I didn't know what I was going to do with my life. I was so confused and I kept hearing three different voices. I thought I was going crazy. Nothing made sense. My parents would tell me to do one thing and then I would go to school and my teachers would tell me to reach for the stars. I was living in two different worlds that kept clashing. I wrote Simply Maria to make sense of all this confusion.

Also, I saw a play by Luis Valdez called "I Don't Have To Show You No Stinking Badges" that dealt with the racism in Hollywood. It opened my eyes and I realized that as a Latina studying theater at the Los Angeles County High School For The Arts I had no future. I could either change my last name to something Anglo or I could do something about it. I decided to start writing to create roles for Latinas and for myself.

I write to empower myself because I grew up feeling very helpless. I grew up feeling like my life as a Latina woman was not important. After I wrote SIMPLY MARIA OR THE AMERICAN DREAM and realized how important my experience is, that of a Mexican-American immigrant woman, I became the protagonist of all my plays and took charge of my life and went on to college. I had to drop out of college three times, but I eventually graduated May 27, 1993.

Josefina López

Los Angeles

April 5, 1996

SIMPLY MARIA OR THE AMERICAN DREAM

A ONE ACT PLAY

CHARACTERS

MARIA   daughter of Carmen and Ricardo; an ambitious Latina with a wild imagination who wants to go to college

CARMEN   Maria's mother; submissive and traditional

RICARDO   Maria's father; a hard-working man, very macho and traditional

JOSE   Maria's macho husband

GIRL 1, MARY   Maria's angel and later her "American Self"

GIRL 2, MYTH   Maria's angel and later her "Writer Self"

GIRL 3, MARIA 2   Maria's angel and later her "Mexican Self"

ENSEMBLE

PRIEST	PERSON 1
CARMEN'S MOTHER	VENDOR 1
WOMAN	VENDOR 2
NARRATOR	BAG LADY
IMMIGRANT 1	PROTESTER
IMMIGRANT 2	MAN 1
IMMIGRANT 3	DIRTY OLD MAN
IMMIGRANT 4	CHOLO 1
STATUE OF LIBERTY	VALLEY GIRL 1
MEXICAN MAN	VALLEY GIRL 2
MEXICAN WOMAN	CHOLO 2
POSTMAN	PERSON 2
PERSON 3	HEAD NURSE

PERSON 4	NURSE 2
ANGLO BUYER	NURSE 3
REFEREE	NURSE 4
ANNOUNCER	BAILIFF
FLOOR MANAGER	JUDGE
HUSBAND	PROSECUTER
WIFE	JUROR 1
SALESMAN	JUROR 2

SETTING

The play begins in a small village in Mexico; moves to downtown Los Angeles and then to East Los Angeles.

TIME: The play takes place over a period of years following the growth of Maria from birth to womanhood.

SCENE ONE

AT RISE: Dim lights slowly come on. RICARDO, a tall, dark, and handsome Mexican man enters. He tries to hide in the darkness of the night. He whistles carefully, trying to make it part of the noises of the night.

CARMEN *(from her balcony).* ¿Ricardo, eres tú?

RICARDO. Yes! Ready?

CARMEN. ¡Sí!

(CARMEN climbs down from her balcony, then runs to RICARDO, kissing and consuming him in her embrace.)

CARMEN. Where's the horse?

RICARDO. What horse?

CARMEN. The one we are going to elope on.

RICARDO. You didn't say to bring one. All we agreed on was that I would meet you here at midnight.

CARMEN. I would have thought that you would have thought to…

RICARDO. Shhh!!!! ¡Mira! *(He points to CARMEN's room.)*

CARMEN. ¡Ayyyy! ¡Mi madre!! Let's go! And on what are we going?

RICARDO. On this. *(He brings an old bike.)*

CARMEN. ¿¡Qué?! On that? No! How could you…? Everyone knows that when you elope, you elope on a horse. Not on a…Ricardo, you promised!

(Offstage CARMEN's MOTHER discovers her missing.)

MAMA. Carmencita! Carmen! She's gone!!!

CARMEN. Oh, no! Hurry! Let's go!

RICARDO *(hops on the bike)*. Carmen, hurry! Get on!

CARMEN. No! We don't fit!

MAMA. ¡M'ija! Where are you?

CARMEN. We better fit! *(She jumps on, and they take off. She falls off the bike, but quickly gets back on.)* Ricardo, marry me! *(Crickets are heard, lights fade.)*

SCENE TWO

AT RISE: Lights come on. THREE WOMEN enter a church with candles. A FOURTH WOMAN, much older, enters with a lighted candle and lights the other candles. The THREE WOMEN then transform into STATUES of saints in the church. The PRIEST comes downstage, waiting for a wedding to begin. CARMEN enters, pregnant.

PRIEST. Will he be here soon?

CARMEN. Soon, he promised.

PRIEST. I was supposed to start half an hour ago.

(A WOMAN enters with a note.)

WOMAN. Is there anyone here named Carmen?

CARMEN. Is it from Ricardo? *(The WOMAN does not know. CARMEN reads the letter.)* "I haven't been able to get a divorce. It's sometime soon, believe me…Just wait. I'm working hard so that I can save money to buy a little house or a ranch for the three of us. If you wait, good things will come." *(To PRIEST.)* There won't be a wedding today.

(CARMEN exits, crying, with PRIEST. The STATUES become WOMEN and they all ad lib malicious gossip about the pregnant bride. The PRIEST enters

and the WOMEN stop gossiping. CARMEN enters again. This time she is no longer pregnant, but is holding her baby.)

PRIEST. Will he be here?

(RICARDO enters.)

CARMEN. He is here.

PRIEST. Good. Now we can begin.

CARMEN *(to RICARDO).* I thought you wouldn't show up. *(RICARDO shushes her. The PRIEST begins his speech which is more or less mumbled and not heard except for:)*

PRIEST. Do you, Carmen, accept Ricardo as your lawfully wedded husband?

CARMEN. I do.

PRIEST. Do you, Ricardo, accept Carmen as your lawfully wedded wife?

RICARDO *(hesitates).* I do.

PRIEST. Under the Catholic church in the holy house of God, I pronounce you man and wife. *(The PRIEST takes the baby from CARMEN and sprinkles holy water on the baby.)* Under the Catholic church, in the holy house of God, this child shall be known as María.

(The PRIEST gives the baby to the OLD WOMAN. CARMEN, RICARDO, and PRIEST exit. The STATUES now transform into THREE ANGELIC GIRLS who begin to hum, then sing beautifully with only the word "María." The OLD WOMAN gives the baby to one of the GIRLS. They come center stage and deliver the following facing the audience.)

ALL. María

GIRL 1. As a girl you are to be:

GIRL 2. Nice,

GIRL 3.   forgiving,

GIRL 1.   considerate,

GIRL 2.   obedient,

GIRL 3.   gentle,

GIRL 1.   hard-working,

GIRL 2.   gracious.

GIRL 3. You are to like:

GIRL 1.   Dolls,

GIRL 2.   kitchens,

GIRL 3.   houses,

GIRL 1.   cleaning,

GIRL 2.   caring for children,

GIRL 3. cooking,

GIRL 1.   laundry,

GIRL 2.   dishes.

GIRL 3. You are not to:

GIRL 1.   Be independent,

GIRL 2.   enjoy sex,

GIRL 3. but must endure it as your duty to your husband,

GIRL 1.   and bearing his children.

GIRL 2. Do not shame your society!

GIRL 3. Never,

GIRL 1.   never,

GIRL 2.   never,

ALL.   never!!!

GIRL 1. Your goal is to reproduce.

GIRL 2. And your only purpose in life is to serve three men:

GIRL 3. Your father,

GIRL 1.   your husband,

GIRL 2.   and your son.

GIRL 3. Your father…

(RICARDO enters carrying a moral with his belongings.)

RICARDO. Carmen, I must go.

CARMEN. Ricardo, don't go. Not after all I've waited.

RICARDO. I don't want to leave, but we need the money. There's no work here. I must go to el norte, so I can find work and send for you.

CARMEN. I don't want to be alone.

RICARDO. You have María. I'm going so that we can have the things we don't have.

CARMEN. I would prefer to have you than the things I don't have.

RICARDO. It's not just for the money, but for me. I want something else besides a life on this farm.

CARMEN. María will not see you.

RICARDO. She will, when I am on the other side. I will send for you, she will be very proud of me.

CARMEN. You promise?

RICARDO. I promise.

CARMEN. Well, then, I will wait. We will wait.

RICARDO. I will write. *(He kisses CARMEN on the forehead.)*

CARMEN. Ricardo, remember that I love you. *(RICARDO leaves.)* Don't forget to write! *(Lights slowly fade.)*

SCENE THREE

AT RISE: Spotlight on NARRATOR.

NARRATOR. Yes, write a lot. They will miss you…And all who are in search of opportunity go to the same place; Amer¬ica. And America belongs to all who are willing to risk.

(Lights come on. A giant sail enters the stage, brought on by some EUROPEAN IMMIGRANTS.)

IMMIGRANT 1. All for a dream.

IMMIGRANT 2. Ciao mia Italia!

IMMIGRANT 3. Auf wiederzein mein Deutschland!

IMMIGRANT 1. Au revoir ma France!

IMMIGRANT 2. Hello, America!

(In the background "America the Beautiful" starts playing. The STATUE OF LIBERTY enters.)

IMMIGRANT 3. The Lady!

IMMIGRANT 1. Up high in the sky…

IMMIGRANT 2. …incapable of being brought down.

IMMIGRANT 3. And like her…

IMMIGRANT 1. …we carry…

IMMIGRANTS 2 & 3. …a similar torch.

ALL. A torch of hope.

STATUE OF LIBERTY. Give me your tired, your poor, your huddled masses yearning to breathe free…

(At the bottom of the STATUE OF LIBERTY appear THREE MEXICAN PEOPLE [RICARDO is one of them] trying to cross the border. They run around hiding, sneaking, and crawling, trying not to get spotted by the border patrol.)

RICARDO. ¡Venganse por aquí!

MEXICAN MAN. ¿Y ahora qué hacemos?

MEXICAN WOMAN. What do we do now?

MEXICAN MAN. ¡Vamonos por alla!

MEXICAN WOMAN. ¡Nos nortearon!

RICARDO. Let's go back. *(They hide behind the EUROPEAN IMMIGRANTS. The STATUE OF LIBERTY composes herself and continues.)*

STATUE OF LIBERTY. I give you life, liberty, and the pursuit of happiness, for the price of your heritage, your roots, your history, your family, your language…Conform, adapt, give up what is yours, and I will give you the opportunity to have what is mine.

MEXICAN MAN. Pues bueno, if we have to.

MEXICAN WOMAN. Sounds good.

IMMIGRANT 3. Look, fireworks!

RICARDO. ¡Lo hicimos!

("America the Beautiful" becomes overwhelming, lights flash representing the

fireworks. A few seconds later the same lights that adorn the celebration for the EUROPEAN IMMIGRANTS become the lights from the border patrol helicopters hunting the MEXICAN PEOPLE. Hound dogs are heard barking, and the MEXICAN PEOPLE scatter and try to hide.)

RICARDO. ¡La migra!

MEXICAN MAN. ¡Corranle! *(The EUROPEAN IMMIGRANTS and the STATUE OF LIBERTY all keep pointing at the MEXICAN PEOPLE so they can be caught. The STATUE OF LIBERTY uses her torch to light every place the MEXICAN PEOPLE run to hide. The MEXICAN PEOPLE run offstage, and with the sail tilted down, they charge after them. Lights fade.)*

SCENE FOUR

AT RISE: Spotlight on POSTMAN who throws in paper airplane.

POSTMAN. Air mail for Carmen García.

(CARMEN runs onstage and picks up the letter from the floor. She reads the letter out loud.)

CARMEN. "Mi Querida Carmen, how are you? How is María? I've sent you some more money. This is the last letter I write to you because I am now sending for you. I fixed my papers with the help of a friend, and I got an apartment where we can live. Tell María I love her, and to you I send all my love…" María!!… "Leave as soon as possible…" María, ¡ven aquí!

(MARIA enters.)

MARIA. Yes, Mamí.

CARMEN. María, get ready, we're going.

MARIA. Going where?

CARMEN. To join your father in the city of the angels.

MARIA. Angels? *(MARIA puts on her coat for the journey. Lights fade.)*

SCENE FIVE

AT RISE: The following is the making of a city. Actors will work as an ensemble to create many roles. It will be organized chaos. Noises of police and fire truck sirens, along with other common city noises are heard. The stage lights up with vendors selling on the streets and all sorts of unusual and not so

*unusual people found in downtown L.A. on Broadway Street. CARMEN and
MARIA become engulfed in the scene, appalled to see what they have come to.*

PERSON 1. Broadway! Downtown L.A.!

VENDOR 1. Cassettes, cartuchos, dos dolares!

MAN 1. Hey, you wanna buy a gold chain?

CARMEN. Perdone señora, could you tell me…

BAG LADY. Get out of my way!

PROTESTER. Homosexuality is wrong! No sex! ¡Se va acabar el mundo!
The world is coming to and end! *(The PROTESTER comes between
CARMEN and MARIA and separates them. MARIA becomes lost. CARMEN
searches frantically for her.)*

CARMEN. María! María, where are you?!

MARIA *(crying)*. ¡Mamí, Mamí!

WOMAN 1. Buy this. Sombras para verte como una estrella de cine.

WOMAN 2. Hair brushes, all kinds, a dollar!

WOMAN 3. You want to buy a handbag?

WOMAN 1. ¡Aguas! Here comes the police! *(All the street VENDORS run
away.)*

MAN 1. Jesus loves you! He died for our sins! *(MAN 1 hands CARMEN a
pamphlet.)*

CARMEN. ¿Qué?

WOMAN 1. That RTD bus is always late!

DIRTY OLD MAN. Hey! Little girl! You want to get married? The world is
coming to an end and you shouldn't die without having done it.

CARMEN. María, ¡¿dónde estás hija mia?!

CHOLO 1. East L.A.!

TWO VALLEY GIRLS. We love it!

CHOLO 2. Hey vato!

TWO VALLEY GIRLS. Party and let party!

CHOLO 2. ¡Hoye mi carnal!

PERSON 2. ¡Viva la huelga! Boycott grapes!

PERSON 3. Chicano Power!

TWO VALLEY GIRLS. We love it!

PERSON 3. Chicano Power!

TWO VALLEY GIRLS. We love it!

PERSON 4. A little culture for the gringitos.

ANGLO BUYER. ¿Cuanto? ¿Salsa? ¿Cerveza?

CARMEN. María!

(MARIA runs scared and bumps into CARMEN. They hug each other. RICARDO, dressed in a charro outfit enters and gives some yells as if ready to sing a corrido. All the chaos of the city stops, and all the city people recoil in fear. RICARDO becomes the hero rescuing CARMEN and MARIA from their nightmare.)

TWO VALLEY GIRLS. We love it!

CARMEN. ¡¡Ayy!! What a crazy city! It's so awful! People here are crazy! *(CARMEN is about to cry, she embraces RICARDO instead.)* But Ricardo, I'm so happy to be here.

MARIA *(trying to get his attention)*. An ugly man chased me!

RICARDO. But are you all right?

MARIA. Sí. Now that you are here.

RICARDO. Carmen, we are finally together like I promised.

CARMEN. Ricardo, where's our home?

RICARDO. Follow me. *(They exit. Lights fade.)*

SCENE SIX

AT RISE: Spotlight on NARRATOR.

NARRATOR: They are going home to the housing projects… Pico Aliso, Ramona Gardens, Estrada Courts. No one likes it there, but it's cheap, "Ta barato." *(Announcing.)* The little house in the ghetto.

(Lights come back on to a small apartment where RICARDO, MARIA, and CARMEN enter.)

RICARDO. Here we are.

CARMEN (disappointed). ¿Aquí?

RICARDO. Yes, I hope it's all right. It's only for now.

MARIA (smiling). I like it! Look, Mamí! There are swings and grass.

RICARDO. There are a lot of kids in the neighborhood who you can play with.

MARIA. Really, Papí? Would they want to play with me?

RICARDO. Sure. (Noticing CARMEN's displeasure.) What's wrong? You don't like it?

CARMEN. Oh, no. I'm just tired from the trip.

RICARDO How was the trip?

MARIA (cutting in). It was great!

CARMEN. Great? You threw up on me the whole way here.

MARIA. Except, I don't understand why the bus never got off the ground. Where are the angels? And where are the clouds? And the gate? And the music…Like in the stories Mamí used to tell me. I thought we were going to heaven. I thought you had been called to heaven because you are an angel. Are you an angel, Papí?

RICARDO. Yes, I'm your angel always.

MARIA. So if this isn't heaven and you're an angel; what are we doing here?

RICARDO. María, I brought you here so that you can have a better life. It wasn't easy for me to get here. One time I was hiding in a truck with a lot of other people for hours. The coyote had left us there until someone came with money to claim us. It was so hot and humid that we were sure we were going to die. But I told myself I was going to make it because I knew I had a daughter to live for. I did it for you. In los Estados Unidos I hear the education is great. You can take advantage of all the opportunities offered to you. You can work hard to be just as good as anybody. You can be anything you want to be! (Pause.) Carmen, let me show you the kitchen. (CARMEN and RICARDO exit.)

MARIA. Estados Unidos, I don't even know you and I already love you! You're too generous. Thank you. I'll work hard. I can be anything I want to be! (MARIA starts changing clothes and ends up wearing a casual shirt and pants when she finishes the following:) Estados Unidos, I'm ready to play the game. I'm gonna show the boys in this neighborhood how to really play

football!

(MARIA makes some football moves. She then runs out. CARMEN enters. CARMEN shouts out through an imaginary window.)

CARMEN *(angrily)*. María,¡ven aquí!

(MARIA runs in.)

MARIA. Yes, Mamí?

CARMEN. La Señora Martinez told me you were playing football with the boys.

MARIA. Yes, Mamí. I was.

CARMEN. I don't want you to be playing with the boys. It's not proper for a señorita.

MARIA. But I'm good at sports. I'm better than some of the boys.

CARMEN. It doesn't look right. ¿Qué van a decir?

(In the background appear the THREE GIRLS who are only heard and seen by MARIA. They whisper to her.)

GIRL 1. Never shame your society.

GIRL 2. Never,

GIRL 3.   never,

All.   never!!!

MARIA. But my Papí said…

CARMEN. You are not to play with boys. *(CARMEN exits.)*

MARIA. I don't understand. Papí tells me to compete, Mamí tells me it doesn't look right.

(MARIA exits to her room. RICARDO enters.)

RICARDO. María, come here.

(MARIA comes out of her room.)

RICARDO. Who were you walking home with?

MARIA. A friend.

RICARDO. A boyfriend?

MARIA. No, just a friend I have in my last class who lives close by.

RICARDO. I don't want you walking home with and talking to boys. Study!

MARIA (*dares to ask*). Papí, why?

RICARDO. You're thirteen and you are very naive about boys. The only thing on their mind is of no good for a proper girl. They tell girls that they are "special." Knowing that girls are stupid enough to believe it. Then they make pendejas out of them. They get them pregnant and what a shame it is for the parents.

MARIA. Papí, how do you know?

RICARDO. Go to your room!

(*MARIA goes to her room. There, the THREE GIRLS appear again and whisper to MARIA.*)

GIRL 1. Never shame your society!

GIRL 2. Never, (*GIRL 3 does not continue, but slowly walks away from the TWO GIRLS.*)

GIRL 1. never,

GIRL 1 & 2. never!!

(*Spotlight on MARIA. MARIA goes to the mirror, GIRL 3 appears in the mirror. MARIA brushes her hair and so does GIRL 3. Then GIRL 3 begins to touch herself in intimate ways, discovering the changes through puberty, while MARIA remains still, not daring to touch herself. Finally, when MARIA does dare to touch herself, CARMEN comes into the room and catches her. Lights quickly come back on.*)

CARMEN. María, what were you doing?

MARIA. Nothing.

CARMEN. María, were you...? (*Before MARIA can answer.*) It's a sin to do that. Good girls don't do that.

GIRL 3 (*goes behind MARIA. Whispers*). Why? Why? Why?

MARIA. Why?

CARMEN (*shocked*). Because it's dirty. Sex is dirty.

GIRL 3. Why is it dirty? What makes it dirty?

MARIA (*suppressing and ignoring GIRL 3*). I'm sorry I didn't know what I

was doing.

CARMEN. María, I'm telling you for your own good. Women should be pure. Men don't marry women who aren't unless they have to. Quieren virgenes. It's best that way, if you save yourself for your own wedding night. Be submissive.

GIRL 3. Why? Why? Why?

MARIA. Yes, but…why?

CARMEN. That's the way it is. I know it's not fair, but women will always be different from men. Ni modo. *(CARMEN exits to kitchen.)*

MARIA & GIRL 3. I don't understand. Why must a woman be a virgin? Why is sex dirty?

(GIRL 1 appears.)

GIRL 1. María, stop questioning and just accept.

GIRL 3. No, María! God gave you a brain so you can think and question. Use it!

GIRL 1. But it is not up to us to decide what is right and wrong. Your parents know best, María. They love you and do things for you.

GIRL 3. María, they are not always right…

(RICARDO enters, he is in the kitchen.)

RICARDO *(interrupting the argument)*. María! Come and help your mother with dinner right now!

MARIA. All right! *(She goes to the kitchen.)*

RICARDO. What do you do in there all that time?

MARIA. I was doing my homework.

RICARDO. It takes you all that time? *(He has the mail and pulls out a letter from the pile.)*

MARIA. Yes, I want my work to be perfect so that I can win an award…

RICARDO. All for an award? How about if I give you a trophy for washing the dishes when you are suppose to, and for doing the laundry right? *(He begins to read the letter. MARIA searches for her mail. She finds a letter, reads it, and becomes excited.)*

CARMEN *(to RICARDO)*. Who's the letter from?

RICARDO. My cousin Pedro.

CARMEN. So what are you going to tell him?

RICARDO. The truth. I'm going to tell him his Martita did a pendejadita and is due in three months. (*To MARIA.*) What do I tell you?

CARMEN. ¡Que verguenza!

RICARDO. ¡Tanto estudio y para nada! It's such a waste to educate women. How is all that education helping her now that she's pregnant and on welfare…What's that smell?! The tortillas are burning!!!

MARIA. ¡¡¡Ayyy!!!

CARMEN. When you get married what is your husband going to say?

MARIA. I'm sorry, I completely forgot.

CARMEN. You can't cook, you can't clean…

MARIA. I try to do all the chores you ask…

CARMEN. You can't do anything right. Not even the tortillas.

MARIA. I really try…

RICARDO. No Mexican man is going to marry a woman who can't cook.

CARMEN. You're almost eighteen. (*Looks to RICARDO.*) I married your father when I was eighteen and I already knew how to do everything.

MARIA. Mamá, Papá, there are more important things… (*MARIA holds the letter, but decides not to say anything.*) I just don't care for housework.

(*MARIA goes to her room. Spotlight on MARIA. She looks at the letter and GIRL 3 appears. They look at the letter and GIRL 3 reads.*)

GIRL 3. "Congratulations! You are eligible for a four-year scholarship… Please respond as soon as possible…" (*MARIA jumps up in excitement. She then gets her typewriter and begins to type her response. The typewriter is not working. She goes outside to look for her father. Lights fade.*)

SCENE SEVEN

AT RISE: RICARDO is in the kitchen reading the newspaper. MARIA brings the typewriter to the kitchen.

MARIA. Papá…¿Esta ocupado?

RICARDO. I'm reading the paper.

MARIA. Do you think...well...maybe when you have finished reading you can fix this for me? Here's the manual. (*MARIA shows it to him. He pretends to look, but cannot understand it because he cannot read.*)

RICARDO. Go get my toolbox. I'll do it my way.

(*MARIA exits to get the toolbox. RICARDO checks the typewriter carefully. MARIA brings back the toolbox and looks attentively and also tries to think of a way to introduce the subject of college. GIRL 1 appears behind them.*)

GIRL 1. There is no one who can take the place of my father, who loves me but cannot express it any other way. If I wasn't scared I would hold you. I love you, Papí.

(*RICARDO finishes fixing the typewriter and hands it to MARIA. MARIA exits to her room to continue typing. CARMEN enters with a basket full of clean clothes.*)

CARMEN. ¡Ayy, que floja! Ricardo, where's María?

RICARDO. She's in her room typing.

CARMEN. She was suppose to pick up the clothes. (*CARMEN goes to MARIA's room.*)

CARMEN. María, come help me fold the clothes!

MARIA. I'm busy.

CARMEN. Busy?! Busy?! Can't it wait? I have things to do too.

MARIA. All right. (*MARIA goes to the kitchen to help her with the clothes. They sit at the table with RICARDO. CARMEN and MARIA begin to fold clothes.*)

CARMEN. María, your birthday is almost here. Do you want me to make you a beautiful dress for your birthday? Maybe you can wear it for your graduation? Oh, our neighbor told me that her daughter Rosario is graduating from a good business school. She says she already has a good job lined up for her as a secretary that pays eight dollars an hour, fíjate.

MARIA (*gets the hint*). Mamá, Papá. I don't want to be a secretary. (*Pause.*) I want to go to college.

RICARDO. What?

CARMEN. It's too expensive.

Photo by Hector Rodriguez

Maria is told by her parents they want her to be a secretary.

MARIA *(quickly)*. I was awarded a big, four-year scholarship!

RICARDO. ¿Qué? College? Scholarship?

MARIA. I want to be educated. *(Courageously.)* I want to be an actress.

RICARDO. You want to go to college to study to be an actress?! ¡¡Estás loca?!

CARMEN. Are you crazy? You don't know what you want to do.

RICARDO. I didn't know you had to study to be a puta.

CARMEN. What have we done to make you want to leave us? We've tried to be good…

MARIA. Nothing. It's not you. I want to be something.

RICARDO. Why don't you just get married like most decent women and be a housewife?

CARMEN. That's something.

RICARDO. That's respectable.

MARIA. I don't understand what you are so afraid of…

RICARDO. I don't want you to forget you are Mexican. There are so many people where I work who deny they are Mexican. When their life gets better they stop being Mexican! To deny one's country is to deny one's past, one's parents. How ungrateful!

MARIA. But you said that with an education I could be just as good as anybody. And that's why you brought me to los Estados Unidos.

RICARDO. No. Get married!

MARIA. I will. But I want a career as well. Women can now do both.

RICARDO. Don't tell me about modern women. What kind of wife would that woman make if she's so busy with her career and can't tend to her house, children, and her husband?

MARIA. And that's all a woman is for? To have children? Clean a house? Tend to her husband like a slave and heat his tortillas?!

RICARDO. ¡Que atrevida! Why do you make it seem like it's some sort of a nightmare? *(Sarcastically.)* Women have always gotten married and they have survived.

MARIA. But surviving is not living.

CARMEN. María, listen to your father.

MARIA. Papá, I listened to you. That's why! You encouraged me when I was young, but now you tell me you can't. Why?

RICARDO. Because…you are a woman.

MARIA. That's not fair!

RICARDO. Get out of my face! *(MARIA runs to her room, crying.)*

CARMEN. Ricardo, why don't you even let her try, por favor?

(RICARDO angrily leaves. CARMEN goes to Maria's room. Lights change to Maria's room.)

CARMEN. María don't cry. Don't be angry at us either, and try to understand us. M'ija, we are doing this for your own good. We don't want you to get hurt. You want too much, that's not realistic. You are a Mexican woman and you can't change that. You are different from other women. Try to accept that. Women need to get married, they are no good without men.

MARIA. Mamá, I consider myself intelligent and ambitious, and what is that worth if I am a woman? Nothing?

CARMEN. You are worth a lot to me. I can't wait for the day when I will see you in a beautiful white wedding dress walking down the aisle with a church full of people. That is the most important event in a woman's life.

MARIA. Mamá, we are in los Estados Unidos. Don't you realize you expect me to live in two worlds? How is it done? Can't things be different?

CARMEN. No se. That's the way your father is. Ni modo.

MARIA. ¿Ni modo? ¡Ni modo! Is that all you can say? Can't you do anything? *(Gives up and explodes at CARMEN.)* Ahhh! Get out! Get out!!! *(CARMEN leaves and MARIA continues to pound on her pillow with rage. MARIA slowly begins to fall asleep. Lights slowly fade.)*

SCENE EIGHT

AT RISE: GIRL 2, who will now portray "MYTH," appears. She wears a spring dress and looks virginal. She goes to MARIA.

MYTH *(shaking MARIA lightly)*. María, get up and come see.

MARIA. Who are you?

MYTH. I'm Myth. María, come see what can be.

MARIA. What do you mean? What's going on?

MYTH. María, you are dreaming the American dream. You can be anything you want to be. Follow me. *(The sound of a horse is heard.)*

MARIA. Is that a horse I'm hearing?

MYTH. See…

(A PRINCE appears and he and MYTH dance to a sweet melody. Just as they are about to kiss, the fierce sound of a whip accompanied by loud and wild cries of a horse running off are heard.)

PRINCE *(in a very wimpy voice)*. My horse! My horse!!! *(He runs off to chase after his horse.)*

MARIA. What happened?

MYTH. I don't know.

(Another crack of the whip is heard, but now GIRL 3, who will portray "MARY," appears with the whip.)

MARY. Sorry to spoil the fairy tale, but Prince Charming was expected at

the castle by Cinderella… Hello, María.

MARIA. And who are you?

MARY. My name is Mary. It's my turn now, so get lost, Myth! (*MARY snaps her fingers and a large crook pulls MYTH offstage.*)

MYTH. You're such a bitch!

MARY. Control, that's the thing to have. So come along and follow me!

MARIA. Where are you taking me to?

MARY. To liberation! Personal independence, economic independence, sexual independence. We are free. María, in America you can be anything you want to be. A lawyer. A doctor. An astronaut. An actress! The Mayor. Maybe even the President…of a company. You don't have to be obedient, submissive, gracious. You don't have to like dolls, dishes, cooking, children, and laundry. Enjoy life! Enjoy liberation! Enjoy sex! Be free!

(*GIRL 1, who will now portray "MARIA 2," appears brandishing a broom.*)

MARIA 2. You bad woman! You puta!

MARY. I'm not!

MARIA 2. You American demon. You are. You are. You just want to tempt her then hurt her! (*MARIA throws MARY the whip to defend herself.*)

MARIA. Mary, catch!

MARY. Thanks! Now we will see!

(*MARIA 2 and MARY have a quick duel, until a MAN blows a whistle and becomes a REFEREE for a wrestling match. The REFEREE takes away the broom and the whip from the WOMEN.*)

REFEREE. All right, c'mon girls. I want this to be a clean fight. (*The WOMEN push him away and charge at each other. MARY tries some dirty tricks.*) I told you I wanted this to be a clean fight. (*To MARY.*) What were you using?

MARY. Nothing. I'm so innocent.

REFEREE. Now come on over here and shake hands.

MARIA 2 (*asking the audience*). Should I? Should I? (*MARIA 2 gets MARY's hand and twists it. They wrestle wildly, with MARY winning, then MARIA 2. The REFEREE finally steps in and proclaims MARIA 2 the winner.*)

REFEREE. Break! Break! (*He holds MARY and pulls her out.*)

MARY *(barely able to speak).* María, before you are a wife, before you are a mother, first you are a human being!! *(MARY is dragged out. MARIA 2, having won the fight, acknowledges the cheers of the crowd, then gestures for MARIA to kneel and pray. MARIA 2 puts a wedding veil on MARIA.)*

MARIA 2. A woman's only purpose in life is to serve three men. Her father, her husband, and her son...Her father...

(RICARDO enters, he picks up MARIA and escorts her to the church. The bells and the wedding march are heard. MARIA walks down the aisle. The groom enters.)

MARIA 2. Her husband...*(The couple kneels and a wedding lasso is put around them.)*

PRIEST. Dearly beloved, we are gathered here, under the Catholic church, in the holy house of God, to unite these two people in holy matrimony. Marriage is sacred. It is the unification of a man and a woman, their love and commitment, forever, and ever, and ever, no matter what! Well, then let's begin...María, do you accept José Juan Gonzalez García López as your lawfully wedded husband to love, cherish, serve, cook for, clean for, sacrifice for, have his children, keep house, love him, even if he beats you, commits adultery, gets drunk, rapes you lawfully, denies your identity, money, and in return ask for nothing? *(MARIA thinks about it and then turns to her parents who mouth to her "I do.")*

MARIA. I do.

PRIEST. Very good. Now, José. Do you accept María García Gonzalez López as your lawfully wedded wife to support?

JOSE. Simón, que yes.

PRIEST. Good. Well, if there is anyone present who is opposed to the union of these two people, speak now, or forever hold your truth. *(RICARDO stands up, takes out a gun, and brandishes it to the audience.)* Do you have the ring? *(JOSE takes out a golden dog collar. The PRIEST gives it his blessings.)* 5, 6, 7, 8. By the power vested in me, under the Catholic church, in the holy house of God, I pronounce you man and wife. *(The THREE GIRLS take away MARIA's veil and bouquet. They place the dog collar around MARIA's neck. Then they get the wedding lasso and tie it around her to make the collar seem and work like a leash. PRIEST speaks to JOSE.)* You may pet the bride. *(The lasso is given to JOSE. He pulls MARIA, who gets on her hands and knees. They walk down the aisle like dog and master. The wedding march plays, people begin to leave. Lights fade out.)*

SCENE NINE

AT RISE: A table and two chairs are center stage. MARIA, pregnant, walks uncomfortably in. She turns on the television, then the ensemble creates the television setting, playing roles of t.v. producer, director, make-up people, technicians, as if the actual studio is there. Brief dialogue is improvised to establish on-set frenzy.

ANNOUNCER. And here is another chapter of your afternoon soap opera, "Happily Ever After." Our sultry Eliza Vasquez decides to leave Devero in search of freedom!

FLOOR MAN. Okay everyone, tape rolling, stand by in 10 seconds. 5, 4, 3, 2, *(Cue).*

ACTRESS. Devero, I'm leaving you.

ACTOR. Eliza, why?

ACTRESS. I don't love you anymore. Actually, I never did.

ACTOR. Eliza, but I love you.

ACTRESS. I faked it, all of it. I did it because I had to. But now I must go and be free! (MARIA claps loudly in excitement for her.)

FLOOR MANAGER. Cut! *(To MARIA.)* What are you doing here?

MARIA. This is my living room.

FLOOR MANAGER. Oh, sure it is. Well, go into the kitchen, make yourself a snack, we'll have the carpet cleaned for you in about an hour. (Pushes MARIA aside.) I know, I'm sorry…Stand by. 5, 4, 3, 2, 1.

ACTRESS. …But now I must go and be free!

ACTOR. You can't do this to me!

ACTRESS. Oh, yes I can!

ACTOR. But I've given you everything!

ACTRESS. Everything but an identity! Well, Devero, Devero, Devero. I've discovered I no longer need you. There are unfulfilled dreams I must pursue. I want adventure.

FLOOR MANAGER. And…cut! That's a take. Roll commercial. 5 seconds. 4, 3, 2, 1.

(The soap opera ends. MARIA claps approvingly. A commercial quickly begins, with the ensemble creating a similar on-set frenzy. In the commercial a MAN

comes home with a can of Ajax as a gift for his WIFE.)

HUSBAND. Honey, I'm home! I brought you something. *(He hides the can of Ajax treating it as if he had flowers.)*

WIFE. Hi, darling! *(They give each other a peck on the mouth from a distance.)* How was work?

HUSBAND. Fine…Ta-dah! *(Presents the can.)*

WIFE. You shouldn't have. Oh, thank you! I need all the cleaning power I can get!

HUSBAND. I can smell you've been cleaning.

WIFE. Yes! I've mopped the floors, did the dishes, the laundry, this house is spotless.

HUSBAND. What a wife! *(They give each other another peck on the mouth from a distance.)* You're a good wife!

(The doorbell rings. MARIA turns off the television. She goes to answer the door. It's her HUSBAND, he comes in and sits at the table.)

JOSE. María! María! I'm home. I'm hungry.

MARIA. José, how was work? Dinner is ready. I made your favorite dish. Do you want to eat now? *(JOSE doesn't answer.)* Well, I'll serve you then. *(MARIA walks off to the kitchen. She returns with a plate. She places it on the table.)* My mother came to visit today and she asked me what we are going to name the baby. She thought it would be nice to call her Esperanza.

JOSE *(with a smirk on his face).* ¿Qué?

MARIA. Of course it isn't going to be a girl. It's going to be a boy, and we'll name him after you. That would be nice, wouldn't it? *(MARIA feels pains.)* ¡Ayyy! How it hurts. I hope after the baby is born, I will be better. I've been getting so many pains, and I have a lot of stretch marks…I know you don't like me to ask you for money, but I need the money to buy a dress that fits me. I have nothing I can wear anymore.

JOSE *(eats a spoonful).* My dinner is cold.

MARIA. Oh, is it cold? I'll heat it up right now. It will only take a minute. *(MARIA runs to the kitchen. JOSE leaves the table and stares at the bed.)*

JOSE. María, ¡mi amor! Come here, baby!…Come on, m'ijita. I won't hurt you.

(JOSE gets on top of the bed. MARIA returns from the kitchen and sees him.)

MARIA. Jose, I don't feel so good.

JOSE. Oh, you'll feel fine in a second. *(He continues to persuade her. Eventually he gets his way. Then, MARIA gives out a loud scream of pain.)* What is it?

MARIA. The baby! *(Lights fade out.)*

SCENE TEN

AT RISE: Lights come on. MARIA goes into labor. JOSE walks her to the hospital. MARIA sits down and spreads her legs wide open. She is covered with a white sheet. THREE NURSES run in. A SALESMAN in a plaid jacket also enters.

SALESMAN. Here we have it. Direct from Mexico. The "Reproducing Machine." You can have one by calling our toll-free number. Get your pencil. It's 1-800-AJUU-AAAA!

HEAD NURSE. Now, relax. Just breathe like this. *(Exemplifies.)* Ahh!!! All in good rhythm. Good! Don't worry, millions of women have Mexican children, especially Mexican women, they have millions. But you'll get use to it. After your fourth child they'll just slide right on out.

MARIA. ¡¡Amá!! ¡¡Mamá!!

HEAD NURSE. There's nothing she can do. She went through it herself. Now, isn't that pain great? You're giving birth! Why it's the most satisfying feeling a woman can feel. Okay, I think it's coming! Push, push, push! *(A baby pops up, flying into the air. It is caught by one of the NURSES. She presents it to the HEAD NURSE.)*

HEAD NURSE *(disappointed)*. Oh, it's a girl.

NURSE 2 *(presents the baby to JOSE)*. Here's your baby daughter.

JOSE. A daughter? *(To MARIA.)* How could you do this to me? I'll have to call her "Sacrifice."

MARIA *(screams again)*. There's another one inside; I can feel it!

HEAD NURSE. Nahhh! Well, I'll check just in case. *(The HEAD NURSE peeps inside the sheet.)* Well. I'll be! Yeah, there's another one. Push! Push! Push! *(Another baby pops into the air. The baby falls to the floor and NURSE 3 chases after it and picks it up. She passes it on to NURSE 2. NURSE 2 presents the baby to JOSE.)*

NURSE 2. Here's another lovely daughter.

JOSE. Another daughter?! I'll have to call her "Abnegation."

SALESMAN. Here we have it! The world renowned Reproducing machine! *(MARIA screams again.)*

HEAD NURSE. What is it?

MARIA. There's another one!

SALESMAN. Ahh, but if you were watching earlier, you saw the other amazing function. It can also be used as a sex object.

HEAD NURSE. Push! Push! Push! *(Another baby pops up.)*

NURSE 1. I'll get it! *(The baby lands someplace far.)*

SALESMAN. Yes siree! You can be the boss. It's at your disposal and control. Hours of pleasure. And if it ever does go out of control, a kick and a few punches will do the job, and it will be back to normal.

NURSE 2. Here's another one.

JOSE *(to MARIA).* Another girl? Why are you doing this to me? I'll call her "Obligation."

SALESMAN. It's made in Mexico. It's cheap! It cooks! It cleans! *(MARIA screams again.)*

HEAD NURSE. Push! Push! Push! *(Three babies pop up into the air. Some land in the audience. All the NURSES collect them.)*

SALESMAN. Its stretch marks can stretch all the way from here to Tijuana. Not even a Japanese model can beat this one.

NURSE 2 *(to JOSE).* Guess what?

JOSE. No, don't tell me; another girl?

NURSE 2. Surprise! Surprise! Surprise!

JOSE. Three girls?! I'll call them "Frustration," "Regret," and "Disappointment."

SALESMAN. It delivers up to twenty-one children. It feeds on beans, chile, and lies.

HEAD NURSE. Are there any more babies in that Mexican oven of yours?

MARIA. I don't think so.

Photo by Hector Rodriguez

Maria gives birth to six babies all at once

HEAD NURSE. See you in nine months for your next Mexican litter.

SALESMAN. You can have your own reproducing machine! 1-800-AJU-AAAA! *(Blackout.)*

SCENE ELEVEN

AT RISE: Lights rise after a brief pause. On the stage is a table which serves as a crib for six crying babies. MARIA tries to quiet the babies by holding them each one at a time, then by the bunch. CARMEN, RICARDO, and JOSE enter. They stand behind her like demons.

JOSE. Shut those babies up!

CARMEN. You're a bad wife!

RICARDO. This house is a mess!

CARMEN. You can't cook, you can't clean!

RICARDO. Look at your children!

JOSE. Where's my dinner?

RICARDO. The dishes?

JOSE. My tortillas?

RICARDO. You're a bad wife!

CARMEN. I did it all my life!

JOSE. Bad wife!

MARIA. No! I'm not! I'm a good wife! I try. I really do! (*MARIA gets the laundry and begins to fold it quickly, but nicely and carefully. Suddenly, the clothes begin to take on a life of their own. There is a giant coat, and a pair of pants surrounding MARIA. They start pushing her around, then her wedding dress appears and heads for MARIA's neck. They wrestle on the ground.*)

CARMEN. Martyr! (*MARIA manages to get away, and runs upstage. As she is running, a giant tortilla with the Aztec Calendar emblem falls on her, smashing her to the ground.*)

MARIA. Help!

RICARDO. Martyr! (*MARIA manages to get out from under the giant tortilla. As she escapes, she is attacked by a storm of plates.*)

MARIA. Help!

RICARDO, CARMEN & JOSE. Martyr!!! Martyr!!! Martyr!!!

MARIA (*becomes uncontrollably angry*). ¡Ya basta! Enough! Do you want your dishes cleaned? I've got the perfect solution for them. (*MARIA goes offstage into the kitchen and loud sounds of dishes being smashed are heard.*) Now you don't have to worry. I'll buy you a million paper plates! Ohhh!!!!! And the tortillas, Mamá! I'm going to show you how they should be done. (*MARIA gets a bag of tortillas and begins tossing them into the audience like frisbees.*) Are these good enough? I hope so! I tried to get the top side cooked first; or was it last? Anyway, who cares! Here are the tortillas! (*She attacks her MOTHER with the tortillas.*) I hate doing the dishes! I hate doing the laundry! I hate cooking and cleaning! And I hate all housework because it offends me as a woman!!! (*There is a piercing moment of silence.*) That's right. I am a woman…a real woman of flesh and blood. This is not the life I want to live; I want more! And from now on I am directing my own life. Action!

(*Lights come fully on. TWO GIRLS grab and pull MARIA harshly to take her to another place. The stage now becomes a courtroom. MARIA is seated next to the JUDGE. The courtroom is filled with people who create a lot of*

commotion. *The JUDGE, the BAILIFF, and the PROSECUTOR enter.)*

BAILIFF. Please rise, the honorable hang judge presiding.

JUDGE *(banging his gavel).* Quiet in my courtroom! I am warning you, anyone who causes any such commotion like this again will be thrown out! Is that understood?! Let's begin!

BAILIFF. We are here today to give trial to María who is being accused by her husband of rebellion toward her implied duties of marriage.

JUDGE. How do you plead?

MARIA. Plead? Innocent! Guilty! I don't know!

JUDGE. Are you making a joke out of my question?

MARIA. No...sir.

JUDGE. It sounds to me like you wish to challenge these laws.

MARIA. I don't understand why I am on trial. What real laws have I broken?

JUROR 1. She knows what she's guilty of.

JUROR 2. She knows what laws not to break!

MARIA. Who are they?

BAILIFF. Your jury.

MARIA. But they are women, Mexican, traditional...They can't possibly be objective.

BAILIFF. They are a good jury.

MARIA. This is unjust! I must speak up to this...

BAILIFF. You have no voice.

MARIA. Where's my lawyer? I do get one, don't I? *(The courtroom fills with cruel laughter, which quickly stops.)*

JUDGE. No, you defend yourself.

MARIA. How do I defend myself when I can't speak?

JUDGE. Destiny, oh pity. Now let's begin. Mister Prosecutor, could you please state the objectives of this trial?

PROSECUTOR *(to audience).* This trial is meant to help preserve the institution of marriage. Ladies and gentlemen of the jury...in this case ladies of the jury. A man's home is his castle where he has his foundation. It is the place where he comes home to his family, and becomes the king of his castle. But this poor man comes home one evening and finds his children unattended, his house a mess, his dinner unprepared, and his wife sitting back, watching soap operas!

MARIA. I object!

JUDGE. You have no voice.

MARIA. You said I was to defend myself.

JUDGE. Not now!

PROSECUTOR. What we are going to try to do is prove the guilt of this woman…

MARIA. I object!

JUDGE. Shut up!

MARIA. I won't!

JUDGE. Mister Prosecutor, call your first witness!

PROSECUTOR. I call Ricardo García to the witness stand.

(*RICARDO takes the stand.*)

PROSECUTOR. Tell us about your daughter.

RICARDO. She was very obedient when she was young, but when she came to the United States she began to think herself "American." …She studied a lot, which is good, but she refused to do her chores because she thought herself above them.

PROSECUTOR. Could you please tell us what happened that evening your daughter rebelled?

RICARDO. I'd rather not…That evening María was hysterical. She threw dishes, tortillas, enchiladas…!

PROSECUTOR. Thank you, that will be all…My next witness will be Carmen García.

(*CARMEN takes the stand.*)

PROSECUTOR. Tell us about your daughter.

CARMEN. She's really a good girl. She's just too dramatic sometimes. She's such a dreamer, forgive her.

PROSECUTOR. Could you tell us what you saw that evening?

CARMEN. Well, she was a little upset, so she did a few things she didn't mean to do.

MARIA. No, Mamá! I meant it!

JUROR 1. She admits it!

JUROR 2. She's guilty!

BAILIFF. Guilty!

ALL. Guilty!

CARMEN. No, she's just unrealistic!

MARIA. I'm guilty then! *(The whole courtroom becomes chaotic. Everyone yells out "guilty." CARMEN becomes so sad she cries.)* Mamí, don't cry! *(Lights begin to fade.)*

SCENE TWELVE

AT RISE: The lights go on and off and everyone disappears. MARIA begins to regain consciousness and wakes up from her dream. She was awakened by CARMEN's actual crying, which continues and grows. MARIA gets up and listens to CARMEN and RICARDO arguing in the kitchen.

RICARDO. ¡Callate! Don't yell or María will hear you.

CARMEN. Then tell me, is it true what I am saying?

RICARDO. You're crazy! It wasn't me.

CARMEN. Con mis propios ojos, I saw you and la señora Martinez meet in the morning by the park. You have been taking her to work and who knows what! Tell me, is it true? Because if you don't I'm going to yell as loud as I can and let this whole neighborhood know what's going on.

RICARDO. Okay. It was me! ¿Estás contenta?

CARMEN. ¡¿Por qué?! Why do you do this to me? And with our neighbor? She lives right in front of us!

RICARDO. Look, every man sooner or later does it.

CARMEN. Do you think I don't know about all of your other affairs before la señora Martinez? She is not your first! I never said anything before because I was afraid you would send us back to Mexico. But now I don't care! You break it with that bitch or…I'll kill her and you. ¡Ayyy! Ricardo, I've endured so much for you. I knew you were no angel when we ran off together, but I thought you would change. You would change, because you loved me. I love you, Ricardo! But I can no longer go on living like this or I'll be betraying myself and I'll be betraying María. *(CARMEN runs offstage crying.)*

RICARDO. Carmen, ¡ven aquí! Carmen, wait!

(RICARDO goes after her. MARIA is in shock, not believing what she just heard. The THREE GIRLS enter. GIRL 3 hands MARIA a piece of paper and a pen. GIRL 1 gets MARIA's jacket. GIRL 2 gets MARIA's suitcase. MARIA sits at the kitchen table and begins to write. The THREE GIRLS stand behind her as she writes the following:)

MARIA. "Dear Mamá and Papá. Last night I heard everything. Now I know that your idea of life is not for me—so I'm leaving. I want to create a world of my own. One that combines the best of me. I won't forget the values of my roots, but I want to get the best of this land of opportunities. I am going to college—and I will struggle to do something with my life. You taught me everything I needed to know. Good-bye."

GIRL 1. Los quiero mucho, nunca los olvidare.

GIRL 2. Mexico is in my blood…

GIRL 3. …and America is in my heart.

MARIA. "Adiós." *(MARIA finishes the letter. She gets up and picks up her suitcase. The THREE GIRLS stand behind her and she puts on the jacket. The THREE GIRLS create the image of wings in flight. The THREE GIRLS leave through the door. MARIA follows them and before she leaves she stops and looks back, then exits.)*

The End

SIMPLY MARIA OR THE AMERICAN DREAM

GLOSSARY SPANISH

Adiós - goodbye

¡Aguas! - Watch out! / Look out!

¡¡Amá!! - Mom!!

¿Aquí? - here

¡¡Ayy!! - Oh!!

¡Ayy, que floja! - Oh, how lazy you are!

¡Ayyy, mi madre! - Oh, it's my mother!

¡Callate! - Shut up!

cartuchos, dos dolares - cassettes, two dollars!

charro - Mexican cowboy

chile - hot peppers

Con mis propios ojos - With my own eyes

¡Corranle! - Run! Get away!

corrido - Mexican ballad that tells a story

¿Cuanto? ¿Salsa? ¿Cerveza? - How much? Salsa? Beer?

¿Dónde estás hija mia?! - My daughter where are you?

el norte - the north, U.S.A.

Esperanza - Hope

¿Estás contenta? - Are you happy now?

¡¿Estas loca?! - Are you crazy?

fijate - look

gringitos - Anglos

¡Hoye mi carnal! - Hey, homeboy!

¡La migra! - the border patrol

la Señora - Mrs.

¡Lo hicimos! - We did it!

Los quiero mucho, nunca los olvidare - I love you very much, I will never forget you.

Mamá - mother

Mamí - mommy

¡mi amor! - my love

Mi querida - My dear

¡M'ija! - My daughter!

¡Mira! - Look!

moral - a traditional Mexican bag made of cloth

Ni modo - Nothing can be done about it.

No se - I don't know.

¡Nos nortearon! - they confused us, lost us

Papá - father

Papá, ¿Esta ocupado? - Father, are you busy?

Pendejadita - stupid mistake

Perdone señora - Excuse me, lady

Por favor - please

¡¿Por qué?! - Why?!

Pues bueno - well, all right

puta - whore

¿Qué? - What?

¡Que atrevida! - How dare you!

¿Que van a decir? - What are they going to say?

¡Que verguenza! - How embarrassing!

quieren virgenes - they want virgins

¿Ricardo, eres tú? - Ricardo, is that you?

¡Se va acabar el mundo! - The world is coming to an end!

Señora - Mrs.

señorita - a young lady

¡Sí! - Yes!

Simon, que - Yeah, sure

Sombras para verte como una estrella de cine - Eye shadows to make you look like a movie star.

'Ta barato - It's cheap

¡Tanto estudio y para nada! - All that education and for nothing.

¡Vamonos por alla! - Let's go that way!

vato - Home boy / guy

¡ven aquí! - come here

¡Venganse por aquí! - Come this way!

¡Viva la huelga! - Long live the boycott!

¿Y ahora qué hacemos? - What do we do now?

¡Ya basta! - Enough!

Artwork by Gaby Lopez @ soapdesign.com

They're sexy, curvy, dangerous, and now they're confessing...Latinas from Boyle Heights.

CONFESSIONS OF WOMEN FROM BOYLE HEIGHTS

A comedic collage of monologues, written & directed by
Josefina Lopez, author of *Real Women Have Curves*

MARCH 14-23, 2003 / FRI & SAT AT 8PM, SUN AT 7PM
CASA 0101 THEATRE ART SPACE – COURAGE PRODUCTIONS
TIX: 323.263.7684 / www.casa0101.org / 2009 E. First Street, LA, CA 90033

Artwork by Gaby Lopez @ soapdesign.com

CONFESSIONS OF WOMEN FROM EAST L.A.

PLAYWRIGHT'S NOTES

Latina women have always been categorized and portrayed as "virgins, mothers, and whores" in plays, movies, and television. I don't like that because I am none of them. I am a combination of all of them. I have a little of the mother, the virgin, and the whore. However, Latinas are much more than that. Latinas are complex, diverse and powerful. All these women that I have written about are me and my mother. They all represent a certain confession at a different stage in my life and her life. When you put them all together you will get to understand the Latina that I am.

Josefina López
Los Angeles
1996

CONFESSIONS OF WOMEN FROM EAST L.A.

A ONE ACT COMEDY

SETTING

Various places in East Los Angeles and Little Tokyo.

TIME: The present.

The stage is bare except for an altar at the center with four candles and several items. The altar is mobile with several compartments and will become an intricate part of the show. There are also four coat racks on four opposite corners of the stage with several costumes. On top of the coat racks are the names of famous streets in East Los Angeles such as: Cesar Chavez Boulevard, Whittier Boulevard, First Street, Soto Street, Indiana Street, Fourth Street and St. Louis Street. Next to the racks are four chairs.

CHARACTERS

MARQUEZ-BERNSTEIN Ph.D.   35, an energetic Latina feminist who encourages Latinas to marry Jewish men in her "How To Be A Super Latina" seminar.

DOÑA CONSEPCION 55, a widowed grandmother. After her husband's death, she is forced to come to terms with her homosexuality when she discovers her husband has given her AIDS.

DOLORES "LOLITA" CORAZON   25, a "Hot Señorita" type who teaches and punishes men with her powerful sexuality.

CALLETANA   40, a street vendor who sells corn on the cob on the street and challenges City Hall for her right to earn a living.

YOKO MARTINEZ   28, a Latina trying to pass for Japanese

ROXIE 30, a self-defense instructor

TIFFANY   20, a Valley Girl and Chicana activist. Accidentally attacks a man who was merely going to ask her for the time.

DOÑA FLORINDA   45, a soap opera addict in recovery. Finds courage and strength in Frida Kahlo's paintings.

VALENTINA   26, a Chicana activist. She is trying to organize her people to fight against Proposition SB1070.

SETTINGS FOR THE MONOLOGUES

MARQUEZ-BERNSTEIN Ph.D. - A fancy hotel suite

DOÑA CONSEPCION - A church

LOLITA CORAZON - The pharmaceutical section in K-mart

CALLETANA - A street

YOKO MARTINEZ - A sushi restaurant in Little Tokyo

ROXIE - The Hollenbeck Police Station

TIFFANY - A Chicano Studies Class at East L.A. College

DOÑA FLORINDA - An apartment in a housing project

VALENTINA - Basement taco shop/hair salon by day and a revolutionary's secret gathering place by night

Lights fade out. After a few seconds lights fade in slightly. Four WOMEN enter from different directions. They are all wearing black. They gather at the altar and light up some sage which they pass around circling in the air, one by one. After they have finished, they push the altar upstage and transform it into a podium. Then three of the WOMEN sit on the chairs. One WOMAN exits.

The lights fade in completely and the three WOMEN become young, shy, Latina students waiting for a seminar to begin. A woman wearing a dressy blazer carrying a large designer bag rushes in as though she were late. She is VICTORIA MARQUEZ-BERNSTEIN, PH.D.

MARQUEZ-BERNSTEIN, PH.D. ¡Hola muchachas! Bienvenidas! Welcome to my seminar. How have you liked the "The High School Latina Leadership Conference" so far? Pretty informative? Eye-opening? Shocking? Well, just get ready to change your lives! Oh, it's nice to see that all of you were able to join me this evening. First of all let me introduce myself. My name is

Doctora Victoria Marquez-Bernstein, Ph.D.

STUDENT #1. A doctor?

MARQUEZ-BERNSTEIN, PH.D. No, I am not a medical doctor, my Ph.D. is in Social Psychology. That's why I decided to teach this seminar, because I am a "Super Latina." Check it out! *(MARQUEZ-BERNSTEIN pulls out a brown and lavender satin cape just like Superman's. It bears the emblem "S L" on it. She puts it on and models it for them.)* You like it? You like it? My mother gave this to me after I got my Ph.D. That's when I became a Super Latina…But for those of you who don't know me, I'm a best-selling author of several self-help books written especially for the Latina of today, like you. I brought a few copies to show you and at the end of the seminar you may purchase them at a discount…All right pues. *(She picks up the books and shows them to her students.)* Now, my first book came out two years ago. "Ten Pendejadas Latinas Do To Mess Up Their Lives," I've done practically all ten, but I'm still here. My next book "La Llorona Complex" deals with the victim persona Latinas adopt. And my mother's favorite, "Latinas Who Don't Complain Enough." I'm also presently working on my second Ph.D. dissertation entitled: "Lorena Bobbitt, The Latina Revolution Begins: Volume One." *(She puts the books aside and stands at the very front of the conference room.)* All right pues. I'd like to see by a show of hands, how many of you Latinas believe you can be a "Super Latina." Aver, aver, everybody raise your hand or get out of my seminar because I don't want you here just occupying space. I want you to participate. Don't be shy. Oh, come on now, you've been taught all your life to be quiet, but today I want you to speak up. What you think matters. Shyness is a sin! *(STUDENT #2 does the sign of the cross.)*

All right, let me put it to you this way! How many of you would like to make $30,000 dollars a year?…*(The three STUDENTS raise their hands.)*

Oh, put your hands down! That's not good enough! *(The three STUDENTS lower their hands.)*

…How many of you would like to make $70,000?…Oh, that's not even close. How many of you would like to make $120,000 a year? Okay, muchachas, all of you raise your hands! Because that's how much money I make. And you see that Mercedes out there, that's mine. So you see, instead of living for weekends waiting for your boyfriend to pick you in his Chevy, mi'jitas, go to college and you can pick him up in your Mercedes! *(She snaps her fingers.)* All right pues. Oh, before we get started, I'm going to share a little secret with you that's gonna save you a life¬time of grief. *(Whispering with a New York Jewish accent.)* Marry Jewish men. They're so giving, they work so hard that they'll do anything to please. And if you're into women, marry a Jew, that works too. But if anybody asks you where you heard it, you didn't hear it from me…All right pues. (*She lifts up her arm and points to the upper interior part of it.*) What do I have underneath here? Do all of you know what I have here? Well you should know. It's a Norplant contraceptive. Now, I'm not here promoting the Norplant, I just want you to take responsibility for your fertility. One of the 10 Pendejadas Latinas do to mess up their lives is get pregnant. So don't get pregnant, get a Norplant and you can give yourself five years to complete your education, child-free. You know what, boys/men are nothing but trouble, so if you can avoid them, do so. Learn how to masturbate. Empower yourself with the knowledge…(*All the STUDENTS become embarrassed.*)

Oh, I forgot, I'm not supposed to talk about masturbation. The people who hired me don't want me to mention or say the word masturbation. But if I'm going to talk about preparation, and determination, we should be able to talk about masturbation. But I understand so I won't talk about masturbation. (*Aside.*) Anybody interested in learning, meet me after the seminar. (*She opens her attache case and takes out a piece of paper.*) All right pues, I'm going to read you a poem from a graduate of my seminar. When I met her she had very little self-esteem, she didn't like herself. She was involved with a man who would abuse her. So after she took my seminar, she wrote this poem and sent it to me. It's called, very appropriately, "My Low Self-Esteem Days"…

"Si te quise fue porque I had low self-esteem.

If I swore I'd always be by your side,

Was because I had nothing better to do.

Si te dije you were a great lover,

Was because I had nothing to compare it to.

If I said you and me were meant to be,

Was because I thought I couldn't find any better.

Si te dije que te amaba con toda mi alma,

Was because I hadn't found myself.

If you think that now that time has passed,

And my low self-esteem days are gone,

That I'm a bitch, a whore, a liar.

Well then go ahead!

'Cause you ain't my master, my father, my hero, my lover…

Shit! I ain't even gonna bother…

To address your remarks.

Time has proved me stronger,

I don't need your approval any longer.

So today, I ain't even gonna bother…

To let you know how good it's been…

Without you"

(She takes a dramatic breath of fresh air and lets it go, however her enthusiasm is still there.)

If anybody would like a copy, I'll have them out at the end of the seminar… You know, I could have written this myself. My husband, Murray, as sweet as he was, he took off with the maid. She was a simple girl from Guatemala. Oh, that's the second pendejada Latinas and all women do is to take off with somebody else's husband and then they wonder how he could have left them. So why am I telling you this?…Well, before you can become a "Super Latina" there are a few things you need to know and accept…You see, my father died when I was twelve and although he worked very hard, he never saved any money. He left my mother with nothing but debts and six children and I swore that I would never be that helpless. And I swore that I would do everything in my power not to be like her. Even though I got what I wanted, it didn't guarantee me happiness…It's lonely at the top. But it's better to be lonely and successful than to be lonely and unsuccessful. Your career can't hug you back, but your career will never leave you, will never cheat on you, will never insult you, will never abuse you. Whatever you've invested in your career you will get back, but it will be lonely, because when you've chosen to follow your dreams, people will not be able to identify with you. People won't like you. Men won't like you because as soon as you start asserting yourself in life, pretty soon you're going to be telling him, "A little to the left, a little more to the right, I need some more cunnilingus before I can reach my plateau of excitation…" Oh, I forgot, I'm not supposed to talk about cunnilingus either. All right, fine, we won't talk about cunnilingus anymore. *(Aside.)* Look it up in the dictionary when you get home and you'll forever thank me…Know that the odds are against you, but your spirit has to be strong. Because people will always question your right to get an education. People will assume that because your last name ends with "ez" as in *(She reads name tags.)* Martinez, Chavez, Sanchez, Lopez, and Ramirez, that you got into college or you got your position because of your last name. So you must know what you want and you must know without a doubt that you deserve it. That you deserve to be happy, that you deserve everything in the world. To have money, to have shelter, to have food. You deserve to have hope. I have hope that maybe one of you will not be the same after today. But if you haven't learned anything, remember this. Choose to be the heroine of your life, because, Mi'ijita, ain't no man gonna rescue you. Because as Latinas we don't get to play the role of "Cinderella" and "Snow White." No. As Latinas all we get to play are the roles of virgin, mother, whore, and the pinchi maid. (*She changes gears and becomes energetic and animated once again.*) So stand up if you want to be a "Super Latina" and put on your cape. (*The THREE YOUNG STUDENTS get up and open their arms as though they were wings and follow MERCEDES-BERNSTEIN as she circles the stage.*

(*Aside.*) Have your mother make you one or you can get one at K-mart for $5.99 in the toy section…and follow me, my caped crusaders. Follow me as we take the first step of the beginning of the rest of your lives! (*She stops suddenly and faces them. The three STUDENTS smash into her. She adjusts herself and stands erect. Immediately the three STUDENTS imitate her heroic pose.*)

Now let's go check out my Mercedes so you can decide what features you want when you get yours. ¡Vamonos! (*She charges out like "Superman" with her three STUDENTS, their arms stretched out like capes. Lights fade out.*)

(*Lights fade in. We are now in St. Mary's Church. The podium has become an altar again. There are two chairs centered facing opposite directions. One WOMAN sits on the chair facing upstage, her back is turned and she becomes a PRIEST. Two other WOMEN are on their knees praying next to their chairs. One WOMAN begins singing "Ave Maria" off key as the fourth WOMAN becomes: DOÑA CONSEPCION, wearing a black lace veil over her head.*)

DOÑA CONSEPCION (*with a raspy smoker's voice*). Ya parale, Gorgoñia, ya ni la friegas. You sound like a broken record. (*The WOMAN stops singing and continues praying. DOÑA CONSEPCION walks up to the altar and says a short prayer silently and does the cross. She then walks over to the empty chair next to the PRIEST.*)

Forgive me, Padre, for I have sinned…It's been 25 years since my last confession. My husband died a month ago and I feel so guilty because I'm happy he's dead…He died of lung cancer. I would tell him to stop smoking or he was going to kill me too with secondhand smoke and de adrede he'd smoke some more…Padre, I feel so guilty, but for the first time I can go to sleep without being woke up every 15 minutes by my husband's snoring… Padre, I feel so guilty, but for the first time I can have the TV and the remote control all to myself…Padre, I feel so…I miss him…Who's going to take out the garbage at night? Who's going to take the dogs to the park? Who's going to eat the leftovers?…He wasn't a bad husband, I don't want you to think

that's why I'm happy…I don't want to imply that, because that would be a lie and at this age I've told too many lies…I loved him, as much as I could… He wasn't hard to love because he was handsome and a good father. I had eight children with him, and he took care of us well…I can't even say he was a borracho or anything bad like that aside from his smoking. He never hit me…He came close once when I forgot to mention how much chili powder I had accidentally put on his food and his tongue got irritated. Se enchilo tanto that he wanted to hit me. But aside from that he never raised his hand to me. He never said a mean word to me…Pues, now that I think about it, he never said that much to me…So how can I be happy he's dead? I don't want to be, but I am…I don't know how I can possibly be, but I am…Padre, are you listening? *(She looks closer, checking to see that there is a PADRE there listening. The PADRE is falling asleep.)*

…I went for a medical check-up to check my diabetes and that's how I found out I have AIDS. *(The PADRE moves his chair to give himself some distance just to be safe.)*

I know he gave it to me because I've never slept with anyone but him. I was a virgin when we got married and I never cheated on him…I'm not happy he's dead because he gave me AIDS…I don't want you to think that. I don't really blame him because I never liked sex. It was boring and sometimes painful and I hated getting pregnant. After my eighth child I didn't want to have sex with him anymore. So el pobrecito would have to go get it somewhere else. And I knew that, and I let him. I never said anything about it because what else could he do…Every time he made an attempt to caress me or kiss me I would be disgusted by it and I would push him away…I often wondered why he didn't just divorce me. I even told him to leave me if he wasn't happy. But he wouldn't. I guess I was a good mother and wife even though…It must have been very difficult for my children never to see their parents kissing or touching. I never did that, because…*(She pauses and can't go on…She looks up to God and around her.)* Padre, I've been gay all my life! *(The PADRE raises his hands up to God in disbelief.)*

So in a way I blame myself…I wish I didn't have to tell you this, Padre, but I can't tell anyone else, and my husband's death left me so broke I can't afford a therapist…Maybe I have to come out to you first because it was God who was there with me when I lost my virginity and felt nothing. I thought it was normal not feeling anything the first time, but later on in my marriage, having sex with him seemed unnatural…It was also God who was with me when I had my first, how shall I say…"wet dream," about being with a girl at the age of six. So I just want to tell you to tell God that I have finally accepted what he knew all along…*(She checks to see if the PADRE is listening.)* I also want to tell my children and grandchildren because the doctor told me I have two years to live and I want them to know. But I know this will tear them apart. My husband's death has been hard on them…It's been hard on me because I have to pretend I'm a suffering widow. I don't want to pretend anymore. I cannot smile when I'm around them. I cannot enjoy anything when I'm around them and they never leave me alone! They're always asking me how I'm doing? Sending flowers, greeting cards, men in gorilla outfits with balloons, bringing cakes, cleaning my house, doing my chores; all the things I wanted them to do when they were kids. But now, when I want to be left alone to gather my thoughts about what I'm going to do with my life, my children won't leave me alone. They worry I'll get depressed and die of depression in two years like most spouses who have been married for years and their spouse dies. So they keep bringing their kids over and we have lots of family dinners to keep "Nana" company. We have quality time, we communicate our love for each other, we share all the feelings that we couldn't express when my husband was alive, and I just want to tell them to get the hell out of my house and leave me alone!…(*The PADRE grumbles.*)

See, that got your attention…Padre, how do I tell my children? I wish I could tell them…Do I tell them I'm gay and let them find out I have AIDS when my hair starts falling out, I'm losing weight, and I'm wearing adult Pampers before my time? Or do I tell them I have AIDS and they'll feel so bad for me that they won't mind I'm gay? Or should I even tell them at all? I can just let them believe I died of depression…I don't have to tell them!… Oh, yes, I do…I never told my husband and I robbed him of his chance to find a woman who would satisfy him and make him feel wanted. I might have even saved his life. Maybe he wouldn't have smoked so much if he didn't feel so sexually frustrated and resentful of me…I killed him…

PADRE/PRAYING WOMEN *(shocked)*. You killed him?!

DOÑA CONSEPCION. I killed his spirit…I took away his happiness… *(She cries.)* I never wanted to hurt him. I never wanted to hurt anybody, but I've already hurt everybody by living this lie. The least I can do is hurt everybody with the truth. But how do I tell my grandchildren, "Nana's gay and she's got AIDS." I feel so embarrassed for my family, because this isn't supposed to happen. I'm not supposed to be gay, I'm not supposed to get AIDS, not at this age! Ask God why it happened to me, Padre. If it's punishment, then I understand…If it's a lesson…then I'm grateful because now I can't hide what I've always been. I've got two years to live, I'll at least die having found myself. Even as I'm dying, I'm living every day the way I should have done all my life…I think I'll tell my children and my friends everything tonight. I hope they understand. Y si no. ¡Que se vallan a la chingada! This is my life…Thank you, Padre, thank you, God, thank you, God…Amen… *(DOÑA CONSEPCION does the cross and gets up and walks out. Lights fade out.)*

(Lights fade in. The altar is upstage left and has been transformed into a counter in the pharmacy section of K-mart. There is a little sign on the altar that reads: "PHARMACY." There are two chairs next to each other facing the audience. One WOMAN goes behind the altar and becomes the PHARMACIST. One WOMAN sits at a chair in her corner. One WOMAN enters: She is DOLORES CORAZON, a shy Latina wearing a plain pastel floral print. DOLORES walks up to the PHARMACY counter with a doctor's prescription and hands it to the PHARMACIST.)

DOLORES. Here's my prescription…My name is Dolores Corazón.

LOLITA *(offstage)*. Her real name is Lolita.

DOLORES. How long is it going to take?

PHARMACIST. Fifteen minutes.

DOLORES. Fifteen minutes?!

LOLITA *(offstage)*. Dang! *(The PHARMACIST leaves. DOLORES picks a box of female condoms.)*

DOLORES/LOLITA. Female condoms?…Female condoms.

(LOLITA "CHINGONA" CORAZON enters. She is flamboyant, a sexy Latina who is not afraid to express her opinions and doesn't need anybody's approval. She wears her hair high and loose. LOLITA snaps her fingers and DOLORES and the PHARMACIST freeze.)

LOLITA. Female condoms? Female Condoms! Tsss! The day I start wearing a female condom is the day the Equal Rights Amendment is passed; women are no longer raped and beaten up in this country; baby girls in China stop getting killed for being born female; brides in India stop being burned alive; women in Africa stop having their clitorises cut out; women in Brazil stop getting killed by jealous husbands who get away with it; and young women all over the world have equal opportunity to get an education and get fed properly. 'Til then, shit! The least men can do is wear a condom, know what I mean, prieta? *(She snaps her fingers and DOLORES and the PHARMACIST unfreeze.)*

K-MART ANNOUNCER *(voice-over)*. Attention, K-mart shoppers, the wait is over! You can now apply for your own K-mart Credit Card. And as a Blue Light Special bonus, if you apply within the next fifteen minutes you'll get a discount coupon for your next Lay-away. *(DOLORES walks over to a chair and she and LOLITA sit simultaneously.)*

LOLITA. Sure you do, that little bruise on your face didn't come from no bump. So put down those female condoms and get him some! The cheap kind. The ones that make his pito itch…Besides you only get three in a box for three times the amount for men's condoms. And they look "Uuugly"… But why am I complaining, I don't even use condoms…*(DOLORES looks around wondering if anybody else can hear LOLITA. LOLITA looks herself up and down realizing she looks like the biggest slut and should be using condoms.)* I don't need to…I know you think I'm a slut, I know you do so don't deny it…You're probably looking at me thinking that of all people here in K-mart, I should be counting the minutes before these fat, "Fiesta" colored condoms become the next "Blue Light Special," right?…No, that's o-kay, people call me a slut…Now, do I look like a slut to you? Of course I do, I work at it. But you can be one or just look like one, but I ain't one. I'm a chingona! I like that better. Matter of fact, I don't know what a puta is, I don't think I've ever met one…Oh, yeah, wait, yeah, once. This one stupid chick who was having sex for all the wrong reasons. She was trying to keep her boyfriend from leaving her. She had no respect for herself. I, on the other hand, respect myself and I do what I do for all the right reasons. For fun. And I don't use condoms, 'cause I don't need any. I'm what some men call a "tease." And it don't bother me. I know men look at me and they go in their minds, "Yo, I bet she's easy." They put on their macho airs and they give me their packaged crap about how sexy I look and how I remind them of their sisters. Their sisters! These losers can't even come up with original lines. And they also tell me how they saw me in their dream the night before and it was destiny that we met and shit like that. Then they rub up against me, and if they don't already have a hard-on I give them one when I look at them and smile. I give them that idiotic look they love and make them think they're so clever and funny, so funny that I'm wet all over. They think I'm easy but what they don't know is that I'm hard. Harder to breaker, harder to dominate, harder than their dicks. *(LOLITA turns to DOLORES and gives her a serious look.)*

So, Prieta, let me ask you, why do you want to cheat on your boyfriend? Yeah, I know you do, so don't deny it. 'Cause otherwise you wouldn't be checking out the condoms if you were in a "happy monogamous relationship" like you claim to be…No, don't tell me, don't tell me… Your boyfriend promised you he would never raise a hand to you, he'd rather die than to do a thing like that again, right? But, mi'jita, he will. So now you're seeking the comfort of a stranger to caress those wounds, huh? Yeah, I know I'm good, I still could be a psychoanalyst if I wanted to, you know? But, mi'jita, when your boyfriend finds out, he's gonna kick your ass… *(LOLITA waits for a response, then she enthusiastically proceeds to share her knowledge.)* Okay, pues! You're gonna need some tips on how to be a slut.

(LOLITA snaps her fingers and lights fade. They are now in a discotheque. LOLITA leans against the bar, acting "cool," enjoying the music.)

LOLITA. Okay, first thing, Prieta, make eye contact. Any guy you want, you can get. Look around. Pick one. Make eye contact. Stare a little longer than you should, then, turn away…You got him. Then the game begins. So have fun. Just don't touch…I usually don't pick up men. Unless I find one challenging enough, then maybe, maybe, I'll go with him to his apartment.

(LOLITA snaps her fingers, lights change to an apartment setting. She does several seductive poses.)

LOLITA. They kiss me and I let them play with my breasts. I whisper all the dirty things they want to hear. "Ayy, Papi, como me gustas. Ayy, que grandototote estas, chulo." And if they're gringos they go crazy for this one, "Eres mi rey. You are my king. Can I have a bite of your big and meaty burrito? Que rico, suave…" *(To the audience.)* Gerardo stole that line from me, all right…"¡Sabroso!" Then I get all hungry and want to leave to go buy some tacos, but I can't because they got me all wrapped up with their hands…Then when they get as hard as a brick and they're burning up inside, their pelvis' start trembling. My hand goes inside their pants. I barely touch it and they become little boys…And that's when the real acting begins. *(LOLITA puts up her hand to her forehead very dramatically like an innocent virgin in distress.)*

"Oh, no, I can't do this. I can't. I'm a virgin!…I have to go home," I tell them. They're so hard and excited, their faces turn yellow. The misery of ending up with blue balls hits them and they beg me to stay. "I can't. I shouldn't be doing this," I say with the voice of a total virgin. And they believe me and lower their expectations, 'cause they're so horny by now they'll settle for me pulling on their dicks. But I won't even do that, 'cause I'm a virgin. *(LOLITA laughs, indulging in the lie.)*

So I'm practically out the door and sure enough they're so pissed-off at me by now they accuse me of being "a tease." Then I stop and I look at them all sincere and shit. "I'm not a tease…Well, I can't have sex with you, but what if…What if…What if you masturbated for me. Oh, I bet you look so beautiful when you come." And the guys fall for it. Yeah! Yeah! They do! They're so horny they settle for masturbating for me. So I watch. They make these faces. I imagine kinda like the faces they would be making as they were being born. They look like children screaming for their lives. They look so vulnerable, so delicate, like I could take them into my arms and crush the life out of them…Sometimes I touch their faces and hold them while they come. I watch their faces and I get more excited than if I were to have sex with them. *(She starts to make facial expressions. She looks excited but then she stops, frightened. She walks over to DOLORES who is now sitting and stands behind her as if whispering this story to her.)*

I remember the first time I had sex. I went with him to his apartment, I was so excited and scared. But when he stuck his hand in my panties and his finger entered me I told him, "Oh, no, I can't do this. I can't. I'm a virgin!" He kept pressing it in and he thought I was being a tease. He got on top of me, penetrated me, humped me. He made faces, like he enjoyed it even though I was screaming. I kept screaming because I felt like he was tearing me inside. With every scream and grimace I made, I got glimpses of his face. I couldn't understand his look. How could he look like an angel, happy and peaceful, when he was hurting me? (*DOLORES doesn't want to hear anymore so she runs away from LOLITA. Lights fade in. DOLORES and LOLITA sit across from each other simultaneously.*)

Yeah, I know not all men are assholes. I actually met a "redeemable male" a few months ago…I hate to admit it, but I love him. Why do you think I'm checking out the condom section? He's kinda nice, but I like him too much to seriously consider giving it up to him…No, not my virginity, some dickhead already took that…But I don't think I'm ready yet. It's tough to let a man see you lose control, and that's just one thing I gotta have…

PHARMACIST. Dolores Corazón, your prescription is ready.

DOLORES/LOLITA. That's me!

LOLITA. Good luck…I hope your boyfriend doesn't kick your ass, again. (*LOLITA gets up and leaves. DOLORES looks for LOLITA but can't see her anymore.*)

PHARMACIST (*voice-over*). Second call for Dolores Corazón. (*DOLORES goes to the counter. LOLITA stands behind her. They both pick up the prescription simultaneously. Lights fade out.*)

(*Lights fade in. One WOMAN goes to the altar and removes the "PHARMACY" sign. She takes the altar from the side and pushes it forward like a shopping cart. This woman becomes: CALLETANA "LA ELOTERA", a short, dark, very indigenous-looking woman with a long black braid. She is dressed plainly, wearing an apron, knee-highs, a colorful dress, pants, and a red baseball cap.*)

CALLETANA. ¡Elotes! ¡Elotes! ¡A un dolar! Andele, seño, buy a corn. Ayy, what diet, for what? Your old man is fat too. Eat one and you'll feel much better. Anyway, who is going to want to steal your husband? He's fat and bald… No, no, no. No mucho. Not a lot. Not enough for a pretty little girl in need of a green card to be repulsed, but enough to keep them away… Andele, compreme uno…A, bueno…How do you want it? With mayo and everything? (*CALLETANA starts preparing the corn first with lemon, mayo, then goat cheese, butter, chili powder. She gives the corn on the cob to a member of the audience and speaks to the audience.*)

I've worked here on this corner of the street for five years now. It's my anniversary and to celebrate it, I am having a special. Two corns for $1.99. No, no, no mas 'stoy bromiando, just kidding. Ni me crea...I came from Mexico and I brought my three daughters with me because my husband, viejo rabo verde, left me for a tiny squincla mal pintada. A twenty-year-old mensa. And I came here and worked as a maid until I got tired of being treated like a slave...No, no. Now don't go thinking that I'm scared of hard work, because I'm not. By selling corn on the street I can provide for myself and my daughters. And the good thing about it is that I am the boss. I don't want nobody feeling sorry for me. Because if people do, I'd rather just shoot myself right now. Why be a burden on society? I don't like it when they say that Mexicans are lazy, because we are not. Prietos y sensillos tal vez, pero lazy no. Because we didn't cross a river and risk our lives to get here just to be tourists. We came here to work. N'ombre, I'm not scared of work, eso si que no. Cochina y mal hablada yes, pero lazy no. I used to have a grandmother who would wake up every morning at five a.m. to prepare the nixtamal and she would make the tortillas by hand like a real woman... ¡Elotes, elotes, con mucho chile! (*She prepares another corn. Taking her time and doing it with a certain pleasure. She sings a love song in Spanish. A police squad car is heard in the distance.*)

What I didn't like when I first started was that I would be selling corn and the police would pass by and they would tell me it was illegal what I was doing. That they would have to arrest me. But because I reminded them of their mothers they wouldn't arrest me. So then I would move. But in a little while I'd come back. Every week they would do this and I just acted like a mensa and I'd tell them "Yes, mister! Okay, okay." Then they'd leave, but I'd always come back. One day, they finally caught me. And in front of everybody they put handcuffs on me and put me inside their police car... That was a very interesting night, my first time in jail. I spent it with the prostitutas. I learned a thing or two, that I can't mention in front of children, that might come in handy one of these days when I meet my galan de cine. (*She prepares a corn.*) Ah, you think because I'm old and my chichis almost touch the floor I don't get an itch down there once in a while. But like they say, mejor que la gosen los humanos a que se la coman los gusanos, eh? (*The corn on the cob all of a sudden becomes a phallic symbol. She continues singing the love song.*)

But the next day after they let me out of jail, I returned to my corner and another vendor was there. Un viejo chancludo, peludo, a hairy man selling sour mangos. He stole my corner. And worst of all he kept coming on to me. A whole year at my corner and on my one-year anniversary they threw me in jail and I lost my corner. I liked that corner because it was close to a bar and when men got drunk they would buy their girlfriends a corn to impress them. And the prostitutas, when they were done for the night would be very hungry and would buy some corn. *(The other WOMEN take out a dollar from their brassiers and buy a corn from CALLETANA.)*

Pero gueno, so I left and I joined the tamale vendors at a church nearby. And one day this young woman, who called herself a Chicana, but I called her a cochina because she was dressed up like a hippie, started telling me about what was going on in City Hall and that if I was interested in telling my story to try to convince the politicians to legalize street selling. "No, no." I told her. I didn't want to go, pero mi hija, my twelve-year-old daughter, mi chatita, she gave me the saddest look when she asked me why they took me to jail. "What did I do wrong?" I told her "nothing," but it got me angry that she doubted me. It broke my heart. And I started thinking to myself and asked myself, "What is my crime?" I have not robbed anyone. What is my crime; trying to survive? Why don't they go arrest those welferosos who only sit on their ass, breeding, robbing the government. When I know I haven't done anything wrong, I'm not scared of anything, not even the devil…

(She quickly crosses herself, almost contradicting herself. Lights fade. CALLETANA takes her "cart" to the center and turns it around. It is now a podium. CALLETANA shyly approaches the podium. Spotlight on her.)

We are here to tell you that we are just trying to survive. We are not taking away any big profits from the stores where we sell at because whatever we make is only to get by. To feed our families. We are not on the streets robbing, committing crimes, or hurting the economy like we are blamed. But just because we're "illegal aliens," as you call us, doesn't mean we have no voice. But why are we "illegal"? I don't understand. What is our crime? Wanting to survive and feed our children? That is the right of every human being. Because even if we are undocumented we are part of this city and we contribute to the economy. Today I come to remind you that the streets, the land, and the sun belong to no one. They belong to all of us. And that's why I come to ask you that you give us the right to earn a living…Gracias. *(CALLETANA walks away from the podium feeling relieved and proud. She goes back to her cart and continues preparing corn with even more pride.)*

I was really nervous, but I told them what I thought they should know. And el Mr. Councilman Woo, ese buen hombre, he tried helping us and everything came out okay. We won the right to sell…I have a dream that one day we will have a union like Cesar Chavez did for los Campesinos. That's what that Chicanita, la hippie, told me…I would like to have a union between all the street vendors and have medical benefits. I know it's almost impossible, pero bueno, dreaming is free, ¿qué no? Maybe one day we will have a union and the police and the gangs will leave us alone. Because there

are a lot of us and maybe with a union things would be different…¡Elotes! ¡Elotes! ¡Elotes con mucho chile! *(Lights slowly fade out.)*

(Lights fade in. One WOMAN takes the altar from center to her corner, upstage right. She turns around and puts on a Japanese kimono and carries a Japanese fan. She becomes: YOKO "I THINK I'M TURNING JAPANESE" MARTINEZ, The other three WOMEN take their chairs and sit in three different locations onstage. They put on identical "Noh" masks. YOKO walks gently forward, taking small steps.)

YOKO. Irasshaimase! Tokyo Housu e youkoso. Welcome to Tokyo House of Sushi. *(YOKO runs to MRS. ITO #1 fanning herself.)* Teburu e otsure shimasu. Kore wa anata no menu de gozaimasu. *(YOKO runs to MRS. ITO #3 fanning herself.)* Watashi wa Yoko tomoushimasu. You can call me Yoko. Konban no osusumi wa uni to ikura desu. Tonight's specials are uni and ikura. *(YOKO runs to MRS. ITO #2 fanning herself.)* Nani o nomini narimasu ka. What would you like to drink? *(YOKO runs to MRS. ITO #1 fanning herself.)* Go chyumon wa. What would you like to order? *(YOKO runs to MRS. ITO #2 fanning herself.)* Hai! Arrigato gozaimasu.…What did you say Mrs. Ito?…You want me to list the names of all the fish used in sushi, in Japanese? Sure! Hai! Maguro, Toro, Katsuo, Saba, Shake, Tai, Hirame, Tako, Suzuki, Ebi, Uni, Hamachi, to…to…ah… ah…ah….*(YOKO has difficulty remembering the rest. She tries to remember, but can't. She breaks out of character.)*

¡Ah, que la chingada! ¡Se me olvido! I forgot! What's it called? I know, I know, I was supposed to have learned all my Japanese lingo by now, but it's hard remembering all those "K" sounds. I'm a Latina, I like things to flow. How do people learn this stuff? How do people make love in this language when it sounds like you're constantly constipated?…¡Ay, dios! *(YOKO gets carried away and then stops herself when she realizes she's putting her foot in her mouth. YOKO runs to MRS. ITO #2 and bows.)* Gomen nasai! *(YOKO runs to MRS. ITO #3.)* Wait, wait, I can learn this language! Please give me one more chance to prove to you I can do it, Mrs. Ito. Please, really, really, onegaishimasu!…*(YOKO bows very low in front of MRS. ITO #3. Beat.)* You see, you see. I do know Japanese…I need this job! You don't know what I've been through. I tried getting a job at a French restaurant but they were so rude I had to quit. Then I went to a Brazilian restaurant but they said I needed to be darker, but I don't tan, I burn. Then I worked at an Italian restaurant, but the owner kept pinching me in the ass, and I had to quit because I told his wife, and she got the restaurant in her settlement. So you see I really need this job!! *(She does a physical Kabuki theater movement to show how distressed she is.)* You see, you see. I do know Japanese culture. Did you just get that Kabuki theater reference thing I just did for you? *(YOKO gives herself away.)*

Okay, okay. I don't actually need this job. I just want it to increase my chances of meeting Japanese men. You see, I've been working in Mexican restaurants too long and all I meet are Mariachis, day laborers, soccer players, busboys, dishwashers, relatives of all of the above, and I just don't want to end up marrying…a Latino man. I want something different. It's not like I'm looking for a man with a Ph.D. and a Rolls Royce and a mansion, or nothing. I just want my life to be different. I want somebody different. I want a man who is gentle, kind, who doesn't scream. I'm tired of men screaming at me…So you see, Mrs. Ito, since I've never seen Japanese men screaming, except like in them Bruce Lee movies…(*MRS. ITO(s) lifts her face, upset.*) Oh, they're Chinese, huh? Well, see, I figure they're gentle enough. I can deal with the sexism and the tiny penises. Watachi wa anata no chinco o aishitemasu. See, see, I just said in Japanese "I love your dick." Look, I'll say it again. (*YOKO runs to MRS. ITO #3.*) Watachi wa anata no chinco o aishitemasu. I'll say it again. (*YOKO runs to MRS. ITO #2.*) Watachi wa anata no chinco o aishitemasu. I mean, not to infer that all Japanese men have small penises, I mean, who cares, it's not like it's the most important thing. Small, medium, large, they're all the same to me. Fune okisawa mondai dewa nakute yarikata no mondai desu. It's not the size of the ship, but the motion of the ocean. But you know what I mean? Wakarimashita ka…I just can't deal with screaming. It's not the actual screaming that bothers me, it's the face of a man screaming, it's his expression, it's his aggression, it's his fist screaming at me… I just don't want to end up marrying my father…(*YOKO is about to start crying. Then, she strikes a Kabuki theatre crying pose instead.*)

Did you get this Kabuki reference thing, too?…Yeah, I guess I could easily just marry a white guy, but they're passionless…No! No, not to say that all white men are passionless, it just turns out that all the white guys I've been with have been passionless. They didn't have what Latinos call "las chispas," or as you would say "hibana," sparks. They were very nice men, who were more open-minded, but something was missing. Like in bed there were no "Te amo mi'jita," "Ti amo carrina," You know Italian is such a beautiful language, but Italian men are just like Mexican men…(*YOKO runs to MRS. ITO #3.*) Mrs. Ito, I know I don't look Japanese. I know that by the very fact that I have large breasts practically disqualifies me from passing for Japanese, but I'll tie them up; no one will know I'm a 36D, I swear!…Oh, I'm sorry, no I didn't mean to imply that Japanese women have small breasts. No, I mean, who cares. The French have a saying, "Les femme qui n'ont pas de poitrine sont le meilluers. Les homme puet etre plu porche a leur cuore." They say that French men, I heard this one Japanese woman claim, prefer flat-chested women because they can get closer to their hearts…(*YOKO runs to MRS. ITO #2.*) Look Mrs. Ito. I'm Mexican, and aside from having large breasts I've also got huge hips and sometimes I wish I were Japanese so

I'd eat a lot of fish and rice and not have to worry about my weight. I mean, I'm on a diet right now, but I'm Mexican, so that's impossible…You know the secret to good Mexican food is la grasa, or as you'd say "abura," grease. You see, that's another reason I want this job. So I can go on a diet, eat lots of fish, and get down to a marriageable size…*(YOKO runs to MRS. ITO #3.)* Mrs. Ito, Mrs. Ito, aside from the Japanese, I'm a great waitress. I've been a waitress all my life. In fact, it's the only thing I know how to do, aside from some Kabuki theater and a little Flamenco. Otherwise, if I could I…I know I'm not that smart, but I know how to take orders, I smile, and I don't spill water. Please give me one more chance, onegaishimasu. I don't know what else to tell you but the truth…I just need a chance. *(After a few seconds of waiting for a response, YOKO lowers her head and is about to go into the kitchen. MRS. ITO(s) rise. YOKO stops and is surprised.)* You will?! Okay. Ah, just for today. No, okay. I'll get started right away…*(YOKO excitedly runs, then she stops and turns to them.)* Mrs. Ito, Mrs. Ito…Domo arrigato gozaimasu. *(YOKO bows her head gratefully. MRS. ITO(s) bow back. Lights fade out.)*

(Lights fade in. The altar has been moved upstage center. We are at the Hollenbeck Police Station. One WOMAN enters and becomes: ROXIE "THE SELF-DEFENSE INSTRUCTOR," a tough-looking Latina, wearing jeans, cowboy boots with steel heels, and a sleeveless blouse that shows off her tattoos. She could easily be mistaken for a "butch" lesbian, but she's not. Her core is very feminine, her exterior is very masculine. She sits in handcuffs trying to explain her side of the story. She is frustrated and tries to control her anger. Three WOMEN sit in their chairs, they become POLICE OFFICERS listening to ROXIE.)

ROXIE. I can't believe you're really going to book me, officer. I did it out of self-defense. I thought he was going to attack me so I attacked him before he tried it. How was I supposed to know he wasn't going to attack me? So what that he claims he wasn't going to attack me. Of course! What's he going to say? "Yeah I was going to attack her, rape her, and leave her for dead, but she hit me in the balls before I had a chance to throw her on the floor and punch her face"? I'm innocent! Why would I attack a man for no reason? *(She knows she's not convincing anybody.)*

Okay, let me explain…But first, take these handcuffs off of me. I'm gonna need to demonstrate what I did…

POLICEWOMAN #1 *(muttering)*. Fuckin' dyke…

ROXIE. I'm not a lesbian and what has that got to do with it? *(One POLICEWOMAN removes the handcuffs from her. One POLICEWOMAN gestures with her hand to ask if she was drinking.)*

No, I wasn't drinking. Oh, yeah, I did. I drank a "7-Up," and, yeah, I know I'm not supposed to be walking by myself at night. I'm a self-defense instructor, I teach these things…Yeah, I'm not joking. I got harassed so much by men. I got tired of their threatening remarks so I took a self-defense class. I got so good at it I decided to teach it… Yeah, I'm angry, wouldn't you be if men constantly grabbed at your breasts? You're walking down the street and some man just slips his hand in and grabs your breasts and when you cuss him out he laughs…I can see you wouldn't understand…I'm not saying you're flat-chested, I just think the police uniform makes you look it…I'm not a lesbian, and I haven't been looking at your breasts… *(ROXIE stands up with her hands at her waist with her breasts sticking up.)*

You know I wasn't always like this…Really…When I was young I was flat-chested, *(Aside.)*…too. I wasn't that young, about eleven, twelve. I remember I was a real tomboy back then…

(Lights fade a little and ROXIE reminisces and becomes the 12-year-old she used to be.)

One day, I remember I was waiting in line to borrow a football and this guy ahead of me turned around, checked me out, and said out loud so that all the other boys could hear him, "Hey, flat-chested!" I knew he was talking to me but I ignored him. He knew I heard him and he got closer and stared at my chest…He was right. I was flat. *(She sits.)*

So that day, I remember sitting on the toilet staring at my chest. "It's hopeless!" I thought. "I'm one of the few girls in sixth grade who still doesn't have chichis"…After getting tired of looking at my ugly, tiny, minuscule, nipples, I got up and went to my older sisters' drawers and started looking for a bra. I got the smallest I could find and I put it on, but it was still too big. I stuffed some toilet paper in both cups and it felt so good to have breasts. I raced my hands up and down my new breasts, enjoying the pleasure they gave me. But I stopped because I knew God was watching…So I took off the bra and sat back on the toilet…*(She looks up to God, then she slowly gets on her knees.)*

And it occurred to me that if God was watching, God would also be listening. I closed my eyes and I prayed. "Dear God, please give me breasts. I will be a good human being…I will do your will, I will be an honest person, I will be good."

(We hear holy music and ROXIE slowly stands up from her praying position and raises her arms to God then lowers them as though they were wings and finally points to her breasts. The older ROXIE is now back.)

...I believe there is a God. I got breasts quickly after that. So the next time I saw that guy, he didn't even recognize me...I love having big breasts. I'm not saying I'm a better woman for having them, I just think they're a beautiful part of me...Sometimes my sisters and girlfriends make fun of me because of their size, I don't mind. I love my breasts. They are my connection with God. Thank you, God, for making me a woman!...I used to have boyfriends who were atheists. But I made believers out of them. Or at least I think so, because they used to say, "Oh, my God, they're so big!" I would tell them, when you touch them, let them be your reminders that there is a God...I wonder if God is a woman?...So when men just walk by and grab my breasts like it's their right, in my eyes they're committing a sin against God! They are taking away my connection with God. They are desecrating my nipples—I mean temples. Because this body belongs to me!!! The last time a jerk grabbed my breast I felt so helpless. I cried for an hour when I got home. Then the next day I went to my first self-defense class...Soon after I was teaching my own self-defense class...

(Lights fade in completely. ROXIE is standing erect and strong, teaching her own class.)

In order to not be a victim, you have to stop acting like one! Lift your heads high, walk with confidence. Defending yourself is only a matter of using your five weapons. Your hands, fingers, knees, legs, and your voice against his five vulnerable parts. His eyes, nose, throat, groin, and knee. It only takes forty pounds of pressure to dislocate a knee. Not every woman here will be attacked, but one out of three women will be raped within her lifetime. When it comes to defending yourself, any woman can...The first thing we will learn is your basic hand release...*(She demonstrates by holding one of her hands at the wrist with the other.)*

When a man has grabbed you by the wrists...First of all, never let a stranger invade your personal space. Your personal space is the space at arm's length around you...So if you're being pulled by the wrists, don't pull. Just make a fist and twist against his thumb because it is the weakest part of the hand and the hand will release. Then you run and yell "fire." Don't yell "rape" because people might not come. Yell "fire" as loud as you can or if you're in L.A. you can also try yelling earthquake. People will come look only when it concerns them...So everybody get up and let's do it!

(Lights fade a little. ROXIE is no longer the self-assured and confident instructor.)

But even with all the knowledge and training I still got raped...I didn't know that I had gotten raped until I read a magazine article that said that when a man has sex with a woman when she is not conscious, it is rape. I wasn't drunk, I was just falling asleep. I was so tired. I wanted to spend the night in bed with him just talking and then he was on top of me. I couldn't yell "fire," I couldn't kick or fight back. He kept wanting it and I just submitted. It was so casual that when I woke up I just thought it was unpleasant…*(She shakes her head and becomes the tough woman that she is.)*

So I don't let any man get into my personal space. That man should have known better following a woman at night and asking for the time! That's just plain stupid!…No, I'm not saying he was "asking for it." I just think some men have to be sympathetic and aware of the fear they provoke in women. All the rest already know and they laugh when they see it in us…So that's it. That's my confession. Are you gonna let me go? *(She waits, anticipating resistance. Then their response surprises her.)*

POLICEWOMAN #2. You can go.

ROXIE. I can go?! I can go! I'd knew you'd understand…

POLICEWOMAN #3. He dropped the charges.

ROXIE. He dropped the charges? Oh, I'm glad…

POLICEWOMAN #3. But you gotta apologize…

ROXIE. I have to apologize?! Apologize? Apologize!…Do I legally have to?…*(Sarcastically.)* Oh, I should, after all I attacked him…Oh, no, I'm very grateful to him! *(ROXIE feels like punching something or somebody. She finally controls herself and makes a deal with herself.)*

Sure, I'll apologize…I just want to get the hell out of here! Man, either way, we lose!…Where is he?! *(ROXIE marches out angry, but contained. Lights fade out.)*

(Lights fade in. We are in a Chicano Studies class. One WOMAN walks up to the altar and brings it center stage. She turns the altar around and it becomes a podium. Two FEMALE STUDENTS are seated on the floor. One WOMAN is at the podium finishing her speech. The fourth WOMAN becomes: TIFFANY "THE BORN-AGAIN CHICANA." TIFFANY is light, with light brown hair. She is at the front of the class, seated, wearing trendy clothes and lots of jewelry. TIFFANY is a born-again Chicana who grew up in the valley. TIFFANY is waiting to go on next. STUDENT #1 is at the podium finishing her speech.)

STUDENT #1. Thank you for listening to my speech…¡Viva la Raza!… Oh, Tiffany is next. *(TIFFANY hesitantly goes to the front of the podium and begins reading her speech. It is in Spanish and she is having difficulty with her pronunciation.)*

TIFFANY *(with Valley Girl accent)*. Las razónes que nuestra raza debe

resistir éste racismo es que, es que, es que…No, I can't do it! I know, I know. I signed up to give a speech to denounce Proposition 187, but, I can't do it in Spanish! Well, maybe I can, I just can't get the "Rrrr's" right…Okay, okay, I'll try it again…Las razones que… (TIFFANY takes a moment and breathes deeply.) I can't do it! Like I'm not in the right frame of mind…I just got into an argument with my boyfriend…

STUDENT #2. Again?

TIFFANY. Yeah, again, sooo! We argue a lot because I think it like turns me on. Julio is a Brown Beret and he can debate the hell out of people. Anyway, last night I heard the bad news…

STUDENT #1. Oh, what's that?

TIFFANY. Well, it was for me, okay? So like I had to deal with it, all right? Last night I heard that Madonna purchased the film rights to the biography of Frida Kahlo and wanted to star in the role. Like when I heard that, I thought it was perhaps like a bad episode of the "Twilight Zone." Like ¡o mi dios! Oh, my God! How outrageous! And then they, Hollywood, wanted Julia Roberts to star in the role but she like turned it down because of the controversy it would create. I was really glad Julia showed some conscience. Now I know who is going to play the role and my mind aches, in disgust, disbelief, and insult. I mean, like last night I couldn't go to sleep…I mean, because I thought there is something I have to do. Like someone should tell Frida…because like she should know. If she were alive she'd be cursing in disbelief. (In bad Spanish.) "¡Pos que chingados, éstos pinches gringos!" So last night I began writing to her. I know, I know, how ridiculous, huh? But I had to do it…

STUDENT #2. Are you going to mail it?

TIFFANY. Am I going to mail it?! Don't make fun of me, my fellow Chicano hermana.

STUDENT #3. Where are you going to address it to?

TIFFANY. Where am I going to address it to?! Oh, ha, ha, ha…Like the world beyond. Like 666 Death Row. Like the cosmos. Like the Kingdom of God. Like I don't know!…I just wanted to share this letter with the class, being that if I don't do my speech I'll fail the class. All right? Can I do this instead, Professor? (She waits for approval. Then she proceeds to prepare herself to share her letter.)

Okay, cool…But wait, Professor, can you like remove that insensitive "Chicanosauraus Rex" before I start? No, oh, well, could you at least fail her if she laughs? Really, you will? ¡Orale! (TIFFANY clears her throat.)

"Dear Frida…Dear Frida, I'm writing to you because I think you need to know. Ayy, Frida, last night I found out this Italian chick is gonna play you in a Hollywood movie. Not that there's anything wrong with being Italian. You know, I used to think I was Italian several years ago when I was 'in denial about being Mexican,' or at least that's what my Chicano boyfriend has convinced me I did… Okay, you know, like that wasn't my fault, all right? My mom married an Anglo man when she lived in Texas. And she stopped speaking Spanish because the teachers would punish her for doing it and she didn't want me to suffer the way she did. My mother became a Republican to fit in with my father's family. So, Julio still blames me for lacking the conscience. I mean, he quotes Marx to me. `It is not a man's conscience that determines his existence, but it is the existence of a man that determines his conscience.' So I like argue back that despite my existence I can still gain a Chicano conscience, right?…Okay, fine, like that's another story…" *(TIFFANY continues with her letter.)*

"Why should they cast an Italian chick? Why not a Mexican, or Chicana, or Latina actress? What are they doing to you? *(Beat.)* Every time I see your image I cringe because I know Madonna wants to play you. She paid three million for the film rights to your biography. I can just imagine Madonna dressing up as you and including you in her dance and song act. Dressing up with flowers in her head and exploiting our indigenous fashion heritage. Like I'm…" shhhh!!!…Julio thinks I should stop wearing these clothes or I should dye my hair black and get some sun because I'm too pale. I remember when I thought I was better because I was a light-skinned Mexican, but now I wish I had like jet black hair, like brown, brown skin, and like really full, full lips…Okay, fine!…*(TIFFANY gets back on track and continues with her letter.)*

"Now everybody loves you. People worship you, you're a fad. They have `discovered' you like they `discovered' the Americas. You're a newfound treasure, and your paintings are selling in the millions. And it doesn't bother anyone you were bisexual or that you had a moustache. People love you even more…" Love, you know, like what is love? I think I love Julio, but I don't think he loves me. Or at least it seems he's always saying like I should be something else. Like he's in love with what I could be but not with what I am…*(TIFFANY becomes serious and continues reading the letter more passionately. Her Spanish has gotten a lot better now.)*

"But you were my inspiration first. My first ray of hope when I had no self-esteem. When I had no role models. Your paintings gave me courage because I could identify with your coraje. I liked you immediately because you weren't 'beautiful.' But you had an attitude and a sense of humor that made your physical predicament less painful to yourself and those around you. And I'm writing to tell you that when the hype is over, I will still have

those images from your paintings imprinted in my conscience and…I know they can't take you away from me, because you'll always be en mi corazón… Sincerely, Tiffany." *(Her fellow STUDENTS applaud. TIFFANY gains confidence.)*

Professor, could I like do the speech for you? I think I can do it now. *(She takes a moment to breathe and begins.)* Las rasones que nuestra raza debe resistir este racismo es que la Proposicion 187 es un ataque contra todos. Primero comienzan con los Latinos, despues con los Asiaticos, y todos los demas que no son Anglo-Saxones. ¿Qual es la differencia entre Wilson and Hitler? ¡Si como Hitler que se encargo de tratar de desacerse con toda una raza, asi Wilson quiere desacerse de nuestra raza! ¡¡Por eso todos los Latinos debemos luchar contra la Proposicion 187!! *(TIFFANY makes a realization.)* Excuse me, but like, I have to go break up with my boyfriend…*(TIFFANY walks out. Lights fade out.)*

(Lights fade in a little. The altar is in front of one WOMAN. She opens a compartment in the altar. A little light inside of it flickers giving the illusion that it is radiating an image like a television. The WOMAN, sitting back watching television with the remote control in her hand, becomes: DOÑA FLORINDA "THE TV SOAP OPERA ADDICT," short, large, with auburn hair; its roots showing, wearing a floral tent dress, and knee-high stockings. THREE WOMEN also sit in front of their imaginary television, each with a remote control. We hear soap opera music as DOÑA FLORINDA gets up from her chair and walks C. The THREE WOMEN put their remote controls down and become part of the support group. DOÑA FLORINDA stands alone in silence. She stares at the audience for a minute before she finally speaks.)

DOÑA FLORINDA. My name is Florinda…

SUPPORT GROUP. Hola, Florinda.

DOÑA FLORINDA. and…I'm a…addicted to…I am a TV soap opera addict…But only the Spanish ones! I don't get "Ryan's Hope" or "General Hospital" or "One Life To Live." No le hallo el chiste. They go on for years and if you ask me I think they stole the plots from the Spanish telenovelas. I did watch "Santa Barbara" for a while when that Latino hunk A. Martinez was on it. Ayy que papasito. But then that gringa wife of his got so annoying. She was such a chillona and I stopped watching it. Pero eso si, even the soaps in Spanish—I only watch the Mexican ones. No me gustan las de Venezuela or Puerto Rico or with *(Disgusted.)* prietos and mulatos. I don't know why…Oh, but the Brazilian ones are the best even though they have mulatos. So, I'm not really an addict addict…Oh, no, I'm "rationalizing," I'm sorry…*(Reciting.)* "The road to recovery is acceptance"…so I must accept that I am a telenovela addict and unless I deal with my illness I will continue to ruin my life, waste away, gain more weight, lose my children and my third husband, and my hemorrhoids won't get any better. *(DOÑA FLORINDA breaks down crying. Her crying is very dramatic, as if she were in a soap opera herself. A short time later she collects herself and finds the courage to continue.)*

My husband, who is Cuban, who looks like the galan in my favorite Spanish TV soap "Juan Del Diablo," told me I had to get help or he would leave me…He always says that "Spanish TV soaps, telenovelas, are the 'opium of the Latino masses,' the work of the CIA to keep Latin America pacified through the transmission of subliminal messages and micro x-rays which in the long run deteriorate brain cells at a rate faster than marijuana and alcohol"…I don't know what he means. All I know is that telenovelas have ruined my life…*(DOÑA FLORINDA breaks down crying again. She falls to the floor dramatically. The THREE WOMEN go to her aid with their remote controls and press them as if zapping her with imaginary rays that give her a feeling of comfort.)*

I've lost two husbands because of this. I didn't start out watching soaps in my marriage, but every time my husband and my children would ignore me after I took care of their needs I would watch the telenovelas so I wouldn't get bored. Then I got so involved with the telenovelas I neglected my husbands and my kids. Both my husbands warned me to quit it. So I started hiding in the bathroom watching them on my TV Walkman. When my husbands found out, they'd break them. But that didn't stop me. It got so bad I even learned how to operate and program a VCR so I could tape them and watch them at midnight when my husbands were sleeping. So I wouldn't sleep at night and during the day I was a zombie. I would just sleep and my youngest son Tomas would go hungry. I'd give him money for fast food or heat him a frozen meal. He is twelve years old and weighs two hundred and fifty pounds and no one invites him to their birthday parties…*(DOÑA FLORINDA breaks down crying again, by now her crying is annoying. She walks back to her chair next to the TV.)*

One day I got so upset because my telenovela was interrupted by a newsbreak only to find out my daughter was holding up a K-mart and she was holding the "Blue Light Special" announcer hostage. *(The THREE WOMEN go to her aid and sit around DOÑA FLORINDA trying to comfort her, but they all get hooked on the telenovela.)*

Then another day I was switching channels from one telenovela in a commercial break to my other telenovela and I saw my son as a "transvestite who wants to get a sex change" on the talk show "Cristina." He kept telling Cristina that all he wanted was his mother to give him some attention; to connect with me. He kept calling out my name, begging Cristina to tell me, just in case I was watching, that he loved me. And you know what I did? I

changed the channel and continued watching my telenovela. *(She blows her nose. The THREE WOMEN go back to their chairs.)*

If I'm supposed to say "no" to telenovelas then what do I say "yes" to? Why would I want to give them up when I've got nothing else in my life. As stupid or as dumb as telenovelas are accused of being, they are still more interesting than my life. All I have to say "yes" to is regret. I followed my mother's advice and I did everything she told me…She told me not to elope with a man because he was poor and a…mulato. He loved me con una passion, but my mother thought he was beneath me, muy poca cosa, "What kind of a life" would I have with him? "What will people say?" *(Her tears are gentle, she's no longer annoying or dramatic.)* I didn't go with him when he came for me that night…Mi negrito, my beautiful mulato pleaded with me to go with him, but I listened to my mother…So I got the kind of life I never wanted…When I watch tele¬novelas I'm the bad girl. I'm the puta. I'm the woman who steals the men, who cheats, who makes her mother suffer, who throws acid at beautiful girls' faces…I'm all of them except la santa. *(She smiles and feels relieved.)*

I am here because I need help. I must give them up before my 12-year-old explodes. Before my daughter gets out of jail from "juvi," and before my son decides he's going to have the sex change. ¡Que drama! My life has gotten to be like a telenovela. Especially since I appeared on "Cristina" last week and confronted my son publicly and discovered my husband was having an affair with la vecina, and my daughter is pregnant. All my neighbors saw it and the chisme on my block has gotten out of hand. Hijole, the rumors people are spreading about me! It's actually exciting! Ah, miren, someone should make a telenovela about my life and get Charro to play me or someone like her, ¿qué no? And maybe it could be called "Por Un Hombre Guapo," "Tres Veces Casada," "A Woman And Her TV"…Oh, I'm sorry, I'm "rationalizing" again…*(Pause.)* I'm doing my best and I am taking one day at a time. I'm down to only watching one tele¬novela a day. "Juan Del Diablo." It will be over next week so it's not that bad, but I can't wait to find out what's going to happen!…*(She looks at her watch.)* ¡Hijole! Ya va a empezar la telenovela de las ocho. Ya me tengo que ir! I'm sorry, but I have to go…*(DOÑA FLORINDA quickly goes back to her chair, pulls out the remote control, and watches TV. The THREE WOMEN also take out their remote controls and watch TV. Lights fade out.)*

(Lights fade in. The altar has been moved center stage and is now a podium. We are at "Killer Tacos" basement, a taco shop/hair salon by day and a revolutionary's secret gathering place at night. THREE WOMEN are seated in their chairs enthusiastically talking about current events in the news. One WOMAN enters and becomes: MARISA "LA VALENTINA" CHAVEZ, a Chicana, who is fed up with Republicans and racism. She is dressed in black

pants, a red t-shirt, and black combat boots. She walks to the center, takes command, getting everyone's attention.)

VALENTINA. Everybody settle down!! We're going to start now because I don't believe in Latino Time. Thank you for coming. Welcome to "Killer Tacos," I know the basement is not the best place to hold a meeting but since it was last-minute, and since being a revolutionary is a 24-hour job in public and in private, I hope you don't mind the basement. So I'm glad to see that most of you are here instead of dancing the night away at "Peppers." My name is…Valentina. Named after "La Valentina," for those of you who haven't taken a Mexican History course, take one…She was the Mexican woman general that fought alongside Pancho Villa…

WOMAN *(whispers to another WOMAN)*. Is that her real name?

VALENTINA. No, that's not my real name, I can't give you my name because I'm planning to start a riot today! I'm going to set fires. I'm going to set fires in you. You know what was wrong with the L.A. riot? It was unorganized! That's what a riot is. Unorganized rage! Think of all that anger, all the passions, all that belief that justice was not being done. All the civil disobedience. Imagine what could have been accomplished instead, if all that anger, all that rage, and passion was focused, united, like a laser beam… But all that was accomplished was brute violence…Oh, and by the way, anybody got any stereo or video equipment they can donate to the East L.A. Community Center?… Thought I'd ask…*(She looks around, but no one makes an offer.)*

Today I heard something very disturbing and I wanted to cry, but tears don't change things; action does. It's 1996 gente, raza, but before we know it, with all the Republicans in office, it will be 1950 again! Women won't be able to get safe and legal abortions, affirmative action will be gone, under-represented people like us won't have equal access to jobs…All that was fought for and accomplished in the '60s will be lost. People will get so desperate they'll have nothing to lose because everything will have been taken away from them. People are gonna get themselves a white person and shoot them. When I found out Pete Wilson was going to go after affirmative action that's what I wanted to do. When I saw the beating of the defenseless undocumented woman by a sheriff in Riverside on National TV, that's what I wanted to do.

…Gente, I'm telling you, we can no longer just sit back and say, "Oh, they're just trying to scare us." Before we know it, if we continue with that attitude, we'll all be on a train, but not to Mexico. To a desert somewhere, like they did to the Japanese-Americans. And they're not just going to hold us there, they'll send us to the ovens like the Nazis did to the Jews. You think I'm exaggerating? You think I'm shitting you? You think it's 1996 and this can't

happen? Well, yeah, it's 1996, and the ERA, the Equal Rights Amendment, twenty-four fucking little words that say women will be equal under law can't get passed and added to the fucking U.S. fucking Constitution, and yes, it's 1996! Let me tell you, when Republicans or any other racist force start making motions and policies in the name of God, family values, "contract with America," start preparing yourself for the worst. "Manifest Destiny" lives on! And in the words of Martin Luther King, "It is not so much the fault of the bad people, but of the good people who stood by watching and let it happen." Are we going to just sit back and let it happen? No! No! Repeat after me, no!!! *(She throws her fist up in the air and starts doing the Chicano clap. Someone interrupts her.)* What?…Now?… You want me to do it now?…But I had something going here?…All right, a deal's a deal…*(She takes out a cardboard sign that reads: "KILLER TACOS of EAST L.A. Over 1 Million Served.")*

Gente, in exchange for the space, I promised my friend Freddie Lechuga that I would promote his restaurants. And don't anybody accuse me of being a vendida 'cause I know people like to throw that word around like it was a tortilla…So Freddie's passing flyers with coupons for your future visits. Support raza-owned establishments and they will support us. The chips and salsa are also courtesy of him…Let's give him a big Chicano clap to thank him. *(She claps.)* So just remember: "Killer Tacos, if the salsa doesn't kill you, the dog meat will"…Just kidding, Freddie. *(VALENTINA "kicks back" for a minute, then resumes as leader.)*

Okay, everybody, settle down, get your chips and your tamarindo drinks quickly because I have a confession to make…I've lived in this country 23 years…For 15 years I was undocumented, and for 8 years I've held off becoming a U.S. citizen because I didn't feel I was part of this country. It wasn't until I started to read the history of the U.S. and the Americas did I see how our contributions, the contributions of my gente, made this country. It is then that I realized "I am part of this country." The blood, sweat, and tears of my people is what paved the roads for me to get here and claim this country as my own…*(She pulls out an application form and shows it to the group.)*

Do all of you know what this is?…It's an application for U.S. citizenship… Last week I applied to become a citizen. For most of you Chicanos who were born here, it might not be a big deal. But the people who became Chicanos recently, this might be very painful. It was to me… There are two questions in here that took me some time to answer. It asks, "Are you willing to renounce your country of origin for the privilege of becoming a U.S. citizen?" It asks, "Are you willing to fight against any country in defense of the U.S. of A?" I was going to lie and just mark "yes." I'm applying to be a U.S. citizen because I want to vote. I can go to all the rallies, marches, and protests and scream "¡Si se puede!" 'til I turn blue. Pero no se puede unless we can vote. There have been two elections where I could have voted against Bush, against Republicans, but I didn't. I couldn't answer those two simple question...I still can't. "Will you renounce your country of origin?" Can I? Ah...Yes, but my Mexico, the Mexico that only exists in black and white movies, the only one I got to know, will always be showing in the movie theatre of my mind... "Will I fight against any country in defense of the U.S.?" ...Yes, as long it's not Mexico or any in Latin America, or any people of color, because brothers killing brothers, I'll have none of that, I've already seen too much of that...I will, someday...But I am willing to give up my country in defense of myself, in defense of my spirit...(*She puts the application down on a table and takes a minute to collect herself.*)

I brought you all here, the "MeCHA's," my "Chicana/ Latina Feminist Support Group," the "Rebels Without A Cause Group," the "Latina Lesbian Alliance," and many others of you that I met at K-mart in the hair-bleaching or condom section. At the parking lot of McDonald's with nothing better to do. At the bus stops stealing movie posters or vandalizing them with the words "Hollywood Sucks." At Little Tokyo trying to pass for Japanese. At "Peppers" waiting in line. At the "Telenovela Addicts Anonymous Meeting." At churches coming out of confession or selling elotes. I even invited "The Machos Against Change Coalition," because I need your help. Our Raza needs your help. Times are getting scarier and dangerous for us. If you don't believe me, just open your eyes. Because we are coming to a point in this country where it is going to come down to voting or violence...Gente, raza, I want you to stand up and turn to one another...So what if she's a lesbian. So what if he's a macho. So what if she's speaking to you in Japanese...Turn to one another and hug each other...Because today the revolution begins...I know you're probably thinking, "How can we start a revolution when we couldn't even get our act together to vote against 187"? I don't know. I just know it is a historic time in the state of California. For the first time we are a majority, but that means nothing if we don't vote. Nothing if we don't vote. This is no longer a "white America," and that is why there is a backlash against us. The closer we get to reaching our goals to liberate ourselves, the more afraid people in the establishment get. And it doesn't matter if you're already a citizen. With Proposition 187 everybody is a suspect. Your brown hair makes you a suspect. Your brown eyes make you a suspect. Your brown skin makes you a suspect! Does it have to come down to that? What will it take for the sleeping giant to awaken? What will it take for our spirits to rise? Voting or violence, now it's one or the other. Awake, my raza, awake! Awake, my raza, awake! Awake, raza!! (*The WOMEN begin to sing a song of unity. They circle her, clapping, while VALENTINA climbs on a chair and does the "Chicano clap." She then walks over to the altar and lights up a stick of sage. The WOMEN continue clapping until they come together at the altar.*

Lights fade. In the darkness VALENTINA circles the sage in the air and passes it on. Each woman does the same and lights fade out.)

The End

CONFESSIONS OF WOMEN FROM EAST L.A.

GLOSSARY
SPANISH

(F) French - (I) Italian - (J) Japanese translations

A, bueno… - Oh, well…

¡A un dolar! - For one dollar!

(J) abura - lard

Ah, miren - Oh, look

¡Ah, que la chingada! - Oh, shit!

Andele, compre me uno… - Come on, buy one…

Andele, seño - Come on, Ms.

Aver, aver - Let's see, let's see.

¡Ay, dios! - Oh, God!

¡Ayy - Oh

Ayy, Papi, como me gustas - Oh, Daddy, how I like you

Ayy, que grandototote estás, chulo - Oh, how big you are, cutie

Ayy, que papasito - Oh, what a babe!

¡Bienvenidas! - Welcome!

borracho - drunk, alcoholic

Chicanita - Chicana term of endearment

chichis - slang: tits, breasts

chillona - cry baby

Chingóna - (playwright's word:) kick-ass, fighter, femme-fatal

chisme - gossip

cochina - dirty girl

Cochina y mal hablada - Dirty and bad spoken

corazón - heart, soul

de adrede - on purpose

Doctora - Doctor

Dolores - Pains

(J) Domo arrigato gozaimasu - Thank you very much

Doña - Mrs., a sign of respect for an older woman

el pobrecito - my poor husband

¡Elotes! - Corn!

¡Elotes, elotes, con mucho chile! - Corn, corn, with lots of chili pepper!

en mi corazón - in my heart

Eres mi rey - You are my king

ese buen hombre - that good man

eso si que no - that, no way

galan - hero, beau

galan de cine - movie star

gente, raza - (both mean:) my people

Gracias - Thank you

gringa - white woman

gringos - whities, Anglo-Saxon

hermana - sister

Hijole - Oh man

Hola - Hello

¡Hola muchachas! - Hello gals!

Juan Del Diablo - Juan of the Devil

la - the

La Elotera - The corn lady

La Llorona - The crying woman; a famous Mexican legend about a woman who killed her children, threw them into a river, and then committed suicide. However, God would not let her into heaven until she found her children, so her spirit roams the rivers of Mexico looking for her children.

la santa - the saint

la vecina - the neighbor

las chispas - sparks

Las razónes que… - The reasons are…

Las razónes que nuestra raza debe resistir éste racismo es que, es que, es que… - The reasons our people must resist this racism is that, is that, is that…

Las razónes que nuestra raza debe resistir este racismo es que la Proposicion 187 es un ataque contra todos. Primero comienzan con los Latinos, despues con los Asiaticos, y todos, los demas que no son Anglo-Saxones. ¿Qual es la differencia entre Wilson y Hitler? ¡Si como Hitler que se encargo de tratar de desacerse con toda una raza, asi Wilson quiere desacerse de nuestra raza! ¡Por eso todos los Latinos debemos luchar contra la Proposicion 187!! - The reasons our people must resist this racism is that Proposition 187 is an attack against all of us. First they begin with Latinos, then with the Asians, and then everyone else who is not an Anglo-Saxon. What is the difference between Wilson and Hitler? Like Hitler, who took charge of getting rid of a group of people, Wilson would like to get rid of our people! That is why all Latinois must fight against Proposition 187!!

(F) Les femme qui n'ont pas de poitrine sont le meilluers. Les homme puet etre plu porche a leur cuore - Women who don't have breasts are the best. Men can get closer to their hearts.

Lolita - nickname derrivative of Dolores

los campesinos - the farmworkers

Machos - traditional Mexican men who behave as though they are superior to women

mejor que la gosen los humanos a que se la coman los gusanos - better that humans enjoy it than the worms eat it

mensa - dummy

mi chatita - my flat-nosed one, (term of endearment)

Mi'jita - my darling

mi'jitas - my little daughters, darlings

mi negrito - my little black one, (term of endearment)

mulatos - black/dark people

Ni me crea - Don't believe me

Nixtamal - cornmeal

No le hallo el chiste - I don't get it.

No me gustan - I don't like them.

No mucho - Not much.

No, no, no mas 'stoy bromiando - No, no, I'm only joking.

N'ombre - No way man.

¡O mi dios! Oh my God

(J) Onegaishimasu! - Please, I beg of you!

¡Orale! - Cool! Yeah!

Padre - Father, priest

Papi - Daddy

pendejada - stupidty

pendejadas - stupidities

Pero eso si - However/But

pero bueno - but, oh well

pero mi hija - but my daughter

Pero no se puede - But we can't do it…

pinchi - expletive, stupid

pito - slang: dick

Por un Hombre Guapo - For a Handsome Man

¡Pos que chingados, éstos pinches gringos! Oh, those damned whities!

prieta - dark one, (mestiza)

prietos - darkies

Prietos y sensillos tal vez, pero - Dark and simple-looking, maybe, but

prostitutas - prostitutes

pues - then

puta - slut, whore

¡Qué drama! - What drama!

¿Qué no? - Don't you think?

Que rico, suave - How delicious, smooth…

¡Que se vallan a la chingada! - then they can go to hell!

raza - our people

Sabroso - tasty

Se enchilo tanto - The salsa got to him, his tongue got irritated by the salsa

¡Se me olvido! - I forgot!

Señorita - Miss, lady

¡Si se puede! - Yes we can do it!

Si te dije… - If I told you…

Si te dije que te amaba con toda mi alma… - If I told you that I loved you with all my soul…

Si te quise fue porque… - If I liked you it was because…

Squincla mal pintada - an over-painted slutty girl

Te amo mi'jita - I love you my darling

(J) Teburu e otsurue shimasu. Kore wa anata no menu de gozaimasu - This way to your table. Here is your menu.

telenovelas - soap operas

(I) Ti amo carrina - I love you darling

Tres Veces Casada - Three Times Married

Un viejo chancludo, peludo - A hairy, dirty old man

¡Vamonos! Let's go!

vendida - sell-out

viejo rabo verde - dirty old man

(J) Wakarimashita ka - Do you understand?

welferosos - slang: welfare recipients

Y si no - And if not

ya ni la friegas - you messed it up

Ya parale - Stop it already

Ya va a empezar la telenovela de las ocho. ¡Ya me tengo que ir! - The eight o'clock soap opera is about to start. I have to go now!

They're sexy, curvy, dangerous, and now they're confessing...Latinas from Boyle Heights.

CONFESSIONS OF WOMEN FROM BOYLE HEIGHTS

A comedic collage of monologues, written & directed by Josefina Lopez, author of *Real Women Have Curves*

MARCH 14-23, 2003 / FRI & SAT AT 8PM, SUN AT 7PM
CASA 0101 THEATRE ART SPACE — COURAGE PRODUCTIONS
TIX: 323.263.7684 / www.casa0101.org / 2009 E. First Street, LA, CA 90033

Artwork by Gaby Lopez @ soapdesign.com

Center photo is of Michael Ruesga

CASA 0101 is proud to present

A DAY OF THE DEAD
CELEBRATION

with Two One Acts by Josefina Lopez:

Food for the Dead   *Unconquered Spirit*

November 5-21, 2010

Artwork by Gaby Lopez @ soapdesign.com

FOOD FOR THE DEAD

PLAYWRIGHT'S NOTES

My father and my brothers used to tease my little brother because he didn't want to play sports. My father would often say that if one of his sons ever turned out to be a homosexual he would rather die than live with the shame. Then I began to wonder what would happen if one day my little brother came home and announced he way gay. I thought, "All hell would break loose!"

So there came the idea for Food for the Dead. I wrote it when I was 19 as a protest to my younger brothers bullying while I was at New York University studying dramatic writing. At that time I felt very alienated. I was the only Latina in my writing class and I felt like no one understood where I was coming from. I was experiencing so much cultural shock that I wanted to write something that celebrated my culture. Also, I had a friend who was Latino, gay and a playwright, but he wouldn't write about being gay and neither would a couple of other Latino gay playwrights I also knew.

So I attempted to write about it. Since I'm not gay and didn't do any research I ended up making a lot of innocent mistakes and some of the actors from the University of California, San Diego production were "offended." One of the leads dropped out because "it went against his religion" (but 5 years later I discovered he was gay and in the closet). The gay Anglo actor playing "Fernando" said to me "gays don't want to marry – that's a heterosexual paradigm."

At one meeting with the actors I was given so many notes and complaints that I told my mentor Professor Jorge Huerta, "I'm not going to

write anymore." He encouraged me not to give up being a writer. I'm glad I took his advice. Twenty two years later that same actor may still believe that gays do not want to marry, but I am happy this play was ahead of its time and is now so topical with that horrible Prop 8. In fact, so much has happened in the last weeks concerning gays in the military and the bullying of gay youth that it's now a part of our conversation and conscience.

I dedicate this play and performance to that young man who was the victim of bullying named Tyler Clementi. May his soul find peace.

Josefina López

Los Angeles

November 2010

FOOD FOR THE DEAD

A ONE ACT PLAY

SETTING:

Candela's dining room in Montebello, California.
TIME: Halloween night.

CHARACTERS

CANDELA	late 40s, the mother of four children
JOSE	late 20s, the oldest son
ROSARIO	late 20s, the oldest daughter
GLORIA	early 20s, the youngest daughter
JESUS	early 20s, the youngest son
FERNANDO	late 20s, Jesus' Anglo lover
RUBEN	early 50's, Candela's deceased husband
SARA	late 50s, Candela's comadre (friend)

AT RISE: The stage is dark. Lights fade in a little to reveal the figure of a WOMAN wearing a black shawl over her head, we cannot see her face. The WOMAN enters from the offstage kitchen carrying a plate with food. She places the plate on a small altar. She lights the candles on the bottom of the altar, and more light reveals that it is an altar in memory of her dead husband RUBEN. The altar contains a black and white portrait of him as well as personal belongings and other religious ornaments. The WOMAN kneels and

begins to pray. She then does the sign of the cross and says "Amen." The lights fade in fully and the WOMAN takes off her shawl. She is CANDELA. She adjusts her sexy dress and looks at her watch. She walks toward the table and begins to set it. CANDELA places six plates then she stops to look at the sixth plate. She retrieves it, and a few seconds later puts it back. CANDELA looks at her watch again then goes to the mirror and looks at herself. She exercises her mouth and says the vowels out loud.

CANDELA. The rain in Spain falls mainly on the plain. Hello. How do you do? I'm fine, thank you. You like my dress? Yes. It's from the Jacklyn Smith Collection. *(The doorbell rings. She runs to the door and opens it.)*

KIDS *(offstage)*. Trick-or-treat!!!!!

CANDELA. ¡Ayyy! *(She gets a bowl of candy next to the door and distributes it.)* Oh, how cute! Here's for you. A nice chocolate bar. And for you…What are you supposed to be? *(Awaits an answer.)* A giant condom?! Oh, well, here's for you…What? You don't want it?…You want a chocolate bar just like your little brother? All right…*(She gives him a chocolate. She gets more candy and is about to give it away.)* You want a chocolate too just like your best friend? But I don't have any more chocolate bars…I don't…No, I'm not lying…Your costume is just as cute… Look. *(She sticks out the bowl to show him. The KIDS begin to pull on the bowl.)* I can't give you all the candy! *(They continue to pull on the bowl until all the candy flies out from her bowl and hits her face. She kicks the door shut.)* ¡Dios mio, que esquincles! *(CANDELA picks up the candy. She goes to the mirror and straightens herself. The doorbell rings again. She rushes to the door excitedly.)*

KIDS. Trick-or-treat!!!!!! *(CANDELA grabs the bowl of candy and tosses it out the door.)*

CANDELA. ¡Bolo! *(CANDELA shuts the door. She goes offstage to the kitchen to check on the food. The doorbell rings. She runs again, but then she looks at the empty bowl.)* Who is it?

JOSE *(off)*. Jose!

(CANDELA quickly opens the door to JOSE.)

JOSE. ¡Madre!

CANDELA. ¡Hijo! *(They hug and kiss on both cheeks.)* Come in. Come in. Esta es tu casa.

JOSE. Oh, the food smells great! *(He heads for the kitchen.)*

CANDELA. Of course. I made it.

JOSE (*stops and notices the altar*). And that?

CANDELA. It's a little altar for your Papá...I got so embarrassed putting it around his grave, especially with all the food I cooked for him. So I brought it here. There was this nosy gringa who asked me when Ruben was going to come out from the world beyond to eat dinner. I told her, "The same time your dead husband comes to smell your flowers." I shut her up. But I thought it would look better here at least for tonight.

JOSE. You used to put it by his grave? I never knew that.

CANDELA. Yes. I've been doing it for eight years. This is my ninth year and my last. Tonight will be the end of my novenario. Because I am going to say good-bye to Ruben and hello to the new me!

JOSE. So what's for dinner?

CANDELA. It seems the only thing the men in this family ever think about is food.

JOSE. I'm sorry, Amá. I'm really excited for you, that you're experiencing your freedom and all that, I'm all for it. I mean it. I'm modern, I understand. It's just that I haven't had a decent meal for months. My wife can't cook for beans. I wish she'd quit her job at the clinic and stay home so that she can learn how to cook like you.

CANDELA. So where are Martha and the boys? Why didn't you bring them?

JOSE. Ah...They're fine. I told them it was a small, private family dinner...

CANDELA. And Martha didn't mind? Oh, it's all right. They can come. Let me go call them and invite them over. I haven't seen my grandchildren since...(CANDELA walks to the phone.)

JOSE. No!...Don't call them. They're not home...Martha took the kids trick-or-treating by now.

CANDELA. That's too bad.

JOSE. It's all right. The boys wanted to go trick-or-treating instead. Amá, I want this night to be special for you.

CANDELA. So do I...Except...

JOSE. What?

CANDELA. Do you think Jesus is coming?

JOSE. Amá, he left...I'm sort of hoping he won't come. All he'll do is get you

upset.

CANDELA. Bueno, come to the kitchen with me and I'll give you a probadita of my tamales. *(They walk toward the kitchen, then the doorbell rings.)* I'll be right there.

(CANDELA opens the door. Her two daughters, ROSARIO, very much a Huppy, (Hispanic Young Urban Professional) and GLORIA, very mellow and somewhat of a hippie, enter.)

ROSARIO. ¡Amá! How nice you look! You look like you could be my sister.

CANDELA. ¿De veras? Oh, flattery will get you anywhere with me. *(GLORIA and CANDELA hug and kiss on both cheeks.)*

GLORIA. Ma, you look so beautiful and thin. And you're wearing make-up!

CANDELA. Sí, I became good friends with the Avon lady.

ROSARIO. What have you done to the house? It looks so different. It looks so, so, clean. Don't you think so, Gloria?

CANDELA. I've been doing repairs on it myself. And it's clean because there's no one here to make a mess…Pero diganme, how are both of you doing? Gloria how is UCLA?

GLORIA. School's fine. 'Cept I've got this totally uncool professor who doesn't understand why I want to be a Transcendental Psychologist. And it's a drag living in the dorms. Ma, I need to get my own space.

CANDELA. But can you afford it?

GLORIA. I could if I got a roommate…

ROSARIO. I just started working at this firm owned by Elizabeth Taylor's divorce lawyer. It's a big deal to be working for them.

CANDELA. What exactly do you do?

ROSARIO. Amá, I've told you, I'm a divorce lawyer.

CANDELA. They have specialized lawyers for that?

ROSARIO. Oh, yes! There is a large demand for divorce lawyers. I handle the divorces for our Hispanic clients. It's an advantage to speak Spanish where I work. It's too bad people don't think before they get married. Too bad for them, but good for me. But it is emotionally draining. Especially when there are kids involved. Poor children get separated…*(She gets over-emotional.)* But I'm making big bucks, oh, yeah. Those seven years of college are really starting to pay off. *(The doorbell rings. "Trick-or-Treat" is heard outside.)*

CANDELA. Bueno, bueno, pasense.

GLORIA. Wo, Ma! What's that?

CANDELA. It's an altar for your Papá.

(CANDELA goes to answer the door. ROSARIO and GLORIA take off their jackets and make themselves at home. JOSE comes out of the kitchen and they all catch up on the latest.)

VOICES. Trick-or-treat!!!

CANDELA. I'm sorry! No more candy!

VOICES. Trick-or-treat!!!

CANDELA. No candy!

VOICES. No candy?!

JESUS *(offstage)*. ¡Mamá!

CANDELA. Jesus, is that you?!!

(JESUS hugs CANDELA and kisses her on both cheeks. Immediately after they finish kissing, FERNANDO enters.)

CANDELA. Jesus, who is this?

JESUS. Mamá, this is my best friend Fernando.

CANDELA. Your best friend? Oh. Nice to meet you, Fernando. Mi casa es su casa.

FERNANDO. What did you say?

CANDELA. Mi casa es su…You don't speak Spanish?

FERNANDO. No, I'm afraid I'm American and only know one language. But Jesse is teaching me some Spanish… "Muchas gracias," "mucho gusto," "mucho macho." *(They laugh.)*

CANDELA. Well, make yourself at home.

FERNANDO. Gracias.

CANDELA. Everyone, look who is here!

ALL. Jesus!! *(CANDELA exits to the kitchen. GLORIA runs up to JESUS. They hug.)*

GLORIA. What a surprise! What a trip to see my little brother. I was so worried about you. I didn't think you would show up.

JESUS. I wouldn't miss it for anything…Everyone, I want you to meet my best friend Fernando.

GLORIA. Your best friend? Oh, right. It's a real pleasure to meet you, Fernando. Welcome to our family gathering.

FERNANDO. Gracias.

ROSARIO. So, Jesus, how was New York? Was it fun being a starving artist? Was it as romantic as you imagined it to be?

JESUS. Yes and no. It was very romantic, but I hate being poor. I've decided to come back to California. Maybe I'll go back to school and get a job like you, dear sister.

ROSARIO. You're finally coming to your senses, little brother…Did you all see my new BMW parked outside? I've only been out of college a year and…

JESUS. Was that your BMW outside? Oh, my God! I think one of the little trick-or-treaters was stealing your hub caps…

ROSARIO. Why, Jesus, didn't you know? BMWs don't have hub caps. *(ROSARIO walks away triumphantly).* You haven't changed.

JESUS. Neither have you.

JOSE *(extending his hand).* Hello, Jesus. I thought you had broken all ties with this family. You changed your mind. I wonder why.

JESUS. It's nice to see you again, big brother. Why do you think I came back?

JOSE. You ran out of money?

JESUS. You don't know me as well as you think.

JOSE *(whispering).* Why did you bring your friend here? This is only for family. You know how much this means to Mamá.

JESUS. I know what I'm doing. Fernando is my friend.

(CANDELA enters from kitchen with food.)

CANDELA. Okay, everyone, take your seats at the table so we can begin our dinner. *(ALL sit around the table in their designated seats. FERNANDO is left standing, waiting to be seated.)* Oh, I'm sorry…(CANDELA looks around for a chair.) Ah…Sit…Sit, right over there.

JOSE. But that's Papá's chair.

FERNANDO *(to JESUS)*. I thought your father was dead?

JESUS. He is.

FERNANDO *(suddenly realizing)*. Oh, oh, oh. Forgive me. Ah…I'll just sit over here close to Jesse…

JOSE. Jesse? You mean Jesus?

CANDELA. No. You can sit there. It's fine. You're our guest.

FERNANDO. I don't want to interfere…

JOSE *(muttering)*. You already have.

CANDELA. No. I insist. I don't want you to think that Mexicans are unfriendly people.

FERNANDO. Oh, I understand, but I really don't want to get in the way of any primitive rituals you're about to perform.

ROSARIO. Primitive rituals?

CANDELA. No problem. I insist.

FERNANDO. Only if it's no problem.

CANDELA. Sit down! *(FERNANDO falls into a chair.)* Let's begin.

GLORIA. I'm so glad that we're all here together. I've been so busy with my studies that I have not even called.

CANDELA. I've been busy with my studies too. I missed you all. This house is too big for me. I think it's haunted. Sometimes at night I swear I can hear everybody's voice. It's as if the walls have absorbed each one of you and I hear all the laughter and the crying…And sometimes I can hear your father's voice. *(ALL look toward the altar.)*

FERNANDO. Spooky! Maybe you should move.

CANDELA. Oh, no. This house is finally mine. I just made the last payment on the house last week.

ROSARIO. That's great, Amá. Maybe you can sell it and move to a better neighborhood.

CANDELA. But all of my comadres live around here.

FERNANDO *(notices the altar)*. What is that?

CANDELA. Oh, don't you know?

FERNANDO. Well, it sort of looks like an Aztec pyramid or something, pardon my ignorance…Ahh, it's an altar!

CANDELA. It's a Mexican custom for the "Day of the Dead."

FERNANDO. How curious!

JOSE. Amá, let's begin.

CANDELA. Who wants to say the prayer?

JESUS. Mamá, you say it, como siempre.

CANDELA. All right…(*They bow their heads, except for FERNANDO. CANDELA is about to begin. She notices FERNANDO.*) Is something wrong?

FERNANDO. Oh, please go right ahead. Don't mind me.

ROSARIO. You don't believe in prayer?

GLORIA. What religion do you practice?

JOSE. Are you an atheist?

FERNANDO. No. I'm agnostic…Please. I don't want to keep interfering. Go right ahead.

CANDELA. Bueno. (*She bows her head to begin prayer.*) Padre nuestro que estás en los cielos te damos las gracias por ésta comida… (*JESUS coughs, hinting for her to continue in English.*) Ah…And we ask that you bless this food that we are about to eat…(*JOSE coughs hinting for her to continue in Spanish.*) Tambien te pidemos que nos cuides de todo lo malo y de la tentacion… (*JESUS coughs again.*) Please take care of my husband wherever he may be. Forgive us for our sins…(*JOSE coughs again.*) Tambien te damos las gracias por darnos la salud para poder estar aquí como una familia…(*JESUS coughs.*) Please give us peace…(*JOSE coughs.*)…y armonia. (*GLORIA coughs to show her disapproval of JOSE's cough.*) Give us…(*Pretty soon everyone is coughing, even FERNANDO. They fade out CANDELA' praying. She finally gives up.*) ¡Amen! (*They stop coughing and try to continue as if nothing happened.*)

JOSE. Let's eat. I'm hungry.

ROSARIO. What did you make for us?

CANDELA. You know, the usual.

ROSARIO. I'm so hungry I could eat my briefcase. I miss your cooking so much, Amá. Where I live you can only get tortillas in the frozen section.

CANDELA. You really like my food?

JOSE. I love it! It's greasy and salty, and very bad for you. Can we eat now?! *(He doesn't wait to be served.)*

GLORIA. Ma, you should open a Mexican restaurant.

CANDELA. You really think so?

FERNANDO. Definitely! You should open it in New York. There are so many yuppies making a big fuss over the pseudo-Mexican restaurants.

JOSE. I especially like your tamales.

GLORIA. Did you make any sugar ones with raisins?

FERNANDO. What are ta-ma-les? *(ALL stop for a second and stare at him.)*

ROSARIO. You don't know what tamales are?

CANDELA. Pues denlo uno, give him one.

GLORIA. Jesus has never taken you to a Mexican restaurant?

FERNANDO. I'm afraid I've been an ignorant American for so many years…

JESUS. Don't be so hard on yourself.

FERNANDO. Yes, I have been, but I'm trying not to be… That's why I'm so happy I met Jesse…*(They pass the tamales to ROSARIO. She serves him one. All eyes are on him, awaiting his reaction.)* Oh, no.

ALL. What?!

FERNANDO. It has meat in it.

GLORIA. You're a vegetarian?

FERNANDO. Yes.

CANDELA. There are some sugar tamales. Aver dale otro. How about some Spanish rice or beans?

JOSE. You do know what beans are, don't you?

FERNANDO. Of course. Jesse shared a burrito with me one day…

JOSE. So, Mamá, you look so nice and young.

FERNANDO. Yes. She looks so young and sexy.

JOSE. She's not sexy! She looks beautiful, for an older woman.

CANDELA. Ayyy, thank you. I've been buying a lot of nice make-up and learning how to put it on. My comadre Sara started working for Avon. She's been so nice to me and she is trying to convince me to work for Avon. But I want to continue going to community college. Did you notice that I don't have such a thick accent anymore? (ALL laugh quietly, being that her accent is pretty thick even with the improvement.) I have a very good speech class.

FERNANDO. That's excellent that you have gone back to school and continued your education. You're still young, you can start a new life. You could even remarry.

JOSE. Of course not! My mother is not interested in remarrying.

CANDELA. I don't know about that. Maybe. It gets kind of lonely…

ROSARIO. ¡Amá!

CANDELA. Who knows, I might…I've been so lonely without Ruben and it's taken a lot of courage and strength to go on living alone.

FERNANDO. I bow my head to you. (He begins to clap for CANDELA, they ALL join him.)

JESUS. Yes, Mamá, we're so proud of you!

CANDELA. Thank you! But enough about me. Jesus, you've been so quiet. I want to know how New York was. I want to know everything.

JESUS. Everything?

CANDELA. Did you go to the art school after all?

JESUS. Yes, but I've decided not to continue.

GLORIA. Why not?

CANDELA. Is it because of money?

JESUS. No…I just haven't been able to do any artwork. When I first got to New York I was full of inspiration and was working on many projects. I began to take photographs of New York City, the buildings, the people. I couldn't believe I was there. There are so many people with diverse backgrounds, beliefs, and lifestyles. So many people living together in one city, sometimes in peace, sometimes not. Each day I met and took a picture of a different person. And one day I took a picture of myself…

JOSE. Do we have to listen to this?

ROSARIO. Gloria, can you pass me the rice?

GLORIA *(passes the rice to her)*. And what happened, Jesus?

JESUS. I developed the photograph, but I wasn't on the picture.

JOSE. What do you mean, you weren't there? Maybe you just took it the wrong way.

CANDELA. Really, Jesus? That happened to me too. After Ruben died I swear I looked into the mirror to brush my hair and I couldn't see myself.

ROSARIO. So, Gloria, what classes are you taking?

GLORIA. Clinical psychology, Abnormal psychology, Developmental psychology...So, Fernando, is this your first time in California?

FERNANDO. Yes, it is.

CANDELA. So what do you think about Los Angeles?

FERNANDO. People are very friendly here.

ROSARIO. As opposed to New York?

FERNANDO. No. They're just more easy-going. But it's such a big city and it seems so segregated.

JOSE. And what's wrong with that?

FERNANDO. People here don't have to mix with other people unlike themselves and they're not exposed to other ways of living...

JOSE. I think it's fine the way it is. If you want to live with the Asians you live in Monterey Park. If you want to live with the blacks, you go to Compton. And if you want to be around gays, you go to West Hollywood. If you want to be around us, you stay in East L.A. *(GLORIA and ROSARIO quickly try to change the conversation. GLORIA distracts FERNANDO and ROSARIO distracts JOSE. They begin separate conversations which are not heard, but seen during CANDELA's conversation with JESUS.)*

JESUS. Something was missing. I couldn't paint because my paintings reflect who I am. And I had left half of me behind.

CANDELA. His death took all of me because there was no one left except an old woman who couldn't take care of herself.

JESUS. I came back for you Mamá, not for Jose, or Rosario, maybe for Gloria, but I must come to terms with you or I am blocked.

CANDELA. I need to say good-bye to Ruben.

JESUS. I met Fernando at school. He inspires me. He's more than my best friend. He is someone who knows me. I respect him, even admire…

CANDELA. I've been learning a lot about myself in my sociology class and I want to understand. I've grown so much. I am a reflection of my growth.

JESUS. And so am I!

CANDELA. And I have come to love myself.

JESUS. And I love Fernando.

ALL. What?!

JESUS. Mamá, Jose, Rosario, Gloria, and Papá. Wherever the hell he may be. Fernando and I are lovers. *(CANDELA is shocked and tries to hold back the tears. JOSE chokes on his tamale, ROSARIO is disgusted, and GLORIA is excited.)*

CANDELA. ¿Pero cómo puede ser?

JOSE *(to FERNANDO)*. I knew there was something about you I didn't like. You're gay!

GLORIA. Finally!

ROSARIO. But that's…Yuuuckkk!!!

JESUS. Fernando, I love you.

(Lightning strikes in the living room, and all the lights go out except for the candles on and around the altar. RUBEN's portrait glows. From the bottom of the altar the candles spit fire and the ground opens up. Loud Mexican music comes from the hole, then RUBEN crawls out of the hole. He is wearing a red Mariachi suit, tail and horns, trumpet included. He plays the trumpet announcing himself. On his leg are chains made out of large, red, chile peppers. Before he can finish his trumpet solo a skeleton pulls on his leg trying to drag him back to hell. RUBEN pulls his leg, kicks the skeleton, then finally throws the trumpet and hits the skeleton on the skull. The skeleton falls back to hell.)

CANDELA. Ruben!!!

JOSE. ¡Papá!

FERNANDO. ¡Mucho Macho!

ROSARIO. Papá, is that you?

RUBEN. The one and only! I'm back!! *(CANDELA runs toward him in excitement. She tries to hug him but quickly moves away from his burning*

Photo by Josefina Lopez

Ruben, Candela's dead husband, loses his temper.

body. Conceitedly:) Candela, keep a distance. I'm too hot to touch.

GLORIA. Wo! ¡Pa! Like, you're dead!

RUBEN. Only my body, but my spirit is still alive in this house. I always told my compadres that if one of my sons ever turned out to be a homo…That! I'd rather die than live with the shame. But since I'm already dead I had to come back and stop this cochinada! Candela, is this what you have allowed our son to become? A maricón!!!

CANDELA. I had no idea, Ruben!

JESUS. I knew you would all react this way, but I came because I didn't want to hide it from you anymore. I came hoping that just maybe you would understand and accept me. Fernando and I are leaving now. Even though you may not like who I am, I'm happy. *(JESUS and FERNANDO walk towards the door. RUBEN flips his wrist and the door locks.)*

FERNANDO *(trying the door knob).* It's locked!

RUBEN. You're not getting out of here yet. You'll either come out of here a complete man, or a woman.

MEN *(quickly shield their crotch).* Oooooohhhhh!!!!!!!

RUBEN. Get away from the door! I've got you locked in. *(RUBEN goes to the door. FERNANDO and JESUS move away from it. The doorbell rings.)*

165

KIDS. Trick-or-treat! *(Doorbell rings again.)*

FERNANDO & JESUS. Help!!!!

KIDS. Trick-or-treat!! *(Doorbell rings again.)*

RUBEN. Shut up! *(Doorbell rings once again.)* I'll give them a treat, all right! *(RUBEN opens the door and steps outside. Offstage he transforms into a monster and scares the little KIDS, who scream and run away. RUBEN comes back in holding a small Burger King paper crown on his head and a handful of candy.)* Candy anyone?

JESUS. What are you going to do with us?!

RUBEN. I'm going to beat the maricón out of you! *(He is about to strike JESUS, but he begins to smell the food from the table and he slowly backs away from JESUS.)* Candela, what's for dinner?

CANDELA. Tamales, arroz, frijoles fritos…

GLORIA. Didn't they feed you in hell?

RUBEN. Yes, but in hell all the Mexican restaurants are full. I'm starving!… I'll beat it out of you right after I eat dinner, so don't go away. Ha, ha, ha, ha!!! *(He notices the altar.)* For me? Thank you, Candela, for worshipping me all these years. ¡Todavia soi el rey de esta casa! Candela, be a good wife and go fetch me some more food. I want my food hot, I think the food on this table is already cold.

GLORIA. Can't you heat it up yourself with your little finger?! Don't you have a special magic trick to do it?

RUBEN. I probably do, but I want Candela to heat it up for me. Andele mi Candelita, sea bonita and run to the kitchen to get my tortillitas.

CANDELA *(complying)*. All right, Ruben. Anything you say. I'm happy you're back. I don't know how to deal with this kind of family problem. *(CANDELA starts for the kitchen like a submissive servant, anxious to please.)*

ROSARIO. Don't go to the kitchen! Don't let him boss you the way he always did. You're not married to him anymore. He's dead!

CANDELA. But your father is hungry from his trip from hell. *(Exits.)*

GLORIA. So! Let him starve. Don't let him tell you what to do!

RUBEN. ¿Qué paso hijas? Aren't you happy to see me? What's wrong? You're not married yet? Is this what has become of my sweet daughters…Come, let's all sit around the table and continue with dinner.

JESUS *(telling FERNANDO)*. That's an order.

RUBEN. Hey, everyone, smile! Aren't you happy to see me?

JOSE. I am, ¡Papá! I got married and I have three sons!

RUBEN. ¡Que macho! And you, Rosario? Are you married yet?

ROSARIO. No. I'm a divorce lawyer and I'm too busy…

RUBEN. You better hurry. You're almost thirty and not very pretty.

GLORIA. So how did you do it, to come from the world beyond? Do you have some sort of pass? When does it expire?

RUBEN. And you? Have you gotten married yet?

GLORIA. I'm only twenty-one.

RUBEN. Yes, but you're getting fat.

GLORIA. I haven't gotten married because I don't want to get stuck with a macho. I'm going to marry a modern man.

RUBEN. You'll probably have to support him.

GLORIA. I'd rather support him than have him beat me.

RUBEN. Shut up!

JOSE. So, Papá, what did you do in hell?

RUBEN. Watched reruns…of my life…Candela, ¡apurate con la comida! Don't forget the hot salsa. And bring some tequila while you're at it.

(CANDELA enters carrying a lot of plates.)

CANDELA. There is no tequila. I have no liquor in this house.

RUBEN. No liquor? Hmmm. So how have you been without me? Tonight you and I are going to celebrate. You can bet our bed is going to be on fire tonight…Fire. Get it? Laugh! *(They all make forced laughter and stop at the same time.)*

CANDELA. I've been wonderful. I made the last payment on the house last week. I'm going to community college…

RUBEN. Are you wearing make-up?

CANDELA. Yes, do you like it?

RUBEN. I've told you never to wear make-up. Women who wear make-up look cheap. You're my wife and a mother.

CANDELA. I'm studying English. I can speak on the phone and order merchandise with my credit card and not get nervous. I got an American Express a month ago. I remember when I used to think that an American Express was a "Greencard"...

RUBEN. You got an American Express? I guess they're giving them to anybody now.

CANDELA. I lost twenty pounds and I fixed up the house. I went to the library and read my first American novel.

RUBEN. This food tastes like shit. What did you put in it? Shit?

CANDELA. I went to my first play. I saw A Doll's House. I wore a tight dress without a bra.

RUBEN. Candela, stop talking all that nonsense and get my tortillas!

CANDELA. Aren't you happy for me?

RUBEN. Yeah, yeah, but I'm starving! *(He eats, barely chewing, gulping his food. Everyone is disgusted watching him.)*

CANDELA. Why is it that every time I tried to talk to you, you were always too hungry to listen to me? You eat too much. Your arteries are going to clog up and you're going to have a heart attack!

RUBEN. Candela, I did and I died, so shut up!

CANDELA. You did? I never knew how. Nobody told me. They just kept saying I didn't want to know. What happened? How exactly did you die?

JESUS. Yes, Papá, tell her! Prove to us just how macho you are!

RUBEN. Ahh....

CANDELA. What does he mean?

FERNANDO. Jesse, what did your father do? And why did he end up in hell?

RUBEN. None of your business!

ROSARIO. That's right, why are you in hell?

RUBEN. Ahhh...*(They corner him.)*

JOSE. What happened?

GLORIA. What are you hiding?

RUBEN. Nothing!

CANDELA. Tell me, Ruben!

ALL. Tell us! Tell us! *(The doorbell rings.)* Who the hell is it?!!

WOMAN *(offstage)*. The Avon lady! *(Pause.)*

CANDELA. No! My comadre Sara!

SARA *(offstage)*. Candela, I've got something to show you!

CANDELA. I can't let her in! She's such a chismosa!

RUBEN *(runs to the door)*. Sara!

(He quickly opens the door to SARA.)

RUBEN. Hello. Come in. Welcome.

SARA. Hello…Who are you?

RUBEN. I'm Ruben—Rubento. Candela's younger brother.

SARA. I didn't know she had a younger brother.

RUBEN. Yes, you see I come from another world, I mean country. I'm from Mexico. We got separated when we were very young, and come in…

SARA. Thank you…Hello, Candela…I'm interrupting! That's right. I forgot your family reunion. I'm sorry. I'll come back another time. I'll leave you my little book.

CANDELA. Sí, sí, please.

RUBEN. No. You're not interrupting anything. Please stay and join us for dinner and have some tamales. Have you ever tried Candela's tamales? They're delicious. *(He holds SARA by the arm and pulls her to the table.)*

SARA. You know, you look familiar.

RUBEN. I do?

SARA. You look like Candela's husband.

RUBEN. I do?

SARA. But you couldn't be, he's dead. *(ALL laugh in relief.)* How come you're dressed like that?

RUBEN. Ah…Ah…

FERNANDO. Halloween!

RUBEN. Yeah! Please have something to eat.

SARA. I just came to show Candela a new type of make-up that arrived today.

CANDELA. I would like to see it, but not now.

RUBEN. Candela, don't be rude. She's our guest. Andale, Sara, show us your stuff.

SARA. I need some room on the table to put my suitcase.

RUBEN. Candela, clear the table…(*They clear the table quickly. SARA places her suitcase on the table and opens it.*)

SARA. It's called Lucifermagic. It's great to cover up black eyes, scars, scratches, cuts on the face. It's selling like hotcakes. Women in East L.A. are placing large orders. It's in demand. Let me show you. (*SARA applies the make-up all over her face. ALL watch silently as she applies it and suddenly she transforms into a monster from beyond.*)

MONSTER/SARA. I've come back to get you, Ruben!

FERNANDO. It's the devil! (*ALL scatter. CANDELA gets a cross from the altar. The others also get one or make one with their fingers.*)

GLORIA (*with her fingers crossed*). ¡Cruz!, ¡Cruz!

RUBEN. Candela, don't let it take me! (*CANDELA attacks the devil fearlessly with the cross.*)

DEVIL/SARA. Coward! Coward!

RUBEN. I'm not a coward!

DEVIL/SARA. Then why did you escape? You couldn't stand the reruns of your life and watching all the pain you caused those that love you! Coward! (*They keep pushing the DEVIL away. Finally CANDELA pushes the DEVIL back into the pit. They throw their crosses in.*)

RUBEN. Thank you, Candela!

CANDELA. Only I have the power to save you, isn't it true, Ruben? It's because of me that you're still here.

RUBEN. Which only proves that after all these years you still need me and love me.

CANDELA. I think the only reason I saved you is because I want to know how you died.

RUBEN. I can't tell you. I don't want to tell you. It's been nine years!

Photo by Josefina Lopez

Candela confronts her dead husband.

CANDELA. Then don't you think I've waited long enough?

RUBEN. I'm ashamed.

JESUS. Ashamed? Is that part of your macho vocabulary.

RUBEN. All right…I had a heart attack…during orgasm… while having sex with your cousin Ramón. *(ALL gasp.)*

ALL. Ramón!!!!! *(Then they ALL burst into laughter, except for CANDELA.)*

CANDELA. You see this altar? I made it for you. Every year since your death I've been taking food to your grave. I've been loyal, but you were never faithful. *(CANDELA tries to hold back her pain and anger. She goes to the altar and gets his photo and throws it at him. She grabs his shoes and pants from the altar and also throws them at him.)*

RUBEN. Please forgive me.

CANDELA. No…I can't go back to the way it used to be. You died and my life was shattered. The mirrors shattered because I couldn't see myself. I had no identity, no self, I didn't exist. I've been putting the pieces of this mirror back together. It's taken me more than seven years to recover, but now I like what I see…I like who I am. I love my life… without you…You didn't come back to try and stop Jesus, you came back to try and stop me. My independence threatens you. You want to continue dominating me, but I've

171

come too far to let you stop me…And, as for Jesus, I can't reject him because if I am rejecting his sexual liberation then how can I feel justified in my own liberation? He is my son. And although I don't understand why he is gay, I'd rather live with the truth then deny what has always been there. Ruben, ¡yo soy la reina de esta casa! It's my house, I paid for it. The papers say so, and I say so! So, Ruben, you go to hell! *(CANDELA pushes him back into the pit. The pit closes and the smoke disappears. CANDELA collects herself.)* Good! Now let's finish eating. Eat as much as you like, because the next time I'll be charging you for it.

GLORIA. Why?

CANDELA. Because I think I might open that Mexican restaurant you were suggesting. I think I'll call it "La Reina de la Casa."

JESUS. Mamá, did you really mean what you told Papá about me?

CANDELA. Sí, hijo. I think I understand…I've taken a few psychology classes myself.

GLORIA. In that case, Ma, I think I should tell you that I'm moving into a commune with my boyfriend Siddhartha.

ROSARIO. Amá, I want to have a child and not get married. I am looking for a potential biological father to impregnate me.

JOSE *(about to cry)*. Mamá, Martha wants to get a divorce from me and she wants to take the house!

ROSARIO. Does she need a lawyer?

FERNANDO. I think I'll try a raisin tamale.

CANDELA *(looks to God)*. It's going to be hell being a new-age mother, but I'll try. *(Lights fade out.)*

The End

CASA 0101 is proud to present

A DAY OF THE DEAD
CELEBRATION

with Two One Acts by Josefina Lopez:

Food for the Dead   **Unconquered Spirit**

November 5-21, 2010

Artwork by Gaby Lopez @ soapdesign.com

UNCONQUERED SPIRITS

PLAYWRIGHT'S NOTES

"History should be looked at through everyone's subjective experience," said historian Jose López who spoke to a college group of Latino students who couldn't agree whether to call themselves "Latin" or "Hispanic" Alliance. For me this was no longer an issue because I had resolved to call myself a Chicana. This was the first time I had heard a historian mention the importance of everyone's experience in history, including women. He added, "We should see the conquest of Mexico, not as an invasion by Spain of Mexico, but as the rape of thousands of Native American women by Spanish men." I was blown away because for the first time I felt the experience of women was being validated. "The same goes with slavery in the United States. We should look at the experience of all the enslaved women who were raped during this period of history," he added. That day, I left school feeling empowered by this point of view and the overwhelming amount of facts and information that shattered so many myths about Columbus' glorified "discovery of America."

This excitement led me to do more research and in my investigation of the histories of Latin America and religion, I "discovered" a few things. I discovered history is always told through a man's point of view. "His-story" is also always told by the winner. Women and their bodies have always been the battlefield on which personal and political wars (rape) are fought. Women represent a man's most valued "possession," therefore her body also represents the prize, thus making her the loser.

No matter who wins the battle, women will always lose (i.e. rape, impregnation, or loss of children). And since she is always the "loser," "her-

story" is never told. History is therefore devoid of "her" experience, "her" point of view, and "her-story." It's as if all these men who have discovered, created, and destroyed, throughout history had no mother, (well maybe Hitler didn't). Women are not included in history, are not given credit, and worst of all we are blamed for so many things. Interestingly, one man commands the dropping of atomic bombs on hundreds of thousands of human beings, but no one blames him or "malekind." One woman kills her children or gives a man an apple to eat and women will never hear the end of it. When we look at history we must ask ourselves who is telling the story and why. I am telling this her-storical drama through my point of view, a feminist and Chicana's point of view, in my attempt to pose a "What if...?"

A couple of years before I started calling myself a Chicana, I use to call myself "Hispanic," (only because I had been to New York City and rather than let people refer to me as "Spanish," I preferred to call myself "Hispanic"). I stopped calling myself Hispanic when it was pointed out to me that "Hispanic" only makes reference to the Spanish side of my mestizo heritage. I had never stopped to think about this before because all my life I took for granted that I had Spanish blood.

I was born with light features and this was always seen as something positive by my relatives. I never meant to be in "denial" about my identity, because I have always been proud of being Mexican, but I was ignorant about my indigenous heritage. I adopted the title of "Chicana" because I wanted to recognize the indigenous side of who I am. Even though, "Chicano" has a negative connotation, ("Chicanos are hippies who wear bandannas and start riots" according to my older sibling), by taking on this title I hope to dispel myths about Chicanos as being uneducated, angry, confused, and with a "chip on their shoulders."

With this play I hope to give recognition to my "mother," which is Mexico. I wrote this play for Mexico and for my great-great-great-..."grandmother" who was Aztec and was raped by the Spaniards. I am recognizing her and accepting her because she is just as important as my Spanish great-great-great-..."grandfather." The Chicano was born out of rape and hatred. This play was born out of love and acceptance...and "What if..?"

Josefina López
Los Angeles
April 28, 1995

176

UNCONQUERED SPIRITS

ACT ONE

CHARACTERS

JUANA   late 30s, Xochimilco's mother. Tells Xochimilco the legend of La Llorona

XOCHIMILCO *as a young girl.*   As a 10-year-old Mestiza, she has an enormous curiosity and a zest for life, curious, playful, and courageous

TONANTZIN   the mother of the Aztec Gods

SOLDIER   a Spanish soldier

FRAY BARTOLOME   a kind man, who wishes to convert the natives to Christians

FRAY FRANCISCO   an evil man who hates the natives

OLLIN   an old native man

XOCHITL   early 20s, a naive girl who wants to be baptized

TEXCOCO   a young native who is part of the resistance movement

TIXOC   one of the last Aztec priests

TLALOC   an Aztec deity

PARTERA   a mid-wife

LA LLORONA   the crying woman spirit

XOCHIMILCO, *as a grown woman, 35 years old.*   As a woman who looks older than her years, she is defeated, jaded, and angry

MALINA   10, Xochimilco's daughter

LOLA late 30s, Xochimilco's co-worker and friend. Curious and courageous

PETRA late 50s, Xochimilco's co-worker and friend

EMMA 21, an intelligent woman who is a communist

CHRIS supervisor at the pecan factory, Xochimilco's lover

SERAFINA a woman who performs abortions

PRIEST He takes Xochimilco's last confession and punishes her for the abortion

ANGELS Xochimilco's saviours and helpers

BAILIFF he takes Malina away from Xochimilco

SCENE ONE: MEXICO, 1913

(The lights come on to a small wooden shack. The moon is full, illuminating the mountain peaks. center stage is a giant tree with several branches that stick out as though they were the arms of women reaching out of the tree. This tree is 500 years old and it stands firm, delicate as nature can be, but strong like a cannon or a phallus, erect towards heaven. The wind blows and whistles throughout the night. JUANA, looking older than her years, wearing an old dress and a dirty apron, comes out of the small shack. She takes off her apron and looks out to the tiny lake close by.)

JUANA. Xochimilco! Xochimilco! Get in here! ¡Ven aqui! ¡Ahorita! *(She waits for a response. She walks further downstage to the lake.)* Ya es tarde. It's late! You have to finish packing!

(XOCHIMILCO, 10 years old, enters.)

XOCHIMILCO *(enthusiastically)*. No! I don't want to go!

JUANA *(goes to XOCHIMILCO, pulling her by the ear)*. Go inside the house and pack your things. Stop being a little diablita, do what I say and be an angel, porfavor.

XOCHIMILCO. But angels don't have any fun! *(XOCHIMILCO pulls away and runs from her. She covers her ears and challenges JUANA.)* Mamí, try catching me now!

JUANA. ¡Ayy, diabla! ¡Vas a verlo! When you have a daughter she's going to be just like you de traviesa, you'll see.

XOCHIMILCO *(Whining)*. I already packed my bags…Can I go back down to the water?

JUANA. No, you're going to turn into a sirenita, or a little duck. *(JUANA catches XOCHIMILCO and tickles her tummy. They laugh.)*

XOCHIMILCO. Are there lakes where we are going?

JUANA. Si. Your aunt tells me it's nice. And you'll have your cousins to play with. You'll like it over there.

XOCHIMILCO. Mamí, I don't want to leave. Why do we have to leave Mexico?

JUANA. Because there's nothing here for us.

XOCHIMILCO. What about my Papí? What if he returns from la revolucion and doesn't find us here?

JUANA. Xochimilco, get inside the house now and get ready for bed! Hasme caso.

XOCHIMILCO. No! I don't want to go!

JUANA. ¡Ahora si vas a verlo! If your father were here…! *(JUANA breaks out crying. XOCHIMILCO tries to hold back her own tears.)*

XOCHIMILCO. Mamí, my Papí isn't coming back, is he? *(JUANA stops crying unsure what to say.)* Is that why that letter you got last week made you cry so much? *(JUANA nods painfully. XOCHIMILCO tries to be strong for her mother.)* I'll be good. Don't cry, Mamíta. *(XOCHIMILCO comforts her mother.)* Mamíta, in my prayers I ask God to take care of my Papí…Mamí… Where is heaven?

JUANA. Up there?

XOCHIMILCO. Where is hell?

JUANA. Sometimes I think it's right here on earth. Xochi, mi'ijita, for the last time, get inside the house and get ready, or…or…

XOCHIMILCO. Or what?

JUANA. Or…La Llorona will get you!

XOCHIMILCO. What? Who?

JUANA. La Llorona. I'm surprised you haven't seen her yet. *(JUANA sits down nonchalantly.)* La Llorona is the spirit of a woman all dressed in white who roams by the rivers of Mexico looking for her dead children who she killed a long time ago…An uncle of mine saw her many years ago when he was herding sheep one night. She came to him and asked him for water. He said she was very beautiful with long golden hair and a pale face. He asked her what she was doing there so late and she simply said she usually walked

by there at night. She thanked him for the water and walked away. From a distance she screamed "¡¡Ay mis hijos!!" and then disappeared.

XOCHIMILCO *(Intrigued and scared).* Why did she kill her children?

JUANA. Are you sure you want to know? You might not want to go down to the lake after you hear the story…Let me see if I can remember it…A long time ago, there was a very beautiful Indian woman and a handsome Spaniard who fell in love. They loved each other very much and had children. Then he left her and went off to Spain to marry another woman. When he returned to Mexico the Indian woman went to a big ball and saw them dancing happily together. She was so angry that she went home and killed her children. She cut them into little pieces and threw them into a river. Then she killed herself. But when her spirit reached the gates of heaven, God would not let her in until she found her children. So her spirit roams the rivers of Mexico looking for her children, screaming, "¡¡Ayy mis hijos!!" *(XOCHIMILCO, screams. JUANA laughs.)*

XOCHIMILCO. But how could she kill her children?

JUANA. She lost her mind, se volvio loca, and did it out of revenge.

XOCHIMILCO. Maybe it was an accident.

JUANA. No, she was a bad woman and a terrible mother… And when she sees little girls like you misbehaving she goes to their bed, pulls them out, and takes them away.

XOCHIMILCO. She won't take me, will she, Mamí?

JUANA. She will if you continue to disobey me. Asi es que siguele. I'll tell her to come and get you. I'll even give you to her. Who needs a bad little girl? *(XOCHIMILCO starts crying.)* No, no, no te apures, I was just trying to scare you. Don't be scared, if you're a good girl, nothing's going to happen to you…All right, you can go down to the water for a little bit, if you still want to. Just remember, we have to wake up early to catch the train. *(JUANA kisses her on the forehead and leaves. XOCHIMILCO, who was pretending to be crying, quickly changes expressions. She is about to run back into the water when she stops to reconsider.)*

XOCHIMILCO. Ah…No, I think I'll just lie here, just in case La Llorona passes by…Not that I'm scared or anything… but it's getting late, it's cold… and I'm sleepy. *(She goes to her bed and lies down, and gets ready to go to sleep. She starts praying.)* Padre nuestro que estás en los cielos, forgive me because I am not on my knees, but I don't want La Llorona to get me…God, if you can really hear me, please take care of my Papí. I know he is in heaven with the angelitos. God, please take care of my Mamíta and me…Amen.

(XOCHIMILCO does the sign of the cross and goes to sleep. Lights fade out slowly.)

SCENE TWO: TENOCHTITLÁN, 1521

(TONANTZIN, the Aztec Goddess of the earth, screams from the very top of the Pyramid of the Sun as Tenochtitlán is being destroyed. The shadows of fire are seen. All around her is chaos.)

TONANTZIN. ¡¡Ayy mis hijos!! Look how they are destroying Tenochtitlán! Look how the flowers are dying. ¡¡Ayy mis hijos!!

(TWO SPANISH SOLDIERS capture TONANTZIN and tie her to a cross. The pyramid is quickly transformed into a Mission. They place the cross on the top of what used to be the Pyramid of the Sun to establish the new reign. As the lights fade out we hear the following along with angelic music.)

BISHOP *(Voice-over)*. The true and universal God, our Lord, Creator and dispenser of being and life, as we have been telling you in our sermons, has a character different from that of your Gods. He does not deceive; He lies not; He hates no one, despises no one. There is nothing evil in Him. He is perfectly good. He is the essence of love, compassion, and mercy. And He showed his infinite mercy when He made Himself man here on earth like us; humble and poor, like us. He is eternal, He created heaven and earth and hell. He created us, all the men in the world, and He also created the devils whom you hold to be Gods and whom you call Gods, and who did not support you in the slightest, while the true and omnipotent God has allowed his faithful servants, the Spaniards, to conquer Mexico...

SCENE THREE: (MEXICO), NEW SPAIN, 1559

(The angelic voices of a Native American children's choir bring peace to the horror of the destruction and genocide of the Natives of Tenochtitlán.

Lights fade in.

Several years later, in the same Mission, a group of Native Americans listen to a sermon on their knees. Some of them have difficulty staying on their knees for so long. A SPANISH SOLDIER comes by and whips their backs so they will sit up.)

BISHOP. This true God is everywhere. He has his Kingdom, which He began in the beginning of the world. He would have you enter it now, and for this you should consider yourselves blessed. *(The BISHOP finishes his*

181

sermon.) You may stand.

(The BISHOP leaves. Two friars, FRAY BARTOLOME and FRAY FRANCISCO take over.)

FRAY BARTOLOME. Tomorrow you will be baptized. We know that our training was done quickly, but there is urgency to save your souls. Be ready to recite and know the credo, Our Holy Father, the ten commandments, the immortality of the soul, original sin, heaven and hell, what are good and bad angels, and Lucifer's descent from heaven. To make sure you are prepared we are going to test you. Who would like to be first?

(No one volunteers. FRAY BARTOLOME looks around. He stares at an OLLIN, an older Native American man who is very shy.)

FRAY BARTOLOME. You. Come here. I want you to recite the credo.

OLLIN *(Comes forward).* Yo creo en Dios, todo poderoso, creador de los cielos y de la tierra. *(OLLIN forgets the rest of the prayer.)*

FRAY FRANCISCO. Yes…Continue…

OLLIN. Ah…Ah…I forgot it.

FRAY FRANCISCO. Repeat after me…I believe in Jesus Christ his only son…

OLLIN. Yo creo en Jesus Cristo…

FRAY FRANCISCO. His only son…

OLLIN. Su unico hijo…

FRAY FRANCISCO. Our Lord, who was created…What is wrong with you?! Repeat it! *(OLLIN doesn't say anything.)* Are you so stupid! Can't you hear? *(OLLIN remains still. FRAY FRANCISCO loses his patience and is about to strike him when FRAY BARTOLOME stops him. He takes him aside.)*

FRAY BARTOLOME. Brother Francisco, we are here to save souls, not break bones…Patience, patience.

FRAY FRANCISCO. Why should we save their souls? They are savages, idiots! They are not human.

FRAY BARTOLOME. Think of them as children. They may lack the knowledge of the mind, but they can gain the knowledge of the soul. Could the gates of the Kingdom of God be closed to these simple souls, full of good will? No. That is why we are here. To educate them about human morality… Let me deal with him. *(FRAY BARTOLOME walks up to OLLIN.)* In order to enter the kingdom of God you must renounce your false Gods. Are you prepared to do that? *(OLLIN shakes his head "no.")* Then I am forced to show you what happens to those who do not renounce their false gods.

(The following ritual is a theatrical presentation by the FRIARS. They blow out the candles illuminating the Mission, and bring in the darkness. They light a huge fire and throw chickens and small animals into the flames. The Native Americans hear the animals howling and screeching and become very frightened.)

FRAY BARTOLOME. Where do you want your soul to end up? In there or in God's paradise?

OLLIN *(very scared).* In paradise.

FRAY BARTOLOME. Then you will learn your prayers. *(FRAY FRANCISCO and FRAY BARTOLOME turn off the fire and light the candles.)*

FRAY FRANCISCO. Recite for me the credo.

OLLIN. Yo creo en Dios todo poderoso, creador de todos los cielos y la tierra, y Jesus Cristo, su unico hijo…

(XOCHITL, a Native American woman, whispers the credo to OLLIN when he forgets it.)

FRAY FRANCISCO. That's enough. I know that you will have it memorized by tomorrow.

FRAY BARTOLOME. Let this serve as an example to you. God is merciful, but He won't tolerate the adoration of false Gods…Tomorrow you will be baptized, your knowledge of our Lord and his Son will be tested. Be here at eight in the morning, ready, and in your best clothes…You can leave.

(The frightened Native Americans leave. XOCHITL is on her way out. FRAY BARTOLOME approaches her. TEXCOCO, one of the Native American, stops and listens to their conversation on the side.)

FRAY BARTOLOME. Xochitl, you are very special. Our Lord is very proud of your servitude and the commitment you show by helping others to better serve and understand our Lord.

XOCHITL *(Embarrassed).* It is nothing. I do it out of love for my Lord. I am only thankful that you are helping me and my people save our souls.

FRAY BARTOLOME. Your soul is worth saving, hija. Tomorrow will be a very special day for you. It will be the beginning of your membership into the house of God.

XOCHITL. I look forward to tomorrow. *(She walks away, shyly.)*

FRAY BARTOLOME. Don't forget that it is your turn to decorate the altar tomorrow.

XOCHITL. No, Padre. I am on my way right now to get the flowers.

FRAY BARTOLOME. Very good, hija. Then be with God. Adiós.

XOCHITL. Adiós. *(She kisses his hand and walks away. TEXCOCO casually follows her out. Lights fade out.)*

SCENE FOUR

(Lights fade in. In the background is a hill full of large stones. XOCHITL enters carrying two large baskets full of white flowers (calla-lilies). She sits down on the ground to rest and catch her breath.)

XOCHITL. Dear Lord, all these souls that lie here, open your heaven to them. I will do your will so that their souls and maybe mine will be saved…

(TEXCOCO sneaks up behind her.)

TEXCOCO. Don't pray so hard. Don't you know that God is deaf when it comes to our prayers?

XOCHITL. How can you talk that way? You're supposed to be ready for baptism tomorrow!

TEXCOCO. They're going to have to kill me before they baptize me.

XOCHITL. You don't mean that! I can help you. I can make you understand.

TEXCOCO. You act like such an angel, but don't you know angels aren't brown.

XOCHITL. I'm not trying to do anything, but serve my Lord.

TEXCOCO. Do you really believe them? They enslaved our people and treat us like animals. And yet they're supposed to serve a loving and compassionate God…If their God created all men, then we belong to Him, and we are brothers with the Spaniards, but why are we looked down on as though we weren't even human? Have you thought about this?

XOCHITL. I can only try to teach you what I know. The faith is up to you.

TEXCOCO. You can't answer me, can you?

XOCHITL. I am late, I have to go…Excuse me.

TEXCOCO. Hermana, have they stolen your soul already?

XOCHITL (*picks up the baskets and starts walking away*). See you tomorrow at the baptism…The Lord be with you, Hermano.

TEXCOCO (*runs after XOCHITL*). Stop praying to your false God. If He were so compassionate and loving He wouldn't have sent them here to kill all of our people and your parents. It is a lie that they are the servants of God. They didn't come to serve God, they came to serve themselves. They came to rob us of our gold, our land, our souls! Why are you believing their lies as the truth?

XOCHITL. Get away from me!

TEXCOCO. Hermana, I only tell you because I'm scared to lose you. They've already killed most of us by poisoning our bodies with their diseases. Now they are poisoning our souls by baptizing us into permanent slavery.

XOCHITL. Stop it! Stop it! Leave me alone! You're a demon! I know about you. You're a bad angel sent to test my faith. Get away, demon…Lord, give me strength…(*She starts praying "Our Heavenly Father."*)

TEXCOCO. Pray as much as you want, but I won't disappear, and now that I've entered your mind, this doubt will never leave you.

XOCHITL. I don't want to hear anymore! Stop confusing me! I'm supposed to be ready for my baptism.

TEXCOCO. Floresita, I didn't mean to be so cruel. I'll leave you alone. But ask yourself why this God would want us to live in fear of him and his servants. Why he would allow us to suffer this way? (*XOCHITL runs away from him. TEXCOCO watches her, disappointed. Lights fade out.*)

SCENE FIVE

(*Lights fade in faintly. The Mission is lit up by only a few candles. XOCHITL enters. She proceeds to the altar and kneels in front of the statue of the crucifixion.*)

XOCHITL. Dear Lord…Forgive me, but I have doubts. I don't understand…

(*FRAY FRANCISCO enters.*)

FRAY FRANCISCO. What is it you don't understand? (*He has frightened her.*)

XOCHITL. I'm embarrassed…I'm ashamed to admit it to you.

FRAY FRANCISCO. Come here. I will listen. Whatever you can say to our Lord, you can say to me because I am his servant. *(XOCHITL walks toward him, shyly.)* Don't be scared. *(She walks closer to him.)* Now tell me. What do you have doubts about? *(He innocently puts his arm around her shoulder.)*

XOCHITL *(Hesitantly)*. If…If our Lord made all men…*(His arm slowly slides down to her waist.)*

FRAY FRANCISCO. Yes…

XOCHITL. And he created the Pope and our Emperor King Charles I, you and me…

FRAY FRANCISCO. And you are certainly a divine and beautiful creation.

XOCHITL *(Shyly smiling)*. …and my people…Then why…?

FRAY FRANCISCO. Why what? *(He pulls her closer to him. XOCHITL closes her eyes now.)*

XOCHITL. Then if we are all God's children, why would God let me and my people be enslaved and be treated like animals, and suffer this way?

FRAY FRANCISCO. It is because we are here to suffer. Only when we suffer do we prove to God how worthy we are of his paradise. Your people need to suffer, to repent for all of your sins, for all your human sacrifices and worship of false gods. Only after you have suffered on earth can you truly deserve to enter through the gates of heaven. Do you want to be saved? *(XOCHITL nods "yes" as she looks sadly to her feet.)* Then you must suffer. *(His hand is now between her legs, rubbing on her. XOCHITL holds back her tears. She passively and defenselessly awaits his other hand. He puts his hand in her blouse and she does nothing. Blackout.)*

SCENE SIX

(Lights fade in. There is a full moon. Clearly it has a face, that of a crying woman. XOCHITL runs in, barely able to stand up. She is crawling on the ground. She is silent for a few seconds, then she begins to whimper.)

XOCHITL. Dear God, I know you exist, because even after what has happened I still have the strength to love you. But dear God, what is your name? Is it Jesus or Tlaloc, or does it matter what your name is as long as you are mine and are above me and everywhere? I want you to love me as your child, but how can this be your will?

(TEXCOCO appears.)

TEXCOCO. Why do you cry, Floresita?

XOCHITL. You must be a demon! Because you only appear when I am praying.

TEXCOCO. It's because your crying can be heard all throughout Tenochtitlán and your tears even make the moon cry.

XOCHITL. I'm not crying!

TEXCOCO. Did you find the answer? Is that why you're crying?

XOCHITL. No!…

TEXCOCO. Are you still going to be baptized tomorrow?

XOCHITL (Gasping for air). What do you want from me? Leave me alone!

TEXCOCO. I can't…To see you cry that way makes me want to cry too… What is wrong? (He tries to hold her, but she pushes him away.)

XOCHITL. Nothing! There's nothing wrong with me!

TEXCOCO. Then you must be rejoicing because tomorrow you will be "saved." (XOCHITL bursts out in more tears. She falls to the ground as if wanting to bury herself in the dirt. She claws the ground with rage.)

XOCHITL. I want to die! (TEXCOCO tries to lift her from the ground. She pulls herself down.)

TEXCOCO. You can't die! Xochitl, you're not a coward.

XOCHITL. You don't know me, how can you say that?

TEXCOCO. Because you are my hermana. And our fathers and mothers were not cowards. The Spaniards would like us all to die and finally disappear so they can do whatever they want with our land and gold, but we have to live. Our Gods gave us our will to live. (XOCHITL lifts herself up. She takes his hand and sits up on a rock. She wipes her tears away and regains her strength.)

XOCHITL. I asked Fray Francisco to tell me why…why… they treat us this way…and he…(She cries.) He told me I had to suffer…And he…he…(She covers her face in shame.) But I let him!! I didn't do anything. I didn't scream; I didn't run. I didn't fight! I laid on the ground, looking up to the cross. And I kept thinking that if…if I endured, that the Lord would love me more.

TEXCOCO (Hugs her). I'm sorry…I'm sorry you had to find out that way, but will you still get baptized tomorrow?

187

Photo by Josefina Lopez

Texcoco comforts Xochil after her rape.

XOCHITL. Do we have a choice?!

TEXCOCO. No, but we can do it our way.

XOCHITL. How?

TEXCOCO. Can I trust you? Will you feel this way tomorrow and always?

XOCHITL. Yes, I think so.

TEXCOCO. Come with me. I have to show you something.

XOCHITL. What is it? Where will you take me?

TEXCOCO. Trust me, Xochitl. *(He extends his hand out to her. She considers it carefully, then takes his hand. They walk towards the moon. Lights fade out.)*

SCENE SEVEN

(TIXOC, one of the last Aztec priests, makes fire and lights up copal which he places on a small altar. He prays silently. TEXCOCO lights a candle. XOCHITL follows him.)

TIXOC. Who's there?

TEXCOCO. It's me, Texcoco. *(Another candle is lit.)*

TIXOC. Who is she?

TEXCOCO. This is Xochitl.

TIXOC. Ah, good…You finally convinced her to come.

XOCHITL. Where are we?

TIXOC. You must first swear that you will never tell anyone what you see here tonight or else you will put our lives in danger.

XOCHITL. I swear.

TIXOC. Do you swear not to tell even if you are tortured?

XOCHITL *(Freezes in contemplation, then answers him).* I swear.

(TIXOC leads them in the darkness. He reaches a spot and lights up a torch. The room, a temple, is illuminated. On the walls are murals depicting the ceremonies of the Aztecs as well as the different deities.)

XOCHITL. What is this?

TIXOC. When the Spaniards came, they destroyed every temple and idol they could find. All the temples were destroyed, but this one was spared because it was built underground. But lake Texcoco is leaking through the cracks. *(TIXOC illuminates a mural that exemplifies the Fire Ceremony.)*

XOCHITL. What is this?

TIXOC. These are the murals illustrating the history of our ceremonies. This one is the Fire Ceremony.

XOCHITL. When did it happen?

TIXOC. You are too young to know about it because it only happens every fifty-two years. Our ancestors believed that a sacred period of time was fifty-two years and they held a New Fire Ceremony to mark the end of a

cycle and the beginning of a new one. They would break all their pots, and start with new. They would start a new fire and relight the entire city after it was in darkness for days. The last time it happened was almost fifty-two years ago. *(TIXOC takes them further inside the temple. Visible are three large statues of Tlaloc, Quetzalcóatl, and Tonantzin. TIXOC lights up sticks of copal.)* After the destruction of Tenochtitlán we had to smuggle and store all the sacred idols and objects. It is a sacred place where we worship our God Tlaloc, Quetzalcóatl, God of Culture, and Tonantzintlalli, our mother earth. Do you see how those demons have come and disrespected and destroyed our mother earth? That is why our Gods have ordered us to rise up against the Spaniards. We have to continue our resistance if we are to survive. Xochitl, I have asked Texcoco to bring you here because you can help us with our resistance. *(TEXCOCO brings forth a small gold statue of Tlaloc. He presents the statue to her.)*

TEXCOCO. Tomorrow before the baptism, when you are decorating the altar, you will be the only one there. Xochitl, when no one is looking, you will hide Tlaloc behind the crucifixion. So that when we are being baptized, we are accepting and praying to our God, Tlaloc.

XOCHITL. I can't do that…If they catch me I'll be thrown to the pit of hell or tortured.

TEXCOCO. You won't get caught.

XOCHITL. But if I do?!

TEXCOCO. It's already hell on earth for us, how bad can it be?

XOCHITL. I can't…

TEXCOCO. If their God is, as they claim to be, a loving and forgiving God, he'll forgive you. Our ancestors believed that you went to hell or heaven based upon the way you died. If you get caught, you will die as a heroine, and go to heaven.

XOCHITL. It's a sin to worship false gods.

TEXCOCO. Then which ones are false? Their god; or ours? *(XOCHITL walks away. TEXCOCO follows her.)* Where are you going?

XOCHITL. Back to the Mission.

TEXCOCO. How can you go back? What are you going back to, Fray Francisco? He'll be glad to give you more lessons on suffering. *(XOCHITL freezes and turns around.)* Take the statue with you. Think about it. If you don't want to risk it, then swear to me you will not show it to anyone, or tell anyone where you got it and you will give it back to me. *(XOCHITL gives*

TEXCOCO *an angry look, but she grabs the statue from him and hides it in her moral. Lights fade out.)*

SCENE EIGHT

(Lights fade in faintly. XOCHITL enters wearing a white dress and carrying the two baskets of flowers (calla-lilies). She walks up to the altar. From the basket she gets a bunch of flowers and begins to decorate the altar. She brings the other basket next to the altar. She looks around nervously and gets the statue from the basket. Concealed in a large bunch of flowers, she is getting ready to hide the statue when FRAY BARTOLOME appears.)

FRAY BARTOLOME. What are you doing?

XOCHITL *(Jumps up and screams)*. I'm sorry, Padre, you scared me.

FRAY BARTOLOME. I heard someone and I came to see.

XOCHITL. I came to prepare the flowers.

FRAY BARTOLOME. So early? Xochitl, you are truly a little angel sent from heaven. You are so dedicated.

XOCHITL *(Smiles)*. It is nothing.

FRAY BARTOLOME. I see so much good in your heart. I am always filled with joy when I see you show so much devotion. *(FRAY BARTOLOME takes the bunch of flowers from XOCHITL and places them down on a counter. He grabs her hands and squeezes them with his.)* God bless you, hija.

XOCHITL. Thank you.

FRAY BARTOLOME. Hija, I will see you in a couple of hours. I'm going back to finish my prayers.

XOCHITL. Yes, Padre, I will see you later. *(She watches FRAY BARTOLOME walk away. She stands still, unsure what to do. Finally, she grabs the bunch of flowers from the counter and proceeds with her plan. Lights fade out.)*

SCENE NINE

(A boys' choir sings in the background. The lights come on to the same Mission, now beautifully decorated. FRAY BARTOLOME has a Native American man, AUGUSTIN, on his knees in front of the holy water. XOCHITL and other Native Americans are waiting to be baptized. FRAY BARTOLOME taps the Native American's forehead with water.)

FRAY BARTOLOME. I baptize you in the name of the father, the son, and the Holy Spirit…Augustín De Los Arroyos…From this day forward you will be another member of the Catholic church.

AUGUSTIN *(Rises and bends to kiss FRAY BARTOLOME's hand).* Thank you, Padre.

FRAY BARTOLOME. God bless you.

(AUGUSTIN leaves and XOCHITL is the next person to get baptized. TEXCOCO enters the Mission. XOCHITL reaches for his hand and holds it. She smiles at him and carefully looks toward the statue of the Crucifixion. FRAY FRANCISCO sees their exchange and walks up to her. TEXCOCO gets in front of the line. XOCHITL shyly looks to her feet.)

FRAY BARTOLOME. Come forward, hijo, and kneel before our Lord. *(TEXCOCO kneels, and pretends to be happy and obedient.)* Please recite "Our Heavenly Father." *(TEXCOCO stutters purposely throughout the prayer. XOCHITL secretly laughs. FRAY BARTOLOME is annoyed by his stutter.)* That's enough! I'm convinced that you know it. *(He wets his hand with the holy water and taps TEXCOCO's forehead.)* I baptize you in the name of the Father, the Son, and the Holy Spirit…Miguel…Miguel…Tartamudo. From this day forward you will be another member of the Catholic Church. *(FRAY BARTOLOME extends his hand out to him. TEXCOCO gives his hand a wet kiss. FRAY BARTOLOME dries it with his robe. TEXCOCO leaves the altar. XOCHITL steps forward, ready to be baptized by FRAY BARTOLOME.)*

FRAY FRANCISCO. Brother Bartolomé, please let me have the honor of baptizing her.

FRAY BARTOLOME *(Surprised).* Ah…If you'd like…

FRAY FRANCISCO. Very much so…*(XOCHITL steps back, afraid of him.)* Come forward and kneel before our Lord. *(XOCHITL steps forward, but looks at her feet. He grabs her chin and makes her look up.)* Look at me. *(She raises her head.)* I want you to recite the credo. *(XOCHITL recites the credo. Midway through it she begins to cry.)* Why are you crying?

XOCHITL *(Looks him in the eye).* Because I am feeling the love of God. *(FRAY FRANCISCO looks away. He wets his hand with holy water and taps her forehead.)*

FRAY FRANCISCO. I baptize you in the name of the Father, the Son, and the Holy Spirit, Maria Isabella De Las Flores. From this day forward you are another member of the Catholic Church. *(He extends his hand to her waiting for it to be kissed. She kisses it with disgust.)*

XOCHITL. Thank you, Padre.

FRAY FRANCISCO. You may stand…May God bless you. *(XOCHITL stands and walks away. TEXCOCO follows her. FRAY FRANCISCO stares at them as they leave together. Lights slowly fade out.)*

SCENE TEN

(In the darkness of the night, several figures enter from all sides of the stage. TEXCOCO and XOCHITL sneak in carefully. TIXOC enters carrying a lit torch. The several Native Americans surround him and await the new era. TIXOC passes on the fire from his torch to another torch until the fire spreads throughout the stage. All the Native Americans in their excitement embrace each other. TEXCOCO embraces XOCHITL.)

TEXCOCO. Tixoc has prophesied that you will be my wife. *(XOCHITL takes his hand and raises it up along with all the others. The Native Americans have joined hands in a circle and raise them to give thanks to the deities for life.)*

TIXOC. With this new era let it bring more unity in our battle to regain our motherland from those white demons. *(As quietly as can be done, they break several pots and other pottery. TIXOC lights his torch and passes it on to another.)*

XOCHITL. Then it will be true. *(After some time of passing on the fire, in the distance, horses and Spaniards are heard approaching. They scatter and disappear into the darkness.)*

SCENE ELEVEN

(Lights fade in. In the Mission, FRAY BARTOLOME and FRAY FRANCISCO are instructing some Native Americans on how to repair the roof. One Native American man is holding a large piece of wood. When he turns around he accidentally knocks off the statue of the Crucifixion. FRAY BARTOLOME immediately strikes the man.)

FRAY BARTOLOME. Stupid savage! Look what you've done!!

FRAY FRANCISCO. Fray Bartolomé! "We are here to save souls, not break bones," remember, my brother?

FRAY BARTOLOME. Yes, but sometimes it is easy to forget…Help me pick it up. *(FRAY FRANCISCO picks up the statue and finds the dusty gold statue of Tlaloc.)*

FRAY FRANCISCO. Brother Bartolomé, look!

FRAY BARTOLOME. What in the devil?! What's the meaning of this? *(FRAY BARTOLOME looks closely at the dusty gold statue.)* This is an idol of the devil himself!! We have been made fools by those savages!! They took the oath, but they are still practicing paganism! We must find those responsible now before their resistance increases! *(FRAY BARTOLOME spits at the statute in disgust. He stares at it for some time. The spit has removed some of the dust and he soon realizes the statue is made of gold. FRAY BARTOLOME is excited.)* My God! It's gold! Pure gold! *(FRAY BARTOLOME is so thrilled by the little treasure, he kisses the statue and holds it tightly next to his heart. FRAY FRANCISCO and FRAY BARTOLOME quickly go to the altar, and without realizing it, destroy it in search of other idols. They find small gold statues of Tonantzin and Quetzalcóatl.)* There must be more where these came from.

FRAY FRANCISCO. I think I know who is responsible…Go call the soldiers and follow me. *(Blackout.)*

SCENE TWELVE

(In the darkness we can see two figures lying together. There is groaning coming from one of them. XOCHITL sits up. She is wearing a white dress and is visibly pregnant.)

TEXCOCO. What's wrong?

XOCHITL. The baby is coming.

TEXCOCO. I'll go get the partera. *(TEXCOCO runs out. Several seconds later he returns.)* Xochitl, run!! We've been found out. Go hide in the temple! Run! No matter what, don't let them catch you alive! *(She runs out.)*

(FRAY FRANCISCO and FRAY BARTOLOME enter with TWO SOLDIERS.)

FRAY BARTOLOME. Where is Isabella? *(TEXCOCO doesn't answer.)*

FRAY FRANCISCO. Take him! *(The SOLDIERS tie him up and take him. Fade out.)*

SCENE THIRTEEN

(Lights fade in. On one side of the stage where XOCHITL is squatting, she is ready to give birth. The PARTERA holds her hand as XOCHITL pushes the baby out. On the other side of the stage, TEXCOCO is tied up in a torture

chamber, lying on a table. FRAY BARTOLOME and FRAY FRANCISCO are around him. FRAY FRANCISCO handles him by the hair.)

PARTERA. ¡Respira y empuja! Push!

FRAY FRANCISCO. Where is Isabella?!!

FRAY BARTOLOME. Where did you get the idols? *(TEXCOCO is tortured with sticks, which have been resting in a fire, by a SOLDIER. TEXCOCO screams in pain. XOCHITL screams too.)*

PARTERA. ¡Empuja con toda tu fuerza! With all your strength so that your child will be valiente. *(XOCHITL pushes with all her might.)*

FRAY BARTOLOME. Miguel, if you tell us where you're hiding the idols we'll let you go.

TEXCOCO. My name is Texcoco and my life means nothing to you. I will die whether I tell you or not!

FRAY BARTOLOME. Tell us where the gold—I mean the idols, are!

FRAY FRANCISCO. Burn his feet, maybe then he'll talk. *(A SOLDIER holds a torch to his feet. TEXCOCO cries in pain. XOCHITL does too.)*

PARTERA. It's coming. Just push a little harder!

FRAY BARTOLOME. Remove the torch. I want him alive. I want all those idols destroyed once and for all. Tell us where you have them! *(TEXCOCO remains silent. They torch his feet again.)*

TEXCOCO. I will never tell you!!! Even if you find them and destroy our temples and idols, you will never break our spirits. You can kill me, but you cannot kill our hopes of being free!

FRAY BARTOLOME. Then kill him! *(FRAY FRANCISCO plunges a dagger into TEXCOCO's heart. TEXCOCO screams as he reaches death. XOCHITL screams as she gives birth.)*

PARTERA. It's a boy. *(She spanks the baby. The baby cries. XOCHITL keeps pushing.)*

XOCHITL. There's another life in me! *(The PARTERA helps the baby out. She spanks the second baby.)*

PARTERA. It's another boy. *(The PARTERA wipes the baby clean and studies it. She brings the candle closer to the baby's face.)* Your children are white. *(XOCHITL cries.)* There's no need to be ashamed. So many of our hermanas have had the same thing happen to them…No matter who wins the battles, we always lose…Relax.

(A young Native American MAN comes running in.)

HUETZIN. Xochitl! They have killed Texcoco! *(XOCHITL screams in pain and rage.)* No, there's no time to cry! They are looking for you! You must run! *(XOCHITL stands up. Her white dress is stained with blood.)*

PARTERA. ¡Core, largate! Or you'll put us all in danger.

XOCHITL. Which way should I leave?

PARTERA. Por el lago, by the way of the lake! *(XOCHITL picks up her two sons to take them with her.)* Leave them here.

XOCHITL. No. I don't want them to find my children and baptize them. *(XOCHITL runs out with them. Lights fade out.)*

SCENE FOURTEEN

(The moon is out, it has the face of a crying woman. XOCHITL runs in with her children. She is running towards the lake. Nearby is the giant tree.)

XOCHITL. Oh, my children, where will I take you? There's nowhere to go… *(XOCHITL climbs the tree with the babies, reaching the top.)* Lake Texcoco, how peaceful you look. Your water looks so clean and pure. Pure enough to cleanse my children of the poison. My Tenochtitlán, this is where you began and here is where my life ends. *(Faint sounds of footsteps are heard coming towards her. XOCHITL places one of the babies on the tree. She holds the other baby up towards the sky.)* Tonantzin, my mother earth, can you hear me?

(TONANTZIN appears at the bottom of the lake.)

XOCHITL. Mother earth, to you I give this child. I return him to you to cleanse his body so that his soul will not be conquered. *(She throws the baby into the lake. TONANTZIN catches him and water splashing is heard. XOCHITL picks up the other baby and holds it up toward the sky.)* Tlaloc, can you hear me?

(TLALOC appears at the bottom of the lake.)

XOCHITL. Tlaloc, I give this child to you as my sacrifice, so that you never abandon my people. Continue to give us strength and courage in our fight! *(She throws the baby and TLALOC catches him and water splashing is heard.)* ¡Ayy mis hijos! It is because I love you that I've returned you to a better place where you won't be a half-breed, a mestizo, conquered and enslaved, but free souls. Ayyy mi Tenochtitlán, all of your beauty is being destroyed. All of your flowers are dying. *(Footsteps are heard coming closer.)* Ayy mis hijos. It is time for me to join you.

SOLDIER 1 *(Voice-over)*. There she is!

SOLDIER 2 *(Voice-over)*. She's killed her children!

SOLDIER 1 *(Voice-over)*. Get her!

XOCHITL. ¡Qué viva Tenochtitlán!

(XOCHITL dives into the lake. As XOCHITL reaches the lake and drowns herself, LA LLORONA, a horrific and monstrous woman with golden hair and a deformed face, comes out of the tree.)

SCENE FIFTEEN: MEXICO, 1913

(At the lake. XOCHIMILCO still sleeps. Spotlight downstage on LA LLORONA who screams loudly, waking up XOCHIMILCO.)

LA LLORONA. ¡¡¡Ayyy mis Hijos!!!

(XOCHIMILCO freezes as she stares at LA LLORONA. LA LLORONA extends her hands to XOCHIMILCO as if calling out for her to come. LA LLORONA walks toward XOCHIMILCO. XOCHIMILCO screams and hides under her blankets. JUANA goes to her and holds her. XOCHIMILCO screams again thinking LA LLORONA is holding her.)

La Llorona appears to Xochilmilco.

Photo by Josefina Lopez

JUANA. ¿Qué paso?

XOCHIMILCO. I saw her! I saw her! La Llorona was in my dream and then she came out of the lake!

JUANA. You had a nightmare.

XOCHIMILCO. No, she was here! ¡Aquí estába!

JUANA. Ya, ya. She's gone. I wouldn't let her take you. You imagined her.

XOCHIMILCO. But she screamed and woke me up.

JUANA. No, I was calling for you to wake up. We have to hurry, apurate, because the train will be leaving soon. Ten, put on your coat. *(JUANA hands XOCHIMILCO her coat. XOCHIMILCO puts it on while JUANA walks aside to pray.)* Dios mio, take care of us on our journey to el norte. Let us have a better life than the one we've had here…Our lives, nuestras vidas, are in your hands… Amen.

(They pick up their belongings, packed in morales and Mexican cookie boxes. JUANA walks ahead as XOCHIMILCO slowly follows. XOCHIMILCO turns back to get one last look at her home and LA LLORONA is there. LA LLORONA walks toward her. She sticks out her hand, which is bloody, to XOCHIMILCO who stands watching her, mesmerized. As LA LLORONA gets closer, XOCHIMILCO finally awakens from the spell and screams. XOCHIMILCO tries to catch up to JUANA. She keeps turning back and LA LLORONA is still there with her hands up as if calling for her. JUANA and XOCHIMILCO head upstage and disappear in the darkness. Lights slowly fade out as we see LA LLORONA rubbing her bloody hands together and looking towards heaven.)

END OF ACT ONE

UNCONQUERED SPIRITS

ACT TWO

SCENE ONE: U.S.A., SAN ANTONIO, TEXAS 1938

(Lights fade in. XOCHIMILCO, who is now 35 years old, but looks older from hard work, is on her knees. She is at the bedside of her daughter, MALINA, the oldest of her five children, whom she is tucking into bed. XOCHIMILCO kisses MALINA on the forehead and turns out the lights. On a wall there is a little altar for JUAN, her deceased husband. She lights a candle for him and begins her prayer.)

XOCHIMILCO. Juan, if you were here I probably wouldn't have thought about it, but I have to do it. It's for the best… Que descanses en paz. Mi querido Juan como te estraño. *(She grabs her purse and sweater and begins to go out the door. MALINA hears her and quickly sits up.)*

MALINA. Where are you going, Mamíta?

XOCHIMILCO. I'm…I'm going out.

MALINA. But where?

XOCHIMILCO. Just for a little walk.

MALINA. You're not going to leave us, are you? *(XOCHIMILCO is so surprised by her question, she immediately comes back to reassure her.)*

XOCHIMILCO. Mi'ijita, why would you ask me that? Of course not!

MALINA. It's just that I see you sad all the time. Papí looked like that

before…he left.

XOCHIMILCO. But how can you remember his look? You were so young.

MALINA. I remember him.

XOCHIMILCO. And your father; your father didn't leave you. If it would have been up to him, he would have lived until you were all grown up…No, cariño, I'm not going to leave you.

MALINA. Do you promise?

XOCHIMILCO. Pues, if God gives me permission, I promise I won't leave you.

MALINA. Mamíta, I love you.

XOCHIMILCO. Yo tambien te amo a ti…I have you in my corazón. I have all of your hermanitos, right here tambien…Bueno, ya. You better go to sleep.

MALINA. No, Mamíta. I don't feel like going to sleep.

XOCHIMILCO. You have to. Tomorrow is a school day.

MALINA. But I don't want to go to sleep. I don't want to go to school anymore!

XOCHIMILCO. Why not?

MALINA. They keep calling me a "wetback" and they tell me I should go back to where I belong.

XOCHIMILCO. But you do belong, you were born here.

MALINA. Three boys keep picking on me and it gets me so angry. I wish I could hit them back when they spit at me.

XOCHIMILCO. Just ignore them and walk faster. Now please go to sleep, I'm going to be late.

MALINA. For what? Who are you meeting?

XOCHIMILCO. Mi madre would always tell me, "Vas a verlo, when you get married and have children, you're going to have a daughter just like you." So, I must deserve you, Malina.

MALINA (Stalling for time). Tell me a bedtime story.

XOCHIMILCO. I don't know any.

MALINA. Make one up.

XOCHIMILCO *(Thinks about it seriously).* Hmm…I know one, but it's very scary.

MALINA. I can take it. Tell it to me.

XOCHIMILCO. It's about La Llorona.

MALINA. La what?

XOCHIMILCO. La Llorona. La Llorona is the spirit of a woman, all dressed in white, who roams by the rivers looking for her dead children who she killed a long time ago…I think I remember my mother telling me that an uncle of hers saw her many years ago when he was herding sheep one night in Mexico. She came to him and asked him for water. He said she was very beautiful with long golden hair and a pale face. He asked her what she was doing there so late and she simply said she usually walked by there. She thanked him for the water and walked away. From a distance she screamed, "¡¡Ay mis hijos!!" and disappeared. *(MALINA screams.)* So wherever there are rivers, she roams by, looking for her children. And when she sees children misbehaving, she comes and pulls them out of their beds by their feet and takes them with her.

MALINA. But there aren't any rivers around here, are there?
(XOCHIMILCO nods "yes." MALINA gasps in fear. She covers herself under the blankets.)

XOCHIMILCO. No, don't worry, if you behave, I won't let her take you…Ya me voy.

MALINA. Aren't you scared La Llorona will get you?

XOCHIMILCO. No…I'm a good girl. Buenas noches. *(XOCHIMILCO exits through the door. Lights fade out.)*

SCENE TWO

(The moon is out, and it is the only light XOCHIMILCO has to guide her through the streets. As she walks by herself the wind whispers and "¡Ayyy mis hijos!" can almost be heard. XOCHIMILCO searches for an address written on a small paper she is holding. She finds the address. She is more disappointed than happy she found it.)

XOCHIMILCO. What am I doing?…*(Lights fade out.)*

SCENE THREE

(FLASHBACK: Lights fade in. In the center of the stage is a large table full of pecans and tin cylinders. There are several women in the factory. It's very hot and they are busy shelling pecans. There is a table downstage with four chairs and three women. PETRA, LOLA and EMMA.)

LOLA. Last night my husband took me to see a movie con mi galan, my Clark Gable. ¡Ayyy, que guapo ese pinche viejo!

PETRA. A mi ni me gustan nadita esos Americanos. The one I like is Pedro Infante. Ese merito viejo condenado. For that man I'd be willing to leave my husband.

LOLA. Ayy sí, ni te creo.

PETRA. Pues one of these days don't be surprised if you get a postcard from Hawaii from me and Pedro Infante. *(They laugh together.)* Y tu, Emma, how come you're so quiet?

EMMA. Huh? Oh, I was just thinking about a book I read last night. It was exceptional, but I didn't understand it completely…*(Whispering.)* Do you know who Karl Marx is?

LOLA. ¿Quién? Who?

EMMA. Karl Marx. He wrote, "It is not the conscience of man that determines his existence. It is his existence that determines his conscience…" What do you think? Do you agree?

PETRA. Ayy, mi'ijita, n'ombre, don't talk to me about books, mejor cuentame de novelas. Lola, did you hear last night's novela episode?

LOLA. Pos si, how could I miss it. ¡Se 'sta poniendo bien seria la cosa!

(XOCHIMILCO enters from U. She screams, facing U as she comes in.)

XOCHIMILCO. ¡Viejos cochinos! ¡Sin verguenzas! ¡No tienen madres!

LOLA. What happened?

XOCHIMILCO. I went behind the bushes to go do number 1 and number 2 and there were these two viejos rabo verde looking to get an eyeful.

LOLA. I know who they are. When I went to the bushes allí estában de mensos los idiotas.

PETRA. That guy with the Emiliano Zapata moustache and the crooked eyes?

LOLA. ¡Ese merito!

XOCHIMILCO. I'm tired of having to go to the bushes to shit! Why haven't they fixed the women's toilet? It's been broken for months and they still don't do anything about it.

EMMA. Why don't we go complain together, that way they'll listen to us.

PETRA. It won't help. They'll just tell us that a plumber is coming next week.

LOLA. So what did you use to wipe your nalgas?

XOCHIMILCO. I found a newspaper, and cleaned myself with Clark Gable's face.

LOLA. Ay, why did you have to do that? Why didn't you save it for me so he could have kissed my ass.

PETRA (*Somewhat disgusted*). Ayy, que grosera y mal hablada eres pinche, Lola.

LOLA. Talking about grosera…Do you know the joke about…(*EMMA throws some pecans in her mouth.*)

PETRA. Don't eat them! Or they'll take them away from your wages.

EMMA. I thought they already did. They pay us so little at least I can have a free lunch on them. (*She continues eating them.*)

XOCHIMILCO. So what's the joke?

LOLA. There were these two men who were trying to cross the border. One was named Juan and the other Ondenasio. Ondenasio had to go to the bathroom so bad he went behind a big rock. Soon after, a pinche gringo de la migra came up to him and asked him in his terrible Spanish, "¿On-de na-cio?" Juan tells him he's behind that rock. The gringo doesn't understand, so he asks him "¿Tiene papeles?" Juan tells him, "No. Usa piedras." (*XOCHIMILCO and PETRA barely chuckle.*) Ora pues, I know a funnier one. There once was a…

(*The supervisor, CHRIS, an Anglo, walks in on them. They instantly become silent and work faster. CHRIS walks around them watching them work. They can feel his eyes staring down their necks. CHRIS stares at PETRA. She becomes very nervous.*)

CHRIS. You work too slow. (*PETRA works faster. CHRIS stares at XOCHIMILCO. XOCHIMILCO tries to ignore him, then she stares at him.*)

XOCHIMILCO. Is something wrong?

CHRIS. Did I say something was wrong?

XOCHIMILCO. No, but you're looking at me like there's something wrong. (*XOCHIMILCO looks away from him and continues working. He continues to stare down at her. XOCHIMILCO raises her head once again.*) We want to know when you're going to fix the women's toilet?

CHRIS. Next week…You women have to stop talking and work faster. This table is always turning in less pounds then the rest of the tables. If this continues I'm going to have to separate you or even fire one of you. (*CHRIS writes a short report on his clipboard. He walks away to the other tables.*)

LOLA. Ahhh, Perro que ladra no muerde. He's all talk, but he's got no power.

EMMA. I think he likes you, Xochi.

LOLA (*Joking*). Que se me hace. You like white men, Xochi?

XOCHIMILCO (*Annoyed and disgusted*). Por favor. (*PETRA stops working. She presses her hands trying to remove the pain.*) Don't work so hard…They will still pay you the same miserable wage. Don't go killing yourself for them. You're not a mule or an animal…My husband worked hard all of his life thinking that if he worked hard he would be promoted. He wasn't…He died of overwork…¡Asi que se chingen ellos!

LOLA. Pues si, they're never gonna fix that toilet, anyway…

EMMA. Yes, they will. If all the women working here got together and demanded that, they'd fix it. And not just the toilet. We could even demand higher wages.

PETRA. Where do you get those ideas, niña? From your books? It's her first week on the job and she already wants to cause trouble.

XOCHIMILCO. Leave her alone, Petra. It's not her fault she's young. She should want better.

PETRA. Pos si, uno de viejo ya que le importa. I'm so old I'm just waiting around to pass out and die. (*The WOMEN look at PETRA then look at each other knowing she'd like some sympathy. Lights slowly fade out.*)

SCENE FOUR

(*FLASHBACK: In a dimly lit motel room, CHRIS and XOCHIMILCO are on the bed in an embrace. XOCHIMILCO is wearing a black camisole and CHRIS is wearing only trunks. CHRIS kisses her neck as he undoes her braid*

behind her. XOCHIMILCO rests on him and stares off.)

XOCHIMILCO. I don't like pretending we hate each other.

CHRIS. It works. *(He grabs her breasts.)* I love your tits, Catheleen.

XOCHIMILCO. Catheleen? Why did you call me Catheleen?

CHRIS. I said that?…Oh, it's because I don't like your name. "Xochi" reminds me of a poodle. *(She bops him on the head and they laugh. They kiss.)*

XOCHIMILCO. Can you stop picking on Petra? Poor woman, she reminds me of my mother.

CHRIS. I'm just doing my job.

XOCHIMILCO. So when is the toilet going to get fixed?

CHRIS. Will you cut it out with that!

XOCHIMILCO. Fine! I won't mention it again. *(Hurt, XOCHIMILCO, turns away from him. He touches her chin and brings her face to his.)*

CHRIS. I told my boss twice about fixing the toilet, and he said that it would cost "too much." They're not going to fix it. Not now, not ever. He asked me why I was so concerned about it. He asked me if I was a "spic lover."

XOCHIMILCO. So what did you tell him?

CHRIS. I told him "no"…I'm in love with you, but you're different.

XOCHIMILCO. I'm no different than any of the other women…

CHRIS. Stay away from Emma. There are rumors that she is a communist.

XOCHIMILCO *(In disbelief, laughs)*. What? She's not a communist. She's just too smart to be working there and she's probably going to find herself a better job soon. She's got a high school education.

CHRIS. That's what I'm worried about…I just found out that my bosses are going to cut the pay by 1 cent per pound. What do you think your people are going to do?

XOCHIMILCO. I don't know…

CHRIS. Do you think they'll go on strike?

(XOCHIMILCO thinks about it. Then LA LLORONA appears before her. She gasps. She disappears soon after.)

XOCHIMILCO. I just saw…No, nothing…Are you going to marry me?

CHRIS. What? Not this again? What is it with you today? You're just full of questions and demands.

XOCHIMILCO. Are you going to marry me or are we just going to mess around until my tits get so saggy you'll get tired of them and leave me?

CHRIS. I can't marry you.

XOCHIMILCO. Why not?

CHRIS. Because…

XOCHIMILCO. Why? You love me, I love you…It's my children, isn't it?

CHRIS. No, I can't marry you because…you're Mexican. I'll lose my job.

XOCHIMILCO. I can't stand hiding like this. I feel like a traitor, screwing the supervisor…Let's get away together!

CHRIS. Where can you and I go and be together without it being a problem? Without getting death threats. I won't be able to get a job anywhere with you as my wife. Look, neither of us was looking for this, but it happened. A love like this isn't supposed to happen, but it did. *(XOCHIMILCO gets off the bed. She picks up her panties and puts them on. She picks up her other clothes and puts them on.)* What are you doing?

XOCHIMILCO. I'm too old to play your whore. I've got five kids waiting for these "tits"!

CHRIS. Xochi, don't leave like this! *(XOCHIMILCO angrily exits. Lights fade out.)*

SCENE FIVE

(FLASHFORWARD: Lights fade in. XOCHIMILCO is in the same lonely street as before, squatting on the floor like a little kid unsure what to do. A light turns on and an old woman, SERAFINA, sticks out her head.)

SERAFINA. Buenas noches…What are you doing all by yourself outside my door? Did "La Rescatera" send you?

XOCHIMILCO. Yes, how did you know?

SERAFINA. All the women who come to me, sometimes wait outside unable to come in. Some leave, some come in. Pasate, hija. *(XOCHIMILCO enters SERAFINA's quaint, dark, and eerie house.)* ¿Hace mucho frio afuera?

XOCHIMILCO *(Shyly)*. Yes, it's kind of chilly.

SERAFINA. Did you have any difficulty finding my house?

XOCHIMILCO. No.

SERAFINA. Are you sure you want to do this? *(XOCHIMILCO thinks about it and takes her time to come up with an answer. Lights slowly fade out.)*

SCENE SIX

(FLASHBACK: Lights fade in. Inside the pecan factory, XOCHIMILCO, EMMA, LOLA and PETRA are busy shelling pecans.)

PETRA. Lola, come me with me to the bathroom so you can throw rocks at all those viejos cochinos trying to get an eyeful.

LOLA. Ayy, doña Petra, at your age who is going to bother looking.

PETRA. You never know. Just because I'm old doesn't mean que no tengo pegue. *(LOLA laughs to herself. PETRA and LOLA walk offstage together. EMMA carefully observes them leave, then turns to XOCHIMILCO.)*

EMMA. Xochi, have you ever heard of the Workers Alliance?

XOCHIMILCO. No.

EMMA. I am recruiting members for the Workers Alliance and I wanted you to join—

XOCHIMILCO. I'm not getting involved in anything you're doing.

EMMA. Did Chris warn you not to get involved with me?

XOCHIMILCO. Chris? Why would you say that?

EMMA. He wants to get me fired more than anyone else. I need to be here long enough to get all the women to join the Workers Alliance…and get you to help me.

XOCHIMILCO. Why would you want me to help you?

EMMA. Because you would make a good leader, you're an angry woman, and you don't have a husband.

XOCHIMILCO. Do you have any children?

EMMA. No and I don't plan to have any as long as things continue to be this bad for Mexicans.

XOCHIMILCO. So you think you have everything figured out?

EMMA. No...Xochi, I respect you. The women listen to you, and you're going to help me.

XOCHIMILCO. What makes you so sure I'm going to help you?

EMMA *(Thinks about it for a minute)*. Did you know Chris is married?

XOCHIMILCO. What do you want from me?

EMMA. You didn't know he was married?

XOCHIMILCO. Oh, so now I'm supposed to be so jealous and enraged that I will help you out of revenge?

EMMA. It's the truth. Her name is Catheleen, they have two children... *(XOCHIMILCO breaks down crying. She quickly remembers she's in public and covers up her pain. XOCHIMILCO begins to recover.)* Xochi, I'm sorry, I didn't mean to be so cruel. *(XOCHIMILCO stares at her and then slowly gives in to EMMA.)*

XOCHIMILCO. He told me they're planning on cutting the pay on the pound by 1 cent.

EMMA. When?

XOCHIMILCO. I don't know when they're going to announce it.

EMMA. By the time they do, we can be preparing for a strike.

XOCHIMILCO. I'm not going to go on strike!

EMMA. So then you're just going to put up with it? Keep praying? Leave it in God's hands so that things will change, like a good little Mexican?

XOCHIMILCO. No, I don't believe in God! I don't even believe in the church or praying...It's just not going to work!

EMMA. And the reason things never change is because with Mexicans like you, they don't have to beat us down, we do that ourselves. *(XOCHIMILCO can't refute her. She thinks about it.)*

XOCHIMILCO. How do you want me to help you? *(Lights fade out.)*

SCENE SEVEN

(FLASHBACK: Lights fade in. At the pecan factory the bell rings and the women are done for the day. They rise and get ready to leave. LOLA, XOCHIMILCO, and PETRA walk out together.)

PETRA. Do you really think that's going to work? Because I told my viejo and he wasn't too crazy about the idea, but he agreed to let me go and take care of my esquincles as long as I made dinner first.

LOLA. Then we'll meet you at 7:00. Do you want us to bring dinner?

XOCHIMILCO. No, just get there on time and invite any of the women who don't know.

PETRA. But do you really think it's going to work?

XOCHIMILCO. We'll never know until we try it…My purse? I almost forgot it…I'll see you. (*XOCHIMILCO runs back into the factory room for her purse. The lights are turned off in the factory. XOCHIMILCO calls out.*) Hello! Anyone there? Can you turn on the lights? I forgot my purse.

(*CHRIS comes in from the darkness holding her purse.*)

CHRIS. Is this yours? (*XOCHIMILCO is frightened by him. She hides her fear. She walks up to CHRIS.*)

XOCHIMILCO. Yes, it is. Thank you.

CHRIS (*Pulls away the purse from her reach, flirting*). I need you to beg a little harder.

XOCHIMILCO. I'm not going to beg for it. It's mine. Give it to me. (*She lunges for her purse, he holds on to her. She fights him playfully.*) Let me go. (*He starts kissing her neck, she tries to resist him, but she gets caught up in his affection and falls for his kisses. He reaches for her breasts, then she grabs his hands.*) Did you miss them?… How do they compare with your wife's? Do Catheleen's tits sag?

CHRIS. Who's Catheleen?

XOCHIMILCO. If you would have told me you were married I still might have screwed you, but at least I wouldn't have hoped that you and I could have…!

CHRIS. What are you talking about? Who told you I was married? Emma? Is she trying to manipulate you, brainwash you, into believing I'm the enemy? Has she turned you against me? Do you believe I could do that to you?

XOCHIMILCO. You have two children! I was the "other woman"! No wonder I felt like a whore all along! You lied to me!

CHRIS. There are rumors going around that there's going to be a strike after we announce the cutbacks. How did Emma find out? I told you to stay away

from her, but you told her! You betrayed me!

XOCHIMILCO. I don't know what you're talking about…

CHRIS. Why are you women gathering tonight? What are you going to talk about?

XOCHIMILCO. A friend of ours is going to have a baby. We're planning a baby shower.

CHRIS. Which friend?

XOCHIMILCO. You don't know her…Now give me my purse?…Please! I have to go. My children are waiting for me.

CHRIS. No…Xochi, I miss you…This whole week without you, it's…I'll leave my wife for you…*(XOCHIMILCO is very scared, but she acts indifferent.)*

XOCHIMILCO. You're just saying that.

CHRIS. No…Take me back. *(CHRIS extends his hand with the purse, defenselessly. XOCHIMILCO carefully takes it. She sees he is sincere and approaches him.)*

XOCHIMILCO. You would leave your wife for me? *(He nods. They stare at each other for a few seconds and she seductively pushes him against the table. She puts the purse on the side of the table and gets on top of him. They begin kissing passionately and aggressively, rotating being on top. They begin to disrobe, but then XOCHIMILCO freezes. She pushes him off.)* No. Stop. Get off of me… This isn't going to work. Even if you marry me, one of us will lose our job. And we can't go anywhere together without it being a problem. It can't work, remember?

CHRIS. We can try.

XOCHIMILCO. No. I know what you're going to do. You're going to keep me hanging on with the promise that you're going to leave her. But you won't. Men like you don't leave their wives for someone like me. And if you did I wouldn't want to marry you. Because if you could cheat on your wife and leave her, you'll do the same to me. I'm too old to be that stupid. *(XOCHIMILCO reaches for her purse. He snatches it from her.)*

CHRIS. No.

XOCHIMILCO. Then keep it. *(XOCHIMILCO starts to walk away.)*

CHRIS. Are you sure about that? You're willing to give up your green card so easily? If the Immigration Patrol catches you without one, they're going to take you back to your backward country, you little commie.

XOCHIMILCO. What did you call me?

CHRIS. Now, I understand what you were doing. You were just screwing me to get me to tell you things to tell Emma!

XOCHIMILCO (*sarcastically*). Yeah, that's what I was doing! All this time I was plotting with Emma. I would leave my children at night so I could screw you and serve the communist party as a spy! (*Laughs.*) Yeah, and you know what we're going to do? We're going to organize a strike and run this company into the ground. And you're going to lose your job. And you won't be able to boss us around anymore and you're going to be nothing! So give me my goddamn purse! (*She lunges and they fight for it. He holds her.*) Let me go!

CHRIS. Don't go! I want you back.

XOCHIMILCO. But I don't want you! I don't need you. You're nothing!

CHRIS. I love you!

XOCHIMILCO (*stops fighting him*). You do?

CHRIS. Yes. (*XOCHIMILCO kisses him. He closes his eyes, refreshed by her affection. Then, she kicks him in the groin, grabs her purse, and makes a run for it.*) You stupid bitch! (*CHRIS catches her. He drags her to a table by the hair and "slaps" all the tin cylinders and pecans off the table to clear it. He throws her on the table where he pins her down. She fights back with all of her might. CHRIS puts his hand over her mouth and unzips his pants.*)…Let's see how much of a fighter you are after I get through with you…(*Blackout. In the darkness we hear moaning and muffled screams.*)

SCENE EIGHT

(*Still in the darkness we hear XOCHIMILCO's screams. Lights fade in and XOCHIMILCO is lying on a table with her legs spread open. SERAFINA is in between her legs inserting a wire clothes hanger. XOCHIMILCO bites into a cloth when she can't stand the pain.*

The present: A light shines on XOCHIMILCO's head. PETRA, EMMA, and LOLA appear behind her and look down at her.)

LOLA. What's wrong?

PETRA. How come you're acting this way?

EMMA. What happened to our plans? We waited for you all night, but you didn't show up.

PETRA. ¿Porqué ya no nos hablas? What happened to you? *(PETRA, EMMA, and LOLA disappear.)*

(SERAFINA drops the remains of the aborted fetus into a bucket by the table.)

SERAFINA *(Reflecting)*. We used to throw them in rivers, now we throw them in buckets…

XOCHIMILCO. What?

SERAFINA. Nothing. *(SERAFINA cleans her hands after she finishes.)* I think you were going to have twins.

XOCHIMILCO. Please don't tell me that. *(XOCHIMILCO begins crying. SERAFINA finishes the abortion. She washes her hands with water and picks up her instruments.)*

SERAFINA. Ya acabe. Rest a little. But when you feel ready you must get up and go home and rest for a couple of days. *(XOCHIMILCO slowly gets up. She is pale and weak. She puts on her panties and her sweater. She tries to bend and pick up her purse but it hurts too much. SERAFINA picks up the purse and hands it to her. XOCHIMILCO opens it and takes out money.)*

XOCHIMILCO. Gracias. *(XOCHIMILCO gives SERAFINA money. SERAFINA takes it and gives her a piece of paper.)*

SERAFINA. I've listed some of the hierbas you can use to help the pain. If you start feeling worse, go to the emergency room. *(XOCHIMILCO nods. She starts to walk out.)* Cuidate.

XOCHIMILCO. Adiós. *(Lights fade out.)*

SCENE NINE

(The moonlight illuminates XOCHIMILCO's pale face. She walks slowly holding on to anything she can. She is in a terrible condition and has to rest on the ground. LA LLORONA appears behind XOCHIMILCO.)

XOCHIMILCO. ¡Ayyyy mis hijos! *(Startled, gets up and runs for her life. LA LLORONA follows after her. Lights fade out.)*

SCENE TEN

(Lights fade in faintly. XOCHIMILCO runs to and enters through the doors

of a little church. She leans on the doors trying to catch her breath. She slides down slowly and crawls to the front of the church to the altar. She starts praying silently. A PRIEST appears behind her.)

PRIEST. What is wrong with you? Are you all right, hija?

XOCHIMILCO. I have to confess, Padre.

PRIEST. What is your urgency?

XOCHIMILCO. I'm dying.

PRIEST. When was your last confession?

XOCHIMILCO. Three years ago.

PRIEST. Why has it been so long?

XOCHIMILCO. My husband died and I stopped believing in God because God abandoned me.

PRIEST. I will hear your confession. *(Lights change to create a more intimate feeling. XOCHIMILCO gets on her knees.)*

XOCHIMILCO. Forgive me, Padre for I have…I've had an abortion. I have five children and like I said, my husband died three years ago and I just couldn't have another one.

PRIEST. That's no reason for committing such a sin!

XOCHIMILCO. Pero, Padre…I resisted, and it was against my will…

PRIEST. That was not the child's fault.

XOCHIMILCO. Yes, it wasn't their fault…

PRIEST. Their?

XOCHIMILCO. They were twins.

PRIEST. Twins!

XOCHIMILCO. I'm sorry! *(XOCHIMILCO falls lower. Lights change, and so does XOCHIMILCO's reality. The PRIEST takes out a whip and starts whipping her.)*

PRIEST. Scream for your children! *(He whips her harder. XOCHIMILCO cannot escape. She gets whipped for every attempt to flee. Blood drips between her legs.)* Scream for your children, sinner! *(XOCHIMILCO tries to walk out of the church.)*

XOCHIMILCO. ¡¡¡Ayyy mis hijos!!!

PRIEST. Louder! Louder so that everyone can hear you! *(The PRIEST whips her even harder.)*

XOCHIMILCO. ¡¡¡¡¡Ayyy mis hijos!!!! *(XOCHIMILCO falls to the floor. She is left on the floor, bloody and lifeless. Blackout.)*

SCENE ELEVEN

(A small light pierces the darkness. It becomes overwhelming and through the light two ANGELS, male and female, in brown angelic gowns, enter. They walk to XOCHIMILCO's corpse. They remove her dress and wipe off the blood. They cleanse her naked body. They wake her up.)

ANGELS. Get ready to meet your God.

XOCHIMILCO. My God?…I thought I had no God. Where is my God? I thought you had abandoned me.

Photo by Josefina Lopez

La Llorona looks over Xochimilco who recovers from her illegal abortion.

GOD'S VOICE *(A man and a woman)*. Xochimilco, I have not abandoned you.

XOCHIMILCO. Then why have you allowed all these horrible things to happen to me and my people? So many crimes committed against my people, all in your name, and you allowed them! So I began to think that I must have no God or you would have protected me. Or they would have stopped and seen that I too was a child of God!

GOD. I protected you by giving you the strength to remind them of your humanity.

XOCHIMILCO. But they only hate me more.

GOD. They don't hate you. They're afraid of you. They're afraid to discover in themselves the same pain, the same longings and dreams that you have. They fear the anger and the hatred of all your people whom they have hurt… I'm going to let you live…Go home and take care of the children you do have.

XOCHIMILCO. I am not sorry. I have given them back to you.

GOD. You are still my child.

XOCHIMILCO. I am?

GOD. Don't forget that.

(The light slowly fades. God disappears and LA LLORONA appears. XOCHIMILCO is no longer afraid of LA LLORONA, who is merely a woman. LA LLORONA extends her hand out to her. XOCHIMILCO reaches for it. LA LLORONA helps her walk and becomes her crutch for the way home.

The sun's rays light the stage where XOCHIMILCO's children are still asleep. LA LLORONA enters holding XOCHIMILCO's lifeless body. She places her down on her bed and tucks her in. LA LLORONA disappears. After a few minutes MALINA uncovers her face, and crawls out of the blankets. She taps XOCHIMILCO's face to wake her up. XOCHIMILCO awakens.)

MALINA. Mamíta, you came back! I prayed all night that you would. *(Lights fade out.)*

SCENE TWELVE

(FLASHFORWARD: Lights fade in on the pecan factory where LOLA, EMMA, and PETRA are busily working. XOCHIMILCO walks in ready to work although she is still pale and weak. The WOMEN are surprised by her

presence. They stare at her, not sure what to say.)

LOLA. He came earlier looking for you.

EMMA. Where have you been?

PETRA. ¿Qué te Pasa Xochi? Why didn't you come yesterday or the day before?

XOCHIMILCO. I've been very sick…I went to La Rescatera…She told me where I could get an abortion. *(LOLA and PETRA grimace in disbelief. EMMA is shocked. PETRA reaches out for her and holds her. XOCHIMILCO remains still and stoic.)*

LOLA. Why didn't you tell us!

XOCHIMILCO. Because…I was ashamed.

LOLA. How did it happen?

(CHRIS enters. He immediately notices XOCHIMILCO. He walks up to her breaking the interchange between PETRA and XOCHIMILCO.)

CHRIS. Why do you even bother showing up today? You've missed two days already. You were fired. There are a lot of other women who'd be happy to have your job.

PETRA. Please let her stay. Pobrecita, she's been sick.

LOLA. She's the fastest worker you've got. Let her stay!

CHRIS *(Thinks about it)*. She can stay…Just don't be absent another day or you're fired. And don't talk back to me anymore or else…

EMMA. Or else what?

CHRIS. I'm not talking to you.

EMMA. I want to know what the "or else" means!

CHRIS. Shut up! You've got a big mouth!

EMMA. Does anyone else want to know what "or else" means?!

CHRIS. All right, that's it. I'm going to fire one of you. Let's see. Who should I pick? Petra, how would you like to be fired? Or Lola, how about you?

XOCHIMILCO. I'll leave! *(XOCHIMILCO picks up her purse and sweater and begins to walk out.)*

PETRA. ¿Pero qué estas haciendo? He's offered to give you your job back, just stay.

LOLA. No seas orgullosa. You need this job.

EMMA. No, Xochi, keep walking!

CHRIS. Yeah, keep walking! What are you going to feed your children? Pride?

XOCHIMILCO *(Turns around).* No! But I can teach them not to let people treat them like you've treated me! Why don't you show them what "or else" means?

CHRIS. Get out of here! You're fired!

XOCHIMILCO. No! I want you to show them. You bastard! Coward! *(She slaps him. He raises his hand to strike her, but he can't slap the face he's caressed before. The WOMEN stop to look at him.)* Come on! *(She "slaps" the pecans and the tin cylinders off the table and throws herself on the table with her legs spread open.)* Do it to me again! Show all these women what happens to a woman with a big mouth. Do it right here!!...See if you can do it without us killing you first! *(CHRIS is now surrounded by all the WOMEN. He cannot meet the challenge and backs away. XOCHIMILCO stands on the table. She is crying.)* And don't you ever touch any of my hermanas like that! Because one of these nights when you're asleep, I will sneak into your bed, and when you think you're safe, snuggled in your bed like a baby, I will choke you until you reach the hell that you've put me through. And you'll have to beg me to remember that I believe in God! *(He tries to ignore her. The WOMEN look at him with disgust and he can't ignore her.)* I will never work here again. *(To the WOMEN.)* And you shouldn't work here either! *(XOCHIMILCO walks out of the factory crying. All the WOMEN look at one another. EMMA starts chanting.)*

EMMA. ¡Huelga! ¡Huelga! *(LOLA joins in the chanting, then PETRA. Pretty soon all the WOMEN are chanting "Huelga." EMMA walks out and the rest of the WOMEN slowly follow. Lights fade out.)*

SCENE THIRTEEN

(Lights fade to Xochimilco's apartment. XOCHIMILCO enters, frantic.)

XOCHIMILCO. Diosito, what have I done?

(She paces nervously. MALINA enters. Her face is painted with white paint. XOCHIMILCO cannot believe her eyes.)

XOCHIMILCO. What happened?

MALINA. I did what you told me to do. They called me a "wetback," I

ignored them and kept walking. But they grabbed me and told me I was a dirty Mexican and the only way I could be clean was if I were white. *(MALINA stops to cry. XOCHIMILCO holds her and begins to remove the paint from her face.)*

XOCHIMILCO. No mi'ijita, God made you the way you are for a reason. *(XOCHIMILCO sits MALINA. down as she wipes off the paint.)* Did I ever tell you the story of how God made people? *(MALINA shakes her head "no.")* Well, Diosito was making cookies in the shape of little people. It was God's first time making cookies so God made the dough from scratch. God put all these magic ingredients into the dough. God put the cookie dough in the oven, but forgot about it. When God remembered, God took out the cookies and they were all burnt. So these became the black people. Then God put some more cookie dough to bake. But God was so anxious not to burn them that God took out the cookies before they were ready and they came out raw. So these became the white people. Then God wanted to try one more time. So God put some more dough in the oven determined to get it right. God was patient, and when God took out the cookies God was so happy because they came out golden brown, just right. And these became the brown people…You see how you're special?

MALINA. Then why did they do this?

XOCHIMILCO. Because you know something they don't know.

MALINA. What's that?

XOCHIMILCO. They're afraid of you because they don't know that you're a good person. That your heart is full of love and hopes just like everyone else's. *(There is a loud knock at the door.)*

PETRA *(Offstage)*. Xochi! ¡Abre!

(XOCHIMILCO lets PETRA in.)

PETRA. They're looking for you! The police are on their way!

XOCHIMILCO. What did I do?

PETRA. They're accusing you of being a communist or no se que otra pendejada. But they're gonna get you. Mira, my brother is waiting for you. Go with him and he'll take you to my compadre who will take you to Mexico. ¡Pero apurate!

XOCHIMILCO. But what about my children?

PETRA. I'll go pick them up at school and send them later.

XOCHIMILCO. Malina, pack some clothes, quickly!

MALINA. Why are we leaving?

XOCHIMILCO. Just go! Do it! (*XOCHIMILCO starts collecting some personal belongings.*)

MALINA. Why are the police looking for you? What did you do wrong?

XOCHIMILCO (*Stops packing*). Nothing. I did nothing wrong. Do you believe me?

MALINA. Yes…(*XOCHIMILCO continues packing.*) Then why are we leaving? (*XOCHIMILCO can't answer. She stops packing.*)

XOCHIMILCO. Petra, I'm not going.

PETRA. ¿Qué? No, no. You don't have a choice! They're going to arrest you and they're going to find you guilty!

XOCHIMILCO. But I'm innocent!

PETRA. Who cares if you're innocent? There is no justice pa' nostra gente, you know that. Your husband died trying to get it, so don't be a martyr. You're not going to change things.

XOCHIMILCO. I can't leave, Petra! My husband and I worked hard so that we could give our children a better life. Why do I have to leave this country? Esta tierra tambien es mia. It belongs to my children, and I'm not going to take it away from them.

PETRA. If you don't leave, they'll put you in jail and they'll take away your children.

XOCHIMILCO. No puedo.

PETRA. ¡Terca como una…! I wish I could drag you by the hair…(*PETRA embraces XOCHIMILCO when she realizes she can't change her mind.*) Entonces mi amiga, que Dios te bendiga, porque te van a joder. (*PETRA kisses her on the cheek.*)

XOCHIMILCO. Aquí me quedo. I'll wait for them.

PETRA. Should I take Malina?

MALINA. No. I want to stay with you. (*PETRA leaves. XOCHIMILCO stands with MALINA as she holds her. They anxiously await the police. Lights fade out.*)

SCENE FOURTEEN

(FLASHFORWARD: XOCHIMILCO and MALINA remain standing together. They are in a courtroom. There is a spotlight on both of them.)

RADIO REPORT *(Voice-over).* In the news today, February 1, 1938, at the peak of the pecan shelling season, thousands of shellers walked off their jobs after management cut rates by 1 cent a pound. At City Hall, a thousand picketers were tear-gassed and some even jailed. Management justified the lack of increase in wages by saying, quote, "If Mexicans earned more, they would just spend it on tequila and on worthless trinkets in the dime store..."

JUDGE *(Voice-over, omnipotent).* This court finds you guilty of unlawful gathering, destruction of property, conspiracy to riot, conspiracy to do harm, espionage, and subversive activities aimed to overthrow the government of the United States. You are a communist and you are a national threat. Therefore it is justifiable to sentence you to 10 years in prison for the crimes you have committed against the government of the United States of America.

EMMA *(Voice-over).* She's innocent!

(A BAILIFF approaches XOCHIMILCO to take MALINA from her. MALINA fights to hold on.)

MALINA. No! No!

XOCHIMILCO *(Holds her tight).* Don't worry for me.... *(Tenderly, trying to comfort a crying child.)* Ten years go fast. When you see the little birds flying, those pretty swallows coming back for spring, always think of me. Because that's where I'll be, with them.

MALINA. I love you, mamita!

XOCHIMILCO. ¡Ayy mi hija! Take care of your brothers. Tell them the truth about their mother so they don't believe the lies. I will be all right if you promise me you will never be ashamed to be what you are, my daughter.

MALINA. I promise. *(They kiss each other before MALINA is taken away. XOCHIMILCO is left alone. Lights begin to fade out.)*

XOCHIMILCO *(Whispering).* Ay mis hijos.

(Lights slowly fade out as the tree is simultaneously lit and now on the tree appear TONANTZIN at the top, XOCHITL, and LA LLORONA. They call out to XOCHIMILCO who slowly walks toward the tree and climbs on it to join the other WOMEN there. They hold each other's hands and they lie on the tree.)

The End

UNCONQUERED SPIRITS

GLOSSARY SPANISH

Aztec & Mayan Names:

XOCHIMILCO [So-chi-mil-co] - Flowered field, also name of a lake in Mexico city

TEXCOCO [Te-ch-co-co] - name of the lake where Tenochtitlán was founded

TIXOC [Tichoc] - the Mayan word for love

LA LLORONA - the crying woman

Abre - Open

Adios - Goodbye

Ahh, perro que ladra no muerde - Ah, a dog that barks doesn't bite

¡Ahora si vas a verlo! - Now you're really going to get it!

¡Ahorita! - Now!

alli estaban de mensos los idiotas - there they were those dumb idiots

A mi ni me gustan nadita esos Americanos - I don't even like those Anglos

apurate - hurry

¡Aquí estába! - It was here!

Aqui me quedo - I'll stay here

Asi es que siguele - So go ahead!

¡Asi que se chingen ellos! - So to hell with them!

Ay - Oh, (any kind of expression)

Ayy, mi'ijita, nombre - Oh, little girl, don't

Ayy mis hijos - Oh, my children

Ayy que grosera y mal hablada eres pinche, Lola - Lola, you are so nasty and crude

¡Ayy que guapo ese pinche viejo! - Oh that damn man is so handsome!

Ayy si, ni te creo - Yeah right, I don't even believe you

Buenas noches - Good night

compadre - my buddy (male)

con mi galan - with my leading man

corazón - heart

¡Core, largate! - Run, get out of here!

corre, vete - run, go

Cuidate - Take care of yourself

de traviesa - naughty

diablita - little devil

Diosito - Dear God

el norte - the north

¡Empuja con toda tu fuerza! - Push with all your strength!

Entonces mi amiga, que dios te bendiga, porque te van a joder. - Then my friend, God bless you,

because they're going to screw with you.

Ese merito - That one

Ese merito viejo condenado - That damned old man

esquincles - children, brats

Esta tierra tambien es mia - This land also belongs to me

Floresita - Little flower

fuerza - strength

Gracias - Thank you

grosera - nasty

¿Hace mucho frio afuera? - Is it very cold outside?

Hasme caso - Listen to me

Hermana(s) - Sister(s)

hermanitos - little brothers

Hermano - brother

hierbas - herbs

hija - daughter

hijo - son

Huelga - Strike

"La Rescatera" - "The Rescuer"

Mama - Mother

mejor cuentame de novelas - better tell me about soaps

mestizo - half-Spanish, half-Native American

mi'jita - my dear daughter

Mi querido Juan como te estraño -

My dear Juan how I miss you

moral - backpack

nalgas - buttocks

No cariño - No darling

No puedo - I can't

no se que otra pendejada - I don't know, some other stupidity

No seas orgullosa - Don't be proud

No te apures - Don't worry

No, usa piedras - No, he uses rocks

novela - soap opera

nuestras vidas - our lives

¿On-de-nacio? - Where were you born?

Ora pues - well then

Padre - Father

Padre nuestro que estás en los cielos - Heavenly Father who art in heaven (prayer)

pa'nostra gente - for our people

Papi - Daddy

partera - midwife

Pasate, hija - Come in my child

Pero apurate - But hurry

¿Pero qué estás haciendo? - What are you doing?

pinche gringo de la migra - a stupid Anglo immigration officer

Pobrecita - poor little one

Por el lago - By the lake

Por favor - Please

¿Porqué ya no nos hablas? - Why don't you talk to us anymore?

pos si - well yes

Pos si, uno de viejo ya que le importa - Well yes, when one gets old it doesn't matter anymore

pues - well

Pues si - Well yes

Que descanses en paz. - May you rest in peace.

que no tengo pegue - that I don't have "it"

¿Que paso? - What happened?

Que se me hace - I think possibly

¿Que-quien? - Wa-what, who?

¿Qué te pasa, Xochi? - What's going on with you, Xochi?

¡Que viva Tenochtitlán! - Long live Tenochtitlán!

¿Quién? - Whom?

Respira y empuja - Breathe and push

Se 'sta poniendo bien seria la cosa - things are getting juicy

se volvio loca - She went crazy

sirenita - little mermaid

Su unico hijo - her only son

tambien - also

Ten - Here

Terca como una... - Stubborn like a...

¿Tiene papeles? - Does he have papers?

valiente - brave

Vas a verlo - You'll see

¡Ven aqui! - Come here!

viejo - old man

Viejos cochinos. Sin verguenza. No tienen madres. Dirty, shameless old men. You don't have mothers.

viejos rabo verde - dirty old men

Y tu - And you

Ya acabe - I finished

Ya es tarde - It's late already

Ya me voi - I'm leaving now

ya, ya - now, now

Yo creo en Dios todo poderoso, creador de todos los cielos y la tierra, y Jesus Cristo, su unico hijo... - I believe in

God almighty, creator of the heavens and the earth, and Jesus Christ, his only son...

Yo tambien te amo a ti... - I love you, too...

CASA 0101

PRESENT ACTIVITIES

Every year, CASA 0101 produces live stage productions, and two 10-week sessions of classes in acting, screenwriting and playwriting. These classes are free to youth and teens ages 7 to 18, $10 for adults, and $5 for adult residents of the 90023, 90033, and 90063 zip codes. However, no one is turned away for lack of money. These courses all culminate in a performance or presentation that is open to the general public.

CASA 0101 has been honored to produce world premieres of works by our emerging Latino writers such as *Hoop Girls* by Gabriela López, *You Don't Know Me* by Patricia Zamora and *Little Red* by Anthony Aguilar and Oscar Basulto. CASA 0101 will continue to provide affordable and accessible programs in theater, film music, art and culture to teens and adults. In addition, CASA 0101 will further expand collaboration with community-based organizations to take CASA's programming to senior centers, high schools, and local health organizations throughout Boyle Heights. These programs will culminate in public performances.

THE ORIGINS OF CASA 0101

CASA 0101 was founded in 2000 by Josefina López who grew up in Boyle Heights to fulfill her vision of an artistic renaissance in East Los Angeles. From its modest beginnings CASA 0101 has grown into a respected theater with a team of dedicated artists that provides regular programming, including full length theater productions, an annual film festival and classes in acting, writing, production and performance/play development.

In June 2011 the new CASA 0101 Theater opens at 2012 E. First, Los Angeles, CA 90033. Please support it with your donations and efforts.

Thank you, Josefina López

THEATER
FILM MUSIC
ART
CULTURE
PASSION

STAFF:
JOSEFINA LÓPEZ

EMMANUEL DELEAGE
Director of Development

MARK KRAUS
Administrator

OUR MISSION

CASA 0101 is dedicated to providing vital arts, cultural, and educational programs—in theater, digital film-making, art and dance—to Boyle Heights, thereby nurturing the future storytellers of Los Angeles who will someday transform the world.

For more information go to **www.CASA0101.org**

WHY THE NAME "CASA 0101"?

CASA means house and/or home in Spanish. 0101 is the original language of computers. It can also mean nothing and everything, yin and yang, male and female, life and death, individual and group, the self and the creator-self. It is a commitment to exploring the world and oneself, the good and the bad, the light and the darkness of our soul and our world to the point where there are no borders and "0" and "1" are one.

CASA 0101
BOARD OF DIRECTORS:

JOSEFINA LÓPEZ
Artistic Director

GERARDO ALVAREZ
Treasurer

EMMANUEL DELEAGE

GINA LINN ESPINOZA

ALLEN GOLDEN

GIOVANII JORQUERA

GABRIELA LÓPEZ DE DENNIS
Secretary

MIGUEL MOUCHESS

EMMA NAVA

EDWARD PADILLA
President

MARIO PADILLA

LUZ VAZQUEZ-RAMOS
Vice-President

WPR BOOKS
is dedicated
to improving
protrayals and
expanding
opportunities for
Latinos in the USA

A WIDE VARIETY OF OPPORTUNITIES

WPR BOOKS, formerly known as WPR Publishing, has been publishing books and directories since 1983. Our best selling book has gone through 7 editions and over 120,000 books.

Latino Print Network, **WPR BOOKS** sister organization, works with over 625 Hispanic newspapers and magazines. These publications have a combined circulation of 19 million in 177 markets nationwide.

Latino Literacy Now is a 501(c)3 organization that has produced 48 **Latino Book & Family Festivals** around the USA since it's founding in 1997. Over 800,000 people have attended these events. It also has carried out the **International Latino Book Awards** since 1997 and the **Latino Book into Movies Awards** since 2010.

Hispanic Marketing 101 is a twice-weekly enewsletter that provides a variety of helpful information. A subscription is free at **www.HM101.com**

We have these and other programs that may be of interest to you. For more information please go to **www.WPRbooks.com** or call us at 760-434-1223.

JOSEFINA LÓPEZ

Josefina López is best known for authoring the play and co-authoring the film Real Women Have Curves, a coming-of-age story about Ana, a first-generation Chicana torn between pursuing her college ambitions, a personal goal, and securing employment which is a family expectation. Along the way, Ana confronts a host of cultural assumptions about beauty, marriage and a woman's role in society. Although Real Women Have Curves is López' most recognized work, it is only one of many literary and artistic works she has created since her artistic career began at 17. Born in San Luis Potosi, Mexico in 1969, Josefina López was five years old when she and her family immigrated to the United States and settled in the East Los Angeles neighborhood of Boyle Heights. Josefina was undocumented for thirteen years before she received Amnesty in 1987 and eventually became a U.S. Citizen in 1995.

Josefina has been an activist and has been doing public speaking for over 20 years and has lectured on various topics including Chicano Theater, Women's History Issues, Minority representation in Cinema at over 200 universities such as Yale, Darmouth, and USC. She also has a magazine column called "Ask A Wise Latina". She has been the subject of countless TV & Radio interviews in which she has passionately discussed immigration issues and other controversial subjects concerning women and minorities.

Josefina is the recipient of a number of other awards and accolades, including a formal recognition from U.S. Senator Barbara Boxer's 7th Annual "Women Making History" banquet in 1998; and a screenwriting fellowship from the California Arts Council in 2001. She and Real Women Have Curves co-author George LaVoo won the Humanitas Prize for Screenwriting in 2002, The Gabriel Garcia Marquez Award from L.A. Mayor in 2003, and the Artist-in-Residency grant from the NEA/TCG for 2007.

Even though she is best known for the success of Real Women Have Curves, Josefina has had more than 80 productions of her plays throughout the United States. In addition, Josefina also paints, writes poetry, performs, designs, lectures on writing, Women's Studies, and Chicano theater. She currently resides in Silver Lake, and is the founder of "Casa 0101 Theater Art Space" in Boyle Heights, where she teaches screenwriting and

playwriting and nurtures a new generation of Latino artists. Josefina is actively working to create an Artist District in Boyle Heights where theater, arts, music can flourish and create opportunities for the many talented artists who reside in Boyle Heights or grew up in Boyle Heights and want to return to contribute.

Josefina is presently developing the musical version of Real Women Have Curves. Her first novel titled Hungry Woman in Paris came out last spring. She wrote a play to protest SB1070 titled Detained in the Desert, which she is currently making into a film. She is working on her next novel Summer of San Miguel and opening a cultural center in Boyle Heights where she plans to continue celebrating women and Latinos! For more information please go to www.josefinalopez.com, www. hungrywomaninparis.com & www.casa0101.org.

JORGE A. HUERTA, PH.D.

Prof. Huerta is a Chancellor's Associates Professor of Theatre Emeritus at the University of California, San Diego, where he began teaching in the department of Theatre and Dance in 1975. He has directed in regional theatres throughout the United States, including New York City's Puerto Rican Traveling Theatre, Gala Hispanic Theatre in Washington, DC, Seattle's Group Theatre and the San Diego Repertory Theatre. Huerta is also a leading authority on contemporary Chicana/o and US Latina/o theatre who has lectured throughout the US, Latin America and Western Europe. He has published many articles and reviews in journals and anthologies and has edited three collections of plays.

Prof. Huerta published the first book about Chicano theatre, Chicano Theatre: Themes and Forms in 1982; his last book, Chicano Drama: Performance, Society and Myth, was published by Cambridge University Press in 2000. Dr. Huerta was inducted into the College of Fellows of the American Theatre in 1994 and elected National Association of Chicana and Chicano Studies, (NACCS) Scholar, in 1997. In 2007 Huerta was awarded the Association for Theatre in Higher Education (ATHE) "Lifetime Achievement in Educational Theatre Award." In 2008 he was recognized as the "Distinguished Scholar" by the American Society for Theatre Research (ASTR), the Society's highest annual honor.

Enjoy more of Josefina's work in
DETAINED IN THE DESERT
& OTHER PLAYS BY JOSEFINA LÓPEZ,
a WPR Books: Latino Insights publication

CPSIA information can be obtained
at www.ICGtesting.com
Printed in the USA
BVHW071202080920
588050BV00001B/88

THE BIOCHEMISTRY
of the TISSUES

THE BIOCHEMISTRY
of the TISSUES

W. Bartley
Professor of Biochemistry,
University of Sheffield

L. M. Birt
Professor of Biochemistry,
School of General Studies,
Australian National University

P. Banks
Lecturer in Biochemistry,
University of Sheffield

JOHN WILEY & SONS LTD
LONDON   NEW YORK   SYDNEY

Made and Printed in Great Britain by William Clowes and Sons Limited,
London and Beccles

This book is dedicated to
Professor Sir Hans Krebs, F.R.S.
by three of his grateful students

Preface

This book is based on a course of lectures given to medical students at Sheffield in preparation for the 2nd M.B. examination. Although it is primarily intended for medical students, it will probably be of use also to students of physiology and pharmacology, as well as being a supplementary book for students of biochemistry who are interested in the more physiological aspects of the subject. It presupposes a knowledge of chemistry somewhat more than 'A' level and may require reference to a standard textbook, for example, *Organic Chemistry* by Fieser and Fieser and *Textbook of Biophysical Chemistry* by West.

The book is intended as an introductory text rather than a comprehensive treatment of the subject and although we feel it may be of interest to the medical practitioner it will require supplementation by a text of clinical biochemistry to meet postgraduate needs.

Although the length of the book and the topics discussed have been limited by the needs of the 2nd M.B. course we have endeavoured in all cases to relate biochemical pathways to the functioning of some specific tissue or to the whole organism. Our experience suggests that students view biochemistry as something separate from the cells themselves. We have tried to show that the physiological and structural properties of cells and tissues follow from the metabolism which provides their energy, the materials from which they are made and the control required for their proper functioning. In this way we hope we have moved from the consideration of biochemistry as a series of arbitrary chemical reactions to an attitude in which biochemistry is another viewpoint of the total anatomy and physiology of the living organism.

W. BARTLEY
L. M. BIRT
P. BANKS

Bibliography

A bibliography will not be provided at the end of each chapter as we have reason to believe that it would not be used to any great extent. Furthermore such bibliographies soon become outdated. Instead we propose to give a single list of periodical publications that provide summaries of the current state of the art in the various areas of biochemistry together with references to the literature.

Publications giving reviews especially suitable for non-specialists
British Medical Bulletin
Essays in Biochemistry
Harvey Lectures
Physiological Reviews
Science Journal
Scientific American

Specialist Reviews and Original Papers
Advances in Chemotherapy
Advances in Clinical Chemistry
Advances in Drug Research
Advances in Enzyme Regulation
Advances in Enzymology
Advances in Pharmacology
Advances in Protein Chemistry
Advances in Teratology
Advances in Virus Research
Annals of the New York Academy of Science
Biochemical Society Symposia
Brookhaven Symposia
Ciba Foundation Study Groups
Ciba Symposia
Cold Spring Harbor Symposia on Quantitative Biology
International Review of Cytology

International Review of Neurobiology
Progress in Biophysics
Progress in Brain Research
Progress in Nucleic Acid Research
Symposia of the Society for Experimental Biology

Annual Reviews—reviews giving extensive references to the literature
Annual Review of Biochemistry
Annual Review of Medicine
Annual Review of Microbiology
Annual Review of Pharmacology
Annual Review of Physiology

Abstracts of the Literature
Index Medicus
International Abstracts of the Biological Sciences

Acknowledgements

We are indebted to Dr. W. Ferdinand, Dr. J. R. Guest and Dr. D. Bellamy for reading the manuscript and for making many helpful suggestions. We would also like to thank Mrs. M. Stuart-King for her expert typing of the several drafts, and all the other members of the department at Sheffield who contributed to the production of the book in various ways.

W.B., L.M.B., P.B.

Contents

Introduction

Biochemistry is a subject which has now penetrated into all other biological disciplines, partly because the exploration of life often requires biochemical techniques. The use of these techniques shows that life in all its different forms tends to use the same chemical devices for achieving its goals.

Although this book is concerned with the biochemistry of the human, it must not be supposed that this is something very different from that of other species. Most of the major metabolic pathways described are common to all mammals and, a great number of them, to all life.

Biochemistry is an attempt to describe life in chemical terms, but it does not stop at the simple statement of the analysis of the living material and of the various reactions whereby the components of life are synthesized and degraded. It is also concerned with how the interlocking systems of chemical reactions are controlled, so that there is growth in infancy, maintenance in maturity, and degeneration in old age.

Besides the chemical pathways, the biochemist is much concerned with the rate at which the chemical changes take place. Probably life, as we understand it, is possible only because reactions which are inherently slow can be made fast enough to supply energy at a comparatively low temperature. The catalysis of the reactions is brought about by special proteins called enzymes. These are simply catalysts that happen to be proteins, and therefore their properties reflect their protein nature. Although enzymes are very important they require the cooperation of other molecules before they can act as controllers of the chemistry of life, and the study of the flow of chemical information to enzymes, and their response to this information, is becoming an increasing part of biochemistry.

Apart from the normal chemical pattern of life, there is the disordered biochemical pattern of disease. Ultimately all diseases can be considered as reflections of a change in the normal biochemistry of the organism, which produces sufficient dysfunction to make the organism markedly inefficient. Changes in the rates of comparatively few metabolic reactions can produce changes in the functioning of the organism, since ultimately all the body's metabolic reactions are interconnected and interdependent. Changes in the rates of metabolic reactions result from some change in function or quantity of an enzyme. Measurements of enzyme activity are now therefore important tests in medicine, supplementing the more usual tests of the gross quantities of inorganic and organic substances in blood, urine and other body fluids. Enzymes may slowly change as a result of chronic disorders, or there may be abrupt changes associated with an acute condition such as myocardial infarction. The pattern of enzymes in a particular tissue is characteristic of the tissue and so, on damage, for example to the heart muscle, the tissue will liberate its characteristic pattern of enzymes into the blood stream, thus altering the normal pattern of enzymes characteristic of the blood. It is now possible in some cases, by studying the pattern of enzymes in the blood, to distinguish which of the organs is damaged. Further, the change in the pattern of enzymes with time gives a prognosis of the course of the disease since, when the lesion heals, tissue enzymes are no longer liberated into the blood.

Biochemistry is not therefore simply a subject which must be learned on the road to medical qualification; it is a subject of increasing use and relevance in the practice of medicine. It is the aim of this book to illustrate the relevance of biochemistry to the understanding of the dynamic pattern of chemical reactions that we call 'The Human.'

CHAPTER 1

The quantitative man

Biochemistry has now passed from the state of a descriptive science to a stage where quantitative problems are becoming more important. Thus a biochemist is always interested in the following things about a metabolic sequence:

(1) The description of the enzymes and chemical changes that comprise the metabolic sequence.
(2) The rate at which material can be transformed by the sequence.
(3) The amounts of material that are utilized by the sequence in the living organism.
(4) The nature of the control mechanisms which adjust the amounts of material utilized by the sequence.

Apart from (1) the considerations are all of a quantitative nature.

The basic biochemistry of all cells is very similar and certain fundamental pathways of utilization of cellular foodstuffs are common to all cells. Very roughly the contributions to the body's metabolism of the different tissues that comprise the human are proportional to the weights of the tissues. As shown in Table 1.1 the skeletal muscle is far and away the largest contributor to body weight with bone, adipose tissue and intestines making the next most substantial contribution.

However, it is not the sheer mass of tissue which determines its quantitative contribution to metabolic activity. A better correlation is the protein content of the tissue because, as we shall see later, the activity of a tissue is determined by its enzyme content and all enzymes are protein in nature. As shown by Table 1.1, the protein content of adipose tissue and bone is much lower than might be expected from the weights of the tissues. However, the protein content of the tissues is not a complete guide since not all the protein is specifically concerned with metabolism; for example, the haemoglobin of the blood has the function of carrying oxygen but does not enter into other metabolic sequences and much of the protein of bones and skin is the inert supporting protein collagen. If we add together the contributions of active protein of skeletal muscle, intestines

Table 1.1. Weights of tissues in a 70 kg man

	Wet weight (kg)	Protein content (kg)
Skeletal muscle	30	6·6
Adipose tissue	13·2	0·92
Stomach and intestines	7.25	1.34[a]
Liver	1·6	0·35[b]
Brain	1·36	0·136
Kidneys	0·29	0·05
Heart	0·29	0·06[a]
Adrenals	0·014	?
Blood	6·4	1·02
Skin	4·9	? ⎫ collagen
Bone	12·0	1·23 ⎭

[a] Assumed protein content as in skeletal muscle.
[b] Assumed protein content as in rat liver.

(which are largely muscle) and heart, we can see that the greater part of the body's metabolism is concerned with muscle. We shall therefore look at the biochemistry of muscle first, making a start with skeletal muscle.

SECTION 1

The Biochemistry of Muscle, the Tissue of Movement

Structure and enzymology of muscle; proteins and enzymes. Biochemical energetics. Muscular contraction

The structure of muscle tissue

Muscle is a device for producing the mechanical work necessary for movement and is, therefore, a tissue which must change its shape. This change of shape is a function of each muscle cell and, ultimately, of some of the molecules which the cell contains.

In the electron micrograph of muscle, shown in Figure 1.1, the characteristic disposition of filaments in the fibrils of a muscle cell is apparent. The thin dark transverse lines are called 'Z lines'; between pairs of Z lines lie the 'I bands' (where there are thin filaments only), the 'A bands' (where there are both thick and thin filaments) and the 'H bands' (where there are thick filaments only). If the fibril is examined under higher magnification, the presence of arrays of thin filaments extending from the Z lines into the spaces between the thick filaments and of cross linkages between the overlapping filaments can be detected (Figure 1.2). These different structures can interact to produce a shortening of the muscle ('contraction'), probably by the sliding of adjacent filaments over each other.

The protein of muscle cells

Two proteins make up the bulk of the muscle tissue, myosin and actin. If muscle is extracted with a salt solution, the A bands disappear and, as myosin is soluble in salt solution, it is thought that the A bands contain myosin which is located in thick filaments. The thin filaments contain the actin, which can exist in two forms, G actin (a globular protein, see p. 11) or F actin (a fibrous protein, see p. 11). Even after isolation from the muscle a mixture of myosin and F actin retains the ability to contract. It is

5

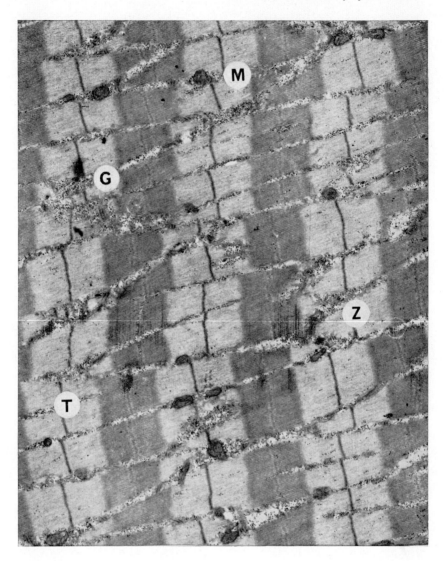

Figure 1.1. An electron micrograph of skeletal muscle. The small number of mitochondria (M) in this field reflects the lower oxidative capacity of this tissue compared with heart muscle (Figure 1.24). All the mitochondria are located near the Z bands (Z) in the general area of the triad system (T) where ATP is required to pump Ca^{2+} ions into the terminal cisternae of the sarcoplasmic reticulum in order to bring about relaxation. Glycogen granules (G) located close to the contractile apparatus are able to provide a ready source of ATP predominantly via glycolysis. By kind permission of Mr. R. Hardy

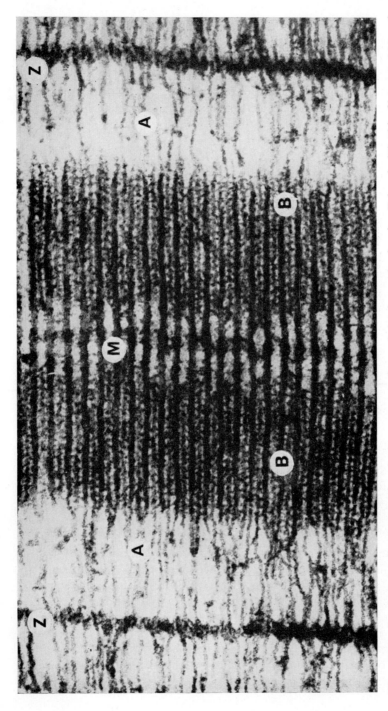

Figure 1.2. An electron micrograph of a single sarcomere from skeletal muscle showing Z bands (Z), thin filaments (A) and thick filaments (M). Note the region of overlap between the thick and thin filaments (A band) and the cross bridges (B) between the thick and thin filaments. By kind permission of Dr. H. E. Huxley, F.R.S.

possible to combine these two proteins in a test tube to form a very viscous solution, or gel, of actomyosin (which may also be present in the living cell, formed at the junction of the thick and thin filaments). The actomyosin solution can be made into threads by squirting it through a narrow nozzle into a dilute salt solution. If the compound adenosine triphosphate (ATP)

is added to the actomyosin threads, they contract and hydrolyse the ATP into adenosine diphosphate (ADP) and inorganic phosphate.

The breakdown of ATP is a process used very frequently to meet the cell's requirements for energy (see p. 308) and it is the immediate energy source for muscular contraction; as long as ATP is available in the muscle, it is capable of contracting.

The catalytic function of muscle protein

An aqueous neutral solution of ATP kept at 40° hydrolyses only slowly, with a life of about four weeks; but in muscle (also at 40° and presumably at pH 7) which contains 34 mg ATP/100 g tissue, the life of the available ATP is only 2 sec. This hydrolysis of ATP is catalysed largely by acto-myosin, which besides being a contractile protein is also responsible for bringing about the conversion of the chemical energy of the ATP molecule to the mechanical energy of muscle contraction at a rate sufficient for the needs of the organism. Compounds which, like actomyosin, act as biological catalysts are called 'enzymes'.

Proteins and enzymes

The function of enzymes

Enzymes are proteins which enable the essential chemical reactions to occur with sufficient rapidity at the temperatures at which living things can survive. The acceleration of the hydrolysis of ATP by actomyosin is an illustration of this property. The explanation of its catalytic action revolves around an understanding of why the solution of ATP without actomyosin does not hydrolyse more rapidly than it does, and involves the concept of the 'activation energy' of a reaction. For pairs of molecules to react they

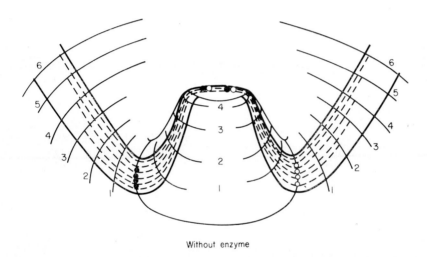

Without enzyme

Figure 1.3. Diagrammatic representation of the energy relationships in an uncatalysed bimolecular reaction. The reactant molecules (○ and ●) are present initially at different energy levels (the contour lines 1–6). Only those at the highest levels (5 and 6) are capable of surmounting the barrier provided by the energy of activation (centre contour lines 1–4)

must possess between them a certain amount of energy at the instant of their collision. In any collection of molecules, there will be a range of energy levels and only those pairs above a certain level will react. The energy required for reaction is called the activation energy; it will vary with different reactions. Thus in the aqueous solution of ATP, the rate at which hydrolysis occurs is proportional to the number of colliding ATP–H_2O

pairs with an energy content greater than the activation energy for hydrolysis and the reaction can be speeded up by warming the solution and increasing the kinetic energy of the molecules. If the temperature is raised from 40 to 50°, the rate of breakdown of ATP is doubled. Alternatively, if the activation energy for the reaction is decreased, the rate will increase without any need to increase the temperature. Enzymes function by lowering the activation energy. For example, the hydrolysis of cane sugar (producing glucose and fructose) has an activation energy of 25 kcal/mole and in aqueous solution this sugar is stable almost indefinitely, as almost none of the molecules have the requisite activation energy; but in the presence of the enzyme invertase, the energy of activation drops to about 9 kcal/mole and hydrolysis proceeds to completion in a few minutes. The difference between catalysed and uncatalysed reactions is summarized in Figures 1.3 and 1.4.

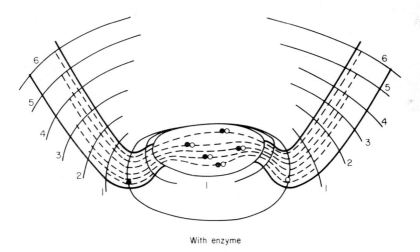

With enzyme

Figure 1.4. Diagrammatic representation of the energy relationships in an enzyme-catalysed bimolecular reaction. The energy of activation is much lower than that in the corresponding uncatalysed reaction (Figure 1.3) and a greater number of reactant molecules (those initially on contours 2–6) have sufficient energy to interact

The nature of enzymes: protein composition and structure

As all known enzymes are proteins, an understanding of many of the properties of enzymes depends on familiarity with the structure and properties of proteins. Basically proteins consist of repeating units of amino

acids joined together by peptide linkages, $-\overset{\overset{\textstyle O}{\|}}{C}-NH-$, to form polypeptide chains.

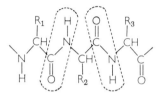

The various R groups represent the side chains of some 20 different amino acids (see Figure 2.15). As the molecular weight of proteins is usually greater than 10,000 there will be at least 90 amino acids joined end to end; in the larger proteins there may be as many as 10,000 constituent amino acids. As well as the end-to-end linkages, there are also cross linkages between adjacent amino acids of the polypeptide chains. If these cross links join groups of extended chains in a fairly stable and rather insoluble structure a fibrous protein is formed; the myosin of muscle is of this type. If the cross links hold a single polypeptide chain in a configuration in which it is extensively folded and bent back on itself, a globular protein is formed; G actin of muscle and most enzymes belong to this class.

The final complex structure of a protein is conveniently described as follows. The 'primary structure' of the protein is the order in which the amino acids occur in the polypeptide chains, i.e. it is the amino acid sequence. The shapes of the amino acids and of the bonds joining them in the peptide links are such that the chain has a natural twist often forming a right-handed corkscrew structure (Figure 1.5). This spiral arrangement, an example of 'secondary structure', is stabilized by a regular array of hydrogen bonds between the carbonyl and imido groups of the peptide bonds (Figure 1.5). Such bonds can join two electronegative elements with the hydrogen serving as a bridge; their formation involves a polarization with a partial loss of an electron from the hydrogen which, as the hydrogen ion, can attract a pair of anions. The extensive coiling and folding of the polypeptide chain into a globular form (the 'tertiary structure') is stabilized by the variety of bonds described in Figure 1.6 and produces a structure of great complexity, as for example in myoglobin (Figure 1.7). The tertiary structure is most important for the catalytic properties of proteins, as it determines the overall shape of the molecule. Lastly, the protein may have a quaternary structure which results from the association of a number of individual folded chains to give the final form of the protein (Figure 1.8).

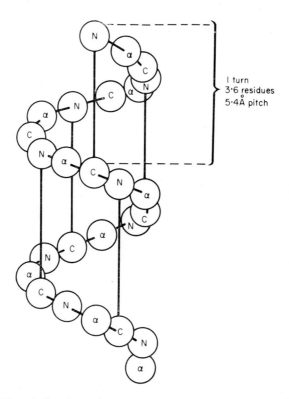

I turn
3·6 residues
5·4Å pitch

Figure 1.5. The α helix of proteins. H bonds, each comprising Ⓝ—H····O=Ⓒ, are represented by the vertical black bars; atoms in the chain are distinguished as N (peptide bond nitrogen), C (peptide bond carbon) and α (α-carbon atom bearing side chain)

The isolation of proteins

As the detailed study of an enzyme (or other protein) often involves its isolation in pure form, a variety of special procedures has been designed for this purpose. One of the commonest is the stepwise addition of ammonium sulphate to a solution of protein, which, by removing water from the surface of the protein molecules, allows them to aggregate and precipitate. This process, known as 'salting out', can be used to separate those proteins which precipitate in different concentrations of ammonium sulphate. Proteins can also be precipitated selectively by altering the pH of the solution as they often have different 'isoelectric points', i.e. pH values at which the protein will not move in an electric field and at which the solubility is minimal. Finally, proteins may be selectively adsorbed onto materials such as calcium phosphate gels or columns of cellulose derivatives (carboxymethylcellulose and diethylaminoethylcellulose) from which they can be eluted by solutions of different salt concentration or pH.

Another technique of considerable value, gel filtration, depends on the separation of proteins from one another or from other compounds on the basis of their molecular dimensions. An artificially cross-linked dextran

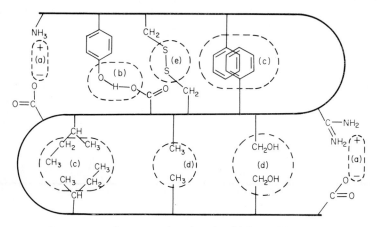

Figure 1.6 Some types of non-covalent bonds which stabilize protein structure: (a) electrostatic interaction; (b) hydrogen bonding between tyrosine residues and carboxylate groups on side chains; (c) interaction of non-polar side chains caused by the mutual repulsion of solvent; (d) van der Waals interactions; (e) a disulphide linkage, a covalent bond. From C. B. Anfinsen, *The Molecular Basis of Evolution*, Wiley, New York, 1959

provides a suitable filter. The holes within the dextran network allow the entry of small molecules and exclude the large; therefore smaller molecules are entrapped in the dextran while larger molecules pass through. A number of grades of suitable dextrans (marketed under the trade name of Sephadex) are available for separating compounds of molecular weight from about 4000 to 200,000.

Testing the physical homogeneity of isolated proteins

A number of techniques may be employed to test the purity of an isolated protein. One method used extensively is to see whether the protein sediments in an homogeneous way in a high centrifugal field developed in

an ultracentrifuge; this instrument can also give information about the
molecular weight, shape, size and density of the protein. The centrifuge
cell spins fast enough to sediment the larger dissolved molecules under
forces of 5×10^5 g and by measuring the change in refractive index across
the cell it is possible to detect the point at which a solute 'boundary' is

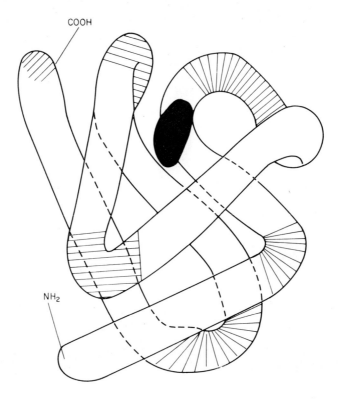

Figure 1.7. Diagrammatic representation of helical (unshaded) and non-
helical (shaded) parts of the molecule of myoglobin. Also shown are N-terminal
(NH_2) and C-terminal (COOH) ends of the structure and the position of the
haem group (black) (see p. 165)

separating from the solvent. If the protein solution has a number of components they will sediment at different rates and a number of peaks
(corresponding to the changes in the refractive index) will be observed.
Although a pure protein solution should sediment as one peak, it does not
follow that if a single peak is found the protein must be pure, as proteins
sometimes associate and sediment as a complex.

Another technique for testing the purity of a protein depends on the fact that all protein molecules are charged, the sign of the net charge depending on the pH of the solution. Thus, if a protein molecule in solution is subjected to an electric field it will tend to move towards one or the other pole, depending on the sign of its charge. Hospital laboratories commonly perform electrophoresis using a gel (of starch or polyacrilamide) as the

Figure 1.8. A tetramer of protein units illustrating the quaternary structure of a complex protein. From E. E. Conn and P. K. Stumpf, *Outlines of Biochemistry*, Wiley, New York, 1963

medium through which the protein migrates. Figure 1.9 illustrates the separation of various forms (termed 'isoenzymes' or 'isozymes') of the enzyme lactic dehydrogenase in human plasma; these isozymes vary in proportion in different diseases. The illustration shows two characteristic patterns of isozymes which occur in infectious hepatitis and myocardial infarction.

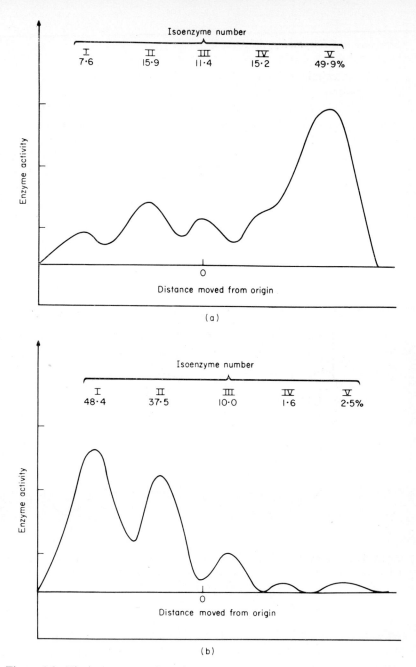

Figure 1.9. The isoenzymes of serum lactic dehydrogenase separated by electrophoresis in agar gel. After electrophoresis each pattern contains 5 isoenzymes, their activities being detected by allowing the enzyme in the gel to react with pyruvate and $NADH_2$, and measuring the decrease in optical density (at 366 mμ) resulting from the oxidation of the $NADH_2$. Pattern (a) infectious hepatitis; pattern (b) mycardial infarction. From J. Kamaryt and Z. Zazvorka, *Science Tools*, 1963

Immunological tests

Proteins purified until they give only one peak in the ultracentrifuge under a variety of conditions and which migrate as a single peak during electrophoresis in a range of buffers are usually considered as pure proteins. However, immunological examination of preparations from different organs can reveal differences in proteins which behave in the same way in all these physical tests. These procedures measure the overall statistical properties of the molecule, e.g. a protein of moderate molecular weight may contain about 300 amino acid residues selected from the 20 common amino acids. Even if exactly the same numbers and sorts of amino acids were selected, the arrangement within the molecule could be tremendously varied and still produce the same physical properties (sedimentation velocity, net charge). Nevertheless, two apparently identical proteins of this type injected separately into animals may produce two separate sets of antibodies, which can be detected by precipitation when antigen and antisera are mixed. Such a test is probably the most sensitive method of distinguishing between proteins which differ only slightly in their structure.

Determination of the sequence of amino acids in proteins

Once a protein has been isolated in a highly purified form, it is possible to determine the sequence of its component amino acids. This has been done for a number of proteins, firstly for insulin (Figure 1.10) by Sanger, who was awarded the Nobel Prize for this work. Obviously, simple hydrolysis of the protein into its constituent amino acids tells nothing about their arrangement, though if the protein is first reacted with some compound which labels an amino acid by virtue of its position in the molecule, subsequent hydrolysis and identification of the labelled amino acid will be useful. The compound 1-fluoro-2,4-dinitrobenzene reacts with free amino groups in proteins, giving the coloured dinitrophenyl (DNP) derivatives which after hydrolysis can be isolated and identified by paper chromatography.

Such a procedure indicated that the insulin molecule had an N-terminal glycine and an N-terminal phenylalanine residue and that there was one lysine residue. Thus each molecule consisted of two linked polypeptide chains (the A and the B chain). As the protein contained cystine and, when treated with a mixture of formic acid and hydrogen peroxide (which splits disulphide bridges), broke down into A and B chains (which could be isolated and purified), it was apparent that these two chains were linked by disulphide bridges (Figure 1.10).

The sequence of amino acids within the two separated chains was determined by partial hydrolysis, identification of the N-terminal residues of each resulting polypeptide chain as the dinitrophenol derivative followed

2+

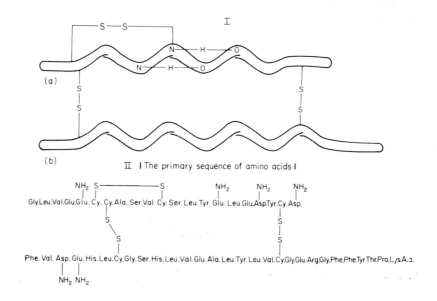

Figure 1.10. A diagrammatic representation of the primary structure of the protein molecule insulin, as worked out by Frederick Sanger and his coworkers. The protein is composed of two polypeptide chains, designated (a) and (b). The two polypeptide chains are held together by two prominent sulphur-to-sulphur (disulphide) bridges. A similar disulphide bridge exists between two amino acids on the (a) chain. (The abbreviations are the initial letters of the names of the constituent amino acids: Glu—NH₂, Asp—NH₂, Cy—S—S—Cy represent glutamine, asparagine and cystine, respectively.) Modified from C. B. Anfinsen, *The Molecular Basis of Evolution*, Wiley, New York, 1963

by complete hydrolysis to give the amino acid composition of the poly-peptides. The results obtained, together with the proportions of amino acids in the entire chain and its molecular weight, could be used to deduce the particular sequence.

The use of specific hydrolytic enzymes for the initial cleavage of the protein has made such analyses somewhat easier. The hydrolytic enzymes used are of two kinds, firstly the *exopeptidases*, which remove amino acids from either the N-terminal end (aminopeptidase) or the carboxyl end (carboxypeptidase) of the protein; and secondly *endopeptidases* which attack the protein specifically wherever certain groupings are present in the molecule (Figure 1.11). Thus pepsin cannot act at positively charged residues in the chain (lysine or arginine) whereas trypsin acts only in this situation. Pepsin and chymotrypsin both require an aromatic amino acid

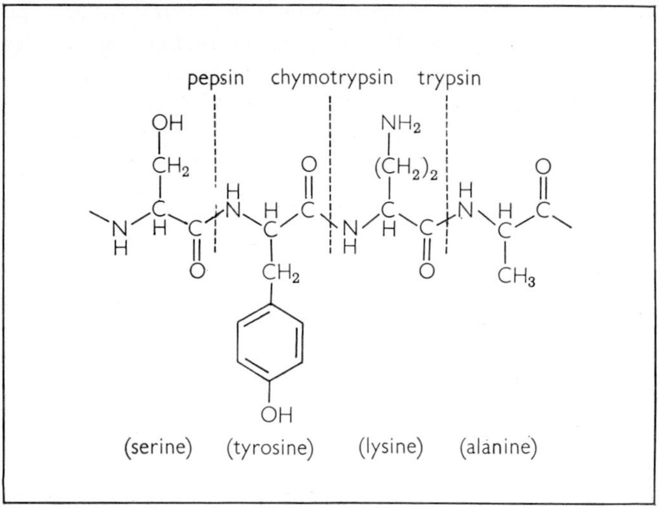

Figure 1.11. The bond specificities of pepsin, trypsin and chymotrypsin at the linkage; for pepsin the aromatic residue must provide the —NH group of the peptide bond, for chymotrypsin it must provide the C=O group.

The complete three-dimensional structure of proteins

The structure of a protein available in crystalline form can also be explored by x-ray crystallography. Photographs of the x-ray diffraction pattern are taken at all possible angles and from the diffraction patterns the position of the atoms in the molecule can be calculated. This technique has provided a complete three-dimensional structure of the molecule of myoglobin and a detailed picture of haemoglobin. X-ray crystallography has also been used to determine the structure of the complex vitamin B_{12} (see p. 106).

Properties of protein catalysts

The specificity of enzyme action

From the preceding discussion of the structure of proteins it is clear that the organization of an enzyme molecule in space will be extremely precise with the polypeptide chain being folded in a certain way and in consequence having particular amino acids present at particular positions on its surface. Thus the enzyme in its cellular environment will have a certain characteristic shape or conformation which in a certain region provides those chemical groupings essential for specific interaction with its 'substrate' (the compound whose transformation is being catalysed). These points of interaction are called 'active sites' and a most important and striking property of enzymes is the selectivity of the binding of substrate in relation to these active sites, i.e. the *specificity* of the reaction catalysed by the enzyme. Commonly a small group of substances of similar chemical nature act as substrates for the enzyme though one compound reacts at a greater rate than the others and is often regarded as *the* substrate utilized by the enzyme *in vivo*. For example, the enzyme alcohol dehydrogenase will react with a wide variety of alcohols, transforming them to the corresponding aldehydes, but ethanol is the substrate utilized most rapidly.

$$\underset{CH_3}{\overset{CH_2OH}{|}} + NAD \rightleftharpoons \underset{CH_3}{\overset{\overset{H}{\diagdown}\overset{O}{\diagup}}{\underset{|}{C}}} + NADH_2$$

With some enzymes, the range of substrates is very wide; for example, the enzyme esterase hydrolyses any carboxylic ester to the corresponding alcohol and acid.

Many organic compounds have a centre of asymmetry and exist in D and L forms. Enzymes acting on such compounds usually exhibit complete optical specificity, reacting with only one of the two isomers. Thus kidney contains two enzymes each oxidizing a wide range of amino acids and producing α-keto acids, ammonia and hydrogen peroxide. One enzyme attacks only the D amino acids, the other only the L forms. In mammals enzymes attacking the D configuration of amino acids are rare, possibly because mammalian protein is built up from the L amino acids series, the D series being confined almost entirely to bacteria. There is, however, a small group of enzymes that has both the optical isomers as substrates. These enzymes, the racemases, convert one isomer into the other.

Sometimes an enzyme may act on only one of a pair of *cis–trans* isomers. For example, fumarase catalyses the formation of malic acid from fumaric acid (the *trans* isomer) by adding water across the double bond; this enzyme will not react with the *cis* isomer, maleic acid.

fumaric acid

maleic acid

Some enzymes appear to have such a restricted specificity that only one substance will serve as a substrate. Thus urease, found in the plant kingdom and also in the mammalian gut because of the resident population of microorganisms, attacks only urea to form carbon dioxide and ammonia.

$$\begin{array}{c} NH_2 \\ \diagdown \\ C{=}O + H_2O \longrightarrow 2NH_3 + CO_2 \\ \diagup \\ NH_2 \end{array}$$

Another enzyme arginase, essential for urea formation, reacts only with arginine

$$\begin{array}{ccc} NH{=}C{-}NH_2 & & NH_2 \qquad\qquad O{=}C{-}NH_2 \\ | & & | \qquad\qquad\qquad | \\ NH \qquad + H_2O \longrightarrow & & (CH_2)_3 \qquad\qquad NH_2 \\ | & & | \\ (CH_2)_3 & & NH_2{-}CH{-}COOH \\ | & & \\ NH_2{-}CH{-}COOH & & \\ \text{arginine} & & \text{ornithine} \qquad\qquad \text{urea} \end{array}$$

Some enzymes previously regarded as specific for one naturally-occurring substrate have been found to act also on substances synthesized by organic chemists. Acetylcholinesterase, which is responsible for hydrolysing acetylcholine to acetic acid and choline (thereby ensuring that the transmission of impulses from nerve to muscle lasts for a brief time only), also hydrolyses synthetic analogues such as carbamylcholine, although at a much slower rate. These analogues are very useful when a prolonged parasympathetic effect is required.

The influence of temperature on enzyme action

The rate of chemical reactions approximately doubles for each temperature rise of $10°$ ($Q_{10} = 2$). Within limits, enzyme-catalysed reactions behave in the same way but their behaviour is complicated by the protein nature of the catalyst. It will be recalled that the activity of the enzyme depends on the existence of a particular conformation of the protein. This conformation, which may not be the most probable one, is maintained by the elaborate cross linkages of hydrogen bonds, salt links, hydrophobic bonds and covalent bonds between the amino acid side chains. Such a structure may be very delicately poised and heating the molecule may impart sufficient energy to it to break some of the bonds holding particular side chains in juxtaposition. If these side chains then become randomly oriented there is little likelihood of the specific conformation of the enzyme molecule being restored on cooling and the protein is said to be 'irreversibly denatured'. In this condition it is catalytically inactive. The rate of

denaturation of proteins is high and becomes progressively higher with
increased temperature. At 70–80°, the Q_{10} for denaturation may be of the
order of hundreds. Such behaviour produces the kind of change in the
activity of an enzyme with temperature shown in Figure 1.12. Initially, as
the temperature rises, the rate of reaction increases with a Q_{10} of about 2.
When the temperature is high enough to permit conformational change in
the protein the overall rate expresses a balance between the rate of the
reaction at that temperature and the rate of removal of active enzyme by

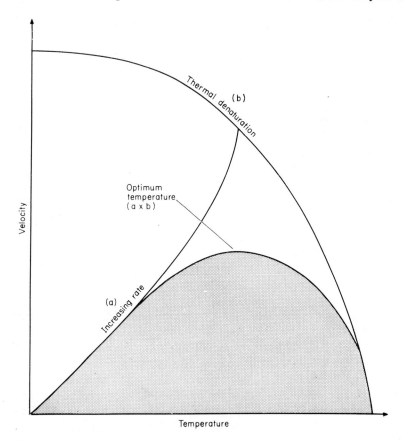

Figure 1.12. Effect of temperature on reaction rate of an enzyme-catalysed
reaction: (a) represents the increasing rate of a reaction as a function of
temperature; (b) represents the decreasing rate as a function of thermal
denaturation of the enzyme protein. The shaded area represents the combination of (a) × (b). From E. E. Conn and P. K. Stumpf, *Outlines of Biochemistry*,
Wiley, New York, 1963

denaturation of the protein. Since the Q_{10} of denaturation increases so rapidly with temperature, the activity of the enzyme soon shows a precipitous fall. It is also clear that the optimum temperature (at which the rate of reaction is maximal) may well depend on the time for which the enzyme is kept at each temperature; if the exposure lasts only a few seconds the optimum temperature will be higher than if heating continues for long periods.

Influence of pH on enzyme activity

The side chains of the amino acids of a protein may contain groups which act as acids or bases depending on the pH; these are commonly the carboxyl groups of glutamic and aspartic acids and the amino groups of lysine, the guanido group of arginine and the imidazolyl group of histidine. Such groups are capable of interacting with each other and by so doing help to establish and maintain the characteristic conformation of the protein. Thus both these interactions and the shape of the protein molecule vary with the pH; it follows that the ease with which a substrate molecule is correctly oriented on the enzyme surface will also be influenced by the pH. Many of the substrates of enzymes are themselves substances which can ionize and the enzymes may interact only with the ionized or the unionized form. All these interactions will result in an influence of pH on the rate of the reaction. Finally, extremes of pH often result in denaturation of the enzyme, as does heating.

As a consequence of the interplay of these effects of pH most enzymes have an optimum pH, that is a particular value of pH at which they work most rapidly. There is a wide range of these values (from about pH 2 to about pH 10) and it follows that many enzymes in the body cannot be working at their optimum pH since, except in the stomach, extremes of pH are not met; the pH range in the body is from about 6·4–7·5. There is surprisingly little information about the rates of enzyme reactions at physiological pH values. Although the pH of some tissues is known as an average it is possible that local variations in pH may occur, at least for short times, in the immediate vicinity of the enzyme molecule, producing large changes in rates in this circumscribed area. These localized pH changes may act as a type of control mechanism (see Section 8).

Quantitative description of enzyme action

It is often desirable or essential to describe the behaviour of enzymes not only qualitatively (as has already been done) but also in more precise quantitative terms. As a preliminary to this description of enzyme action it may be useful to recall some quantitative aspects of reversible chemical reactions since all that enzymes do is to catalyse the attainment of an equilibrium.

Equilibria

A reaction such as A + B → C + D, proceeds at a rate proportional to the product of the concentrations of A and B. However, this proportionality does not tell us exactly how many molecules of A and B are reacting, i.e. whether or not the reaction is inherently fast or slow under the test conditions. For this purpose, the rate constant must be used; it is defined so that the product of the concentrations of the reactant and this constant gives the absolute number of moles/litre reacting in unit time. Thus $[A][B] \times k_1$ = the number of moles/litre of A + B reacting in unit time and $[C][D] \times k_2$ = the number of moles/litre of C + D reacting in unit time. At equilibrium the same number of molecules of A and B disappear and appear in unit time as do those of C and D so that

$$[A][B]k_1 = [C][D]k_2$$

or

$$\frac{k_1}{k_2} = \frac{[C][D]}{[A][B]} = \text{a constant, } K, \text{ the equilibrium constant.}$$

Free energy changes during reactions

In addition to describing the equilibrium position of a reaction it is often desirable to be able to make predictions about the possibility of a reaction occurring in a particular system. Chemists have been able to define a criterion for the feasibility of a reaction. The fundamental property used in this way is *entropy*, which is a measure of the extent to which the constituents of the system under consideration are in a particular pattern or order. As a universal generalization of experience, it is held that the order in the entire reacting system and its surroundings always decreases—this is expressed by saying that entropy has increased.

As it is often difficult or impossible to determine precisely the overall entropy change, another way of determining the feasibility, applicable to individual isolated reactions, has been devised. This is called the 'free energy change' and is the algebraic sum of the change in the heat content and in the entropy of the reactants and products at a particular temperature: thus $\Delta G = \Delta H - T \Delta S$ where ΔG is the change in the free energy, ΔH is the change in the heat content and ΔS is the change in entropy at the temperature T of the reacting system. Its definition is such that a reaction may proceed if ΔG is negative; if it is positive, the reverse reaction is the feasible one; and if it is 0 the reaction is at equilibrium. The equation implies that a 'spontaneous reaction' (ΔG negative) may be driven by either of two types of change in the energy content of the system. The first is a decrease in the heat content (ΔH negative). It is well known that many reactions which occur readily do so with the liberation of heat. For example, hydrogen and oxygen gases react to produce water with a considerable evolution of heat.

$$2H_2 + O_2 \rightarrow 2H_2O \qquad \Delta H = -68,400 \text{ cal/mole}$$

In such reactions, the magnitude of the decrease in H is sufficient to ensure that ΔG is negative also. The second is a decrease in the order in the system (expressed as an energy term by multiplying the entropy change by the temperature of the system, i.e. $T \Delta S$). If this decrease is sufficiently large, it may be decisive in making ΔG negative, i.e. in driving the reaction. For example, if ice is held at a temperature of $0°$, it absorbs heat spontaneously from its surroundings (ΔH is positive) and melts (to form water at the same temperature). The reaction proceeds because the increase in entropy (ΔS) is sufficiently great to make ΔG negative, i.e. the reaction is driven by the decrease in the order of the molecules as water is formed.

ΔG is called the change in 'free energy' because it is a measure of the change in the amount of energy available from a reacting system for the performance of work (the energy 'freed' for work). Obviously it may be greater or less than the heat energy change in the same reaction; but whenever heat energy is absorbed by a system, only a fraction of it can be recovered again ('freed') as work. Thus, although the ice melting at a temperature of $0°$ absorbs heat, this energy cannot be recovered as work, as ΔH is equal to $T \Delta S$ at this temperature, i.e. $\Delta G = 0$. In physical terms, this implies that the water at this temperature has acquired no potentiality for doing work that was not possessed equally by the ice at the same temperature.

As the change in free energy is a measure of the change in heat content (determined largely by the making and breaking of chemical bonds) and in the order (determined largely by the molecular pattern) of the system, it is clear that its magnitude will depend on the total number of molecules reacting. Nevertheless, it is convenient to consider the change resulting from the reaction of those molecules present in a unit volume of the reacting system, i.e. to relate the free energy change to the concentrations of reactants and products. In fact it can be shown that for the reaction $A + B \rightarrow C + D$,

$$\Delta G = RT \ln \frac{[C] \times [D]}{[A] \times [B]} + \text{a constant.}$$

2*

Each individual reaction will have a particular value for the constant, i.e. suppose that [A], [B], [C] and [D] are all equilibrium concentrations, then $\Delta G = 0 = RT \ln K + $ a constant (where K is the equilibrium constant), i.e. $-RT \ln K = $ a constant $= \Delta G^0$, the standard free energy change. Thus

$$\Delta G = \Delta G^0 + RT \ln \frac{[C] \times [D]}{[A] \times [B]}$$

and ΔG^0 is the free energy change when reactants and products are at unit concentration. Biochemists often make use of the term $\Delta G^{0'}$, which is the standard free energy change at pH 7, i.e. when the concentration of H^+ ions is 10^{-7} M but all the other reactants are at unit concentration.

In summary, for any change which occurs, ΔG is always negative. On the other hand, each individual reaction has a characteristic value for ΔG^0 which may be positive ($K < 1$), 0 ($K = 1$) or negative ($K > 1$) and which is proportional to the logarithm of K. It is important to understand that neither of these values tells us anything about the rate of the reaction; as previously discussed this depends on the energy of activation (see p. 9).

Illustration of the dependence of free energy changes on the concentration of reactants

The importance of the concentration of the reactants in determining the free energy change in a reaction can be illustrated with the conversion of glucose-1-phosphate to glucose-6-phosphate (see p. 44), for which the equilibrium constant is 19, i.e. at equilibrium there are 95 parts of glucose-6-phosphate and 5 parts of glucose-1-phosphate so that

$$\Delta G^0 = -1400 \times \log 19 = -1800 \text{ cal/mole*}$$

Now if we mix glucose-1-phosphate (0·01 M) and glucose-6-phosphate (0·001 M) we can calculate ΔG as follows:

$$\Delta G = \Delta G^0 + RT \ln \frac{[\text{glucose-6-P}]}{[\text{glucose-1-P}]}$$

$$= -1800 + 1400 \log \frac{0 \cdot 001}{0 \cdot 01}$$

$$= -1800 + 1400 \times -1$$

$$= -3200 \text{ cal/mole}$$

Thus the amount of glucose-6-phosphate will increase and that of glucose-1-phosphate decrease, with a free energy yield of 3200 cal/mole transformed.

* $RT \ln x = 2 \cdot 3 RT \log x \simeq 1400 \log x$ at 30°.

Conversely if the initial concentration of glucose-1-phosphate is 0·0001 M and of glucose-6-phosphate 0·01 M, ΔG will equal 1000, i.e. the reverse reaction proceeds and the amount of glucose-1-phosphate increases with a yield of 1000 cal/mole. The effect of concentration is often important in biological systems as materials are constantly being formed and used. Nevertheless the range of concentrations feasible in living matter is limited, with most metabolites having a concentration of about 1 mM. If ΔG^0 for any reaction is large and negative (about -5 kcal/mole) then the reaction is for all practical purposes irreversible. This follows because, to reverse the reaction, ΔG must be larger than and opposite in sign to ΔG^0

$$\Delta G = \Delta G^0 + RT \ln \frac{[C][D]}{[A][B]}$$

Now, in order to reverse the reaction when $\Delta G^0 = 5000$ cal/mole, ΔG must $\geqslant 5000$ cal/mole

$$\therefore \ 1400 \ln \frac{[C][D]}{[A][B]} \text{ must} \geqslant 5000$$

$$\therefore \ \ln \frac{[C][D]}{[A][B]} \geqslant \frac{5000}{1400} \quad \text{or} \quad 3·6$$

$$\therefore \ \frac{[C][D]}{[A][B]} \geqslant \text{antilog } 3·6 = 7000$$

Therefore, to reverse the reaction $[C] \times [D]$ must be at least $7000 \times [A] \times [B]$. Thus if $[A]$ and $[B]$ are about millimolar, $[C]$ and $[D]$ would have to be in the 0·1 M range, which is most unlikely.

Equilibria in redox reactions

The consideration of equilibria can also be extended to oxidations and reductions. An atom or molecule that loses electrons becomes oxidized, an atom or molecule gaining electrons is reduced. Such transfers of electrons are reversible processes and are subject to the laws of equilibrium. However, it is difficult to work in terms of electron concentrations and instead the values for electrode potential are used. A potential exists when two different concentrations of electrons are separated and the magnitude of the potential is expressed thus:

$$E = E^0 + \frac{RT}{nF} \ln \frac{[\text{oxidant}]}{[\text{reductant}]}$$

where F is the Faraday (96,000 coulombs); n is the number of electrons transferred in the reaction; and R is the gas constant (8·3 joules/degree/mole). E is an expression of the useful potential of the system and depends on the relative concentrations of oxidant and reductant. E^0 is the 'standard electrode potential'; if its value is high, the substance is a relatively powerful oxidizing agent; it will accept electrons from all components of lower E^0. By convention, the more powerful the reducing agent, the more negative is its E^0 value.

The energy made available during an electron transfer depends on the difference in the values of E^0 and also often on the pH of the reacting system, as many redox reactions involve the evolution or absorption of a hydrogen ion. It is convenient when dealing with biological systems to use the term $E^{0'}$, which replaces E^0 when the pH is not 0 (i.e. when protons are not at unit concentration) and which is defined for each pH. The values most frequently given are for pH 7. The relationship between the difference in $E^{0'}$ values of the reactants and the standard free energy change for the reaction is $\Delta G^{0'} = -nF\Delta E^{0'}$ (to obtain $\Delta G^{0'}$ in calories, $nF\Delta E^{0'}$ must be divided by 4·18 to convert joules to calories). As an illustration of this relationship, we may consider a reaction which is involved in the oxidation of many biological substrates, and in which pairs of hydrogens are transferred to the acceptor nicotinamide adenine dinucleotide (NAD) to give the reduced coenzyme $NADH_2$ which is finally reoxidized by molecular oxygen; much of the energy available to the cell is freed during this oxidation of $NADH_2$ (see p. 79). The $E^{0'}$ for $NADH_2$ is -0.32 V and for oxygen 0.82 V. The difference is 1.14 V. Therefore the free energy produced when 1 mole of $NADH_2$ is oxidized is calculated as

$$\Delta G^{0'} = -\frac{\Delta E^{0'}nF}{4\cdot8}\ \text{cal/mole}$$

$$= -\frac{1\cdot14 \times 2 \times 96{,}500}{4\cdot18}$$

$$= -52{,}636\ \text{cal/mole}$$

Rates of enzyme catalysed reactions

The simplest way to study the rates of enzymic reactions is to see what happens to the initial rates when the relative concentrations of substrate and enzyme are varied.

(A) If the substrate is present in large excess and the quantity of enzyme is varied there is a strict proportionality between the amount of substrate transformed in unit time and the concentration of the enzyme (Figure 1.13).

(B) The situation when the enzyme concentration is high and the substrate concentration is increased is shown in Figure 1.14. The greatest rate of increase occurs when the substrate concentration is low; as the concentration is increased a point is reached eventually when the reaction rate no

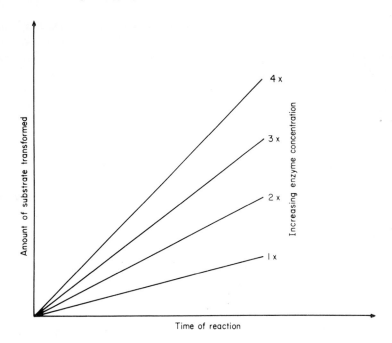

Figure 1.13. Effect of enzyme concentration on reaction rate

longer increases and the enzyme is said to be 'saturated'. Thus, at low concentrations of substrate, the reaction is a first order reaction as it is dependent on the concentration of only one reactant, the substrate. At higher concentrations the reaction is zero order, as it is independent of the concentration of the substrate. It was suggested in 1913 by Michaelis and Menten that behaviour of this kind would be explained if the substrate first combined with the enzyme before catalysis occurred. Figure 1.15 provides an illustration of this concept: here the enzyme is supposed to have four centres ('active sites') with which substrate can combine. When the substrate concentration is low only a few sites will be occupied; when the concentration is raised, all the sites are occupied and no further increase in rate is possible. There is now direct evidence that some enzymes and substrates do interact in this way. Most of the information comes from spectroscopic experiments, spectral changes in the absorption or fluorescence of the enzyme being apparent when the combination occurs.

The plot of initial velocity of enzyme reaction against substrate concentration (Figure 1.14) indicates that there is a particular substrate concentration which allows the enzyme to act at half its maximum rate, in other words, half the available sites are occupied at any moment (Figure 1.15). This concentration is known as the 'Michaelis constant' (the K_m) for the enzyme and is given in terms of molar concentration. A low K_m means the

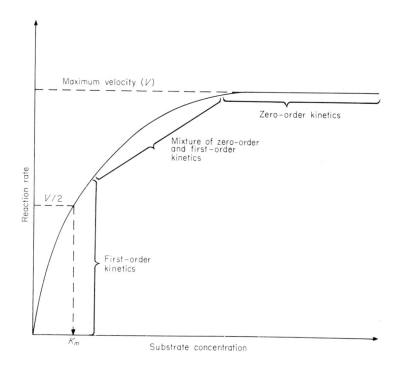

Figure 1.14. Effect of substrate concentration on reaction rate

enzyme will be working at maximum rate with low substrate concentrations and, under natural conditions, may always be working as fast as possible. An enzyme of this kind is not likely to be important in exerting control over metabolism by changes in its activity due to changes in substrate concentration. Enzymes with higher K_m values have a wider scope as controlling elements.

Another useful quantity characteristic of particular enzymes is their 'turnover number'. This is the number of molecules of substrate transformed/mole of enzyme/second. As an illustration of the magnitude of turnover numbers, catalase can utilize 4.2×10^4 moles of hydrogen peroxide/mole/second of enzyme.

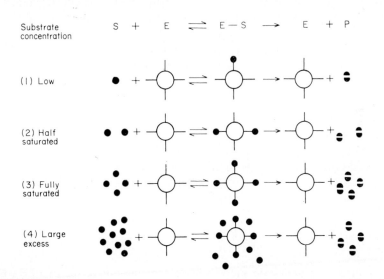

Figure 1.15. Diagrammatic demonstration of the effect of substrate concentration on saturation of active sites on enzyme surface. Note that for a unit time interval cases (3) and (4) give the same amount of P despite the large excess of substrate in case (4). From E. E. Conn and P. K. Stumpf, *Outlines of Biochemistry*, Wiley, New York, 1963

Inhibition of enzyme action

The Michaelis–Menten concept of enzyme substrate interaction can also be used in descriptions of the inhibition of enzymes. Enzymes are often very sensitive to the composition of their immediate environment as the description of the effects of temperature and pH have indicated. The substances now to be considered as inhibitors are those which because of their chemical nature alter the enzyme so that it can no longer work at its optimum rate. There are two main kinds of inhibitors. The first kind, the non-specific inhibitors, exert their influence in a general way, for example by denaturing the enzyme protein; the salts of heavy metals and trichloracetic acid are in this group. The second kind, the specific inhibitors, can be subdivided into two types, the non-competitive and the competitive inhibitors. To understand these two types of inhibition we must recall the concept of the active centre of the enzyme as the area on the surface of the enzyme molecule specially adapted for interaction with the substrate. The non-competitive inhibitor interferes in an irreversible way with the reaction between substrate and the active site. Such inhibitors may be considered to remove a proportion of the enzyme so that the effective quantity of active enzyme is decreased. The interference of the competitive inhibitors can be reversed by adding more of the substrate.

A striking example of competitive inhibition is the action of malonate on succinic dehydrogenase. Succinic dehydrogenase catalyses the following reaction:

$$HOOC \cdot CH_2 \cdot CH_2 \cdot COOH \longrightarrow HOOC \cdot CH{=}CH \cdot COOH$$
$$\text{succinic acid} \qquad\qquad\qquad \text{fumaric acid}$$

The malonic acid molecule has the same general shape as that of succinic acid but since it does not have adjacent CH_2 groups it cannot be dehydrogenated in the same way as succinate. We can represent the interaction of succinate (at a concentration S_1) and malonate (concentration S_2) with the dehydrogenase by the following equations, as the combination with both compounds is reversible.

$$E + S_1 \rightleftharpoons ES_1$$
$$E + S_2 \rightleftharpoons ES_2$$

In a mixture of malonate and succinate, the amounts of the two ES compounds will depend on the concentrations of, and the respective K_m values for the two acids. These K_m values measure how readily the two compounds interact with the enzyme; for example, if the affinity of the inhibitor for the enzyme is 10 times that of the normal substrate then at equal concentrations of substrate and inhibitor there will be 10 inhibitor molecules associated with the enzyme for every substrate molecule. However, if the concentration of the substrate is increased tenfold (so that there are 10 substrate molecules for every inhibitor molecule) then the substrate and inhibitor compete on equal terms and equal amounts of the two types of molecule will interact with the enzyme. Thus in competitive inhibition the K_m of the enzyme for its substrate will apparently increase as a higher concentration of the compound is required to allow the reaction to go at half maximal rate. On the other hand, non-competitive inhibitors produce no change in the K_m but decrease the maximum velocity of the reaction in proportion to the amount of enzyme which has been effectively removed. These differences can be illustrated conveniently by a plot of the reciprocal of the rate $(1/V)$ against that of the substrate concentration $(1/S)$ as shown in Figure 1.16.

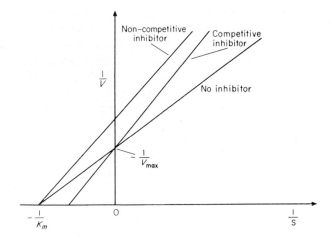

Figure 1.16. Kinetic patterns for enzyme action. V, initial velocity; S, the substrate concentration; K_m, the Michaelis constant; V_{max}, the maximum velocity

The classification of enzymes

The rapid discovery of new enzymes has demanded a rational classification of enzyme types and this has recently been standardized by an international convention. This body has defined 6 classes of enzymes.

(1) The oxidoreductases—all enzymes catalysing oxidations and reductions.

(2) The transferases—enzymes which transfer a chemical group from one compound to another. Many different types of chemical groupings are transferred by enzymes of this class.

(3) The hydrolases—enzymes which catalyse the hydrolytic cleavage of substrate.

(4) The lyases—enzymes which cleave substrates non-hydrolytically.

(5) The isomerases—enzymes bringing about intramolecular re-arrangements.

(6) The ligases—enzymes linking two molecules at the expense of the free energy released from the breakdown of another compound, frequently ATP.

Sources and use of energy for muscle contraction

We must now return to our starting point, namely the concept of the use of the free energy of ATP for the contraction of muscle. We have described the general properties of enzymes and proteins and we know that actomyosin is both a contractile protein and an enzyme that specifically hydrolyses ATP, making use of the energy of hydrolysis for muscle contraction. The reactions responsible for the onset of muscle contraction and the subsequent relaxation are not understood in detail at present. However, the model developed by R. E. Davies and outlined below accounts for many established observations and has predicted some more recent findings.

Figures 1.1 and 1.2 show that skeletal muscle consists of arrays of thick filaments interdigitating with arrays of thin filaments in the region of overlap. The thick filaments are composed of myosin, a part of which, H meromyosin, forms the cross bridges. The thin filaments are composed of actin. It is supposed that ATP is bound to a mobile polypeptide chain which forms part of the H meromyosin and that there is a fixed negative charge at the base of the chain. The repulsion between this charge and the one unneutralized negative charge on the terminal phosphate of the ATP tends to hold the polypeptide chain in a non-helical extended configuration (Figure 1.17).

When the sarcolemma is depolarized by an action potential and the depolarization is transmitted into the muscle by the T system (Figure 1.1), Ca^{2+} ions are released from storage sites in the sarcoplasmic reticulum. These ions form links between the ATP on the extended polypeptide chains and ADP bound to the adjacent actin filaments. Thus, the excess negative charge on the ATP is neutralized so that the coulombic repulsion within the H meromyosin polypeptide is abolished. The extended chain then contracts to form an α helix stabilized by hydrogen bonds and hydrophobic bonds. This process develops a tension which will overcome the external load if sufficient interactions of the same kind develop simultaneously. When the polypeptide chain is fully contracted, the ATP which it carries is brought into contact with an ATPase on the H meromyosin (Figure 1.17). By hydrolysing the terminal phosphate group of the ATP, this enzyme breaks the link between actin and myosin. When the ATP is reformed the coulombic repulsion will be reestablished so that the peptide chain will again extend towards the actin and reenter the cycle of contraction. The entire cyclic process of contraction will end when the free Ca^{2+} ions are pumped back into the vesicles of the sarcoplasmic reticulum at the expense of ATP when the stimulation of the muscle ceases.

This dependence of contraction and relaxation on ATP is a particular example of a universal requirement for this compound as a source of energy in living matter.

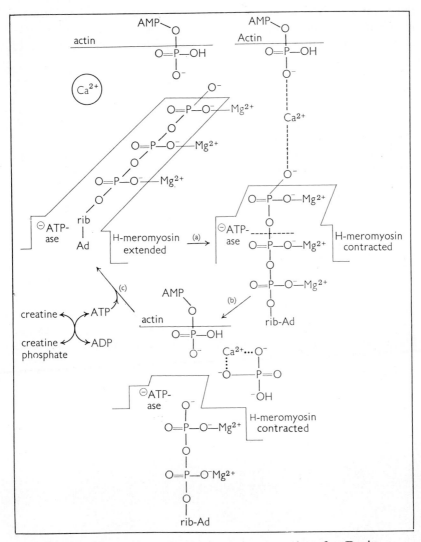

Figure 1.17. Molecular basis of muscle contraction after Davies

Energy supply by ATP

All living processes depend in some way on a continuing supply of energy. This is true not only for the performance of work by muscles but also for biosynthetic reactions and for the constant maintenance of the complex chemical structure of the cell. In purely chemical terms, living things have evolved in such a way that this requirement for energy is manifested as a continuing necessity to carry out phosphorylation reactions, i.e. the transfer of phosphoryl groups from one compound to

$$
\overset{\displaystyle O}{\underset{\displaystyle OH}{\overset{\|}{+P}\text{—OH}}}
$$

another. These phosphorylations are vital to the chemical economy of the cell as they ensure that certain key reactions proceed with high yields of their product, that is, with a favourable equilibrium position. It follows that cells must be able to generate an efficient phosphorylating reagent.

The organic chemist, faced with the problem of performing a synthesis involving the transfer of an acyl group, commonly uses the appropriate acid anhydride; thus for acetylations (transfer of an acetyl group) reagents like acetic anhydride or acetyl chloride may be used. Living cells have adopted the same chemical principle, as they use an anhydride of phosphoric acid for the essential phosphorylation reactions. The particular compound is ATP. We may consider it as having a chemical grouping serving as a chemical 'handle' (AMP) to which is attached the phosphoric anhydride (Figure 1.18). The essential function of this compound can be illustrated by considering the formation of the ester glucose-6-phosphate

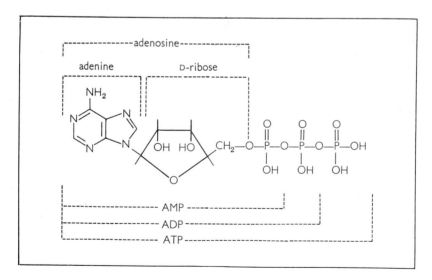

Figure 1.18. Adenosine mono-, di- and triphosphates

from the sugar glucose, a reaction which initiates most of the physiologically important transformations of glucose.

The equilibrium constant for the reaction glucose + phosphoric acid → glucose-6-phosphate + water is 0·0045 whereas that for the reaction glucose + ATP → glucose-6-phosphate + ADP is 5500. Thus it is clear that the yield of the sugar phosphate is greater when the donor of the phosphoryl group is ATP than when it is phosphoric acid. This property of ATP is sometimes described by saying that it has a relatively high 'phosphoryl group transfer potential', higher than that of phosphoric acid. Cells contain a great number of other phosphate compounds, some of which are more efficient phosphorylating reagents than ATP, some less. Because of the importance of phosphoryl transfers in living processes, biochemists have found it convenient to draw up a relative order of phosphorylating ability which enables them to make predictions about the direction of transfer of phosphoryl groups between various compounds. This can be done quantitatively by measuring the ease of transfer to a standard acceptor, water; and for arithmetical convenience, instead of using the equilibrium constants, the free energy changes for the transfer reactions to water ('free energy of hydrolysis', $\Delta G^{0'}$) are preferred. Table 1.2 illustrates the range of $\Delta G^{0'}$ values found.

Table 1.2. Free energies of hydrolysis of some biologically important phosphates

	$\Delta G^{0'}$ (kcal)
Phosphoenol pyruvic acid + H_2O → pyruvic acid + Pi	−13
1,3-Diphosphoglyceric acid + H_2O → 3-phosphoglyceric acid + Pi	−12
Creatine phosphate + H_2O → creatine + Pi	−11
ATP + H_2O → AMP + PP	−8
ATP + H_2O → ADP + Pi	−7
ADP + H_2O → AMP + Pi	−6
Glucose-1-phosphate + H_2O → glucose + Pi	−5
Fructose-1-phosphate + H_2O → fructose + Pi	−4
Glucose-6-phosphate + H_2O → glucose + Pi	−3
Glycerol-1-phosphate + H_2O → glycerol + Pi	−2

Pi inorganic phosphate; PP pyrophosphate
Values are based on those given by M. R. Atkinson and R. K. Morton in *Comparative Biochemistry*, Vol. II (Eds. H. S. Mason and M. Florkin), Academic Press, New York, 1960.

These values can be used readily to make predictions about phosphorylation reactions. For example we can predict that (a) 1,3-diphosphoglyceric acid will form ATP and (b) ATP will form glucose-6-phosphate, rather than the reverse, as the following equations show:

(a) 1,3-diphosphoglyceric acid + $H_2O \rightleftharpoons$ 3-phosphoglyceric acid
$$+ \text{ phosphate } \quad \Delta G^{0'} = -12$$
$$\text{ATP} + H_2O \rightleftharpoons \text{ADP} + \text{phosphate} \quad \Delta G^{0'} = -7$$
i.e. 1,3-diphosphoglyceric acid + ADP $\rightleftharpoons$ 3-phosphoglyceric acid + ATP
$$\Delta G^{0'} = -12 - (-7) = -5$$

(b) glucose-6-phosphate + $H_2O \rightleftharpoons$ glucose + phosphate $\quad \Delta G^{0'} = -3$
$$\text{ATP} + H_2O \rightleftharpoons \text{ADP} + \text{phosphate} \quad \Delta G^{0'} = -7$$
i.e. glucose + ATP $\rightleftharpoons$ glucose-6-phosphate + ADP
$$\Delta G^{0'} = -7 - (-3) = -4$$

Note that these calculations relate only to the equilibrium positions of reactions; they do not give any information about the rates of reaction or the molecular mechanism. In describing these and similar reactions it is customary to refer to ATP as a 'high energy phosphate' compound; this terminology, derived from the evaluation of the free energies of hydrolysis as described, will be used throughout this book.

The provision of ATP for muscle contraction

Although the discussion of the function of ATP makes it clear that a contracting muscle must have a continuous supply of this compound, the amount of ATP in muscle tissue is sufficient for about two seconds' work only. It follows that the supply of ATP must be continually replenished. To anticipate the final picture, this replenishment comes largely from the energy made available during the breakdown of glucose (see Chapters 3, 4 and 5), but as the demands on the energy supply in muscle are unpredictable and often very large, it follows that an immediately accessible store of energy must be available to buffer an immediate stress. The substance which acts as the buffer store in mammalian muscle is phosphocreatine (creatine phosphate). This compound is able to transfer a phosphate group to ADP in the presence of the enzyme creatine phosphokinase thus

Creatine phosphate is one of a class of compounds called guanadino phosphates. Creatine is formed from the amino acids glycine, arginine and

$$
\underset{\text{arginine}}{
\begin{array}{c}
NH_2 \\
| \\
C{=}NH \\
| \\
NH \\
| \\
(CH_2)_3 \\
| \\
NH_2{-}CH{-}COOH
\end{array}}
\; + \;
\underset{\text{glycine}}{
\begin{array}{c}
NH_2 \\
| \\
CH_2 \\
| \\
COOH
\end{array}}
\longrightarrow
\underset{\text{ornithine}}{
\begin{array}{c}
NH_2 \\
| \\
(CH_2)_3 \\
| \\
NH_2{-}CH{-}COOH
\end{array}}
\; + \;
\underset{\text{glycocyamine}}{
\begin{array}{c}
NH_2 \\
| \\
C{=}NH \\
| \\
NH \\
| \\
CH_2 \\
| \\
COOH
\end{array}}
$$

$$
\underset{\text{glycocyamine}}{
\begin{array}{c}
NH_2 \\
| \\
C{=}NH \\
| \\
NH \\
| \\
CH_2 \\
| \\
COOH
\end{array}}
\; + \;
\underset{\text{methionine}}{
\begin{array}{c}
S{-}CH_3 \\
| \\
(CH_2)_2 \\
| \\
NH_2{-}CH{-}COOH
\end{array}}
\longrightarrow
\underset{\text{creatine}}{
\begin{array}{c}
NH_2 \\
| \\
C{=}NH \\
| \\
N{-}CH_3 \\
| \\
CH_2 \\
| \\
COOH
\end{array}}
\; + \;
\underset{\text{homocysteine}}{
\begin{array}{c}
SH \\
| \\
(CH_2)_2 \\
| \\
NH_2{-}CH{-}COOH
\end{array}}
$$

methionine; the guanadino group is transferred from arginine to glycine producing ornithine and glycocyamine which receives a methyl group from methionine to form creatine.

As the free energy of hydrolysis of the phosphate group of creatine phosphate is about $-11,000$ cal/mole, this compound is a high energy phosphate. The phosphate group can therefore be transferred from creatine phosphate to ADP to form ATP. Phosphorylation of creatine is favoured at relatively high pH (the optimum being about 9) whereas the maximum rate of ATP formation from creatine phosphate is obtained at pH 6–7. The pH of the muscle itself varies and, when it is working hard, lactic acid accumulates producing a pH change which is favourable in ensuring that free creatine does not compete so well for the terminal high energy phosphate of ATP.

One other way that the muscle can obtain immediate energy is by utilizing the energy of the terminal phosphate bond of ADP. The free energy of hydrolysis of this bond (see Table 1.2) is about the same as that of the terminal bond of ATP, but ADP cannot serve as a direct energy supply for muscle. However, the enzyme myokinase (or adenylate kinase) catalyses the reaction 2ADP = AMP + ATP (where AMP is adenosine monophosphate). The pH optimum for this reaction is 7·5 and the equilibrium constant

$$
K = \frac{[\text{AMP}][\text{ATP}]}{[\text{ADP}]^2}
$$

is 0·3 without magnesium, 1·1 at a magnesium concentration of 5×10^{-4} M and 0·7 when the magnesium concentration is 10^{-3} M. Thus the concentration of magnesium ion can alter the balance between ATP and ADP. The K_m for ADP is about three times that for either ATP or AMP, ensuring that ADP will not be degraded to AMP, unless the need to provide ATP becomes overriding.

The utilization of the energy of the buffer system of phosphocreatine and the terminal phosphate of ADP provides sufficient energy for 8–10 seconds' work. (The actual time varies somewhat, since the breakdown of the high-energy phosphate is proportional to the work done by the muscle and not to the amount of contraction, i.e. a single contraction with a small load will not hydrolyse as much high-energy phosphate as a single contraction with a large load.) Subsequently energy is supplied by the breakdown of carbohydrate. If we attempt to build up a picture of the changes occurring in the energy reserves of a contracting muscle it is important to realize that steady state levels of many of the components are established, reflecting the balance between loss and replenishment and depending on the rate at which the muscle is working. Thus as soon as ATP is hydrolysed by actomyosin, it is immediately resynthesized from phosphocreatine which in turn is reformed by high-energy phosphate from ATP generated during the breakdown of glycogen to lactic acid. In summary, when a muscle contracts we observe (1) an unchanging ATP level; (2) a fall in the creatine phosphate level; (3) a rise in free creatine; (4) appearance of inorganic phosphate in an amount equal to that of the creatine phosphate disappearing; (5) a fall in the glycogen level; (6) an accumulation of lactic acid. When the muscle ceases contracting the following changes occur (1) the ATP level remains unchanged; (2) the creatine phosphate level increases; (3) free creatine disappears; (4) an equal amount of inorganic phosphate disappears; (5) glycogen levels fall even further; (6) more lactic acid accumulates. The extra glycogen breakdown and the equivalent increase in lactic acid is required to provide the ATP which is used to resynthesize creatine phosphate. Oxygen does not enter into any of these reactions and a muscle can continue to contract without oxygen until virtually all the glycogen is broken down to lactate. However, oxygen is needed when energy is to be produced from the degradation of lactic acid, as discussed in pp. 59–82.

This description of the changes occurring in the phosphates of contracting muscle provides no clear indication that ATP breakdown is the immediate source of energy. This has, however, been demonstrated with 1-fluoro-2,4-dinitrobenzene, a specific inhibitor of the enzyme creatine phosphokinase. As this compound combines with free amino groups in proteins (see p. 17) it seems that the active site of the enzyme must contain either lysine or an N-terminal residue of the constituent polypeptide chains. Muscle treated with fluorodinitrobenzene can contract about three times before exhaustion and during this time ATP is broken down while the store of phosphocreatine remains intact, that is, ATP itself is the immediate source of energy for contraction. The evidence that creatine phosphate is closely concerned in maintaining the supply of ATP in the muscle was obtained as long ago as 1930 when Lundsgard showed that contraction could occur for a short time in the presence of another inhibitor iodoacetate. During contraction creatine phosphate disappeared but no lactic acid was formed, contradicting the previous belief that the formation of lactate from glycogen was necessarily linked with contraction. Iodoacetate is a useful inhibitor reacting fairly specifically with SH groups present in enzymes.

$$R—SH + CH_2 \cdot I \cdot COOH \longrightarrow R—S—CH_2—COOH + HI$$

Thus the inhibitor will block enzymes with a free sulphydryl group in the active site and in muscle tissue the most sensitive enzyme is glyceraldehyde phosphate dehydrogenase, which is a key enzyme in the breakdown of glycogen to lactate. Thus the experiments of Lundsgard also made it clear that the continuous provision of ATP for contraction and recovery of muscle must come from utilizing the energy produced during the degradation of glycogen. This process is called 'glycolysis'.

CHAPTER 3

Glycolysis

Throughout the animal kingdom the main source of energy under anaerobic conditions is the breakdown of carbohydrate. In mammalian muscle, the chief store of energy is the polysaccharide glycogen; in addition, there is a small mobile store of glucose. Both of these compounds yield energy on being degraded to lactate. With glucose, the energy released is about 47 kcal/mole; each equivalent 6-carbon unit from glycogen releases 52 kcal. The series of reactions bringing about this degradation in living things is called glycolysis.

The structure of glycogen

Figure 1.19 illustrates the structure of glycogen; each circle represents a glucose equivalent. In each molecule, there is only one glucose unit with carbon 1 free to act as a reducing agent; this forms the 'reducing end' of the molecule. The presence of two different chemical links in the structure

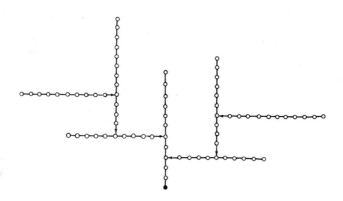

Figure 1.19. Diagram of glycogen molecule: ●, glucose residue carrying free reducing group; ○, glucose residues; ⬆, α1,6 bonds

is apparent from Figure 1.20; thus, linear arrays of glucose molecules joined by 1–4 linkages are connected at branching points formed by 1–6 linkages. The frequency of branching is such that the average number of glucose residues between the branches is about 5.

The degradation of glycogen to glucose-6-phosphate

The first step in the breakdown of glycogen involves the enzyme phosphorylase (see pp. 110, 281, 319), which catalyses the reaction

α-D-glucose-1-phosphate

Here phosphate behaves in the same way as water in a hydrolytic reaction; on the enzyme surface the terminal 1–4 bond of the glycogen molecule is broken, the phosphoric acid providing the phosphate attached to carbon 1 of the glucose-1-phosphate released. The equilibrium constant at pH 7 is 0·3. The reaction is readily reversible and its direction is determined by the ratio of the concentrations of glucose-1-phosphate to phosphoric acid. The concentration of glycogen is not involved since every terminal glucose removed leaves an exactly equivalent terminal residue.

The glucose-1-phosphate is isomerized to glucose-6-phosphate by the enzyme phosphoglucomutase, which is present in muscle in high concentration (about 2% of the water soluble protein). Phosphoglucomutase requires glucose-1,6-diphosphate as a cofactor:

$+ H_2PO_3—enz \xrightleftharpoons{Mg^{2+}}$

glucose-1-phosphate · phosphoenzyme · glucose-1,6-diphosphate · $+ enz$

$+ enz \xrightleftharpoons{Mg^{2+}}$ · glucose-6-phosphate · $+ H_2PO_3—enz$

Sum: · $\xrightleftharpoons{Mg^{2+}}$ · glucose-1-phosphate · glucose-6-phosphate

The enzyme carries a transferable phosphate attached to a serine residue. This phosphate can be donated to either glucose-1- or glucose-6-phosphate to produce glucose-1,6-diphosphate. At equilibrium at pH 7, there is about 19 times as much glucose-6-phosphate as glucose-1-phosphate (see p. 26).

Interrelations between glucose and glucose-6-phosphate

Although glucose is the transportable form of carbohydrate it is important to realize that glucose itself cannot take part in any important metabolic conversion in the cell. It must be phosphorylated before it can enter into pathways of synthesis or degradation. For each mole of glucose phosphorylated, one mole of ATP is required to provide the phosphate for attachment to carbon 6. The energy relationship may be illustrated as follows. The hydrolysis of phosphate from glucose-6-phosphate yields 3 kcal ($\Delta G^{0'} = -3$ kcal/mole). The free energy of hydrolysis of the terminal phosphate of ATP is about -7 kcal/mole. Therefore, the phosphorylation of glucose by ATP is strongly exergonic, to the extent of about -4 kcal/mole; consequently, the equilibrium constant is large ($K = 10^3$).

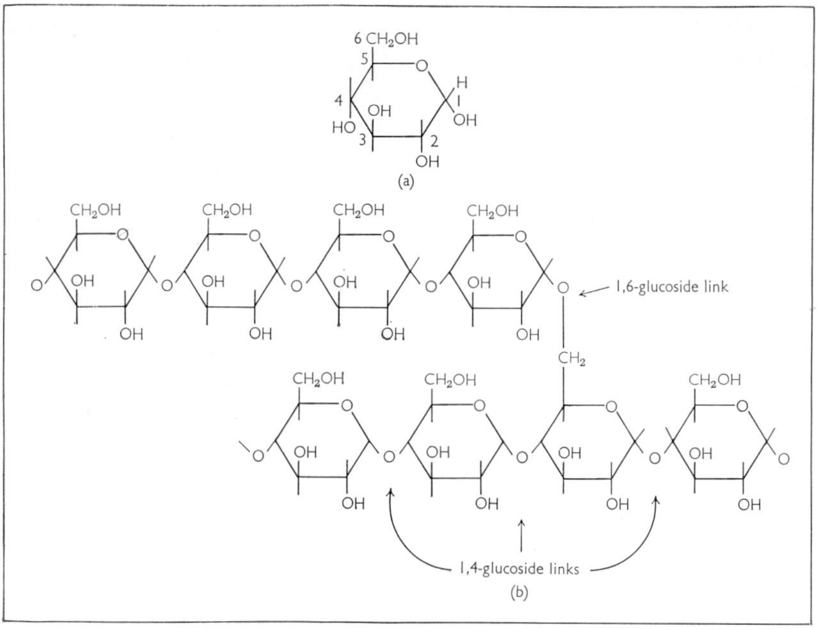

Figure 1.20. Glucosidic links in glycogen (b). The glucose molecule is represented by (a). The numbers refer to the C atoms; all C valencies with unspecified groups are occupied with H

Thus, the animal must 'pay' 4 kcal in terms of energy loss for each mole of glucose-6-phosphate formed from glucose; when glucose-6-phosphate is hydrolysed, with an energy loss of 3 kcal/mole, it gains, on the other hand, a substance which can pass through cell membranes that are impermeable to glucose-6-phosphate.

The formation of glucose-6-phosphate from glucose and ATP is catalysed by the enzyme hexokinase:

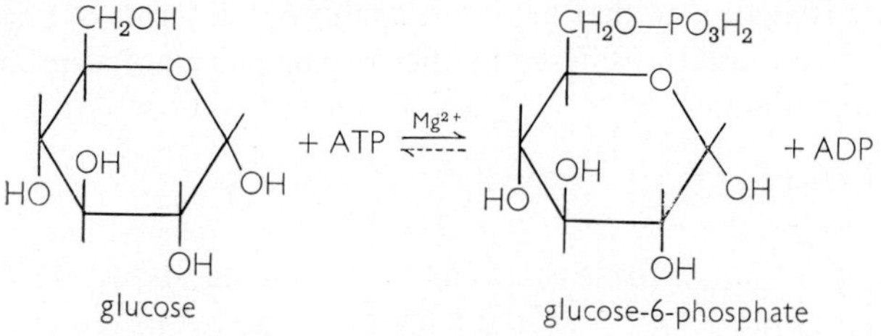

'hex' refers to the six carbon sugars suitable as substrates and 'kinase' refers to the process of transfer of phosphate from ATP. In the hexokinase reaction, a phosphoryl group is transferred from ATP to glucose.

In common with many other phosphokinases, hexokinase requires magnesium. It is a relatively unspecific enzyme, phosphorylating many hexose sugars other than glucose; it has a very low K_m (37 μM) for glucose; and is inhibited by the product of its own reaction, glucose-6-phosphate. There is another enzyme, glucokinase (present in the liver), catalysing the same reaction; but this is specific for glucose, has a much higher K_m (15 mM) and is not influenced by glucose-6-phosphate. The concentration of glucose in the blood is about 5 mM and, although the concentration in the cell is somewhat variable, it is likely that the hexokinase is always saturated with glucose and is therefore working at its maximum rate. The characteristic properties of glucokinase are such, however, that it would seem to be ideally suited for removing any excess glucose that may be formed by converting it to glucose-6-phosphate (see p. 301).

The conversion of glucose to triose phosphate

Glucose-6-phosphate formed either from glycogen or, with the expenditure of a molecule of ATP, from glucose, is now converted into other sugar phosphates. The next step is isomerization to fructose-6-phosphate by the enzyme phosphohexoisomerase (or 'isomerase'). No cofactor is required and the equilibrium constant is about 0·5, so that no great energy changes are involved.

glucose-6-phosphate   fructose-6-phosphate

The succeeding conversion of fructose-6-phosphate to fructose-1,6-diphosphate is again one that has to be 'paid for' in terms of expenditure of ATP. This reaction is catalysed by the enzyme phosphofructokinase and requires magnesium.

fructose-6-phosphate   fructose-1,6-diphosphate

Again, as in the formation of glucose-6-phosphate, the high energy of the ATP is used to phosphorylate the sugar hydroxyl on carbon 1; the ester formed has a low energy of hydrolysis. Thus the reaction is accompanied by a liberation of free energy ($\Delta G^{0'} = -4 \cdot 2$ kcal/mole) and is not readily reversible. The enzyme is influenced by a number of important metabolites and is a key enzyme in controlling the rate of glycolysis; thus, it is inhibited by excess ATP and this inhibition is overcome by ADP, AMP, phosphate and fructose-1,6-diphosphate (see Section 8).

The diphosphorylated sugar is now cut in two by the enzyme aldolase. This reaction produces two triose phosphates, glyceraldehyde-3-phosphate and dihydroxyacetone phosphate; note that the reactive form of the hexose diphosphate is represented as a straight chain in the equation.

The position of equilibrium favours the formation of the hexose diphosphate—and the enzyme is called 'aldolase' because in forming fructose-1,6-diphosphate it catalyses an aldol condensation.

The mixture of triose phosphates that accumulates is equilibrated by an enzyme triosephosphate isomerase, the reaction being similar to that carried out by the phosphohexose isomerase.

The enzyme is very active and although there is 22 times as much of the ketose as the aldose present at equilibrium, the rate of equilibration is so fast that even when glyceraldehyde phosphate is removed by the subsequent reaction at a very high rate, the two trioses remain virtually in equilibrium.

The oxidation of triose phosphate and the reduction of NAD

All the reactions considered so far have been either rearrangements of molecules or phosphorylations, but the next step involves an oxidoreduction and the coenzyme nicotinamide adenine dinucleotide (NAD). (It is also called 'Coenzyme I' or diphosphopyridine nucleotide—DPN—but the modern designation is NAD, as shown by the formula, Figure 1.21.)

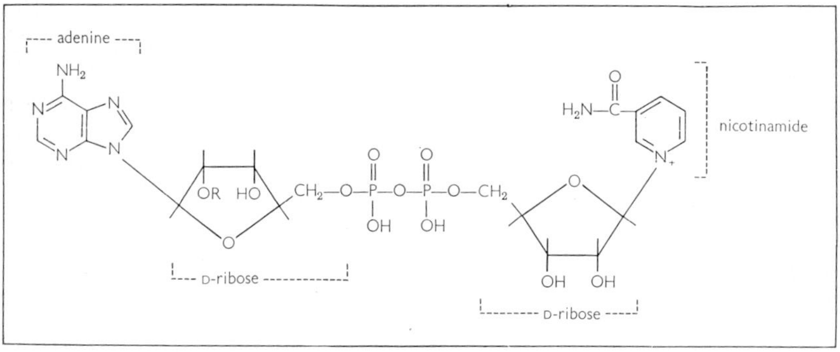

Figure 1.21. The nicotinamide coenzymes (oxidized form). NAD, R = H; NADP, R = PO_3H_2. Nicotinamide is a derivative of the vitamin niacin (nicotinic acid)

This dependence of an enzyme reaction on the availability of another reactant called a coenzyme is common in living things. The coenzyme may be thought of as a chemical 'handle' for carrying a reactive chemical group from one molecule to another in metabolic transformations. NAD is a 'chemical handle' for the transport of 'reducing power' around the cell for utilization at another point. The movement may be only from one part of the enzyme molecule to another part close at hand, or it may be out of one cell organelle, right across the cell and into another cell organelle. The reducing power is carried in a form equivalent to a pair of hydrogens.

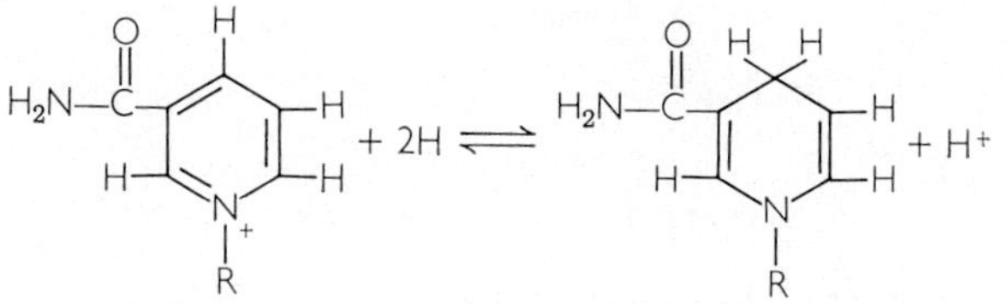

NAD (oxidized) NADH$_2$ (reduced)
(NAD$^+$) (NADH + H$^+$)

The $E^{0'}$ (see p. 28) of the NADH$_2$/NAD couple is -0.32 V and, there-fore, the hydrogens of the substrate must be at a negative potential of at least this magnitude to permit effective transfer to the coenzyme. With many substrates, this condition is met, but there are some important compounds like succinate, in which the hydrogens do not have a sufficiently negative potential and which transfer to another coenzyme called flavin adenine dinucleotide (FAD; $E^{0'}$ -0.22 V) (see Figure 1.29).

The oxidation of glyceraldehyde-3-phosphate, catalysed by glycer-aldehyde phosphate dehydrogenase ('triosephosphate dehydrogenase') results in the reduction of NAD.

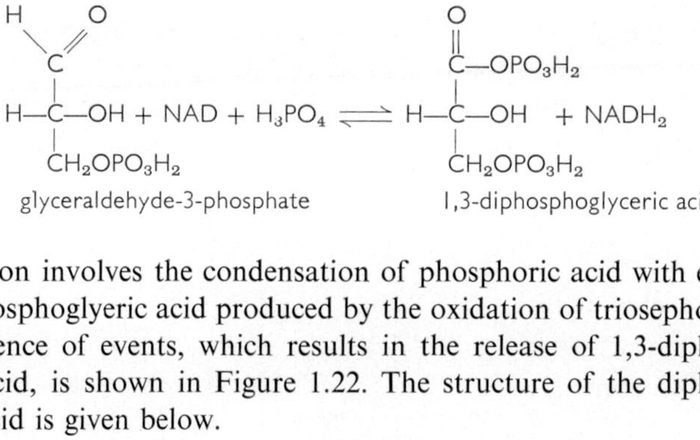

glyceraldehyde-3-phosphate 1,3-diphosphoglyceric acid

The reaction involves the condensation of phosphoric acid with enzyme-bound phosphoglyeric acid produced by the oxidation of triosephosphate. This sequence of events, which results in the release of 1,3-diphospho-glyceric acid, is shown in Figure 1.22. The structure of the diphospho-glyceric acid is given below.

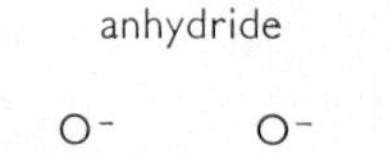

anhydride

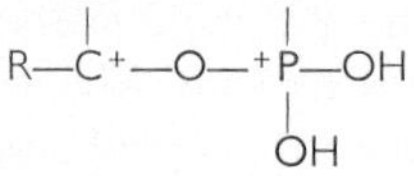

acyl phosphate (mixed anhydride)

3+

$$PO_3H_2-OCH_2-\overset{\overset{\displaystyle OH}{|}}{\underset{\underset{\displaystyle H}{|}}{C}}-\overset{\overset{\displaystyle O^-}{|}}{C}{}^+-O-{}^+\overset{\overset{\displaystyle O^-}{|}}{\underset{\underset{\displaystyle OH}{|}}{P}}-OH$$

1,3-diphosphoglyceric acid (mixed anhydride)

It is an acid anhydride like most of the so-called high-energy compounds; the proximity of the positive charges on the carbon and phosphorus atoms leads to a pronounced thermodynamic instability, which manifests itself in a large heat of hydrolysis (see Table 1.2). Thus the formation of this compound represents a conservation of some of the energy made available during the oxidation of the triose, in the form of a high-energy phosphate compound.

Phosphoglyceraldehyde dehydrogenase is somewhat unusual in that the reduced coenzyme ($NADH_2$) must be replaced by a molecule of NAD before the phosphorylation step can occur (see Figure 1.22); this figure also illustrates the essential role of a sulphydryl group in the enzyme during catalysis. The sulphydryl group is the point of action of iodoacetate (see p. 41).

The utilization of 1,3-diphosphoglyceric acid

Thus, phosphoglyceraldehyde dehydrogenase produces two compounds; $NADH_2$, whose utilization is considered later (see p. 53 and Chapter 4); and 1,3-diphosphoglyceric acid, which is dephosphorylated in the next step of the glycolytic sequence, catalysed by phosphoglyceric acid kinase.

$$\underset{\substack{\text{1,3-diphosphoglyceric} \\ \text{acid}}}{\overset{\displaystyle \overset{O}{\|} \atop \displaystyle C-OPO_3H_2 \atop \displaystyle \underset{|}{H-C-OH} \atop \displaystyle CH_2OPO_3H_2}{}} + ADP \overset{Mg^{2+}}{\underset{}{\rightleftharpoons}} \underset{\substack{\text{3-phosphoglyceric} \\ \text{acid}}}{\overset{\displaystyle HO \diagdown \quad O \atop \displaystyle C \diagup\!\!\!\!\diagup \atop \displaystyle \underset{|}{H-C-OH} \atop \displaystyle CH_2OPO_3H_2}{}} + ATP$$

The free energy change in this reaction is about -4 kcal/mole, i.e. the equilibrium is far to the right. As the $\Delta G^{0\prime}$ for the hydrolysis of the terminal phosphate of ATP is about -7 kcal/mole, the $\Delta G^{0\prime}$ for the hydrolysis of the acyl phosphate group of 1,3-diphosphoglyceric acid is $(-7 + -4.7)$ kcal/mole or about -12 kcal/mole. Thus the organism 'pays the price' of losing about one third of the available energy in the diphosphoglyceric acid for the privilege of ensuring that ADP is phosphorylated quantitatively to ATP, a price similar to that 'paid' for ensuring that glucose was phosphorylated quantitatively to glucose-6-phosphate.

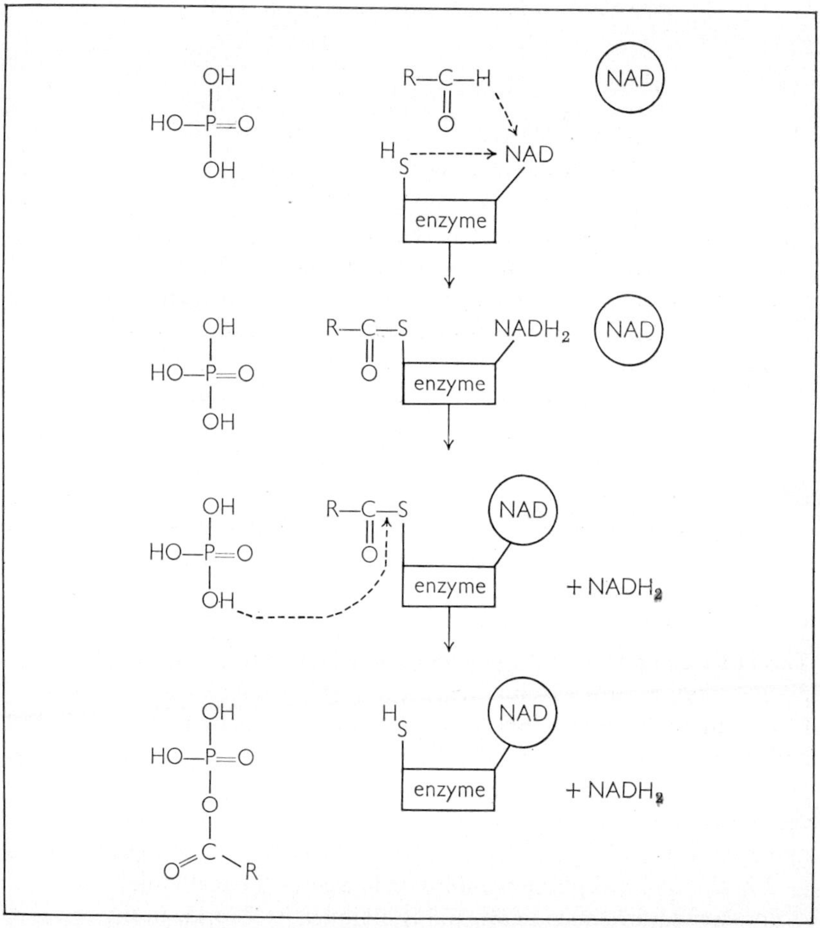

Figure 1.22. Mechanism of action of glyceraldehyde-3-phosphate dehydrogenase

Reactions yielding phosphorylated metabolites able to act as the donor of a phosphoryl group for the synthesis of a nucleoside triphosphate, are called 'substrate level' phosphorylations, to distinguish them from the phosphorylations linked to the respiratory chain (see p. 80).

The formation and utilization of phosphoenolpyruvic acid

3-Phosphoglyceric acid produced by phosphoglyceric kinase is isomerized to 2-phosphoglyceric acid by the enzyme phosphoglyceromutase.

$$
\begin{array}{ccc}
\underset{\text{3-phosphoglyceric acid}}{
\begin{array}{l}
\text{HO}\diagdown \quad \diagup\!\!\diagup\text{O} \\
\qquad \text{C} \\
\qquad | \\
\text{H}-\text{C}-\text{OH} \\
\qquad | \\
\text{CH}_2\text{OPO}_3\text{H}_2
\end{array}}
&
\overset{\text{Mg}^{2+}}{\rightleftharpoons}
&
\underset{\substack{\text{2-phosphoglyceric}\\\text{acid}}}{
\begin{array}{l}
\text{HO}\diagdown \quad \diagup\!\!\diagup\text{O} \\
\qquad \text{C} \\
\qquad | \\
\text{H}-\text{C}-\text{OPO}_3\text{H}_2 \\
\qquad | \\
\text{CH}_2\text{OH}
\end{array}}
\end{array}
$$

Since the equilibrium constant is about 0·17, no great energy change is involved; the reaction is an almost precise analogy to the formation of glucose-6-phosphate from glucose-1-phosphate and, as might be predicted from this analogy, requires 2,3-diphosphoglyceric acid as a cofactor.

The next enzyme in the series is called enolase; this removes water from 2-phosphoglyceric acid to give phosphoenolpyruvic acid.

$$
\begin{array}{ccc}
\underset{\substack{\text{2-phosphoglyceric}\\\text{acid}}}{
\begin{array}{l}
\text{HO}\diagdown \quad \diagup\!\!\diagup\text{O} \\
\qquad \text{C} \\
\qquad | \\
\text{H}-\text{C}-\text{OPO}_3\text{H}_2 \\
\qquad | \\
\text{CH}_2\text{OH}
\end{array}}
&
\overset{\text{Mg}^{2+}}{\rightleftharpoons}
&
\underset{\substack{\text{phosphoenolpyruvic}\\\text{acid}}}{
\begin{array}{l}
\text{HO}\diagdown \quad \diagup\!\!\diagup\text{O} \\
\qquad \text{C} \\
\qquad | \\
\qquad \text{C}-\text{OPO}_3\text{H}_2 + \text{H}_2\text{O} \\
\qquad \| \\
\qquad \text{CH}_2
\end{array}}
\end{array}
$$

This latter compound is the phosphorylated derivative of the enol form of pyruvic acid, a form which is relatively unstable compared with the keto form. Although the equilibrium constant for the enolase reaction is only 3 and the reaction is freely reversible, involving little energy change, the rearrangement of the molecule has redistributed the internal energy so that the phosphate may now be considered as a high-energy group. This is apparent from the different heats of hydrolysis of 2-phosphoglyceric acid (-3 kcal/mole) and phosphoenolpyruvic acid (-13 kcal/mole).

Enolase requires magnesium and is inhibited by fluoride in the presence of inorganic phosphate due to the removal of magnesium as a complex magnesium fluorophosphate.

The final step in the glycolytic pathway is one in which the high-energy phosphate of phosphoenolpyruvic acid is used to form ATP and which requires the enzyme pyruvic kinase.

$$
\begin{array}{ccc}
\underset{\substack{\text{phosphoenolpyruvic}\\\text{acid}}}{
\begin{array}{l}
\text{HO}\diagdown \quad \diagup\!\!\diagup\text{O} \\
\qquad \text{C} \\
\qquad | \\
\qquad \text{C}-\text{O}-\text{PO}_3\text{H}_2 + \text{ADP} \\
\qquad \| \\
\qquad \text{CH}_2
\end{array}}
&
\overset{\text{Mg}^{2+},\text{K}^+}{\underset{\text{- - - - -}}{\rightleftharpoons}}
&
\underset{\substack{\text{pyruvic}\\\text{acid}}}{
\begin{array}{l}
\text{HO}\diagdown \quad \diagup\!\!\diagup\text{O} \\
\qquad \text{C} \\
\qquad | \\
\qquad \text{C}=\text{O} + \text{ATP} \\
\qquad | \\
\qquad \text{CH}_3
\end{array}}
\end{array}
$$

The equilibrium constant of $2 \cdot 6 \times 10^4$ indicates that phosphopyruvate and ADP are converted almost quantitatively to pyruvate and ATP. Again, the penalty of a loss of about 6 kcal/mole of the available energy is paid to ensure that the yield of ATP is high. This reaction concludes the glycolytic sequence proper, but the problem of the regeneration of NAD from the $NADH_2$ formed by the action of phosphoglyceraldehyde dehydrogenase must still be considered.

The regeneration of NAD and the formation of lactic acid

The necessity for regenerating NAD efficiently if glycolysis is to continue is obvious since the concentration of the coenzyme is strictly limited, being about 1 mM in the tissue water. The muscle of the 70 kg man, which amounts to some 30 kg of wet tissue, has about 21 kg of water (70% of the wet weight). This water will contain 21 m moles of nicotinamide nucleotide, which will have a total 'hydrogen capacity' equivalent to that released from 10·5 m moles of glycolysed glucose. Some 50 kcals are obtained from each mole of glucose degraded to pyruvate, i.e. 50 cal/m mole. Therefore, something like 532 calories can be obtained from the amount of glucose required to saturate all the NAD of the muscle with hydrogen. If the man is undertaking moderate exercise (for example, running), he may be using about 10 kcal/min, or 167 cal/sec, and, therefore, without reoxidation, his NAD store will suffice for only about 3 sec of exercise. As most 70 kg men can exercise for considerably longer than 3 sec it follows that the hydrogen must be removed continuously from $NADH_2$ to allow glycolytic energy production to continue. One solution to this problem is to oxidize the hydrogen with atmospheric oxygen to give water—the process of respiration. The second solution, however, permits an anaerobic regeneration of NAD by the enzyme lactic dehydrogenase.

Lactic dehydrogenase transfers the hydrogens of $NADH_2$ to pyruvic acid to form lactic acid and NAD.

The equilibrium is in favour of lactate production ($\Delta G^{0'} = -6$ kcal/mole) and therefore the enzyme is efficient in regenerating NAD. The cyclic nature of the utilization of the coenzyme during the conversion of glucose to lactic acid, as shown in Figure 1.23, makes it apparent that the availability of NAD may limit the rate of the complete pathway.

Thus, the result of glycolysis is the production of two molecules of lactic acid for every glucose unit degraded (see Figure 1.23), the conserva-

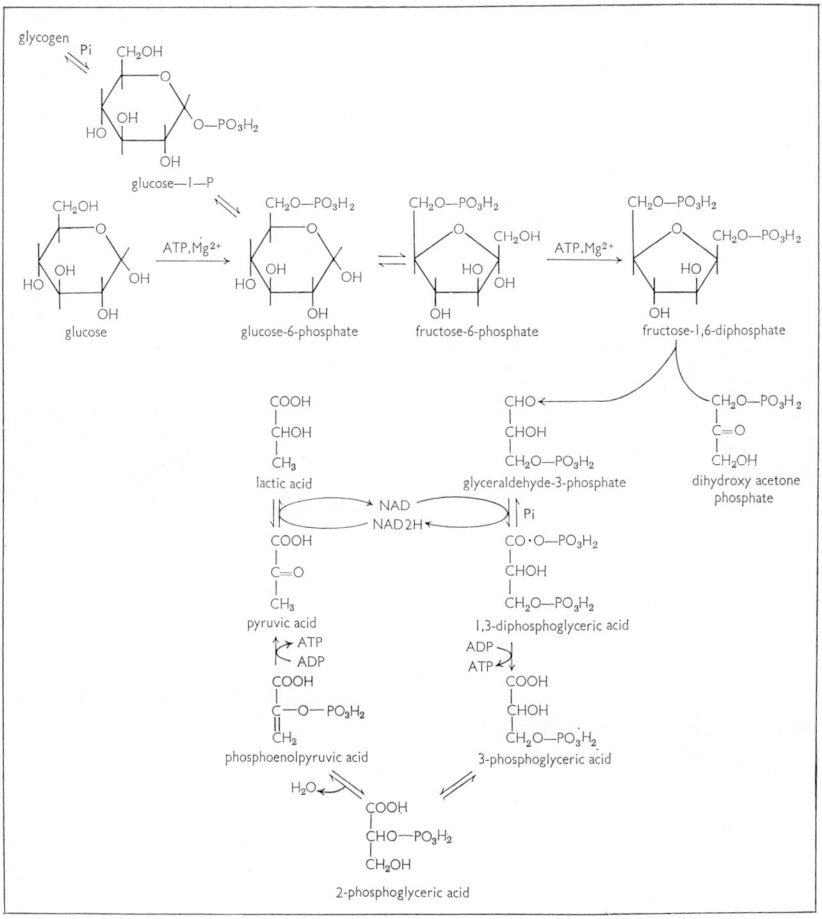

Figure 1.23. The glycolytic pathway

tion as ATP of some of the energy made available, and dissipation of some of the energy as heat. Moreover, the availability of ADP will limit the rate of the glycolytic process, since neither 1,3-diphosphoglyceric acid nor phosphoenolpyruvate can be broken down unless ADP is available to accept the high-energy phosphates. Thus there is a strict 'coupling' of the utilization of ATP with its production in the glycolytic path (see Section 8).

The energy balance of glycolysis

The energy balance from the glycolysis of either glycogen or glucose can be expressed in terms of ATP molecules used or gained, or in terms of the total energy lost as heat or conserved as chemical energy. The values for the balance with ATP are as follows:

Glycolysis from glycogen
(per 6 carbon unit)

ATP used	ATP gained
1 to phosphorylate fructose-6-P	2 from triose phosphate
	2 from phosphopyruvate

Net gain   3 ATP per glucose unit

Glycolysis from glucose

ATP used	ATP gained
1 to phosphorylate glucose	2 from triose phosphate
to glucose-6-phosphate	2 from phosphopyruvate
1 to phosphorylate fructose-6-P	

Net gain   2 ATP per glucose unit

Thus either two or three ATP molecules are synthesized as a net gain, depending on the substrate used.

The energy balance sheet is as follows (Table 1.3).

Table 1.3. Energy balance sheet from glycogen to lactate

	cal
Fed into the system ΔG for formation of lactic acid (56,700 cal) + energy of terminal phosphate of one ATP (11,300 cal). Total available, 68,000 cal.	
Expenditure at phosphorylation of fructose-6-phosphate	−4,300
Expenditure in formation of ATP from 1,3-diphosphoglyceric acid	−9,500
Expenditure in formation of ATP from phosphopyruvate	−10,000
Expenditure in formation of lactate from pyruvate	−12,000
Energy change in all other steps	+13,000
Total known expenditure	−22,800
Energy saved as ATP (4 × 11·3)	45,200 approx

ΔG values are for 0·2 atm O_2, 0·05 atm CO_2, pH 7 and 10 mM concentration of all reactants other than glycogen. 'Expenditure' refers to energy loss as heat. Data from Burton, K., and Krebs, H. A., *Biochem. J.*, 1958.

Assuming that the 'value' of each ATP molecule is 11·3 kcal (at the concentrations of reactants defined in Table 1.3) and that the net gain of ATP is 3 per mole of glucose unit degraded, the efficiency of the process of energy conservation from anaerobic glycolysis is $33·9/56·7 = 60\%$.

Glycolytic enzymes in muscular dystrophy

One disease of muscle in which there is a considerable disturbance of the enzymes of the glycolytic pathway, coupled with a breakdown of the tissue, is muscular dystrophy. This is a progressive wasting disease and, as shown in Table 1.4, there is an appreciable loss of enzymes from the muscle, sufficient to cause a marked drop in the glycolytic rate of the tissue.

Table 1.4. Enzyme content of muscle

	Phosphorylase	Phospho- glucomutase	Aldolase	Total rate of glycolysis
Normal	23	11	19	2.9
Dystrophic	8·6	4·4	6·3	0·8

The values for the enzyme activity are expressed as millimoles of glucose equivalents transformed/g of protein/h.

Whether this loss precedes muscular degeneration, or vice versa, is not known but there is an accompanying rise in the amounts of the enzyme in the blood plasma. Aldolase, in particular, is an enzyme which apparently passes through cell membranes comparatively easily and the rise of aldolase activity in the plasma may be used as a method of diagnosis of the disease.

Universality of the glycolytic pathway in living matter

Although the discussion of the process of glycolysis has centred around its role in muscular tissue, the same pattern of changes is exhibited by an enormous variety of cells—animal, plant and microbial. Many cells capable of extensive glycolysis, however, while preserving the same general pattern, regenerate NAD by reducing a compound other than pyruvate; noteworthy examples are the production of ethanol from acetaldehyde by yeasts and of α-glycerophosphate from dihydroxyacetone phosphate in the flight muscle of some insects.

Disposal of lactic acid

The process of glycolysis described in this chapter results in an accumulation of lactic acid and a loss of glycogen and glucose. Since lactic acid is not excreted in the urine and does not accumulate continuously in the blood during exercise, there must be processes disposing of some of the lactate formed. (There is, of course, some rise in blood lactate after exercise, from a resting level of about 19 mg/100 ml of blood to about 80 mg/ 100 ml.) In the intact animal much of the muscle lactate passes into the blood and thence to the liver where it is resynthesized to glucose and glycogen. The remaining lactate is oxidized to carbon dioxide and water (see Chapter 4).

Organs differ greatly in their ability to oxidize lactate. The venous blood of skeletal muscle under all conditions contains more lactate than the arterial blood; thus, skeletal muscle always makes a net contribution to blood lactate. By contrast, the venous blood of the heart contains less lactate than the arterial blood; thus the heart is a net consumer of lactate. The reason for this difference can be understood in terms of the different functions of the two sets of muscles. Skeletal muscle undertakes only intermittent activity, but for a time this activity may be beyond the capacity of the blood stream to supply oxygen and substrate. Therefore, provision must be made for a large-scale production of energy from anaerobic pathways. On the other hand, the heart works continuously and must rely on aerobic mechanisms to make the most efficient use of the energy in the oxidizable substrates. This difference in function is also reflected in different properties of the lactic dehydrogenases found in the two tissues. That of the heart muscle is inhibited as the concentration of pyruvate rises above about 1 mM and further lactate formation is prevented so that this tissue is not a net exporter of lactate. The enzyme of skeletal muscle is almost unaffected by physiological changes of pyruvate concentration and consequently this tissue always exports lactate to the blood (see p. 310).

Energy yields from carbohydrate in respiration and glycolysis

For each mole of hexose glycolysed to lactic acid, only about 45 to 50 kcal become available to the cell, whereas the total free energy change during the complete oxidation of a mole of glucose to carbon dioxide and water is about 700 kcal. To obtain this same amount of energy anaerobically, the amount of substrate decomposed would need to be about 15 times greater. Only in exceptional circumstances can tissues afford to consume carbohydrate in this way and the great majority of cells possessing both aerobic and anaerobic mechanisms for energy transformation rely on respiration rather than glycolysis for the production of most of their ATP.

However, under special conditions, anaerobic reactions are of advantage even to those cells of animal tissues which are generally dependent on respiration. The substrate for glycolysis can be stored in the tissues in the

3*

form of glycogen, up to several per cent of the wet weight. The additional substrate required for respiration, molecular oxygen, can be stored only in very limited quantities—bound to myoglobin—and respiration is dependent therefore on a continuous supply of oxygen from the circulating blood. Hence, when there is a need for the rapid provision of energy (as, for example, in skeletal or cardiac muscle making an acute effort) this energy can be supplied more effectively for short periods by glycolysis. This may be illustrated by the following calculations, for the energy supply available to a muscle suddenly cut off from the circulation.

Muscle may contain over 1% of available carbohydrate, most of it as glycogen. However, if the circulation ceases, the increasing acidity due to lactic accumulation will prevent the complete glycolysis of this carbohydrate. Assuming that for each 1 g wet weight of muscle, 5 mg of glycogen are broken down (i.e. about half the total amount present) then $\frac{5000}{180}$ μmoles of glucose units (mol. wt. 180) are degraded, i.e. 27·8 μmoles. The free energy yield for the fermentation of one glucose unit of glycogen to lactate is 52 kcal/mole, or 0·052 cal/μmole. Therefore, for the 27·8 μmole degraded by 1 g of tissue the total yield of energy would be about 1·4 cal.

Under aerobic conditions (but with no influx of oxygen from the blood) the oxidation would be limited by the total oxygen stored in the tissue. For each gram of muscle there will be:

   5 μl of dissolved oxygen
   40 μl of oxygen combined with myoglobin (this corresponds to 10^{-4} g of myoglobin iron per g muscle)
   10 μl of oxygen combined with haemoglobin (this assumes that 5% of the tissue consists of arterial blood)

Thus the total oxygen available from all sources is 55 μl/g tissue, i.e. 2·45 μmoles. For each mole of oxygen used when glucose is the substrate, there is a yield of 114·3 kcals or 0·1143 per μmole of oxygen. Therefore, the 2·45 μmoles of oxygen available will be sufficient to release only 0·28 cal from glucose oxidation, or about one-fifth of that available from the anaerobic source.

CHAPTER 4

The oxidation of lactic acid by muscle tissue; the citric acid cycle

The complete degradation of glucose to carbon dioxide involves the oxidative disposal of the lactic acid (or pyruvate) formed during glycolysis. As heart muscle is an efficient oxidizer of lactic acid the process will be considered in relation to this organ, whose structure is shown in Figure 1.24. The most striking difference between this tissue and skeletal muscle (Figure 1.1) is that the latter is composed very largely of the contractile proteins and relatively few mitochondria, whereas in the heart there are rows of rounded mitochondrial structures between the muscle fibres. These mitochondria are responsible for the large oxygen uptake of the heart and its utilization of lactate.

Besides the enzymes responsible for catalysing the reaction with oxygen, mitochondria contain the integrated complex of enzymes responsible for the process called the citric acid cycle which achieves the final oxidative breakdown of lactate and pyruvate (the products of glycolysis) and of other components (fatty acids and amino acids) capable of being converted to intermediates of this cycle. The mitochondrion is thus a striking example of the segregation of a series of complex enzyme sequences in a special cell compartment or organelle. Sometimes the continuation of a metabolic pathway may require the passage of intermediates from one cell compartment to another, as, for example, the movement of the end products of glycolysis (which occurs outside the mitochondrion) into the mitochondria for oxidative degradation.

The oxidation of lactate to pyruvate

The first step in the disposal of lactate is a reversal of the last glycolytic reaction catalysed by lactic dehydrogenase. This enzyme is found mainly outside the intracellular organelles in what is called the 'soluble phase' of the cell. What this means exactly in the muscle cell is far from clear—it is

59

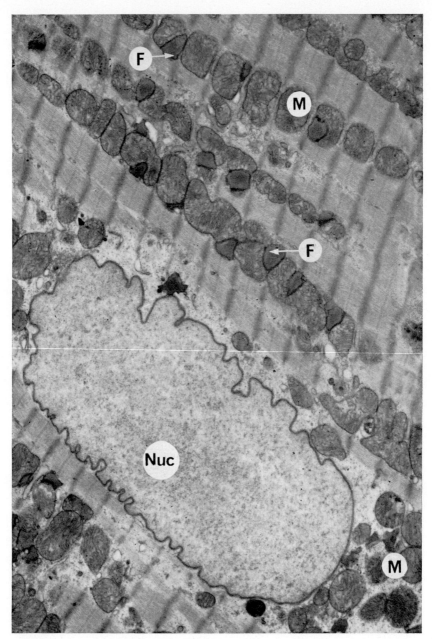

Figure 1.24. An electron micrograph of heart muscle. The abundance of mitochondria (M) and their dense arrays of cristae reflect the predominantly aerobic metabolism of this tissue. Note the location of mitochondria close to the region of overlap between the thin and thick myofilaments. The close association of fat droplets (F) with the mitochondria illustrates the ability of the heart to use fatty acids as a major metabolic fuel. By kind permission of Mr. J. H. Kugler

not known where the enzymes of glycolysis are located in respect to the muscle fibres, though they are certainly extramitochondrial.

As the equilibrium for the reaction lactate $+$ NAD $\rightarrow$ pyruvate $+$ NADH$_2$ favours the production of lactate ($\Delta G^{0'}$ is 6000 cal/mole) the reaction can be reversed only if the concentrations of the products are kept low. In muscle this may be achieved by the rapid consumption of both NADH$_2$ and pyruvate by the mitochondria. The hydrogen from NADH$_2$ is finally oxidized to water, the pyruvate to water and carbon dioxide. For the moment we will consider only the oxidative breakdown of the carbon skeleton of pyruvate by the citric acid cycle.

The citric acid cycle

The postulation of this cycle (also known as the Krebs cycle) in 1937 by Krebs and Johnson was based on observations of oxygen uptake by preparations of minced pigeon breast muscle, incubated with various oxidizable substrates. These experiments were possible at that time only because of a previous development (1902–1926) of a device (the Warburg respirometer) for measuring volumes of gas used (oxygen) or produced (CO_2) in given periods of time by respiring tissues. The instrument shakes tissue samples suspended in a suitable liquid medium in a small flask (the 'cup') immersed in a constant-temperature bath and connected to a sensitive pressure measuring device (the 'manometer'). The gas phase in the apparatus is closed to the atmosphere and, if formation or absorption of a gas occurs during the reaction, its volume can be estimated from the pressure change recorded by the manometer. Changes in the amounts of oxygen and CO_2 can be differentiated by absorbing CO_2 in alkali contained in a glass well in the cup.

Using this instrument Krebs and Johnson observed that the oxygen uptake of the muscle preparation was increased by adding citrate and that the magnitude of the increase was greater than could be accounted for by the complete oxidation of the added substrate, i.e. its addition *catalysed* the oxidative degradation of some other substances in the preparation. Further experiments suggested that the other substances were derived from carbohydrate. Similar catalytic stimulations of oxygen uptake were found with added succinate, fumarate, malate and oxaloacetate, and it seemed that the oxidation of citrate itself involved the following compounds in order: α-oxoglutaric, succinic, fumaric, malic and oxaloacetic acids. Oxaloacetic acid could be converted into citric acid by combination with some unknown compound, thus completing a cyclic series of changes. This cycle was found in a great number of animal tissues. The compound required for the reaction with oxaloacetate to form citrate was shown subsequently to be an activated acetic acid, called acetyl coenzyme A. This compound is formed from (a) pyruvate by an energy-yielding process, (b) long-chain fatty acids by a complex series of reactions also with a net yield of energy, and (c) free acetate by a reaction in which ATP must be consumed.

Formation of acetyl CoA from pyruvate

This reaction, catalysed by a complex of enzymes, is a three-step reaction.

Reaction 1a (pyruvate dehydrogenase)

$$CH_3-\overset{O}{\overset{\|}{C}}-COOH + TPP \longrightarrow CH_3-\overset{O}{\overset{\|}{C}}-H-TPP + CO_2$$

  pyruvic acid   thiamine   α-hydroxyethyl-thiamine
                pyrophosphate   pyrophosphate

Reaction 1b (pyruvate dehydrogenase)

$$CH_3-\overset{O}{\overset{\|}{C}}-H-TPP + \text{(oxidized lipoic acid)} \rightleftharpoons \text{(acetylhydrolipoic acid)} + TPP$$

            oxidized   acetylhydrolipoic
          lipoic acid   acid

Reaction 2 (lipoyl acetyltransferase)

$$\text{(acetylhydrolipoic acid)} + CoASH \rightleftharpoons CH_3-\overset{O}{\overset{\|}{C}}-S-CoA + \text{(dihydrolipoic acid)}$$

        coenzyme A   acetyl-S-CoA   dihydrolipoic
                                                    acid

Reaction 3 (lipoyl dehydrogenase)

$$\text{(dihydrolipoic acid)} + NAD \rightleftharpoons \text{(oxidized lipoic acid)} + NADH_2$$

Each of these steps requires the presence not only of the enzyme and its substrate but also of the appropriate coenzymes.

Reaction 1 is the oxidative decarboxylation of pyruvic acid catalysed by pyruvic dehydrogenase. We may picture this reaction as occurring in two stages. Firstly the pyruvate reacts with the coenzyme thiamine pyrophosphate (TPP or cocarboxylase—see Figure 1.25—derived from

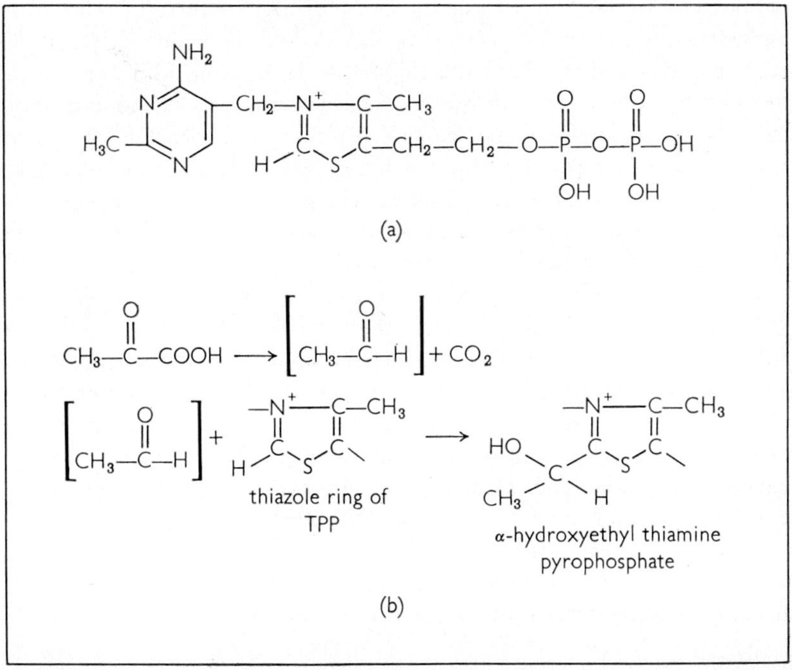

Figure 1.25. (a) Thiamine pyrophosphate (TPP). During the decarboxylation of α-oxo acids the thiazole ring acts as an acceptor for the decarboxylation product; the compound formed may be regarded as an adduct of the TPP and an aldehyde, e.g. with pyruvic acid the reaction may be represented as shown in (b). Thiamine is also known as vitamin B_1

vitamin B_1). The thiazole ring of TPP forms addition complexes with keto compounds; these react with the ion produced by the dissociation of the hydrogen on the carbon lying between the nitrogen and sulphur of the thiazole ring. CO_2 is released from this complex forming hydroxyethyl-thiamine pyrophosphate (HETP). In mammals the second stage is the reaction of HETP with the coenzyme lipoic acid (Figure 1.26). Lipoic acid

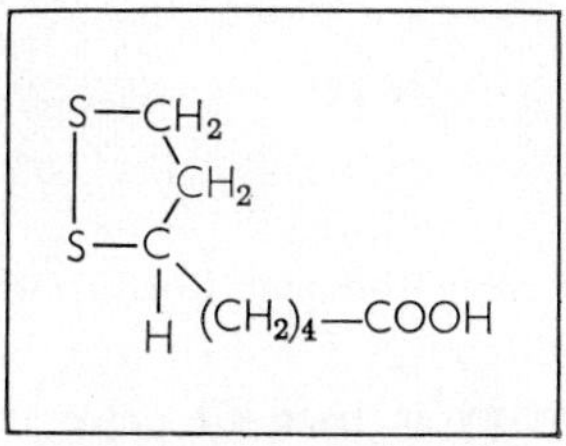

Figure 1.26. Lipoic acid

contains two sulphur atoms existing in the disulphide form or reduced to sulphydryl groups (when it may be considered as a derivative of N-octanoic acid, hence its other name thioctic acid). Arsenite inhibits pyruvate oxidation by combining with the two sulphydryl groups of reduced lipoic acid. The exact details of the reaction of lipoic acid with HETP are not known, but it is supposed that the hydroxyethyl group ('active acetaldehyde') reacts with the oxidized lipoic acid and that rearrangement of the resulting compound forms the acetyl derivative of reduced lipoic acid. This is the stage in which the decarboxylation product of pyruvate (acetaldehyde) is converted to the oxidation level of acetic acid (as the acetyl group) and which reforms free thiamine pyrophosphate.

The second reaction involves the enzyme lipoyl acetyltransferase and is the transfer of the acetyl group to coenzyme A (CoASH). The group involved in the coenzyme is the sulphydryl group of the pantothenic acid residue (Figure 1.27). The products of the reaction are acetyl CoA and reduced lipoic acid. The third reaction catalysed by lipoyldehydrogenase reoxidizes the lipoic acid and produces $NADH_2$.

Thus the overall products of the reaction are acetyl coenzyme A, $NADH_2$ and carbon dioxide; as the decarboxylation is virtually irreversible, the entire reaction sequence is also irreversible.

The reactions of the citric acid cycle

The reactions involved in this cycle are summarized in Figure 1.31, p. 72. The first step is the condensation of acetyl coenzyme A with oxaloacetate to form citrate, catalysed by the 'condensing enzyme' or citrate synthetase.

The thioester linkage between the acetyl group and the sulphydryl group of the coenzyme is a high-energy bond (it may be thought of as a mixed acid anhydride); the energy is used to drive the reaction so that the equilibrium constant is far to the right ($\Delta G^{0'}$ is -7500 cal/mole).

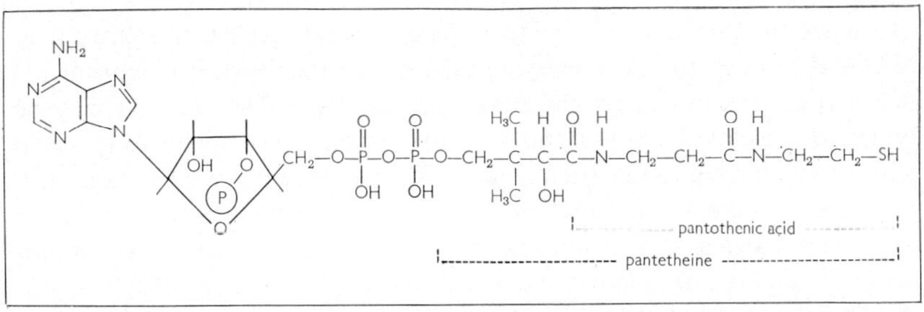

Figure 1.27. Coenzyme A (CoASH). Pantothenic acid is one of the B group of vitamins. $\textcircled{P} = PO_3 H_2$

Citrate is equilibrated with two other acids, isocitrate and *cis*-aconitate by the enzyme aconitase. This reaction probably involves the formation of an enzyme-bound common intermediate, so that the change from citrate to isocitrate does not necessarily pass through *cis*-aconitate.

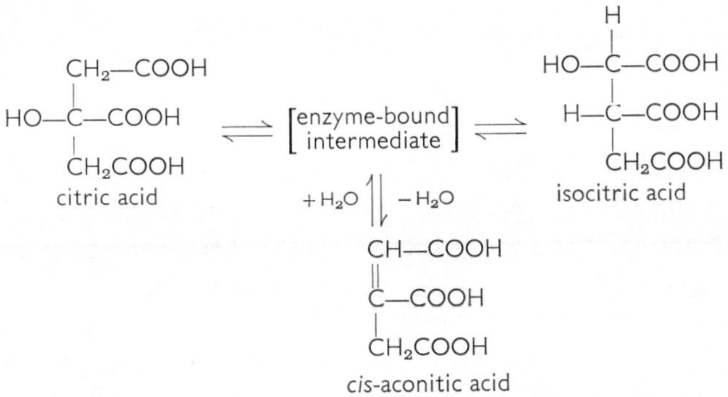

Aconitase requires iron which is apparently vital for the formation of the common intermediate. Formally, the reaction may be written as if water were removed from citric acid to produce *cis*-aconitic acid which can then be rehydrated to produce isocitric acid.

Isocitric acid is oxidized and decarboxylated by isocitric dehydrogenase.

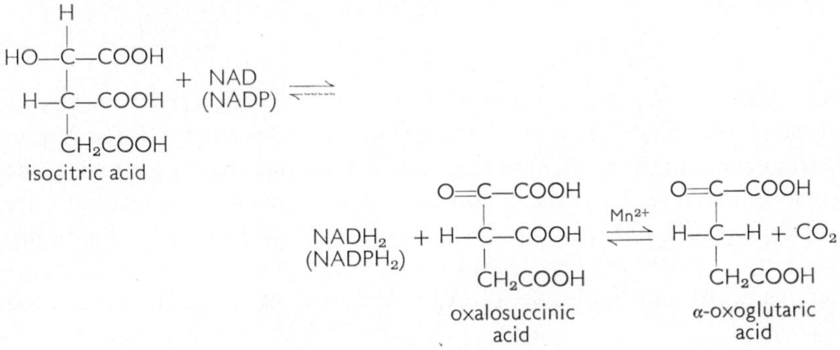

There are two forms of this enzyme, one of which transfers hydrogen to NAD, the other to the closely related coenzyme NADP (Figure 1.21) which functions in exactly the same way as NAD. The reaction may be understood as involving first the oxidative formation of oxalosuccinic acid which remains bound to the enzyme surface; and secondly the manganese-dependent decarboxylation of this bound acid to form α-oxoglutarate.

α-Oxoglutaric acid is converted to succinyl coenzyme A by a complex series of reactions analogous to that oxidizing pyruvate to acetyl coenzyme A. The same cofactors are required and coenzyme A again acts as the recipient of the acyl group formed, and the reaction is inhibited by arsenite.

$$\begin{array}{l} \text{COOH} \\ | \\ \text{C}{=}\text{O} \\ | \\ \text{CH}_2 \\ | \\ \text{CH}_2 \\ | \\ \text{COOH} \end{array} + \text{NAD} + \text{CoASH} \xrightarrow[\text{lipoic acid}]{\text{TPP, Mg}^{2+}} \begin{array}{l} \text{COOH} \\ | \\ \text{CH}_2 \\ | \\ \text{CH}_2 \\ | \\ \text{C}{=}\text{O} \\ | \\ \text{S}{-}\text{CoA} \end{array} + \text{NADH}_2 + \text{CO}_2$$

α-oxoglutaric acid   succinyl CoA

The products are $NADH_2$, carbon dioxide and succinyl coenzyme A, which is a high energy compound that can be used to drive the formation of ATP from ADP and inorganic phosphate. This synthesis (a substrate-level phosphorylation, see p. 51) occurs in two steps. Firstly, succinic thiokinase forms GTP (guanosine triphosphate, which is a nucleoside triphosphate like ATP though containing the base guanine instead of adenine; see Figure 1.28) at the expense of the succinyl CoA.

$$\begin{array}{l} \text{CH}_2\text{COOH} \\ | \\ \text{CH}_2 \\ | \\ \text{C}{-}\text{S}{-}\text{CoA} \\ \overset{\|}{\text{O}} \end{array} + \text{GDP} + \text{H}_3\text{PO}_4 \rightleftharpoons \begin{array}{l} \text{CH}_2\text{COOH} \\ | \\ \text{CH}_2\text{COOH} \end{array} + \text{GTP} + \text{CoA}{-}\text{SH}$$

succinyl CoA   succinic acid

The reaction is readily reversible (K is 3·7). Secondly, GTP transfers its terminal phosphate to ADP, forming ATP and releasing GDP for further participation in the thiokinase reaction. The enzyme required is nucleoside diphosphokinase. Thus the products of this entire series of reactions are succinate, ATP, CO_2 and $NADH_2$; the 6-carbon acid formed at the beginning of the cycle has been degraded to a 4-carbon acid by two decarboxylations while one molecule of ATP and two of $NADH_2$ have been

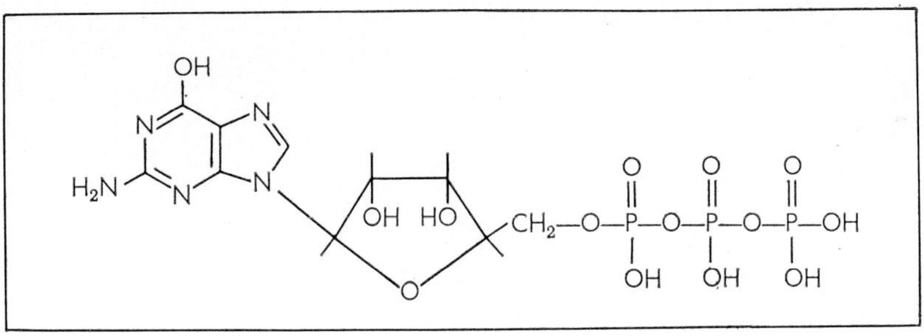

Figure 1.28. Guanosine triphosphate

accumulated. The oxidative decarboxylation of α-oxoglutarate is virtually irreversible and ensures that the cycle as a whole operates in one direction only.

Succinic acid is oxidized to fumaric acid by succinic dehydrogenase which forms part of the membranous framework of the mitochondrion.

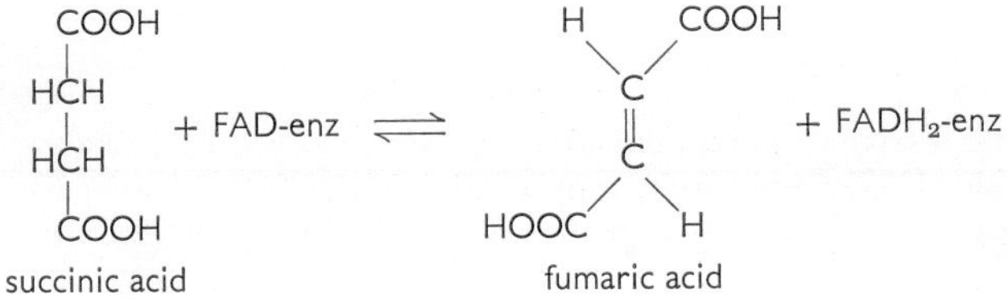

The hydrogen acceptor for this enzyme is FAD (Figure 1.29) which is firmly attached to the enzyme structure (it is a prosthetic group). Enzymes like succinic dehydrogenase are called flavoproteins and the coenzyme is called a flavin. The necessity for dehydrogenases with flavins as hydrogen acceptors arises from the fact that the nicotinamide nucleotides ($E^{0'} = -0.32$ V) are unsuitable as coenzymes for certain oxidations, for example, that of succinate ($E^{0'} = 0$ V), i.e. for reactions involving substrates which do not have hydrogen atoms of sufficient reducing power for transfer to NAD.

Fumarate is hydrated by the enzyme fumarase to form L-malic acid.

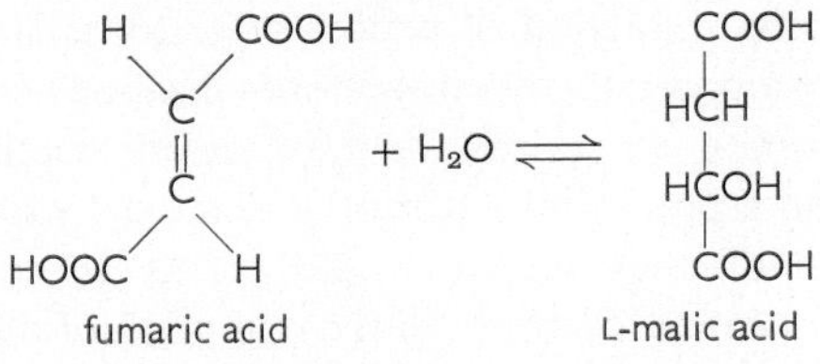

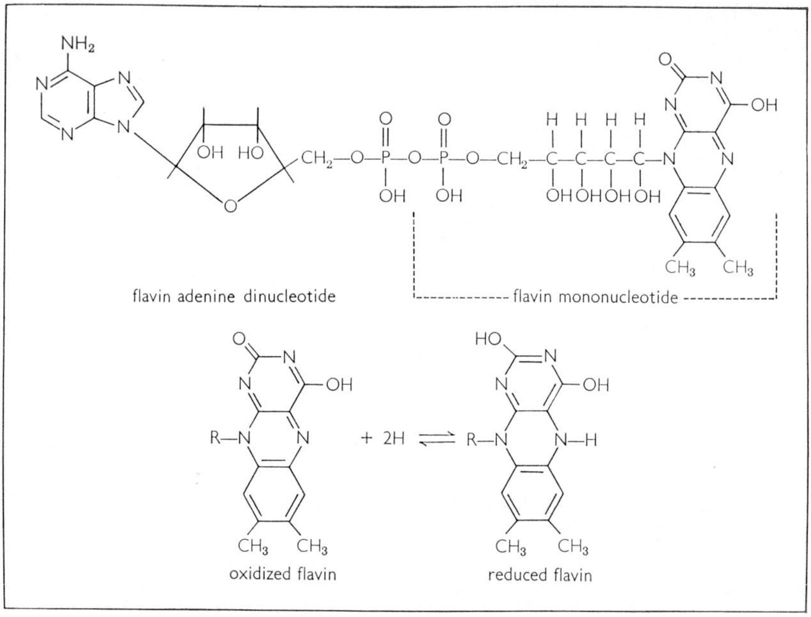

Figure 1.29. Flavin mononucleotide. Flavin nucleotides: flavin adenine dinucleotide (FAD) and flavin mononucleotide (FMN). FMN is the phosphorylated derivative of the vitamin riboflavin (vitamin B_2)

The equilibrium constant is 4·5 so that the reaction is readily reversible.

Malic acid is converted to oxaloacetate by malic dehydrogenase, NAD being reduced.

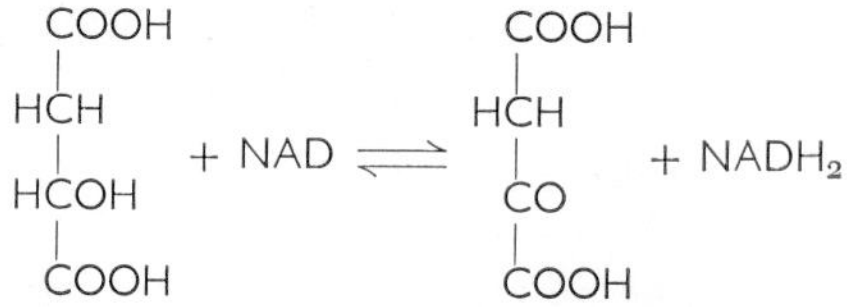

L-malic acid oxalacetic acid

At neutral pH, the equilibrium lies very much to the left ($K = 1{\cdot}3 \times 10^{-5}$) and, in addition, the reduction of oxaloacetate to malate is a very rapid reaction so that oxaloacetate added to tissues disappears in a few seconds. Although oxaloacetate is required for the constant operation of the citric acid cycle it is also a potent inhibitor of succinic dehydrogenase and thus any accumulation of oxaloacetate would act as an automatic cut-out, preventing its own formation through the operation of the cycle.

Asymmetric reactions in the cycle

Studies of the conversion of citrate to α-oxoglutarate and of fumarate to malate have produced valuable information about the mechanism of action of some of the enzymes of the cycle and about the mode of attachment of enzymes and substrates. When citrate formed by reacting acetate and oxaloacetate, labelled in the β-COOH group with ^{14}C,

$$\overset{*}{C}OOH$$
$$\beta \ CH_2$$
$$\alpha \ C{=}O$$
$$COOH$$

is converted in the cycle to α-oxoglutarate, the ^{14}C is always found in the α-COOH group of α-oxoglutarate. It was difficult to account for the fact that the enzymes involved in its metabolism (both citrate synthetase and aconitase) could treat citrate as if its two —CH_2—COOH groups were distinguishable. However, Ogston pointed out that such observations could be explained by assuming an asymmetry of the enzyme–substrate complex. For this to be so, the substrate must be attached to the enzyme in a specific orientation, which will be achieved if the attachment at the active site occurs at not less than three points (Figure 1.30).

Subcellular localization of the enzymes of the cycle

Succinic dehydrogenase is located exclusively in the mitochondria. The α-oxoglutaric dehydrogenase and pyruvic dehydrogenase complex, the condensing enzyme and NAD-dependent isocitric dehydrogenase are probably present only in the mitochondria. Aconitase, NADP-dependent isocitric dehydrogenase, fumarase and malic dehydrogenase are found both in the soluble part of the cell and the mitochondria.

The rate of operation of the cycle

It is possible to calculate the approximate rate of operation of the citric acid cycle from the following considerations. Suppose that a man at rest after exercise is oxidizing lactic acid; two-thirds of his oxygen consumption will come from the TCA cycle and one-third from preliminary reactions. Table 1.5 shows the hydrogen equivalents of the oxygen used.

The oxygen consumption at rest is about 300 ml per minute, i.e. 13·4 m mole of oxygen/minute. The amount required by the citric acid cycle ($\frac{2}{3} \times 13·4$) is 8·8 mM or 17·6 m atoms of oxygen, which is equivalent to

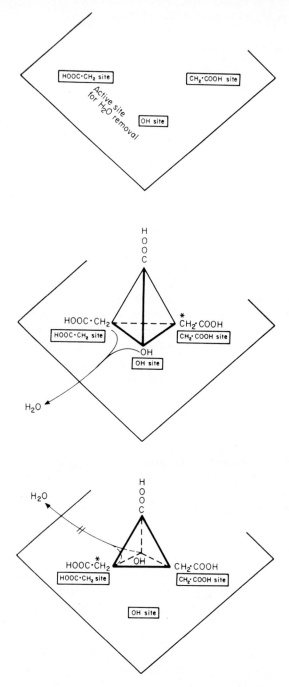

Figure 1.30. Three-point attachment of citrate to the surface of aconitase. The planar surface represents the enzyme, the tetrahedron citric acid; * indicates the $CH_2 \cdot COOH$ group derived from acetate

Table 1.5

Reaction		Number of hydrogens
Lactate	→ pyruvate	2
Pyruvate	→ acetyl-*S*-CoA	2
Isocitrate	→ α-oxoglutarate	2
α-Oxoglutarate	→ succinate	2
Succinate	→ malate	2
Malate	→ oxaloacetate	2
	Total hydrogens in cycle	8
	Total hydrogens before cycle	4

35·2 m atoms of hydrogen oxidized to water; thus $35 \cdot 2/8 = 4 \cdot 4$ m mole of acetyl CoA pass through the cycle/minute, or 264 mg of acetate/minute.

To calculate the frequency of operation of this cycle, we must consider in addition the concentration of oxaloacetate which limits the number of acetyl CoA molecules that can be accepted at any one time. Usually this concentration is about 1 μM, i.e. 1 litre of tissue contains 1 μ mole of oxaloacetate. If we subtract from the weight of the 70 kg man the weight of the blood and bone (neither of which contain oxaloacetate available for the citric acid cycle) the mass of tissue remaining is about 52 kg, with a density of 1·1. Thus the volume of tissue containing oxaloacetate is $52 \div 1 \cdot 1 = 47$ litre, and there will be 47 μmoles of oxaloacetate available at any one time for condensation with acetyl coenzyme A. Therefore, as 4·4 m moles (= 4400 μmoles) of acetyl coenzyme A are consumed/minute, and they pass through the cycle 47 μmoles at a time, the cycle must turn $\frac{4400}{47}$ times/minute, i.e. about 100 times/minute.

The cycle as a common pathway for the degradation of carbohydrate, fatty acids and amino acids to CO_2

Besides oxidizing acetate derived from the pyruvate formed in glycolysis, the citric acid cycle is also involved in the conversion of fatty acids and the carbon skeletons of many amino acids to CO_2. Fatty acids may enter the cycle after being broken down to acetyl CoA units (see p. 123). Many amino acids, after removal of their amino group by transamination or deamination (see pp. 137, 140) can enter the cycle. For example, deamination of alanine, glutamic and aspartic acids produces pyruvate, α-oxoglutarate and oxaloacetate respectively.

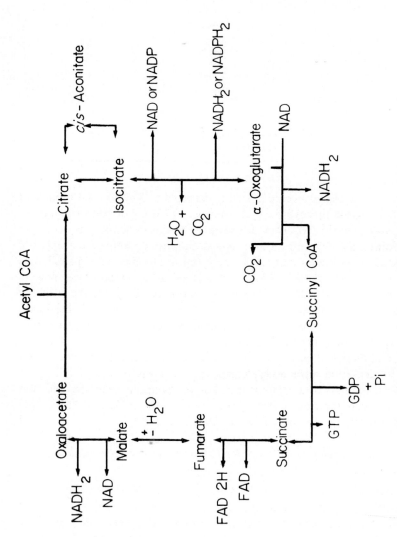

Figure 1.31. Summary of the reactions involved in the tricarboxylic acid cycle

Summary of the functions of the citric acid cycle

The functions of the citric acid cycle may be summarized as follows. Its operation, which begins with acetic and oxaloacetic acids, produces a series of organic acids some of which are used as building blocks for providing essential cell constituents, reduced nicotinamide and flavin coenzymes and GTP. These compounds are formed at the expense of the conversion of one molecule of acetic acid to carbon dioxide so that the net transformation during one turn of the cycle may be represented as follows:

$$CH_3COOH + 2H_2O + 3NAD + FAD\text{-}enz + GDP + Pi \longrightarrow$$
$$2CO_2 + 3NADH_2 + FADH_2\text{-}enz + GTP$$

Much of the energy made available during the degradation of acetate (and indeed during the complete degradation of glucose) is retained in these reduced coenzymes. This is apparent from the values in Table 1.6.

Table 1.6. Energy transformation during the degradation of glucose

Substrate	Energy level of substrate (kcal)	Energy lost from substrate (kcal)	Energy conserved in Reduced coenzymes	ATP
Glucose	700	—	—	—
2 Pyruvate	550	150	100	40
2 Acetate ($+2CO_2$)	440	110	100	0
$6CO_2$	0	440	300 ($NADH_2$) 80 (reduced flavin)	20
		700	580	60

The values[a] are calculated on the following assumptions:

glucose + $6O_2$	$\rightarrow$ $6CO_2 + 6H_2O$	$\Delta G^{0'} = -700$ kcal/mole
$NADH_2 + O$	$\rightarrow$ $NAD + H_2O$	$\Delta G^{0'} = -50$ kcal/mole
reduced flavoprotein + O	$\rightarrow$ flavoprotein + H_2O	$\Delta G^{0'} = -40$ kcal/mole
ATP + H_2O	$\rightarrow$ ADP + phosphate	$\Delta G^{0'} = -10$ kcal/mole

P/O ratios for the oxidation of $NADH_2$ and reduced flavoprotein are 3 and 2 respectively.

[a] All values have been expressed to the nearest 10 kcal to simplify the calculations.

These reduced coenzymes are utilized for the production of ATP by the process of oxidative phosphorylation. In this process, the hydrogens removed from the substrates of the citric acid cycle are finally oxidized to water by a series of components comprising the respiratory chain; the energy made available is used to drive the synthesis of ATP from ADP and inorganic phosphate.

CHAPTER 5

The respiratory chain and oxidative phosphorylation

The respiratory chain is a series of enzymes and cofactors located in the mitochondria which catalyses a stepwise transfer of hydrogen from substrate to oxygen, reducing it to water. Information about the composition of the chain has been obtained largely from an examination of the characteristic light-absorbing properties of many of its component parts (using a variety of elaborate spectrophotometric methods) and by fragmentation of mitochondria and mitochondrial membranes followed by chemical and spectrophotometric analyses. While some doubt exists about the exact role of certain components, it is possible to draw up a generalized scheme for the composition of the chain (Figure 1·32).

The components of the respiratory chain

All the components of this chain except NAD are embedded more or less firmly in the mitochondrial membrane. There are two main points of entry for substrate hydrogen into the chain, one through flavins (for succinate and fatty acids), the other through NAD (for α-oxoglutarate, fatty acids, etc.). $NADH_2$ is also oxidized by a flavoprotein which in heart tissue contains FMN as its prosthetic group. Reducing equivalents entering through either of these two separate pathways are available for reducing all the remaining components which, therefore, constitute a final common pathway to oxygen. There is a third point of entry, which permits hydrogen from $NADPH_2$ to pass to oxygen; this is via the enzyme transhydrogenase, which is firmly bound to the framework of the mitochondria and catalyses the reaction

$$NADPH_2 + NAD \rightleftharpoons NADP + NADH_2$$

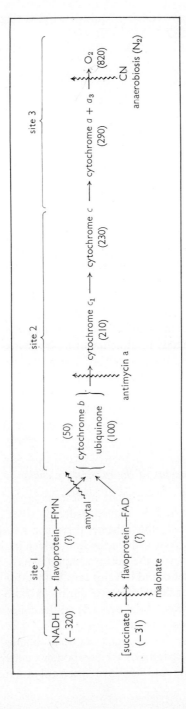

Figure 1.32. The respiratory chain. The values in parentheses are the redox potentials of the components at pH 7 in mV. The values for the flavoproteins are uncertain, but are probably about 0 mV. The portions of the respiratory chain in which phosphorylation may occur are indicated as sites 1, 2 and 3. Points of inhibition are indicated thus: ⤳

In the common pathway reducing equivalents pass through a quinone (ubiquinone or coenzyme Q)

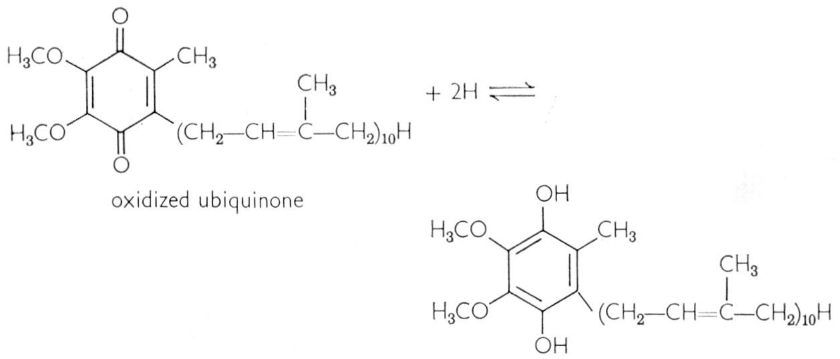

oxidized ubiquinone

$+ 2H \rightleftharpoons$

reduced ubiquinone

and then a series of cytochromes. These are iron-containing proteins with different redox potentials, transferring single electrons with a corresponding change in the valency of the iron. The protein of the molecule is attached to a porphyrin group to which the iron in turn is attached. There is a family of such compounds (the cytochromes a, b and c) differing from one another in the mode of attachment of porphyrin to protein and in the chemical structure of the porphyrins. The porphyrin of cytochrome c (Figure 1·33) is identical to that of the haem group of haemoglobin (see p. 165) and is attached to the protein as shown in Figure 1·34. The cytochromes of the b group have the same porphyrin structure but the mode of attachment to the protein is different; the cytochromes of the a group have a different porphyrin.

The sequence of the components of the respiratory chain

Considerable progress has been made in describing the order in which these compounds function and the sequence already given (Figure 1·32) is the one generally accepted. In this scheme, there is a steadily descending potential down which electrons will readily flow, which indicates that such an order is probable. However, the potentials quoted have been measured on isolated redox components and it is not certain that, for example, when NAD is firmly bound to its dehydrogenase during oxidation this potential remains the same. Also the potential depends on the concentrations of the oxidized and reduced forms present.

More direct evidence for the sequence has been obtained by measuring changes in the absorption spectra of the components under different conditions. The very elaborate and sensitive spectrophotomteric techniques developed by Chance permit the estimation of the extent of reduction and the rates of reaction of different components present in the respiratory chain. Chance has shown that cytochrome $a + a_3$ (also called cytochrome oxidase) is the terminal cytochrome because it is oxidized most rapidly when anaerobic mitochondria are oxygenated; that cytochrome b is the first cytochrome because it is the only cytochrome reduced when substrate is added to mitochondria poisoned with antimycin a; that cytochrome c precedes cytochrome a because substrate added to mitochondria extracted

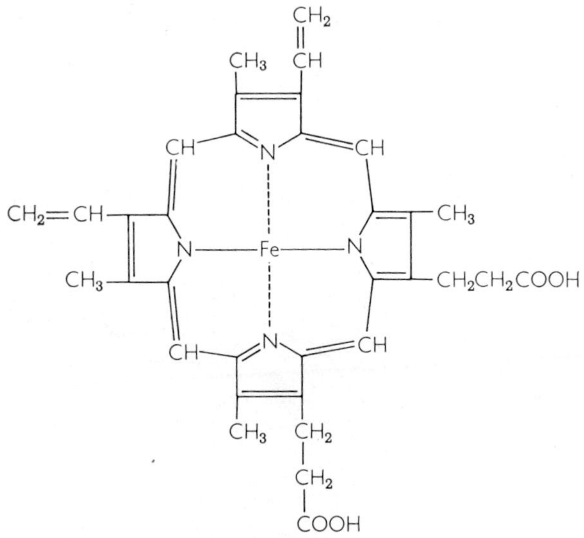

Figure 1.33. The haem prosthetic group of cytochrome c and haemoglobin

with salt (which preferentially removes cytochrome c) reduces cytochrome b and c_1 but not $a + a_3$; and that flavoprotein (and probably ubiquinone) are reduced by added substrate before the cytochromes. Many extensions of this approach have been used, often with inhibitors of respiratory activity. For example, if malonate is added to mitochondria oxidizing succinate, the flavin is not reduced. Amytal (a barbiturate) prevents the oxidation of $NADH_2$ generated by added malate, but does not prevent the oxidation of succinate (indicating that the two flavoproteins of the chain are distinct). Cyanide, by inhibiting cytochrome $a + a_3$, permits all the carriers to be reduced by added substrate. The points of action of the inhibitors of the electron transport chain are shown in Figure 1·31.

The functioning of the respiratory chain

There is little detailed information about the mechanism of the redox reactions in the chain. While it is certain that many of the enzymes reducing NAD do so by transferring one of the hydrogen atoms from the substrate together with an electron to the coenzyme and that a similar

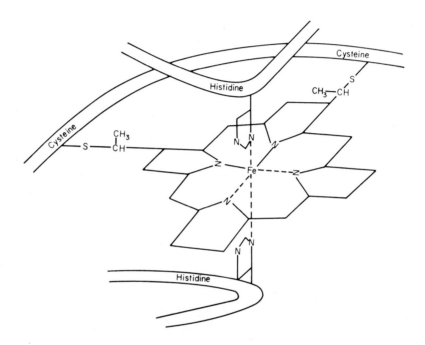

Figure 1.34. Diagrammatic representation of the binding of the prosthetic group in cytochrome *c*. The porphyrin ring is linked covalently to two cysteine residues in the protein; the Fe is linked to N in both the prosthetic group and the protein (the imadazole side chains of the two histidine residues)

movement of hydrogen atoms occurs with a few flavoproteins, the mechanism of redox transfers by the flavoproteins and cytochromes of the respiratory chain is not understood. Nevertheless, the assumption that electrons are transferred between these components has led to the use of the term 'electron' transport chain as a synonym for respiratory chain. What is certain, however, is that maximal respiratory activity depends on the maintenance of the structure of the mitochondrial membranes containing the respiratory carriers. These membranes contain a number of non-enzymic or structural proteins and phospholipids which are essential for the transfer of reducing equivalents.

Respiratory chain phosphorylation

During the transfer of hydrogen from substrate to oxygen by the respiratory chain, sufficient energy is made available to drive the synthesis of ATP from ADP and phosphate. This process, first reported in the 1930s, is called 'respiratory chain' or 'oxidative' phosphorylation and, like the citric acid cycle and the respiratory chain, is localized in the mitochondria.

Energy transformations in the respiratory chain

The change in free energy during the oxidation of hydrogen depends on the energy level of the hydrogen in the substrate. Hydrogen gas, on oxidation to water, yields about 57 kcal/mole. In biological dehydrogenations, hydrogen is transferred to give $NADH_2$ or reduced flavoprotein and less energy is made available when these are oxidized, 53 kcal/mole during the oxidation of $NADH_2$ and 41 kcal/mole for the reduced flavin. It appears to be a fact of life that the production of about 10–12 kcal/mole in one reaction is about the maximum that living things can handle. Reactions such as the oxidation of $NADH_2$ or reduced flavin by oxygen which produce more than this amount of energy are therefore routed through a series of steps, which liberate the energy in smaller 'packets' with which the cell can deal. The respiratory chain is a good example of such a series and it is possible to calculate the magnitude of the release of energy at its different stages. For the synthesis of ATP, there must be sites in the chain where the redox drop is sufficient to free about 8 kcal/mole. Using the equation

$$\Delta G^{0'} = - \frac{\Delta E^{0'} n F}{4 \cdot 18}$$

(see p. 28) and the potentials listed in Figure 1.31, it can be seen that this occurs between NAD and flavoprotein ($\Delta E^{0'} = 0 \cdot 32$ V), cytochrome b and cytochrome c ($\Delta E^{0'} = 0 \cdot 18$ V) and cytochrome c and oxygen ($\Delta E^{0'} = 0 \cdot 53$ V). Therefore at least three molecules of ATP could be formed during the oxidation of one molecule of $NADH_2$ and at least two during the oxidation of reduced flavoprotein in the respiratory chain. This conclusion is supported by quantitative analysis of oxidative phosphorylation.

The coupling of respiration to phosphorylation

Carefully prepared mitochondria, incubated aerobically with substrate under conditions where all the necessary cofactors are available except ADP, have a low rate of respiration. Addition of ADP accelerates the respiratory rate; the rate of respiration increases with increasing concentration of added ADP until a maximum rate is reached. The respiration falls to a low level when almost all the ADP has been converted to ATP. Under these circumstances respiration is said to be 'coupled' to phosphorylation. The mitochondria are also said to show 'respiratory control by ADP', that is, the rate of respiration is controlled by the rate at which ADP is made available (*in vivo* by the utilization of ATP). This simple control mechanism has the obvious advantage of diminishing respiratory activity when there is no need to synthesize ATP (see Section 8).

The quantitative relationship between oxygen uptake and phosphorylation

Not only is there a qualitative relation between oxidation and phosphorylation but there is also a relation between the quantities of oxygen consumed and of ATP synthesized. This has become apparent in many experiments in which the amounts of oxygen respired and ATP produced have been measured. Most of the practical difficulties in such experiments arise because the ATP formed can be utilized for other reactions by the mitochondrial preparations, i.e. the particles have an 'ATP-ase' reaction. To avoid this difficulty, the ATP is often 'trapped' by conversion to glucose-6-phosphate (formed by added glucose and hexokinase) and the glucose-6-phosphate is estimated by a suitable specific method. An additional difficulty is that not all the oxygen uptake of such preparations is coupled to phosphorylation; there may be a built-in 'leak' of respiration. This may be allowed for by measuring the rate of oxygen uptake with a limited amount of phosphate in the absence of the 'glucose–hexokinase trap' (the unstimulated rate), then adding glucose and hexokinase to release ADP from the ATP in the system and measuring the amount of oxygen taken up in the time interval before the respiratory rate returns to its unstimulated value. When this rate is restored, all the phosphate is used up. From such experiments, the ratio

$$\frac{\mu\text{moles phosphate incorporated into ATP}}{\mu\text{atoms oxygen consumed}}$$

can be calculated; this is termed the P/O ratio. When such ratios are measured with intermediates of the citric acid cycle and related compounds the following values are obtained; for pyruvate, approaching 3; for isocitrate, 1–2; for α-oxoglutarate, about 4; for succinate, about 2; for malate, about 3. The most obvious difficulty in interpreting these values is that the addition of any of these substrates initiates the whole series of reactions of the cycle. However if β-hydroxybutyrate, which can be oxidized only to acetoacetate by liver mitochondria, is added to a suspension of these particles P/O ratios of about 3 are obtained. Thus it seems that all substrates which transfer hydrogen to NAD have a P/O ratio of the same value, about 3; this has been confirmed directly by measuring the P/O ratio with $NADH_2$ itself as the substrate. On the other hand, with succinate and other substrates reducing the flavoproteins, less energy is available during the oxidation of the hydrogens and the P/O ratio is only 2. The value listed above which is not explained is the P/O ratio of about 4 for the oxidation of α-oxoglutarate. However, this oxidation involves the formation of ATP from the GTP synthesis during the deacylation of succinyl coenzyme A (see p. 66), as well as from the oxidation of the $NADH_2$ generated, the P/O ratio for the entire reaction is therefore 4. The addition of dinitrophenol, which prevents oxidative but not substrate-level phosphorylation, accordingly diminishes the P/O ratio for this reaction to about 1.

The sites of phosphorylation

The initial consideration of the redox properties of the components of the respiratory chain suggested certain possible sites for ATP synthesis (see p. 79), and there is direct experimental support for the conclusions. Thus the respiratory chain can be reduced at the level of cytochrome c by using ascorbic acid as a substrate and when the reduced cytochrome c is oxidized by oxygen, P/O ratios of rather less than 1 are obtained. If succinate is used as a substrate under anaerobic conditions and the reduction of cytochrome c (added as an acceptor of the reducing equivalents) is measured spectrophotometrically, the P/O ratio (actually P/2e ratio) is about 0·5; with β-hydroxybutyrate as substrate under the same conditions, the ratio rises to between 1·5 and 2. Therefore, it is generally agreed that there is one phosphorylation site between NAD and flavoprotein, one between flavoprotein and cytochrome c and one between cytochrome c and oxygen (Figure 1.31).

The dissociation of respiratory activity and phosphorylation

Although the process of electron transfer and phosphorylation are normally coupled, it is possible to dissociate or 'uncouple' them so that respiration continues without phosphorylation. Uncoupling may result from a variety of physical or chemical treatments of mitochondrial preparations and only a few will be considered.

4+

An uncoupler frequently used is 2,4-dinitrophenol, a drug popular some time ago for reducing weight, until it was found to be toxic. If administered to whole animals, it increases the basal metabolic rate and in many ways mimics hyperthyroidism. When added to mitochondrial suspensions it produces a complete loss of the ability to phosphorylate ADP and, often, an increase in the rate of oxygen consumption. The particles so treated are 'uncoupled', i.e. respiration proceeds at a rate controlled only by the ability of the respiratory chain to transfer electrons and by the amount of oxidizable substrate available.

Phosphorylation can also be prevented without uncoupling. For example, if respiration is blocked in a coupled system by adding antimycin or cyanide then phosphorylation also ceases, because electron transport has ceased.

The mechanism of oxidative phosphorylation

Much ingenuity and effort has been expended in attempting to describe the details of the reactions which link electron transfer in the respiratory chain to the phosphorylation of ADP to form ATP. Unfortunately, little substantial progress has been made. Most workers are agreed that there are probably specific chemical intermediates (possibly proteins) which connect the two processes and refer to them as 'coupling factors'. Various lines of evidence point to their existence, perhaps the most compelling being experiments with oligomycin which, while it prevents ATP formation in respiring mitochondrial preparations, does not inhibit a number of other energy-dependent mitochondrial reactions. Therefore, it is argued, there must be at least one high-energy compound (the coupling factor) formed as the result of respiratory activity and capable of driving the synthesis of ATP or (in the oligomycin inhibited system) the other energy-dependent reactions. Obviously the problem of isolating and identifying such reactive intermediates from the organized and extremely complex structure of mitochondria is very great and no universally acceptable formulation of the process of phosphorylation has been proposed.

An alternative scheme for oxidative phosphorylation which does not require the participation of coupling factors has been proposed by Mitchell. In essence, it envisages that electron transport causes a vectorial movement of protons which generates an ionic gradient across the mitochondrial membrane and that this gradient provides the energy to phosphorylate ADP.

CHAPTER 6

Inhibitors of mitochondrial function: A summary

As we have seen, the main function of mitochondria is to oxidize food-stuffs and produce chemical energy. This requires the cooperation and interaction of three mitochondrial systems—the citric acid cycle, the respiratory chain and the phosphorylation mechanism. Each of the three systems has its own characteristic inhibitors, which have been used to elucidate the various sequences. This section discusses the most important inhibitors of each pathway.

Inhibitors of the citric acid cycle

Fluoroacetate: $CH_2F \cdot COOH$ occurs naturally in some South African plants and has been used extensively as a rat poison; a closely related compound fluoroacetamide has also been used as a systemic insecticide in plants. However, recent information about their extreme toxicity has produced legislation restricting their use. When injected into rats, fluoro-acetate causes large increases (up to seventyfold) in the concentration of citrate in many tissues. α-Oxoglutarate does not accumulate, suggesting that fluoroacetate prevents the conversion of citrate to α-oxoglutarate. It has also been found that fluoroacetate could be converted to fluorocitrate by the condensing enzyme, which does not distinguish between acetate and fluoroacetate, and that fluorocitrate is a potent inhibitor of aconitase. Thus fluoroacetate is poisonous because of a 'lethal synthesis', in which the body poisons itself by using its own enzymes to synthesize a toxic substance.

Arsenite: $\begin{smallmatrix} HO \\ HO \end{smallmatrix} AS{=}O$, inhibits oxidative decarboxylation of pyruvate and α – oxoglutarate by combining with the dithiols of lipoic acid (see p. 63).

Malonate: $HOOC \cdot CH_2 \cdot COOH$ (see p. 32) inhibits succinic dehydrogenase competitively and may cause accumulation of succinate if injected into the intact animal.

$$\text{O} \qquad \text{HO}$$

Parapyruvate: $\text{HOOC}-\overset{\text{O}}{\underset{}{\overset{\|}{\text{C}}}}-\text{CH}_2-\underset{\underset{\text{CH}_3}{|}}{\overset{\text{HO}}{\overset{|}{\text{C}}}}-\text{COOH}$, is a fairly specific in-

hibitor of α-oxoglutaric dehydrogenase. It is formed by the condensation of two molecules of pyruvic acid and may be considered a structural analogue of α-oxoglutarate.

$$\text{O}$$

Oxaloacetate: $\text{HOOC}-\overset{\text{O}}{\overset{\|}{\text{C}}}-\text{CH}_2-\text{COOH}$, although part of the citric acid cycle is itself a potent competitive inhibitor of succinic dehydrogenase. The inhibition amounts to about 50% at a concentration of $10^{-5}-10^{-6}$ M. Oxaloacetate is a labile substance, breaking down readily to pyruvate and carbon dioxide, while at the same time it is essential for the functioning of the cycle. Both the equilibrium of malic dehydrogenase and the inhibition of succinic dehydrogenase ensure that oxaloacetate is conserved. Despite this, there is always some loss of oxaloacetate, which must be replaced. In muscle, the most important replenishment probably comes from the conversion of glutamate to α-oxoglutarate (and hence to oxaloacetate) by glutamic dehydrogenase which is found in mitochondria. Its activity is not very high, but is probably sufficient to make good the loss of citric acid cycle intermediates. Certainly, free glutamate is one of the most common amino acids found in muscle; its concentration in isolated muscle mitochondria may be upwards of 1 mM.

Inhibitors of electron transport

Barbiturates (e.g. amytal, see p. 77) stop respiration by preventing the oxidation of NADH_2. Thus with barbiturates the oxidation of NAD-linked substrates is lowered whilst succinate oxidation is unaffected.

Antimycin is an antibiotic too toxic for clinical use. It is effective at a concentration of less than 0·1 μg/ml and interferes with the reduction of cytochrome c_1.

Inhibitor of transphosphorylation

Oligomycin is a fungicide which, when added to a mitochondrial suspension, inhibits the respiration coupled to phosphorylation. Thus it has no effect on respiration occurring in the absence of phosphate and phosphate acceptor, but inhibits completely the stimulated respiration brought about by adding a phosphate acceptor such as ADP or hexokinase and glucose. The amount of respiration left after addition of oligomycin is a measure of the tightness of coupling of the mitochondria. The inhibition of respiration is completely relieved by the addition of dinitrophenol. It is suggested that oligomycin does not prevent the formation of high-energy intermediates in the oxidative phosphorylation sequence, but does prevent the use of these intermediates in the phosphorylation of ADP to ATP.

Inhibitors of oxidative phosphorylation: uncoupling agents

Nitrophenols (like dinitrophenol) and *halophenols* are uncouplers. Pentachlorophenol has been extensively used in the study of oxidative phosphorylation. *Thyroxine* may be active as an uncoupler because of its ability to disorganize the mitochondrial framework, a property shared by other substances such as detergents (for example, deoxycholate) which also uncouples oxidation and phosphorylation.

Dicoumarol is an uncoupler whose mode of action is not understood. It is formed naturally during the fermentation of hay and other green vegetable matter, giving rise to the haemolytic disease of cattle called sweet clover disease. In structure it is closely related to vitamin K but the effects

dicoumarol   vitamin K_3

of dicoumarol and vitamin K are antagonistic and the uncoupling due to the former may be reversed by the latter. The uncoupling effect of dicoumarol has nothing to do with its antibloodclotting action.

Unsaturated fatty acids, present in tissues, may act as uncouplers. They are effective at concentrations of about 1 mM, probably by acting as detergents. Clearly the uncoupling effect presents a problem to the tissues, since fatty acids are one of the main transportable forms of energy. This problem is solved by binding them firmly to the serum protein albumin so that the mobile fatty acid of the blood is transported in this combination with albumin. Oleic acid, one of the commonest unsaturated fatty acids found in the body, is bound particularly firmly. Addition of serum albumin to a mitochondrial suspension uncoupled by fatty acids restores oxidative phosphorylation.

Calcium is a potent uncoupler, probably because it alters mitochondrial structure. The concentration of calcium required to uncouple a mitochondrial suspension varies with the magnesium concentration; thus, potentially, at low magnesium concentrations, small changes in calcium concentration could have large effects on respiration. Here again the problem is solved by binding most of the calcium to a protein. However, changing the amount of free ionic calcium in the cell could result in uncoupling.

As it is likely that there is a strict coupling of respiration and phosphorylation it is probable that there are natural uncouplers which allow respiration to proceed slowly, even when there is no great demand for ATP. A promising candidate for this role is *carbon dioxide* which has a marked effect in the physiological range of concentrations. It may be the accumulation of CO_2 that initiates respiration in tightly coupled mitochondria.

Arsenate uncouples by replacing phosphate in the high-energy compound which normally transfers its phosphate group to ADP to yield ATP. The arsenate analogue is readily hydrolysed by water so that energy is lost rather than conserved.

SECTION 2

The Biochemistry of Liver and Adipose Tissue: the Chemical Factories

Intracellular anatomy of liver: separation and metabolic properties of isolated cell organelles

The intracellular organization of liver

The liver may be regarded as the great chemical factory of the body since it is responsible for almost all of the bulk syntheses and transformations involving proteins, carbohydrates and lipids.

Compounds synthesized in bulk by the liver

Plasma proteins	Glucose
Triglycerides	Glycogen
Cholesterol	Bile acids
Ketone bodies	Urea

Some special bulk syntheses occur in other organs, digestive enzymes in exocrine glands and haemoglobin in the erythropoietic tissue of the bone marrow, for example; however, no other organ exhibits such diverse capabilities for synthesis as the liver. An electron micrograph of rat liver is shown in Figure 2.1. The cytoplasm contains an array of membranes enclosing tubules and cisternae which are known collectively as the endoplasmic reticulum or the ergastoplasmic membranes. Attached to the surface of these membranes are small granules (ribosomes) composed of ribonucleic acid and protein, which are concerned with the biosynthesis of proteins (Figure 2.2) (see Section 6). Ergastoplasmic membranes are abundant in cells synthesizing proteins for export, such as those of the liver and acinar region of the pancreas. During tissue homogenization the membranes of the endoplasmic reticulum are fragmented to yield particles called microsomes which can be isolated by differential centrifugation (see p. 94). Microsomes derived from tissues that secrete proteins are densely studded with ribosomes giving the fragmented membranes a rough

4*

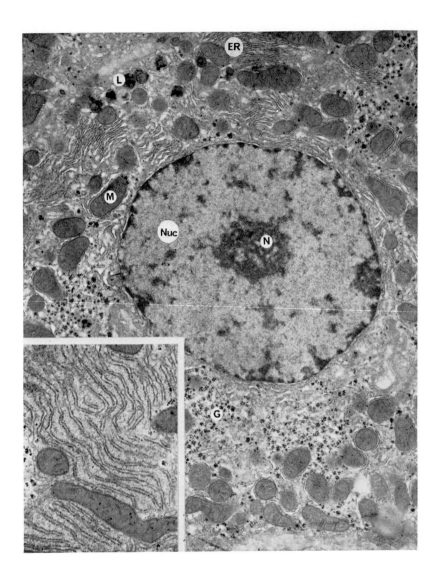

Figure 2.1. An electron micrograph of a liver parenchyma cell showing mitochondria (M), lysosomes (L), glycogen granules (G), endoplasmic reticulum (ER), nucleus (Nuc) and nucleolus (N). The insert, at a higher magnification, shows profiles of the endoplasmic reticulum bearing ribosomes on their outer surface. By kind permission of Mr. J. H. Kugler

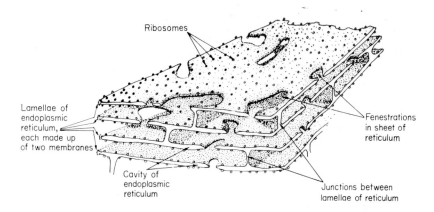

Ribosomes

Lamellae of
endoplasmic
reticulum,
each made up
of two membranes

Fenestrations
in sheet of
reticulum

Cavity of
endoplasmic
reticulum

Junctions between
lamellae of reticulum

Figure 2.2. Stereogram to show general structure of granular endoplasmic reticulum, made up of parallel lamellae which are joined to adjacent lamellae and penetrated by large fenestrations. From S. W. Hurry, *The Microstructure of Cells*, Murray, London, 1965

appearance. In contrast, microsomes derived from tissues not involved in bulk protein synthesis are largely free from ribosomes and have smooth surfaces.

Cells are bounded by a single membrane which may, according to some workers, be reflected inwards to form the tubules of the endoplasmic

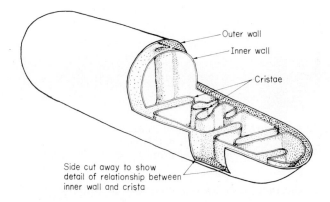

Outer wall

Inner wall

Cristae

Side cut away to show
detail of relationship between
inner wall and crista

Figure 2.3. Stereogram of a single generalized mitochondrion to show the relationships of inner and outer membranes and the cristae. From S. W. Hurry, *The Microstructure of Cells*, Murray, London, 1965

reticulum. These tubules, penetrating the cytoplasm and continuous with the extracellular space, may give access to the nucleus via the space bounded by the nuclear envelope. Observation of the endoplasmic reticulum by phase-contrast microscopy has revealed that it is continuously changing its conformation and position.

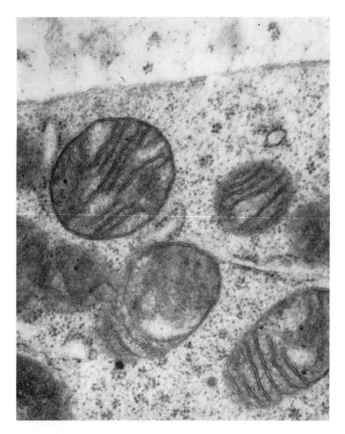

Figure 2.4. An electron micrograph of mitochondria from a leucocyte. Note the small number of cristae in each mitochondrion (cf. Figure 1.24). By kind permission of Professor R. Barer

Between the tubules of the endoplasmic reticulum lie the oval or rod-shaped mitochondria. These organelles conform to the same general plan irrespective of their tissue or organism of origin. A typical mitochondrion, as shown in Figure 2.3 in diagrammatic form, is bounded by a double set of membranes; the inner membrane is highly convoluted to form the cristae and is enveloped by the outer membrane. Thus mitochondria are divided into two compartments, one between the two membranes, and the other, bounded by the inner membrane, into which the cristae project. The membranes, which are thought to have a lipid core sandwiched between two layers of protein, carry the enzymes associated with electron transport and oxidative phosphorylation (see Section 1). The main variation in mitochondrial structure is in the abundance of cristae. In tissues

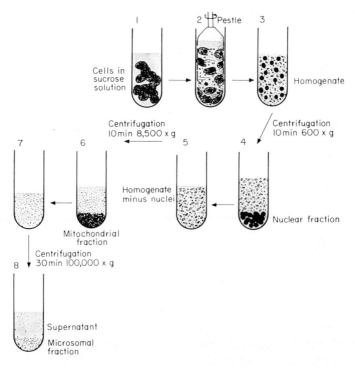

Figure 2.5. Differential centrifugation

having a high oxygen uptake the cristae are tightly packed and numerous, whereas in tissues of low oxidative capacity the cristae are few in number (see Figure 1.24 and Figure 2.4).

The separation of intracellular organelles

In order to isolate cell organelles, the cells must be broken open without damaging the subcellular components. Tissue fragments are suspended in a roughly isoosmotic medium (often 0·25 M sucrose) in a smooth glass tube. By the rapid rotating of a tightly fitting pestle, the cells are disrupted due to the liquid shear forces developed between the rotating pestle and the walls of the tube. If chemical and biochemical studies are to be made on subcellular organelles, the various particles present in the tissue homogenates must be separated from one another on a fairly large scale. The main technique used for this purpose is differential centrifugation, which is based on the fact that particles having the same density will sediment in a centrifugal field at rates which depend upon their sizes. For spheres, the rate of sedimentation varies with the square of the radius. It is clear that differential centrifugation will be unsuccessful if there is a continuous range of particle sizes as it depends upon there being sharp discontinuities in size between one class of particles and another, as exists between nuclei and mitochondria, for example. Figure 2.5 shows the stages involved in fractionating a tissue homogenate. Particles having similar sizes but differing in density can be separated by density gradient centrifugation (see p. 193).

Metabolic properties of isolated cell organelles

Subcellular organelles provide compartments in which enzymes, metabolites and ions can be concentrated, and surfaces on which multienzyme systems are arranged. A polyphasic system, such as that encountered in cells, allows a much more complex pattern of reactions to occur than would be possible in a single phase system. For example, it is difficult to imagine the efficient organization of respiratory chain processes and oxidative phosphorylation without suitable membranes to carry the enzymes. In the absence of cell membranes, across which ionic gradients can be established, the system of signalling by propagated action potentials could not have developed and the whole metabolic integrity of the cell would be threatened if the intracellular proteolytic enzymes (cathepsins) and acid nucleases were not retained within lysosomes (see p. 97).

The following survey outlines some of the metabolic properties and functions of the most common subcellular particles.

Mitochondria

Within mitochondria are located all the enzymes necessary to carry out the reactions of the tricarboxylic acid cycle, the oxidation of fatty acids and oxidative phosphorylation. The last two processes are confined exclusively to mitochondria and whilst enzymes of the citric acid cycle can be found in other cell fractions, pyruvate can be oxidized to CO_2 and H_2O by isolated mitochondria at a rate that is sufficient to account for the total oxygen uptake of the tissue. Of the Krebs cycle enzymes, only isocitric dehydrogenase is at a lower concentration in mitochondria than in whole cells. There are two species of isocitric dehydrogenase in liver, one requiring NAD as cofactor and the other NADP. Mitochondria carry both of these enzymes but only the NADP-dependent form is found in the cytoplasm. The role of the cytoplasmic enzyme may be to provide NADPH$_2$ for the synthesis of fatty acids. Both mitochondria and cytoplasm contain NAD and NADP but in different proportions. NAD is distributed evenly between mitochondria and cytoplasm whilst NADP is about one-and-a half times more concentrated in the former than in the latter. Attached firmly to the membranes of mitochondria is the enzyme transhydrogenase that catalyses the transfer of hydrogen atoms between NADPH$_2$ and NAD. This enzyme permits NADPH$_2$ produced inside mitochondria to pass its hydrogen on to the electron transport chain.

The lipid composition of mitochondria is quite characteristic, and the high content of polyglycerol phosphatide (cardiolipin) is especially noteworthy.

$$H_2COOCR \qquad\qquad H_2COOCR$$
$$R'COOCH \qquad\qquad R'COOCH$$
$$H_2CO-\overset{O}{\underset{OH}{\overset{\|}{P}}}-O-H_2C-CHOH-CH_2O-\overset{O}{\underset{OH}{\overset{\|}{P}}}-O-CH_2$$

cardiolipin

This phospholipid is present in high concentration wherever electron transport chains occur. More than 80% of the fatty acid content of mitochondrial cardiolipin is accounted for by linoleic acid, one of the essential fatty acids.

Nuclei

It has been found that isolated nuclei are permeable to molecules as large as haemoglobin and the basic nuclear proteins (the protamines and histones). On the other hand, they retain some low molecular weight substances, such as ATP and sodium, with surprising tenacity, presumably by a binding mechanism. In order to minimize this leakage of material, calcium is often added to media used for the isolation of nuclei; it probably exerts its effect by increasing the stability of the nuclear membrane.

The main constituents of isolated nuclei are nucleohistones (containing deoxyribonucleic acids, DNA (see p. 242), ribonucleic acids, RNA (see p. 245) and histones) and 'residual proteins'. Several enzyme activities have been found in nuclei including those responsible for the synthesis of the important coenzyme NAD. Other enzymes concentrated in nuclei are arginase and adenosine-5-phosphatase. Glycogen and glycolytic enzymes are also present and the glycogen can be degraded to yield ATP via the glycolytic pathway.

One of the more interesting properties of nuclei is their ability to incorporate radioactive L-amino acids into protein. This ability to engage in protein synthesis depends upon the presence of DNA since it is impaired if the nuclei are treated with DNA-ase. The inhibition becomes progressively greater as more and more of the DNA is depolymerized. An unusual feature of amino acid incorporation into the protein of nuclei is its dependence on the sodium concentration of the medium; when all of the sodium is replaced by potassium only 15% of the activity remains.

Microsomes

The microsomal fraction, as isolated by differential centrifugation, consists of particles (diameter of about 0.1μ) derived from intracellular membranes, together with attached and detached ribosomes. The ribosomes contain almost 50% of the total RNA of the cell. Treating microsomes with detergents such as deoxycholate dissolves the lipoprotein of the membranes without affecting the RNA-granules and can be used as a convenient method for dissociating the ribonucleoprotein particles from the membranes during their purification.

A number of enzymic activities are associated with the microsome fraction; it is characterized by its high content of glucose-6-phosphatase, which forms glucose from glucose-6-phosphate. In the liver, the glucose that is made available in this way is used to keep the level of blood glucose constant. Other enzymic activities located in the microsomal membranes include those responsible for acetate incorporation into cholesterol, bile acid activation, esterase, sulphatase and cholinesterase, as well as those involved in detoxication processes. The enzymes responsible for the incorporation of activated amino acids into protein are probably confined to the ribonucleoprotein particles (see Section 6).

It is likely that some smooth surfaced parts of the endoplasmic reticulum, particularly in the Golgi region, are concerned in forming the membranes of secretory granules. It is of some interest, therefore, that the rate of incorporation of radioactive phosphate into certain phospholipids is stimulated in exo- and endocrine glands during periods of secretory activity, and that about two-thirds of this increment can be located in microsomal material soluble in deoxycholate. Thus phospholipids in the endoplasmic reticulum may be involved in some aspects of secretion.

Lysosomes

Lysosomes are subcellular organelles containing a number of hydrolytic enzymes (having their maximum activities at about pH 5) which are responsible for intracellular digestion and the autolysis of cells. These particles were discovered by De Duve and his associates in experiments involving very refined methods of centrifugation. It was found that the acid phosphatase present in conventional preparations of mitochondria could be liberated by lowering the osmolarity of the suspending solution.

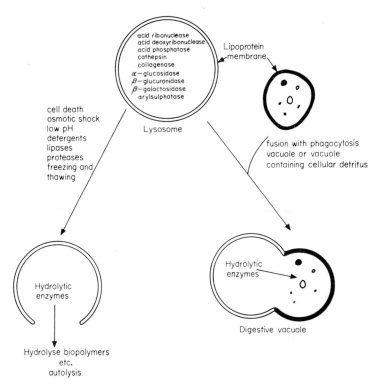

Figure 2.6. Lysosome, structure and function

When the phosphatase and cytochrome oxidase activities were measured in a number of different mitochondrial preparations, the ratio of the two activities to one another varied; as the oxidase activity rose, phosphatase activity fell and vice versa, suggesting that the 'mitochondria' were of more than one type. The two enzymic activities were almost completely separated from one another by density gradient centrifugation (see p. 193) and it was concluded that the acid phosphatase was confined to particles devoid of oxidative enzymes and distinct from mitochondria. Further investigations showed that ribonuclease, deoxyribonuclease, cathepsins and arylsulphatase were isolated together with the acid phosphatase by the centrifugation procedure and were released from the particles in a soluble form by the same types of treatment (decreasing the osmolarity or pH of the suspending medium or by adding detergents). The particles were termed lysosomes and are regarded as inert storage granules bound by a lipoprotein membrane. The enzyme content of lysosomes is summarized in Figure 2.6.

Lysosomes have been identified in kidney, brain, spleen, thyroid and adrenal medulla, as well as other tissues.

In experiments on whole animals and on tissue slices it has been shown that anaerobic conditions produced, for example, by ligation of the blood supply or incubation under nitrogen, cause the release of the lysosomal hydrolases in the soluble form. However, incubation of isolated lysosomes in nitrogen does not liberate more enzymes than incubation in oxygen. It seems likely that the fall in the pH of the tissues that occurs under anaerobic conditions facilitates the release of lysosomal enzymes *in vivo*; certainly the hydrolases are released from isolated lysosomes when the pH is reduced to 5 at 37°. Hence lysosomal enzymes could be responsible for the autolysis of cells once the pH has fallen sufficiently to disrupt the lysosomes. The spectrum of enzymic activities contained within the particles is sufficiently broad to catalyse the degradation of most of the polymers found in cells.

There is also evidence that lysosomes are concerned in the formation of digestive vacuoles in normal cells (see Figure 2.6).

CHAPTER 8

The carbohydrate metabolism of liver

The glucostatic function of the liver; the synthesis of carbohydrate and fixation of CO_2

The brain is sensitive to changes in the concentration of glucose in the blood because glucose is by far its most important source of energy and cannot be replaced by the other major fuels of respiration, fats and ketone bodies. The glucostatic activity of the liver is the principle means for buffering the glucose concentration of the blood against metabolic changes. Following a meal, blood glucose rises to about 130 mg/100 ml and then falls over a period of one to two hours to the fasting level of between 70 and 100 mg/100 ml. Part of this fall is accounted for by the removal of glucose from circulation by the liver, which converts it to glycogen. Between meals the fasting level of blood glucose is maintained at the expense of the stores of glycogen in the liver. The stores of glycogen present in muscle, although totalling 245 gm in a 70 kg man against only 108 gm in the liver, cannot contribute directly to the glucose content of the blood because glucose-6-phosphatase is absent from muscle.

Carbohydrate synthesis

Glycogen is synthesized from glucose originating from a number of sources. Glucose may be derived from the diet together with two other sugars, fructose and galactose, both of which can be converted into glucose. Glucose can also be synthesized from the carbon skeletons of some amino acids and from the glycerol of triglycerides. However, one of the major sources of liver glycogen and glucose is the lactate produced during the contraction of skeletal muscles and transported to the liver via the blood. Muscles, unable to use lactate in this way, synthesize most of their glycogen from glucose absorbed from the blood and originating in the liver. This cycle (muscle glycogen → blood lactate → liver glycogen → blood glucose → muscle glycogen) is called the Cori cycle after its discoverers.

Although the synthesis of glucose or glycogen from lactate should be possible by simply reversing the reactions of glycolysis, this is not the pathway used. Some of the component reactions have unfavourable positions of equilibrium and consequently present large energy barriers to such a simple reversal. If we consider the formation of glucose, there are three reactions that provide substantial energy barriers to the reversal of the glycolytic sequence of reactions. The formation of phosphopyruvate from pyruvate and ATP has an equilibrium constant of $2 \cdot 6 \times 10^4$ in favour of the formation of pyruvate which is equivalent to an energy barrier of 6200 cal. The formation of fructose-6-phosphate from fructose-1,6-diphosphate also involves a large positive free-energy change equal to about 4200 cal. The hexokinase reaction must be reversed as well and this requires 4200 cal since the equilibrium constant is 10^3. If glycogen, rather than glucose, is to be synthesized this last reaction is not required. It is clear from these considerations that appreciable amounts of carbohydrate cannot be synthesized by the direct reversal of glycolysis with the known concentrations of glycolytic intermediates found in the cell. There must, therefore, be some way around these energy barriers. In addition, if we look at the concentrations of ATP and ADP that are required for the three reactions just discussed we find that reversal of both the hexokinase and phosphofructokinase reactions requires high ADP and low ATP concentrations. On the other hand, the reversal of the pyruvic kinase reaction requires low ADP and high ATP concentrations. These two opposite conditions cannot be present simultaneously in the same part of the cell. The solution to these problems is the use of different pathways for the difficult reactions and the segregation of the reactions into different cell organelles.

The conversion of lactate into phosphopyruvate is a prerequisite for its conversion to glucose. Oxaloacetate can be converted to phosphopyruvate in the mitochondria of liver and kidney (and in the liver cytoplasm of some mammals) by phosphoenolpyruvate carboxykinase.

$$
\begin{array}{l}
\text{COOH} \\
| \\
\text{C}{=}\text{O} \\
| \qquad + \text{ GTP} \xrightarrow[\text{carboxykinase}]{\text{phosphoenolpyruvate}} \\
\text{CH}_2 \\
| \\
\text{COOH}
\end{array}
\qquad
\begin{array}{l}
\text{COOH} \\
| \\
\text{C}{-}\text{OPO}_3\text{H}_2 + \text{CO}_2 + \text{GDP} \\
\| \\
\text{CH}_2
\end{array}
$$

GTP is the high energy compound that is formed during the conservation of energy from succinyl CoA in the Krebs cycle; it is also maintained in equilibrium with ATP by the enzyme nucleoside diphosphate kinase.

$$\text{GDP} + \text{ATP} \rightleftharpoons \text{GTP} + \text{ADP}$$

Thus, if there is a plentiful supply of oxaloacetate in the mitochondria and a high level of ATP arising from respiration, phosphopyruvate will be formed. Normally, however, oxaloacetate is not in plentiful supply; the natural tendency is for it to drift out of the citric acid cycle as it decarboxylates spontaneously to give pyruvate and also provides the carbon skeleton for aspartic acid. Since lactate must be the chief precursor of liver glycogen because it is the only substance available in sufficient quantity to account for the observed synthesis, the ways in which lactate can be converted to oxaloacetate prior to yielding phosphopyruvate are now examined.

Lactate is first oxidized by lactic dehydrogenase to pyruvate which is then converted to either malate or oxaloacetate by the addition of a C_1 unit.

$$
\begin{array}{l}
\text{COOH} \\
| \\
\text{CHOH} + \text{NAD} \\
| \\
\text{CH}_3
\end{array}
\underset{\substack{\text{lactic} \\ \text{dehydrogenase}}}{\rightleftharpoons}
\begin{array}{l}
\text{COOH} \\
| \\
\text{C}{=}\text{O} + \text{NADH}_2 \\
| \\
\text{CH}_3
\end{array}
$$

The C_1 unit used is carbon dioxide and if this is to be attached to pyruvate, energy must be supplied to drive the carboxylation. Carboxylation of pyruvate can be achieved by means of two different reactions which use different energy sources and take place in different parts of the cell. The first of these reactions, catalysed by the malic enzyme, is the formation of malate from pyruvate, CO_2 and $NADPH_2$. The energy for this reaction is provided by the oxidation of $NADPH_2$ to NADP.

$$
\begin{array}{l}
\text{COOH} \\
| \\
\text{C}{=}\text{O} + \text{CO}_2 + \text{NADPH}_2 \\
| \\
\text{CH}_3
\end{array}
\underset{\substack{\text{malic} \\ \text{enzyme}}}{\rightleftharpoons}
\begin{array}{l}
\text{COOH} \\
| \\
\text{CHOH} + \text{NADP} \\
| \\
\text{CH}_2 \\
| \\
\text{COOH}
\end{array}
$$

The malic enzyme is found in the soluble fraction of the cell together with many enzymes that generate $NADPH_2$, for example, the NADP-dependent isocitric dehydrogenase and the pentose phosphate pathway (see p. 112). Malate, synthesized in the cell sap, can be converted to oxaloacetate and hence to phosphoenolpyruvate in both mitochondria and cytoplasm for subsequent conversion to glucose and glycogen. By using this pathway, the cell has replaced an essentially irreversible reaction by two reactions with favourable free-energy changes, the carboxylation driven by $NADPH_2$ and the combined decarboxylation and phosphorylation driven by GTP. In this way the energy barrier is broken down into two parts, each of which can easily be overcome with the driving forces at the cell's disposal. It must be emphasized that the energy required to pass from pyruvate to phosphopyruvate via oxaloacetate and malate is precisely the same as if the pyruvic kinase reaction were reversed directly.

Besides permitting the formation of phosphopyruvate from oxalo-acetate, the phosphoenolpyruvate carboxykinase reaction is important because it allows phosphoenolpyruvate produced during glycolysis to supply oxaloacetate when the latter is in short supply; for example, when citric acid cycle intermediates are being tapped off for synthetic purposes.

The other energetically favourable reaction available for the formation of oxaloacetate from pyruvate is catalysed by a mitochondrial enzyme called pyruvic carboxylase.

$$CH_3 \cdot CO \cdot COOH + CO_2 + ATP \xrightarrow[\text{acetyl CoA}]{Mg^{2+}} HOOC \cdot CH_2 \cdot CO \cdot COOH + ADP$$

ATP provides the energy to drive the carboxylation. Acetyl CoA, acting as a cofactor rather than a substrate, is thought to be an allosteric activator. That is to say, by combining with some region of the enzyme other than the active site it causes some configurational change that enhances the activity of the enzyme. Thus when the concentration of acetyl CoA is high the formation of oxaloacetate is stimulated. This, in turn, allows the excess acetyl CoA to be oxidized in the citric acid cycle after combining with oxaloacetate to give citrate. Furthermore, it diminishes the supply of acetyl CoA from glucose by allowing pyruvate to be reconverted to glucose via oxaloacetate and phosphopyruvate. In this way acetyl CoA formation from glucose will be slowed down until the excess has been removed by increased oxidation or synthetic processes.

There are thus three possible routes to phosphopyruvate from pyruvate.

Route 1

pyruvate + ATP $\rightleftharpoons$ phosphopyruvate + ADP

Route 2

pyruvate + $NADPH_2$ + CO_2 $\rightleftharpoons$ malate + NADP
malate + NAD $\rightleftharpoons$ oxaloacetate + $NADH_2$
oxaloacetate + GTP $\rightleftharpoons$ phosphopyruvate + GDP + CO_2

Route 3

pyruvate + CO_2 + ATP $\rightleftharpoons$ oxaloacetate + ADP + Pi
oxaloacetate + GTP $\rightleftharpoons$ phosphopyruvate + GDP + CO_2

The first is by the reversal of the pyruvic kinase reaction; the second is via the reactions catalysed by the combined actions of malic enzyme, malic dehydrogenase and phosphopyruvate carboxykinase whilst the third requires pyruvic carboxylase and phosphopyruvate carboxykinase. The question now is which is the more important of these pathways *in vivo*? A substantial reversal of the pyruvic kinase pathway appears to be very unlikely, not only owing to the unfavourable equilibrium, but also because there is only sufficient of the enzyme to account for 1% of the observed rate of glycogen synthesis, even if it worked at maximum capacity. The K_m of pyruvic kinase for pyruvate is around 10^{-2} M whilst the concentration of this substrate in the cell is only 10^{-3} M. At this concentration of pyruvate, the enzyme would be working at only one-twentieth of its maximum capacity. These considerations rule out pyruvic kinase as a significant enzyme in phosphopyruvate synthesis.

So far as the second route is concerned, phosphoenolpyruvate carboxykinase is present in liver at fifteen times the concentration necessary to account for the observed rate of glycogen synthesis and its K_m values for oxaloacetate and GTP are probably less than their physiological concentrations. However, malic enzyme is not as satisfactory in this respect. The potential activity of the enzyme is about two to three times that required to account for glycogen synthesis but the K_m values for CO_2 and pyruvate are both in the region of 10^{-3} M, which, at best, means that the enzyme would be working at a quarter of its maximal activity under physiological conditions. From these data it appears that the malic enzyme can make a contribution, albeit not a major one, to glycogen synthesis. Furthermore, phosphopyruvate can be synthesized from pyruvate in mitochondria which are devoid of malic enzyme so that this enzyme cannot be obligatory for its formation.

Pyruvic carboxylase and phosphoenolpyruvate carboxykinase have a capacity for phosphopyruvate synthesis that is ten to twenty times in excess of requirements and can operate at maximal activity using physiological concentrations of the substrates. The concentration of CO_2 required to half saturate pyruvic carboxylase is 4.8×10^{-5} M, which is much lower than the 10^{-3} M required by both the malic enzyme and phosphoenolpyruvate carboxykinase. This third pathway would therefore appear to be the most important for the formation of phosphopyruvate from pyruvate.

In some circumstances (for example, if the activity of the mitochondrial phosphoenolpyruvic carboxykinase is insufficient to meet the cell's demand for phosphoenolpyruvate for gluconeogenesis) the rate of synthesis of phosphopyruvate may be limited by the rate at which oxaloacetate can leave the mitochondria. In such cases, more rapid transport may be achieved by conversion of oxaloacetate to the more readily diffusable malate or aspartate (see Figure 2.7) which subsequently are reconverted to oxaloacetate in the cytoplasm.

The second energy barrier to carbohydrate synthesis is encountered in the conversion of fructose-1,6-diphosphate to fructose-6-phosphate, and is by-passed by substituting an hydrolysis, catalysed by fructose-1,6-diphosphatase, for the reversal of the phosphofructokinase reaction.

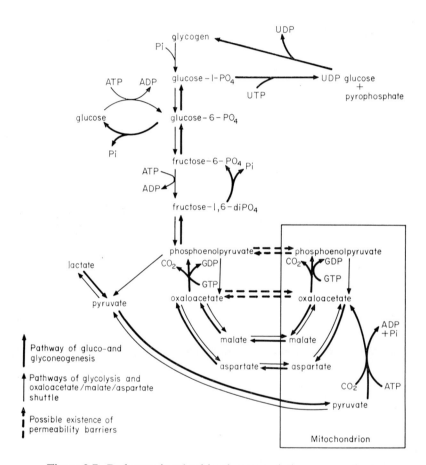

Figure 2.7. Pathways involved in glucose and glycogen synthesis

The energy barrier between glucose-6-phosphate and glucose is also by-passed by a phosphatase, glucose-6-phosphatase, which hydrolyses glucose-6-phosphate to give glucose and phosphate.

The final point of divergence between the glycolytic and glyconeogenic pathways is at the stage of converting glucose-1-phosphate to glycogen.

Despite the ease of reversal of the phosphorylase reaction ($K = 0.3$), the synthesis of glycogen from glucose-1-phosphate *in vivo* is by a group transfer reaction involving the high energy compound uridine triphosphate or UTP. Besides driving the formation of glycogen, this route makes possible a more flexible control of glycogen synthesis and breakdown (see Section 8).

UTP combines with glucose-1-phosphate to give uridine diphosphate glucose (UDP-glucose) and to eliminate pyrophosphate, in a reaction catalysed by a specific pyrophosphorylase. The pyrophosphate is then split by pyrophosphatase, thereby pulling the freely reversible reaction in favour of UDP-glucose formation.

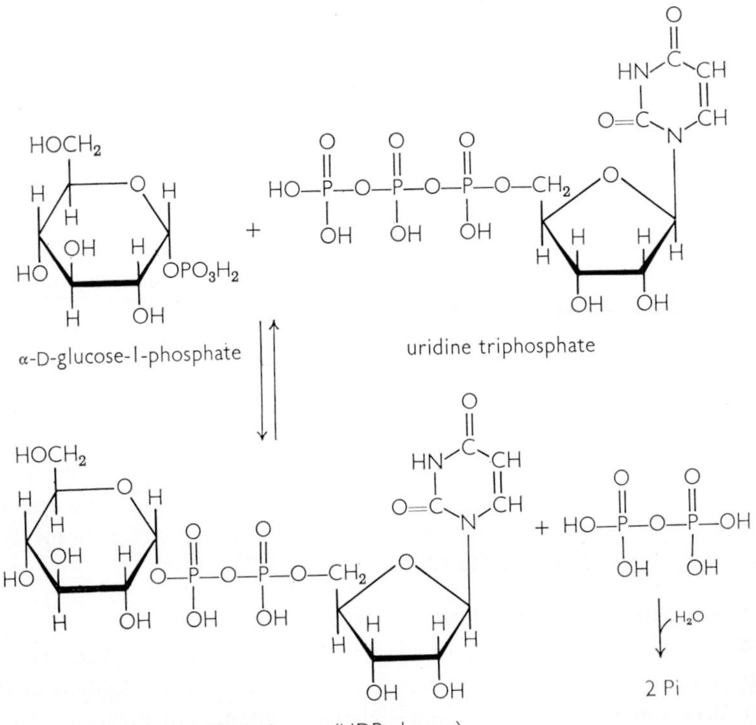

α-D-glucose-1-phosphate

uridine triphosphate

uridine diphosphate glucose (UDP-glucose)

The UDP-glucose transfers its glucose moiety to a terminal glucose residue in a glycogen molecule to lengthen the glucosyl chain. This transfer is effected by glycogen synthetase. Uridine diphosphate can be reconverted to UTP at the expense of ATP. The reactions leading to glucose and glycogen synthesis from lactate are shown in Figure 2.7.

Oxaloacetate formation from propionate

Besides those already mentioned, there is another reaction involving CO_2 fixation that can provide a supply of C_4 dicarboxylic acids. Propionyl CoA can react with CO_2 and ATP to give methyl malonyl CoA which can be isomerized to form succinyl CoA, an intermediate in the citric acid cycle.

$$ATP + CO_2 + CH_3 \cdot CH_2 \cdot COSCoA \xrightarrow[\text{biotin}]{Mg^{2+}} ADP + Pi + \underset{\underset{COSCoA}{|}}{\overset{\overset{COOH}{|}}{CH_3-CH}}$$

$$\underset{\underset{COSCoA}{|}}{\overset{\overset{COOH}{|}}{CH_3-CH}} \xrightleftharpoons[\text{vitamin } B_{12}]{} \underset{\underset{COSCoA}{|}}{\overset{\overset{COOH}{|}}{\underset{\underset{CH_2}{|}}{CH_2}}}$$

The carboxylase requires biotin, one of the B group of vitamins, as a co-factor; this is converted into a carboxy derivative in a reaction involving ATP and CO_2. The enzyme-bound carboxybiotin can then transfer its CO_2 onto propionyl CoA. (Pyruvic carboxylase also requires biotin as a co-factor. It is characteristic of biotin-containing enzymes that they are inhibited by a protein from egg white, called avidin, which binds biotin strongly.) The enzyme responsible for converting methyl malonyl CoA to succinyl CoA is methyl malonyl CoA isomerase which requires vitamin B_{12} as a cofactor.

Thus if propionyl CoA is available, liver and muscle can form succinyl CoA by the combined action of propionyl CoA carboxylase and methyl malonyl CoA isomerase. The major source of propionyl CoA in man is from fatty acids of odd chain length which account for some one to two per cent of the total fatty acids of the lipids stored. In ruminants about a quarter of the total intake of calories is accounted for by propionic acid formed by the bacteria of the rumen.

Milk and honey: the metabolism of galactose and fructose

Besides glucose, fructose and galactose are two other monosaccharides that make an important contribution to the carbohydrate content of the diet. Fructose occurs in honey and is also a component of the disaccharide

sucrose

sucrose which is the widely used cane- or beet-sugar. Galactose is a constituent of lactose, the disaccharide present in milk. Sucrose and lactose are

β-lactose

hydrolysed during digestion to give glucose and fructose, and glucose and galactose respectively. Fructose can be phosphorylated by hexokinase to fructose-6-phosphate which enters the glycolytic pathway. However, this reaction is slow and a special kinase, called fructokinase, is present in liver which phosphorylates fructose to give fructose-1-phosphate. This enzyme is not found in the foetal liver, but develops soon after birth (see p. 257). Fructose-1-phosphate can be split by an aldolase to form dihydroxy-acetone phosphate and glyceraldehyde. The former is an intermediate of the glycolytic pathway whilst the latter has to be phosphorylated before it can take part in glycolysis.

Fructose-1-phosphate can also be phosphorylated by 1-phosphofructo-kinase to give fructose-1,6-diphosphate, but again, this reaction is comparatively slow.

Galactose, like other hexoses, must be phosphorylated before it can be metabolized. Its conversion to galactose-1-phosphate is effected by galactokinase, an enzyme present in only small amounts in foetal liver but which increases in concentration after birth (see p. 257), when milk provides the diet.

galactose   galactose-1-phosphate

Galactose-1-phosphate can react with UDP-glucose to give UDP-galactose and glucose-1-phosphate; the enzyme catalysing this reaction is galactose-1-phosphate uridyl transferase.

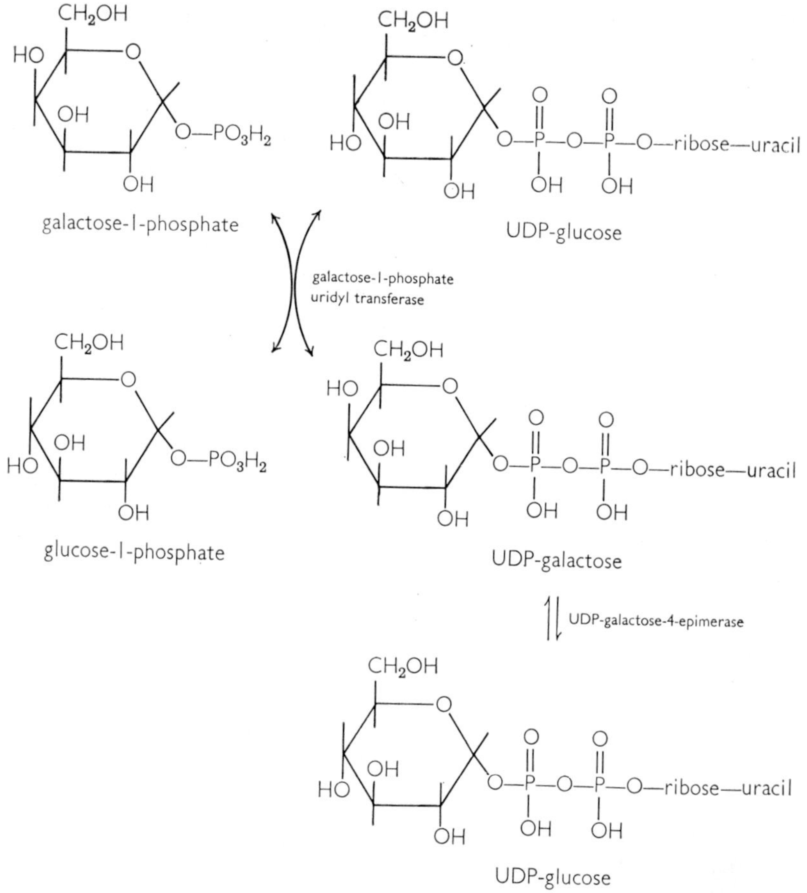

galactose-1-phosphate

UDP-glucose

galactose-1-phosphate
uridyl transferase

glucose-1-phosphate

UDP-galactose

UDP-galactose-4-epimerase

UDP-glucose

UDP-galactose is epimerized to form UDP-glucose by an enzyme called UDP-galactose-4-epimerase which alters the configuration at carbon 4 in the galactose residue. The UDP-glucose formed in this way reacts with more galactose-1-phosphate and thereby initiates its conversion to glucose-1-phosphate so that it gains access to the glycolytic and other pathways.

Diseases of carbohydrate metabolism

Fructosuria

This is a rare and harmless disorder of metabolism in which the ability to use fructose is impaired with the result that it is excreted in the urine. Feeding 50 g of fructose to a fructosuric patient produces a blood fructose level of 50 to 60 mg/100 ml, whilst in a normal individual the same dose gives rise to a blood fructose level of only 10 to 20 mg/100 ml. At present, the evidence suggests that the condition is caused by a deficiency of liver fructokinase.

Galactosaemia

This is an hereditary disease (see Section 6), transmitted by a recessive gene; the homozygote is unable to convert galactose to glucose. The symptoms of the patient are entirely due to the administration of galactose and if this is removed from the diet the symptoms disappear. As might be expected, the symptoms of galactosaemia appear soon after birth and are caused by the galactose component of lactose. The infants appear normal at birth, but rapidly become ill with vomiting and diarrhoea which lead to dehydration, and unless milk is removed from the diet, the infant will die. However, if the diagnosis is made before the disease is too far advanced and galactose is removed from the diet, recovery may be complete. Any delay in treatment may be accompanied by irreversible mental deterioration of the child. Galactosaemia is caused by the congenital absence of galactose-1-phosphate uridyl transferase and may be diagnosed by estimating the transferase activity in the red cells of suspected galactosaemics. In the absence of this enzyme, galactose-1-phosphate accumulates in tissues. Why the accumulation of galactose-1-phosphate should cause such serious effects is not understood, although there are indications that it may inhibit glucose-6-phosphate dehydrogenase activity and thus impair the supply of $NADPH_2$ and pentose sugars (see p. 112).

Another enzyme metabolizing galactose-1-phosphate is UDP-galactose pyrophosphorylase which catalyses the reaction:

$$UTP + galactose\text{-}1\text{-}phosphate \rightleftharpoons UDP\text{-}galactose + pyrophosphate$$

This enzyme is absent in the newborn child but increases in activity in the adult; this increase in activity may explain the somewhat greater tolerance towards galactose shown by adult galactosaemics. Even in the adult the activity of the pyrophosphorylase is only about one-sixth of the normal activity of the transferase, so that adult galactosaemics must still avoid galactose in their diets.

Glycogen storage diseases

There are six, clearly recognized, hereditary diseases that result in the excessive deposition of glycogen in the liver or muscle which can be ascribed to the absence of a particular enzyme. In order to understand these diseases we must examine the way in which branches are introduced into glycogen molecules during synthesis and removed during gly-cogenolysis. The branched structure of glycogen has been shown in Figure 1.19.

When a chain of α 1,4 linked glucose units reaches a certain length during the synthesis of glycogen, a portion of the chain is transferred to an α 1,6 linkage in another part of the chain. In this way α 1,6 branch points are introduced into the molecule with a frequency of about one to every five or so glucose units. The enzyme catalysing this transfer, amylo-(1,4 → 1,6)-transglucosylase, is commonly called the branching enzyme.

When it comes to the breakdown of glycogen, phosphorylase prunes the outer branches residue by residue until the fourth glucose residue before the α 1,6 linkage is reached. The three residues before that carrying the α 1,6 linkage are then removed to another part of the molecule by a trans-glucosylase. In this way the glucose residue engaged in the α 1,6 linkage is exposed and can be liberated as free glucose by the debranching enzyme, amylo-1,6-glucosidase. This liberates the last glucose residue in each branch as free glucose, not as glucose-1-phosphate. Something like 8% of the total glucose residues in glycogen are liberated as free glucose in this way.

Type I: von Gierke's disease

In this disease the abdomen is distended by the liver which is greatly enlarged owing to its excessively large content of glycogen. Patients suffer-ing from the disease have abnormally low fasting levels of blood glucose (between 0 and 15 mg/100 ml against the normal value of 70 to 100 mg/ 100 ml). There is also a greatly elevated level of plasma lipids which may account for 10% of the plasma volume. Biopsies show that the liver con-tains more than 4% of its wet weight as glycogen and that the structure of the polysaccharide is normal. The biochemical lesion responsible for the disease is the absence of glucose-6-phosphatase. Thus, whilst glycogen can be synthesized via the UDP-glucose pathway and broken down by phosphorylase, it cannot provide sufficient glucose to maintain the con-centration of blood glucose at its normal value. The low level of blood glucose that is found is probably maintained by the hydrolytic action of the debranching enzyme and tissue amylases on the glycogen stores.

It is interesting to note that glycogen is not formed in the liver until shortly before birth when the branching enzyme makes its appearance. In the normal individual glucose-6-phosphatase activity develops at birth and the stored glycogen is used rapidly.

Type II: Pompe's disease

This disease is characterized by extreme muscular weakness, a greatly enlarged heart, and a high concentration of glycogen in the heart, muscles and liver. It is believed to be caused by a congenital absence of lysosomal acid maltase which is able to remove glucose residues from the external branches of glycogen. Thus it would appear that glycogen breakdown by the acid maltase of the lysosomes, as well as by phosphorylase, is of physiological importance.

Type III: Forbes' disease

In contrast to von Gierke's disease, this condition is characterized by an excessive deposition of glycogen in the heart and muscles as well as in the liver. The disease is caused by the absence of the debranching enzyme. When glucose is available, the synthesis of glycogen proceeds normally and a branched molecule is formed. However, when the glycogen is broken down (by the combined action of phosphorylase and the transglucosylase) glucose residues can only be removed until the next branching point is reached because the debranching enzyme is absent. As glucose becomes available again chain extension continues, and, once another α 1,6 linkage is introduced, all the glucose residues between the two branching points are trapped and the glycogen molecule has irreversibly grown in size.

Type IV: Andersen's disease

This is a rare disease believed to be caused by the absence of the branching enzyme.

Type V: McArdle's disease

This disorder is characterized by the inability of skeletal muscles to carry out normal work. For example, under ischaemic conditions only 10 to 20% of the normal amount of work can be performed by the forearm and hand muscles. Also the concentration of lactate and pyruvate falls in the venous blood coming from the muscle during exercise, whereas under normal conditions the concentrations of these two acids rise. The glycogen content of the muscles is greatly increased above the normal values and homogenates of muscle prepared from biopsy specimens are unable to form lactate from the glycogen stores, although they can do so from added glucose-1-phosphate. These observations are in complete agreement with the finding that phosphorylase is absent from the muscles. Since glycogen deposition is still proceeding, this disease provides evidence to support the view that phosphorylase is not involved in the biosynthesis of glycogen. Furthermore the pathway leading to glycogen synthesis via UDP-glucose is operative in patients suffering from McArdle's disease. Liver phosphorylase, in contrast to muscle phosphorylase, is unaffected and therefore the liberation of glucose into the blood from liver glycogen stores can still be elicited by the injection of adrenaline.

Type VI: Her's disease

In this disease liver phosphorylase is missing whilst muscle phosphorylase activity is unaffected.

Congenital absence of glycogen synthetase

This is a very rare condition and is characterized by an inability to maintain the level of blood glucose under fasting conditions owing to the lack of stored carbohydrates; the hypoglycaemia can be prevented by regular feeding.

The pentose phosphate pathway

Besides the glycolytic pathway there is another important pathway that provides an alternative metabolic route for the degradation of glucose-6-phosphate. This is the pentose phosphate pathway, by whose overall activity three molecules of glucose-6-phosphate and six molecules of NADP can be transformed into three molecules of CO_2, two of fructose-6-phosphate, one of glyceraldehyde-3-phosphate and six of $NADPH_2$. Thus, this method of dealing with glucose provides a supply of $NADPH_2$, which is necessary for, amongst other things, the synthesis of fatty acids. The successive transformations of glucose-6-phosphate involve several phosphorylated five-carbon sugars. Of these ribose-5-phosphate is of particular importance as it provides the ribose moiety of the ribonucleic acids.

The pentose phosphate pathway can most simply be considered in two parts, an oxidative part and a non-oxidative part. The oxidative part (Figure 2.8) consists of two dehydrogenations and a decarboxylation. Glucose-6-phosphate is dehydrogenated to give 6-phosphogluconic acid by glucose-6-phosphate dehydrogenase, with NADP taking part as the hydrogen acceptor. The 6-phosphogluconate is then oxidatively decarboxylated in a reaction, again involving NADP as hydrogen acceptor, to give D-ribulose-5-phosphate and CO_2. In the non-oxidative part of the pathway, some of the ribulose-5-phosphate is epimerized to form xylulose-5-phosphate and some is enolized to give ribose-5-phosphate. These last

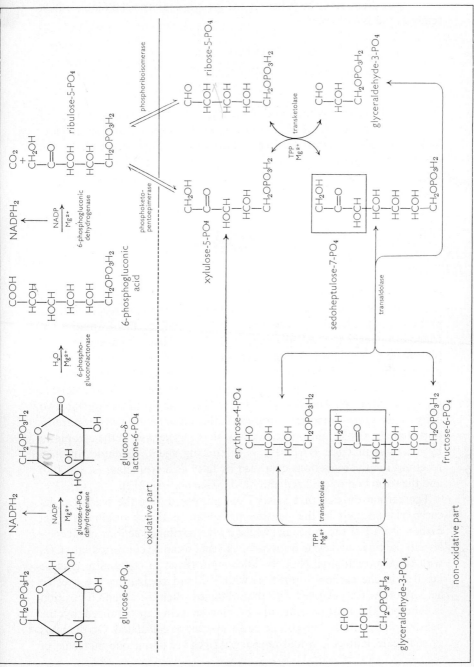

Figure 2.8. Pentose phosphate pathway

5+

two sugars then react together in the presence of transketolase, which removes the ketol group

$$
\begin{array}{c}
CH_2OH \\
| \\
C{=}O \\
|
\end{array}
$$

from xylulose-5-phosphate and attaches it to the aldehyde group of ribose-5-phosphate, to form sedoheptulose-7-phosphate and glyceralde-hyde-3-phosphate. Transketolase requires thiamine pyrophosphate, the pyrophosphate derivative of vitamin B_1, as the coenzyme that binds the ketol group. Transaldolase then catalyses the removal of the aldol group

$$
\begin{array}{c}
CH_2OH \\
| \\
C{=}O \\
| \\
CHOH \\
|
\end{array}
$$

from sedoheptulose-7-phosphate to glyceraldehyde-3-phosphate to make erythrose-4-phosphate and fructose-6-phosphate. The final reaction in the pathway is catalysed by transketolase and involves the formation of fructose-6-phosphate and glyceraldehyde-3-phosphate from erythrose-4-phosphate and xylulose-5-phosphate. The reactions of the pentose phosphate pathway are shown in Figure 2.8. The final products of the pathway, fructose-6-phosphate and glyceraldehyde-3-phosphate, can both enter the glycolytic pathway. $NADPH_2$ formed in the cytoplasm during the two dehydrogenations cannot be oxidized via the mitochondrial electron transport chain to any significant extent. NADP is regenerated in the cytoplasm by reactions that use $NADPH_2$ as a reducing agent. Examples of such reactions are the reductions catalysed by fatty acid synthetase (see p. 120) and the reduction of oxidized glutathione (see pp. 169, 212).

The carbon dioxide that arises from glucose during the oxidative de-carboxylation step in the pentose phosphate pathway originates from carbon atom 1 of the molecule, whilst by the combined actions of glycolysis and the citric acid cycle both carbons 1 and 6 can be converted into CO_2 with equal probability. Thus, by allowing a tissue to metabolize glucose labelled in the carbon 1 position with ^{14}C and comparing the specific activity of the CO_2 evolved with that obtained when the carbon 6 position is labelled, the relative amounts of glucose being metabolized by the pentose phosphate and glycolytic pathways can be calculated. On the basis of such calculations it would appear that in liver about one molecule of glucose in sixteen passes through the pentose phosphate pathway. However, these calculations can only be regarded as approximations since progressive randomization of the carbon atoms, for example, in the citric acid cycle, makes interpretation of the results very difficult.

Glucuronic acid formation

By contrast with the oxidation of the aldehyde group of glucose which yields gluconic acid (found in a phosphorylated form in the pentose phosphate pathway), oxidation of the primary alcoholic group at the C_6 position of D-glucose to a carboxyl group yields D-glucuronic acid.

D-glucuronic acid

D-Glucuronic acid is a component of many mucopolysaccharides, for example, hyaluronic acid, chondroitin sulphate and heparin (see p. 231); it also forms conjugates with some steroid hormones and bilirubin prior to their excretion. The formation of glucuronic acid is essentially a divergence from the pathway of glycogen synthesis. UDP-glucose can be oxidized by a NAD-linked dehydrogenase to yield UDP-glucuronic acid. This compound, like the parent UDP-glucose, has a high free energy of hydrolysis and is able to take part in those reactions leading to polymer formation and detoxication processes. The overall pathway from glucose to glucuronic acid is:

glucose $\longrightarrow$ glucose-6-phosphate $\longrightarrow$ glucose-1-phosphate $\longrightarrow$

UDP-glucose $\longrightarrow$ UDP-glucuronic acid $\longrightarrow$ glucuronic acid

The involvement of UDP-derivatives in the biosynthesis of polysaccharides illustrates an important aspect of biochemical energetics. The formation of any polymer from its constituent monomers requires an input of energy. In biological systems this requirement is fulfilled by converting the monomers to derivatives that are able to condense together, in reactions having negative free-energy changes, to yield the polymer. In order to form such reactive monomers a nucleoside triphosphate is used to provide energy that is conserved in the activated monomers. The conserved energy is liberated when the activated monomers link together.

UDP-glucuronic acid can also be hydrolysed to give free glucuronic acid which, in many animals, can be converted into ascorbic acid (vitamin C). In man, the higher apes and guinea-pigs an enzyme involved in this conversion is missing so that these animals have what amounts to a genetic defect affecting the whole of their species and manifesting itself by a requirement for vitamin C.

In man, glucuronic acid can be converted, by a number of reactions including a decarboxylation, into L-xylulose. Most people are able to transform this sugar into D-xylulose (see p. 112). This transformation involves the reduction of L-xylulose by $NADPH_2$ to give the pentahydric alcohol xylitol which is then oxidized by NAD to form D-xylulose:

$$
\begin{array}{ccccc}
\begin{array}{c} CH_2OH \\ | \\ C{=}O \\ | \\ HCOH \\ | \\ HOCH \\ | \\ CH_2OH \end{array}
&
\begin{array}{c} NADP \\ \rightleftarrows \\ NADPH_2 \end{array}
&
\begin{array}{c} CH_2OH \\ | \\ HOCH \\ | \\ HCOH \\ | \\ HOCH \\ | \\ CH_2OH \end{array}
&
\begin{array}{c} NAD \\ \rightleftarrows \\ NADH_2 \end{array}
&
\begin{array}{c} CH_2OH \\ | \\ C{=}O \\ | \\ HOCH \\ | \\ HCOH \\ | \\ CH_2OH \end{array}
\\
\text{L-xylulose} & & \text{xylitol} & & \text{D-xylulose}
\end{array}
$$

Individuals suffering from the harmless hereditary condition known as essential pentosuria excrete large amounts of L-xylulose in their urine. These patients are unable to convert L-xylulose to xylitol with the result that the former passes into the urine. Pentoses can sometimes be detected in the urine of normal individuals, usually following over-indulgence in plums or cherries; however, in such instances the chief sugar concerned is arabinose rather than L-xylulose.

CHAPTER 9

The metabolism of fat; the relationship between adipose tissue and liver

Because the metabolism of carbohydrates is often studied before that of lipids, it is commonly believed that the provision of energy by the oxidation of fatty acids is of secondary importance compared with the oxidation of carbohydrates and is only associated with unusual physiological states such as starvation. This view is wrong; the provision of energy from both carbohydrates and fats proceeds simultaneously and the relative importance of these two groups of compounds as sources of energy at any instant depends upon the interaction of many complex nutritional, metabolic and hormonal factors. In terms of the total energy reserves of the body, fat is of much greater quantitative importance than carbohydrate. On a weight for weight basis, triglycerides are able to supply, by oxidation, about two-and-a-half times more ATP than carbohydrates. Furthermore, whilst the glycogen reserves in muscle and liver total some 400 g, the adipose tissue of a normal 70 kg man contains about 10 kg of triglyceride.

The metabolism of the body can be understood only when the differing roles played by the various organs are appreciated. For example, the liver synthesizes glucose from the lactate produced by skeletal muscles and exports it for use by the brain and other tissues, including muscles. In addition, skeletal muscle, being a net producer of lactate, provides a metabolic fuel for the heart which is a net consumer of lactate. In the same general way, the overall pattern of lipid metabolism can only be understood in terms of the different contributions made by a variety of tissues.

Metabolism of adipose tissue

Triglycerides are stored in the fat cells of adipose tissue which is located in the abdominal cavity, beneath the skin and between skeletal muscle

117

fibres. Contrary to older ideas, these fat stores are in a state of continuous metabolic flux that involves the synthesis, rearrangement and degradation of the triglycerides.

Triglyceride synthesis

Triglycerides are synthesized from long chain fatty acids and L-α-glycerophosphate by the following series of reactions:

$$3R \cdot COOH + 3CoA \cdot SH + 3ATP \longrightarrow 3R \cdot COS \cdot CoA + 3AMP + 3\,\text{Pyrophosphate}$$

$$
\begin{array}{l}
CH_2 \cdot OH \\
| \\
CH \cdot OH \qquad + 2R \cdot COS \cdot CoA \longrightarrow \\
| \\
CH_2 \cdot OPO_3H_2
\end{array}
\qquad
\begin{array}{l}
CH_2 \cdot OCR \ (\overset{O}{\overset{\|}{})} \\
| \\
CH \cdot OCR \ (\overset{O}{\overset{\|}{})} \qquad + 2CoA \cdot SH \\
| \\
CH_2 \cdot OPO_3H_2
\end{array}
$$

(L-α-glycerophosphate)   (phosphatidic acid)

$$
\begin{array}{l}
CH_2 \cdot OCR \ (\overset{O}{\overset{\|}{})} \\
| \\
CH \cdot OCR \ (\overset{O}{\overset{\|}{})} \qquad + H_2O \longrightarrow \\
| \\
CH_2 \cdot OPO_3H_2
\end{array}
\qquad
\begin{array}{l}
CH_2 \cdot O \cdot CR \ (\overset{O}{\overset{\|}{})} \\
| \\
CH \cdot OCR \ (\overset{O}{\overset{\|}{})} \qquad + H_3PO_4 \\
| \\
CH_2 \cdot OH
\end{array}
$$

(phosphatidic acid)   (diglyceride)

$$
\begin{array}{l}
CH_2 \cdot OCR \ (\overset{O}{\overset{\|}{})} \\
| \\
CH \cdot OCR \ (\overset{O}{\overset{\|}{})} \qquad + R \cdot COS \cdot CoA \longrightarrow \\
| \\
CH_2 \cdot OH
\end{array}
\qquad
\begin{array}{l}
CH_2 \cdot OCR \ (\overset{O}{\overset{\|}{})} \\
| \\
CH \cdot OCR \ (\overset{O}{\overset{\|}{})} \qquad + CoA \cdot SH \\
| \\
CH_2 \cdot OCR \ (\overset{O}{\overset{\|}{})}
\end{array}
$$

(diglyceride)   (triglyceride)

Before they can react with L-α-glycerophosphate, long chain fatty acids are converted into their reactive acyl-CoA forms at the expense of ATP. This reaction probably involves the intermediate formation of acyl adenylate derivatives which remain bound to the enzyme, thiokinase, in much the same way as do the amino acyl adenylates involved in protein synthesis (see Section 6). Two molecules of activated fatty acids then react with a molecule of L-α-glycerophosphate to form 1,2-glycerophosphatidic acid (phosphatidic acid) which in turn loses its phosphate group to yield a 1,2-diglyceride. By reacting with a further molecule of activated fatty acid the diglyceride is converted into a triglyceride. The three acyl residues in a triglyceride frequently differ from one another in both chain length and degree of saturation.

In adipose tissue glycerol cannot be converted into L-α-glycerophosphate because the necessary enzyme, glycerokinase, is absent. Thus, the only source of L-α-glycerophosphate is from dihydroxyacetone phosphate (an intermediate of glycolysis, see p. 47) via a reduction catalysed by L-α-glycerophosphate dehydrogenase.

$$
\begin{array}{ccc}
CH_2OH & & CH_2OH \\
| & & | \\
C{=}O \quad + NADH_2 \rightleftharpoons & HOCH & + NAD \\
| & & | \\
CH_2OPO_3H_2 & & CH_2OPO_3H_2
\end{array}
$$

This dependence upon dihydroxyacetone phosphate and hence upon glucose as the source of L-α-glycerophosphate is of particular significance in the regulation of triglyceride release and synthesis by adipose tissue (see p. 121).

Fatty acid synthesis

Adipose tissue obtains long chain fatty acids from the chylomicra (see p. 127), lipoproteins (see p. 123) and free fatty acids (FFA) of the plasma, and by *de novo* synthesis from carbohydrates. Whilst mitochondria are known to engage in fatty acid synthesis and chain extension to some extent, it now appears that the major pathway for fatty acid synthesis is located in the cytoplasm and differs in its detailed enzymology from that of fatty acid oxidation. Glucose supplies C_2 units in the form of acetyl-CoA by glycolysis and pyruvic decarboxylase and these provide the basic units from which long chain fatty acids are formed.

Acetyl-CoA is converted into malonyl-CoA by an ATP-dependent carboxylation reaction that requires biotin (one of the B group of vitamins) as a coenzyme for acetyl-CoA carboxylase.

$$
\text{enzyme–biotin} + CO_2 + ATP \longrightarrow \text{enzyme–biotin—}CO_2 + ADP + Pi
$$

$$
\begin{array}{l}
\text{enzyme–biotin—}CO_2 + CH_3{\cdot}COSCoA \longrightarrow \\
\end{array}
\quad
\begin{array}{l}
COSCoA \\
| \\
CH_2 \quad + \text{ enzyme–biotin} \\
| \\
COOH
\end{array}
$$

In yeast, and probably in mammals, the entire process of conversion of malonyl-CoA to long chain saturated fatty acids is catalysed by a multi-enzyme system, called fatty acid synthetase. Yeast fatty acid synthetase bears two sulphydryl groups concerned with this reaction sequence; the

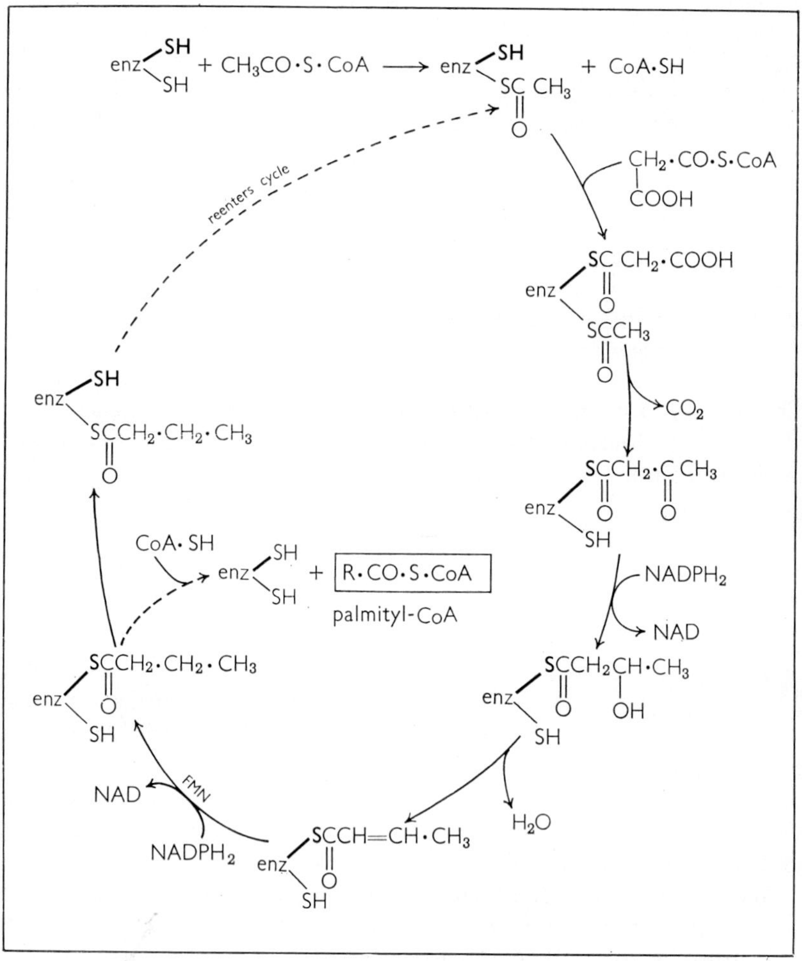

Figure 2.9. Fatty acid synthesis

enzyme system is primed when acetyl-CoA reacts with one of these and malonyl-CoA with the other (Figure 2.9). The acetyl group is transferred to the malonyl group which condenses with it and simultaneously loses carbon dioxide. In this way an acetoacetyl derivative of the enzyme is formed in a reaction that is rendered irreversible by the accompanying decarboxylation. The acetoacetyl enzyme is reduced by $NADPH_2$ to give the D-(−)-β-hydroxybutyryl derivative. This is dehydrated and then reduced by $NADPH_2$, in a reaction involving flavin mononucleotide (FMN, see Figure 1.29) as a bound coenzyme, to yield the butyryl enzyme. The butyryl group is next transferred back to the SH group with which the acetyl-CoA originally reacted. The cycle is repeated once the enzyme has combined with more malonyl-CoA. This sequence of reactions is continued until a fatty acyl enzyme is formed (in which the acyl group has about 16 carbon atoms). Fatty acyl-CoA is then released by a reaction involving free coenzyme A. Fatty acid synthetase is inhibited by its products, namely long chain fatty acyl-CoA derivatives; furthermore, acetyl-CoA carboxylase is stimulated by citrate. Thus, when fatty acids are in plentiful supply their rate of synthesis is decreased, and when citrate (and hence acetyl-CoA) is readily available it is increased. Most of the $NADPH_2$ required for both of the reductions catalysed by fatty acid synthetase is provided by the pentose phosphate pathway which is particularly active in adipose and mammary tissue (but see Section 8).

The utilization of triglycerides

Triglycerides arriving at adipose tissue as components of chylomicra or β-lipoproteins are hydrolysed to give free fatty acids and glycerol by a lipoprotein lipase, termed the clearing factor lipase, which requires heparin as a cofactor. The exact location of this enzyme within adipose tissue is uncertain (although in the mammary gland it is attached to the cell membrane) and it is not entirely clear whether hydrolysis is intra- or extracellular. The lipoprotein lipase is responsible for clearing the plasma of chylomicra after a fatty meal, a process that is usually complete after one or two hours.

The balance between net triglyceride synthesis and breakdown in adipose tissue is determined chiefly by two factors, the availability of glucose and the activity of the adrenaline-sensitive lipase, an enzyme not to be confused with the clearing factor lipase.

The triglycerides of adipose tissue are continuously hydrolysed by the adrenaline-sensitive lipase to yield fatty acids and glycerol. Provided there is an adequate supply of glucose, this hydrolysis can be matched by resynthesis because glucose supplies the L-α-glycerophosphate needed for triglyceride formation. However, if the supply of glucose is limited, as, for example, during insulin deficiency or starvation, the provision of L-α-glycerophosphate will be diminished and hydrolysis of triglyceride will outstrip its synthesis. Hence free fatty acids and glycerol will accumulate
5*

in the cells; glycerol can pass into solution in the plasma as do the free fatty acids provided plasma albumins are present with which they can form water-soluble complexes. Persons with a congenital deficiency of plasma albumins have an impaired ability to mobilize fatty acids.

The activity of the adrenaline-sensitive lipase is stimulated by a number of hormones and especially by adrenaline. When adrenaline reaches the adipose tissue after release from the adrenal medulla, fatty acids are mobilized; in addition, glucose is released from glycogen stores in the liver and muscles. There is now good evidence that adrenaline exerts its effect upon the lipase by stimulating the synthesis of cyclic 3′,5′-AMP (see p. 281) which is a cofactor for this enzyme as well as for phosphorylase. Glucagon and ACTH also stimulate the lipase; glucagon appears to act in a similar manner to adrenaline whereas ACTH has both intrinsic activity and a facilitating effect upon the action of adrenaline.

Brown adipose tissue is characterized by a high content of mitochondria. In contrast to white adipose tissue it does not respond to catecholamines by a net release of free fatty acids into the circulation. Instead most of the fatty acids are used for the resynthesis of triglyceride within the tissue, the remainder are oxidized in the mitochondria to provide ATP for the resynthesis. This cycle of hydrolysis and resynthesis constitutes an ATPase evolving heat. Thus the physiological role of the brown adipose tissue is to provide heat for the maintenance of body temperature rather than to supply metabolic fuels for use by other parts of the body.

Fat metabolism of the liver

Albumin-bound fatty acids and glycerol in solution pass from adipose tissue to the liver and muscles where they can be metabolized. The liver is also able to take up triglycerides from β-lipoproteins and chylomicra although it does not possess clearing-factor lipase. During starvation clearing-factor lipase disappears from adipose tissue with the result that most of the available triglyceride is taken up by the liver rather than the fat depots.

In the liver long chain fatty acids can be metabolized via three main pathways: oxidation to CO_2 and H_2O to provide energy, conversion to acetyl CoA and synthesis to triglyceride. The acetyl CoA may give rise to acetoacetate or it may be used to synthesize other compounds such as cholesterol (see p. 286). Synthesis to triglyceride proceeds as in adipose tissue but in liver glycerol, as well as glucose, can provide the necessary L-α-glycerophosphate because glycerokinase is present to carry out the reaction

$$\text{glycerol} + \text{ATP} \longrightarrow \text{L-}\alpha\text{-glycerophosphate} + \text{ADP}$$

Under normal conditions the liver does not store the triglycerides which it synthesizes but instead exports them as water-soluble β-lipoproteins to other tissues. Thus, if the liver is to dispose of its triglycerides in this manner it has to be able to synthesize an adequate supply of β-globulins to incorporate into β-lipoproteins together with the triglycerides, phospholipids and cholesterol.

Oxidation of fatty acids

Oxidation of long chain fatty acids to CO_2 and H_2O takes place in mitochondria and is accomplished by degrading the acids to form acetyl-CoA residues that can be further oxidized via the citric acid cycle. The pathway of fatty acid oxidation starts when the fatty acid is activated by combination with coenzyme A in the thiokinase reaction (Figure 2.10). The activated fatty acid is dehydrogenated by acyl-CoA dehydrogenase with FAD as hydrogen acceptor to form an $\alpha:\beta$ unsaturated acyl-CoA

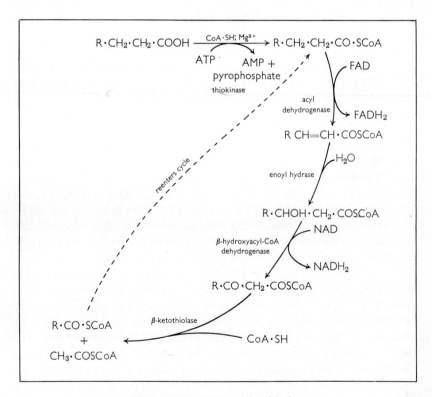

Figure 2.10. Fatty acid oxidation

derivative. As with the succinic dehydrogenase reaction in the citric acid cycle, methylene hydrogen atoms do not have a sufficiently negative redox potential to reduce NAD so that a hydrogen acceptor of more positive potential [FAD] has to be used.

Water is then added across the double bond to give an L-($+$)-β-hydroxy-acyl-CoA compound which in turn is oxidized by β-hydroxyacyl-CoA dehydrogenase with NAD as hydrogen acceptor to form the corresponding β-ketoacyl-CoA. This reaction is formally similar to the malate dehydrogenase reaction. In the final reaction of the sequence, catalysed by β-ketothiolase, coenzyme A reacts with the β-ketoacyl-CoA to yield acetyl-CoA and an acyl-CoA that is two carbon atoms shorter than the original fatty acid. Acetyl-CoA can enter the citric acid cycle and be completely oxidized to H_2O and CO_2, whilst the shortened acyl-CoA can reenter the pathway of fatty acid oxidation. Eight repetitions of this 'β-oxidation' pathway allow stearic acid (C_{18}) to be converted into nine molecules of acetyl-CoA.

Only a limited number of fatty acid molecules are activated at any given time and no more are attacked until the original molecules are completely degraded. This is because there is only a limited amount of coenzyme A available for the activation and β-ketothiolase reactions. Thus, there is an orderly consumption of fatty acids and not a random attack in which all the acids become somewhat shorter.

Comparison of the pathways of synthesis and oxidation of fatty acids

The degradative pathway, although theoretically reversible, is of minor importance in fatty acid synthesis because the concentrations of reduced coenzymes ($NADH_2$ and $FADH_2$) needed to drive it are not available in mitochondria. Although the equilibrium of the β-ketothiolase reaction is also unfavourable, the formation of acetoacetyl·CoA from two molecules of acetyl-CoA by reversal of this reaction may be readily accomplished because the concentration of acetyl-CoA available is sufficiently high. However, during the next turn of the cycle, when butyryl-CoA has to react with more acetyl-CoA to give β-ketohexanyl-CoA, the equilibrium is against synthesis because butyryl-CoA is present in only low concentrations. Thus, further chain extension by reversal of the oxidative pathway becomes progressively hampered owing to the fact that successive long chain acyl-CoAs are increasingly rare. In contrast, in fatty acid synthesis the condensation step is accompanied by a decarboxylation which pulls the reaction in the direction of synthesis and allows the synthetic pathway to engage in chain extension beyond four carbon units. Another difference is that the reducing power for synthesis is provided by $NADPH_2$, rather than by NADH$_2$. Finally, in fatty acid biosynthesis the intermediates acylate the SH groups of the synthetase rather than that of coenzyme A.

As with glycogen synthesis and breakdown, the existence of separate pathways for the oxidation and synthesis of fatty acids allows flexibility of control and the simultaneous operation of both pathways.

Ketone bodies

Acetyl-CoA residues derived from fatty acids can condense to form acetoacetyl-CoA. This can be deacylated in the liver to yield acetoacetate both directly and via β-hydroxy-β-methyl glutaryl-CoA (Figure 2.11). Acetoacetate so formed leaves the liver (which is unable to reactivate it because the appropriate kinase is not present) and passes to other tissues

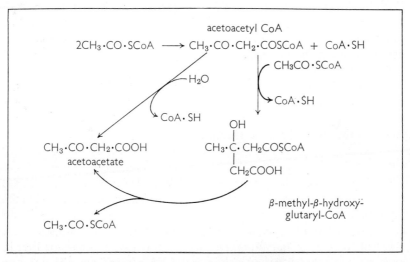

Figure 2.11. Formation of acetoacetate

able to reconvert it to acetoacetyl-CoA and use it as a metabolic fuel. In heart, the enzyme thiophorase reactivates acetoacetate by transfering the CoA group from succinyl-CoA (formed in the citric acid cycle) to aceto-acetate. Many tissues, for example, heart muscle, can obtain as much as 70% of their total energy by the oxidation of acetyl-CoA residues derived from acetoacetate. Also acetoacetate decarboxylates spontaneously to give acetone and can be reduced by β-hydroxybutyrate dehydrogenase to D-(−)-β-hydroxybutyrate with NADH$_2$ as hydrogen donor. Acetoacetate, β-hydroxybutyrate and acetone are the 'ketone bodies'. It should be noted that the β-hydroxybutyryl-CoA formed during fatty acid oxidation is the L (+) isomer whilst the ketone body and the β-hydroxybutyryl derivative of fatty acid synthetase are the D $(-)$ isomers. These observations indicate that the ketone body D-$(-)$-β-hydroxybutyrate cannot be derived directly from the L-$(+)$-β-hydroxybutyryl-CoA formed during fatty acid oxidation.

Energy yield of triglyceride oxidation

During each turn of the fatty acid oxidation spiral a molecule of FAD and a molecule of NAD are reduced. The reoxidation of these coenzymes by the electron transport chain can be coupled to the formation of 5 molecules of ATP. Thus, during the eight turns of the spiral needed to convert stearic acid to acetyl-CoA, 40 molecules of ATP can be produced, giving a net yield of 39 since one molecule of ATP is required to activate the fatty acid initially. Moreover, as each acetyl-CoA is oxidized a further 12 molecules of ATP can be formed. Thus the net yield is $39 + (12 \times 9) = 147$ molecules of ATP per molecule of stearic acid oxidized. This may be compared with 117 molecules of ATP formed during the complete oxidation of three glucosyl residues from glycogen, which also contain 18 carbon atoms.

Glycerol liberated by adipose tissue can be oxidized by the liver with a net yield of 22 molecules of ATP. However, during starvation the glycerol of triglycerides may assume more importance as a source of glucose to maintain the level of plasma glucose.

Fatty livers

Under normal conditions the rate of triglyceride synthesis by the liver is balanced by the rate at which triglycerides are released into the blood in the form of β-lipoproteins. Thus fatty livers may arise when there is an imbalance between triglyceride synthesis and the synthesis of β-lipoprotein.

During periods of starvation free fatty acids (FFA) arrive at the liver in larger amounts than usual since the rate of FFA release from adipose tissue increases as the level of blood glucose falls. To some extent the liver is able to compensate for this increased arrival of FFA by increasing the rates of the various pathways able to metabolize fatty acids, including triglyceride synthesis and export. However, during even moderate starvation there is a tendency for triglyceride to accumulate in the liver.

Similarly in uncontrolled diabetes, glucose cannot enter adipose tissue as easily as usual because insulin is not available to facilitate its transport across the cell membrane. Therefore the synthesis of L-α-glycerophosphate, and consequently of triglyceride, is diminished and there is a net loss of FFA from the tissue as a result of the continuous activity of the adrenaline-sensitive lipase. Under these conditions the liver is again faced with the problem of processing large amounts of FFA and, despite increased metabolic activity, triglycerides accumulate causing a fatty liver to develop. A further consequence of increased FFA metabolism by the liver is the increased production of ketone bodies that characterizes both starvation and diabetes.

Reduced synthesis of β-globulins, even with normal plasma fatty acid concentrations, will also result in fatty livers. An example of this is the fatty liver occurring in carbon tetrachloride poisoning. This damages the endoplasmic reticulum and inhibits protein synthesis. Similarly, the absence of choline from the diet can also lead to the development of a fatty liver. This is probably because choline can act as a source of methyl groups to reconvert homocysteine to methionine (see p. 151), an essential amino acid required for β-globulin synthesis.

Small intestine and plasma

After a meal triglycerides (resynthesized in the mucosal cells of the small intestine from absorbed long chain fatty acids and L-α-glycerophosphate derived from blood glucose) are discharged into the lymphatic system in the form of chylomicra. These pass into the blood stream via the thoracic duct and give the blood a characteristic milky appearance. The chylomicra are droplets of fat about 1 μ in diameter which are wrapped up in a membrane of phospholipid and cholesterol; they contain only 2% of their weight as protein compared with 7% in β-lipoproteins. More than 80% of the weight of the chylomicra is accounted for by triglyceride; consequently the particles have a low density and float to the surface like cream when blood is centrifuged. Possibly some β-lipoproteins also originate from the intestinal mucosa.

Summary

The interrelationships between adipose tissue, liver, muscles and small intestine are illustrated in Figure 2.12.

Metabolism of phospholipids

The triglycerides discussed in the preceding sections are important as energy stores. The phospholipids are essential components of the lipoprotein membranes of subcellular structures. These lipids differ from triglycerides in possessing both polar and non-polar regions which enable the molecules to be orientated at interfaces with the polar, water-soluble groups in the aqueous phase and the non-polar groups in the non-aqueous

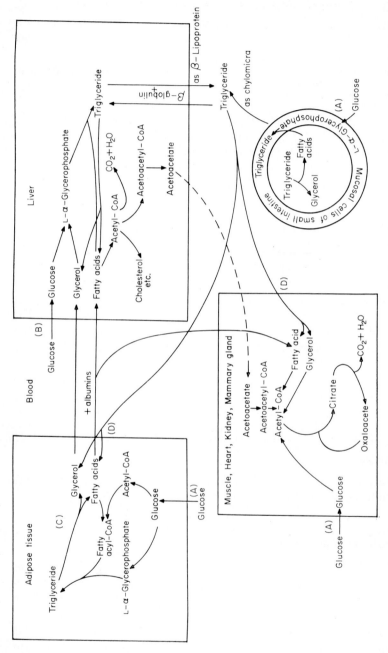

Figure 2.12.   Tissue interrelationships in lipid metabolism. (A) Site of action of insulin; (B) Insulin not required for glucose entry; (C) Hormone-sensitive lipase; (D) Clearing factor lipase

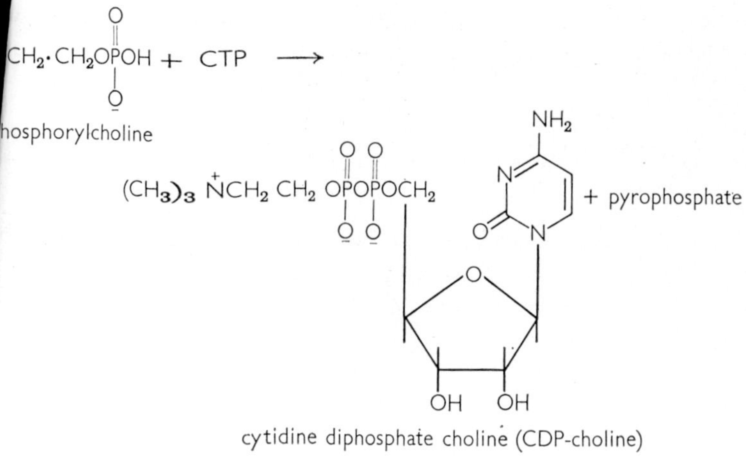

$$CH_2 \cdot CH_2 O \overset{O}{\underset{O}{\overset{\|}{P}}} OH + CTP \longrightarrow$$

phosphorylcholine

$$(CH_3)_3 \overset{+}{N}CH_2 CH_2 \ O\overset{O}{\underset{O}{\overset{\|}{P}}}O\overset{O}{\underset{O}{\overset{\|}{P}}}OCH_2 \quad + \text{ pyrophosphate}$$

cytidine diphosphate choline (CDP-choline)

line reacts with **ATP** to give phosphorylcholine which is then con-
ed into cytidine di**p**hosphate choline by further reaction with cytidine
phosphate (**CTP**). **CTP** is a high energy phosphate compound similar to
P but having the **a**denine group replaced by the pyrimidine cytosine
p. 243). The rea**ct**ions involved in choline activation are expensive

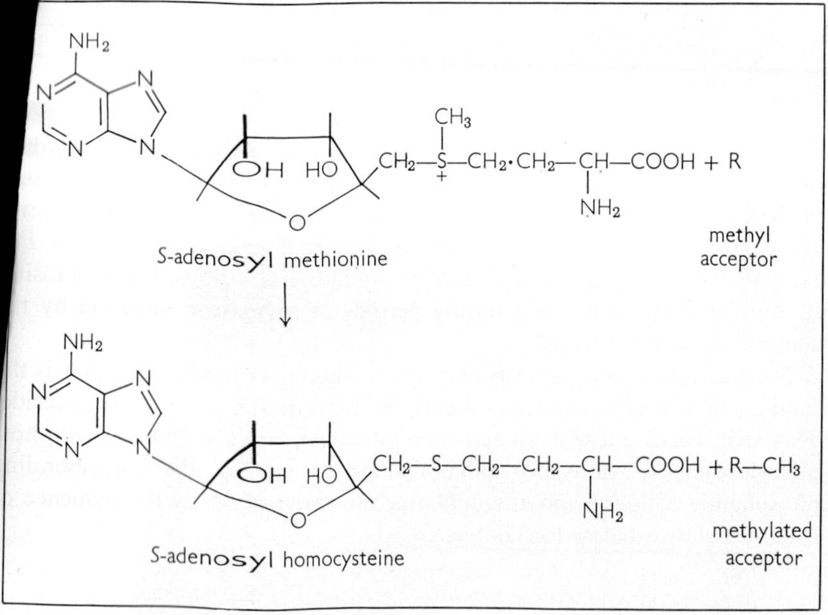

$$S\text{-adenosyl methionine} \quad CH_2{-}\overset{CH_3}{\underset{+}{S}}{-}CH_2 \cdot CH_2{-}\overset{}{\underset{NH_2}{CH}}{-}COOH + R$$
methyl acceptor

$$S\text{-adenosyl homocysteine} \quad CH_2{-}S{-}CH_2{-}CH_2{-}\overset{}{\underset{NH_2}{CH}}{-}COOH + R{-}CH_3$$
methylated acceptor

Figure 2.13. **A**ctivation of methionine by reaction with ATP

phase. The formulae of some phospholip
water-soluble groups indicated, are show

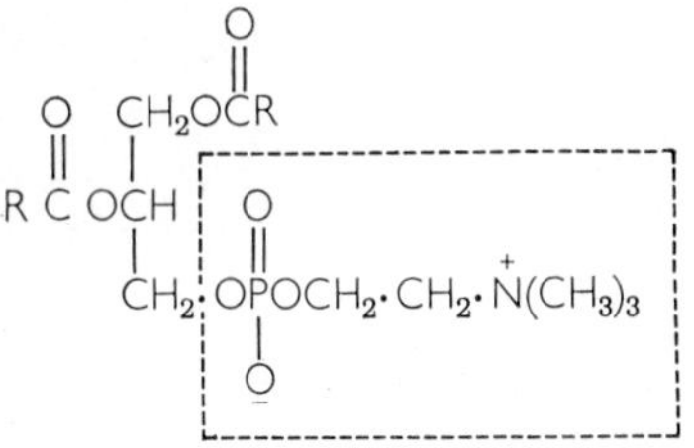

$(CH_3)_3\overset{+}{N}$

phosphatidyl choline
(α-lecithin)

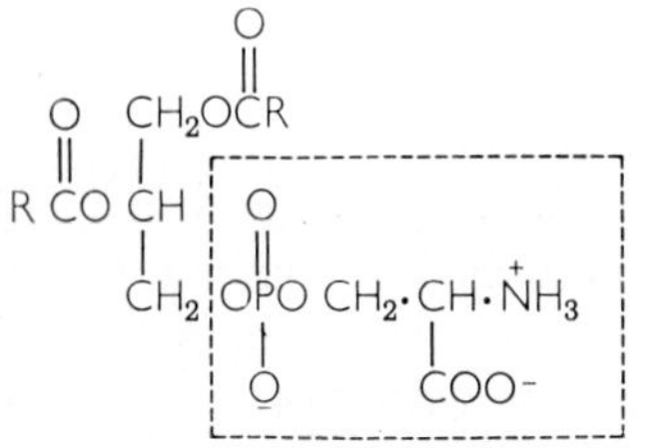

phosphatidyl serine
(cephalin)

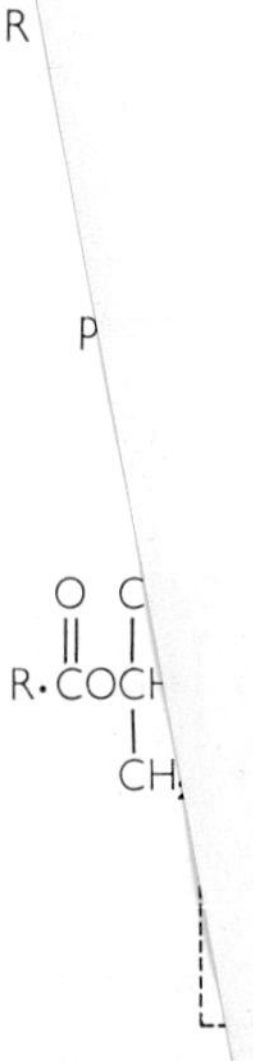

Cho
vert
trip
AT
(se

phos

Dashed lines enclose the water-soluble groups.

Each is an ester of a phosphatidic acid and a wa
Studies with radioactive phosphate have shown th
phospholipid molecules are continually turning over. T
varies markedly with changes in the physiological activ
example the rate of incorporation of phosphate into ph
is stimulated about ten-fold during periods of amylase
acinar cells of the pancreas.

The pathway of biosynthesis of glycerol-containing pho
same as that of triglycerides as far as the formation of a
This then reacts, not with an activated fatty acid, but with
phorylcholine or phosphorylethanolamine to yield the
phosphatide. Choline and ethanolamine are activated by t
reactions shown below for choline.

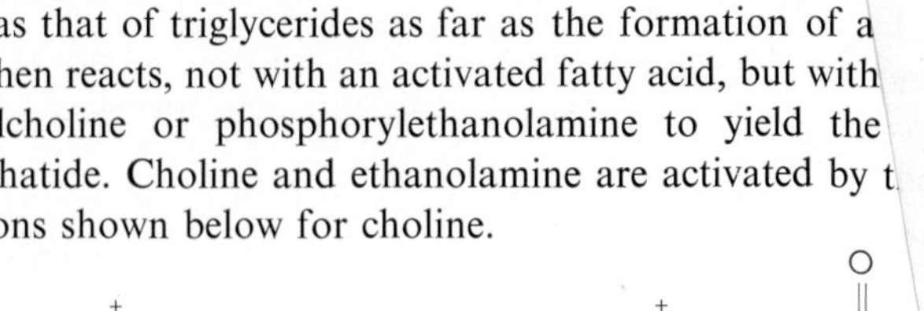

$$(CH_3)_3\overset{+}{N}CH_2 \cdot CH_2 \cdot OH + ATP \longrightarrow (CH_3)_3\overset{+}{N}CH_2 \cdot CH_2 \cdot O\overset{O}{\underset{O^-}{\overset{\|}{P}}}OH$$

choline   phosphorylcholine

from the energetic standpoint because three pyrophosphate bonds are broken (pyrophosphate formed during the synthesis of CDP-choline is cleaved by pyrophosphatase). This high cost of activation is identical with that incurred during the conversion of glucose to glycogen (see p. 105). The activated intermediates for phospholipid synthesis are handled as the high energy cytidine diphosphate derivatives whilst in carbohydrate synthesis uridine diphosphate derivatives are used. Presumably this specificity for cofactors allows control to be exercised over one pathway more or less independently of the other.

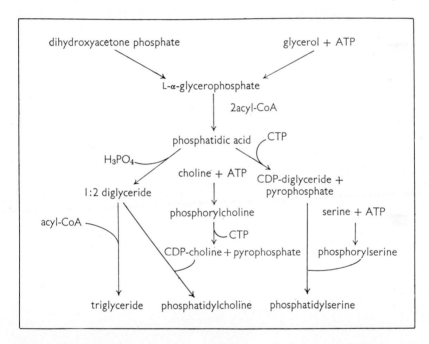

Figure 2.14. Pathways involved in the biosynthesis of triglycerides and phospholipids

The interconversion of ethanolamine and choline and of phosphatidyl-ethanolamine and phosphatidylcholine requires a methyl donor. This is provided by methionine that has been activated by reaction with ATP. In this reaction all the phosphate groups of ATP are lost and the adenosine is attached to the sulphur of the amino acid, forming *S*-adenosyl methionine (Figure 2.13). The transfer of a methyl group from *S*-adenosyl methionine gives rise to *S*-adenosyl homocysteine. Homocysteine may be remethylated by a methyl group attached to tetrahydrofolic acid (see p. 344). The methyl group can arise by the transfer and subsequent reduction of the CH_2OH group of serine to tetrahydrofolic acid with the concomitant formation of glycine.

The formation of phosphatidylserine differs from the pathway outlined above in that phosphorylserine reacts with a CDP-diglyceride in the final reaction. These various pathways are summarized in Figure 2.14.

Certain toxins, for example, some snake venoms and the toxin of the gas gangrene bacillus, contain the enzyme lecithinase. This degrades lecithin to lysolecithin by removing the acyl residue in the 2 position and so produces a powerful detergent able to dissolve cell membranes. Much of the danger of snake bites comes from the haemolysis that occurs when lysolecithin is formed both in the plasma and in the red-cell membranes from preexisting lecithin.

Besides the phospholipids derived from phosphatidic acids there are others derived from the long-chain bases sphingosine and dehydro-sphingosine. These sphingomyelins, as their name suggests, are especially abundant in nerve and brain. They contain a single fatty acid in an amide linkage with the amino group of sphingosine, and are linked through a phosphodiester bridge to choline.

$$CH_3(CH_2)_{12} \cdot CH = CH \cdot CH \cdot CH_2OR'$$

with substituents: OH and NH below the two CH groups; from NH down to $C=O$ and then to R.

Sphingomyelin R = long chain fatty acid
R′ = phosphatidyl choline

cerebroside R = long chain fatty acid
R′ = galactose

Besides phospholipids there are other lipids based on glycerol and sphingosine which do not contain phosphate. These include cerebrosides, gangliosides and sulpholipids.

CHAPTER 10

Nitrogen metabolism in the liver

General metabolism of amino acids

The supply of amino acids

The chief supply of nitrogen in man comes in the form of protein and is supplied to the liver as the hydrolysed products of proteins, i.e. as amino acids (Figure 2.15). In the growing animal, these amino acids are used particularly for the synthesis of the proteins required for the increase in body size; the mature animal can afford to oxidize a larger proportion of the amino compounds. In addition to those available from dietary sources, many amino acids are readily synthesized from the products of carbohydrate metabolism and ammonia. Thus aspartic acid, glutamic acid and alanine can be formed by amination of oxaloacetic, α-oxoglutaric and pyruvic acids respectively.

The essential amino acids

Some amino acids cannot be synthesized at a rate fast enough to meet the needs of the body. Dietary requirements for these special amino acids were first defined for rats which grew normally only if ten particular amino acids were available in their food. These were, firstly, the branched chain amino acids, valine, leucine and isoleucine. The second group, more varied in their chemical structure, were methionine, phenylalanine, histidine, tryptophan, lysine, arginine and threonine. Arginine is included in this list because although rats (like humans) can live and grow without arginine, they develop faster if it is present in the diet.

Essential amino acids are necessary for the synthesis of most proteins and some important non-protein substances. Thus, phenylalanine (or tyrosine) is required for the production of the hormones adrenaline and thyroxine (see Section 7). The hormone insulin has 57% of its constituent amino acids as essential amino acids and the pituitary hormone vasopressin also contains a substantial amount of essential amino acids. These

133

Figure 2.15. The amino acids

Group I Aliphatic

Amino Acids Containing One Carboxyl Group and One Amino Group

Glycine

$$NH_2—CH_2—COOH$$

Glycine, the simplest amino acid, does not possess an asymmetric carbon atom.

L-Alanine

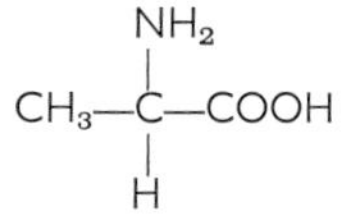

L-Valine

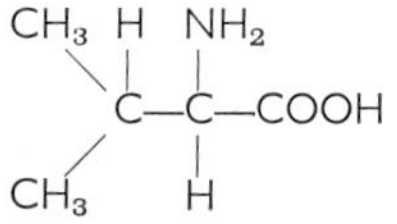

L-Leucine

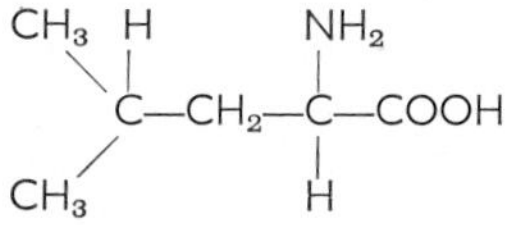

L-Isoleucine

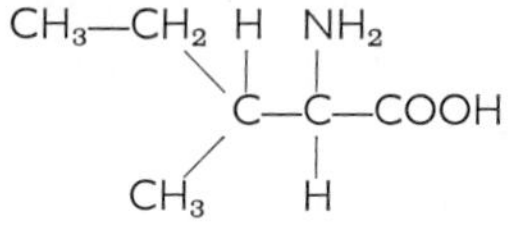

L-Serine

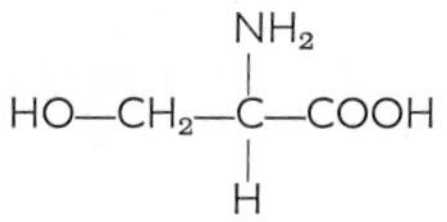

L-Threonine

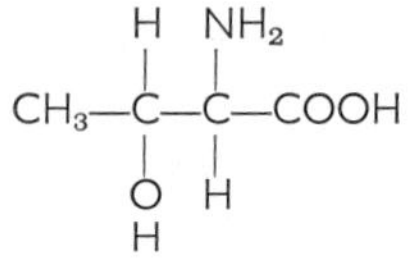

Monamino–Monocarboxylic Amino Acids Containing Sulfur

L-Cysteine

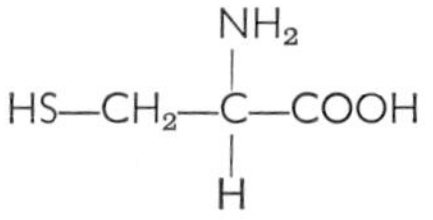

Figure 2.15 (*contd.*)

L-Cystine

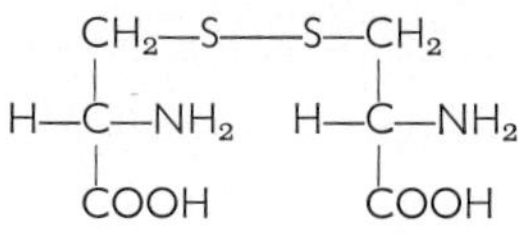

$$CH_2-S-\!\!-\!\!S-CH_2$$
$$H-\overset{|}{C}-NH_2 \quad H-\overset{|}{C}-NH_2$$
$$\underset{COOH}{|} \qquad \underset{COOH}{|}$$

L-Methionine

$$CH_3-S-CH_2-CH_2-\overset{\overset{NH_2}{|}}{\underset{\underset{H}{|}}{C}}-COOH$$

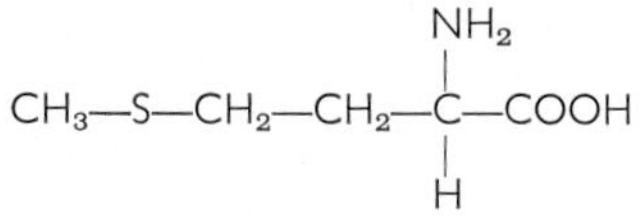

Dicarboxylic Amino Acids

Since these amino acids contain an additional carboxyl group, aqueous solutions of the free amino acid will be acidic.

L-Glutamic acid

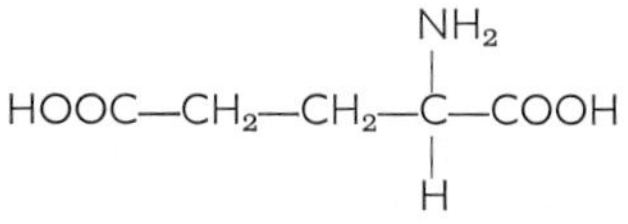

$$HOOC-CH_2-CH_2-\overset{\overset{NH_2}{|}}{\underset{\underset{H}{|}}{C}}-COOH$$

L-Aspartic acid

$$HOOC-CH_2-\overset{\overset{NH_2}{|}}{\underset{\underset{H}{|}}{C}}-COOH$$

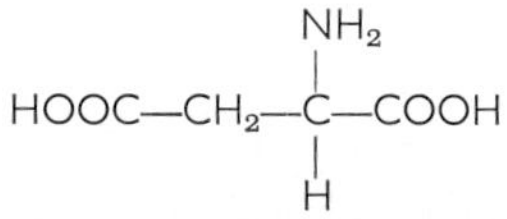

Basic Amino Acids

L-Lysine

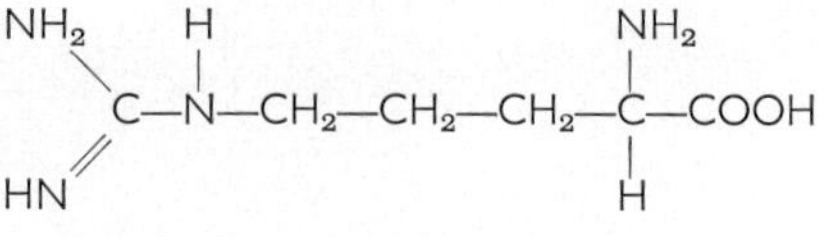

$$NH_2-CH_2-CH_2-CH_2-CH_2-\overset{\overset{NH_2}{|}}{\underset{\underset{H}{|}}{C}}-COOH$$

Aqueous solutions of lysine are basic because lysine has the additional amino group in its structure.

L-Arginine

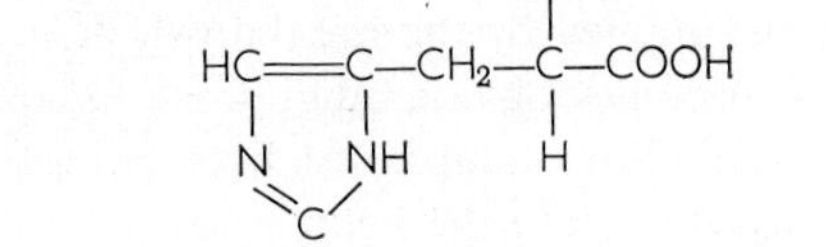

$$\overset{NH_2}{\underset{HN}{\diagdown}}\overset{H}{\underset{}{\overset{|}{C}-N-CH_2-CH_2-CH_2-}}\overset{\overset{NH_2}{|}}{\underset{\underset{H}{|}}{C}}-COOH$$

This amino acid is strongly basic because of its guanidino group.

L-histidine

$$HC=\!\!\!=\!\!C-CH_2-\overset{\overset{NH_2}{|}}{\underset{\underset{H}{|}}{C}}-COOH$$
$$\underset{\underset{\overset{\diagup}{C}}{N\quad NH}}{|\qquad|}$$
$$\underset{H}{}$$

(*continued*)

Figure 2.15. (*contd.*)

Group II   Aromatic amino acids

These amino acids contain the aromatic or benzene ring.

L-phenylalanine

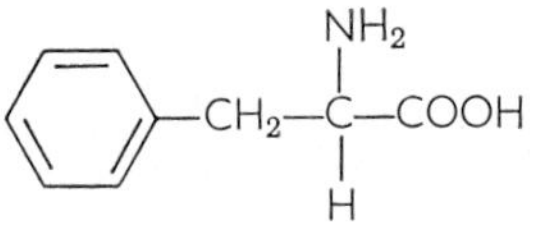

L-tyrosine

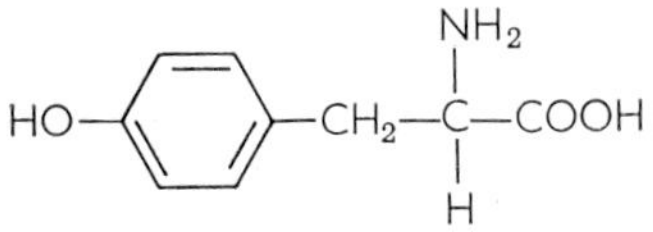

Group III   Heterocyclic amino acids

L-tryptophan

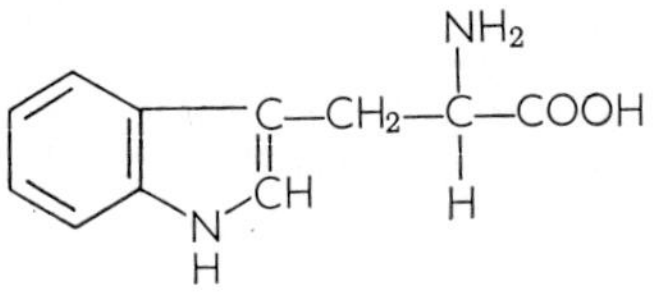

L-proline

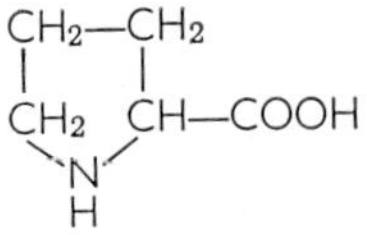

L-hydroxyproline

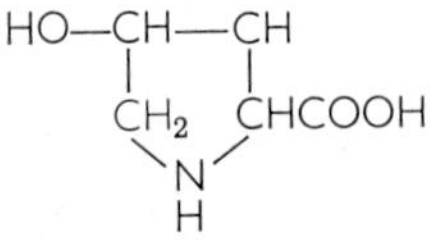

(and other) hormones are such potent substances that they must be removed as soon as they have done their job; consequently, there is a continuing need for their synthesis, and if amino acids are not available from
the diet they must be supplied by the breakdown of other body proteins.
During starvation it becomes obvious that some tissues and proteins are
less essential than others. For example, the liver can lose 50% and skeletal
muscle 30% of its weight, while the heart loses only 3%. Thus liver and
muscle proteins can act as a store of amino acids. When amino acids are
finally degraded their amino groups are converted to urea (see p. 140),

which is excreted in the urine. Therefore by measuring the amount of urea in the urine and the amount of nitrogen in the food, a nitrogen balance sheet can be drawn up. If the amount of nitrogen in the diet equals the amount of nitrogen excreted, the individual is said to be in nitrogen balance. The actual amount of protein required in the diet for nitrogen balance varies with the different types of protein ingested, as some proteins can provide larger amounts of essential amino acids than others and it is the intake of the essential amino acids that is critical. For man, between 30 and 120 g of protein are required per day to maintain nitrogen balance. Positive nitrogen balance, i.e. an excess of nitrogen intake over loss, is found during growth or when tissues are being repaired, for example during pregnancy or after burns. A negative nitrogen balance, when the nitrogen loss exceeds the intake, comes about during starvation and malnutrition. After surgical operation, there is always a period of net nitrogen loss when the liver and muscle protein is depleted.

Transamination and the breakdown of the carbon skeleton of the amino acids

Amino acids may be oxidized to yield energy only after deamination (i.e. when the α-amino group has been removed). Experiments with rats fed with amino acids labelled with ^{15}N have shown that there is a very rapid exchange of the amino group amongst almost all the amino acids. This shuttling of the amino group back and forth between different carbon skeletons is called 'transamination' and is believed to be the most important way of initiating the degradation of amino acids. These transamination reactions enable the amino nitrogen of all the amino acids except lysine and threonine (which do not participate in transamination) to be transferred to oxaloacetate and α-oxoglutarate to form aspartate and glutamate; thereafter the amino group can be removed by either a deamination reaction (for example that catalysed by glutamic dehydrogenase), or by direct transfer from aspartic acid into the urea cycle (see p. 142).

Transaminases present in mitochondria can also be important in determining the rate of glutamate oxidation. In many tissues glutamic dehydrogenase is not very active but glutamate can still be oxidized at a high rate. This is accounted for by the following series of reactions. A little of the glutamate is oxidized to α-oxoglutarate by glutamic dehydrogenase:

$$
\begin{array}{ccc}
\text{COOH} & & \text{COOH} \\
| & & | \\
\text{CH} \cdot \text{NH}_2 & & \text{C} = \text{O} \\
| & & | \\
\text{CH}_2 & + \text{NAD} + \text{H}_2\text{O} \rightleftharpoons & \text{CH}_2 \quad + \text{NADH}_2 + \text{NH}_3 \\
| & & | \\
\text{CH}_2 & & \text{CH}_2 \\
| & & | \\
\text{COOH} & & \text{COOH} \\
\text{glutamic acid} & & \text{α-oxoglutaric acid}
\end{array}
$$

The α-oxoglutarate is then oxidized rapidly in the citric acid cycle to oxaloacetate which transaminates with more glutamate to yield aspartate and α-oxoglutarate:

$$
\begin{array}{c}
\text{COOH} \\
| \\
\text{C}\!=\!\text{O} \\
| \\
\text{CH}_2 \\
| \\
\text{COOH}
\end{array}
+
\begin{array}{c}
\text{COOH} \\
| \\
\text{CH}\!\cdot\!\text{NH}_2 \\
| \\
\text{CH}_2 \\
| \\
\text{CH}_2 \\
| \\
\text{COOH}
\end{array}
\rightleftharpoons
\begin{array}{c}
\text{COOH} \\
| \\
\text{CH}\!\cdot\!\text{NH}_2 \\
| \\
\text{CH}_2 \\
| \\
\text{COOH}
\end{array}
+
\begin{array}{c}
\text{COOH} \\
| \\
\text{C}\!=\!\text{O} \\
| \\
\text{CH}_2 \\
| \\
\text{CH}_2 \\
| \\
\text{COOH}
\end{array}
$$

oxaloacetic   glutamic   aspartic α-oxoglutaric
   acid   acid   acid   acid

The latter, after oxidation to oxaloacetate, can again accept amino groups from glutamate. This mechanism achieves simultaneously a rapid oxidation of glutamate and the preservation of amino groups: it is of special importance in tissues like mammary gland and liver where amino groups are required for the synthesis of milk and plasma proteins.

The transaminases require a derivative of vitamin B_6 as a coenzyme. Vitamin B_6, as originally defined, is pyridoxine, but the coenzymes are the related compounds pyridoxal phosphate and pyridoxamine phosphate:

pyridoxine   pyridoxal   pyridoxamine

pyridoxal phosphate   pyridoxamine phosphate

In the transamination reactions, the α-amino groups of the amino acids are attached to the aldehyde group of pyridoxal phosphate to form a Schiff's base which breaks down to give a keto acid and pyridoxamine phosphate. The amine of pyridoxamine phosphate can then be transferred to another keto acid (Figure 2.16).

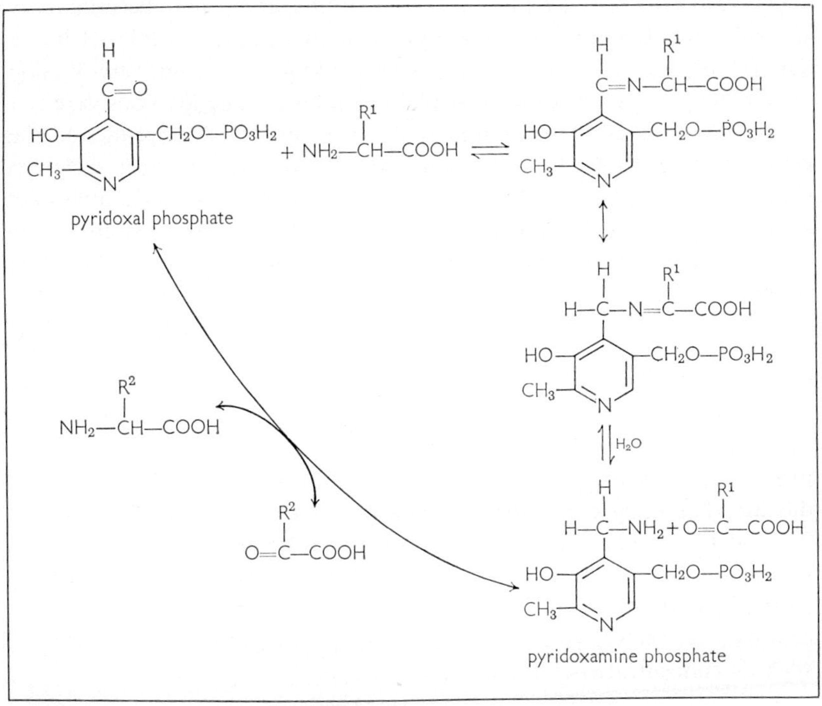

Figure 2.16. The role of pyridoxal phosphate in transamination reactions

Table 2.1. Products of breakdown of amino acids

Glucogenic amino acids		Ketogenic amino acids	
Acid	Product	Acid	Product
Glycine	Pyruvate	Leucine	Acetoacetate
	Succinate	Isoleucine	Acetyl-CoA
Serine	Pyruvate		Propionyl-CoA
Threonine	Propionate	Phenylalanine ⎱	Fumarate
Valine	Propionate	Tyrosine ⎰	Acetoacetate
Histidine	α-Oxoglutarate		
Arginine	α-Oxoglutarate		
Lysine	α-Oxoglutarate		
Isoleucine	Acetyl-CoA		
	Propionyl-CoA		
Cystine	Pyruvate		
Proline	α-Oxoglutarate		
Hydroxyproline	Pyruvate		

The keto acid produced by loss of the amino group may be utilized as an oxidizable substrate or as a biosynthetic intermediate. Table 2.1 lists a number of amino acids whose corresponding keto acids are readily convertible to intermediates of oxidative pathways already considered.

The amino acids are traditionally divided into the glucogenic and the ketogenic (see Table 2.1). The glucogenic acids yield carbon skeletons which can be used to synthesize glucose. The most obvious examples are alanine, aspartic acid and glutamic acid; the other amino acids are not so clearly linked with precursors of glucose and their metabolism is often complex.

Deamination and the urea cycle

Deamination of amino acids produces unwanted ammonia which, because it is extremely toxic, must be converted into a suitable excretory product; this is urea, formed by combination of ammonia and carbon dioxide. The daily elimination of urea in the urine is about 25 g, nearly 90% of the nitrogenous excretion. Urea is formed in the liver, so that hepatectomy prevents its production and causes a constantly mounting level of blood ammonia. It was known from the beginning of the present century that the enzyme arginase, which splits arginine to ornithine and urea, is concentrated in the liver.

However, in an individual in nitrogen balance almost all the nitrogen ingested as protein is excreted as urea, so that all the other amino acids must contribute to urea synthesis as well as arginine. Using thin slices of liver incubated with an oxidizable substrate to provide energy, Krebs and Henseleit found that urea could be synthesized from ammonia and CO_2. In the presence of small amounts of ornithine, citrulline or arginine the rate of urea synthesis from ammonia and CO_2 was stimulated and much more urea was formed than anticipated from the amount of amino acid added. Other common amino acids did not act catalytically although their amino groups could be converted into urea stoichiometrically. In the absence of an oxidizable substrate to provide energy only arginine gave rise to urea. These results led to the formulation of the ornithine cycle as the pathway of urea synthesis.

The reactions involved in the ornithine cycle have been examined more closely and its individual steps can be described in greater detail. The first step is the formation of carbamyl phosphate from one molecule of ammonia and one of CO_2 in a reaction catalysed by carbamyl phosphate synthetase.

$$NH_3 + CO_2 + 2ATP \rightleftharpoons H_2N \cdot CO \cdot O \cdot PO_3H_2 + 2ADP + Pi$$
carbamyl phosphate

This reaction uses two molecules of ATP to drive it in the direction of synthesis and to keep the concentration of ammonia below the toxic level. The activity of the enzyme is increased by *N*-acetyl glutamic acid which takes no direct part in the reaction but which may act as an allosteric activator (see p. 313). Ornithine transcarbamylase then catalyses the transfer of the carbamyl residue to ornithine to form citrulline and liberate inorganic phosphate.

$$
\begin{array}{ccc}
NH_2 & & NH \cdot CO \cdot NH_2 \\
| & & | \\
(CH_2)_3 & CO \cdot NH_2 & (CH_2)_3 \\
| \quad + \quad | & & | \qquad + \ H_3PO_4 \\
CH \cdot NH_2 & O \cdot PO_3H_2 & CH \cdot NH_2 \\
| & & | \\
COOH & & COOH \\
\text{ornithine} & & \text{citrulline}
\end{array}
$$

The second amino group of urea is derived from aspartic acid which reacts with ornithine, forming argininosuccinic acid.

$$
\begin{array}{cc}
NH & NH \qquad COOH \\
\| & \| \qquad | \\
C \cdot OH \qquad COOH & C—NH—CH \\
| \qquad\qquad | & | \qquad\quad | \\
NH \quad H_2N \cdot CH \quad + ATP \rightleftharpoons & NH \qquad CH_2 \quad + AMP + PP \\
| \qquad\qquad | & | \qquad\quad | \\
(CH_2)_3 \qquad CH_2 & (CH_2)_3 \quad COOH \\
| \qquad\qquad | & | \\
CH \cdot NH_2 \quad COOH & CH \cdot NH_2 \\
| & | \\
COOH & COOH \\
\text{citrulline} \quad \text{aspartic} & \text{argininosuccinic} \\
\text{(enol form)} \quad \text{acid} & \text{acid}
\end{array}
$$

This reaction, catalysed by argininosuccinate synthetase, requires ATP and liberates pyrophosphate which is degraded to two molecules of inorganic phosphate by pyrophosphatase. Thus this reaction involves the cleavage of two high energy bonds and is essentially irreversible. Argininosuccinate is split to form arginine and fumaric acid by argininosuccinase.

$$
\begin{array}{ccc}
NH \qquad COOH & NH & \\
\| \qquad | & \| & \\
C—NH—CH & C—NH_2 & \\
| \qquad\quad | & | & HC \cdot COOH \\
NH \qquad CH_2 \rightleftharpoons & NH \quad + & \| \\
| \qquad\quad | & | & HOOC \cdot CH \\
(CH_2)_3 \quad COOH & (CH_2)_3 & \\
| & | & \\
CH \cdot NH_2 & CH \cdot NH_2 & \\
| & | & \\
COOH & COOH & \\
\text{argininosuccinic} & \text{arginine} & \text{fumaric acid} \\
\text{acid} & &
\end{array}
$$

Arginine is finally hydrolysed by arginase to give urea and ornithine which can reenter the cycle by reacting with carbamylphosphate. Fumarate formed during the cycle can be reconverted to aspartate via oxaloacetate and transamination.

$$\begin{array}{l} \text{HC·COOH} \\ \parallel \\ \text{HOOC·CH} \end{array} \quad \underset{}{\overset{\pm H_2O}{\rightleftarrows}} \quad \begin{array}{l} \text{CH}_2\text{COOH} \\ \mid \\ \text{CHOH·COOH} \end{array} \quad \underset{\text{reduction}}{\overset{\text{oxidation}}{\rightleftarrows}}$$

fumaric acid   malic acid

$$\begin{array}{l} \text{CH}_2\text{COOH} \\ \mid \\ \text{CO·COOH} \end{array} \quad \underset{}{\overset{\text{transamination}}{\rightleftarrows}} \quad \begin{array}{l} \text{CH}_2\text{COOH} \\ \mid \\ \text{CH·NH}_2 \\ \mid \\ \text{COOH} \end{array}$$

oxaloacetic   aspartic
acid   acid

The need for ATP makes it clear why oxygen and a substrate were required in the original experiments of Krebs. Each turn of the cycle consumes the equivalent of 4 molecules of ATP, 3 of which can be produced by oxidative phosphorylation during the conversion of fumarate to oxaloacetate. Thus the formation of one molecule of urea leads to the net consumption of one molecule of ATP.

The process of urea formation is a good example of cooperation between different cell compartments. Mitochondria are the main source of ATP in the liver and, as might be expected, the synthesis of carbamyl phosphate and the subsequent reaction with ornithine to give citrulline takes place there. The location of the enzymes forming arginine from citrulline is not known; arginase occurs throughout the cell but is concentrated in the nucleus. Therefore, ornithine must pass into the mitochondria to be converted to citrulline and arginine must pass out of the mitochondria to be efficiently hydrolysed. The oxidation of fumarate to oxaloacetate occurs in the mitochondria, but the transaminases converting aspartate to oxaloacetate are found in both the mitochondrial and the soluble fraction of the cell. Thus, besides the chemical cycle, there is also a cyclic movement of components within the cell.

Other nitrogenous constituents of urine

Creatinine

Apart from urea, the main sources of urinary nitrogen are creatinine (about 1–4 g daily) and uric acid (0·7 g daily). Creatinine is the cyclic anhydride of creatine.

$$\begin{array}{c} \text{CH}_3 \\ \mid \\ \text{HN}=\text{C} \overset{\text{N}}{\diagdown} \text{CH}_2 \\ \mid \quad\quad \mid \\ \text{HN}\text{---}\text{C}=\text{O} \end{array}$$

creatinine

Under normal physiological conditions there is a slow spontaneous conversion of creatine to creatinine in the body and the amount of creatinine excreted by an individual is almost constant, bearing some relationship to the total muscle mass of the body. Normally, creatine itself does not appear in the urine, though it does so if large doses are fed and also during childhood when the muscle mass is changing. There are two important abnormal conditions which also lead to a large excretion of creatine in the urine, amputation of a limb and muscular dystrophy. After amputation, there is a lag before the liver decreases its synthesis of creatine to a level that can be accommodated within the reduced muscle mass available. With the progressive muscular dystrophies the excretion of creatine continues as the muscle mass diminishes.

Formation of uric acid: the degradation of the nitrogenous bases

Nucleic acids contain nitrogenous bases, either purines or pyrimidines, linked to pentose phosphates (see pp. 242–248.)

purines

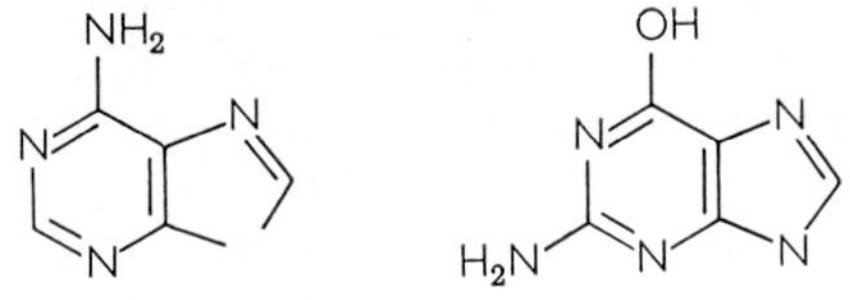

adenine

guanine

pyrimidines

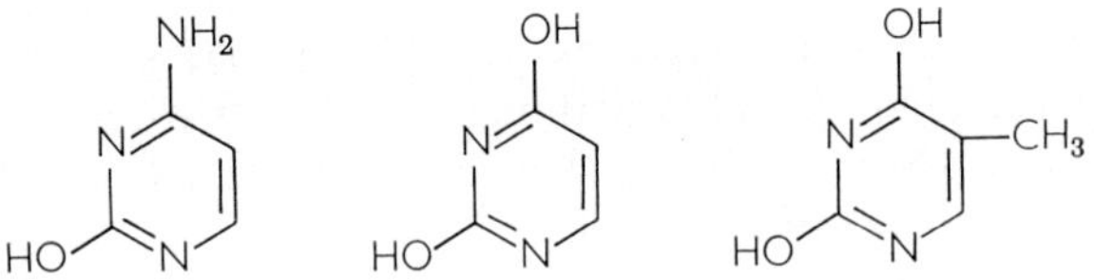

cytosine

uracil

thymine

The breakdown of these acids involves the release of the bases. The pyrimidines uracil, cytosine and thymine are degraded by fission of the ring to form products such as amino acids, ammonia and carbon dioxide. The purines adenine and guanine are not degraded extensively but are excreted by man as uric acid. The adenine ring gives rise to uric acid by deamination either of adenosine (forming inosine which is split to hypoxanthine and ribose) or of adenosine monophosphate (forming inosine monophosphate which reacts with pyrophosphate to form hypoxanthine and phosphoribose pyrophosphate). The hypoxanthine (6-hydroxy-purine) is oxidized by xanthine oxidase firstly to xanthine (2,6-dihydroxy-purine) and then by the same enzyme to uric acid. Guanine (2-amino-6-hydroxypurine) is hydrolysed by guanase, which removes the amino group and gives xanthine directly. The pathways are summarized below:

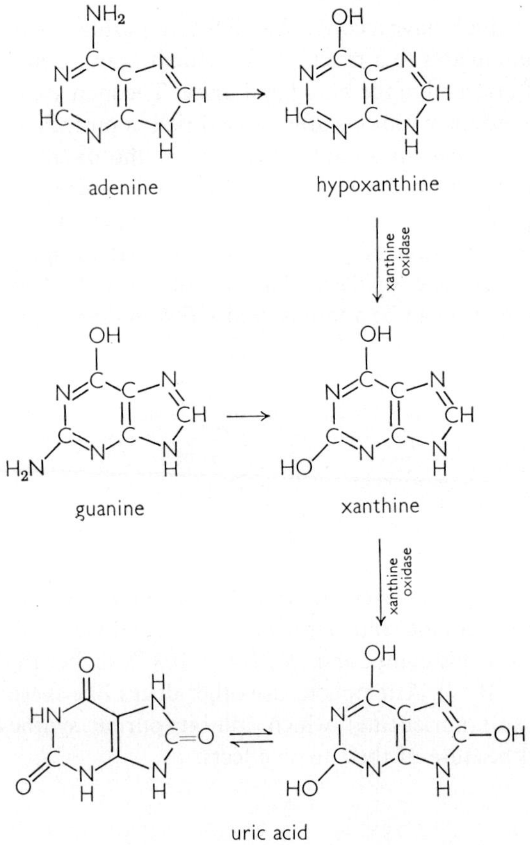

adenine → hypoxanthine

guanine → xanthine

uric acid

The enzyme xanthine oxidase is of special interest since, besides being specific for the oxidation of hypoxanthine and xanthine, it has a quite separate ability to catalyse the oxidation of a wide range of aldehydes to acids. Its presence in milk is apparently concerned with the oxidation of aldehydes. The enzyme has flavin as a prosthetic group and requires molybdenum as a cofactor; it reacts directly with oxygen, producing hydrogen peroxide.

6+

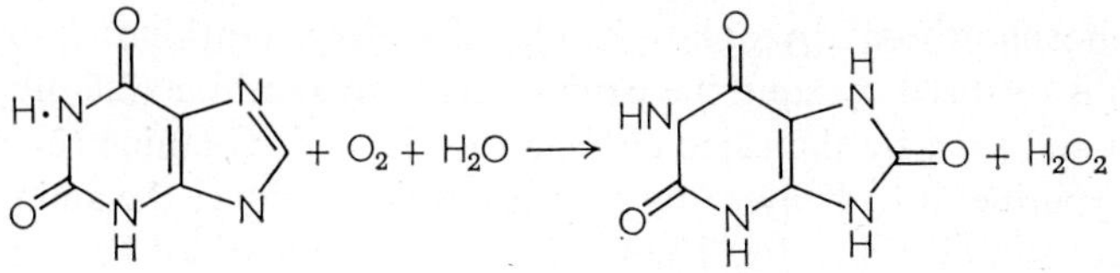

xanthine   uric acid

Some individuals have a congenital defect in purine metabolism in which uric acid accumulates to a much greater extent than normal, resulting in a high level of uric acid in the blood and urine. The increase is similar to that occurring in ordinary subjects after a meal rich in purines (for example one containing fish roes or sweetbreads) but in the diseased condition the level of uric acid is always high and may produce deposition of urates in the joints, giving rise to gout. A recently developed and promising treatment for the condition of gout involves the use of specific and potent inhibitor of xanthine oxidase. This is allopurinol—4-hydroxypyrazole pyrimidine—which can be administered safely in doses of 400–800 mg/day

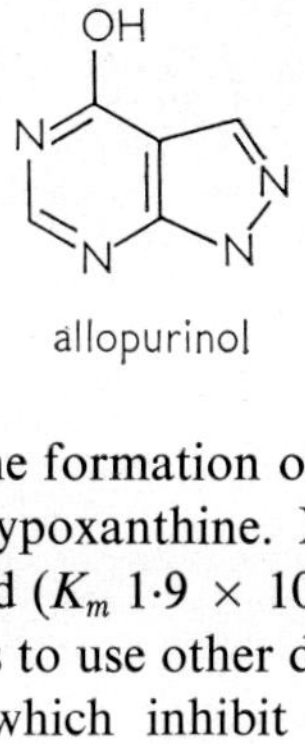

allopurinol

and which greatly decreases the formation of uric acid, though not of the more soluble xanthine and hypoxanthine. Xanthine oxidase has a very high affinity for this compound (K_m 1.9×10^{-7}), higher than for xanthine itself (K_m 5×10^{-6}). Attempts to use other drugs like azaserine and DON (6-diazo,5-oxo-L-norleucine) which inhibit purine synthesis have been unsuccessful because of their toxic effects.

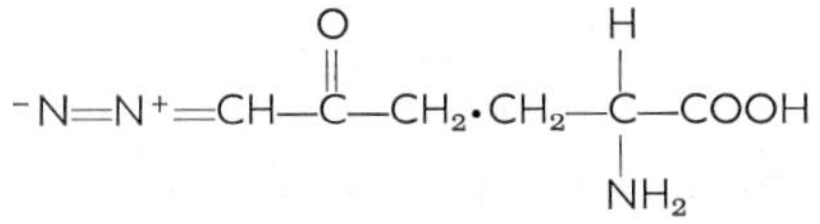

6-diazo-5,oxo-L-norleucine

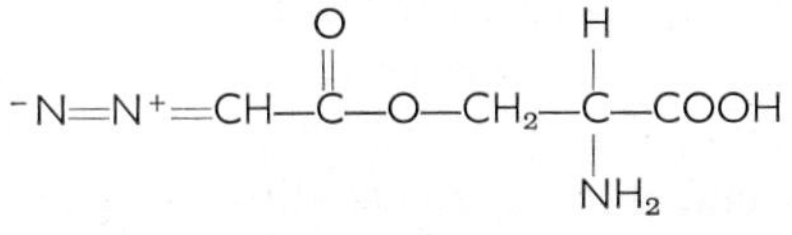

azaserine

Detoxication

In the course of its life an organism may ingest substances which are useless and may in fact be poisonous. A whole series of enzymes has evolved which transforms these substances into something less harmful; for example ammonia, which is very toxic, is converted to urea which is non-toxic; this transformation occurs continually because of the necessity for metabolizing protein. Originally it is probable that most of the detoxifying enzymes had to deal only with toxic substances formed by bacterial action in the gut and with hormones which had fulfilled their function. For the human being, the chemical situation has become much more complicated because of the battery of new drugs to which the body is frequently subjected and the presence in the environment of toxic insecticides and other newly-synthesized substances which are being encountered for the first time. Clearly the organism cannot have enzymes in store to deal specifically with all the new chemicals produced by the organic chemist; the enzymes already available must serve as effectively as possible. Sometimes their action makes matters worse—as with fluoracetate (p. 83).

One of the main difficulties in studying detoxication is to know what is meant by a toxic substance. Many compounds develop toxicity if the dose is sufficiently great and some species are quite resistant to substances which are extremely toxic to others. Also the time of exposure to the toxic substance is important, as is the route by which it enters the body. The complexity of the situation has been summarized by Aldridge thus: 'To attempt to evaluate the dangers to man of chronic exposure to a substance such as an insecticide from a simple toxicity test on rats is rather like expecting to learn a language by opening a dictionary at one page only.' An adequate understanding of the toxicity of a compound can be obtained only after a most exhaustive investigation of its interaction with the enzyme complexes of various organs and tissues.

Almost all the enzymes concerned with detoxication are associated with the membranes of the liver cell and can therefore be isolated in the microsomal fraction during differential centrifuging. Often $NADPH_2$ is a necessary coenzyme even when the detoxication process is an oxidation. The types of chemical reaction involved in detoxication are oxidation, reduction and conjugation.

Oxidation

Probably the commonest way of degrading unwanted material is by oxidizing it. Often the products are organic acids or hydroxylated derivatives. For example, benzylamine is converted to benzoic acid by oxidation of the amino group (presumably by an amine oxidase).

benzylamine   benzoic acid

With aniline (an aromatic amine), the amino group cannot be altered but the ring is hydroxylated (using oxygen and $NADPH_2$) in the *para* position.

aniline   p-aminophenol

A similar hydroxylation is carried out on the drug acetanilide (a common antipyretic substance) forming *para*-acetyl aminophenol

acetanilide   p-acetyl aminophenol

Reduction

Aromatic nitro groups can be reduced to the corresponding amines. Nitrobenzene (a very toxic substance rapidly absorbed through the skin) and picric acid are both treated in this way, giving *para*-aminophenol and picramic acid respectively.

nitrobenzene   p-aminophenol

picric acid   picramic acid

Conjugation

Probably the most versatile method available to the body for removing unwanted substances is to combine them with another compound, in the process of conjugation. Glycine is frequently used as the conjugating substance, reacting with carboxyl groups of acids through its amino group to form a substituted amide. The commonest of these is hippuric acid, the conjugate with benzoic acid. The peptide bond formed in this conjugate requires a preliminary conversion of the benzoic acid to benzoyl CoA. This activation requires ATP.

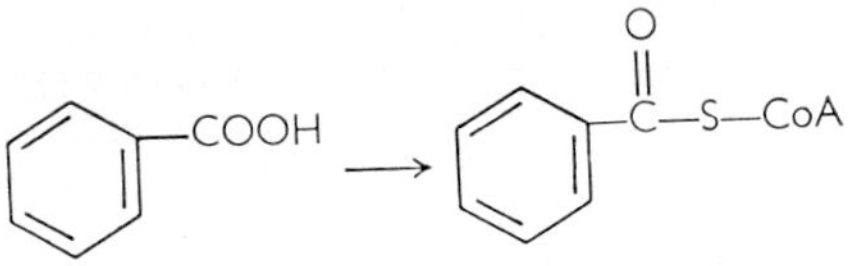

benzoic acid   benzoyl coenzyme A

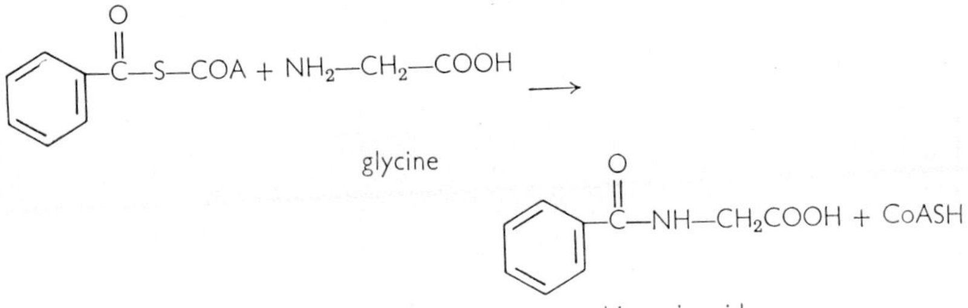

glycine

hippuric acid

The ability to synthesize hippuric acid is the basis of a test for liver function. Sodium benzoate is administered orally or intravenously and the amount of hippuric acid appearing in the urine over a standard period is measured; in the oral test normally about 50% of the 6 g administered is excreted in 4 hours. Salicylic acid (*ortho*-hydroxybenzoic acid)

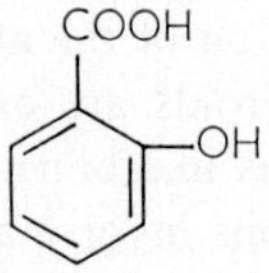

is also excreted as the glycine conjugate; this acid may be formed in the body by hydrolytic deacylation of aspirin (acetylsalicylic acid).

Many substances including unwanted steroid hormones may be con-
jugated as sulphate esters; for example, phenol is excreted in this form. The
synthesis of the ester can occur only after activation of the sulphate by
ATP. The activated sulphate, 3'-phosphoadenosine,5'-phosphosulphate
(PAPS—see Figure 2.17) is formed at the expense of two molecules of
ATP, one to provide the AMP residue for attachment to the sulphate, the
second to phosphorylate the 3 position of the ribose of the adenosine.
PAPS is used not only in detoxication, but also for inserting sulphate into
mucopolysaccharides and in forming the sulpholipids of the brain.

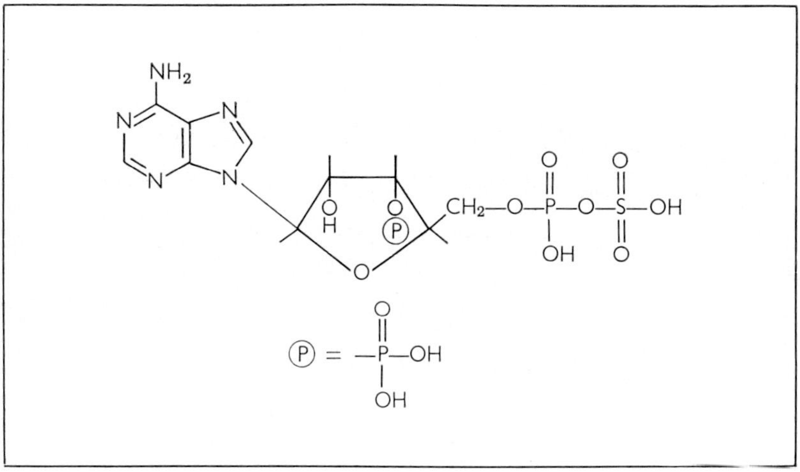

Figure 2.17. 3'-Phosphoadenosine,5'-phosphosulphate (PAPS)

Glucuronic acid may also be used as a conjugating substance, reacting
with phenols through its aldehyde group. The reactive form of the conjugating agent is UDP-glucuronic acid, which can be derived from UDP-
glucose (p. 105) by the oxidation of the alcohol group at carbon 6 of the
sugar. Most of the corticosteroids are excreted in the urine as inactive
glucuronides, as are substances like bilirubin (p. 167).

Some important detoxications involve acetylation, as for example with
sulphonamides. Unfortunately, the acetyl derivatives of the earliest sul-
phonamide drugs (for example sulphanilamide) were very much less
soluble than the drugs themselves and with heavy doses and an insufficient
intake of water it was possible to suffer kidney damage by deposition of

the insoluble acetyl derivative. The enzyme responsible for acetylating sulphonamides is probably the same as that acetylating choline to form acetylcholine.

Finally, conjugation may involve methylation of the toxic substances. This occurs, for example, with pyridine. Methionine acts as the methyl donor after activation with ATP (see Figure 2.13).

All the enzymes involved in detoxication are part of the normal complement of the body and may function to remove a metabolically active substance formed during the normal metabolism of the tissues. Detoxication is thus a part of the natural regulatory mechanism of the body. When a foreign substance is presented to the cell it is largely a matter of chance as to whether the enzymic manipulations that occur produce a substance which is more or less harmful. For example, the oxidation of the side chains of barbiturates and the deamination of amphetamine both produce less toxic substances but the oxidation of the insecticide parathion, itself non-toxic, produces an intensely poisonous anticholinesterase. Similarly, substances like tetraethyl tin or tetraethyl lead, both non-toxic, have one of the ethyl groups removed to give the poisonous triethyl tin and triethyl lead. Thus while it may be accurate to think of the basic reactions of detoxication as 'purposeful', in that they have evolved as part of the complex chemical mechanism of the body, it is not correct to suppose that an organism can deal with new foreign substances in a purposeful way. In this sense the term 'detoxication' is a misnomer.

SECTION 3

The Intestine

CHAPTER 11

The digestion and absorption of food

Most people equate their environment with the part of the world that impinges on their skin. Biochemically this is incorrect. The chemical environment of the skin is something of great stability changing only fractionally in its chemical composition. It is in fact the intestinal lining which bears the brunt of the changing chemical environment and responds to it by transforming, absorbing or rejecting the mixture of chemicals presented to it. No microorganisms or plants suffer the same variety of chemical insults as does the mammalian intestine, and in the case of the human the intestine must cope with the mixed bag of esoteric chemicals that make up the modern doctor's armoury of drugs. The epithelial cells of the intestine (perhaps because of the traumatic conditions to which they are exposed) are rapidly replaced. On average the total lining of the intestine is replaced in somewhat under two days. In weight this amounts to about 450 g, roughly equivalent to 10 g of fat and 40 g of protein daily. Besides this endogenous protein, the pancreatic juice contributes protein amounting to about 100 g daily. This protein and fat is largely reabsorbed. If the intake of food is equivalent to 2500 cal it is likely that at least half of it will come from carbohydrate sources. The remainder will amount on average to about 60 g of protein and 100 g of fat. Thus the intake of protein from endogenous sources is considerably larger than the dietary intake and in the poorer countries where the daily protein intake is less than 30 g, 80% of the protein digested is derived from endogenous sources. Because of the large contribution of endogenous protein the amino acid composition of the gut contents is relatively constant and direct experiments have shown that this amino acid composition is entirely unaffected by the composition of the diet. In spite of this (see Section 8), the proportion of protein in the diet can alter the enzymic make-up of the liver.

Besides removing substances from the lumen of the intestine, the intestine contributes substances to the lumen content. In general the substances contributed by the intestine are required to facilitate the intestine's

Table 3.1. Substances secreted into intestinal lumen[a]

Proteins	Origin	Function
Pepsinogen	Stomach	To yield pepsin which preferentially splits peptide links adjacent to aromatic amino acids (see p. 18).
Amylase	Pancreas	To hydrolyse polysaccharides mainly to maltose.
Trypsinogen	Pancreas	To yield trypsin for the splitting of peptide links mainly between the carboxyl group of lysine or arginine and the amino group of another amino acid.
Chymotryp-sinogen	Pancreas	To yield chymotrypsin for splitting peptide links mainly between carboxyl of aromatic acid and the amino group of an amino acid other than aspartate or glutamate.
Maltase	Pancreas	Splits maltose to glucose.
Carboxy-peptidase	Pancreas	Removes amino acids from carboxyl end of a peptide.
Lipase	Pancreas	Splits triglycerides in stepwise fashion to fatty acid and glycerol at rates depending on the fatty acid composition.
Maltase	Intestinal mucosa	Splits maltose to glucose.
Sucrase (invertase)	Intestinal mucosa	Splits sucrose to glucose and fructose.
Lactase	Intestinal mucosa	Splits lactose to galactose and glucose.
Amino peptidase	Intestinal mucosa	Removes amino acids from amino end of a peptide.
Dipeptidase	Intestinal mucosa	Splits dipeptides to amino acids.
Phosphatase	Intestinal mucosa	Removes phosphate from organic phosphates.
Lecithinase	Intestinal mucosa	Breaks down phospholipids to constituents.
HCl	Gastric mucosa	Stops enzymic actions in the material ingested; converts pepsinogen to pepsin; provides favourable pH for action of pepsin; hydrolyses fructose-containing sugars.
$NaHCO_3$	Pancreatic juice	Brings material discharged by the stomach into the intestine to a roughly neutral pH suitable for the action of the digestive enzymes.
Bile salts	Liver	Emulsifies and solubilizes water-insoluble material.

[a] The list of materials is not comprehensive but includes those which are quantitatively most important. The functions listed are the main functions.

task of absorption. For convenience the bile and the secretions of the pancreas will be considered together with the secretions of the intestine proper. Table 3.1 shows the main substances (excluding salivary amylase) discharged into the lumen by the intestinal tract.

Activities of the digestive enzymes

Within the exocrine cells the proteolytic enzymes pepsin, trypsin and chymotrypsin are stored as the inactive forms pepsinogen, trypsinogen and chymotrypsinogen, presumably to prevent their hydrolysing the cellular protein. Their activation on discharge into the gut lumen consists in re-moving a short peptide. With pepsinogen the gastric HCl can remove the masking peptide and the pepsin thus liberated is also able to activate the remaining pepsinogen. With trypsin the primary activator is an enzyme called enterokinase, present in the intestinal secretion. Once again the trypsin liberated can hydrolyse the remaining trypsinogen. Chymotryp-sinogen has no special activating substance but requires trypsin to remove its masking polypeptide and the chymotrypsin liberated is unable to act as an activator for the remainder of the chymotrypsinogen. The carboxy-peptidase of the pancreatic juice is also secreted in an inactive form and is activated by trypsin, but, whereas the polypeptides removed from the inactive precursors of the other proteinases were comparatively small, in this case a protein of roughly two-thirds the original molecular weight is split off.

Digestion and absorption

Before examining the digestion and absorption of the various foodstuffs, it is worth considering the quantity of food eaten. Table 3.2 shows the average composition of the British diet for an intake of 2500 cal daily.

Table 3.2. Composition of British diet of 2500 cal daily

Foodstuff	Percentage of calories from each foodstuff in diet	Weight of foodstuff (g)	Calories contributed
Fat	35	97	875
Protein	11	70	275
Carbohydrate	54	340	1350

As an example of the amount of food supplying this number of calories, one large brown loaf (28 oz) eaten with ¼ lb butter (comprising about 105 g fat, 68 g protein and 400 g carbohydrate) would provide about

2800 cal. If 4 oz of cheese is eaten as well, the bread ration could be dropped to $1\frac{1}{2}$ small loaves (21 oz) and the composition of the food ingested would be about 142 g fat, 79 g protein and 300 g carbohydrate. For a conveniently carried ration, a 1 lb bar of milk chocolate will supply about 2400 cal consisting of 155 g fat, 24 g protein and 214 g carbohydrate. Suppose on the other hand the meal consists of steak (6 oz), chips (8 oz), green vegetables or salad (4 oz), biscuits and cheese (2 oz of each), all washed down with a pint of good beer, about 1800 cal would be ingested with an intake of 92 g fat, 57 g protein, 143 g carbohydrate and 32 g alcohol. Thus 1 to 2 lb of material may be eaten at a meal and of that about 300 g will be dry solids. The pound or so of food passing into the stomach is met by the gastric juice. In the fasting state this juice is roughly equivalent to $0 \cdot 1$ N HCl and its volume will be about 100 ml although this would be greatly increased if the meal had been pleasurably anticipated. The protein of the meal is a very efficient buffer and the 50 or so grams eaten will mop up the acidity of the HCl with the result that the pH of the stomach contents rises to about 6. Some 300–400 ml more of gastric HCl is required to lower the pH to between 2 and 3. Direct measurements of the pH of the stomach contents during a meal, either with a conventional glass electrode or with the 'radio pill', show that initially the pH is not much below neutrality, but during the next hour or so it falls to about 3. This is still above the pH of about 2, which is usually accepted as the optimum for action of pepsin. However, it appears that the human stomach contains two types of pepsin and that both of these have two pH optima, one around 2 and the other at $3 \cdot 3$. The exact positions of these pH optima depend on the nature of the protein that is being digested. Thus pepsin does not require such acid conditions as hitherto believed for its efficient action.

The secretion of hydrochloric acid

The gastric secretion of HCl (as H^+ and Cl^-) is a special case of the more general problem of ion transport (see pp. 174 and 199). Because of the large differential between the H^+ concentration of the gastric juice and of the blood, the work required for transport is considerable. The oxyntic cells secreting HCl have a very high rate of respiration and appear to be one of the most efficient of chemical transducers. Consequently anaerobic conditions and uncouplers of oxidative phosphorylation are inhibitory for HCl secretion. The Cl^- apparently accompanies the H^+ passively in order to maintain electrical neutrality. Carbon dioxide under the influence of carbonic anhydrase combines with water to give bicarbonate which passes into the blood stream to compensate for its deprivation of chloride. The alkaline tide in blood and urine subsequent to a meal is supposed to be brought about by this compensatory movement of bicarbonate.

Intestinal digestion

The addition of the pancreatic secretion to the lumen contents besides contributing the enzymes listed in Table 3.1 adjusts the pH to the neighbourhood of 6·5. Cleavage of the proteins to amino acids then takes place by the cooperative action of the proteinases and other peptidases listed in Table 3.1. Polysaccharides such as starch and glycogen will be hydrolysed to maltose and glucose by the pancreatic amylase. The disaccharides sucrose, maltose and lactose are apparently absorbed as such into the cells of the intestinal mucosa and are then hydrolysed into their constituent monosaccharides by the appropriate enzymes.

The breakdown of the lipids is somewhat more complicated, being influenced by the composition of the material presented for digestion. It is generally agreed that the formation of both a fine emulsion and micelles aids the digestion and later absorption of fats and their breakdown products. Bile salts and other surface-active agents, such as phospholipids and monoglycerides, are constituents of a mixture which promotes digestion by altering the interaction between water and the normally water-insoluble glycerides. Dietary fat is usually considered to be triglyceride, but in fact phospholipids constitute a substantial, or even the major, fraction of the ingested lipid, depending on the food eaten. For example, fish muscle has about 20% of its lipid as phospholipid, animal skeletal muscle around 30%, bird muscle about 40% and offal about 70%. The breakdown of phospholipids requires the cooperation of three enzymes; phospholipase A (from the pancreas) removes the fatty acid from the β position of the phospholipid to give a lyso compound. The second fatty acid is removed from the α position of the lipid by β-phospholipase to liberate a free fatty acid and, for example, glycerylphosphorylcholine. The latter substance is then hydrolysed by a diesterase to glycerol phosphate and choline. The breakdown of triglycerides by pancreatic and intestinal lipase is best regarded as a stepwise hydrolysis, but with the process becoming slower as each fatty acid is removed.

The absorption of amino acids

The efficiency of amino acid absorption by the intestine is very high; of the total amino acids presented to the intestine only about 5% remains unabsorbed. Apart from glutamate and aspartate the amino acids are absorbed by an oxygen-dependent active process with one amino acid competing with another more or less effectively for the transporting site.

The clear demonstration of movement of the amino acids against a concentration gradient was made by the use of the everted sac technique designed by Wilson and Wiseman. In this technique a segment of intestine is turned inside out and tied at either end after the lumen has been filled with a suitable fluid. Movement of material through the intestinal wall can be assessed by measuring the change in content of substances in the lumen of the sac.

The absorption of carbohydrates

The main dietary monosaccharides presented to the intestine for absorption are glucose, galactose and fructose; a smaller quantity of mannose and the pentose sugars are also utilized, depending on the dietary habits. Of these sugars, glucose and galactose are absorbed by an active process which is characteristically inhibited by phlorizin. Oxidative phosphorylation has been thought to be necessary for the active uptake of the two sugars because the process has been inhibited by uncouplers of oxidative phosphorylation and by anaerobic conditions.

The absorption of lipid

The absorption of fat like that of protein is very efficient; the amount of faecal fat is only about 5% of the amount ingested. Details of the absorption of fat are still obscure, but measurements of the fat composition of the human intestinal lumen has shown that a very substantial part consists of free fatty acids. If glycerides are absorbed, they are apparently broken down to fatty acids within the intestinal mucosa. The absorption process and the constitution of the chylomicra which appear in the blood require the resynthesis of triglycerides. The glycerol split from the triglycerides during hydrolysis is not used for resynthesis, instead glucose supplies L-α-glycerophosphate as in the synthesis of triglycerides in the fat depots (see Figure 2.12). Monoglycerides that are absorbed can also be converted to triglycerides by successive reactions with acyl-CoA derivatives. The passage of resynthesized triglycerides through the cell and their collection to form chylomicra is not well understood. Some electron microscope evidence suggests the triglycerides pass along the fine pores of the endoplasmic reticulum by a process like pinocytosis. Whatever the mechanism, the triglycerides that pass into the blood stream are different from those presented to the intestinal mucosa both in the arrangements of the fatty acids in the glycerides and in the carbon skeletons of the glycerol part of the molecule.

The water solubilities of the fatty acids presented to the intestine are very different. Whereas all the sugars and the amino acids are highly water-soluble, the fatty acids decrease in water solubility until by C_{12} they may be considered water-insoluble. The transport of fatty acids up to C_5 in chain length has been shown to be by an active process inhibited by phlorizin, dinitriphenol and anaerobic conditions. The short chain fatty acids mainly pass through the intestine into the blood stream without forming triglycerides and it is only when they pass as the free fatty acids that the transport is active. Quantitatively these short chain fatty acids are minor components of the diet, for example your intake of acetic acid is probably dependent on the quantity of pickles you eat.

The absorption of water and salt

The intestine transports water very efficiently from its contents to the blood stream. This may be seen from the fact that the water excreted in the faeces (100–200 ml) shows little change irrespective of the amount of liquid consumed. The intestine has to transport not only the fluid ingested but also the fluid contributed by the various secretions of the digestive system. The quantities involved are shown in Table 3.3.

Table 3.3. Contributions to water and salt contents of intestinal lumen

	Daily contribution of water to intestinal contents (l)	Daily contribution of Na$^+$ (g)	Daily contribution of Cl$^-$ (g)
Saliva	1·5	0·8	1·5
Gastric juice	3·0	3·3	15·0
Bile	0·9	4·0	2·9
Pancreatic juice	0·7	2·1	1·7
Shed cells of intestinal lining and other secretions	0·2	0·5	0·6
Total from endogenous sources	6·3	10·7	21·7
Content of food	2·5	4·0	5·0
drink	3·0		
Total exogenous sources	5·5	4·0	5·0
Total all sources	11·8	14·7	26·7
Excreted in faeces	0·2	0·12	0·09
Percentage absorbed of lumen contents	98·5	99·2	99·7

Roughly half the water load of the intestine is contributed by the internal secretions. Besides water, the internal secretions contribute substantial quantities of Na$^+$ and Cl$^-$ to the lumen contents, much more than comes from exogenous sources (see Table 3.3), and again there is an almost quantitative absorption of these substances. Some at least of the movement of these three substances from the intestine into the blood is against a chemical gradient and like the other active transport mechanisms of the intestine they are inhibited by anoxia, by inhibition of oxidative phosphorylation and by phlorizin. It is probable that much of the chloride is passively transported as a counter ion to the actively moved sodium, but there is evidence that at some sites in the intestine there is also an active transport of chloride.

SECTION 4

Transport of Materials and Messages: the Blood and the Brain

CHAPTER 12

Blood cells

Red cells

Haemopoiesis

Red cells arise from mesenchymal cells present in bone marrow. This process of differentiation involves the conversion of cells that are relatively unspecialized, with a wide range of metabolic activities, into highly specialized cells laden with haemoglobin, lacking a nucleus and having a meagre anaerobic metabolism. The absence of a nucleus, and hence of DNA (which can act as a template for the m-RNA needed for protein synthesis; see Chapter 17), means that mature red cells are unable to repair the damage which they suffer during passage through the capillaries. Consequently red cells have a limited life span of about 120 days. Since a 70 kg man contains some 2.5×10^{13} erythrocytes, it follows that roughly 2.5×10^6 must be formed every second to replace those that are removed from the circulation. The rate of production can greatly exceed this value when the oxygen tension of the blood is reduced following haemorrhage or exposure to low atmospheric tensions of oxygen. Low oxygen tensions in the blood cause a protein activator of haemopoiesis, haemopoietin, to be released into the circulation from the kidneys. Recent work suggests that haemopoietin stimulates the differentiation of mesenchymal cells by acting as a 'genetic derepressor'. That is to say, in the presence of haemopoietin, DNA which was previously unable to function is able to act as a template for m-RNA synthesis and so provides the information necessary for the synthesis of certain proteins including globin, the protein component of haemoglobin. The stimulatory effect of haemopoietin on haemoglobin and RNA formation by bone marrow is inhibited by the antibiotic actinomycin D (see p. 254) which is a specific inhibitor of DNA-dependent RNA synthesis.

Synthesis of haem

The protoporphyrin ring of haem, the pigment of haemoglobin, is synthesized from glycine and succinyl-CoA. These two compounds react

165

together to give δ-aminolevulinic acid, two molecules of which combine to form the pyrrole derivative porphobilinogen.

succinyl-CoA	glycine	α-amino-β-oxo adipic acid	δ-amino-levulinic acid

2-δ-aminolevulinic acid   porphobilinogen

Subsequently four molecules of porphobilinogen polymerize to form a cyclic tetrapyrrole which undergoes modification of its side groups to yield protoporphyrin III, the parent compound of haem.

M = —CH$_3$; R = —CH=CH$_2$; P = —CH$_2$·CH$_2$·COOH in protoporphyrin III

R = —CH$_2$·CH$_2$·COOH in coproporphyrin II

Finally the four nitrogen atoms of the tetrapyrrole are able to chelate ferrous iron to form haem (see Figure 1.33). Apparently the body is unable to convert all the porphobilinogen into protoporphyrin and some of it always ends up as coproporphyrin which is useless for the synthesis of haem and is excreted in the urine. The amount of coproporphyrin so excreted is a reasonably constant fraction of the amount of haem synthesized. Therefore when the rate of haemoglobin synthesis is increased, following haemorrhage for example, the amount of coproporphyrin in the urine also increases. There are conditions (some hereditary, some acquired) termed porphyrias, in which porphyrins are synthesized at an excessively high rate so that their level in the blood rises and the urine becomes dark red in colour. Often in these conditions porphyrins are deposited under the skin which then becomes sensitive to light and ulcerates. There can also be mental disturbances and recently it has been suggested that the madness of George III was a result of porphyria.

Bile pigments

When haemoglobin is broken down, the porphyrin ring is opened and converted into the bile pigments biliverdin and bilirubin which are excreted in the faeces.

biliverdin (green)

$\downarrow$ +2H

bilirubin (yellow)

A 70 kg man destroys about 6·25 g of haemoglobin daily, giving a total excretion of bile pigments around 200 mg per day.

The metabolism of iron

The red cells contain about 3 g of iron representing some 60% of the total in the body; the greater part of the remainder is stored in a special iron-containing protein called ferritin. In males, the normal daily loss of iron is about 1 mg and any loss in excess of this is the result of bleeding. Most mixed diets contain between 10 and 20 mg of iron, but only 1 to 2 mg is absorbed unless there is an increased need for iron following blood loss. Most of the dietary iron is in the ferric state which, unlike the ferrous, is not at all well absorbed. It is an old observation that infants may develop anaemia during vitamin C deficiency. The probable reason for this is that ascorbic acid plays a part in reducing ferric iron to ferrous. In the scorbutic infant, probably fed on pasteurized or dried milk, there is a combination of low vitamin C and low iron intake, since cow's milk contains not more than 0·2 mg of iron and 1 mg of vitamin C per 100 ml. The actual quantity of iron absorbed depends on the amount of ferrous iron and ferritin stored in the intestine. If the iron content of the mucosal cells is low, iron is more readily taken up. Once ferrous iron has entered the mucosal cell, it combines with a protein, apoferritin, and is oxidized to the ferric state to form ferritin. In fasting animals the level of apoferritin in the mucosal cells is low but within a few hours of oral iron administration has increased up to fiftyfold. When the level of iron in the plasma falls, some of the iron leaves the ferritin in the mucosa. It then enters the blood in the ferrous form as the iron–protein complex transferrin; the attachment to protein prevents the iron from being lost into the glomerular filtrate. Much of the plasma iron is deposited as ferritin again in the liver, spleen and bone marrow. Iron liberated in the breakdown of haemoglobin is also deposited as ferritin if it is not immediately used for the synthesis of more haemoglobin. With radioactive iron it has been found that about 27 mg of the body's store of 5 g of iron is used daily and 20 mg of this comes from the direct reutilization of iron from broken-down red cells. Since iron is not excreted to any significant extent and its absorption is regulated by the iron content of the mucosal cells, it follows that blood transfusions increase the total iron content of the body in a relatively irreversible manner. Excess iron is deposited in the liver as haemosiderin granules. The accumulation of haemosiderin can cause severe liver damage in patients suffering from haemolytic anaemia who have received many transfusions over a period of years.

Carbohydrate metabolism and drug sensitivity of red cells

Intermediate between the nucleated normoblasts and enucleate red cells are the reticulocytes, which, although not possessing an organized nucleus, retain some basophilic material. These cells contain mitochondria allowing them to obtain succinyl-CoA and energy by oxidative phosphorylation, both of which are required for the synthesis of haemoglobin. During periods of very rapid red cell production, large numbers of these immature red cells enter the circulation. In contrast to the reticulocytes,

mature red cells lack mitochondria and meet their small energy requirement by glycolysing glucose at a rate of 1·5 m mole/kg/h. Some of the
ATP supplied in this way is used to drive the sodium pump which maintains the differential distribution of sodium and potassium ions across the
erythrocyte membrane (see p. 177).

Besides the glycolytic pathway, red cells contain the enzymes of the
pentose phosphate pathway and therefore are able to form $NADPH_2$ in
the reactions catalysed by glucose-6-phosphate dehydrogenase and 6-
phosphogluconate dehydrogenase. Lowering the activity of glucose-6-
phosphate dehydrogenase and hence the ratio $NADPH_2/NADP$ decreases
the stability of red cell membranes and increases their tendency to lyse.
For many years it had been known that some individuals in the Mediter-
ranean and Middle East developed a haemolytic anaemia, termed favism,
after eating fava ('broad') beans. The administration of the antimalarial
drug primaquine was sometimes accompanied by haemolysis of the red
cells and subsequently it was found that sensitive patients also suffered
from a haemolytic attack when given acetanilide or sulphanilamide. It was
discovered eventually that the concentration of glutathione (both total and
reduced) in the red cells of drug-sensitive individuals was lower than
normal. Reduced glutathione is the principal compound containing SH
groups in red cells and a certain minimum concentration of it is required
to maintain the integrity of the cell membrane and to prevent it from
lysing. Oxyhaemoglobin converts reduced glutathione into the oxidized
form which is broken down by red cells and the addition of one of the
sensitizing drugs mentioned above accelerates the rate of this oxidation.
Normally, red cells have the capacity to synthesize sufficient $NADPH_2$ to
reduce oxidized glutathione as soon as it is formed and so prevent its
destruction. However, whilst the activity of glutathione reductase in
drug-sensitive red cells is normal, that of glucose-6-phosphate dehydrogenase is only about one-tenth of the normal value. Hence, the biochemical
lesion causing the drug sensitivity of red cells is an inability to form
sufficient $NADPH_2$ to reduce glutathione and so prevent its degradation.
Drug-sensitivity can now be predicted by measuring the glucose-6-phos-
phate dehydrogenase activity of red cells. $NADPH_2$ is also used to reduce
methaemoglobin (that is haemoglobin having its iron in the ferric state)
back to haemoglobin. Primaquine-sensitive red cells have a diminished
ability to carry out this reduction as they lack an adequate supply of
$NADPH_2$ and recently this defect has also been used to identify persons
likely to suffer a haemolytic attack if treated with the drug.

One curious observation was that the haemolysis of the red cells in
susceptible patients ceased if administration of primaquine was continued.

This is because only old cells are haemolysed; young cells can produce NADPH$_2$ at a rate sufficient to keep their glutathione reduced. Thus when all the old cells are lysed, lysis stops. It is known that the glucose-6-phosphate dehydrogenase of red cells declines with age, presumably because the cells, lacking a nucleus, are unable to replace worn-out enzyme molecules. Since the deficiency of glucose-6-phosphate dehydrogenase is a genetic defect, it might be expected that other types of cells would also be deficient in the enzyme. This is so, but the deficiency is not as great as in red cells, presumably because nucleated cells can constantly synthesize new enzyme as the old is broken down.

The role of glucose-6-phosphate dehydrogenase in red cell metabolism is shown in Figure 4.1.

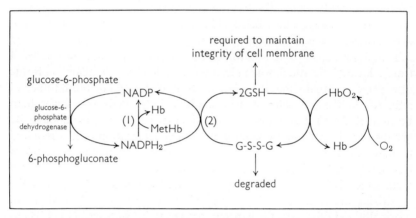

Figure 4.1. Role of glucose-6-phosphate dehydrogenase in red cells. (1) Reduction of methaemoglobin (Fe^{3+}) to haemoglobin (Fe^{2+}) by methaemoglobin reductase. (2) Reduction of oxidized glutathione to reduced glutathione by glutathione reductase

Oxygen and carbon dioxide carriage by haemoglobin

Haemoglobin is one of the few proteins whose amino acid sequence and three-dimensional structure are known (Figure 4.2). It has a molecular weight of about 67,000 and consists of four coiled polypeptide chains. Each subunit contains a cleft formed by the folding of the polypeptide chain into which a haem group is set edgeways and held by hydrophobic bonds and a dative covalent link between a histidine residue and the iron atom.

There are four different species of normal haemoglobin polypeptides in human beings designated as α, β, γ and δ. Most haemoglobin molecules contain two α chains and two β, γ or δ chains, thus haemoglobins A, A$_2$

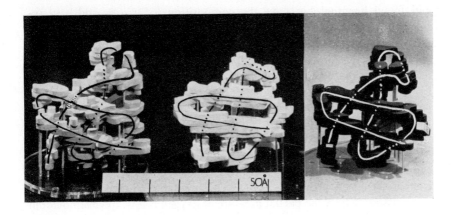

Figure 4.2. Molecular models of haemoglobin and myoglobin. (a) Models of (1) sperm whale myoglobin, (2) horse haemoglobin α-chain, (3) horse haemoglobin β-chain illustrating the similarity in the tertiary structure of the three chains (Perutz and coworkers, 1960). (b) Model of haemoglobin molecule at 5·5 Å resolution, showing the two α-chains (white) and two β-chains (black) tetrahedrally arranged relative to each other (Perutz and coworkers, 1960)

and foetal haemoglobin have the composition $\alpha_2\beta_2$; $\alpha_2\delta_2$ and $\alpha_2\gamma_2$ respectively. Each of the four polypeptides is inherited through a separate gene although they are very similar in structure. Many abnormal haemoglobins have been characterized in which a single amino acid in a particular polypeptide chain is replaced by another owing to a mutation in the gene responsible for determining the amino acid sequence of the polypeptide. The best known of these abnormal haemoglobins is haemoglobin S which occurs in people who suffer from sickle-cell anaemia and those bearing the sickle cell trait (see p. 262).

Oxygen is carried by red cells in combination with haemoglobin; in the capillaries of the lungs oxygen displaces a water molecule attached to the iron of the haem group to form oxyhaemoglobin. In the capillaries of other tissues, where the partial pressure of oxygen is low, oxyhaemoglobin dissociates to give free oxygen which is replaced on the haem group by a molecule of water. It should be emphasized that in the gain and loss of oxygen by haemoglobin the iron always remains in the ferrous state. The extent to which haemoglobin is converted to oxyhaemoglobin depends on the partial pressure of oxygen in a sigmoid fashion (Figure 4.3). Such an S-shaped dissociation curve indicates that haemoglobin can be fully saturated by oxygen over a wide range of oxygen partial pressures. Such behaviour affords some protection against exposure to low oxygen tensions.

The sigmoid shape of the dissociation curve results from a cooperative interaction between the four haem groups which are carried on separate polypeptide chains. The four haem groups are not in contact with one another so that the haem–haem interaction upon which the shape of the oxygen dissociation curve depends must involve very subtle interactions between the four polypeptide chains. The nature of this interaction is not understood, although x-ray crystallographic studies have revealed that conformational changes occur during oxygenation. Suffice it to say that combination of oxygen with one haem group facilitates the combination of oxygen with any one of the remaining three groups. With increasing partial pressures of CO_2 the oxygen dissociation curve is displaced towards the right (Figure 4.3). This phenomenon, known as the Bohr effect, means that oxyhaemoglobin dissociates as the pCO_2 is increased; such behaviour is, of course, well suited to the unloading of oxygen in the tissues where the pCO_2 is high.

Besides carrying 97% of the oxygen present in blood, haemoglobin carries some 20% of the blood CO_2 bound to amino groups (the carbamino-bound CO_2):

$$\text{Hb—NH}_2 + CO_2 \rightleftharpoons \text{Hb—NH·COO}^- + H^+$$

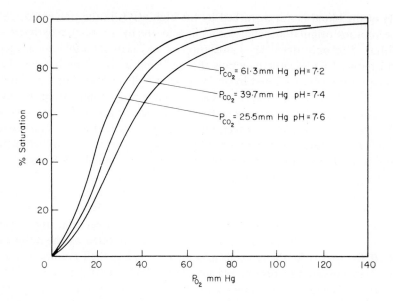

Figure 4.3. Effect of CO_2 tension on the dissociation of oxyhaemoglobin in blood. From White, Handler and Smith, *Principles of Biochemistry*, 3rd ed., McGraw-Hill, 1964

Haemoglobin is also responsible for buffering a further 60% of the total CO_2. Oxyhaemoglobin is a stronger acid than haemoglobin, thus, when blood is oxygenated in the lungs, protons are released from haemoglobin, i.e.

$$HHb + O_2 \rightleftharpoons HbO_2 + H^+$$

These protons react with bicarbonate ions to form carbonic acid which is converted rapidly to CO_2 and H_2O by the carbonic anhydrase present in red cells

$$H^+ + HCO_3^- \underset{\text{carbonic}}{\overset{}{\rightleftharpoons}} H_2CO_3 \rightleftharpoons H_2O + CO_2$$
$$\text{carbonic}$$
$$\text{anhydrase}$$

Owing to the low pCO_2 in the lungs, the blood is able to unload much of its bicarbonate as CO_2 in this way. In the tissues oxyhaemoglobin dissociates and in doing so takes up protons to form reduced haemoglobin which is a weaker acid than oxyhaemoglobin. These protons are derived from the carbonic acid formed by the action of carbonic anhydrase on the H_2O and CO_2 produced by the metabolic activities of the tissue. Thus the pH of the blood is not disturbed by the high pCO_2 in the tissues because the protons originating from carbonic acid are tightly bound by haemoglobin. Not only does the dissociation of oxyhaemoglobin into oxygen and reduced haemoglobin permit the buffering of H^+ ions but the dissociation is itself facilitated by an increase in hydrogen ion concentration. Thus CO_2 buffering by haemoglobin facilitates oxygen unloading by oxyhaemoglobin and vice versa. The Bohr effect can be accounted for only in part by the increase in hydrogen ion concentration that attends increases in pCO_2 as a result of the action of carbonic anhydrase. The bicarbonate ions formed from CO_2 in the red cells are neutralized by K^+ ions that formerly neutralized oxyhaemoglobin.

As a result of the transformations described above, most of the CO_2 entering erythrocytes in the capillaries is converted to HCO_3^- ions with the result that the ratio $[HCO_3^-]/[Cl^-]$ in red cells is larger than the corresponding ratio in the plasma. This imbalance is corrected by the diffusion of HCO_3^- ions from the red cells into the plasma and their replacement by Cl^- ions moving in from the plasma. The chloride shift is reversed when the red cells enter the pulmonary capillaries and begin to take up oxygen and discharge CO_2.

The carriage of oxygen and carbon dioxide by erythrocytes is summarized in Figure 4.4.

Ion transport by red cells

The concentration of potassium in red cells is much higher than in plasma whilst that of sodium is much lower (see Table 4.1).

Table 4.1. Potassium and sodium concentrations in red cells and plasma (mM)

	Red cells	Plasma
$[K^+]$	150	5·4
$[Na^+]$	12–20	144

This uneven distribution of ions was once thought to arise during red cell differentiation and to be maintained in mature red cells because their membranes were impermeable to both Na^+ and K^+. About 1940 this point of view had to be abandoned because experiments with ^{24}Na and ^{42}K indicated that red cell membranes were permeable to both Na^+ and K^+. It was also found that when blood was stored at 2°, the red cells lost K^+ and gained Na^+; furthermore, when the temperature was raised to 37°

the cells slowly regained their lost K^+ and expelled the excess Na^+. However, in the absence of glucose or in the presence of an inhibitor of glycolysis, such as fluoride or iodoacetate, cold-stored red cells were unable to restore their ionic composition to normal when incubated at 37°. These observations indicated that red cells are permeable to Na^+ and K^+ and have to maintain their ionic composition by expelling any Na^+ that enters

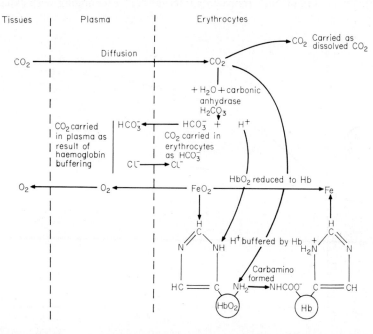

Figure 4.4. Schematic representation of the processes occurring when carbon dioxide passes from the tissues into the erythrocytes. The imizadole ring of histidine is shown as the reactive portion of the haemoglobin molecule. Modified from H. W. Davenport, *The ABC of Acid-Chemistry*, University of Chicago Press, Chicago, 1950

and by taking up K^+ to replace that lost by leakage. Since such ion movements are against concentration gradients they require an input of energy in accordance with the formula:

$$\Delta G' = RT\, n \ln \frac{[Na^+]_{out}}{[Na^+]_{in}} + m \ln \frac{[K^+]_{in}}{[K^+]_{out}} + (n - m)EF$$

where R is the gas constant, T is the absolute temperature, F the Faraday and E the membrane potential which is calculated to be about 10 mV; n is the number of sodium ions expelled and *m* the number of potassium ions taken up.

Evidence now exists that the net transport of Na^+ outwards, which is an active process, is dependent upon the inward movement of K^+. There is also a passive efflux of Na^+ that can be observed in the absence of glucose, or in the presence of glucose but absence of external K^+ (Figure 4.5). This efflux of Na^+ represents internal Na^+ exchanging with external

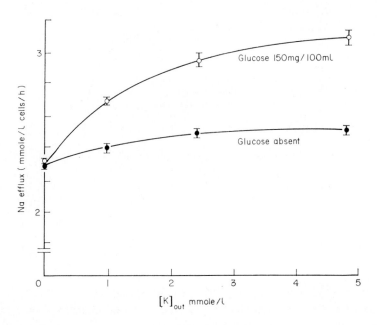

Figure 4.5. The effect of glucose on sodium efflux at different external potassium concentrations. Each point is the mean of three estimations. From Glynn, *J. Physiol.* (*London*), 1956

Na^+ and is abolished if Na^+ is omitted from the external medium. Such a passive exchange produces no net change in concentration so that it does not require an input of energy and can consequently be observed in the absence of glucose. Figure 4.5 shows that in the presence of glucose a potassium-dependent efflux of sodium is superimposed on the passive flux. This potassium-dependent sodium efflux is an active process driven by energy obtained from glucose and is stimulated half-maximally by 1.8 mM K^+.

Potassium influx also consists of two components, one independent of glucose but linearly dependent on the concentration of external potassium and another dependent upon glucose and showing Michaelis–Menten kinetics with regard to K^+ ions with a K_m of about 2 mM. The similarity between the K_m values for potassium of the K^+ influx and K^+-dependent Na^+ efflux adds further support to the view that both processes are mediated by the same system. Recent work suggests that one K^+ is taken up for every Na^+ extruded actively although earlier estimates of the ratio were 2 to 3. That is to say the values of n and m in the equation on p. 175 are probably unity.

Cardiac glycosides such as ouabain prevent the uptake of K^+ and expulsion of Na^+ by erythrocytes. This inhibition is by a direct action on the transport system rather than by interference with the glycolytic pathway and can be overcome by increasing the external concentration of K^+ ions. In addition to inhibiting active transport the cardiac glycosides also decrease the size of the passive fluxes.

Ion transport ATP-ase

Studies on the rate of K^+ influx as a function of the internal ATP concentration provided evidence that the energy required for active transport by red cells is supplied by ATP derived from glycolysis. Further clarification of the role of ATP came when Post and his coworkers reported the existence of an ATP-ase in the membranes of haemolysed red cells that required the presence of Na^+, K^+ and Mg^{2+} for maximal activity. The ATP-ase and ion transport by red cells share many common features.

(1) Both systems are located in the red cell membrane.
(2) Both use ATP but not ITP.
(3) Both require the presence of Na^+ and K^+ together for maximal activity.
(4) The K_m value for Na^+ is similar for both systems.
(5) The K_m value for K^+ is similar for both systems.
(6) Cardiac glycosides inhibit both systems to the same extent.
(7) Excess potassium overcomes glycoside inhibition in both instances.
(8) The activation of both systems by K^+ is inhibited by high concentrations of Na^+.
(9) In both systems NH_4^+ can substitute for K^+ but not for Na^+.

On the basis of these similarities it was concluded that the ATP-ase activity was related to the ion transport system.

Whittam has examined the connection between ion transport and ATP-ase activity by making use of a technique that enables the ionic

7+

composition within red cell 'ghosts' to be defined. Red cells are haemo-lysed in a solution containing 4 mM ATP and the ghosts (ruptured red cells having lost most of their haemoglobin) are resealed by adding 3M NaCl, KCl or tris-chloride. After incubation at 37° has stabilized the ghosts, they are spun down, washed and resuspended in a solution con-taining Na^+, K^+ or choline as the main cation. All the solutions used contain Mg^{2+} in addition to the other ions. In this way it is possible to prepare ghosts with internal concentrations of Na^+ and K^+ that can be varied at will, and which can be suspended in different ionic environments. With ghosts prepared in this way it has been found that the hydrolysis of ATP within the cells is dependent upon the external concentration of K^+ up to 10 mM and upon the internal concentration of Na^+ up to 100 mM but is independent of the external Na^+ concentration. At present it has not been possible to discover whether the ATP-ase activity is independent of the internal K^+ concentration because ghosts free from potassium have not been prepared. The asymmetric activation of the ATP-ase might be anticipated from the fact that ion transport is dependent on the external potassium and internal sodium concentrations. ATP added to the external medium is not degraded and phosphate liberated during the hydrolysis of internal ATP is released into the cells rather than into the medium. Ouabain added to the external medium inhibits activation of the mem-brane ATP-ase by both Na^+ and K^+.

By varying the internal concentration of Na^+ and the external concen-tration of K^+ the rate of ion transport can be altered. Such experiments demonstrated that the activity of the ATP-ase varies directly with the rate of ion transport so that the number of ions transported per molecule of ATP hydrolysed remains constant and is independent of the electro-chemical gradient against which the ions are moved. The free energy made available by the hydrolysis of 1 mole of ATP in red cells has been calcu-lated to be 13 kcal. During the time taken by the ouabain-sensitive ATP-ase to hydrolyse 1 mole of ATP, red cells can expend 9 kcals on ion transport. Thus the amount of energy liberated by the ATP-ase and the amount used for ion transport are similar. This is consistent with the view that ion transport and the ATP-ase form a coupled system.

The activity of the Na^+/K^+-dependent ATP-ase exerts some control over the rate of glycolysis by red cells. Lactate production increases by up to 75% above the basal level when ion transport is stimulated by raising the external K^+ and internal Na^+ concentrations. This extra lactate production is inhibited by ouabain. The control of glycolysis is thought to result from variations in the concentration of ADP formed from ATP by the Na^+/K^+ activated ATP-ase. During periods of increased ion transport the rate of ADP production rises and since ADP is a substrate for the phosphoglycerokinase and pyruvic kinase reactions, glycolysis is stimulated. This provides a further example of the way in which the activity of a pathway supplying energy is adjusted to meet the demands of the work being performed (see Section 8).

Mechanism of ion transport

A carrier, driven by ATP, which picked up a sodium ion at the internal surface of the membrane and transported it to the outer surface where it was exchanged for a potassium ion which was then carried into the cell has been postulated by many workers in an attempt to account for active transport (Figure 4.6). More recently, carriers have tended to become unfashionable and current ideas are focused on enzymes that cause their cofactors to

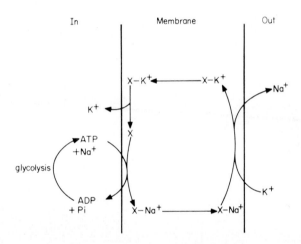

Figure 4.6. Carrier-mediated transport of cations across red cell membrane

move in a vectorial fashion (see p. 82). A simple scheme of this type may be outlined as follows. ATP phosphorylates an enzyme in a reaction that requires Na^+ as cofactor at a site that can be approached only from the inside of the cell. During phosphorylation the conformation of the enzyme changes so that the only path available to the sodium leads to its emergence at the opposite side of the enzyme, that is, the side in contact with the extracellular solution. Dephosphorylation of the enzyme may then require the presence of potassium at a site accessible only from the outside of the cell and lead to the movement of potassium inwards.

White cells

Phagocytosis

One of the special functions of leucocytes is to engulf and destroy bacteria that enter the body. Biochemical studies have shown that the respiration of isolated leucocytes is stimulated by the presence of dead bacteria or small particles and that the increased respiration is more or less proportional to the number of particles taken up. This work has now been set on a quantitative basis by using polystyrene granules of known size. Polystyrene spherules are taken up rapidly at first (Figure 4.7) but

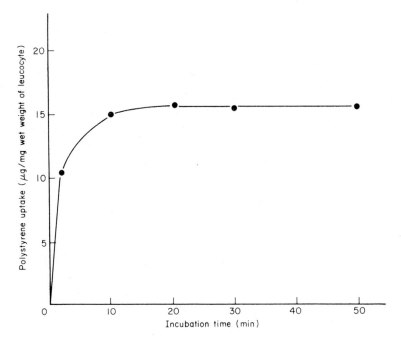

Figure 4.7. Uptake of polystyrene granules by leucocytes. From Roberts and Quastel, *Biochem. J.*, 1963

after 20 min no more are engulfed. The total amount of polystyrene accumulated is independent of the size of the particles. Table 4.2 illustrates this feature of phagocytosis and also shows the three-fold stimulation of respiration that occurs in the presence of the spherules.

Probably the most important factor contributing to the increased oxygen consumption is the oxidation of $NADPH_2$ by a particle-bound $NADPH_2$

Table 4.2. Effect of polystyrene particles on phagocytosis and O_2 consumption by polymorphonuclear leucocytes from guinea pigs. After Roberts and Quastel (1963)

Diameter of spherules (μ)	O_2 uptake in 40 min (μl)	Polystyrene uptake in 40 min (μg/mg wet wt. of leucocyte)
0·088	17·3	7·4
0·264	44·7	30·1
1·305	51·2	34·3
3·04	50·6	35·9
7–14	14·1	0
No polystyrene	14·9	0

oxidase. The $NADPH_2$ is formed by the preferential oxidation of glucose via the pentose phosphate pathway that accompanies phagocytosis. The physiological role of this $NADPH_2$ oxidase is unknown. However, recent experiments suggest that the stimulated consumption of oxygen is subsequent to the accumulation of bacteria or particles by phagocytosis. These processes using oxygen play some part in destroying engulfed bacteria, because the bacteriocidal but not the bacteria accumulating properties of leucocytes are impaired under anaerobic conditions. Furthermore, leucocytes that have been allowed to take up bacteria and have then been washed quickly to remove any extracellular bacteria still exhibit an elevated Q_{O_2} although phagocytosis is clearly impossible. The energy required for phagocytosis appears to be supplied by the glycolytic pathway rather than by oxidative phosphorylation, since the production of lactate increases and the uptake of particles is inhibited by fluoride and iodoacetate but not by cyanide, dinitrophenol or anaerobic conditions.

The rate of incorporation of $^{32}PO_4$ into phosphatidic acids, phosphatidyl inositol and phosphatidyl serine is also increased greatly during phagocytosis. This increased turnover of phospholipids may be related to changes in the organization and amount of cell membrane that are required if particles are to be enveloped (see p. 96).

CHAPTER 13

Plasma

Plasma proteins

The plasma is one of the most inactive parts of the body biochemically, yet it is the material that is most frequently analysed for diagnostic purposes. This is because its composition reflects the activity of other organs in the body and is not distorted by its own metabolic activity. Besides its six main classes of proteins, the plasma contains enzymes that have leaked from the tissues. The six classes of plasma proteins are albumin, α_1-globulin, α_2-globulin, β-globulin, γ-globulin and fibrinogen. Albumins are soluble in water whereas globulins and fibrinogen are insoluble in water but soluble in dilute salt solutions. The various protein fractions are usually separated by paper electrophoresis for clinical examination (Figure 4.8). Most of the plasma proteins enter the blood from the liver where they

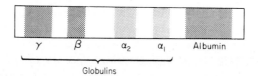

Figure 4.8. Paper electrophoretic pattern of human serum, showing the separation of albumin and globulins (α, β and γ)

are synthesized, although the γ-globulins, which are rich in antibodies, are derived from lymphoid tissue and plasma cells. The presence of plasma proteins results in the development of a colloid osmotic pressure across the capillary walls that opposes the hydrostatic pressure of the blood and so prevents the tissues from becoming oedematous. Under normal conditions the plasma proteins turn over rapidly and must be removed at rates equal to those of their synthesis since their concentration in the plasma remains constant. Proteins removed from the circulation, possibly by pinocytosis, are degraded by intracellular proteinases to their constituent amino acids which can then be incorporated into new proteins. Thus
182

the plasma proteins act as a mobile store of amino acids which is used by the tissues. In prolonged starvation the concentration of plasma proteins in general, and of albumins in particular, falls, and, especially in children, hunger oedema develops. In some cases of extreme malnutrition, albumins are injected intravenously to alleviate the oedema symptoms and to provide a source of amino acids.

Plasma proteins and disease

The concentration of individual proteins in the plasma changes in certain diseases. For example, cirrhosis of the liver leads to the impairment of albumin synthesis and a consequent fall in the level of albumin in the plasma, whilst in nephrosis albumins are lost in the urine. The β-globulins, precursors of β-lipoproteins, increase in quantity during hepatitis, as do γ-globulins in cirrhosis of the liver. Apart from changes in response to disease, there are some inherited abnormalities in the composition of the plasma resulting from an inability to synthesize particular proteins such as fibrinogen, antibodies, albumins and thromboplastic factors.

Besides the normal proteins already considered, the plasma contains small quantities of enzymes that are of growing importance in clinical studies. Damage to tissues frequently results in a leakage of enzymes into the plasma and there is a roughly quantitative relationship between the amount of tissues damaged and the amounts of enzymes liberated. Thus, pathological changes in some tissues are accompanied by marked increases in the activity of characteristic enzymes in the plasma whose measurement can aid diagnosis of the condition. In prostatic cancer, the activity of acid phosphatase in the plasma is elevated, whilst pancreatitis leads to an increase in the amount of circulating amylase. Muscular dystrophy is attended by a rise in the plasma concentration of such enzymes as aldolase and creatine phosphokinase. In myocardial infarction glutamate oxalo-acetate transaminase (GOT), lactic dehydrogenase (LDH) and malic dehydrogenase (MDH) enter the circulation from the damaged tissue.

Some enzymes occur in several distinct forms, termed isoenzymes, that can be separated from one another by electrophoresis. The pattern of LDH isoenzymes found in heart differs from that found in liver. Thus by studying the LDH isoenzymes in plasma following myocardial infarction it is possible to determine whether any secondary damage has occurred to the liver as a result of congestion caused by a diminished venous return.

Not all increases in the activity of plasma enzymes are indicative of pathological changes. Following severe muscular exercise there is an elevated level of aldolase in the plasma and during pregnancy the activity

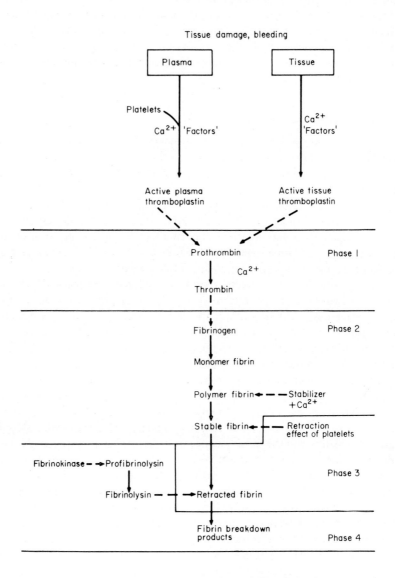

Figure 4.9. Processes involved in the clotting of blood; ➤ is converted to,
➤ acts on. Redrawn from *Documenta Geigy*, 6th ed., 1962

of plasma histaminase increases, presumably to protect the mother from the toxic effects of histamine which is present in high concentration in the foetus.

In addition to aiding diagnosis, measurement of changes in the activity of plasma enzymes can be of use in assessing the progress of recovery. For example, the healing of a cardiac infarction is attended by a decline in the level of enzymes entering the blood from the damaged region.

Blood coagulation

Blood has to remain fluid so that it can be circulated around the body, but at the same time it has to be able to coagulate rapidly if bleeding is to be brought under control. The need to fulfil both of these requirements has led to the evolution of a highly complex series of processes that allow the clot-forming protein, fibrin, to be liberated from its precursor, fibrinogen, only following damage to the blood vessels (Figure 4.9).

When blood is shed, changes occur which result in the formation of a platelet thrombus and the liberation of thromboplastins having proteo-lytic activity from both damaged tissues and plasma. These initial changes involve interactions between many clotting factors, protein and lipid in nature, that are understood only in part. Provided that Ca^{2+} is available, the thromboplastins bring about the conversion of prothrombin to thrombin, a proteolytic enzyme whose natural substrate is fibrinogen. Under the influence of thrombin, fibrinogen is hydrolysed to give 'mono-mer' fibrin and two fibrinopeptides. Fibrin monomers polymerize in the presence of Ca^{2+} and a stabilizer to form a network of proteins, cross-linked by disulphide bonds, called stable fibrin. Platelets cause this fibrin clot to retract, thereby expelling any occluded plasma. Clots are eventually broken down by the fibrinolytic system whose active agent is another proteolytic enzyme termed fibrinolysin.

Coagulation can be inhibited for clinical purposes by heparin which amongst other actions interferes with the prothrombin to thrombin conversion and by vitamin K antagonists such as dicoumarol since the formation of prothrombin depends upon the presence of vitamin K.

7*

CHAPTER 14

The brain

General metabolism

The gross metabolism of a human subject can be described by his oxygen consumption, carbon dioxide evolution, calorie intake and heat production under various physiological conditions. The overall picture obtained indicates nothing of the marked differences in metabolism which exist between the various organs that comprise the body. Similarly, an overall study of the metabolism of the brain illustrates some gross features of cerebral activity, but a deeper understanding can only be achieved when the subtle differences in the structure, metabolism and function of the component parts of the brain are appreciated.

A 70 kg man has a brain weighing about 1·4 kg; this relatively small mass of tissue receives some 15% of the cardiac output and is responsible for about 20% of the total oxygen consumption at rest. The RQ of 0·99, calculated from the concentrations of oxygen and carbon dioxide in the blood entering and leaving the brain, indicates that carbohydrate provides the fuel for respiration. Glucose consumption by the brain is more than sufficient to account for the observed oxygen uptake, the excess being degraded only as far as lactate which can be recovered in the venous blood. Brain differs from other organs in that virtually only glucose can act as a metabolic fuel, therefore the Q_{O_2} falls as the level of glucose in the blood is reduced. (By way of contrast, heart muscle is able to oxidize fatty acids and ketone bodies and in consequence its respiration is largely independent of the level of blood glucose.) Since it has stores of glucose and glycogen sufficient for only ten seconds' activity, the brain is critically dependent upon the glucose supplied by the blood. Small falls in the concentration of blood glucose can be compensated by increases in the cerebral blood flow, but more severe falls (occasioned, for example, by an overdose of insulin) can lead to the onset of a coma that is potentially fatal. Unless the supply of glucose is restored to normal within an hour or so, the brain may suffer irreversible damage. Diabetic comas are caused by acidosis, rather than by the elevated level of blood sugar that characterizes uncontrolled diabetes mellitus.

There are no marked changes in the oxygen consumption of the brain accompanying the transition from rest to mental activity even though marked changes in electrical activity can be observed. In contrast, McIlwain has found that slices of human grey matter have a basal rate of respiration of 55 μmoles O_2/g/h which can increase to 110 μmoles O_2/g/h during electrical stimulation. The reason for this apparent discrepancy is that the cells in different parts of the brain do not show their maximum activity at the same time so that the net effect is for the rate of respiration of the whole brain to remain constant under all normal physiological conditions. Electrical stimulation of brain slices also leads to an increased production of lactate and a momentary fall in their content of ATP, although the latter is quickly replenished as the metabolic rate rises (Figure 4.10).

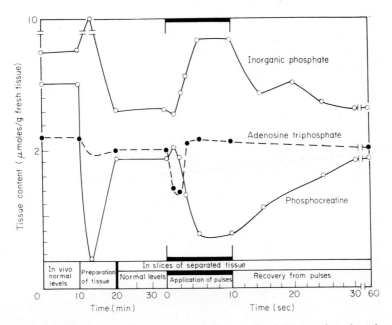

Figure 4.10. Effect of excision and stimulation on the ATP-creatine phosphate and inorganic phosphate content of guinea pig brain. From McIlwain, *Biochemistry of the Central Nervous System*, 3rd ed., Churchill, London, 1966

The metabolism of glutamate and ammonia

Of the amino acids, only glutamate is used by the brain at an appreciable rate; it provides a limited source of energy, acts as a trap for ammonia and is the immediate precursor of γ-amino butyric acid which

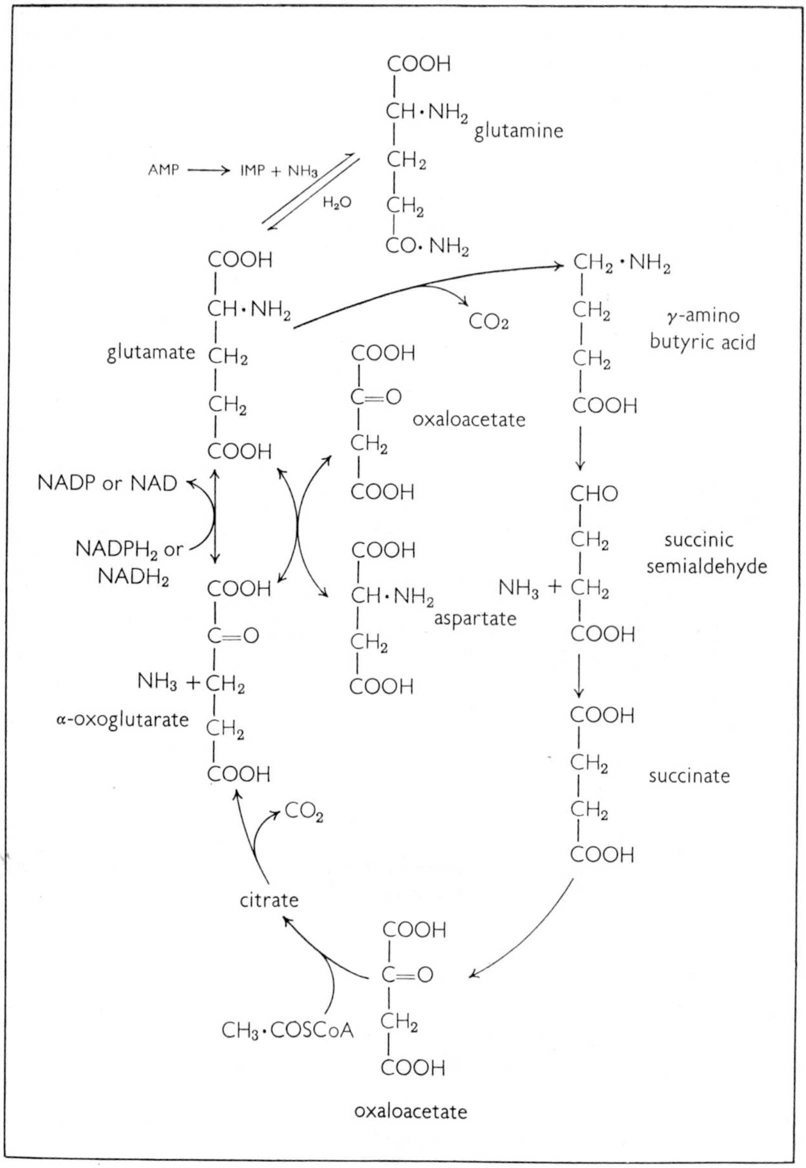

Figure 4.11. Metabolism of glutamate, ammonia and γ-amino butyric acid in brain

has an inhibitory effect on the activity of the central nervous system. Glutamic acid and its amide, glutamine, account for around 80% of the total free amino acids of the brain and are present at a concentration some fifteen times higher than in blood. Transamination between glutamate and oxaloacetate yields α-oxoglutarate (a potential source of energy) and aspartate.

Ammonia is formed in the brain at a very high rate by the deamination of AMP to inosine monophosphate, the hydrolysis of the amide group of glutamine and, to a much lesser extent, by the deamination of glutamate. If the concentration of ammonia in the brain rises appreciably convulsions may result. It follows, therefore, that in the brain ammonia must be removed as fast as it is formed. Any tendency for the concentration of ammonia to rise is counteracted by the conversion of α-oxoglutarate to glutamate by glutamic dehydrogenase and by the conversion of glutamate to glutamine by glutamine synthetase. Both of these reactions require a supply of energy, the first in the form of reduced coenzyme, and the second as ATP. The function of ammonia in the metabolism of the brain is not entirely understood, but it is clear that elaborate chemical devices exist to keep its concentration within close limits. Certainly, isolated brain tissue gives rise rapidly to free ammonia which, if it occurred in the intact animal, would lead to convulsions. Any extensive removal of ammonia converting α-oxoglutarate to glutamate drains away intermediates from the citric acid cycle. Such depletions may be made up by carbon dioxide fixation by the malic enzyme (see p. 101) which allows pyruvate to be converted to malate.

Another conversion undergone by glutamate in the brain is decarboxylation to give γ-amino butyric acid in a reaction that requires pyridoxal phosphate as a coenzyme. Removal of γ-amino butyric acid is effected by deamination to form succinic semialdehyde and ammonia. The succinic semialdehyde can be oxidized to succinate and thence to oxaloacetate which, by condensation with acetyl-CoA, can eventually give α-oxoglutarate again. The ammonia can combine with α-oxoglutarate to give glutamate and hence γ-amino butyric acid (Figure 4.11). Provided that any dicarboxylic acids drained out of the cycle can be replaced by CO_2 fixation, the γ-amino butyric acid cycle will operate as long as C_2 units are supplied.

Vitamins and brain metabolism

Dietary deficiencies of those vitamins that provide coenzymes for reactions supplying energy can lead to the development of nervous disorders. This is hardly surprising when one considers the high rate of metabolism of the brain and the rapid deterioration of brain function when the supply of glucose is restricted.

Thiamine (B₁)

Thiamine pyrophosphate is required for the decarboxylation of pyruvate during its conversion to acetyl-CoA (see p. 62). Thus, in thiamine deficiency, the citric acid cycle (normally the main source of energy for cerebral activity) is inhibited and pyruvate and lactate accumulate. The human brain contains about 5 mμ moles of thiamine/g of tissue and it retains this more tenaciously than any other organ. Thus, during the first 15 days of a diet deficient in thiamine, the brain retains its normal content of the vitamin whilst other tissues have only some 30% of their original content. After 15 days, when the brain thiamine begins to fall, nervous symptoms develop. Beriberi, a disease resulting from a deficiency of thiamine, is endemic in those parts of the world where polished rice provides the staple diet. Two forms of the disease, dry and wet beriberi, are known. The former is characterized by peripheral neuritis, muscular wasting, impaired cardiac function and mental confusion; in the latter a general oedema obscures the wasting. Thiamine deficiency is encountered more commonly in the West as Wernicke's syndrome in alcoholics who have a low intake of normal foodstuffs. Although some of the milder symptoms of this disease may be relieved by giving thiamine, some cerebral lesions cannot be reversed and leave a clinical condition termed Korsakoff's syndrome, which comprises mental confusion and a failure to remember recent events.

Pyridoxal (B₆)

A phosphorylated form of vitamin B₆, pyridoxal phosphate (see p. 138), is involved in several important reactions in brain tissue. The transamination occurring between glutamate and oxaloacetate and the decarboxylations of glutamate to γ-amino butyric acid, of 5-hydroxytryptophan to 5-hydroxytryptamine and of dopa to dopamine all require pyridoxal phosphate as a coenzyme. Vitamin B₆ deficiency is characterized by convulsions which may result from a diminished ability to form γ-amino butyric acid, which has an inhibitory effect on neuronal activity and is able to afford protection against convulsions induced by strychnine.

Nicotinic acid (B₃)

Nicotinic acid is a component of NAD and NADP (see Figure 1.21) and is hence linked intimately with reactions supplying energy for cerebral activity. Mental disturbances, such as depression, are amongst the first symptoms of pellagra and may develop into dementia as a result of a severe niacin deficiency. Other symptoms of pellagra are dermatitis, diarrhoea and magenta tongue.

Biochemical aspects of brain structure

In the preceding part of this chapter certain features of the overall metabolism of the brain have been studied, but before much progress can be made in understanding the working of the brain it will be necessary to discover much more about the detailed anatomy, physiology and biochemistry of its various parts at all levels of organization. Some idea of the complexity of the problems facing research workers can be obtained by considering the diversity of components in the section of cerebral cortex shown in Figure 4.12. From the biochemical point of view the problem can be resolved into four parts; to define the chemical composition of the various areas of the brain, to fractionate the tissue in order to obtain information about the structure and function of subcellular particles, to build up a picture of the metabolism of the individual cell types and, finally, to discover how the activities of the different cells are integrated to produce coordinated nervous activity and to store information in a retrievable form. The remainder of the chapter will be concerned with developing these themes.

Chemical composition of the brain

Since the brain is inhomogeneous in its cellular organization and in its physiological function, it cannot be expected to have a uniform chemical composition. There is, indeed, no more to be said for regarding the brain as a single organ than for thinking of the alimentary tract and its attendant glands as a single organ.

Chemically the brain is characterized by its high content of lipid which accounts for 56% of the total dry weight of the white matter and 32% of that of the grey matter. The lipids themselves are of a special nature, containing a large proportion of sphingomyelins and cerebrosides (see p. 132). Most of the lipid is metabolically inert, especially the sphingomyelins of the white matter, which have a structural rather than a metabolic role. However, there is a small fraction of phospholipids, particularly the phosphoinositides and the phosphatidic acids, that turns over rapidly. This high rate of turnover is shared by brain phosphoproteins and is related to the level of neuronal activity. Unlike the lipids in other parts of the body, those in the brain are not depleted by extreme starvation.

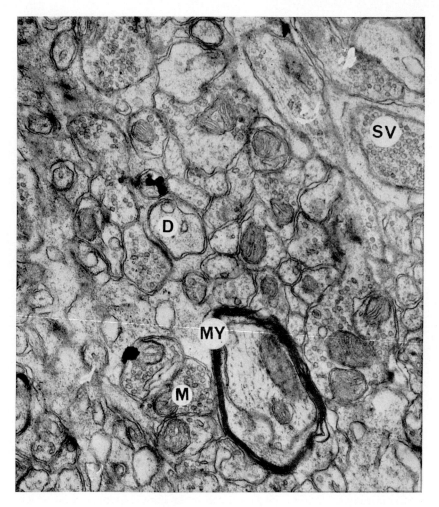

Figure 4.12. A section of cerebral cortex showing myelin sheath (MY), dendrites (D) and numerous nerve endings containing synaptic vesicles (SV), and mitochondria (M). By kind permission of Professor E. De Robertis

The division of the central nervous system into grey matter (largely neurons and neuroglia) and white matter (predominantly myelinated axons and neuroglia) corresponds with marked differences in chemical composition.

The higher concentration of lipids in white matter reflects the high degree of myelinization in that area. Myelin is formed by many layers of

Table 4.3. Composition of white and grey
matter (%)

	White	Grey
Water	70	84
Protein	10	8
Phosphatides	8·5	3·7
Cerebrosides	5	3
Cholesterol	5	0·7
Inorganic	0·8	0·8

cell membrane (derived from Schwann cells) arranged around axons in a spiral fashion. Histochemical methods allow certain substances and enzyme activities to be located in individual neurones, and recently the three types of neurone, containing adrenaline, noradrenaline and 5-hydroxytryptamine respectively have been distinguished by techniques that involve the formation of fluorescent derivatives of the amines. These studies advance the older observations that certain physiologically active compounds are concentrated in different parts of the brain. For example, the hypothalamus and caudate nucleus contain different concentrations of noradrenaline and dopamine.

Table 4.4. Concentration of amines in the hypothalamus
and caudate nucleus of the dog (μg/g)

	Nor-adrenaline	Dopamine	5-Hydroxy-tryptamine
Hypothalamus	1·03	0·26	1·7
Caudate nucleus	0·06	5·90	0·7

Fractionation of brain tissue

Next to liver, brain has been the tissue most frequently subjected to cell fractionation studies. Because of its basic architecture the brain, on homogenization, gives rise to a much wider range of particles than liver, so that it is difficult to isolate pure fractions of its subcellular particles by differential centrifugation. This difficulty can be circumvented to some extent by using the technique of density gradient centrifugation. In this technique the homogenate, freed from unbroken cells by an initial centrifugation at low speed, is layered on top of a sucrose density gradient contained in a centrifuge tube (Figure 4.13). Centrifugation is carried out at high speed until the particles become distributed as bands in the gradient. Each band

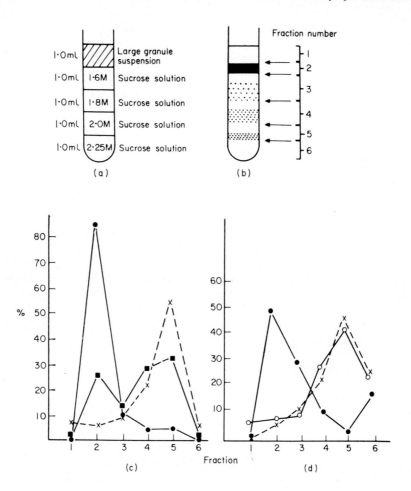

Figure 4.13. Subfractionation of the large granule fraction from the bovine adrenal medulla by density gradient centrifugation. (a) Centrifuge tube before specific gravity gradient centrifugation. The large granule fraction was suspended in 0·3 M sucrose solution. (b) Appearance of the tube after centrifugation in Spinco rotor SW 39 at 145,000 g for 60 min. The arrows indicate the points where the tube was cut. (c) Distribution of succinic dehydrogenase (●—●), catechol amines (× -- ×) and protein nitrogen (■—■) in a specific gravity gradient. In Figs (c) and (d) fractions are numbered as shown in Figure (b). Ordinate: recovery as percentage of recovery in all fractions. (d) Distribution of succinic dehydrogenase (●—●), catecholamines (× -- ×) and ATP (○—○) in a specific gravity gradient. Ordinate: recovery as percentage of recovery in all fractions. From Blaschko and coauthors, *J. Physiol.*, 1957

represents a population of particles having the same density as the sucrose solution in that part of the gradient and is more or less homogeneous depending upon the starting material. Thus, in this technique the subcellular particles are separated by taking advantage of their differences in density, rather than their differences in size. After centrifugation the tube is either pierced and the material allowed to run out slowly into tubes so that each fraction can be collected separately, or the plastic tube is sectioned serially by a special cutter that seals the bottom of each slice of liquid and allows it to be removed quantitatively before the next slice is made.

Fairly pure preparations of brain mitochondria have been prepared by this technique. These mitochondria show a much greater range in size than liver mitochondria and their enzymic composition is somewhat different. For example, about 10% of the glycolytic activity of the cell is sedimented with brain mitochondria and cannot be removed by simply washing with the suspending medium. Treatment with detergents, however, can remove the glycolytic enzymes whilst leaving the enzymes of oxidative phosphorylation firmly attached to the mitochondrial membranes. It may be that the glycolytic enzymes are attached to the mitochondrial surface by a lipoprotein material. Certainly there seems to be no doubt that a great deal of the hexokinase of brain is always associated with brain mitochondria. The endogenous substrates of brain mitochondria are present in much higher concentrations than in liver mitochondria and consist almost entirely of amino acids with glutamine accounting for a substantial fraction of the total quantity.

Table 4.5. Detectable substrates in brain mitochondria (μmoles/g dry weight)

	Rat	Pigeon
α-Oxoglutarate	0·4	0
Glutamate	75·2	46·9
Glutamine	37·5	25·7
Aspartate	27·3	10·5

A band sedimenting in density gradients above that enriched in mitochondria was found to contain much of the acetylcholine, noradrenaline and 5-hydroxytryptamine of brain. Electron microscopic examination showed that this band consisted of pinched-off nerve endings that contained synaptic vesicles and mitochondria and were still attached to their

subsynaptic webs (Figure 4.14). These particles are now called synaptosomes. By subjecting synaptosomes to carefully controlled osmotic shock
it is possible to liberate the synaptic vesicles intact and then to purify them
further by density gradient centrifugation (Figure 4.15). It can then be
demonstrated that the physiologically active amines mentioned above are

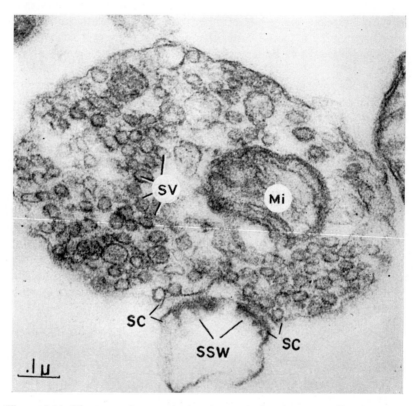

Figure 4.14. Electron micrograph showing an isolated nerve ending (synaptosome) containing synaptic vesicles (SV) and a mitochondrion (Mi). The nerve
ending is still attached to the subsynaptic web (SSW) derived from the post-
synaptic cell. The synaptic cleft is designated SC. By kind permission of
Professor E. De Robertis

concentrated in the vesicles rather than in the cytoplasm of the nerve
endings. Since acetylcholine and noradrenaline function as chemical
transmitters in the peripheral nervous system the finding of these and
other amines (for example, γ-amino butyric acid) concentrated in the synaptic vesicles derived from brain neurones supports the view that they

fulfil a similar role in the central nervous system. It might be expected that a neurone of a given type would yield synaptosomes containing only one species of transmitter substance and that the appearance of several amines in the synaptosome fraction reflects the heterogeneity of the

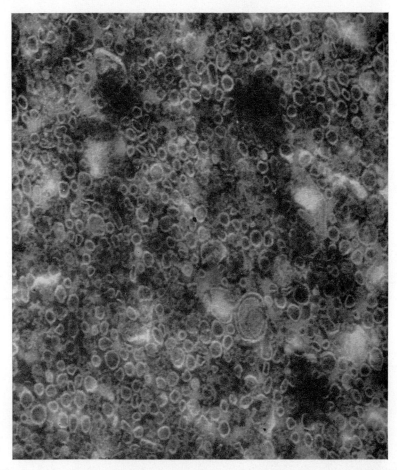

Figure 4.15. Negatively stained preparation of isolated synaptic vesicles. By kind permission of Professor E. De Robertis

neurones in the tissue fractionated. This may be so; however, electron microscopy shows that many nerve endings contain two kinds of synaptic vesicle, one having an electron dense core and the other apparently devoid of electron dense material (Figure 4.16). Possibly these two forms of vesicle contain different transmitters.

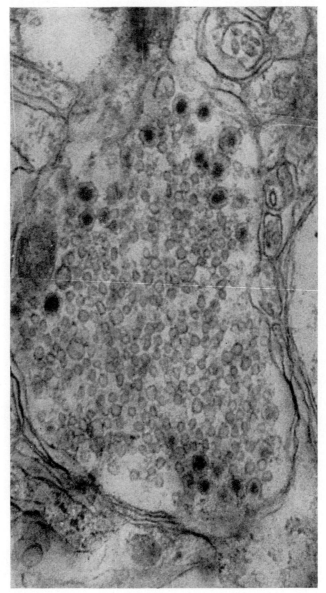

Figure 4.16. Electron micrograph of a nerve ending from the anterior hypothalamus of the rat containing both dense- and light-core vesicles. By courtesy of Professor E. De Robertis from A. Pellegrino de Iraldi and coworkers, 1963

The synaptic vesicles containing acetylcholine

$$CH_3 \cdot C \cdot O \cdot CH_2CH_2N^+(CH_3)_3$$
$$\overset{\|}{O}$$

also carry the enzyme choline acetylase that synthesizes acetylcholine from choline and acetyl-CoA. Acetylcholine esterase, which by hydrolysing acetylcholine terminates its activity, is located in the outer membranes of synaptosomes. Thus the enzymes synthesizing and degrading acetylcholine are segregated into two regions, one in which a store of transmitter is built up and a second in which the transmitter is destroyed when it has been released from the store and fulfilled its physiological function. The choline liberated during the hydrolysis of acetylcholine reenters the nerve ending where it can be reacetylated (see p. 283). The mitochondria present in nerve endings supply ATP which acetylthiokinase can use, together with acetate and coenzyme A, to synthesize acetyl-CoA and hence acetyl-choline. The mitochondria also provide the energy required to expel the increased number of Na^+ entering the nerve ending when the membrane is depolarized by the arrival of an action potential.

Functional aspects of neuronal biochemistry

Membrane potentials and ion transport

One of the basic properties of neurones is their ability to transmit action potentials. In order to describe how such potentials are generated, it is necessary to introduce the concept of equilibrium potentials and then to examine results obtained from experiments on the giant axons of squids and crabs. When two solutions of KCl of different concentrations (C_1 and C_2, where C_1 is greater than C_2) are separated by a membrane impermeable to Cl^- ions but permeable to K^+ ions, a potential

$$E = \frac{RT}{F} \ln \frac{C_2}{C_1}$$

is developed across the membrane so that the more concentrated solution is at a potential E volts more negative than the more dilute solution. This potential exactly balances the tendency of the K^+ ions to diffuse from the more concentrated solution; it is therefore called the *equilibrium potential*.

At rest the inside of a squid axon is at the potential of about -70 mV (the resting potential) with respect to the external sea water. If the nerve is depolarized by 10 to 15 mV, by placing a cathode against the axon membrane, changes in the permeability of the membrane towards sodium and potassium ions occur in sequence so that an action potential is initiated. At the peak of the action potential the inside of the axon becomes some 50 mV positive with respect to the external medium. That is to say, the action potential has an amplitude of about 120 mV. After the action potential has passed, the membrane potential returns to normal via a phase of hyperpolarization (Figure 4.17). These potential changes can be explained

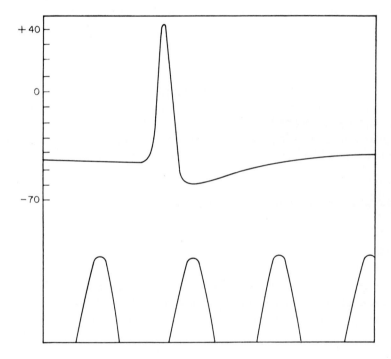

Figure 4.17. Action potential recorded between inside and outside of squid giant axon. The vertical scale indicates the potential of the internal electrode in mV, the sea water outside being taken as zero potential. Time marker, 500 cycles/sec. From Hodgkin and Huxley, *J. Physiol.*, 1945

as follows: the axon has a high internal concentration of K^+ ions and a low internal concentration of Na^+ ions, whilst in the external medium the concentration of Na^+ ions is much greater than that of K^+ ions. Thus if the cell membrane was equally permeable to sodium and potassium ions, the potential across the membrane would be equal to the sum of the equilibrium potentials of sodium and potassium across the membrane, i.e.

$$E_{Na^+} = \frac{RT}{F} \ln \frac{[Na^+]_{out}}{[Na^+]_{in}} = +55 \text{ mV}$$

$$E_{K^+} = \frac{RT}{F} \ln \frac{[K^+]_{out}}{[K^+]_{in}} = -75 \text{ mV}$$

$$\therefore E_{memb} = E_{K^+} + E_{Na^+} = -75 \text{ mV} + 55 \text{ mV} = -20 \text{ mV}.$$

In fact the observed resting potential is -70 mV. This discrepancy between the observed and calculated values can be accounted for by supposing that, at rest, the membrane is considerably more permeable to K^+ than to Na^+ ions. This may be expressed thus

$$E_{memb} = \frac{\alpha RT}{F} \ln \frac{[K^+]_{out}}{[K^+]_{in}} + \frac{\beta RT}{F} \ln \frac{[Na^+]_{out}}{[Na^+]_{in}}$$

where α and β are the permeabilities to potassium and sodium respectively. There is much evidence to support the view that the potassium equilibrium potential makes a greater contribution to the resting potential than the sodium equilibrium potential. For instance, the resting potential can be increased by reducing $[K^+]_{out}$ and decreased by raising $[K^+]_{out}$: on the other hand varying $[Na^+]_{out}$ has very little effect on the resting potential, as is to be expected if the membrane permeability to sodium is low. Furthermore, using perfused squid axons it is possible to vary the resting potential by altering $[K^+]_{in}$, whereas it is scarcely affected by marked changes in the value of $[Na^+]_{in}$.

During the rising phase of the action potential, the permeability of the membrane towards sodium increases rapidly so that at the peak of the potential it is some twenty times greater than that towards potassium (Figure 4.18). Hence, at this peak, the recorded membrane potential approximates closely to that of the sodium equilibrium potential. Shortly before the action potential reaches its peak, the permeability towards potassium begins to rise above its resting level and continues to do so after the peak has passed and the sodium permeability begins to fall. When the permeability towards sodium has returned to its basal level, the permeability towards potassium is still much above its resting value so that a period of hyperpolarization is produced. The resting potential is restored when the membrane permeabilities towards both cations have returned to their original values. The net effect of these changes is that the axon loses a little potassium and gains a little sodium. Unlike that of the resting potential, the magnitude of the action potential depends upon the concentrations of sodium inside and outside the axon; thus increasing the external sodium concentration increases the height of the spike potential.

As the axon is continually losing K^+ and gaining Na^+ (slowly at rest and more rapidly during the propagation of an action potential) it is necessary to restore the ionic gradients by the expenditure of metabolic energy. This is apparently achieved by pumping out sodium ions and

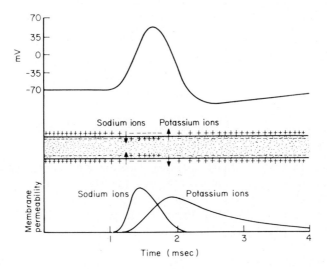

Figure 4.18. Nerve impulse travels along a nerve fibre as a self-propagating wave of electrical activity. The potential across the outer membrane of the fibre reverses and then returns to normal again. These changes are caused by rises in ionic permeability, which permit rapid movement of sodium ions into the fibre, followed by an egress of potassium ions. From Keynes, *Sci. Am.*, 1958

allowing potassium ions to enter the axon passively. The reason for supposing that sodium ions rather than potassium ions are transported actively is as follows. The resting potential across the membrane is about -70 mV, which is approximately equal to

$$\frac{RT}{F} \ln \frac{[K^+]_{out}}{[K^+]_{in}}$$

that is to say, the energy required to move one gram equivalent of K^+ ions into the axon against the concentration gradient is

$$RT \ln \frac{[K^+]_{in}}{[K^+]_{out}}$$

which is approximately equal to EF, the energy gained when a gram equivalent of K^+ moves down its electropotential gradient into the axon. In other words, there is virtually no net change in free energy when a K^+ ion traverses the membrane, because the electrical 'driving force' in one direction is almost exactly balanced by the concentration 'driving force' in the other. However, for sodium

$$\frac{RT}{F} \ln \frac{[Na^+]_{out}}{[Na^+]_{in}}$$

does not equal -70 mV, the observed membrane potential, but is about $+55$ mV. Therefore in order to remove one gram equivalent of sodium ions from the axon, work equal to

$$RT \ln \frac{[Na^+]_{out}}{[Na^+]_{in}} + E_{memb}F$$

has to be done against both the chemical concentration *and* electropotential gradients. This equation differs from that given for the energy requirements of ion transport in the red cell (p. 175) in which neither sodium nor potassium ions are at the same electrochemical potential on either side of the cell membrane. This situation may be summarized thus:

Nerve	Red cell
E_{memb} is *equal to* $\dfrac{RT}{F} \ln \dfrac{[K^+]_{out}}{[K^+]_{in}}$	E_{memb} is *not equal to* $\dfrac{RT}{F} \ln \dfrac{[K^+]_{out}}{[K^+]_{in}}$
E_{memb} is *not equal to* $\dfrac{RT}{F} \ln \dfrac{[Na^+]_{out}}{[Na^+]_{in}}$	E_{memb} is *not equal to* $\dfrac{RT}{F} \ln \dfrac{[Na^+]_{out}}{[Na^+]_{in}}$

Hence in the red cell both sodium and potassium must be actively transported to maintain the observed ionic gradients, whilst only sodium need be pumped by nerve to achieve the same result. The reason for this difference is that nerve has a higher content of non-diffusible anions than red cells, which results in the establishment of a much larger Donnan membrane potential (see below) in nerves than in red cells. In nerves this potential accounts for nearly all of the observed resting potential of -70 mV that opposes the egress of K^+ from the axon. In red cells the size of the Donnan membrane potential is insufficient to retain all of the K^+ ions contained in the cell, so that most of them have to be retained at the expense of metabolic energy.

A Donnan membrane potential is established if a solution of KCl is separated by a semipermeable membrane from a solution containing the potassium salt of a non-diffusible anion, such as a protein. Potassium and chloride ions will diffuse through the membrane into the compartment containing the non-diffusible anion (P^-) until an equilibrium is established.

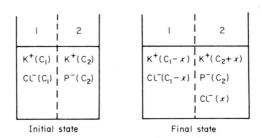

Initial state   Final state

C_1 = initial concentration of KCl in compartment 1
C_2 = initial concentration of KP in compartment 2
x = amount of KCl entering compartment 2 from compartment 1.

Arguments based on thermodynamic principles lead to the conclusion that at equilibrium the products of the concentrations of diffusible ions in both compartments are the same, that is:

at equilibrium

$$[K^+]_1 \times [Cl^-]_1 = [K^+]_2 \times [Cl^-]_2$$

Now since compartment 1 contains only KCl the number of K^+ ions must equal the number of Cl^- ions

i.e. $[K^+]_1 = [Cl^-]_1$

In compartment 2 $[K^+]_2 = [P^-] + [Cl^-]_2$, because all the negative ions must be neutralized by potassium ions.

$$\therefore [K^+]_2 > [Cl^-]_2$$

and as

$$[K^+]_1 \times [Cl^-]_1 = [K^+]_2 \times [Cl^-]_2$$

it follows that $[K^+]_2$ must be greater than $[K^+]_1$.

Thus a concentration gradient of potassium ions is established across the membrane as a result of the presence in one compartment of a non-diffusible anion. This concentration gradient will be associated with a membrane potential equal to $RT/F \ln [K^+]_1/[K^+]_2$ that will render compartment 2 negative with respect to compartment 1 and thus oppose the movement of K^+ ions down their concentration gradient. In nerves the resting potential is attributable to the difference in K^+ ion concentration on either side of the membrane. This concentration gradient of potassium is maintained by a Donnan equilibrium involving non-diffusible anions within the axon. Sodium ions are unable to contribute to the resting potential significantly because they are expelled from the axon by the sodium pump and so play only a small part in establishing the Donnan equilibrium. Effectively the sodium pump renders the membrane impermeable to sodium and hence prevents it coming into equilibrium with the non-diffusible anions.

Since sodium is actively extruded from nerves in order to maintain the gradients of sodium and potassium across the cell membrane, the properties of the sodium pump will now be considered.

If a giant nerve fibre from squid is loaded with $^{24}Na^+$ and then bathed by a continuous stream of a solution containing unlabelled sodium, the amount of $^{24}Na^+$ leaving the fibre can be measured at regular intervals (Figure 4.19). The rate of $^{24}Na^+$ loss falls as the concentration of the isotope within the nerve diminishes (Figure 4.20). If 0·2 mM dinitrophenol (DNP) is added to the bathing solution the efflux decreases dramatically. When the DNP is washed away, the rate of $^{24}Na^+$ efflux is restored to the control value. These observations suggest that sodium efflux depends upon a supply of ATP derived from oxidative phosphorylation. Similar effects on the rate of $^{24}Na^+$ expulsion can be obtained by adding cyanide (CN^-) or azide (N_3^-) to the external medium. Axons are still able to conduct action potentials of undiminished size when the active transport of sodium is inhibited. This is to be expected because the ion fluxes forming the action potential are spontaneous or downhill processes, whilst maintenance of the ionic gradients is an active process. This view is confirmed by experiments in which all the axoplasm is removed from a giant axon and replaced by a solution of KCl. If such an axon is suspended in a solution of NaCl, it is still able to propagate action potentials despite the absence of an energy source. From these considerations it can be concluded that two systems concerned with ion movements exist in the axon membrane, one driven by metabolism and responsible for building up ionic gradients and another, independent of metabolism, responsible for controlling the downhill movement of sodium and potassium ions at rest and when the membrane is depolarized. This is illustrated in Figure 4.21 which also summarizes differences between the two systems. Sodium efflux from axons poisoned with cyanide can be restored by injecting ATP into the axoplasm but not by adding ATP to the external solution. This recalls Whittam's observation (p. 178) that the ion-transport ATP-ase of red cells cannot degrade ATP external to the erythrocytes and that ion-transport is coupled to ATP breakdown inside the cells. As with red cells, the rate of sodium

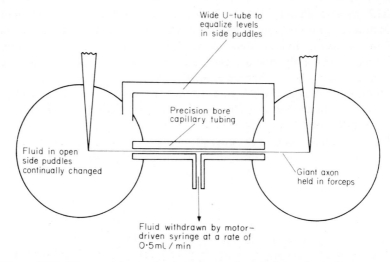

Figure 4.19. The experimental arrangement for studying ionic fluxes across the giant axon. From Hodgkin and Keynes, *Symp. Soc. Exp. Biol.*, 1954

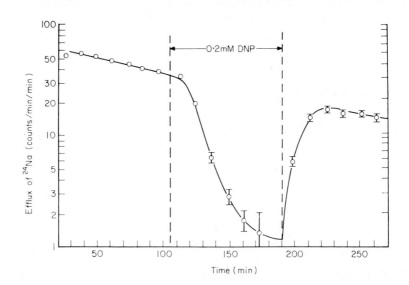

Figure 4.20. Sodium efflux from *Sepia* axon during treatment with dinitrophenol. The internal concentration of sodium had been raised initially by stimulation for 4 minutes at 156/sec in a Ringer solution containing ^{24}Na-labelled sodium. Poisoning the axon reduces the efflux. From Hodgkin and Keynes, *J. Physiol.*, 1953

expulsion from nerves is dependent upon the external concentration of potassium, suggesting that active transport of sodium is coupled to the inward movement of potassium. An ATP-ase that requires Na^+, K^+ and Mg^{2+} for maximum activity has been located in the membrane of crab nerve by Skou; it is inhibited by ouabain and behaves similarly to 'ion-transport' ATP-ases found in other tissues including brain. Such an ATP-ase is probably involved in the active transport of sodium in nerve tissue in a manner similar to that proposed for the ATP-ase of red cells (see p. 177). Indeed, it has been found that the phosphorylation of brain microsomes by ATP requires Na^+ ions whilst dephosphorylation requires K^+ ions.

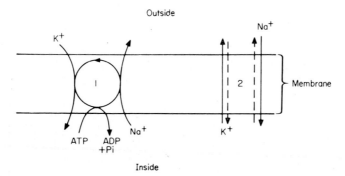

Figure 4.21. Systems regulating the passage of ions across the axon membrane

(1) Processes maintaining ionic gradients	(2) Depolarization fluxes
Inhibited by DNP: CN^-; N_3^-	Not affected by DNP; CN^-; N_3^-
Inhibited by Ouabain	Not affected by Ouabain
Lithium not readily expelled	Lithium can replace Na^+ in the action potential fluxes
Maximum rate of ion movement 50 $\mu\mu$mole/cm²/sec	Maximum rate of ion movement 10,000 $\mu\mu$mole/cm²/sec

Stimulation of frog nerves causes a marked increase in their rate of oxygen consumption and carbon dioxide evolution. It can be calculated that about 2·6 out of every 3 molecules of ATP produced as a result of this extra oxygen consumption must be used to pump sodium out of the axons. A feedback system probably ensures that the supply of ATP increases to meet the demand of the pump at any instant. The faster the pump works, the more rapidly ADP is produced and can act as a phosphate acceptor in a tightly coupled system for oxidative phosphorylation (see Section 8).

As might be expected electrical stimulation of slices of cerebral cortex depolarizes the cell membranes and causes an increase in the sodium content of the tissue which is approximately balanced by a fall in the potassium content (Figure 4.22); at the same time the rate of respiration rises. When stimulation ceases the ionic gradients are reestablished and glucose is consumed. Very low concentrations of chlorpromazine, a drug that is widely used as a tranquillizer, inhibit the effects of electrical stimulation. It is suggested that chlorpromazine depresses cerebral activity by preventing the possible dilation of pores in the cell membrane through which potassium may be lost when the cell is depolarized.

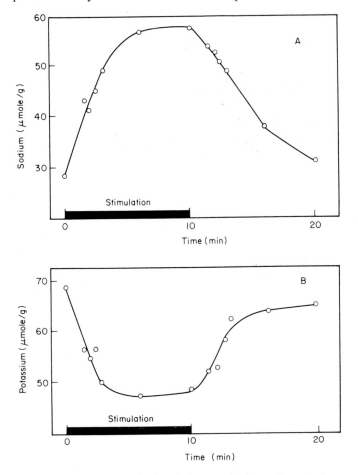

Figure 4.22. Effect of electrical stimulation upon the sodium and potassium contents of slices of guinea pig brain. From McIlwain, *The Biochemistry of the Central Nervous System*, 3rd ed., Churchill, London, 1966

When an action potential arrives at a nerve ending, there is an influx of Ca^{2+} ions into the nerve which causes the synaptic vesicles (see p. 196) to discharge their contents of neurotransmitter substances into the synaptic cleft. These substances then induce the depolarization or hyperpolarization of the post-synaptic cell body.

Optic nerve, superior cervical ganglion, pineal pathway

At present very little is known about the kind of biochemical changes that can be induced in neurones stimulated by neurotransmitters liberated from nearby nerve endings. This is a particularly important field of study because the existence of memory may well require the synthesis of macromolecules in response to a particular pattern of neuronal stimulation; at a later date, such a molecule may be able to modulate neuronal activity in a manner that would allow the memory store to be tapped. An understanding of the complex processes underlying memory has hardly begun to emerge, but one example of how nervous activity can cause profound biochemical changes has been described for the pineal gland. The cells of the pineal synthesize the hormone melatonin (5-methoxy-*N*-acetyltryptamine) which, when released into the circulation, inhibits the onset of the oestrus cycle in rats. Melatonin is synthesized from tryptophan via the following series of reactions:

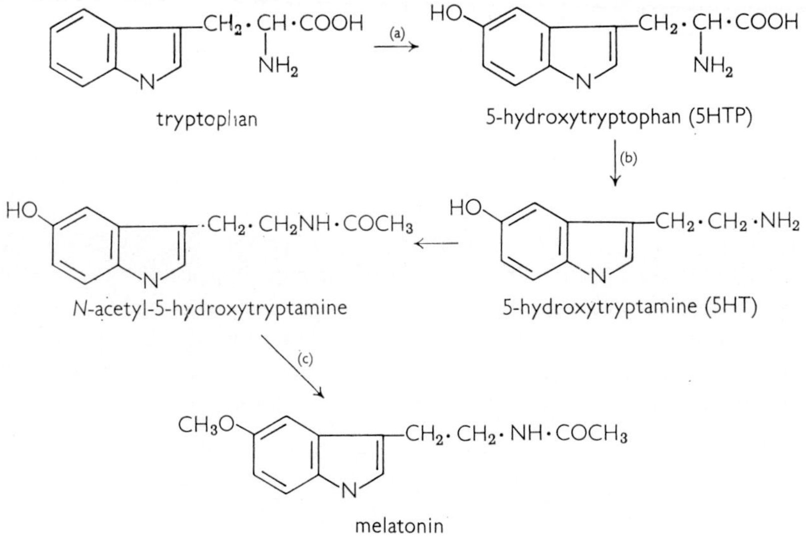

The biosynthetic pathway for melatonin:
(a) tryptophan hydroxylase
(b) 5HTP decarboxylase
(c) hydroxyindole-*O*-methyltransferase

8+

The enzyme introducing the methoxy group in the last reaction to form the physiologically active hormone from its inactive precursor is hydroxy-indole-*O*-methyltransferase or HIOMT. Under natural conditions the onset of the oestrus cycle is controlled by the seasonal variations in light and darkness. Experiments have shown that the onset of oestrus in rats can be induced by subjecting the animals to continuous illumination and retarded by keeping them in darkness or by shielding their eyes from light. Oestrus can also be prevented by removing the superior cervical ganglia through which impulses are relayed to the pineal via sympathetic fibres. It is now known that during periods of darkness HIOMT is synthesized from its component amino acids and catalyses the formation of melatonin. During periods of illumination, provided that impulses can be transmitted from the eyes to the pineal, the synthesis of HIOMT is inhibited so that its concentration falls and the synthesis of melatonin is reduced (Figure 4.23). As the level of melatonin in the blood declines, its inhibitory effect on the ovaries and on the proliferation of the reproductive tract dies away and the processes leading to oestrus can begin.

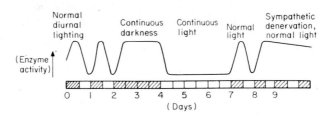

Figure 4.23. The effect of changes in illumination and sympathetic denervation upon the activity of hydroxyindole-*O*-methyltransferase (HIOMT) activity of rat pineal glands

This example indicates that the cells of the pineal respond to the release of a chemical transmitter from sympathetic nerves by altering their rate of synthesis of an enzyme responsible for the formation of a hormone. It is thus clear that, as a result of stimulation, neurones may respond with metabolic changes in addition to electrical responses.

CHAPTER 15

The eye

The eye has a unique job to do in the body and, as might be expected, this is reflected in the biochemistry of its various tissues. Firstly, light falling upon the retina has to be absorbed by special pigments to initiate a series of chemical changes which finally yield an action potential in the optic nerve. Secondly, the lens, which focuses light on to the retina, must be constructed from materials which are transparent to light of a particular range of wavelengths. Normally the skin ensures that the tissues of the body are not penetrated by light and that the enzyme systems of cells are protected from the harmful effects of radiant energy (see Section 9).

The architecture of the eye presents two metabolic problems. If the cornea, lens and humours are to be transparent they cannot be supplied with blood vessels, therefore a strongly aerobic system of metabolism is not possible in those parts of the eye. On the other hand, since the retina is an extension of the brain, with the brain's sensitivity to oxygen lack, it must have a blood supply adequate to provide its high requirements for glucose and oxygen. Even a brief interruption of the blood supply to the retina can cause lasting damage.

The lens

The relationship between structure and carbohydrate metabolism

As the lens has no blood supply, it has to rely on the slowly circulating aqueous humour for its oxygen and raw materials and for the removal of its metabolic waste products. Since the amount of oxygen in the aqueous humour is limited to that held in physical solution, the oxygen supply to the lens is restricted. Furthermore, the lens is unique amongst tissues in that it has no way of removing old cells, which become compressed into its centre. The compressed nucleus of the lens eventually becomes very hard but retains its transparency. The entire lens has a very low rate of metabolism and the compressed inner portion does not have a significant aerobic metabolism because of its isolation from the blood. Experiments

211

carried out *in vitro* indicate that about 90% of the glucose used by the lens is glycolysed to lactate. The remaining 10% is degraded via the pentose phosphate pathway and accounts for the carbon dioxide production by isolated lens. The small oxygen consumption of the lens *in vitro* is probably related to the non-enzymic oxidation of the SH group of glutathione (see p. 169). Glutathione can exist as a reduced monomer, G–SH, and as an oxidized dimer, G–S–S–G. G–SH is present in the lens at high concentration and is responsible for maintaining the SH groups of the lens proteins in the reduced state. Oxidized glutathione can be reduced by $NADPH_2$, produced during the oxidation of glucose via the pentose phosphate pathway.

In vivo the fall in pH that accompanies anoxia causes the lens to become opaque. The opaqueness caused by anoxia is readily reversed when the oxygen tension is restored to normal values.

Cataracts

A lens may be made opaque simply by exposing it to a lowered temperature. For example, if an isolated eye is cooled to 10°, the lens becomes opaque, but on rewarming to 20° the opacity disappears. This reversible opacity is due to some change in the physical properties of the lens fibres, which is most marked in the inner and more dehydrated fibres. Possibly the amount of water associated with the proteins changes, causing an alteration in the refractive index of the lens fibres. Apart from these highly artificial opacities, there are several types of cataract that may be met clinically; of these, two classes will be discussed in detail.

Radiation cataract

Exposure to x-rays and other ionizing radiations can lead to cataract formation. The ability of a given dose of radiation to induce the formation of a cataract is greater in younger animals because the amount of damage appears to be proportional to the number of mitoses occurring during irradiation. There is a latent period before the changes can be seen, the duration of which is shorter the larger the dose of radiation received.

Biochemically the earliest change observed is a fall in the amount of reduced glutathione (GSH) in the lens; this occurs before there is any sign of opacity and continues as the cataract develops. With complete opacity the GSH content falls by about 85%. Subsequent to the loss of GSH there is also a smaller loss of protein SH groups. After irradiation the level of glutathione reductase is less than in the control lens. This enzyme catalyses the reduction of oxidized glutathione with $NADPH_2$

$$GSSG + NADPH_2 \longrightarrow 2GSH + NADP$$

The injection of cysteine or GSH about 30 minutes before exposure to radiation protects the lens against radiation damage.

Cataract resulting from a high level of monosaccharides in the blood

Galactosaemic infants and diabetics are particularly prone to develop cataracts and in diabetics the susceptibility to cataract is greater in the young person than in the old. Cataracts may also be induced in experimental animals by feeding them on a diet rich in galactose or xylose, or by inducing experimental diabetes by injecting alloxan. In all these cases there is an inverse relationship between the concentration of blood sugar and the time taken for a cataract to form; the higher the hyperglycaemia, the sooner the cataract develops. As might be expected, the administration of insulin delays or prevents cataract formation in alloxan diabetes. Phlorizin also prevents diabetic cataract by decreasing the renal threshold for glucose, thereby allowing it to overflow into the urine. Since phlorizin does not ameliorate the other symptoms of diabetes, it can be concluded that cataract is a symptom of high blood sugar and not of a specific metabolic defect of diabetes. Most of the information about the biochemistry of cataract has been obtained from experimental cataracts induced by feeding rats with the pentose sugar D-xylose. When a 21-day-old rat is given a diet containing more than 20% of D-xylose, complete opacity of the lens results in about 3 weeks. The cataract, which closely resembles those caused by feeding galactose or by experimental diabetes, does not appear to be due to precipitation of the lens protein, but to the swelling of the outermost fibres. It is a curious observation that the opacities developed in response to xylose are not permanent or progressive, and, even if the feeding of xylose is continued, the cataracts regress. Formation of the cataracts is accompanied by a marked reduction in the GSH and $NADPH_2$ concentrations in the lens and regression is accompanied by an increase in the level of these two components. Also, by measuring the formation of radioactive carbon dioxide from the Carbon 1 and Carbon 6 atoms of the appropriately labelled ^{14}C glucose, it can be shown that the pentose phosphate pathway has declined in activity at the time when the $NADPH_2$ levels are low. Similarly, the content of soluble protein, which is rich in SH groups, falls at the time when opacities are being produced, as does the level of ATP. With all these carbohydrate-induced cataracts there is this common syndrome, a lowered SH level, a lowered $NADPH_2$ level and a lowered activity of the pentose phosphate pathway. The lower activity of the pentose phosphate pathway decreases the amounts of $NADPH_2$ and GSH (equilibrated with $NADPH_2$ by glutathione reductase) and, consequently, the SH groups of the proteins will become oxidized. Since the solubility and configuration of the proteins are partly dependent on SH groups and determine the refractive index and water content of the lens, the lowering of the $NADPH_2$ level may account for most of the changes leading to cataract formation. The spontaneous recovery of the rat from xylose cataract may be due to the fact that, in many species, the activity of the pentose phosphate pathway is low at birth and during infancy and increases to a maximum at maturity. The mechanism whereby high levels of monosaccharides in the blood interfere with the pentose phosphate pathway is not clear, but it does seem certain that all cataracts are accompanied by a low level of GSH and protein SH groups in the lens.

α- and β-Crystallin

Protein accounts for about 35% of the weight of the lens (a much higher proportion than in any other tissue of the body); 85% of the protein consists of two soluble components, α-crystallin and β-crystallin, which are present in roughly equal amounts. Both proteins tend to be more soluble, and hence more transparent, in the presence of each other than separately. Both the crystallins contain a substantial number of free SH groups, presumably on the side chains of cysteine residues. β-crystallin contains perhaps five times the number of SH groups found in α-crystallin, but the exact proportions are not known because of the practical difficulties in estimating free SH groups. In cataract the amount of β-crystallin decreases. Similarly, in old age the proportion of β-crystallin to α-crystallin decreases and sometimes a senile cataract develops. The importance of free SH groups in maintaining the transparency of the lens may be explained by the finding that the addition of reagents containing SH groups (such as cysteine) increases the solubility of some proteins and prevents the polymerization of others.

Studies of the breakdown and synthesis of the lens proteins have shown that the α-crystallin contains a proteinase and a peptidase, both hydrolysing β-crystallin. Thus in a lens, which is not constantly regenerating its protein, there will be a progressive breakdown of β-crystallin. Between 2·5 and 5% of the protein of the lens is replaced daily and since the rate of protein synthesis in the intact lens is less than half the potential rate of protein breakdown as measured in lens homogenates, it is clear that in life the catabolic reactions must be held in check, thereby allowing the synthetic reactions to maintain the balance.

Summary

It is now possible to advance a general explanation of the biochemistry of cataract as follows (Figure 4.24). Maintenance of the correct proportion

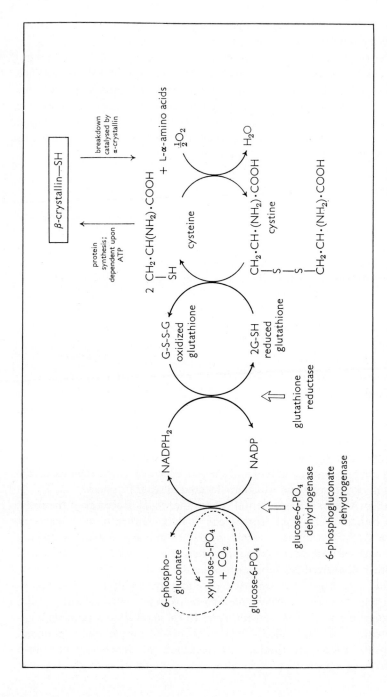

Figure 4.24. Outline of the reactions by which the two oxidative steps of the pentose phosphate pathway maintain the SH groups of β-crystallin in the reduced state

of α- and β-crystallin for lens transparency requires the synthesis of protein against a continuing breakdown. Cysteine in the pool of free amino acids must be maintained in the reduced form, since the protein to be synthesized, chiefly β-crystallin, contains a high proportion of SH groups. The reduction of cysteine is ensured at the expense of reduced glutathione which, in turn, requires $NADPH_2$ generated in the pentose phosphate pathway to keep it in the reduced state. Thus the development of a cataract may be expected following any treatment that inhibits protein synthesis or restricts the availability of reducing power.

The retina

The importance of the retina as the main sensing device of the body can hardly be overestimated; more than a third (about a million) of all the nerve fibres entering or leaving the central nervous system do so by way of the optic nerve. Even with this enormous number of nerve fibres, the number of receptor cells in the retina is much greater, so that each nerve fibre receives the impulses from about 100 photosensitive cells. The biochemistry of the retina may be conveniently considered in two parts, the biochemistry of the visual process and the general metabolism of the retina.

The biochemistry of the visual process

A good deal is known about the biochemistry of the visual process in the rods, which are concerned with vision at low light intensities, whilst very little is known about the biochemistry of the cones, which are responsible for vision at high light intensities and colour vision. Recently, however, evidence has been obtained for the existence of three pigments having their absorption maxima in the red, blue and green regions of the spectrum respectively and which are located in separate cones.

Vitamin A plays a fundamental role in the visual processes of the rods; in the retina its *all trans* isomer can undergo either of two reactions (Figure 4.25). It can be oxidized by NAD in the presence of alcohol dehydrogenase to the corresponding aldehyde called *all trans*-retinene and be further converted by retinene isomerase to $\varDelta^{11}$-*cis*-retinene. Alternatively, *all trans*-vitamin A may isomerize to a form with the *cis* configuration at the $\varDelta^{11}$-position which can also be oxidized by NAD and alcohol dehydrogenase to give $\varDelta^{11}$-*cis*-retinene. In the dark $\varDelta^{11}$-*cis*-retinene combines with a protein called opsin to form the purple visual pigment, rhodopsin. In the light, rhodopsin is bleached and dissociates into opsin and *all trans*-retinene; i.e. light alters the configuration of the retinene from Δ^{11}-*cis*- to *all trans*- and the complex subsequently dissociates. The bleaching of rhodopsin is accompanied by an increase in the number of free SH groups, whilst the resynthesis of rhodopsin is associated with a decrease in the number. These findings suggest that Δ^{11}-*cis*-retinene combines with an SH group in opsin to form rhodopsin. The *all trans*-retinene liberated during the bleaching of rhodopsin can be isomerized by retinene isomerase to give Δ^{11}-*cis*-retinene which is able to reenter the visual cycle. This outline of photochemical events in rod vision leaves unanswered a whole range of important questions. How, for example, are the rearrangement and dissociation of rhodopsin connected with the electrical changes

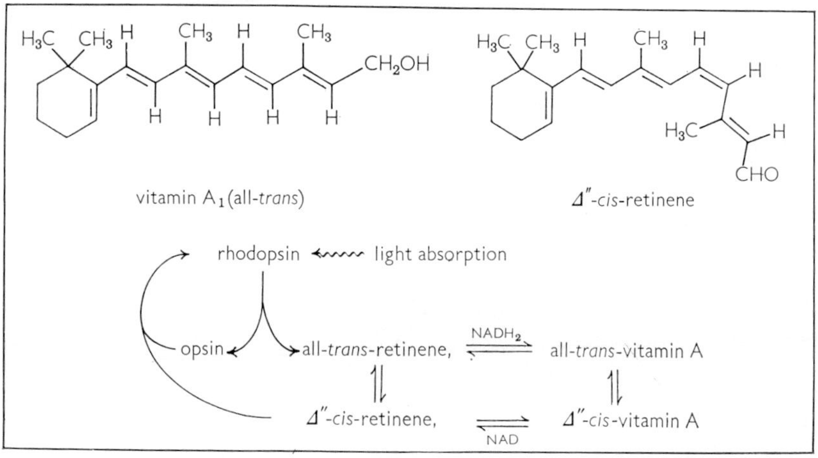

Figure 4.25. Reactions involved in the photo dissociation of rhodopsin

which eventually give rise to an impulse in the optic nerve? At present nothing is known about these dark-reactions with any degree of certainty.

It is clear that a deficiency of vitamin A will lead to defective rod vision. This can be demonstrated by the following experiment. After a preliminary exposure to intense light (to bleach the rhodopsin) the subject is placed in the dark and the lowest light intensity that he can detect is measured from time to time during a period of about an hour. The results obtained in this way are shown in Figure 4.26. First cone adaptation occurs until a plateau is reached which measures the lowest intensity of light to which the cones are sensitive (cone threshold). The cone–rod transition time is a measure of the time taken for sufficient of the opsin to recombine with Δ^{11}-*cis*-retinene for the visual process of rods to operate

8*

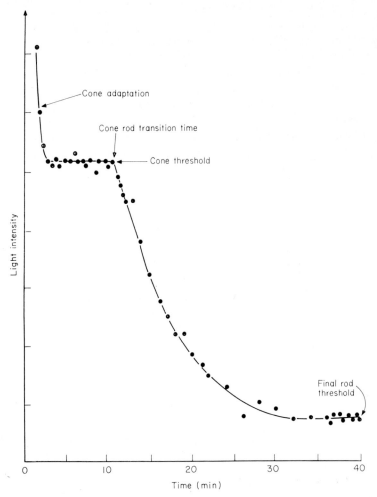

Figure 4.26. Normal curve of dark adaptation showing cone threshold, cone–rod transition time and final rod threshold. From *Vitamin A Requirements of Human Adults*, MRC Special Report Series, H.M. Stationery Office, 1949

after bleaching. The final rod threshold represents the minimum intensity of light that the fully dark-adapted eye can detect. In vitamin A deficiency both the cone–rod transition time and the rod threshold are increased (Figure 4.27). The rate of recombination of opsin and Δ^{11}-*cis*-retinene depends upon the product of the concentrations of the two components and, as the concentration of Δ^{11}-*cis*-retinene is reduced in vitamin A deficiency, it follows that the cone–rod transition time will be lengthened

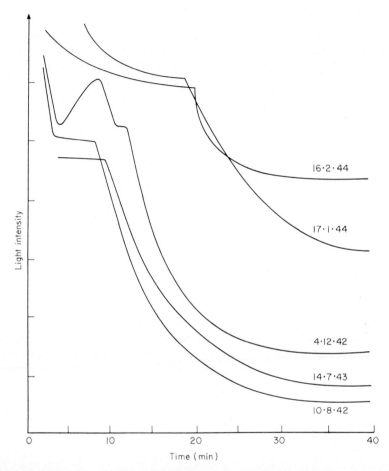

Figure 4.27. Curves of dark adaptation obtained from a subject maintained on a diet deficient in vitamin A from 10 August 1942 until 16 February 1944. From *Vitamin A Requirements of Human Adults*, MRC Special Report Series, H.M. Stationery Office, 1949

in vitamin A deficient subjects. Similarly, in the dark, the sensitivity of the response to test illuminations depends upon the amount of rhodopsin available to be decomposed by the light. In the fully dark-adapted eye of the vitamin A deficient subject, the amount of rhodopsin present is less than in the fully dark-adapted eye of a normal subject; hence, the former has a higher final rod threshold than the latter. It has also been found that the peripheral rods lose their rhodopsin more rapidly than the central rods in vitamin A deficiency.

General biochemistry of the retina

The retina has the highest rate of respiration of any mammalian tissue, and also a higher rate of glycolysis than most other tissues; even under highly aerobic conditions it still accumulates lactic acid. From measurements of the liberation of the carbon 1 and carbon 6 atoms of glucose, it appears as though 20% of the glucose used is metabolized by the pentose phosphate pathway. As in other nerve tissues, the store of glycogen is very small so that continued metabolism is almost entirely dependent upon the supply of glucose in the blood. Interrupting the blood supply to the retina for even a few minutes causes irreversible damage. Retina also has a high rate of CO_2 fixation, which is inhibited by uncoupling reagents and therefore probably involves pyruvic carboxylase (see p. 102).

The effect of alcohols on retinal metabolism is of particular interest. Since alcohol dehydrogenase is a necessary part of the rhodopsin cycle and is a relatively unspecific enzyme, it might be expected that alcohols would interfere with retinal metabolism by competing for this enzyme. It has been shown that drinking ethanol causes an impairment of night vision, even when taken in small quantities. However, from the clinical point of view the effect of methanol on the retina is much more important. Methanol is lethal to man if drunk in sufficient quantity, the fatal dose being about 65 g, and quantities as small as one teaspoonful can cause blindness. It is generally believed that the toxicity of methanol is due not to methanol itself but to formaldehyde which is produced from it metabolically. This is another instance of a lethal synthesis (see p. 151). Formaldehyde is believed to be the toxic agent because it, but not methanol, is an extremely potent inhibitor of respiration and glycolysis in the isolated retina. Table 4.6 shows the effect of methanol, formaldehyde and formate on the respiration of the retina.

Table 4.6. Effect of methanol, formaldehyde and formate on the respiration of ox retina using ^{14}C glucose as substrate

Addition	Conc. (mM)	Q_{O_2}	Inhibition of $^{14}CO_2$ production
Nil	—	7·4	0
Methanol	1000	6·1	0
	2000	5·7	0·9
Formaldehyde	0·5	7·2	27·2
	1·0	6·7	48·2
	2·0	5·7	64·0
	3·0	3·5	76·2
	5·0	2·4	84·2
Sodium formate	100	4·8	49·2
	200	4·4	61·5

The only substance tested which caused inhibition at low concentration was formaldehyde. With isolated retinal mitochondria a concentration of formaldehyde of 1 mM or upwards almost completely abolished oxidative phosphorylation without affecting respiration markedly. Electron microscopy shows that the rods are packed with mitochondria, accounting for the very vigorous respiration of the retina, and suggesting that much of its energy is supplied by oxidative phosphorylation. If oxidative phosphorylation is inhibited by formaldehyde, the supply of ATP will fail and the coupling of the photochemical process with neural transmission will be abolished. Furthermore, it is possible to explain how the administration of ethanol immediately following the ingestion of methanol can prevent the toxic effects of the latter. Ethanol competes successfully with methanol for the available alcohol dehydrogenase, yielding acetaldehyde instead of formaldehyde and acetaldehyde does not uncouple oxidative phosphorylation.

SECTION 5

The Structural Tissues

CHAPTER 16

The biochemistry of structural proteins, mucopolysaccharides and bone

Although it is convenient to consider the body as a set of interconnected organs, this approach leaves out the important question of the shape of the body and the positional arrangement of the organs within the body. The human is draped over its bones and wrapped up in its skin and it is on the type of draping and wrapping that we base most of our ideas of the beauty of the human body. Since the skeleton is the only rigid tissue, it provides the basic shape and points of attachment for other tissues. Much of the material making the necessary attachment between tissues is fibrous, as is much of the wrapping material. The fibrous proteins, collagen and elastin, make most of the connections where organs and bones are held together, and the skin is characterized by another fibrous protein called keratin. On the other hand the ends of bones are kept apart by other polymers of a carbohydrate nature, capable of resisting pressure. These are the mucopolysaccharides as found, for example, in cartilage. Even individual cells are often kept apart by a thin layer of a ground substance, composed mainly of mucopolysaccharide. Since the connective tissue fulfils a passive role it has a rather low rate of metabolism; indeed, much of the tissue is extracellular. Fibroblasts, or cells resembling fibroblasts, are the main cellular components and it would appear that these cells could not be highly aerobic, since they are often embedded in an avascular fibrous material. The biochemistry of the structural polymers and the role of fibroblasts in their formation will be considered briefly.

Keratin

This fibrous protein (which is characteristic of the skin and structures derived from the skin, such as hair and nails) contains a very high proportion of glycine, serine and cystine (each about 15–20% of the total amino acids). It is the cystine which, by cross-linking the protein chains, ensures high tensile strength and low solubility. Treatment of keratin with suitable reducing agents such as thioglycolic acid will cleave the disulphide linkages, greatly increasing the solubility of the protein and reducing its tensile strength. Such softening of hair by reducing agents is used in the artificial waving or straightening of hair, the disulphide links being reestablished after the hair has been arranged in the required form. Unlike collagen and elastin, keratin is synthesized and retained within the cell. During the process of keratinization, cell division takes place parallel to the surface of the skin and the cells move further from the source of nourishment. In the epidermal cells the first sign of keratin formation is the appearance of delicate fibrils. These thicken to about 60 Å, aggregate and coalesce to form the fibrils visible in the light microscope. As the fibrils grow, amorphous granules make their appearance and, in the last stage of formation of the keratin, associate with the fibrils. As with collagen, a soluble monomer, called prekeratin (molecular weight of about 640,000), may be extracted from skin; it contains SH groups but no disulphide bridges. Polymerization (the formation of the fibrils) involves the establishment of these bridges. It seems that a disulphide bridge appears roughly at every 18 amino acid residues.

Collagen

Threads of fibrous protein appear throughout almost all organs. Such threads are particularly plentiful in the connective tissues, including bone, and are usually embedded in an amorphous matrix of mucopolysaccharides (see p. 231). Most of the fibres are rather inelastic and have a high tensile strength. These inelastic fibres, which comprise some 80% of the dry weight of tendons, consist of the protein collagen. Quantitatively collagen is the most abundant protein in the body. Values of from 20% to 40% of the total body protein have been obtained by different workers. In contrast to keratin, virtually all the collagen in the body is extracellular and, as with keratin, devoid of enzyme activity. Because it is outside the cell, collagen is not easily accessible to enzymes and is broken down by the body only very slowly (see p. 229). Table 5.1 shows the approximate quantities of collagen found in some tissues.

As might be expected, skin and bone contain most of the body's collagen, but a substantial amount is also found in skeletal muscle. As a percentage of dry weight, collagen contributes most to tendon, up to 86%; cordae tendinae 84%, skin 79% and cornea 78%. These are all tissues where great toughness is required.

Table 5.1. Approximate amounts of collagen in some human tissues

Tissue	Collagen content mg/g wet weight	Total quantity of collagen in the total tissue (g)
Skeletal Muscle	12·1	363
Liver	1·3	2·2
Kidneys[a]	31·4	9·1
Skin	197	965
Bone[b]	69	830
Lungs	39	39

[a] Analysis for rat kidney. Total quantity calculated for human kidney assuming the same content as in the rat.

[b] Analysis for rat bone. Total quantity calculated for human bone assuming the same content as in the rat.

Formation of collagen

It seems clear that the cells responsible for the production of collagen are the fibroblasts. Figure 5.1 shows collagen fibre from rat tail. These large and insoluble fibres are assembled *in situ* and are not exported as finished products from the cell; rather, a soluble monomer is released which polymerizes outside the cell to give the fibres as illustrated in Figure 5.2. The monomeric molecules are tropocollagen; they consist of three coiled helixes of polypeptide chains. When released from the cell they line themselves up in overlapping ranks forming the fibres which are first stabilized by hydrogen bonding and then by covalent links between the

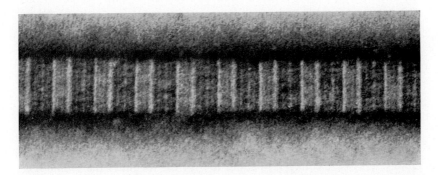

Figure 5.1. An electron micrograph of a single collagen fibre from rat tail; the periodicity results from the staggered alignment of chains of tropocollagen subunits. By kind permission of Professor R. Barer

ranks of monomers. The staggered alignment of the tropocollagen molecules (each 2900 Å long) results in a periodicity (at 700 Å) in the collagen
fibres responsible for the striated appearance. The way in which the extracellular tropocollagen molecules are instructed in the direction in which
they should point, or in the shape of the final fibre, is not at all clear.

The amino acid composition of collagen is most unusual. Not only are
some amino acids present in much higher amounts than in any other
protein, but some unusual amino acids not found in other proteins contribute substantially to the polypeptide chain. Thus one third of the amino
acids of the collagen of human skin is glycine. Alanine, proline and
hydroxyproline each amount to 10% of the total; thus these 3, together
with glycine, comprise 60% of the amino acid content of collagen. Aspartic
acid and glutamic acid together comprise another 10% and arginine and
serine about another 5% each. The remaining 20% is shared amongst the

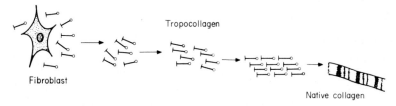

Figure 5.2. Polymerization of tropocollagen

other amino acids, including the unusual amino acid hydroxylysine.
Tryptophan and cysteine are absent. It is generally believed that the
hydroxyamino acids contribute very largely to the hydrogen bonding
mechanism that maintains the collagen as a continuous fibre. Other covalent bonds, possibly ester bonds, provide cross-links which further
stabilize the molecule and which increase in number, as do the hydrogen
bonds, as the collagen ages.

Biosynthesis of collagen

Exchange between the amino acids of the metabolic pool and those of
the collagen molecule is usually very slow. A net increase in the amount of
collagen can be induced experimentally, for example, when a wound in the
skin heals or when a polysaccharide such as carageenan (extracted from
the seaweed called Irish Moss) is injected subcutaneously. In the latter case
granulomas develop at the site of injection and the fibroblasts within
rapidly synthesize collagen to about 10% of the weight of the granuloma.
There seems no doubt that the protein is synthesized by the usual mechanism (see p. 240) but ascorbic acid plays an essential but obscure role in the
process. Many observations have shown that, in the scorbutic wound,

healing is slow or does not occur, and that in scorbutic guinea pigs collagen is lacking in the skin, particularly in regenerating skin. Also in the granulomas induced experimentally by carageenan, there is only a small synthesis of collagen if the animal is scorbutic. There seems no doubt that proline and lysine respectively are the precursors of the hydroxylated compounds (hydroxyproline and hydroxylysine) within the collagen molecule. There is, however, some doubt about the stage in the synthesis of the protein at which the hydroxylation occurs. Some experiments suggest a hydroxylation of the parent amino acid whilst it is attached to soluble RNA; others suggest a hydroxylation subsequent to the formation of the peptide bond. In either case the reasons why some proline or lysine molecules are selected for hydroxylation and not others remains obscure. What is clear is that both oxygen and ascorbic acid are necessary for the hydroxylation process. Under anaerobic conditions, or in the absence of vitamin C, proline is incorporated into collagen but is not converted to hydroxyproline.

Ageing of collagen

It has been established experimentally that the collagen of older people is less soluble than that of younger people. Also, the newly-formed collagen laid down of skin during wound healing is more soluble than the older collagen in the surrounding skin. Part of the ageing process appears to be the establishment of more and more cross links between chains with a consequent stiffening of the molecules. Such changes are thought to be responsible for the degeneration of the elastic tissues in old age, which is irreversible because the collagen of these tissues does not turn over. However, in other tissues collagen does turn over. In rats, for example, the turn-over of the collagen in the liver is about one half that of the other protein of the tissue and there seems to be some relationship between the overall metabolic activity of a tissue and the rate of its collagen turnover.

Elastin

The elastic fibres which are characteristic of ligament are composed largely of the elastic protein, elastin. Elastin is an extracellular, fibrous protein apparently produced by the same cells as collagen. However, it differs in almost every particular from collagen. The fibres are elastic, branched and yellow in colour. The elasticity depends on the presence of water—when dried, elastin is brittle. The distribution is also different from that of collagen; elastin is sparse in skin and tendon, of roughly equal quantity to the collagen in lung and artery, and provides about 80% of the protein in ligament. The amino acid composition is similar to that of collagen, one third of the amino acids being glycine. The four amino acids proline, glycine, alanine and valine comprise 80% of the amino acids but hydroxyproline is present in very small amounts and cysteine is absent. Almost 95% of the side chains of the protein are non-polar. Degradation studies have shown that the yellow colour of elastin is due to the presence of two unusual amino acids desmosine and isodesmosine.

$$COOH$$
$$CH_2 \cdot CH_2CH_2 \cdot CH$$
$$NH$$

$$HOOC\diagdown CH \cdot CH_2 \cdot CH_2 \diagdown \qquad CH_2 \cdot CH_2 \cdot CH \diagup COOH$$
$$H_2N\diagup \qquad \diagdown NH_2$$

$$N^+$$
$$(CH_2)_4$$
$$CH$$
$$H_2N \quad COOH$$

desmosine

$$HOOC\diagdown CH \cdot CH_2 \cdot CH_2 \diagdown \qquad CH_2 \cdot CH_2 \cdot CH \diagup COOH$$
$$H_2N\diagup \qquad \qquad \diagdown NH_2$$
$$CH_2 \cdot CH_2 \cdot CH_2 \cdot CH \diagup COOH$$
$$\diagdown NH_2$$
$$N^+$$
$$(CH_2)_4$$
$$CH$$
$$H_2N \quad COOH$$

isodesmosine

These substances form the bridges between the polypeptide chains of elastin. From isotope studies with lysine it has been shown that the desmosines are formed by reaction between lysine moieties present in the elastin precursor. In copper deficiency elastin is not formed and structures like the aorta or heart valve may rupture. From such deficient animals a protein similar to elastin (but much more soluble) may be extracted which has much more lysine than normal elastin and is deficient in desmosine bridges. Thus it appears that copper is necessary for the condensation of lysine in the elastin precursor to give the desmosine.

Lathyrism

The sweet pea (*Lathyrus odoratus*) contains β-aminopropionitrile. This substance administered to an animal causes loss of tensile strength in the tissues with increased solubility of both collagen and elastin. In both cases the cross linking between the protein chains fails to occur. The precise nature of the effect of the β-aminopropionitrile is not understood, but it is unlikely that the mechanism of action can be the same in both collagen and elastin.

Mucopolysaccharides

The mucopolysaccharides are synthesized by the fibroblasts, or their analogues the chondrocytes. One special mucopolysaccharide, heparin, is synthesized by a special cell (the mast cell) and retained within the cell in granules together with histamine for secretion when required (histamine is synthesized by decarboxylation of histidine; cf. biosynthesis of cate-cholamines, Figure 7.1).

L-histidine   histamine

Other mucopolysaccharides are secreted continuously as they are formed.

There is no clear definition of a mucopolysaccharide, since historically this group of substances (often mucus-like in nature) has comprised polymers containing hexosamine residues, or lacking hexosamine and associated with protein, or not associated with protein. More commonly the term mucopolysaccharides is applied only to those substances which contain a uronic acid residue and hexosamine. Of the many mucopoly-saccharides, only the acidic mucopolysaccharides will be considered, especially the hyaluronic acids and the chondroitin sulphates.

Hyaluronic acid is composed of alternating units of glucuronic acid and *N*-acetyl glucosamine.

hyaluronic acid

Chondroitin sulphate contains glucuronic acid alternating with *N*-acetyl galactosamine in which one of the hydroxyl groups is sulphated as shown.

chondroitin sulphate A

It is likely that mucopolysaccharides are linked more or less firmly with protein *in vivo*; frequently serine appears to be the linking amino acid. The mechanism of the synthesis of the protein–mucopolysaccharide complex is not clear, but it appears that the fibroblast synthesizes the complete molecule. The hyaluronic acid of the synovial fluid has been extensively studied both in the normal and in the arthritic subject. Whilst the normal knee joint may contain only 0·4 ml of synovial fluid, an arthritic joint may contain 20–30 ml of fluid containing a relatively unpolymerized hyaluronic acid and a disproportionately high content of protein.

Biosynthesis of mucopolysaccharides

Electron microscopy and autoradiography have shown that in cartilage fragments ^{35}S accumulates at first in the vesicles of the Golgi apparatus. Later the vesicles move towards the periphery of the cell and ^{35}S appears in the extracellular matrix only after the vesicles discharge their contents. If steel mesh cylinders are implanted under the skin, mucopolysaccharide synthesis is induced and ^{14}C-labelled glucosamine is incorporated into the newly synthesized material. The amount of mucopolysaccharides synthesized is altered by hormones; for example, the skin of alloxan diabetic rats contains only about one half of the amount found in that of normal animals and injection of insulin cures the deficiency. Oestrogens and androgens also markedly alter the amount of mucopolysaccharides found in animals or in tissue preparations, but results with the intact animal are sometimes at variance with those found with isolated tissue preparations. However, cortisone and hydrocortisone suppress the formation of mucopolysaccharides both *in vivo* and *in vitro*.

Role of vitamin A in the metabolism of cartilage and bone

It has been long known that overdosage of vitamin A in growing animals produces softening of the bones and degeneration of cartilage. Some of the mechanisms have been clarified by Honor Fell and her associates working with bone rudiments grown in tissue culture. The explants used were the humeri, femurs and tibiae of embryonic chicks at the 6–6½ day stage. At this stage the rudiments consist of rods of cartilage beginning to ossify at each end and with a very thin enclosing layer of calcified material. In a culture medium containing vitamin A at 3 μg/ml, rudiments cease to grow and become soft and gelatinous and, as shown with labelled sulphate, the explants stop taking up sulphate and begin to lose the material already incorporated. Staining shows that the amount of mucopolysaccharide (chondroitin sulphate) is diminishing. After 6 days cultivation in the medium containing vitamin A, the amino sugar content of the explant is only one half of the controls. Vitamin A induces these changes in two ways. The first is stimulation of the breakdown of the lysosomes in the cartilage with release of the hydrolytic enzymes which degrade the proteins and mucopolysaccharides of the young cartilage. The second is inhibition of the synthesis of components of cartilage such as hexosamine and hydroxyproline. The lysosomal enzymes are liberated at concentrations of vitamin A which do not inhibit the synthesis of hexosamine in the bone explants.

Calcium phosphate deposition in bone

The main supporting material of the body is bone, which owes its strength to the presence of calcium phosphate in the form of hydroxyapatite. The calcium is constantly being laid down by the osteoblasts and eroded by the osteoclasts. The formation of the calcium phosphate is brought about by the enzyme alkaline phosphatase, which liberates phosphate from organic phosphates. The phosphate then reacts with calcium to form the insoluble calcium phosphate. In the inherited disease of hypophosphatasia the bone does not calcify properly and the alkaline phosphatase of the tissues is low. The network of collagen within bone appears to act as a former for the crystallization of calcium salts. Abnormalities of collagen arrangement can lead to abnormalities of the bone structure.

Physical properties of structural tissues

By comparing values in Tables 5.1 and 5.2, it can be shown that the amount of mucopolysaccharide in the tissue is only one tenth to one hundredth of the amount of the fibrous proteins that they envelop.

Table 5.2. Approximate amounts of acid mucopolysaccharides
in some tissues

Tissue	Mucopolysaccharide content mg/g of fresh tissue	Total quantity of mucopolysaccharides in the total tissue (g)
Skeletal muscle	0·1	3
Liver	0·14	0·23
Kidneys	0·36	0·1
Plasma	0·15	0·4
Skin	2·02	9·9
Bone	0·88	10·56
Lungs	0·15	1·54

However, because the mucopolysaccharides trap water within their gel-like structure they probably occupy as large a volume as the structural proteins. Such a mucopolysaccharide gel containing embedded protein fibres may be compared to one of the modern plastics like polythene incorporating within it glass fibres and rubber strands. This material would have considerable tensile strength but would be able to alter its shape and transmit pressures throughout its bulk with ease. Modification of the basic tissue 'plastic' is made by varying the proportions of chondroitin sulphate (rigid molecules) to hyaluronic acid (flexible molecules), by altering the amounts of inelastic fibres (collagen) to elastic fibres (elastin) and finally by adding inorganic filler (hydroxyapatite) to give bulk and rigidity. With these 5 components, structures as different as cartilage (low friction, good elasticity and rigidity due to a high proportion of chondroitin sulphate), synovial fluid (high lubrication and high shock absorption due to a high proportion of hyaluronic acid), tendon (high tensile strength and low elasticity due to a high proportion of collagen) and bone (high load bearing due to high concentration of hydroxyapatite filler) can be made.

SECTION 6

Biochemistry of Reproduction

The reproduction of mammals requires the cooperation of a number of specialized tissues which are responsible for the fertilization of the mature ovum, which provide the appropriate environment for foetal development and which supply carbohydrate, fat and protein for the nutrition of the young animal after birth. The organs most directly concerned are the gonads, the uterus and the mammary glands; in this section, certain aspects of their biochemistry will be considered.

In essence, reproduction consists of the transmission of the characteristic potentialities of a single cell to its progeny: this is true even for the multicellular organism, in which those properties potential in the fertilized egg are expressed in the many-celled complexes of the fully differentiated organism. In biochemical terms, the transmission implies that the parent cell is able to produce daughter cells capable of manufacturing those patterns of enzymes appropriate to their spatial and temporal position in the life history of the organism, since the enzyme complement will determine both the structural development and the metabolic activities of the cells and organs. Therefore a general understanding of the biochemistry of heredity requires a consideration of the mechanism of protein biosynthesis.

CHAPTER 17

The biosynthesis of proteins

The biosynthesis of amides and simple peptides

The biosynthesis of proteins depends on the formation of peptide linkages between the carboxyl group of one amino acid and the amino group
of another (see Section 1). The reaction is the formation of a substituted
amide. The commonest form of amide in the body is glutamine, the amide
of glutamic acid. The attachment of ammonia to the carboxyl of glutamic
acid requires energy and as usual this comes from ATP. It is probable that
an enzyme–phosphate complex of glutamic acid is formed first and that
this is then attacked by ammonia (Figure 6.1). Analogous reactions occur
during the formation of the tripeptide glutathione (Figure 6.2).

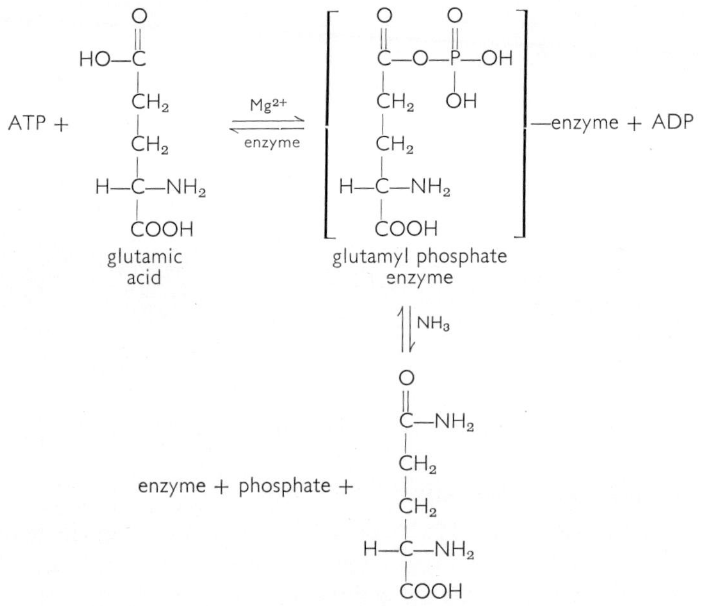

Figure 6.1. Biosynthesis of glutamine. The reaction is catalysed by the enzyme
glutamine synthetase

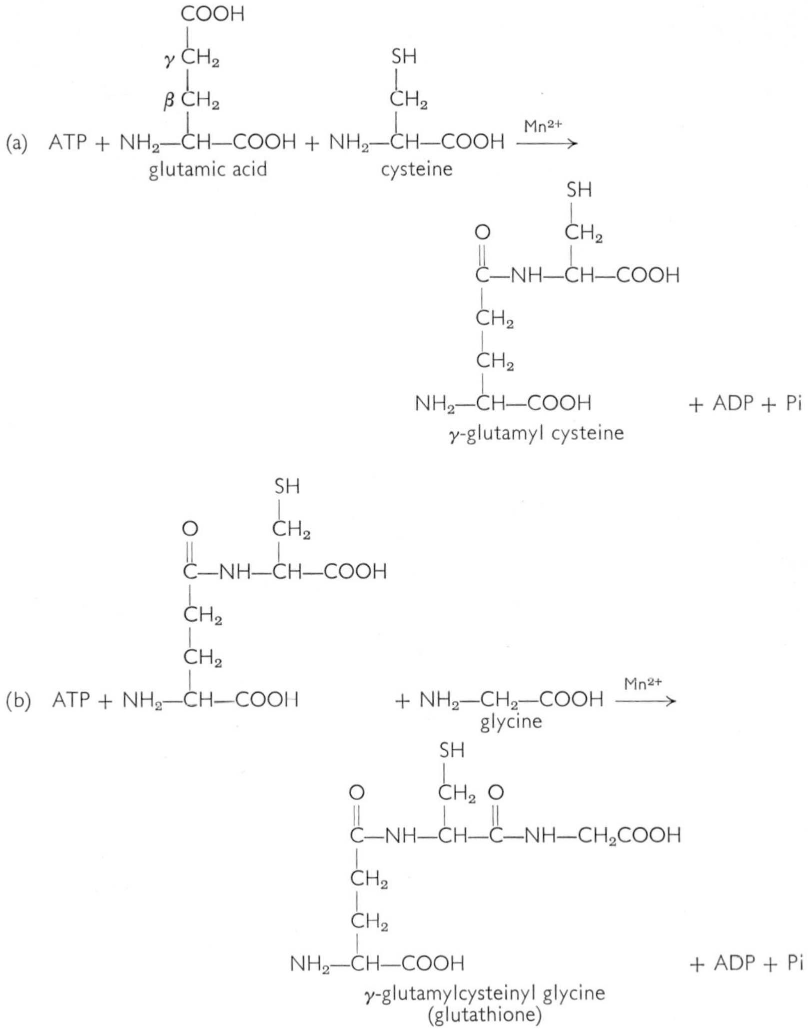

$$
\begin{array}{c}
\text{COOH} \\
|\\
\gamma\ \text{CH}_2 \\
|\\
\beta\ \text{CH}_2
\end{array}
\qquad
\begin{array}{c}
\text{SH}\\
|\\
\text{CH}_2
\end{array}
$$

(a) $\text{ATP} + \text{NH}_2-\text{CH}-\text{COOH} + \text{NH}_2-\text{CH}-\text{COOH} \xrightarrow{\text{Mn}^{2+}}$

      glutamic acid   cysteine

$$
\begin{array}{c}
\qquad\qquad \text{SH}\\
\qquad\qquad |\\
\text{O}\qquad \text{CH}_2\\
\|\qquad\ \ |\\
\text{C}-\text{NH}-\text{CH}-\text{COOH}\\
|\\
\text{CH}_2\\
|\\
\text{CH}_2\\
|\\
\text{NH}_2-\text{CH}-\text{COOH}
\end{array}
\qquad + \text{ADP} + \text{Pi}
$$

      γ-glutamyl cysteine

$$
\begin{array}{c}
\qquad\qquad \text{SH}\\
\qquad\qquad |\\
\text{O}\qquad \text{CH}_2\\
\|\qquad\ \ |\\
\text{C}-\text{NH}-\text{CH}-\text{COOH}\\
|\\
\text{CH}_2\\
|\\
\text{CH}_2\\
|
\end{array}
$$

(b) $\text{ATP} + \text{NH}_2-\text{CH}-\text{COOH} \qquad\qquad + \text{NH}_2-\text{CH}_2-\text{COOH} \xrightarrow{\text{Mn}^{2+}}$

                                        glycine

$$
\begin{array}{c}
\qquad\qquad \text{SH}\\
\qquad\qquad |\\
\text{O}\qquad \text{CH}_2\ \ \text{O}\\
\|\qquad\ \ |\quad\ \ \|\\
\text{C}-\text{NH}-\text{CH}-\text{C}-\text{NH}-\text{CH}_2\text{COOH}\\
|\\
\text{CH}_2\\
|\\
\text{CH}_2\\
|\\
\text{NH}_2-\text{CH}-\text{COOH}
\end{array}
\qquad + \text{ADP} + \text{Pi}
$$

      γ-glutamylcysteinyl glycine
          (glutathione)

Figure 6.2. Biosynthesis of glutathione

Nucleic acids and the biosynthesis of proteins

The early work (1935–1950s) on the formation of peptide bonds in proteins provided the following important clues. The process was shown to be energy dependent, the indications were that one ATP molecule was required for each peptide bond formed and was used to activate the carboxyl group of the amino acid preparatory to its condensation. Further,

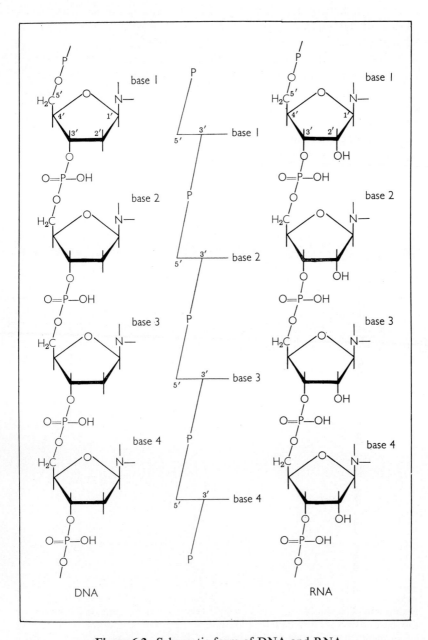

Figure 6.3. Schematic form of DNA and RNA

it was clear that the nucleic acids, both RNA and DNA (see Figure 6.3), were essential for the synthesis of proteins. Evidence for the nuclear localization of DNA and for the movement of RNA from nucleus to cytoplasm led to the concept that DNA, as the genetic material, directed the synthesis of specific forms of RNA which in turn directed the synthesis of specific proteins. This concept visualizes the attachment of particular amino acids to specific transfer RNA molecules (*t*-RNA) and their condensation in an order determined by the interactions of the *t*-RNA amino acid complex with another species of RNA (messenger or *m*-RNA). *m*-RNA transfers the genetic message from the nuclear DNA to the cytoplasmic site of synthesis in the ribosomes.

The structure and biosynthesis of DNA

Much evidence points to the fact that DNA, found in greatest concentration in the nuclei of cells, is the genetic material of the cell carrying the 'hereditary plan' for cell growth. The structure of DNA isolated from

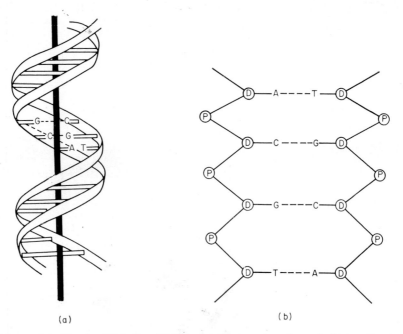

(a)   (b)

Figure 6.4. The double helix of DNA; (a) the two strands are held together by the base pairing described in Figure 6.5. In each strand the sequence of components is as shown in (b), in which P = phosphate residue; D = deoxyribose; A = adenine; C = cytosine; G = guanine; T = thymine

many types of cells conforms to the same general pattern; it contains the purine bases adenine and guanine, the pyrimidine bases thymine and cytosine, the pentose deoxyribose and phosphate. The backbone of the molecule consists of alternating sugar and phosphate units, with the bases linked to the sugar residues (Figure 6.3). X-ray studies of molecules of DNA suggests that they contain two chains which are spiralled around each other, as first proposed by Watson and Crick in 1953 (Figure 6.4a). The nature of the linkage between these chains was deduced from the fact

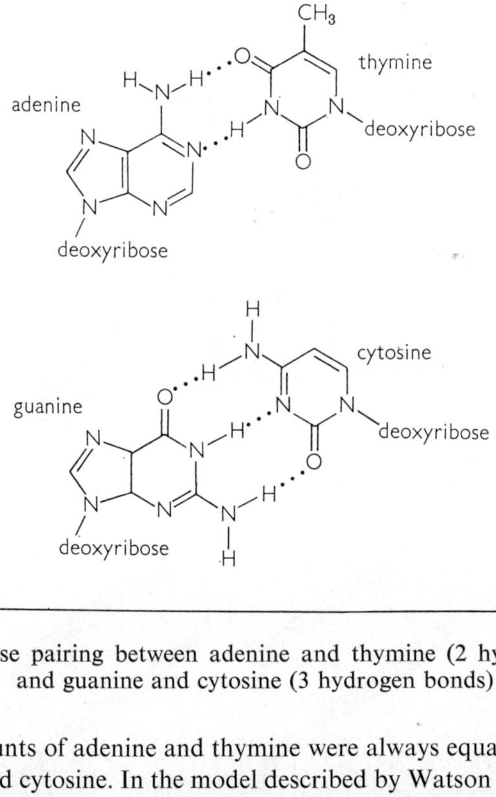

Figure 6.5. Base pairing between adenine and thymine (2 hydrogen bonds) and guanine and cytosine (3 hydrogen bonds)

that the amounts of adenine and thymine were always equal as were those of guanine and cytosine. In the model described by Watson and Crick, this is accounted for by the proposal that the bases are hydrogen-bonded to each other with specific pairings of adenine and thymine, and of guanine and cytosine (Figures 6.4b and 6.5). Such a structure can also account for the all-important conservation of hereditary information during cell division. In principle, it follows from the specificity of the base pairing that each strand of the DNA should be capable of directing the assembly of its complementary strand when DNA synthesis is occurring so that two new double-stranded DNA molecules will be formed of composition identical to the parent molecule and to one another (Figure 6.6).

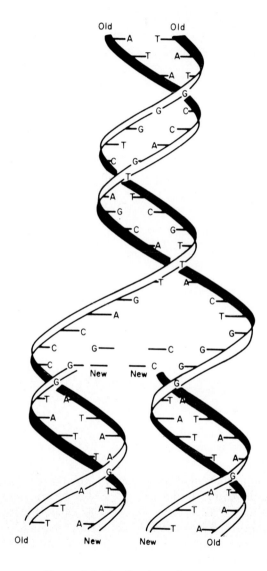

Figure 6.6. Replication of DNA

The synthesis of DNA requires all four deoxyribonucleoside triphosphates, magnesium ions, DNA primer and the enzyme DNA polymerase (Figure 6.7). *In vitro* the DNA synthesized has the same base composition as the primer, which is most active when it is present as single-stranded DNA (i.e. when it has been denatured). The way in which double-stranded DNA is replicated *in vivo* is not understood nor is the process by which it is unwound to expose the individual chains. However, it is certain that each strand is provided with a new complementary strand, in which the bases have been aligned in the correct sequence by the requirements for specific base pairing already described. Thus in each mitotic cycle the daughter cells will receive DNA molecules identical to those of the parent cell. It was suggested that the linear sequence of bases in DNA acts as a chemical 'code', indicating to the cell the order in which amino acids should be strung together to make particular polypeptide chains and

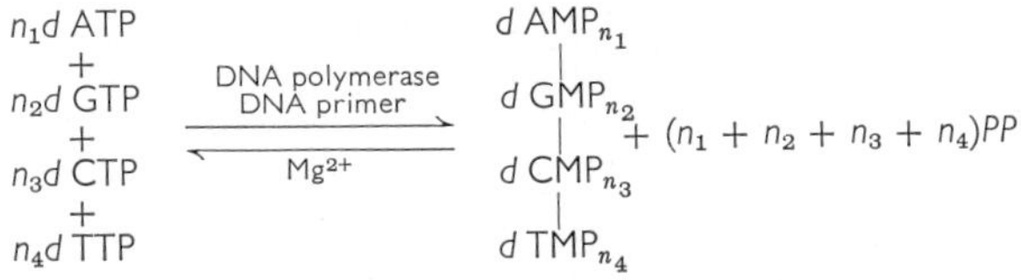

$$n_1 d \text{ ATP} \\ + \\ n_2 d \text{ GTP} \quad \xrightarrow[\text{Mg}^{2+}]{\text{DNA polymerase} \atop \text{DNA primer}} \quad d \text{ AMP}_{n_1} \\ + \\ n_3 d \text{ CTP} \\ + \\ n_4 d \text{ TTP}$$

$$d \text{ AMP}_{n_1} \\ | \\ d \text{ GMP}_{n_2} \\ | \quad + (n_1 + n_2 + n_3 + n_4)PP \\ d \text{ CMP}_{n_3} \\ | \\ d \text{ TMP}_{n_4}$$

Figure 6.7. The synthesis of DNA by DNA polymerase. The dioxynucleotides are represented thus: d ATP adenine dioxyribonucleoside triphosphate; d AMP adenine dioxyribosenucleoside monophosphate, etc; *PP* represents pyrophosphate

therefore particular proteins. As the DNA is largely confined to the nucleus, and as much synthesis of protein occurs in the rest of the cell, it was also clearly apparent that the information in the chemical 'code' must be transmitted to the cytoplasm in some way. An obvious candidate for the 'transmitter substance' is RNA, which occurs both in the nucleus and outside it.

The structure and function of RNA

The RNA content of cells comprises a number of functionally different classes of RNA. All these classes contain the bases adenine, uracil, guanine and cytosine, bonded to chains of molecules of the sugar ribose linked through phosphate diester bonds (Figure 6.3). The bases are capable of the specific pairing reactions, adenine with uracil, guanine with cytosine (Figure 6.8).

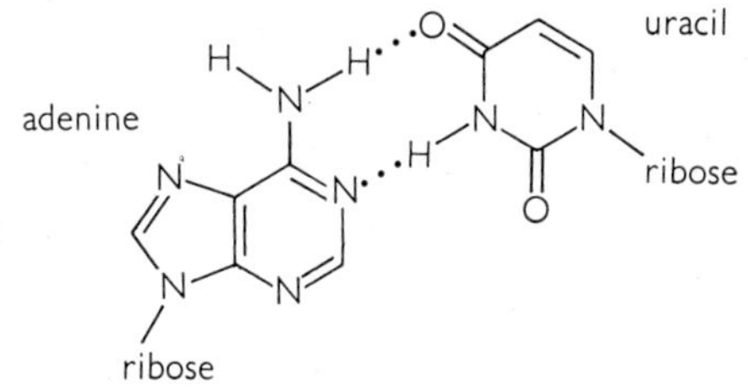

Figure 6.8. Base pairing between adenine and uracil in RNA

Transfer RNA (*t*-RNA); also called soluble RNA (*s*-RNA)

This is a class of RNA of relatively low molecular weight (about 25,000), each molecule containing 75–100 nucleotides. A number of different types of *t*-RNA are present in all cells, each one being capable of reacting with a particular amino acid during protein biosynthesis. One of these, reacting with L-alanine, has been obtained in pure form and its nucleotide sequence (77 bases) determined; the three-dimensional structure of this and other *t*-RNA molecules is uncertain, though it appears likely that the polynucleotide chain is folded back on itself and has a number of regions stabilized by base pairing (Figure 6.9). The end of the chain with which the amino acid reacts has the base sequence AMP–CMP–CMP–; attachment of the amino acid residue involves esterification of the 3' position on the ribose of the terminal adenosine (Figure 6.10). Another region of this molecule has a sequence of three bases which is specific for the particular amino acid and which is complementary to a corresponding set of three bases in a 'messenger' RNA molecule; this is the 'coding region' of the *t*-RNA (Figure 6.9).

Ribosomal RNA

Ribosomes (see p. 96) contain about 60% RNA (ribosomal RNA) and 40% structural protein. During the synthesis of protein the functionally active ribosomes are distinguished from other ribosomal material by their attachment to molecules of 'messenger' RNA to form polysomes.

Messenger RNA (m-RNA)

This type of RNA directs the biosynthesis of a particular protein. Most of the data concerning messenger RNA has come from the study of bacterial systems where it appears to be relatively short-lived, being degraded by hydrolytic enzymes fairly rapidly; in higher organisms, some species of *m*-RNA are much longer-lived. The most important properties of any messenger RNA molecule are its capacity for combining with ribosomes and its possession of a base sequence complementary to some part of the DNA containing the cell's genetic information. During protein synthesis, discrete sections of the information contained in the nuclear store of DNA are transcribed into specific molecules of *m*-RNA by a DNA-dependent

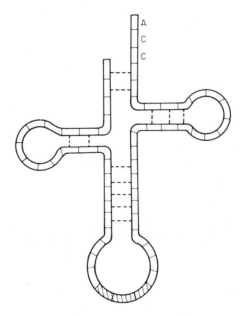

Figure 6.9. Diagrammatic representation of a possible configuration for a molecule of *t*-RNA. The amino acyl group is attached to the end of the chain terminating in cytosine, cytosine and adenine (C····C····A). The 3 bases in the shaded portion occupy the coding region of the molecule (see text). The dotted lines represent the H bonds between base pairs that are responsible for maintaining the structure of the molecule

RNA polymerase which requires Mg^{2+} and all four ribose nucleoside triphosphates. The *m*-RNA provides a programme to direct the assembly of proteins in the ribosomes. A variety of experiments has confirmed the feasibility of such a role for messenger RNA, perhaps the most striking being those in which the synthetic messenger RNA, polyuridylic acid, promotes the synthesis of a polypeptide of one particular amino acid, phenylalanine, when added to a cell-free system capable of protein synthesis. The attachment of ribosomes to the messenger-RNA produces clusters of ribosomes called 'polysomes' or 'polyribosomes'. It is not yet clear whether *m*-RNA leaves the nucleus to combine with ribosomes in the cytoplasm, or whether the ribosomes are programmed with *m*-RNA in the nucleus before they enter the cytoplasm. A further problem that has yet to be solved is how the decision is taken as to which part of the DNA is transcribed at any particular time. It is generally held that there are bio-chemical 'switches' which control the accessibility of a particular part of the DNA for transcription of its information, but the nature of these switches is poorly understood.

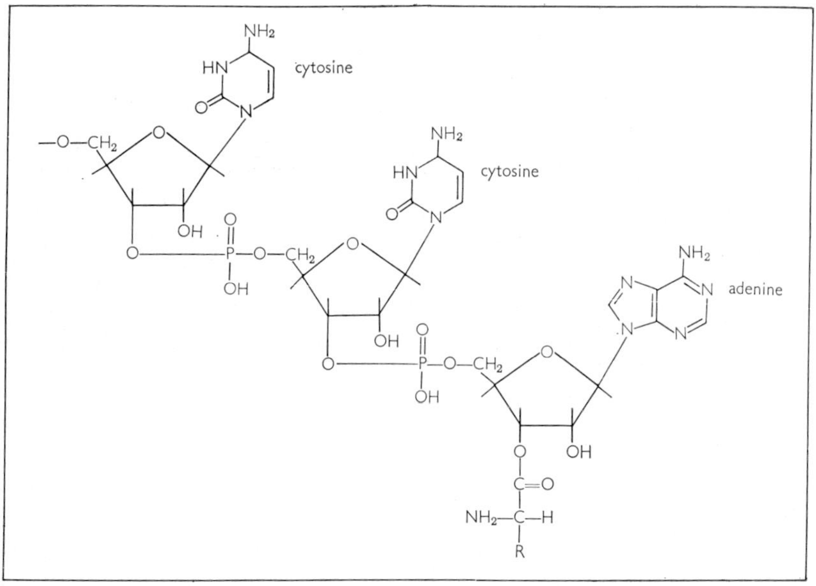

Figure 6.10. The three terminal nucleotides in a *t*-RNA molecule, with the bases adenine, cytosine, cytosine. The amino acyl group is attached to the 3′ position of the ribose in the terminal adenine nucleotide

Polysomes

Polysomes can be separated from other RNA material by centrifuging. A number of ribosomes may attach simultaneously to a single molecule of messenger RNA (Figure 6.11). Each separate ribosome acts as a site for protein synthesis during the period of its attachment to the messenger, which may direct the synthesis of a number of individual protein molecules simultaneously.

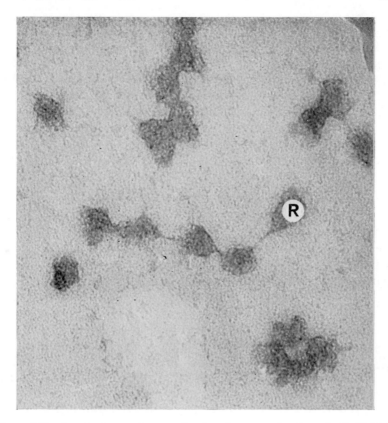

Figure 6.11. An electron micrograph of polysomes showing the individual ribosomes (R) linked together by a fine thread of RNA. Reproduced by kind permission of Dr. H. S. Slayter from *J. Mol. Biol.*, 1963

The description of messenger RNA has indicated that there should be a detectable relationship between the base sequence of the cell's DNA and that of the messenger RNA molecules. There is now good evidence from work with bacterial systems that only one of the DNA strands (the sense strand) acts as a primer for *m*-RNA synthesis *in vivo*, and as might be expected there is complementarity between the base sequence of the *m*-RNA and the sense strand of the DNA.

The biosynthesis of proteins

The activation of amino acids

This requires the attachment of an amino acid to the corresponding *t*-RNA molecule by a transacylation process using ATP thus:

9*

$$\text{AA} + \text{ATP} + \text{enz} \longrightarrow \text{enz—AA—AMP} + \text{PP}$$
$$\text{enz—AA—AMP} + t\text{-RNA} \longrightarrow \text{AA—}t\text{-RNA} + \text{AMP} + \text{enz}$$

(The amino acid (AA) reacts with ATP, the amino acyl–AMP product (AA–AMP) remaining bound to the enzyme surface (enz); pyrophosphate (PP) is released and is hydrolysed to Pi by pyrophosphatase.)

There appear to be separate and specific amino acid-activating enzymes (or amino acyl-t-RNA synthetases) for each L-amino acid found in proteins; they occur in the soluble phase of the cell. The amino acyl–AMP intermediates are bound to the surface of the enzyme throughout the course of the reaction.

The condensation of amino acids: peptide bond formation

This involves the cooperation of the amino acyl-t-RNA complexes, a molecule of messenger-RNA, ribosomes and probably two soluble enzyme systems (Figure 6.12). The first of these enzymes appears to require GTP and Mg^{2+}. It binds the amino acyl-t-RNA to an acceptor site on an active ribosome, attached to a molecule of messenger RNA; the binding will occur only for the particular amino-t-RNA complex whose base sequence at its coding region is complementary to the base sequence of that portion of the messenger RNA at the binding site. Current information indicates that sets of three bases define the association between the messenger and t-RNA molecules, i.e. the 'genetic message' from the DNA is transmitted by a 'triplet code'. Thus at this stage it is a portion of the RNA structure of the amino acyl-t-RNA complex that is recognized by the messenger RNA and not the amino acid structure itself (see Figure 6.13). This was shown conclusively by experiments in which cysteine was attached to its specific t-RNA, then treated with Raney nickel. This treatment removes the SH group of the amino acid, which is converted to alanine, i.e. the product is alanine attached to the t-RNA molecule specific for cysteine. However, in a cell-free protein synthesizing system, the complex behaves as if it still contained cysteine. Considerable progress has been made in determining the triplets of bases coding from individual amino acids, in what amounts to the 'translating' of the 'genetic language' of the cell.

The second soluble enzyme (the peptide synthetase) transfers the growing polypeptide chain, which is itself bound to the ribosomes through a t-RNA molecule, to the amino acyl residue of the incoming amino acyl-t-RNA (Figure 6.12). When the transfer has been completed, t-RNA is released and the messenger RNA is moved across the ribosomes so that its next triplet of bases is positioned at the binding site, prior to the attachment of the next amino acyl-t-RNA molecule. Thus the alternate operation of these two soluble enzymes condenses amino acids into the protein chain, in an order determined by the sequence of the triplets of bases in the messenger RNA.

The finished polypeptide is released from the ribosome when the messenger RNA has passed completely through the binding sites on the ribosome. It appears to assume its final three-dimensional structure spontaneously; it is not known whether this begins during chain elongation or after release.

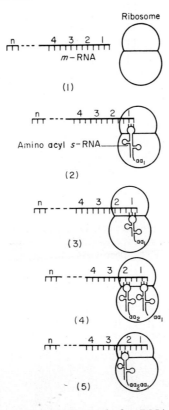

Figure 6.12. (1) Ribosome approaches end of *m*-RNA. (2) Ribosome attaches to end *m*-RNA. Triplet 1 (3 bases) at binding site selects appropriate, specific amino acyl-*s*-RNA; binding involves a soluble enzyme, GTP, Mg^{2+}. (3) Ribosome moves along *m*-RNA for a length corresponding to one triplet, so that the second triplet is opposite the binding site. (4) Triplet 2 at binding site selects appropriate, specific amino acyl-*s*-RNA, which is bound by the action of the enzyme system. (5) The first amino acyl group is transferred to the second with the formation of a peptide bond by a second enzyme system. The first *s*-RNA is released. Steps 3, 4 and 5 are repeated for each new amino acid residue

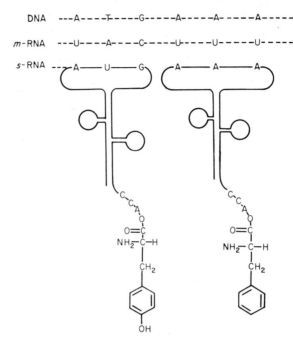

Figure 6.13. The relationship between DNA, *m*-RNA, *s*-RNA and the alignment of amino acyl groups on the *m*-RNA. The amino acid tyrosine has as its 'code word' the base sequence UAC; for phenylalanine it is UUU

In summary (Figure 6.14), DNA provides the fundamental 'message' describing the nature of the protein to be synthesized. This message and the units which implement the message are carried on two separate kinds of RNA, messenger RNA and transfer RNA, to the sites of protein synthesis on the ribosomes which contain their own characteristic form of RNA.

Protein turnover

Even in the mature animal, the need for a protein synthesis continues. Isotope studies have shown that the proteins of the body are in a constant state of flux, being continually built up and broken down and the lifetime of particular proteins in various tissues could be calculated. With the adult in nitrogen balance, when there is little or no change in the protein content of the body, it is possible to equate the rate of breakdown with the rate of synthesis. Table 6.1 gives an approximate idea of the quantities of protein synthesized in different organs of the body.

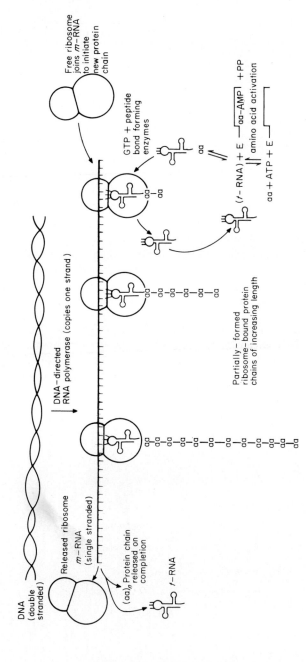

Figure 6.14. Diagrammatic representation of how ribosomes, attached by messenger RNA to form polysomes, participate in protein synthesis

Table 6.1. Daily synthesis of protein in the 70 kg man

	Quantity (g)
Plasma	14
Liver	24
Skeletal muscle	6
Haemoglobin	7
Rest of body	25
Total	76

There are three main factors responsible for protein turnover; the replacement of damaged cells as in the intestinal mucosa and blood, the secretion of proteins by exo- and endocrine tissues and the normal intracellular degradation and resynthesis of proteins.

Although Table 6.1 lists the rates of protein synthesis on a daily basis, this does not imply that these amounts of new proteins must be ingested daily. Man can be in protein balance with as little as 10 g of dietary amino acid per day, provided that he receives the essential amino acids (p. 133) in the right proportions. During periods of restricted protein intake, the body's amino groups are carefully preserved, though there is still a constant synthesis and degradation of all the body's proteins.

Inhibitors of protein synthesis

Actinomycin D is an antibiotic, and also a potent antitumour agent. It inhibits DNA-dependent RNA synthesis by forming a complex with DNA, the site of attachment being the deoxyguanosine residues. By preventing RNA synthesis, it also inhibits protein synthesis.

Puromycin inhibits the formation of proteins, probably by substituting for an amino acyl-*t*-RNA, whose structure it closely resembles (Figure 6.10). It differs in that the amino acyl residue of puromycin is attached to the sugar residue by an amide, rather than an ester, linkage. It is likely that the inhibitory action follows the transfer of the growing peptide chain to the free NH_2 group of puromycin which is bound instead of an acyl-*t*-RNA at the ribosomal site (Figure 6.12). Further transfer is then impossible because of the different mode of attachment of the resulting peptide to the sugar group and the peptidyl puromycin is released from the ribosome.

Chloramphenicol is a potent inhibitor of bacterial protein synthesis, completely preventing the growth of a wide range of species at concentrations of about 10 μg/ml. It interrupts the elongation of the protein by interfering with the transfer of the growing peptide chain to the incoming amino acid.

The *tetracyclines* also inhibit the elongation of the growing peptide chain, though their site of action is probably distinct from that of chloramphenicol. They are effective against a wide range of bacterial species. Tetracycline R_1, $R_2 = H$; Chlorotetracycline (Aureomycin) $R_1 = Cl$, $R_2 = H$; Oxytetracycline $R_1 = H$, $R_2 = OH$.

Streptomycin appears to be bound in such a way to the ribosomes of sensitive bacteria as to 'distort' the messenger RNA, so that the genetic code is 'misread'. The resulting dislocation of protein synthesis produces bacteriostasis.

Cycloheximide (actidione) inhibits mammalian protein synthesis but is ineffective in bacterial systems. It appears to block the formation of the peptide bond.

Certain *amino acid analogues* have also been used as inhibitors e.g. ethionine (replacing methionine) and *p*-fluorophenylalanine (replacing phenylalanine and tyrosine). In some systems, however, protein synthesis continues and active enzymes containing appreciable quantities of the analogues may still be formed.

ethionine   *p*-fluorophenylalanine

CHAPTER 18

Postnatal synthesis of enzymes and inborn errors of metabolism

The expression of hereditary information in a temporal sequence: changes in enzyme patterns at parturition

As previously remarked, hereditary transmission of information in multicellular organisms implies the development of new enzyme patterns in temporal extension during growth and development. A fruitful bio-chemical approach to the understanding of these processes has been to measure the variations in the activity of particular enzymes in developing tissues. Changes occurring in some of the enzymes of carbohydrate metabolism in the livers of foetal and neonatal rats may be used to illustrate the kind of information being obtained.

Before birth, the foetus is supplied with carbohydrate from the maternal circulation; at this time, glucose and glycogen levels in the foetal liver are relatively low. Then, just before birth, there is a very great increase in the amount of glycogen, mainly at the expense of free glucose. The prelimi-nary phosphorylation of this glucose is brought about by hexokinase which works at maximal rate at low glucose concentrations (see p. 46). The accelerated synthesis of glycogen follows the rapid appearance of large amounts of glycogen synthetase in the liver (Figure 6.15); the foetal liver has a high concentration of glucose-6-phosphate, which stimulates the activity of the synthetase.

Immediately after birth, the animal utilizes much of this stored glycogen, and glucose-6-phosphate, to maintain the concentration of blood glucose. This is a consequence of the rapid increase in the activity of phosphorylase and glucose-6-phosphatase before birth (Figure 6.15).

In the succeeding days, enzymes required for gluconeogenesis, e.g. fructose-1,6-diphosphatase, glucose-6-phosphatase, pyruvic carboxykin-ase, increase steadily in amount, as does the glycogen. There is an enhanced ability to synthesize glycogen from galactose, an obvious adaptation to the

257

presence of lactose in the milk. Also during the post-natal period the glycolytic capacity of the liver diminishes with decreased activities of such enzymes as hexokinase, phosphofructokinase and aldolase. The levels of lactate and pyruvate decline reflecting both decreased glycolysis and increased gluconeogenesis. Utilization of lactate for glycogen synthesis may be facilitated by the increase in the amount of the 'skeletal muscle type' isoenzyme of lactic dehydrogenase (see p. 310) which occurs at this time;

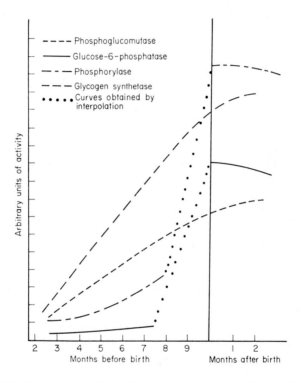

Figure 6.15. Enzyme activities of human liver tissues. From Shutt, 1966

this isoenzyme, as it is not inhibited by pyruvate as readily as the 'heart muscle' type, will be able to channel lactate through pyruvate into the synthetic pathway more effectively.

Almost nothing is known about the way in which such controlled sequential changes in the activities of enzymes are brought about. Taking glucose-6-phosphatase as an example, it is clear that the increased activity in the neonatal liver is due to the formation of new enzyme, as it is prevented by inhibitors of protein synthesis. The synthesis is a response to the changed environment after birth, as it occurs immediately after premature delivery. However, none of a large number of individual components of this changed environment tested has been shown to influence the development of the enzyme.

Genetic defects

The transmission of information to progeny is not always achieved with complete precision. If the offspring in which faulty transmission has occurred are viable, they often exhibit 'genetic defects'. Such defects, influencing the metabolism of carbohydrates, have already been discussed (p. 108). Another particularly instructive group of such defects relates to the metabolism of amino acids.

Phenylketonuria

This is a condition in which phenylpyruvic acid is excreted in the urine. The condition is inherited through a recessive gene and large amounts of phenylalanine accumulate in the tissues. It has been established that phenylalanine hydroxylase (catalysing the conversion of phenylalanine to tyrosine, Figure 6.16) which normally develops in the liver a few weeks after birth, failed to appear; for these patients therefore tyrosine is an essential amino acid. Both sexes are equally susceptible to the disease, which may be detected several weeks after birth, when the plasma phenylalanine concentration increases some thirtyfold over the normal and phenyl pyruvic acid is excreted in the urine, which in consequence gives a green colour when tested with ferric chloride. After about 6 months mental symptoms appear and the majority of the patients are idiots or imbeciles; about 1% of the mentally defective population are phenylketonurics. Besides their mental deficiency the patients are usually undersized, underpigmented, extremely nervous and have a series of persistent limb movements which may continue for hours at a time. In younger children, some of the nerves lack normal myelin. All these symptoms are the consequence of the inability to convert phenylalanine to tyrosine.

The urine of the phenylketonurics does not contain any abnormal metabolites but rather greatly increased concentrations of the normal metabolites, phenylalanine, phenyllactic, phenylpyruvic and phenylacetic acids (the last often conjugated with glutamine). Whether or not suspected persons are heterozygote carriers of the disease can be tested by measuring the plasma tolerance to a dose of phenylalanine. The discovery of the biochemical defect in phenylketonuria has made possible a treatment based

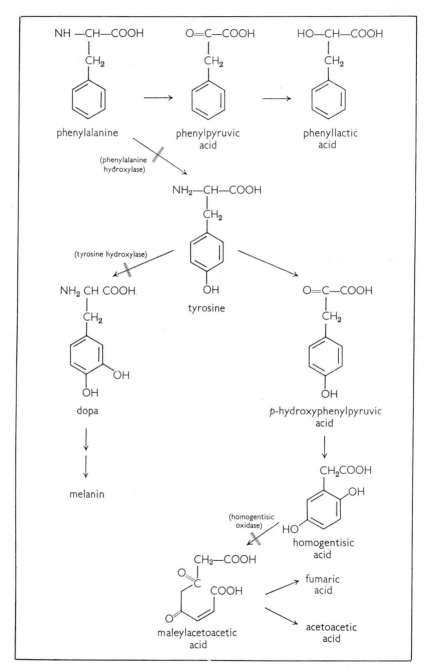

Figure 6.16. Metabolism of phenylalanine and tyrosine

on the limitation of dietary phenylalanine; a difficult procedure as the need to diminish the intake of this amino acid must be balanced against the requirement for phenylalanine for protein synthesis. Only if the controlled diet is begun at a very early age are the clinical symptoms amenable to treatment; pigmentation becomes normal, nervous restlessness diminishes and there is a great improvement in mental capacity. In patients diagnosed and put on a low phenylalanine diet soon after birth, development is apparently completely normal. However, since such treatments were introduced only in 1958, the long-term prognosis is still uncertain. In older patients there is no improvement in the mental condition following restriction of dietary phenylalanine.

Alcaptonuria

This is a rare, hereditary, metabolic disease in which homogentisic acid (a normal metabolite occurring during the metabolism of phenylalanine and tryosine, Figure 6.16) accumulates and is excreted in the urine. The urinary homogentisic acid is often oxidized to a dark, melanin-like substance and thus the urine itself becomes darkly coloured; however, if the urine is acid or contains much ascorbic acid, this darkening is greatly delayed and may not be observed at all. Under these conditions, homogentisic acid may be detected by its ability to reduce copper and silver salts and molybdates. Besides appearing in the urine, the accumulated homogentisic acid may cause pigmentation of the cartilage and other connective tissues and, in later years, arthritis usually develops in the affected areas.

Alcaptonuria is caused by the failure of the enzyme homogentisic acid oxidase (Figure 6.16) to develop in the liver after birth. There is no known treatment for the condition as, even in starvation, homogentisic acid is still formed from the tyrosine and phenylalanine derived from the breakdown of endogenous protein.

Albinism

In this condition the melanocytes fail to synthesize the pigment melanin which is responsible for skin colour; some or all of the melanocytes may be involved. The genetic defect is such that the enzyme tyrosine hydroxylase (tyrosinase) which forms 3,4-dihydroxyphenylalanine (DOPA) from tyrosine is absent (Figure 6.16). As adrenalin synthesis is unaffected, it seems that only the melanocytes are involved directly.

Cystinuria

Cystine is an extremely insoluble amino acid and sometimes gives rise to renal stones. In the inherited metabolic disease cystinuria the urine contains more cystine than normal; it precipitates in the urine and may also be deposited in the kidney to form stones. In this condition there is a defect of reabsorption by the kidney tubules. Lysine, ornithine and arginine are also excreted in these cases, but as these compounds are soluble they normally escape notice.

Sickle-cell anaemia

In this condition the erythrocytes become sickle-shaped; this may be a permanent configuration, in which case the patient is also severely anaemic, or it may develop at a relatively low oxygen tension. The sickle-cell effect is not very marked in the young, but becomes fully apparent only when foetal haemoglobin (haemoglobin F) is replaced by the normal adult haemoglobin A after about 6 months of post-natal development. Electrophoresis of the haemoglobin of the sickle cells from non-anaemic patients revealed two different pigments, haemoglobin A and an abnormal form of haemoglobin (haemoglobin S). This discovery led to the suggestion that the difference between the two types of sickling was that one occurred in individuals homozygous for haemoglobin S, and the other in heterozygotes. Analysis of the haemoglobin pattern of two non-anaemic 'sickle-cell' parents and of their two children confirmed this suggestion. Neither parent was anaemic but their red cells responded to lowered oxygen tension by forming sickles. Hence both parents were considered heterozygous for the sickle-cell trait. The elder child showed no sickling under any circumstances and had normal haemoglobin. The younger had only the sickle-cell haemoglobin and was anaemic.

The sickling of the cells is due to a physical property of the haemoglobin S. The oxygen capacities of haemoglobin S and haemoglobin A are about the same, as are the solubilities of the oxidized forms; however, on reduction, the solubility of haemoglobin A is decreased by about one half, while that of haemoglobin S is diminished fiftyfold so that it comes out of solution in a gel-like mass. The greater the amount of haemoglobin S, the greater the distortion of the cell, so that the tendency for sickling is greater in the homozygote than in the heterozygous carrier. Most of the ill effects of the condition result from the increase in blood viscosity which follows the distortion of the erythrocytes (after gelling of the haemoglobin S) and the destruction of these distorted cells. As the blood viscosity increases, the rate of blood flow diminishes and the extent of deoxygenation increases, so that the sickling becomes more pronounced. If the sickle cells block small blood vessels the resulting stasis will cause a further lowering of the oxygen tension and increase sickling. The blocking of such vessels will prevent blood flow to areas of the tissue which may become necrotic. Finally, the abnormally-shaped sickle cells tend to be engulfed by the reticuloendothelial cells, thus shortening the life span of the affected erythrocytes. One of the oddest consequences of the sickle-cell condition is that in some African countries it appears to offer protection against malignant malaria! This is probably because the erythrocytes infected with the malarial organism tend to stick to the walls of the blood vessels and therefore to become deoxygenated. If the host is a sickle-cell heterozygote, these deoxygenated cells will sickle and because of their changed shape will be phagocytosed. Thus there is a selective removal of the malarial organism in the heterozygotes.

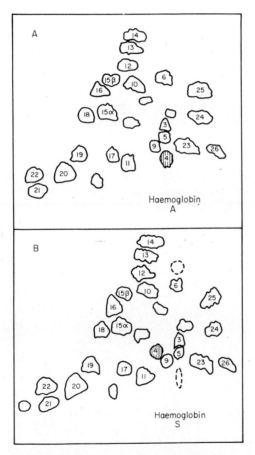

Figure 6.17. Tracings of 'fingerprints' of haemoglobins A and S. The enclosed areas represent peptide fragments of the proteins released by trypsin digestion. The only difference between the two proteins is in the peptide represented by the shaded area. From Baglioni, *Biochim. Biophys. Acta*, 1961

The biochemical differences between haemoglobin A and haemoglobin S were worked out by Ingram. As it was known that the haem group was the same in each, the difference had to be sought in the structure of the globin itself. By treatment with trypsin (see p. 18), the molecules were broken into comparatively large peptides whose amino acid composition could be more readily investigated. About 28 polypeptides were obtained, which were spread out in a characteristic pattern on paper by electrophoresis and chromatography. The pattern is called the 'fingerprint' of the haemoglobin. Figure 6.17 shows the 'fingerprints' of haemoglobin A

Hb A $\overset{+}{\text{NH}_3}$—Val—$\overset{+}{\text{His}}$—Leu—Thr—Pro—$\overset{-}{\text{Glu}}$—$\overset{-}{\text{Glu}}$—$\overset{+}{\text{Lys}}$ . . .

Hb S $\overset{+}{\text{NH}_3}$—Val—$\overset{+}{\text{His}}$—Leu—Thr—Pro—Val—$\overset{-}{\text{Glu}}$—$\overset{+}{\text{Lys}}$ . . .

Figure 6.18. Amino acid sequence at the N-terminal end of the polypeptide chain of haemoglobin. Proteolysis with trypsin splits the chain at the arrow

and haemoglobin S—the shaded areas indicate where they differ. The peptides corresponding to these shaded areas were eluted and their detailed amino acid composition studied. These analyses showed that the only difference between the two haemoglobins is the substitution of a valine for a glutamic acid unit normally found in the haemoglobin A (Figure 6.18). Thus, changing one amino acid in 280 is responsible for the different properties of the two haemoglobins and for all the clinical consequences which arise therefrom. Presumably this difference in turn is brought about by one alteration in the base sequence of the DNA.

CHAPTER 19

The biochemistry of reproductive tissues: sperm, the uterus and the mammary gland

The metabolism of spermatoza

During mammalian fertilization the male's genetic message is carried to the ovum by the spermatozoon. Mature spermatozoa neither grow nor divide and have a stable metabolic pattern. During their maturation, however, there are marked changes in their biochemical composition. The immature sperm contains RNA, which disappears almost completely during maturation because there is then no further requirement for protein synthesis. A group of enzymes concerned with the degradation of RNA (acid phosphatase, alkaline phosphatase and 5′ nucleotidase) also disappear. Glycogen is removed during maturation so that the activity of the mature sperm is largely dependent on external carbohydrate for its energy provision.

Structurally sperm are divided into three parts. The head contains the DNA (about 2·5 to 3·0 × 10^{-9} mg/cell) and a hydrolytic enzyme that enables the sperm to penetrate the ovum. The middle section may be thought of as the sperm 'motor' and is most active metabolically. It consists of a central core of fibres surrounded by mitochondria (Figure 6.19), has a high respiratory rate and provides ATP for locomotion. This ATP is used by the third section of the sperm, the tail, possessing an ATP-ase activity in its contractile fibre which behaves in the same way as the actomyosin fibres of the muscle.

In vivo the sperms live in the seminal plasma, a fluid produced by the combined secretions of several accessory glands. It contains high concentrations of substances found only in low concentration elsewhere in the body. Characteristic components of the seminal plasma are:

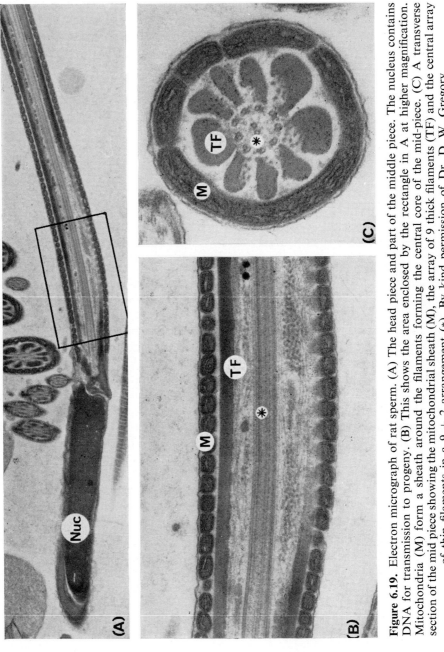

Figure 6.19. Electron micrograph of rat sperm. (A) The head piece and part of the middle piece. The nucleus contains DNA for transmission to progeny. (B) This shows the area enclosed by the rectangle in A at higher magnification. Mitochondria (M) form a sheath around the filaments forming the central core of the mid-piece. (C) A transverse section of the mid piece showing the mitochondrial sheath (M), the array of 9 thick filaments (TF) and the central array of thin filaments in a 9 + 2 arrangement (∗). By kind permission of Dr. D. W. Gregory

(a) Citric acid—derived from the secretions of the prostate gland and present in the semen of man at concentrations of 5–25 mg/ml.

(b) Acid phosphatase. The prostatic fluid is one of the richest sources of acid phosphatase in the body, the amount of the enzyme in the gland increasing about five-hundredfold when the male matures. Normally the enzyme does not pass into the blood stream but it does so in cancer of the prostate or when metastases from a prostatic carcinoma develop in bone. Therefore, measurements of the plasma acid phosphatase are useful as a diagnostic aid during the clinical treatment of prostatic carcinoma. Injections of androgens also increase the blood level of this enzyme whereas castration or estrogens cause large decreases.

(c) Prostaglandins. These are a group of complex acid substances which are potent smooth-muscle contractile agents. They are derived from essential fatty acids such as linoleic acid; a typical structure (prostaglandin E_1) is

$$CH_3-(CH_2)_4-CHOH-CH=CH-\overset{\overset{\displaystyle H}{|}}{C}-\overset{\overset{\displaystyle H}{|}}{\underset{\underset{\displaystyle HO-HC\diagdown_C\diagup C=O}{|}}{C}}(CH_2)_6-COOH$$

$$\underset{H_2}{}$$

(d) Choline, phosphoryl choline, glyceryl phosphoryl choline, presumably derived from the metabolism of the phospholipids of the sperm or the accessory organs.

(e) Spermine, secreted by the prostate gland, is a nitrogenous base present at concentrations of 3–4 mg/ml of semen. Its precise function is unknown, but it has been shown to stabilize preparations of cells, mitochondria, ribosomes, bacteriophage and some enzymes *in vitro*. Some of these effects may be due to its ability, as a polyamine, to complex with nucleic acids.

$$H_2N-(CH_2)_3-NH-(CH_2)_4-NH-(CH_2)_3-NH_2$$
spermine

(f) Fructose. Seminal fructose comes from the vesicular and epididymal secretions and reaches concentrations of about 2–4 mg/ml of semen. It is one of the most important constituents of the semen since it provides the chief metabolizable substrate available for locomotory activity. It is formed by the accessory glands, principally the seminal vesicles. The concentration of seminal fructose reflects the concentration of blood glucose and, as a consequence, is affected by insulin. The conversion of glucose to fructose in the vesicles is dependent on the availability of testosterone and may occur in two ways. Glucose may be phosphorylated to glucose-6-phosphate which is isomerized to fructose-6-phosphate from which fructose is released by a phosphatase. Alternatively glucose may be reduced by $NADPH_2$ and sorbitol dehydrogenase to sorbitol, a sugar alcohol; this can be reoxidized to fructose by an NAD-dependent enzyme (aldose reductase). It appears likely that testosterone increases the amount of both the sorbitol dehydrogenase and the aldose reductase in the vesicles.

The fructose of the seminal plasma provides the energy necessary for motility under anaerobic conditions, as, for example, after deposition in the female reproductive tract. Fructose is converted to fructose-6-phosphate by hexokinase and then utilized in the glycolytic pathway. Under aerobic conditions the lactate formed may be oxidized in the citric acid cycle of the mitochondria in the sperm; this ability to respire (using not only lactate but perhaps also the seminal citrate and fatty acids derived from the phospholipids) will be essential when the supply of fructose deposited with the sperm is exhausted (probably about 20 minutes after ejaculation). In this time, many of the sperm will have moved into the uterus, where oxygen may be somewhat more readily available. Thus the significance of the initial fructolysis may be to enable the sperm to move away from the original concentrated deposit in the genital tract where oxygen tension is relatively low.

The motility of the sperm depends on factors other than the availability of fructose. Firstly the pH optimum is about 7; if the medium is more acid motility decreases, if more alkaline it increases but only for a short time. Secondly sperms in concentrated suspension are inactive, and will become much more active on moderate dilution. Further dilution inactivates them. Sperms are viable for long periods of time if frozen to $-79°$ in 10% glycerol.

Apart from the motility of the sperms (which will affect the number that reach the ova) successful fertilization depends on the ability of the sperm to penetrate the ovum. Although the sperm head contains a hydrolytic enzyme that may function in dissolving the outer coating of the ovum, many sperms are apparently incapable of such penetration. This appears to be due to the deposition on the sperm of a carbohydrate material, possibly a mucopolysaccharide, derived from the seminal plasma. The uterine secretion contains an amylase, which is capable of removing this carbohydrate material so that the uterine secretion itself may determine whether penetration of the ovum by sperms will occur. The glucosamine liberated from the degraded carbohydrate (and also from uterine mucopolysaccharides) can be used by sperm as an energy source, which will be especially important when seminal fructose and citrate are exhausted.

Contraception

Spermicidal substances

Many substances kill spermatoza and have been used as contraceptives. They may be classified as follows:

(1) Electrolytes. Sperm are immobilized and killed in either hypertonic or hypotonic solution. Sodium chloride (5%) in a jelly has been used as a contraceptive.

(2) Enzyme inhibitors such as fluoride, iodoacetate, 2,4-dinitrophenol all kill sperm by blocking essential metabolic pathways.

(3) Substances reacting with SH groups kill sperm very effectively; phenylmercuric acid is used extensively as a contraceptive.

(4) Surface active agents (such as detergents and soaps) suppress fructolysis and motility. They probably remove the lipoprotein coat from the sperm and allow compounds like cytochrome c to diffuse out. The detergent cetyl methyl ammonium bromide (CETAB or cetavalon) at concentrations of 0·001% completely suppresses fructolysis and sperm motility.

Oral contraception

In the last 20 years the possibility of preventing conception by the oral administration of various steroid compounds has been recognized and exploited. These compounds—'oral contraceptives'—are synthetic oestrogens or progesterones which interfere with the normal ovulatory cycle of the female.

Variations in the amounts of collagen and elastin in the uterus

During pregnancy and after parturition, there is a considerable change in the weight of the uterus; one of the most interesting features of this change is that it involves a relatively rapid synthesis and destruction of the fibrous proteins collagen and elastin (see pp. 226, 229). Collagen forms about 6% of the weight of the non-gravid uterus. During pregnancy, the weight of the uterus increases about tenfold, but that of collagen only sixfold, so that, at term, the uterus has 3–4% collagen. After parturition, the weight of the uterus and its collagen content decline rapidly in parallel, falling in some four weeks to about the values present in the non-gravid uterus and continuing to decrease for the next 6–8 weeks. The pattern of changes in the amount of elastin in the uterus is similar; this protein accounts for only about 1% of the weight.

Variations in the amount of uterine cathepsin, which increases about sixfold during pregnancy to a value maintained for the first few weeks after birth, suggest that this enzyme may be concerned with the removal of uterine proteins during involution. Its inactivity before birth suggests a localization in lysosomes (p. 97), from which it may be liberated by hormonal changes or by the partial anoxia which follows the collapse of the uterine blood vessels after birth.

The metabolism of the mammary gland

The metabolic changes which occur in the mammary gland at the onset of lactation are probably larger than those in any other organ during normal development. For each volume of milk secreted, about 400 to 500 volumes of blood are circulated through the gland. When no milk is being secreted metabolism is very low but at the height of lactation each cell is producing in each second 4,000,000 to 6,000,000 molecules of carbohydrate, fat and protein. At the same time there are considerable increases in the activity of many enzymes. The enlargement of existing mitochondria and the formation of new ones at parturition is reflected in a fivefold increase in the activity of succinic dehydrogenase and cytochrome oxidase. The amounts of the enzymes of the pentose phosphate pathway, glutamic dehydrogenase, transaminases and arginase all increase to a maximum during lactation, falling rapidly again at involution. The maximum increase in protein synthesis is accompanied by a large increase in the RNA content of the gland.

Glucose degradation

Glucose utilization by the pentose phosphate pathway is particularly important in the metabolism of the mammary gland. As much as 60% of the total glucose degraded may pass through this pathway, probably to form the $NADPH_2$ required for synthetic processes. Glucose is also glycolysed in the gland and any lactate formed is oxidized to CO_2 and water.

The biosynthesis of lactose

Lactose is a disaccharide in which galactose is joined by a β-linkage to carbon 4 of glucose; it is a reducing sugar as carbon 1 of the glucose is unsubstituted. It is almost confined to the mammary gland and milk, though small amounts may appear in the urine during lactation. Glucose required for lactose synthesis is derived mainly from the blood, though it is probable that other carbon sources are utilized for gluconeogenesis in the gland itself. Glucose is converted to glucose-6-phosphate by hexokinase and then to glucose-1-phosphate by phosphoglucomutase. Glucose-

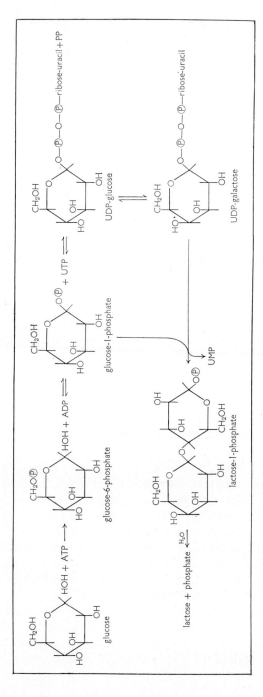

Figure 6.20. The biosynthesis of lactose

1-phosphate and uridine triphosphate form UDP-glucose, in a reaction catalysed by UDP-glucose pyrophosphorylase (the same enzyme as that involved in glycogen synthesis; see p. 105). UDP-glucose-4-epimerase converts the sugar structure from glucose to galactose, giving UDP-galactose which combines with glucose-1-phosphate to form lactose-1-phosphate and UDP. Hydrolysis of the lactose phosphate yields the free sugar (Figure 6.20).

The biosynthesis of milk protein

Casein and β-lactoglobulin make up 90% of the milk protein and, as they do not occur in the blood, must be formed in the gland itself. The source of the amino acids for this synthesis is probably the plasma amino acids, and not the plasma proteins, as the following considerations show. With the rate of blood flow through the gland (400 volumes of blood for each volume of milk secreted) both plasma proteins and plasma amino acids are present in sufficient concentration to provide the amounts of amino acids required; the concentration of plasma peptides is too low for them to function as precursors. Arteriovenous differences across the gland show a significant drop only for the free amino acids, though the magnitude of this drop cannot account for more than about 70% of the observed synthesis of milk protein. However, measurement of radioactivity from plasma proteins and the milk proteins after the addition of a labelled amino acid to the blood shows that amino acids in the milk proteins are always of higher specific activity than the corresponding compounds in the plasma proteins which, therefore, could not be functioning as precursors. From these experiments it can be concluded that 70–90% of the milk proteins is formed from the amino acids of the blood.

The biosynthesis of milk fat

Milk fat (which has a characteristic composition for each species of mammal) comes from two quite separate sources. Part is synthesized in the gland itself, part is transferred directly from the blood. The quantities derived from each source are somewhat variable and depend on the state of nutrition of the animal. Isotope studies have shown that acetate can be used to synthesize fatty acids in the gland; and the substantial arteriovenous differences detected for β-hydroxybutyrate make it probable that C_2 units may also be derived from this compound.

Dietary lipids also make their appearance in the milk. Measurement of arteriovenous differences across the gland show that the chylomicron fraction and the very low density lipoproteins contribute to the milk lipids; free fatty acids of the blood are not involved. During lactation there is a very large increase in the activity of clearing factor lipase, and there is little doubt the triglycerides presented to the gland are first hydrolysed and then resynthesized before entering the milk. Although isotope studies showed that the glycerol of the milk fat came mainly from blood glucose, there is no increase in plasma glycerol in the blood leaving the gland. Therefore the glycerol liberated by the clearing factor lipase is probably oxidized within the gland.

SECTION 7

Actions of Hormones on Cells

When released into the circulation in response to some change in the environment of the cells in which they are synthesized, hormones are able to induce alterations in the metabolism of selected target tissues.

Although the pathways for the biosynthesis of many hormones are known the mechanism of action of hormones on their target cells is not completely understood; the reason for this lies in the highly integrated nature of cell metabolism. All the components of a living cell are in a state of dynamic equilibrium with one another so that a change in the activity or concentration of one component will result in alterations of differing magnitudes in the activities or concentrations of other components. Therefore, since hormones alter the metabolism of their target tissues by reacting with a limited number of cell components, it is clear that other components will be affected indirectly and to varying extents. A consequence of this dynamic balance of cell metabolism is that it is difficult to distinguish the primary change induced by the hormone from the secondary, tertiary and quaternary changes that are consequent upon it.

Many hormones produce physiological responses very rapidly after their administration to whole animals or to isolated organs. For example, noradrenaline and vasopressin cause the blood pressure to rise almost as soon as they are injected intravenously, and oxytocin administered to an isolated uterus rapidly induces a contraction. The concentration of blood sugar begins to fall very shortly after insulin is administered, whilst adrenaline and glucagon cause the rapid mobilization of glucose from glycogen. Other hormones control processes which cause much slower physiological responses. Responses of this type are brought about by the sex hormones that control the onset of puberty and by the growth hormone that exercises control over development. The release of slow-acting hormones depends, to a considerable extent, upon their rate of synthesis, which normally is adjusted to meet the current demand. The demand for fast-acting hormones is met from preexisting stores that are replenished during periods of quiescence. In contrast to the slow-acting hormones which cause a profound metabolic reorganization of their target cells, the fast-acting hormones initiate responses that pass away rapidly and leave the target cells essentially unchanged.

The division of hormones into two classes, fast- and slow-acting, may be an oversimplification; indeed there is good evidence that insulin and perhaps thyroxine and calcitonin have both types of action. It is, however, useful to distinguish between fast and slow responses since they seem to derive from basically different mechanisms of hormone action. The former follow from the activation of preexisting enzymes and the latter are dependent upon the synthesis of new enzymes.

Hormonal regulation of metabolism presupposes that hormonal action can be terminated as well as initiated; thus metabolic pathways exist that can convert hormones into compounds devoid of, or having much reduced physiological activities.

CHAPTER 20

The catecholamines and cyclic 3',5'-AMP

The catecholamines, adrenaline and noradrenaline, are the two fast-acting hormones whose modes of action are understood best. These two compounds are synthesized from tyrosine in the adrenal medulla and in the sympathetic and central nervous system by the sequence of reactions shown in Figure 7.1. Adrenaline and noradrenaline are formed in different cells in the adrenal medulla; presumably the methylating enzyme is absent from those cells that accumulate noradrenaline. Within the cells, the amines are stored in subcellular granules. Chromaffin granules containing adrenaline and noradrenaline may be separated from each other and from mitochondria by density gradient centrifuging of adrenal homogenates (Figure 4.13). Besides catecholamines, the chromaffin granules of the adrenal medulla contain large quantities of both ATP and a characteristic protein. Within the granules these three components probably form a non-diffusible complex. When the cells of the adrenal medulla are stimulated by acetylcholine (released from the endings of the splanchnic nerves), their cell membranes are depolarized and Ca^{2+} enters. These divalent cations probably permit the membranes of the granules to fuse with the cell membrane so that the contents of the granules can be released into the extracellular space by reversed pinocytosis. All fast-acting hormones appear to be stored in subcellular particles and all are probably secreted by a mechanism similar to that proposed for the catecholamines. For example, oxytocin and vasopressin, formed in the cell bodies of the supra-optic and paraventricular nuclei, migrate down the axons in granules which accumulate in the dilated nerve endings that form the neurohypo-physis. It is probable that these two hormones are also formed in separate cells; certainly the supraoptic nucleus has a higher ratio of oxytocin to vasopressin than the paraventricular nucleus. Impulses passing down the fibres depolarize the nerve endings and allow Ca^{2+} to enter which then initiate the secretory response.

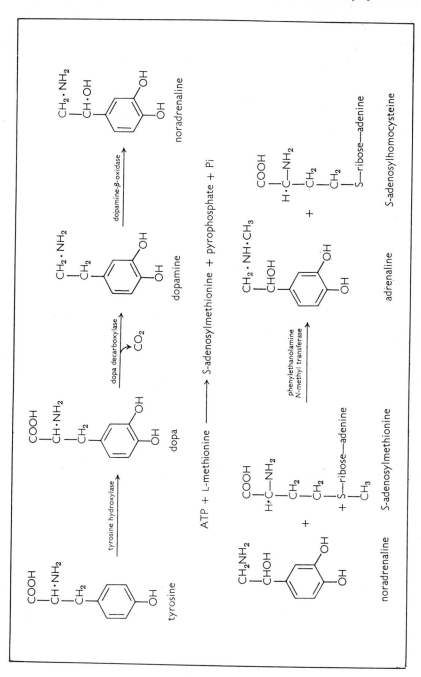

Figure 7.1. Reactions involved in the biosynthesis of catecholamines

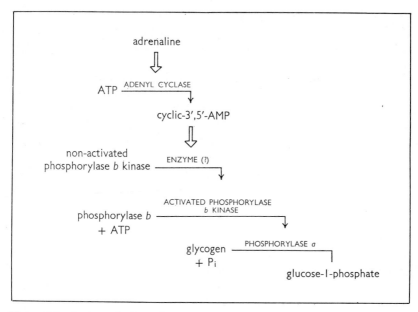

Figure 7.2. Action of adrenaline on glycogen breakdown in muscle. Activated enzymes printed in capitals; ⇩ stimulates; ↓ converted to.

Metabolic effects

The injection of adrenaline is followed by the breakdown of glycogen in liver and muscles (see pp. 111, 319) and by a rise in the level of blood glucose. Glycogen is degraded to glucose-1-phosphate by phosphorylase which exists in two forms termed *a* and *b* (this is true for both liver and muscle phosphorylase despite their being different enzymes). Phosphorylase *a* is much more active than the *b* form from which it is derived by phosphorylation with ATP. This activating phosphorylation, catalysed by phosphorylase kinase, is facilitated by cyclic 3′,5′-AMP which is formed from ATP by adenyl cyclase (Figure 7.2).

cyclic 3′,5′—AMP

The investigations of Sutherland and his coworkers have shown that adenyl cyclase is located in the cell membrane and that it is stimulated by adrenaline. Adenyl cyclase may therefore be regarded as a physiological receptor for catecholamines.

Following the discovery of the role played by adrenaline in the activation of phosphorylase, it was widely suggested that all the physiological responses elicited by adrenaline and noradrenaline were consequences of phosphorylase activation. It is now known that this view cannot be correct. For example without activating phosphorylase and in the total absence of glycogen both adrenaline and cyclic 3',5'-AMP cause the relaxation of the smooth muscle taenia coli and the cessation of its spontaneous electrical activity. It is now apparent that cyclic 3',5'-AMP acts as a cofactor for several enzymes besides phosphorylase *b* kinase and that the variety of physiological responses induced by adrenaline is a result of differences in the levels of those enzymes sensitive to cyclic 3',5'-AMP in the different target tissues. Thus adrenaline stimulates the breakdown of triglycerides in adipose tissues because a lipase sensitive to cyclic 3',5'-AMP is present. In addition to activating phosphorylase *b* kinase, cyclic 3',5'-AMP produced in response to adrenaline causes the conversion of the more active form of glycogen synthetase into the less active form. Thus adrenaline simultaneously stimulates glycogen breakdown and inhibits glycogen synthesis. These synergistic operations prevent the activities of the two enzymes from combining to form a wasteful UTP-ase (see p. 312).

Fast-acting hormones other than the catecholamines stimulate the synthesis of cyclic 3',5'-AMP by adenyl cyclase (Table 7.1), their specificity is

Table 7.1. Tissues in which cyclic 3',5'-AMP formation is stimulated
by hormones

Tissue	Hormone	Physiological response
Liver	Catecholamines Glucagon	Glucose release
Adrenal cortex	ACTH (adrenocorticotrophic hormone	Steroidogenesis
Kidney Frog skin Toad bladder	Vasopressin	Sodium uptake and water reabsorption
Corpus luteum	LH (luteinizing hormone)	Steroidogenesis
Thyroid	TSH (thyrotrophic hormone)	Thyroxine release; I_2 uptake
Adipose tissue	Catecholamines Glucagon ACTH (adrenocorticotrophic hormone) Vasopressin	Free fatty acid release from white adipose tissue. Heat production by brown adipose tissue (see p. 122)
Gastric mucosa	Histamine	HCl secretion
Parotid salivary gland	Adrenaline	Amylase secretion

presumably conferred by the specificity of the adenyl cyclases present in the different tissues. The relationships between these fast-acting hormones, adenyl cyclase and cyclic 3',5'-AMP is summarized in Figure 7.3.

It is by no means true that all rapid responses induced by hormones are mediated via cyclic 3',5'-AMP. Neither the entry of glucose into muscles and adipose tissue which is stimulated by insulin nor the depolarization of nerves and muscles by acetylcholine appears to involve cyclic 3',5'-AMP. The possibility that oxytocin acts via cyclic 3',5'-AMP has not been explored but in view of its structural similarity to vasopressin and of the common evolutionary origin of these two hormones it would seem to be a reasonable supposition. Although there is no evidence for or against the

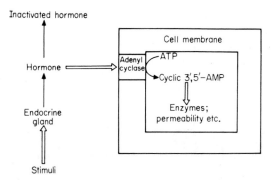

Figure 7.3. Relationship between some fast-acting hormones and cyclic 3',5'-AMP

view that the luteinizing hormone (LH) and the follicle stimulating hormone (FSH) stimulate cyclic 3',5'-AMP formation in the testes and ovaries respectively, such a stimulation might be expected since LH stimulates steroidogenesis in the corpus lutem via cyclic 3',5'-AMP formation.

Inactivation

The most important process involved in terminating the action of catecholamines is probably their restorage in the nerve endings from which they were released. There is now good evidence that the same molecule of noradrenaline may be released and restored several times by sympathetic nerve endings. Circulating catecholamines are also inactivated by catechol-*O*-methyl transferase (COMT) which methylates the *O*-hydroxy group on the benzene ring. Within the cells in which they are produced the catecholamines are destroyed by monoamine oxidase (MAO) if they fail to

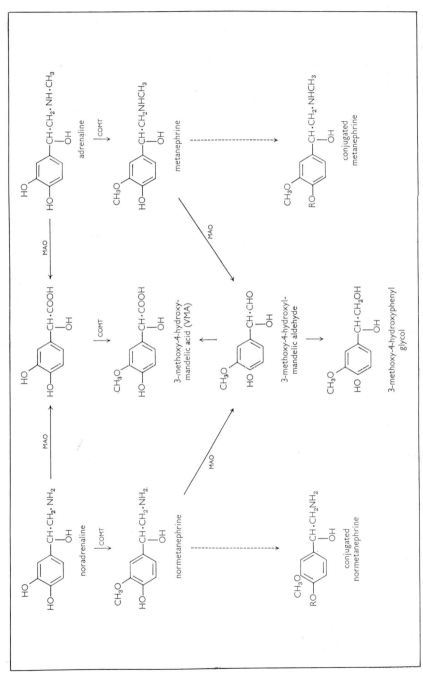

Figure 7.4. Metabolism of catecholamines by monoamine oxidase (MAO), catechol-*O*-methyl transferase (COMT) and conjugation

gain access to the storage granules. Figure 7.4 shows the products formed by the combined action of COMT and MAO. In cases of phaechromo-cytoma (tumour of the adrenal medulla) the content of 3-methoxy-4-hydroxymandelic acid (VMA) in the urine rises markedly and can be used for diagnostic purposes.

CHAPTER 21

Steroids

Biosynthesis of cholesterol

Before considering the actions of the steroid hormones produced by the adrenal cortex, gonads and placenta, it is convenient to discuss the biochemistry of cholesterol, their common precursor.

All the carbon atoms of cholesterol

Source of carbon atoms in cholesterol

○ derived from CH$_3$ group of acetate
● derived from · COOH group of acetate

are derived from acetate by the following series of reactions (Figure 7.5). Acetoacetyl-CoA reacts with acetyl-CoA to form β-hydroxy-β-methyl-glutaryl-CoA (HMGCoA). This compound is reduced to mevalonic acid and then converted, via three phosphorylations and a decarboxylation, into Δ^3-isopentenyl pyrophosphate. Three of these pyrophosphorylated isoprenoid units condense, head to tail, to form farnesyl pyrophosphate. Two molecules of this then condense, tail to tail, to give squalene. Squalene is converted to lanosterol, the first steroid precursor of cholesterol, via a complicated ring closure, and is subsequently transformed into cholesterol.

Cholesterol and atherosclerosis

Besides being synthesized in the liver and appropriate endocrine organs, cholesterol also forms part of the diet, both as the free alcohol and as the

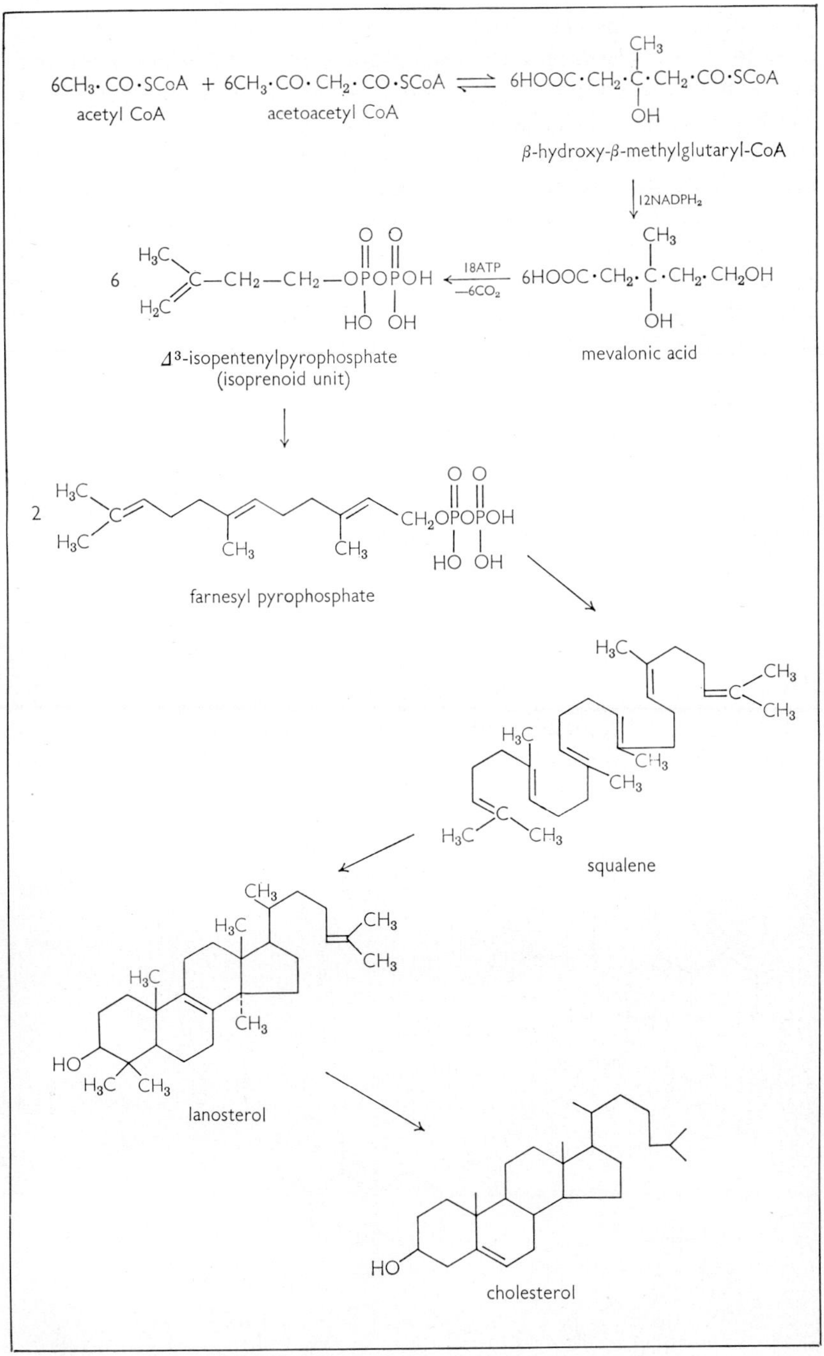

Figure 7.5. Biosynthesis of cholesterol

esters of fatty acids. The disease atherosclerosis is characterized by the deposition of cholesterol in the arterial walls and it has been widely held that a high dietary intake of cholesterol can increase this deposition. Furthermore there is evidence to suggest that such deposition can be reduced if the diet contains an adequate supply of polyunsaturated fatty acids. Whilst cholesterol deposition is clearly of great importance in the development of atheromatous lesions, the factors leading to its occurrence are poorly understood and are almost certainly more complex than the existence of a dietary excess of cholesterol coupled with a deficiency of essential fatty acids. There seems to be no absolute requirement for dietary cholesterol and the level of plasma cholesterol in many people is unaltered by their dietary intake. This is probably because the ingestion of large quantities of cholesterol leads to the formation of a cholesterol lipoprotein complex that depresses the rate of endogenous synthesis by inhibiting the reduction of HMGCoA to mevalonic acid by a reductase located in the microsomal membranes. This feedback mechanism is absent in some cases of human hepatoma. It appears that in most instances a high level of plasma cholesterol is a consequence of an innate high rate of synthesis rather than of an excessively large intake.

Bile acids

The cholesterol content of bile is reasonably constant whilst its content of bile acids such as cholic and deoxycholic acids formed by the oxidation

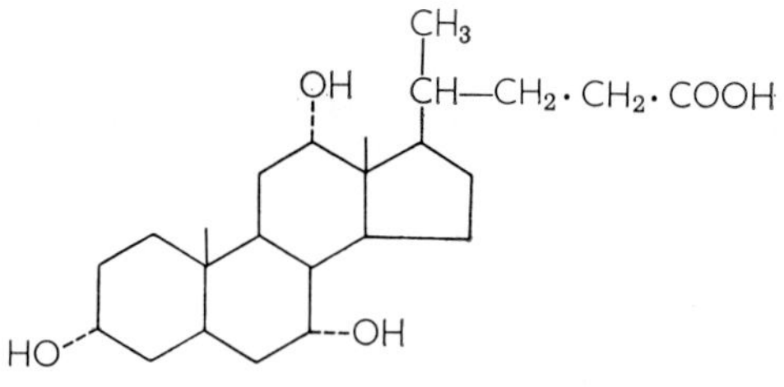

cholic acid

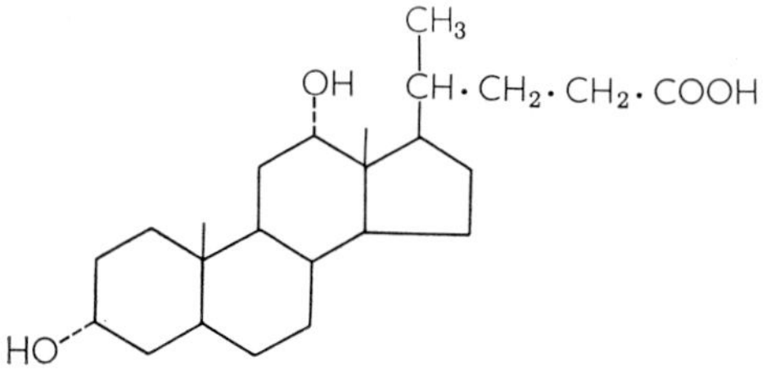

deoxycholic acid

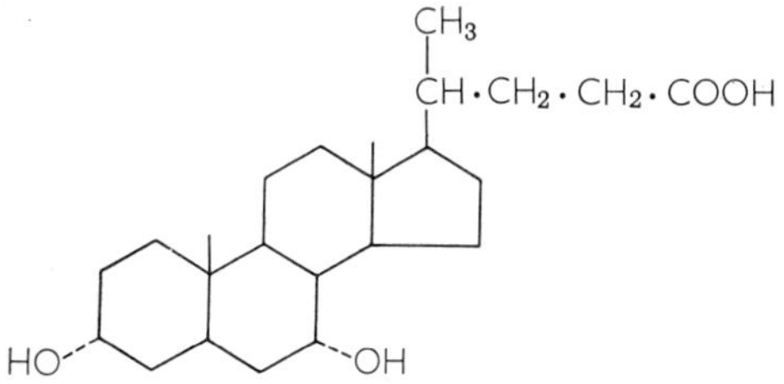

chenodeoxycholic acid

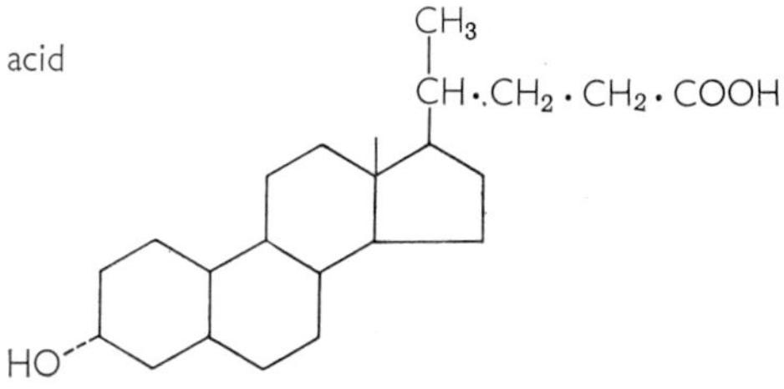

lithocholic acid

of cholesterol, is more variable and reflects the dietary intake of cholesterol. The bile acids are conjugated with taurine and glycine to form the anions of bile salts such as taurocholate and glycocholate. Cholesterol is soluble in hepatic bile because it is able to form water-soluble complexes with the bile acids. In the gall bladder, water and bile salts are reabsorbed so that the concentration of cholesterol in the stored bile increases. If this concentration proceeds too far, cholesterol crystallizes out of solution and can give rise to gall stones.

Synthesis of steroid hormones

The reactions leading from cholesterol to the various steroid hormones are many and complex (see Figure 7.6) and will not be discussed in detail. Suffice it to say that many of the reactions involved are hydroxylations requiring oxygen and $NADPH_2$. This coenzyme is supplied mainly by the two dehydrogenation reactions of the pentose phosphate pathway which is particularly active in all the organs synthesizing steroid hormones.

The rates of synthesis of most of the steroid hormones are controlled by specific trophic hormones released from the pituitary; these are adrenocorticotrophic hormone (ACTH) for the glucocorticoids of the adrenal cortex, follicle stimulating hormone (FSH) for oestrogens, and luteinizing hormone (LH) for both testosterone in the testes and progesterone in the corpus luteum and placenta. The rate of aldosterone formation in the zona glomerulosa of the adrenal cortex is regulated, at least in part, by angiotensin II. Angiotensin II is a peptide liberated from the plasma

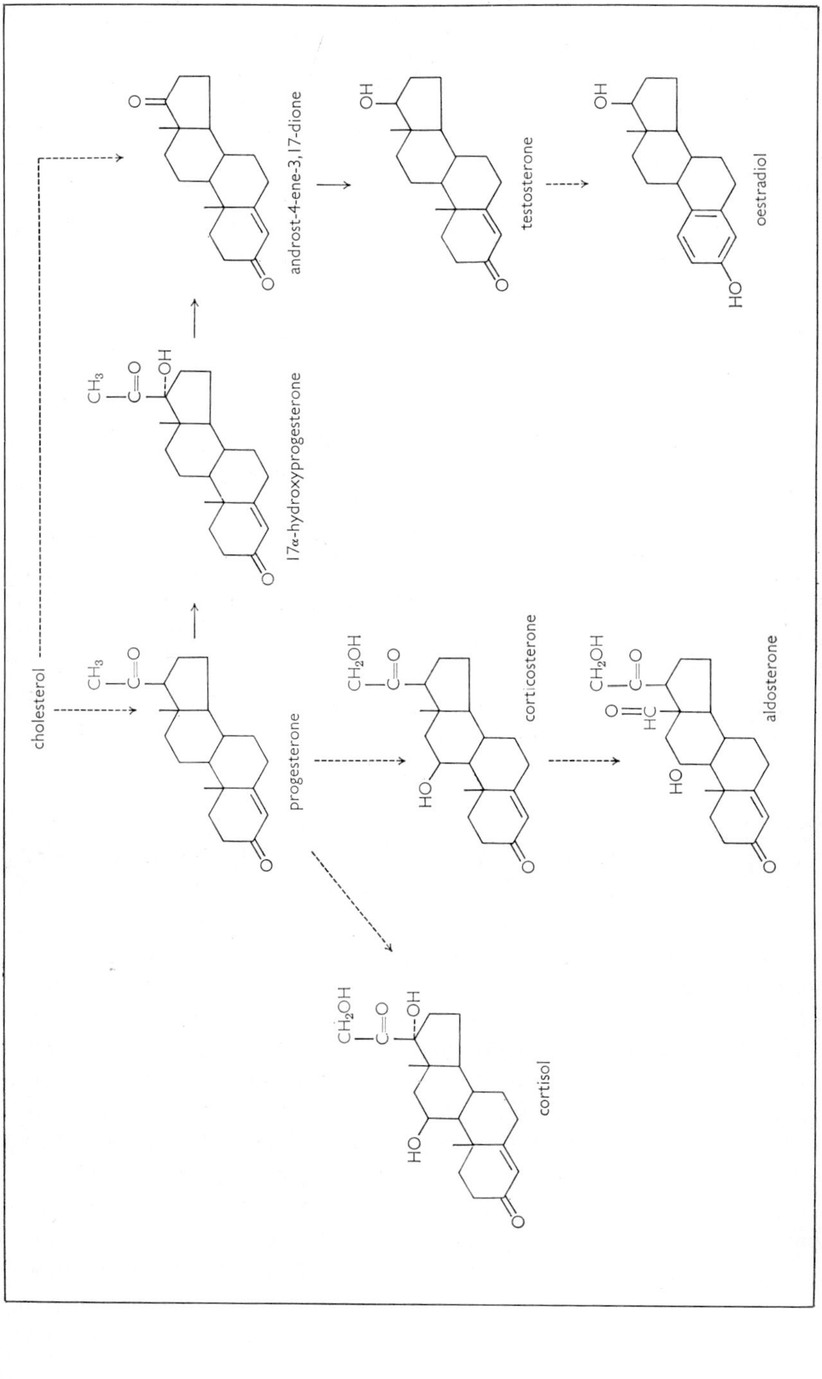

Figure 7.6. Biosynthetic relationships between cholesterol and steroid hormones

protein angiotensinogen, by renin which is secreted by the juxta glomerula cells of the kidney when the blood pressure in the renal artery falls.

Glucocorticoids

The glucocorticoids formed in the zona fasiculata and zona reticularis of the adrenal cortex are concerned with adjusting the metabolism to withstand stress and with gluconeogenesis in particular. The two most important glucocorticoids are cortisol and corticosterone (Figure 7.7). The injection of cortisol induces changes in many physiological parameters of which the most important are:

(1) An increase in the level of blood glucose.

(2) A marked alteration in the metabolic pattern of liver, such that gluconeogenesis is stimulated whilst carbohydrate oxidation is slowed down.

(3) An increase in protein catabolism in peripheral tissues with the result that both the mass and number of cells in the thymus and skeletal muscles are reduced. These involuting tissues provide a source of amino acids which can contribute to the amino acid pool of the liver.

Deamination of these amino acids in the liver causes an increase in the rate of urea synthesis and provides carbon skeletons which can be oxidized to provide energy or (in the case of those derived from glucogenic amino acids) can be transformed into glucose and glycogen. In addition to providing the liver with substrates drawn from involuting tissues, treatment with glucocorticoids leads to changes in the enzyme pattern of the liver such that gluconeogenesis is stimulated whilst carbohydrate oxidation is slowed down. Thus after giving cortisol the rates of RNA and protein synthesis in the liver begin to rise and after about 30 minutes marked increases in the activities of tyrosine-α-oxoglutarate transaminase, tryptophan pyrrolase (which degrades tryptophan) and glycogen synthetase can be measured. Somewhat later, although the exact time depends upon the dosage and glucocorticoid used, the activities of glucose-6-phosphatase, fructose-1,6-diphosphatase, pyruvate carboxylase, phosphoenolpyruvate carboxykinase and alanine transaminase begin to rise. All of these enzymes are involved in the conversion of glucogenic compounds into glucose (see Chapter 8), although the role of tyrosine-α-oxoglutarate transaminase and tryptophan pyrrolase is obscure. These increased enzyme activities are all the result of *de novo* protein synthesis and do not occur in the presence of actinomycin D which prevents the DNA-dependent synthesis of messenger RNA (see p. 247). At present, we can only speculate about the relationships between these various changes. The early increases in enzyme activities probably result from a direct action of the glucocorticoids on protein synthesis; the later changes may be caused by alterations in metabolism that are consequent upon the early changes. In any event the glucocorticoids are slow-acting hormones that modify the enzymic composition of their target tissues.

Aldosterone

Aldosterone (Figure 7.7) is secreted by the zona glomerulosa of the adrenal cortex and causes the cells bordering the distal tubules of the kidney to reabsorb sodium at a faster rate from the modified ultrafiltrate of plasma present in the lumen. This results in the retention of sodium which is accompanied by a retention of water, especially in the extra-cellular compartments of the body. Hence aldosterone has antidiuretic properties whilst aldosterone antagonists such as aldactone are useful as diuretic agents.

aldactone or spironolactone

Besides stimulating sodium reabsorption, aldosterone also stimulates potassium excretion although this effect is not as marked as that on sodium reabsorption.

Experiments on sodium transport by toad bladder indicate that there is a lag period of about 90 minutes following the administration of aldoste-rone before the rate of sodium transport begins to rise and that the rise can be inhibited by actinomycin D. Hence aldosterone is another slow-acting hormone that exerts its effects by stimulating protein synthesis. This may be contrasted with the rapid rise in sodium reabsorption that follows the administration of vasopressin to the same preparation.

The rate of aldosterone synthesis and of its release is controlled by angiotensin II which is formed when the blood pressure in the renal artery falls (see p. 289). By increasing the amount of extracellular water, aldosterone causes the blood volume to rise with a concomitant improve-ment in the blood pressure.

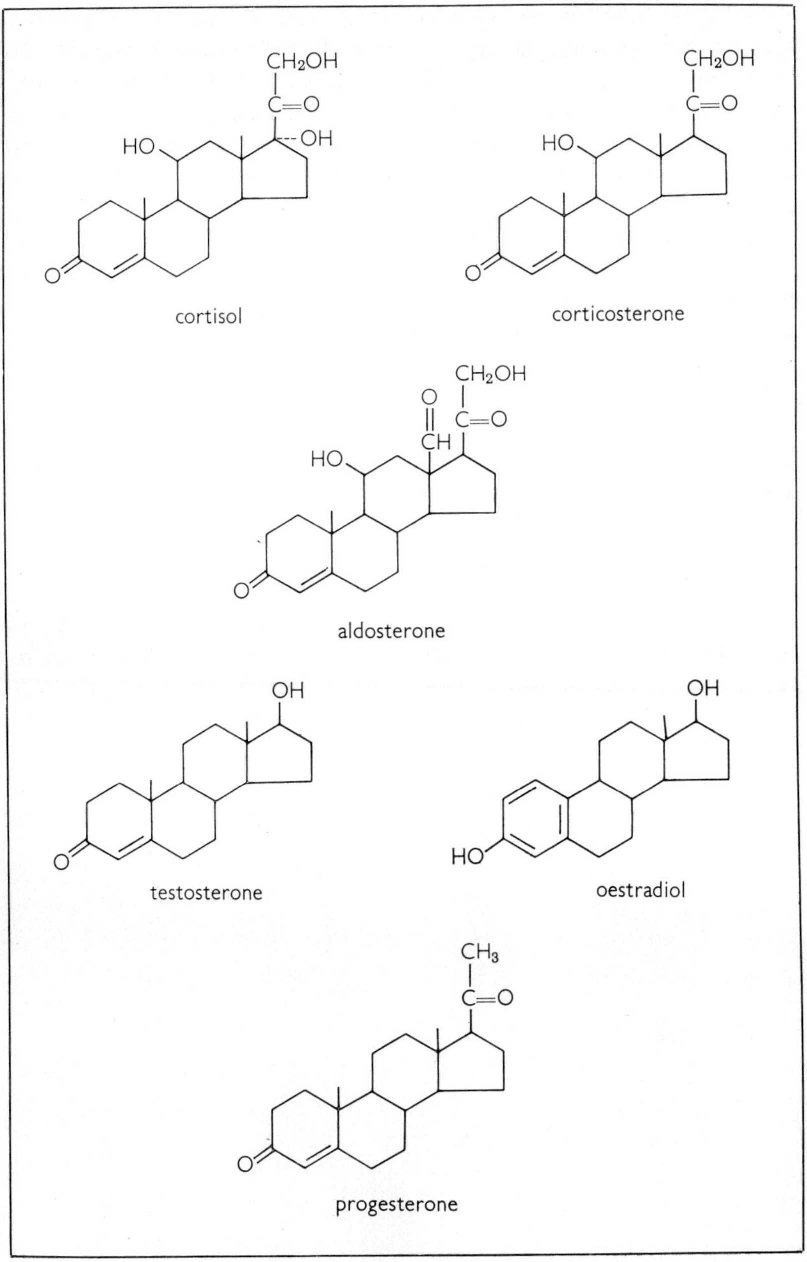

Figure 7.7.

Testosterone, oestradiol and progesterone

These three hormones (Figure 7.7) exert their physiological actions, such as the development of sexual characteristics, preparation of the mammary glands for lactation and the proliferation of the endometrium, by inducing the synthesis of proteins in selected target tissues. For example, testosterone administration increases the production of acid phosphatase by the prostate gland. All the physiological actions of these hormones can be inhibited by actinomycin D and puromycin. Interactions of oestradiol with purified enzymes such as $NADH_2$–NADP transhydrogenase and glutamic dehydrogenase have been described but their physiological significance is obscure.

Summary

In conclusion it is suggested that the steroid hormones alter the enzymic composition of their target tissues by altering the rate of synthesis of particular enzymes.

Inactivation of the steroid hormones

Steroid hormones are inactivated in the liver by reduction and by conjugation, especially with glucuronic acid, and to some extent with glycine and sulphate. The conjugated steroids, in contrast to the hormones, are not well bound by plasma proteins and, in humans, pass into the urine with ease. The conjugated steroids also enter the bile and are voided with the faeces or reabsorbed.

CHAPTER 22

Thyroid hormones

Synthesis

Thyroglobulin is the main component of the colloid that is secreted into the lumen of the follicles by the surrounding cells of the thyroid. In addition to the amino acids commonly found in proteins, thyroglobulin contains a number of iodinated amino acids that exhibit hormonal activity when released by proteolysis. The most potent of these are thyroxine (T_4) and 3,5,5′-triiodothyronine (T_3).

Thyroxine
3,5,3′,5′-tetraiodothyronine (T_4)

3,5,5′-triiodothyronine (T_3)

In the gland the rate of release of thyroid hormones from thyroglobulin by proteolysis and hence of their entry into the circulation is controlled by the thyroid stimulating hormone (TSH) from the pituitary. TSH also regulates the uptake of iodide by the thyroid which amounts to approximately 50 μg per day. Iodide peroxidase converts iodide into an active species of iodine, possibly the iodinium ion (I^+), that is able to iodinate hormonal precursors, such as tyrosine, present in thyroglobulin as amino acid residues. The details of the reactions involved in the formation of thyroxine and T_3 from tyrosine and iodide are unknown although the general outline of the pathways involved is clear (Figure 7.8). Inhibition of iodide peroxidase by thiocarbamides such as thiourea and thiouracil (which have found thiourea

thiouracil

clinical application in the treatment of hyperthyroidism) depresses the rate of synthesis of thyroid hormones.

Thyroxine accounts for most of the organic iodine released by the thyroid with T_3 making up the remainder, possibly up to 20%. In the plasma thyroxine combines with two types of carrier protein, one an α-globulin and the other, of less quantitative importance, an albumin. The greater biological potency of T_3 compared with thyroxine may be a consequence of the former not being bound by plasma protein.

Metabolic effects

Hyperthyroid individuals are characterized by a metabolic rate that may be 50% higher than normal; this in turn causes a marked loss of weight. Other symptoms of hyperthyroidism are tachycardia, high blood pressure, hyperglycaemia and a negative nitrogen balance. In hypothyroidism the reverse obtains; the metabolic rate is depressed and body weight increases. Hypothyroidism at birth develops into cretinism unless thyroxine replacement therapy is given.

Thyroid hormones have been found to affect many biochemical parameters both *in vivo* and *in vitro*, yet, until recently, an understanding of their mode of action had failed to emerge for several reasons. Firstly, many of the effects had been observed only after the administration of excessively large quantities of the hormones to the test system. Secondly, little attention had been given to the time sequence of the various changes that could be observed following the injection of the hormones into thyroidectomized animals. It would appear that the first change that can be observed following the injection of physiological doses of thyroid hormones (20 µg T_3/100 g) to thyroidectomized animals is an increase in the activity of DNA-dependent RNA polymerase in the nucleus. This is followed by an increased incorporation of amino acids into mitochondrial and microsomal proteins (Figure 7.9). Subsequently the basal metabolic rate (BMR) rises in parallel with the activity of cytochrome oxidase. The rise in BMR is not accompanied by an uncoupling of oxidative phosphorylation so that the P:O ratio remains around 2·5. If high doses of thyroid hormones are given (1700 µg T_3/100 g), the BMR increases after a lag period of only 2 hours compared with 30 hours under physiological conditions and the P:O ratio is reduced to 0·7. This agrees with the uncoupling of oxidative phosphorylation that is observed when mitochondria are incubated *in vitro* with relatively high concentrations of thyroxine. Following physiological doses of T_3, the mitochondria of skeletal muscle are found to be enlarged, more numerous and to contain a more dense array of cristae than normal. This is probably the morphological expression of the

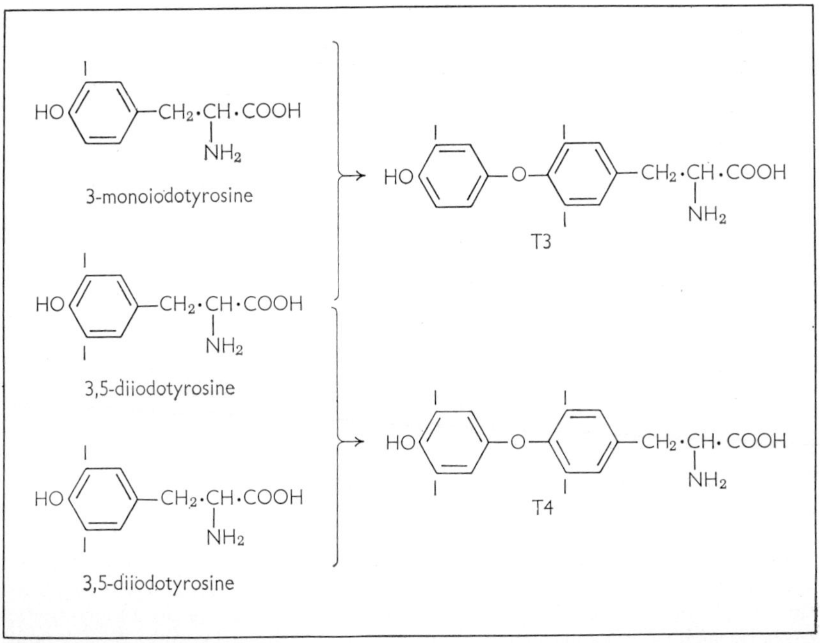

Figure 7.8. Possible pathways for the biosynthesis of thyroid hormones. The reactions are thought to involve amino acid residues present in thyroglobulin

increased incorporation of amino acids into mitochondria and of the increased BMR. Recently evidence has been obtained that thyroxine and some other slow-acting hormones stimulate the formation in the nucleus of both messenger RNA and ribosomal RNA (DNA acts as a template in the synthesis of both these species of RNA) and this leads to an increase in the number of polysomes present in the cytoplasm. The new polysomes (see p. 248) are tightly bound to the microsomal membranes and are more active in protein synthesis than the older, monomeric ribosomes which occur free in the cytoplasm. The increase in membrane-bound polysomes

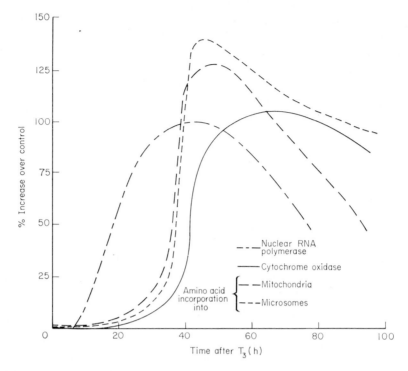

Figure 7.9. Idealized version of the time-course response of some activities in nuclei, mitochondria and microsomes from livers of thyroidectomized rats after a single injection of 20 μg triiodothyronine (T_3)/100 g body weight. The main features are that mitochondrial respiration (here illustrated only by cytochrome oxidase activity) reached a peak value after amino acid incorporation into protein by microsomes and mitochondria; that the protein synthetic capacity of both mitochondria and microsomes increased simultaneously and after a long lag period; that the DNA dependent RNA polymerase in nuclei showed a response several hours before a stimulation was observed in the cytoplasmic protein synthesis and was well within the latent period of BMR stimulation. From J. R. Tata in *Actions of Hormones on Molecular Processes*, Wiley, New York, 1964

is accompanied by an increase in phospholipid incorporation into the microsomal fraction of the cell and to a proliferation of the endoplasmic reticulum.

Inactivation

The thyroid hormones are removed rapidly from the circulation by the liver which converts them to their less active pyruvic acid derivatives by transamination. The hormones and their pyruvic acid analogues can also be deiodinated by a dehalogenase present in liver and skeletal muscle.

CHAPTER 23

Insulin

In addition to lowering the concentration of glucose in the blood, insulin (Figure 1.10) stimulates fat deposition in adipose tissue, glycogen formation in liver and protein synthesis in several tissues; it also reduces the rate of free fatty acid release from adipose tissue.

Effect of insulin on glucose uptake

The uptake of glucose by muscles, adipose tissue and lactating mammary gland is stimulated by insulin. In contrast, the uptake of glucose by liver, brain and non-lactating mammary gland is not affected by insulin.

The glucose concentration within cells other than those of the liver and possibly kidney is low. Thus the movement of glucose into muscle, adipose tissue and brain cells is a spontaneous, downhill process which is restricted only by the poor permeability of the cell membrane; it does not take place against a concentration gradient, hence it does not require an input of energy. It is now generally believed that one of the primary actions of insulin is to increase the permeability of cell membranes so that glucose can move down its concentration gradient more rapidly. Liver cell membranes are freely permeable to glucose with the result that the concentration of glucose inside the parenchyma cells approximates to that in the blood; thus in this instance there is no force causing a net movement of glucose across the membrane in either direction.

It has been suggested that glucose enters cells by combining with some component in the cell membrane which then diffuses across the membrane and liberates the glucose at the internal surface, i.e. glucose enters the cell by carrier-mediated diffusion. Evidence supporting this view includes the demonstration that the rate of uptake of glucose is independent of the external glucose concentration provided that the latter exceeds a certain value; i.e. the uptake mechanism can be saturated in the same way that an enzyme can be saturated by its substrate (see p. 29). Furthermore glucose uptake can be inhibited competitively by some other hexoses and pentoses and finally the mechanism for sugar transport exhibits some

299

degree of specificity; for example glucose but not sorbitol can enter muscle cells. As all these properties are similar to those possessed by enzymes, it is argued that glucose entry must be mediated by an enzyme-like carrier. However, if the diameters of the pores in a membrane approach those of diffusing molecules, the system may show kinetic properties similar to those of a carrier mechanism.

Insulin can be shown to alter membrane permeability by using sugars such as 3-methyl glucose and arabinose which are not metabolized and which therefore accumulate within the cells when their entry is facilitated by insulin.

The way in which insulin promotes the entry of sugars is still unknown. It has been suggested by Randle that, in the absence of insulin, glucose is prevented from diffusing down its concentration grade because a carrier exists in a phosphorylated, inactive form. In the presence of insulin it is imagined that the carrier can no longer be phosphorylated by ATP or some similar compound and is hence able to transport sugars across the membrane. This view is based on the observation that glucose uptake is stimulated by anoxia and dinitrophenol (DNP), both of which reduce the availability of ATP. The control of diffusion through fine pores could also be regulated by phosphorylation and dephosphorylation reactions.

There is also evidence that SH groups on the cell surface react with the disulphide bonds of insulin since the number of titratable SH groups on the membrane falls in the presence of insulin. Furthermore insulin is not bound by isolated diaphragm if the tissue is pretreated with *N*-ethylmaleimide which reacts with SH groups.

The facilitating action of insulin upon the rate of glucose uptake is not inhibited by actinomycin D and may be regarded as a fast response.

Insulin coma

The amount of glucose used by tissues is roughly proportional to their weight. Thus, since the total weight of muscle in a 70 kg man is about 35 kg, whilst the brain and the liver weigh 1·4 kg and 1·6 kg respectively, it follows that muscle will use about 90% of the glucose available to those three tissues. The total quantity of glucose in the blood is 30 m moles and the consumption of glucose by resting muscle in the absence of insulin is about 15 m mole/kg/h. Therefore the 35 kg of muscle will consume the blood's supply of glucose in 3·5 minutes. Since a steady state exists, the rate of glucose utilization by the muscle must be equal to the rate at which glucose enters the blood from other sources, notably the liver. The three-to fourfold increase in the permeability of muscle cell membranes towards glucose that is brought about by insulin means that the muscles can use the blood's supply of glucose in about 1 minute. If the production of glucose is limited, then the blood glucose level must fall until the concentrations of glucose inside and outside the muscle reach values that limit glucose transport into the muscle to the amount that can be produced and passed into the blood. That is, the blood glucose level must fall as the permeability increases. This lowering of the level of blood glucose by the muscles will bring about a fall in the rate of brain metabolism that will culminate in insulin coma and death.

Inhibition of fatty acid release from adipose tissue by insulin

The way in which insulin prevents free fatty acid release from adipose tissue by allowing glucose to enter the cells to provide a supply of L-α-glycerophosphate for triglyceride resynthesis has been discussed in Chapter 9.

Effect of insulin on protein synthesis

For many years insulin has been known to stimulate the synthesis of proteins in liver, adipose tissue, diaphragm, heart and mammary gland. At first it was thought that the action on protein synthesis was secondary to those on carbohydrate metabolism. However, recently it has been found that the stimulation of protein synthesis by insulin can occur in the total absence of glucose.

The administration of insulin to rats made diabetic by treatment with alloxan causes the rate-limiting enzymes of glycolysis (phosphofructokinase and pyruvate kinase) and of glycogenesis (glucokinase, glycogen synthetase) to be synthesized in increased amounts in the liver. Glucokinase catalyses the same reaction as hexokinase but has a much higher K_m (about 15 mM) and is consequently of importance in removing glucose from the circulation when its concentration rises above resting levels, for example, after meals rich in carbohydrates.

In addition to increasing the rate at which glycogen synthetase is formed, insulin also converts the relatively inactive, phosphorylated form of the enzyme into the more active, non-phosphorylated form. This activation by dephosphorylation recalls Randle's views on the action of insulin on the glucose transport system (see p. 300). Besides inducing key enzymes involved in the utilization of glucose, insulin inhibits the synthesis of glucose-6-phosphatase, fructose-1,6-diphosphatase, pyruvate carboxylase and phosphoenolpyruvate carboxykinase. These are the four rate-limiting enzymes involved in the formation of glucose from non-carbohydrate sources.

In adipose tissue insulin stimulates lipogenesis both by allowing glucose to enter the cells to provide L-α-glycerophosphate (see p. 121) and acetyl CoA, and also by inducing the synthesis of the key enzymes of fatty acid synthesis, namely: fatty acid synthetase, acetyl CoA carboxylase and the citrate cleavage enzyme.

Summary

Insulin has both fast and slow actions: the former include the stimulation of glucose uptake and the activation of glycogen synthetase, the latter involve the induction and repression of particular enzymes and are inhibited by actinomycin D. The overall pattern of these changes is to alter the balance of metabolism away from glucose synthesis and towards glucose utilization and storage. From the teleological point of view this makes sense. If insulin is released from the islets of Langerhans it means that the level of blood glucose is high; therefore the peripheral tissues can afford to both degrade and store it. If insulin is not released, the level of blood glucose is low and glucose is in short supply. Under these conditions gluconeogenesis by the liver and kidneys is essential to ensure that the blood glucose can be maintained at a level adequate for the proper functioning of the brain.

Inactivation

Insulin is inactivated by the enzyme glutathione insulin transhydrogenase which uses reduced glutathione to reduce the disulphide bonds in insulin and so split the protein into its component α- and β-polypeptide chains. The site of destruction is primarily in the liver and the half-life of insulin is about 30 minutes under normal circumstances.

SECTION 8

The Control of Metabolic Processes in Cells

The control of the processes whereby cells take up material from their immediate environment, metabolize it, and then dispose of the unwanted material obviously comprises a large field and many of the topics will only be mentioned in passing. In the higher organism comparatively few of the cells of the body make any direct contact with the outside world. Except for the cells of the intestinal mucosa, the individual cells of the multi-cellular organism have a more or less stabilized environment which is the cooperative product of the rest of the cells of the body. Even in this comparatively stable, internal environment, however, there may be changes of sufficient magnitude to cause a large response by the cells. An example of the sort of changed environment that cells may experience is the increase in the amount of lactate in the plasma during exercise, which rises to about four times the value in the resting condition. Another example is the doubling of the glucose content of the plasma after a carbohydrate meal, whilst during starvation, or in response to adrenaline, the free fatty acid content of the plasma can increase about threefold. Also the saline constituents of the plasma can change, reflecting the amount of water loss or of salt ingestion. These variations in internal environment usually last only a matter of hours but the point to be made is that chemically the internal environment is variable. In contrast, the chemical composition of the external environment is relatively constant, as illustrated by the constancy of atmospheric carbon dioxide and oxygen, the gaseous substrates consumed by most organisms. Similarly, the salt concentration in the environment of the fish, or of other marine organisms, is relatively stable compared with the changes in salt concentration that occur in the body fluids of higher organisms.

In the intact animal, therefore, there must be constant adaptation to the changing internal environment. Essentially the only three methods the cell has for selectively altering its pattern of metabolism are:

(1) Selectively altering the permeability of a barrier where this limits the rate of passage of substrate to an enzyme.
(2) Selectively altering the rate at which an enzyme handles its substrate without changing the enzyme quantity.
(3) Selectively altering the quantity of enzyme.

The passage of materials into the cell

Irrespective of the nature of the organism the first thing that must happen when a cell reacts to its environment is for a piece of that environment to be taken up into the cell and it is at the cell membrane that the first opportunity exists for the cell to exercise choice and control.

11+

Although, for example, water passes in and out of cells in response to relative changes in the osmolarity of the intra- and extracellular media, the ease with which it does so will depend on the cross-sectional area available for water diffusion. For example, the hormone vasopressin increases the fraction of the surface area of the toad bladder available for unhampered passage of water. This may be equated with a dilation of water pores in the cell membrane or, alternatively, the hormone may alter the structure of the water in the pores. Water molecules can be considered as forming short-lived clusters which are held together by a network of hydrogen bonds. Some of the molecules have all four possible hydrogen bonds intact; these are the ice-like molecules at the centre of the cluster; some of the molecules at the surface of the cluster have three, two or one hydrogen bonds intact. These clusters are surrounded by the free, non-hydrogen-bonded molecules of water. The clusters are continually melting and reforming so that the whole system is in dynamic equilibrium. It has been calculated that the mean cluster size in water is about 25 molecules and the mole fraction of free water is of the order of 0·01 to 0·1. When non-polar hydrocarbons are introduced into this system there is a shifting of the water clusters to a higher state of order; to a more ice-like structure. The diffusion rate of molecules will be slower when the state is more ordered, since the opening up of holes for the passage of the diffusing molecule will be less frequent. Thus in a pore of a membrane the actual amount of free water available for diffusion of a solute must be much influenced by the various chemical groups which make up the border of the pore. Measurements of the change in diffusion rate and in total amount of water moved through living membranes under the influence of vasopressin strongly suggest an effect on the structure of water within the membrane's pores (Figure 8.1). Thus it appears that the factor limiting permeability to water movement in membranes may well be water itself, but water which is in an organized state. Similar considerations apply to the movement of water within the cell, which will be limited by the permeability of the membranes which surround organelles, or which, like the endoplasmic reticulum, partition off parts of the cell. Moreover, water-soluble materials (such as ATP and ADP) cannot pass freely around cells. Many experiments have shown that the intracellular membranes are effective barriers to free movement; for example, some of the intracellular potassium (which is an essential cation for the process of oxidative phosphorylation) is confined within the mitochondria—a localization which makes sound metabolic sense. Passage of such solutes through membranes will be altered by a change in the structure of water in the membranes and by any changes in the charged groups presented to the diffusion path. Matters are complicated by the fact that the intracellular membranes are composed not of static molecules but of enzymically active proteins intermingled with phospholipids whose conformation and charge are dependent on the metabolic state of the cell. Also, organelles and membranes within a cell do not have fixed positions but are constantly

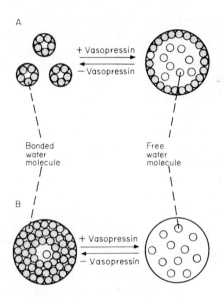

Figure 8.1. Schematic diagram of possible actions of vasopressin. In A the aqueous channels in the bladder are considered to be very small and the frictional force or bonding between water molecules and pore wall is greater than between water and water. Vasopressin is pictured as reversibly making several small channels into one large pore in which the central core of water possesses the physical characteristics of bulk water.

In B the actual confines of the aqueous channels through the bladder are considered fixed but in the absence of vasopressin the channels are clogged by a structured water which is more highly organized than unconfined water at the same temperature. The action of vasopressin is pictured as reversibly 'melting' such a structured water perhaps through an effect on the walls of the pores but without actually altering the confines of the pores. After Leaf and Hays, *J. Gen. Physiol.*, 1962; reprinted by permission of the Rockefeller University Press

moving. Consequently the preferred path of diffusion of a molecule is constantly subjected to spatial and temporal modification. Any detailed analysis of this complex situation has so far proved impossible, but it is known that the permeability of organelles such as mitochondria varies with their content of ATP and NAD, and, since these substances are actually metabolized by the mitochondria, many hypothetical control mechanisms may be devised using this knowledge.

The regulation of energy production

To maintain its life the cell must synthesize its energy currency (ATP) at a rate sufficient for (a) the synthesis of cellular components, (b) the maintenance of cellular organization and (c) the maintenance of the intra- and extracellular solute differentials. For efficiency, the synthesis and demand for ATP must be balanced; only a small reserve is maintained to satisfy urgent requirements during the short period before the pathways of ATP synthesis (glycolysis and oxidative phosphorylation) adjust themselves to the altered situation. The requirement for ATP arising under (a) is roughly equivalent to the rate of synthesis of new macromolecules and this probably makes the most variable demands on the energy supply. The requirement under (b) is not at all clear but the maintenance of cell structure against cellular disorganization will require an input of energy to prevent the natural increase in entropy. In muscle, for example, there may be very large and variable demands for energy for the rearrangement of contractile proteins that accompanies muscular work. Under (c) the requirement for ATP to maintain ionic gradients is probably constant for the body as a whole, although the ionic shifts accompanying the passage of an impulse in excitable tissues will result in local high demands. In isolated tissues it can be shown that the maintenance of ionic concentrations uses ATP and results in the subsequent stimulation of glycolysis or oxidative phosphorylation to produce more ATP. This coupling of ion movement with ATP utilization and production is demonstrated by Whittam's experiments with red cells (see p. 178) which showed that the rate of glycolysis was in part controlled by the rate of ion transport. Similarly, a fraction of respiration in the brain or the kidney is correlated with ATP usage for ion transport. The membrane 'ATP-ase' responsible for transducing the chemical energy of ATP into the potential energy of an ionic gradient produces as its other product ADP. Both the ATP-producing systems (glycolysis and oxidative phosphorylation) function only when ADP is available to receive the 'high energy' phosphate produced by the system. As a first premise we may say that energy utilization (for synthesis, organization or ion movement) is determined by the ATP concentration available in the cell, whereas energy production is determined by the ADP concentration in the cell. The latter may be illustrated by the respiratory control of isolated mitochondria which respire at only a low rate in the presence of oxidizable substrate, unless ADP is also available to receive the 'high energy' phosphate produced. The ratio of the respiratory rate in the presence of excess ADP to the rate, when no ADP is available, is called the 'respiratory control ratio'. A high respiratory control ratio means the tissue will rapidly replenish its store of ATP, whereas with a low respiratory control ratio the process will take longer. It is clear that although control of energy utilization and production depends on the concentration of ATP and ADP respectively, the site within the cell at which the ATP or ADP is located is also extremely important. For example ADP produced at the cell membrane during the process of ion transport cannot accelerate respiration until it has entered the mitochondria. Therefore ADP must go to the mitochondria or the mitochondria must go to the ADP. In fact both processes probably take place. Time-lapse film studies of some tissues have shown a regular movement of mitochondria from nucleus to cell membrane and back again, and electron microscope studies appear to show a movement of mitochondria along nerve axons.

The control of metabolism by tissue specialization

In addition to the effect of the intracellular organization on cell metabolism, the location of special functions within particular tissues exerts a control over the metabolism of the whole organism. Sometimes the metabolic differences between tissues are all or none: for example the liver produces urea, whereas the heart does not. In many tissues the difference is one of degree; for example skeletal muscle is a net producer of lactate, whereas heart muscle is a net consumer of lactate. Tissues also differ in the activities of individual enzymes. Figure 8.2 compares the activities of some of the enzymes concerned with the utilization of glucose-6-phosphate in the liver, the kidney and the adipose tissue. These relative activities result in the net flow of carbon along the pathways shown in Figure 8.3, which are in accordance with the known function of these tissues; thus, for example, the adipose tissue preferentially synthesizes fatty acids, whereas the liver preferentially synthesizes glycogen. Sometimes the all-or-none differences between tissues may rest mainly in the cell organelles. Although the mitochondria from all tissues endow their cells with the capacity for oxidation and phosphorylation, mitochondria from some tissues have metabolic functions appropriate to the characteristic activity of the organs from which they are derived. Thus liver mitochondria contain enzymes which are concerned with the particular metabolic functions of the liver, and these enzymes are not found in the heart mitochondria. One of the main functions of the liver is to produce urea from ammonia and CO_2. This is an endergonic process and, as the ATP required to drive it is produced by the mitochondria, it is not surprising that the carbamyl phosphate synthetase is also located in the mitochondria. Another mitochondrial enzyme drawing on ATP, and one which plays a key role in liver function, is pyruvic carboxylase, which catalyses the initial step in glucose and glycogen synthesis (see Section 2). Again the logic of the localization is clear—a direct tapping of the ATP is possible

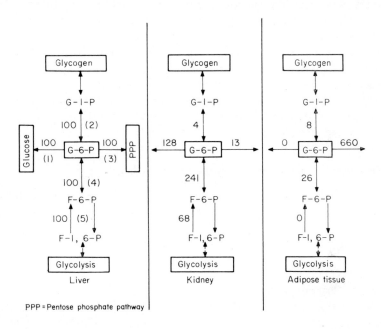

Figure 8.2. Carbohydrate enzyme activities in liver, kidney and adipose tissue in rat. The activities were compared on a percentage basis, taking the values found in liver arbitrarily as 100%. (1) Glucose-6-phosphatase; (2) phosphoglucomutase; (3) glucose-6-phosphate dehydrogenase; (4) phosphohexose isomerase; (5) fructose-1,6-diphosphatase. From Weber, *Advances in Enzymology*, Vol. 1, Pergamon, London, 1963

and carbon dioxide for fixation is produced continuously by the citric acid cycle and by oxidative decarboxylation of pyruvate which also form acetyl CoA, the 'allosteric activator' (see p. 313) of the carboxylase.

Besides the difference in the amounts of enzymes in tissues (see Figure 8.3) there are differences in the quality of an enzyme. An example of this is the difference between the lactate dehydrogenases of skeletal and heart muscle (see p. 57). Since the enzyme in heart is inhibited by low concentrations of pyruvate, it will not form large amounts of lactate from the pyruvate presented to it. By contrast the enzyme in skeletal muscle is not inhibited in this way and will continue to form lactate at relatively high concentrations of pyruvate. Also the heart enzyme is much more active in oxidizing lactate to pyruvate at low concentrations of lactate than the skeletal muscle enzyme. These facts, together with the very much larger numbers of mitochondria found in the heart, explain why heart is a net oxidizer of lactate and skeletal muscle is a net producer.

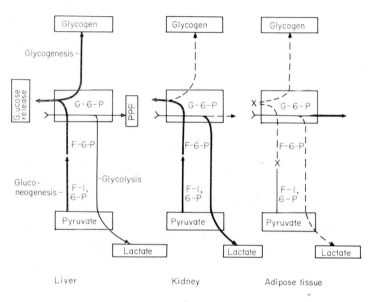

PPP = Pentose phosphate pathway

Figure 8.3. Comparison of carbohydrate metabolism in liver, kidney cortex and adipose tissue. The relative activities of metabolic pathways are indicated by the thickness of the arrows. The interrupted lines indicate pathways of very low activity. The × sign means complete absence of an enzyme activity, showing qualitative metabolic differences. From Weber, *Advances in Enzyme Regulation*, Vol. 1, Pergamon, London, 1963

The control of enzyme activity by metabolites

Although degradative and synthetic pathways are often substantially different, certain intermediates and enzymes are frequently common to both pathways. Yet experiment shows that there is no confusion in the organism as to which course of metabolism is appropriate for meeting the current needs. Frequently ATP is used to direct carbon flow in metabolic pathways. Thus, for example, the use of ATP ensures quantitative conversion of glucose to glucose-6-phosphate and of fructose-6-phosphate to fructose-1,6-diphosphate. The resultant phosphorylated compounds are ester phosphates and the energy gap between such phosphates and ATP ensures the unidirectional nature of glycolysis. This energy gap is circumvented during gluconeogenesis by making use of a different pathway in which specific phosphatases convert fructose-1,6-diphosphate to fructose-6-phosphate and glucose-6-phosphate to glucose. However, difficulties could arise if the kinases and phosphatases were sufficiently close spatially to form an 'ATP-ase'. For example,

$$\text{ATP} + \text{glucose} \longrightarrow \text{glucose-6-P} + \text{ADP}$$
hexokinase or glucokinase

$$\text{glucose-6-P} + \text{H}_2\text{O} \longrightarrow \text{glucose} + \text{Pi}$$
glucose-6-phosphatase

Sum $$\text{ATP} + \text{H}_2\text{O} \longrightarrow \text{ADP} + \text{Pi}$$

Thus, all that would be achieved would be the hydrolysis of ATP. In this instance the problem is solved by spatially separating the relevant enzymes; the hexokinase and the glucokinase are in the soluble fraction of the cell, whilst the glucose-6-phosphatase is bound to the endoplasmic reticulum. Glucose hydrolysed from glucose-6-phosphate by the phosphatase can pass through the membrane into the extracellular fluid and out of reach of the phosphorylating enzymes. Another solution which may be coupled with a spatial separation is the use of a metabolite which inhibits an enzyme in one pathway while stimulating an enzyme operating in the reverse direction. An example of this is the stimulation of phosphofructokinase and the inhibition of fructose-1,6-diphosphatase by AMP.

Problems of regulation also arise when major metabolic pathways intersect at what may be called the cross-roads of metabolism. Glucose-6-phosphate, as already mentioned, is found at such a cross-roads—so are oxaloacetate, acetyl CoA and glutamate. Controlling the flow of substances at these intersections requires complex interrelationships which must be carefully coordinated. Many of the enzymes which are situated at these strategic metabolic points are subject to control by metabolites other than their own substrates. Such control has already been mentioned for succinic dehydrogenase which is inhibited competitively by oxaloacetate (see p. 68). In many cases, however, the controlling substance or effector does not interfere with the active site of the enzyme, but attaches itself to another site now known as the allosteric binding site. With such enzymes and a fixed substrate concentration the plot of activity against effector concentration is sigmoidal, the points of inflection being determined by the relative concentrations of the substrate and the allosteric effector. The net result of this is to fix a narrow concentration range of substrate and effector within which a maximum change of enzymatic activity will occur. Allosteric effectors may cause either inhibition or activation. In all the allosteric enzymes studied in detail, it has been shown that the enzyme is composed of subunits, and in some it has been shown that catalytic and allosteric sites are on different subunits. The ways in which a number of metabolites (not necessarily substrates of the enzyme) influence the activities of some key enzymes controlling breakdown and synthesis of carbohydrate are described in the next section.

Control of the activity of phosphofructokinase

One of the enzymes subject to extensive metabolite control is phospho-fructokinase (Figure 8.4).

$$\text{fructose-6-P} + \text{ATP} \longrightarrow \text{fructose-1,6-diphosphate} + \text{ADP}$$

The two substrates of the enzyme have opposite effects. Fructose-6-phosphate activates the enzyme, whereas increasing the concentration of ATP above certain limits progressively inhibits the enzyme. Of the products of the reaction, ADP stimulates. Thus the enzyme will act as a stabilizer of the ATP/ADP ratio by influencing the overall rate of glycolysis. Consumption of ATP by some energy-requiring process will relieve the

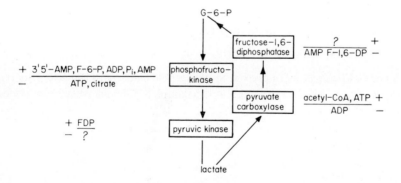

Figure 8.4. Control of allosteric enzymes by small molecules. The figure shows the substances that increase (+) or decrease (−) the activity of the four allosteric enzymes in the pathways between glucose-6-phosphate and lactate.
  The arrows indicate the direction of substrate flow between enzymes

11*

ATP inhibition, and the consequent formation of ADP will further accelerate this process by its stimulatory activity. The resultant increase in glycolysis will restore the ATP concentration and shut off the reaction. A continuing need for ATP will automatically adjust the phosphofructokinase reaction to a rate sufficient to supply ATP through glycolysis. The hydrolysis of ATP yields orthophosphate which also activates phosphofructokinase and so stimulates glycolysis and thus ATP regeneration. Phosphofructokinase is also activated by AMP which is produced during a number of reactions (e.g. by the activation of fatty and amino acids, by the formation of argininosuccinate and by the action of myokinase), thus AMP will also tend to stabilize the ATP/ADP ratio. Cyclic 3',5'-AMP also stimulates phosphofructokinase. This may be explained as an anticipatory change, since the cyclic 3',5'-AMP, by its influence on the phosphorylase system, will stimulate a breakdown of glycogen, and thus phosphofructokinase must be ready to phosphorylate the extra fructose-6-phosphate entering glycolysis.

Finally, since citrate is a potent inhibitor of phosphofructokinase, a control link is established with the citric acid cycle. It is clear that a high rate of glycolysis is not required when the concentration of citrate is high, since this implies that the citric acid cycle is working to capacity. But for the restraint imposed by citrate, acetyl CoA molecules would continue to arise from carbohydrate and since their entry to the citric acid cycle is limited they would condense to give acetoacetate and a ketotic condition.

Control of the activity of fructose-1,6-diphosphatase

Whereas the flow of carbon to lactate is controlled by phosphofructokinase, the reverse flow in the direction of glucose and glycogen is controlled by fructose-1,6-diphosphatase (Figure 8.4).

$$\text{fructose-1,6-diphosphate} + H_2O \longrightarrow \text{fructose-6-P} + Pi$$

Since both enzymes are present in the soluble fraction of the cell, a spatial separation cannot be assumed and a coupled ATP-ase system could be formed.

$$\text{fructose-6-phosphate} + ATP \longrightarrow \text{fructose-1,6-diphosphate} + ADP$$

$$\text{fructose-1,6-diphosphate} + H_2O \longrightarrow \text{fructose-6-P} + Pi$$

$$\text{Sum} \quad ATP + H_2O \longrightarrow ADP + Pi$$

Such wasteful coupling is prevented since fructose-1,6-diphosphatase is strongly inhibited by AMP and by high concentrations of fructose-1,6-diphosphate, both of which stimulate phosphofructokinase. Thus, when there is a demand for ATP synthesis by glycolysis, the concentrations of the effector metabolites are automatically set to favour glycolysis and to restrain gluconeogenesis, i.e. the ATP level is low and there is a rise in the concentration of ADP and also of AMP under the influence of myokinase. Furthermore, the fructose-1,6-diphosphatase is inhibited by the AMP. These effects are amplified by the increase in quantity of fructose-1,6-diphosphate coming from the stimulation of phosphofructokinase by ADP and AMP. Thus glycolysis is favoured and gluconeogenesis is inhibited.

On the other hand, if ATP from oxidative phosphorylation is plentiful, phosphofructokinase will be inhibited and the fructose diphosphatase will be released from its inhibition by the concomitant reduction in the amount of AMP. Under these conditions triose phosphates are condensed by aldolase to fructose-1,6-diphosphate for gluconeogenesis. This process will allow a continued formation of fructose-6-phosphate from fructose-1,6-diphosphate whilst the ATP and presumably citrate concentrations are holding phosphofructokinase in check. These conditions are found when the citric acid cycle is functioning maximally.

When glucose synthesis is required, for example, from blood lactate, the following sequence of events occurs. Lactate is very rapidly oxidized to pyruvate. The $NADH_2$ produced can be oxidized to yield ATP and in doing so it consumes ADP. Since ATP, ADP and AMP are in equilibrium through the myokinase reaction ($2ADP \rightleftharpoons ATP + AMP$) and the total concentration of adenylate nucleotides is constant, it is clear that increasing the amount of ATP at the expense of ADP must also diminish the amount of AMP. Also the NADH and L-α-glycerophosphate dehydrogenase can be used to reduce dihydroxyacetone phosphate to L-α-glycerophosphate. The removal of the dihydroxyacetone phosphate in its turn allows the removal of fructose-1,6-diphosphate by aldolase and thus the rapid oxidation of lactate decreases the concentration of the two substances which inhibit the fructose-1,6-diphosphatase, AMP and fructose-1,6-diphosphate. Subsequently, the steady supply of fructose-1,6-diphosphate at a low concentration allows a continued synthesis of glucose and glycogen.

Control of the pathway of pyruvate metabolism

The blood lactate is one of the chief substrates for the synthesis of liver carbohydrate. It is the difficulty of reversing the pyruvic kinase reaction which provides the first obstacle to carbohydrate synthesis. The enzyme pyruvic carboxylase (Figure 8.4) circumvents this difficulty by catalysing the following reaction:

$$ATP + CO_2 + pyruvate \rightleftharpoons oxaloacetate + ADP + Pi$$

In the next step catalysed by phosphopyruvate carboxykinase, oxalo-acetate reacts with GTP to produce phosphopyruvate.

$$\text{oxaloacetate} + \text{GTP} \rightleftharpoons \text{phosphopyruvate} + CO_2 + \text{GDP}$$

Since phosphopyruvate can be utilized by pyruvate kinase (to give ATP plus pyruvate), the combined action of phosphopyruvate carboxykinase and pyruvate kinase would merely result in the net hydrolysis of GTP.

$$\text{GTP} \longrightarrow \text{GDP} + \text{Pi}$$

In some tissues the problem is solved because the PEP-forming reactions are within the mitochondria, whereas the pyruvic kinase is in the soluble fraction.

Pyruvate carboxylase has an absolute requirement for acetyl-CoA as an allosteric activator. It is a typical allosteric enzyme which can be dissociated into subunits; this dissociation is prevented by acetyl-CoA. Pyruvate carboxylase is inhibited by ADP but this inhibition can be overcome competitively by ATP. Thus the high ATP/ADP ratio required to overcome the energy barriers to carbohydrate synthesis will also stimulate the carboxylase.

Competing metabolic pathways for C_2, C_3 and C_4 units

At this point it is convenient to consider the divergent routes of metabolism open to pyruvate (Figure 8.5) by examining the disposal of two molecules of pyruvate within the mitochondrion. The oxidative decarboxylation of one of the molecules would produce acetyl-CoA, CO_2 and $NADH_2$ which can be oxidized to generate ATP. Pyruvate carboxylase can then fix the CO_2 into the pyruvate utilizing ATP and the acetyl-CoA as activator. Finally, the acetyl-CoA can combine with the oxaloacetate to form citrate. The net result is

$$2 \text{ pyruvate} \longrightarrow \text{citrate}$$

Citrate has been described as an allosteric inhibitor of phosphofructo-kinase but it is also an allosteric activator for the enzyme acetyl-CoA carboxylase which carries out the initial reactions of fatty acid synthesis, i.e.

$$\text{Biotin–enzyme} + CO_2 + \text{ATP} \overset{Mg^{2+}}{\rightleftharpoons} CO_2\text{–biotin–enzyme} + \text{ADP} + \text{Pi}$$

$$CO_2\text{–biotin–enzyme} + \text{acetyl-CoA} \rightleftharpoons \text{biotin–enzyme} + \text{malonyl-CoA}$$

The activation of this enzyme by citrate is very similar to the activation of pyruvate carboxylase by acetyl-CoA and is believed to occur in the same way by the aggregation of subunits. Acetyl-CoA carboxylase is also inhibited by long chain acyl-CoA derivatives, an illustration of end product inhibition. These reactions provide an example of a substance (acetyl-CoA) which stimulates the formation of a product (oxaloacetate) which can combine with acetyl-CoA and thus decrease its effect on the first reaction. This combination produces a substance (citrate) which will stimulate removal of acetyl-CoA by another route to fatty acids and in so doing reduce the production of the stimulator. These changes will all act in a way to damp down oscillations of substrate concentrations.

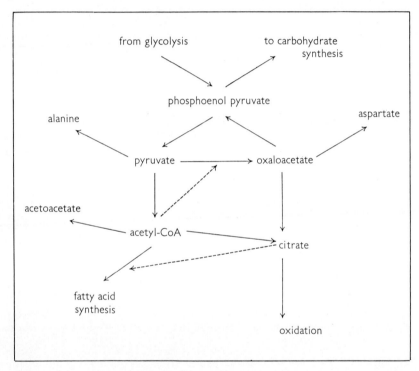

Figure 8.5. Competing metabolic pathways for C_2, C_3 and C_4 units. The dotted lines indicate points where an enzyme can be affected allosterically by the metabolite indicated

Disposal of glucose-6-phosphate; pacemaker reactions

The metabolism of carbohydrate by the mammalian liver is a system which offers an opportunity for studying pacemaker reactions. In the mammal glucose is metabolically inert until it is phosphorylated. Once phosphorylated, there are four possible routes for glucose-6-phosphate metabolism (Figure 8.2). It can simply be dephosphorylated to glucose for transport and utilization elsewhere. It can be converted to glucose-1-phosphate by phosphoglucomutase and then follow the route of glycogen synthesis for storage purposes. Phosphohexose isomerase can transform it to fructose-6-phosphate which then leads to synthesis of fructose-1,6-diphosphate. Finally, by dehydrogenation with glucose-6-phosphate dehydrogenase, it can enter the pentose phosphate pathway as phosphogluconic acid. It appears that only the formation of glucose-1-phosphate is free from metabolic control by a component of another metabolic pathway (Figure 8.6). Phosphohexose isomerase, which catalyses the

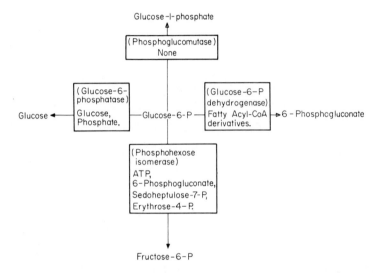

Figure 8.6. Substances inhibiting the metabolic pathways open to glucose-6-phosphate. The enzymes and their inhibitors are given within the boxes

formation of fructose-6-phosphate in the glycolytic pathway is inhibited by 6-phosphogluconate, sedoheptulose-7-phosphate and erythrose-4-phosphate. Thus an active pentose phosphate pathway will tend to reinforce its own claim to glucose-6-phosphate. It must not be supposed that the formation of fructose-6-phosphate is prevented, since this is also a product of the pentose phosphate pathway, but by this route $NADPH_2$ is formed as a by-product. Phosphohexose isomerase is also inhibited by ATP. Thus in times of ATP plenty the pathway of carbohydrate metabolism will be diverted into the pentose phosphate pathway to provide $NADPH_2$ for fatty acid synthesis. However, a restraint on fatty acid synthesis is exercised since glucose-6-phosphate dehydrogenase is inhibited by long chain fatty acyl-CoA derivatives. The remaining pathway (the hydrolysis by glucose-6-phosphatase to give glucose) is subject to product inhibition by glucose and phosphate. Glucose-6-phosphatase has a secondary function acting as a pyrophosphatase for which the phosphate acceptor can be water or glucose. Thus if glucose and pyrophosphate are available, glucose-6-phosphatase can synthesize glucose-6-phosphate. The concentration of pyrophosphate can increase in two ways. After a meal, glucose and fatty acids may enter the liver. The glucose after phosphorylation will be converted in part to glucose-1-phosphate which in turn may react with UTP to give UDP-glucose with the release of pyrophosphate; pyrophosphate can also arise during the activation of the fatty acids. The pyrophosphate can then react with glucose to give still more glucose-6-phosphate. In addition, the glycogen synthetase is specifically activated by glucose-6-phosphate, which further accelerates the deposition of glucose as glycogen. Finally, the orthophosphate liberated by the reaction of glucose with pyrophosphate can inhibit the hydrolysis of glucose-6-phosphate by the phosphatase. Glucose-6-phosphatase is therefore an enzyme capable of directing the conversion of either glucose to glycogen or in starvation glycogen to glucose.

The interconversion of glycogen and glucose-1-phosphate

The breakdown of glycogen to glucose-1-phosphate in muscle is a phosphorolysis catalysed by two distinct but interconvertible enzymes, phosphorylase *a* (a tetramer) and *b* (a dimer). In muscle, the conversion of *b* to *a* is an ATP-dependent dimerization which is catalysed by phosphorylase *b* kinase (see Figure 8.7).

$$2 \text{ phosphorylase } b + 4\,\text{ATP} \longrightarrow \text{phosphorylase } a + 4\,\text{ADP}$$

(Liver phosphorylase is also activated by a reaction with ATP, but without dimerization.) The conversion of phosphorylase *a* to phosphorylase *b* is catalysed by a phosphatase which liberates four phosphate molecules and allows the dimers to separate. Phosphorylase *a* is the more active of the enzymes; except under special conditions it is not activated by AMP but it is inhibited by UDP-glucose and malate. Phosphorylase *b* is less active than phosphorylase *a* and is absolutely dependent on AMP for its activity. Phosphorylase *b* is inhibited by glucose-6-phosphate and ATP, whereas glucose-1-phosphate reinforces the stimulatory effect of AMP. It is clear that the rate of breakdown of glycogen will be dependent on the ratio of the *a* to the *b* form. However, the conversion by phosphorylase *b* kinase of the non-phosphorylated form (phosphorylase *b*) to the phosphorylated form (phosphorylase *a*) is far from simple because the kinase itself exists in an active and an inactive form. The inactive form of the kinase can be converted to the active form by either (1) treatment with ATP, or (2) treatment with Ca^{2+} together with a protein called KAF (kinase activation factor). In the first case, the rate of conversion of the inactive to the active kinase by ATP is greatly accelerated by the presence of cyclic 3',5'-AMP. The formation of cyclic AMP from ATP is brought about by an enzyme called adenylcyclase whose activity is stimulated by adrenaline which also causes a depletion of liver glycogen and an increase in blood glucose. The events following adrenaline injection can therefore be envisaged as stimu-

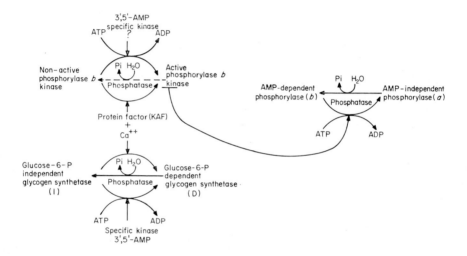

Figure 8.7. The interconversions of phosphorylase *b* and phosphorylase *a* and of glycogen synthetase I and glycogen synthetase D

lation of adenylcyclase—increase in cyclic AMP concentration—activation of the kinase—conversion of phosphorylase *b* to phosphorylase *a*—stimulation of glycogen breakdown. The second method of activating the kinase, by Ca^{2+} and KAF, is probably important for controlling the breakdown of glycogen in muscle, since the electrical stimulation of muscle results in a flood of Ca^{2+} into the muscle cell (see p. 34).

The synthesis of glycogen by glycogen synthetase is governed by regulatory mechanisms which have many points in common with the breakdown process; the same effector molecules are involved but they have the opposite effects. Like the phosphorylase, the synthetase exists in two interconvertible forms. The D (dependent) form of the enzyme which requires glucose-6-phosphate for its activity is less active than the I form (independent) which does not require glucose-6-phosphate except under special circumstances. The conversion of the I to the less active D form may be brought about by phosphorylation with ATP and a specific kinase (contrast the conversion of phosphorylase b to a, where phosphorylation by ATP and a kinase produces greater activity). The specific kinase is activated by cyclic $3',5'$-AMP and, as we have seen previously, the cyclase producing this is controlled by adrenaline. Thus the injection of adrenaline not only stimulates the breakdown of glycogen, but also retards glycogen synthesis by initiating the transformation of the synthetase to the less active D form. A second method of converting the I to the less active D form of the synthetase is by treatment with Ca^{2+} and probably the same KAF protein factor concerned in the activation of phosphorylase b kinase. Once again there is reciprocity between controlling factors for phosphorylase and synthetase activity (Figure 8.7).

The control of fatty acid synthesis in adipose tissue

Adipose tissue converts glucose to fatty acid with high efficiency and the rate of this conversion can be rapidly increased by insulin (see p. 302). The breakdown of glucose yields ATP, reducing power and acetyl-CoA. The synthesis of fatty acids requires ATP to drive the reaction and a balance between the quantity of acetyl-CoA and reducing power available. The restriction imposed on the process is the necessity of having the reducing power in the form of $NADPH_2$, e.g. from the pentose phosphate pathway. It is possible to assess the carbon flow from glucose through the pentose phosphate pathway, the citric acid cycle and into fatty acids by comparing labelled CO_2 production from uniformly ^{14}C-labelled glucose, with that from glucose labelled in position 6 and measuring the quantity and labelling pattern of the fat produced. Administration of insulin, which greatly stimulates fatty acid synthesis, causes a fourfold increase in glucose metabolism via the pentose phosphate pathway, a decrease in the metabolic flow through the citric acid cycle and a stimulation of oxygen uptake probably as a result of an increased oxidation of pyruvate to acetyl-CoA. From the measurements of the carbon flow the relative contribution to reducing power by each pathway can be deduced (Figure 8.8). The increase in reducing power in response to insulin is sufficient for the extra production of fatty acid, but the fraction contributed by $NADPH_2$ is only about 60% of the amount required. Somehow $NADH_2$ must be converted to $NADPH_2$ to remedy this deficit. Experiments with isolated adipose tissue

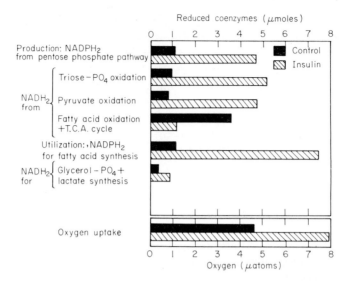

Figure 8.8. The production and utilization of reduced coenzymes in rat adipose tissue during lipogenesis. From Ball, *Advances in Enzyme Regulation*, Vol. 4, Pergamon, London, 1966

have shown that it can convert pyruvate to fatty acids, in the absence of glucose, i.e. when there is no apparent source of $NADPH_2$. Further investigations have shown that adipose tissue has a very high content of malic enzyme. The amount of this enzyme increases as fat synthesis increases in response to changes in diet and treatment with hormones. The situation was clarified by the observation that adipose tissue contains pyruvate carboxylase and the provision of $NADPH_2$ from $NADH_2$ was explained by the following sequence of reactions.

$$\text{pyruvate carboxylase}$$
$$\text{pyruvate} + CO_2 + \text{ATP} \longrightarrow \text{oxaloacetate} + \text{ADP} + \text{Pi}$$

$$\text{malate dehydrogenase}$$
$$\text{oxaloacetate} + NADH_2 \rightleftharpoons \text{malate} + \text{NAD}$$

$$\text{malic enzyme}$$
$$\text{malate} + \text{NADP} \rightleftharpoons \text{pyruvate} + CO_2 + NADPH_2$$

$$\text{Sum} \quad \text{NADP} + NADH_2 + \text{ATP} \rightleftharpoons NADPH_2 + \text{NAD} + \text{ADP} + \text{Pi}$$

These reactions constitute an ATP-requiring transhydrogenase and the demand for ATP to drive this reaction could explain the increased respiration during insulin-induced fatty acid synthesis.

If fatty acids are to be synthesized from carbohydrate, there must be a continuous transport of acetyl-CoA from the mitochondria to the soluble fraction of the cell, where fatty acid synthetase occurs. There seems to be no doubt that acetyl-CoA cannot cross the mitochondrial membrane, but citrate can. However, the soluble fraction of the adipose tissue cell, like the liver cell, contains the citrate cleavage enzyme which carries out the following reaction:

$$citrate + CoA + ATP \longrightarrow acetyl\text{-}CoA + oxaloacetate + ADP + Pi$$

Changes in amount of this enzyme parallel those of the malic enzyme under different dietary conditions, and the synthesis of both enzymes in the mammal appears to be controlled by a single mechanism. Since the soluble fraction of the cell contains a malate dehydrogenase as well as malic enzyme, the oxaloacetate formed by citrate cleavage can be used for the production of $NADPH_2$ and pyruvate (as above). The pyruvate is free to return to the mitochondria, where it can serve as the precursor of either the C_2 or C_4 fragments for further citrate synthesis. Repetition of this cycle of events in the soluble fraction and the mitochondrion provides a continuous supply of acetyl-CoA for fatty acid synthesis.

The necessity for balancing the supply of reducing power with a particular carbon source is illustrated by the fact that when acetate alone is supplied to the adipose tissue, the tissue is unable to synthesize fatty acids because reducing power cannot be provided either by the pentose phosphate pathway or by the malate/oxaloacetate shuttle. If glucose is added, all the glucose flows through the pentose phosphate pathway to produce the $NADPH_2$ required for fat synthesis. Normally when the adipose tissue is supplied with abundant glucose and insulin, the limiting step in fat synthesis appears to be the rate at which acetyl-CoA can be transferred, as citrate, across the mitochondrial membrane.

In the isolated enzyme system the synthesis of fatty acids from acetyl-CoA is limited by acetyl-CoA carboxylase whose activity can be affected by the concentration of citrate (see Figure 8.5). The magnitude of the citrate effect *in vivo* is uncertain but measurements have shown that during starvation the level of citrate in the liver falls to about half, and this may help to explain the decrease in fatty acid synthesis during starvation. The acetyl-CoA carboxylase is also inhibited by long chain acyl-CoA derivatives. The activation by citrate is very strongly inhibited by the CoA derivatives.

The formation of ketone bodies

The major metabolic routes open to acetyl-CoA include the formation of long chain fatty acids, condensation with oxaloacetate to give citrate and the formation of acetoacetate by the condensation of two molecules of acetyl-CoA (see p. 125). The relative flow of acetyl-CoA along these metabolic routes depends on the concentrations of acetyl-CoA and oxaloacetate and on the activity of condensing enzyme. Earlier work suggested that during starvation the concentration of oxaloacetate in the liver was unchanged, at a stage when the ketone bodies of the blood had increased some tenfold. Emphasis was then directed towards the overproduction of acetyl-CoA as the cause of ketosis. With the development of methods for measuring acetyl-CoA, it was shown that the amounts of acetyl-CoA in the liver could be increased from about 20 to 50 mμ moles/g wet wt. by administering a fatty diet or in alloxan-induced diabetes. The level of acetyl-CoA which saturates the condensing enzyme is about 50 μM so the observed increase in acetyl-CoA concentration under these conditions should lead to an increase in the amount of citrate formed. However, with labelled acetate it has been shown that the formation of citrate is actually reduced under conditions leading to ketosis. In recent years, more sensitive methods have been used to reexamine the concentration of oxaloacetate in the liver and it has been found that in diabetes or high fat diet the oxaloacetate concentration (3 mμmoles/g fresh weight) is approximately half the normal concentration (5–6 mμmoles/g fresh weight). This is not due to a decrease in the supply of C_4 acids from pyruvate by carboxylation, because the amount of malate found in the liver showed a substantial rise so that the total amount of malate plus oxaloacetate actually doubled. The fall in oxaloacetate concentration appears to be caused by a displacement of the equilibrium of malate dehydrogenase due to the high concentration of $NADH_2$ produced by the rapid dehydrogenation of fatty acids. Moreover, condensing enzyme is markedly inhibited by long chain acyl-CoA derivatives (as is acetyl-CoA carboxylase and hence fatty acid synthesis (see p. 119)); palmityl-CoA at the concentration normally found in the tissues (10^{-6} M) produced 50% inhibition of the condensing enzyme *in vitro*. This inhibition was competitive with respect to oxaloacetate; and it has been suggested that the acyl-CoA is an allosteric inhibitor. The formation of ketone bodies when fat is being metabolized (during starvation and with high fat diets) could be explained by the inhibition of fatty acid synthesis and of acetyl-CoA entry into the citric acid cycle by palmityl-CoA and other long chain acyl-CoA derivatives. This leaves ketone body formation as the only other important metabolic route which acetyl-CoA can follow.

To compensate for the decreased permeability of skeletal muscle to glucose in the diabetic condition there is a continuous demand for glucose synthesis to increase the concentration gradient from blood to muscle. The resulting overspill of glucose in the urine increases the demand on oxaloacetate for gluconeogenesis. As a result the amount of oxaloacetate available for taking acetyl-CoA into the citric acid cycle is restricted and there is a corresponding increase in the flow of acetyl-CoA into ketone bodies.

Metabolic control by changes in enzyme quantity

So far we have been concerned with modulation of enzyme systems by various metabolites but we have not considered what happens when large changes in substrate concentration occur. In certain circumstances a rapid change in substrate concentrations may saturate the preexisting population of enzymes. This may cause the accumulation of intermediates and an increase in the concentration of the ultimate product of reaction. If these changes in substrate levels are of a temporary nature no adjustment in the enzyme population is necessary.

If the metabolic load on the enzyme system is increased or decreased markedly for a long time, then the actual size of the enzyme population may vary by an 'adaptive change'. There are rate-limiting steps in any metabolic sequence and Krebs has suggested that the enzymes catalysing these 'pacemaker' reactions are those most likely to be involved in such adaptive changes. In the pathways concerned with the metabolism of glucose-6-phosphate the rate-limiting enzymes are the two NADP-requiring enzymes (glucose-6-phosphate dehydrogenase and 6-phospho-gluconic acid dehydrogenase), the two phosphatases (glucose-6-phosphatase and fructose-1,6-diphosphatase) and phosphofructokinase. One might expect these enzymes to be sites for adaptive control, so that during stress their quantities may change to meet the changing circumstances. This can be illustrated by following the events which occur during fasting. Since the glucose concentration of the blood must be maintained, there must be enhanced gluconeogenesis and hormonal mechanisms are brought into play to adjust the amounts of the appropriate enzymes. Such changes in liver enzymes during prolonged starvation are shown in Figure 8.9. The amount of glucose-6-phosphatase is maintained or even increased, whereas the amounts of most of the other enzymes decline. Those concerned with the conversion of glucose to glucose-1-phosphate or phosphogluconic acid decline especially rapidly. The important point is that the four enzymes decline at quite different rates (see Figure 8.9). As might be expected, re-feeding after starvation causes a rapid increase in the quantities of enzymes in the liver, with a specially large change in glucose-6-phosphate dehydrogenase.

To find out whether the changes in the amounts of enzyme result from complete synthesis, or whether they are simply due to the activation of

preexisting but inactive proteins, use has been made of compounds which
induce or inhibit protein synthesis. Cortisone induces enzyme formation in
the whole animal, as illustrated for liver glucose-6-phosphatase in Figure
8.10. The changes in the blood sugar are also shown. If an inhibitor of

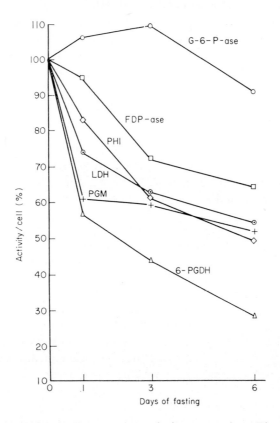

Figure 8.9. Changes in liver enzymes during starvation. The enzymes are
glucose-6-phosphatase (G-6-P-ase), fructose-1,6-diphosphatase (FDP-ase),
phosphohexose isomerase (PHI), lactate dehydrogenase (LDH), phosphoglucomutase (PGM) and 6-phosphogluconate dehydrogenase (6-PGDH).
  From Weber, *Advances in Enzymology*, Vol. 1, Pergamon, London, 1963

protein synthesis (e.g. puromycin or actinomycin—see Section 6) is given
with the cortisone much of the enzyme synthesis is inhibited, as shown in
Figure 8.11. The effects of the inhibitors on cortisone-induced synthesis of
glucose-6-phosphatase and fructose-1,6-diphosphatase indicate that *de*

novo enzyme synthesis is involved. The refeeding of starved animals also causes an increase in enzyme levels, but the pattern of induction is different. Cortisone stimulates formation of the enzymes concerned with the synthesis of glucose, whereas refeeding specifically stimulates production of the enzymes of the pentose phosphate pathway, which will provide $NADPH_2$ for increased fat synthesis. Thus the enzymes of carbohydrate metabolism are in a dynamic state, rapidly responding to the need of the whole animal.

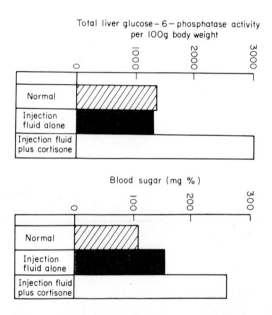

Figure 8.10. Effect of cortisone on hepatic glucose-6-phosphatase activity and blood glucose levels in fed rats. From Weber, *Advances in Enzyme Regulation*, Vol. 1, Pergamon, London, 1963

Control of glucose synthesis in the kidney

It is possible to investigate the adaptive control of a complete process such as glucose synthesis in the whole animal or in a tissue slice. As an experimental material for studying glucose synthesis, kidney has a practical advantage over liver because it has a low glycogen reserve. The blood flow through the kidney is about one-fifth of the heart output, and, since the combined weight of the kidneys is about one-fifth that of the liver, its contribution to body glucose synthesis is quite substantial. The material

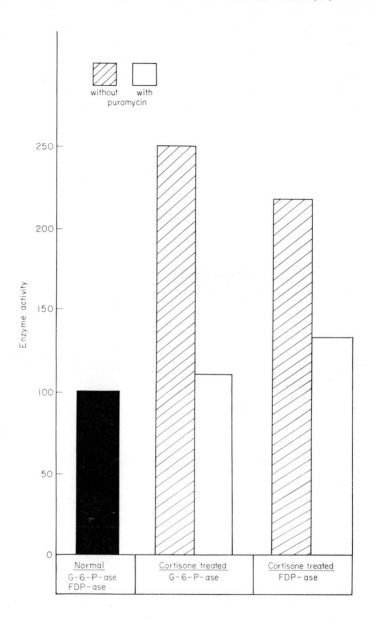

Figure 8.11. Puromycin inhibition of cortisone-induced hepatic enzyme synthesis. G-6-P-ase = glucose-6-phosphatase, FDP-ase = fructose-1,6-diphosphatase. From Weber, *Advances in Enzyme Regulation*, Vol. 1, Pergamon, London, 1963

presented to kidney (and liver) for synthesis of glucose is the lactate produced by muscle glycolysis.

Table 8.1 shows the effect of different diets, and starvation, on the synthesis of glucose from lactate in the kidney.

Table 8.1. Effect of diet on the formation of glucose from lactate in rat kidney cortex slices[a, b]

Substrate added	Glucose formed (μmoles/g dry wt./h)		
	Standard mixed diet	Low-carbohydrate diet (casein–margarine)	Starvation for 48 h
None	$12 \cdot 6 \pm 1 \cdot 46$ (14)	$22 \cdot 8 \pm 1 \cdot 0$ (15)	25 ± 2 (6)
L-Lactate (10 mM)	$110 \pm 3 \cdot 1$ (24)	$200 \pm 4 \cdot 8$ (14)	200 ± 17 (6)

[a] Young rats, 3–4 months old, were used. The low-carbohydrate diet was given for 3–5 days. Slices were incubated for 1 hour. The results are given as means $\pm$ S.E.M. with the numbers of observations in parentheses.

[b] Results taken from Krebs and coworkers, *Biochem. J.*, 1963.

Synthesis is greatly increased during starvation or with a low carbohydrate diet and the changes in the enzyme levels in the tissues are consistent with this. One other condition where an increase of glucose synthesis occurs is during exercise, as shown in Table 8.2.

Table 8.2. Effect of physical exercise (prolonged swimming) on the rate of gluconeogenesis in rat kidney cortex[a]

Substrate	μmoles glucose/g dry wt./h	
	Normal rats	Exercised rats
None	$11 \cdot 2$	20
Lactate	97	171

[a] Results taken from Krebs and coworkers, *Biochem. J.*, 1963.

Here the stimulus for extra synthesis is the high lactate production which demands a rapid resynthesis of glucose, whereas in starvation and on a carbohydrate-low diet the stimulus comes from the lack of carbohydrate.

The effect of diet on the enzyme pattern of tissues

Measurements of the enzyme patterns of animals fed different diets have shown that besides the relative proportions of fat, protein and carbohydrate, the *nature* of the carbohydrate has a large effect in determining the enzyme pattern of liver. As shown in Table 8.3 the activities of pyruvate kinase and glucose-6-phosphate dehydrogenase are much higher when the dietary carbohydrate is sucrose than when it is starch.

Table 8.3. Effect of dietary carbohydrate on the enzyme activity of rat liver

Dietary carbohydrate	Activity of pyruvic kinase (μmoles of substrate transformed/ g protein/min)	Activity of glucose-6-phosphate dehydrogenase (μmoles of substrate transformed/ g protein/min)
Starch	121	14
Sucrose	780	150

As a consequence of these changes, a faster deposition of fat would be expected with a diet rich in sucrose than with one which is rich in starch and such speculations are borne out by experiment. Interaction between dietary protein and carbohydrate is illustrated by the finding that when glucose and casein are given together by mouth glucose-6-phosphate dehydrogenase increases after about 12 hours; neither casein nor glucose alone has this effect. However, glucokinase is induced by feeding glucose without adding casein. The enhanced activities of both the dehydrogenase and the kinase are the result of *de novo* protein synthesis, since giving actinomycin, or puromycin, prevents the increases. Many years ago Pavlov demonstrated that the pancreatic secretion changed in response to the diet (Table 8.4) and later work using controlled isocaloric diets (Table 8.5) has confirmed and extended his findings.

Table 8.4. Long-term effect of dietary composition on proportions of the pancreatic enzymes secreted by dogs (Pavlov, 1902)

	Units secreted/6 h		
	Amylase	Lipase	Protease
Experiment 1			
Bread and milk for 6 weeks changed to	12	—	0·25
Meat for 23 days	2	—	2·5
Experiment 2			
Equal protein diets for 3 weeks then changed to			
Bread	1601	800	1975
Milk	432	4334	1085
Meat	648	3600	1502

Table 8.5. Relative contents of enzymes in rat pancreas after three weeks' feeding of isocaloric diets[a]

Diet fed	Amylase	Lipase	Protease
High carbohydrate	$+41$	0	-55
High protein	-19	$+30$	$+200$
High fat	-65	-12	0

[a] Values are the percentage changes from a balanced diet; from Greengard and Knox.

High protein diets increase the glutamic–pyruvic–transaminase and glutamic–oxaloacetic–transaminase levels by about 100% compared with the normal diet, or by about 500% compared with a protein-free diet. Similarly, starvation (which in many respects is equivalent to a high protein diet except that the protein comes from endogenous sources) produces a marked increase in the transaminase concentration. These changes are not due to adrenal hormones, since they occur in adrenal-ectomized animals. The conditions under which the liver transaminase shows the greatest increases include treatment with cortisone, high protein diet, starvation and alloxan diabetes. The common physiological charac-teristics of these conditions are enhanced gluconeogenesis, increased protein catabolism and a rise in the amino acid pool in the liver. It is reasonable to suggest that increased transaminase activities are directly responsible for the extra gluconeogenesis in the liver. The transaminases feed their products (α-oxoglutarate, pyruvate and oxaloacetate) into the pool of intermediates for making glucose. As might be expected, arginase and urea excretion also increase with a high protein diet and in body wasting. As with the transaminase changes, the increased protein in the diet produces increases in arginase even in adrenalectomized animals. The reason for the higher activity of the arginase, however, is quite different. Arginase has a half-life in the body of about 5 days, but with a high protein diet the half-life is increased considerably. The rate of synthesis of the enzyme shows only a small increase, but its degradation is much slower. It is thought that, because of the increased quantity of substrate available, the enzyme is more frequently in combination with its substrate, and under these conditions is less susceptible to degradation.

Changes in the enzyme pattern of the liver can also be brought about by changes in the fat content of the diet such as that experienced by all mammals during the change from the high fat content of milk to the lower fat content of the adult diet at weaning. (Reference has already been made to some enzyme changes occurring at parturition (p. 257).) Nutritionally the early life of the mammal is characterized by two changes; a sudden one when transplacental alimentation, predominantly carbohydrate, is replaced by a high-fat diet of milk, and a more gradual one when milk is replaced by solid food at weaning. The change at birth is physiologically defined, since the composition of the milk is essentially invariable. In contrast, the change at weaning is not strictly defined because the animals may be weaned to any of a wide range of diets, all of which may be regarded as normal. Figure 8.12 shows how the fat-synthesizing ability of the liver (measured by the incorporation of ^{14}C acetate into lipid) changes after birth and during weaning, and Figure 8.13 shows the changes in

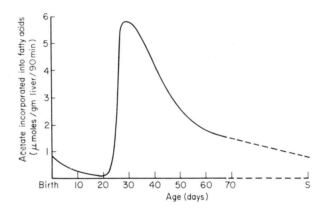

Figure 8.12. Changes in the incorporation of acetate into rat liver lipid before and after weaning (day 20). The value at **S** is for stock fed adults. Unpublished results from Taylor, Bailey and Bartley, 1967

enzyme levels which are associated with changes in fat metabolism. By weaning the animals to a diet rich in fat these changes are largely suppressed.

All these examples emphasize the dynamic nature of the body's enzyme population which is constantly changing to meet the chemical challenges presented to it. The body as a whole and the individual tissues in particular must respond to these chemical challenges in a balanced, compensatory manner. Failure by the body or tissue to make these normal adjustments may be the cause of metabolic disorders. In extreme cases such failures may lead to the death of the cell or they may on the other hand result in uncontrolled cellular proliferation.

Enzyme patterns in tumours

The following examples illustrate how defects in the mechanisms which regulate the enzyme levels and activities in tissues occur during the uncontrolled growth of certain tumours. First, the control of cellular proliferation is partly mediated by the control of *de novo* synthesis of purine nucleotides and of DNA polymerase activity. In hepatomas the synthesis of the purine nucleotides goes on unchecked, and this allows the DNA polymerase to make more DNA, which in turn eventually leads to an increased rate of cell division.

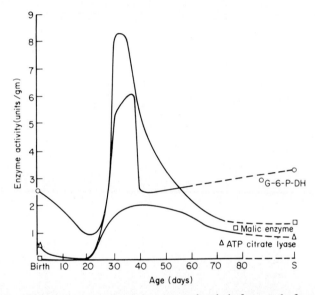

Figure 8.13. Changes in some hepatic enzyme levels before and after weaning (day 20). The values at S are for stock fed adults. G-6-P-DH = glucose-6-phosphate dehydrogenase. From Taylor, Bailey and Bartley, 1967

In rapidly growing liver tumours phosphoenolpyruvic carboxykinase, glucose-6-phosphatase and fructose-1,6-phosphatase are virtually absent. These tumours glycolyse at a high rate but cannot synthesize their own carbohydrate. It is suggested that the synthesis of the three missing enzymes are controlled by the same mechanism and that a single defect affects the synthesis of all three enzymes.

Cholesterol synthesis in liver is controlled by a negative feedback mechanism at a point where β-hydroxy-β-methylglutaric acid is converted to mevalonic acid (see p. 286). The inhibitor which switches off enzyme synthesis is a cholesterol-containing lipoprotein which is located on the ergastoplasmic membranes. In three hepatomas the cholesterol feedback system is missing.

*   *   *

This section has been concerned with illustrations of the mechanisms which control the metabolism of the organism and enable it to supply the necessary integrated responses to various environmental changes. Many of the control mechanisms arise directly from the inherent nature of the chemical substances comprising the body, but others are more indirect and involve modulation of enzyme activity or of enzyme quantity. Although we have not considered the controlling effect on the human of the nervous system, nor the control of behaviour patterns emanating from the higher centres of the brain, it is one of the remaining tasks of the biochemist to explain such controls in terms of the chemical mechanisms set out in this section.

SECTION 9

Radiation Biochemistry

Man is subjected to radiation of varying wavelengths but, in general, his body is constructed in a way that prevents the penetration of radiation. However, some radiations, such as cosmic rays, x-rays, the background radioactivity of the earth, buildings and food, do penetrate. In recent years the advance of technology has increased the level of background radiation and has introduced the possibility of exposure to large doses of harmful radiation by accident, carelessness or warfare.

The damage inflicted by irradiation is related to the amount of energy absorbed by the body; the unit used to express this is called the rad which is equivalent to the absorption of 100 ergs/g of tissue. Workers exposed to ionizing radiations wear badges containing a photographic film mounted behind a light-opaque cover. Radiation penetrating the cover causes a darkening of the film that can be used as a measure of exposure and if this exceeds a statutory value, the worker must cease to expose himself to risk.

As nuclear technology has developed, much effort has gone into research designed to investigate the effects of ionizing radiations on living organisms and on chemicals of biological interest. This work is known as radiobiology.

Radiation and tissue damage

Experiments carried out *in vitro* have shown that most compounds of biological interest are damaged by ionizing radiations. In the dry state and perhaps in solution such compounds can absorb radiant energy directly and therefore undergo chemical change. In solution a further possibility exists, namely that the radiation interacts with water molecules to form free radicals (highly reactive molecular species carrying an unpaired electron)

$$H_2O + \text{irradiation} \longrightarrow \dot{H} + \dot{O}H$$

which in turn react with the solute molecules. In either event the compound of biological interest may be altered within a few microseconds, or less, of exposure to the radiation. In the presence of oxygen the damage inflicted by irradiation is enhanced owing to the formation of $H\dot{O}_2$ radicals which are less reactive and consequently have a longer life than the $\dot{H}$ and $\dot{O}H$ radicals formed in the absence of oxygen. The longer life of the radical permits it to travel further before experiencing an inactivating collision and hence increases its probability of reacting with a solute molecule. Despite the demonstration that irradiation can inactivate enzymes, cause the denaturation of proteins and the degradation of nucleic acids *in vitro*, there is little evidence that radiation damage *in vivo* is initiated by such

12

changes. It even appears that the breakage of chromosomes induced by radiation is not caused by a direct interaction of the chromosome with the radiation but involves indirect biochemical processes.

Intensive investigations have revealed no changes in the general metabolic patterns of animals subjected to a lethal dose of x-rays. Glycogen synthesis by the liver increases but this appears to be a secondary effect attendant upon the arrival of glycogenic precursors from degenerating cells. Although it has been suggested that ionizing radiations exert their effects by oxidizing SH groups, neither inhibition of enzymes having SH groups at their active centres nor a decline in the total concentration of SH groups has been observed *in vivo* after irradiation. In contrast to this, experiments *in vitro* have shown that enzymes containing SH groups are inactivated.

Biochemical changes that have been detected shortly after irradiation and which may underlie the pathological changes observed some hours after irradiation are:

(1) Increases in the activity of acid hydrolases such as DNA-ase, cathepsins and acid phosphatase.

(2) Release of cytochrome *c* from mitochondria.

(3) Uncoupling of oxidative phosphorylation.

(4) Inhibition of ATP synthesis by nuclei.

(5) Inhibition of DNA synthesis.

The first of these changes, the increases in the activity of acid hydrolases, is particularly interesting because radiation never enhances enzyme activity *in vitro*. The most simple explanation of the results obtained *in vivo* is that irradiation releases the enzymes from some restraint upon the expression of their activity. It may be that their release from lysosomes (see p. 97) is facilitated. This simple explanation is complicated by the fact that isolated lysosomes require high doses of irradiation before they become leaky.

It is perhaps significant that the five changes listed above all involve subcellular organelles which are bounded by lipoprotein membranes. There have been suggestions that ionizing radiations could initiate the oxidation of lipids by chain reactions that may lead to marked changes in membrane structure. The ability of ionizations to trigger a chain reaction would allow the original radiation damage to be amplified. Since the total amount of energy transferred to a cell by irradiation, and hence the amount of primary damage, is very small, it should be accommodated easily unless some amplification of the primary change occurred.

It is characteristic that radiation damage *in vivo* increases as the density of ionization increases. That is to say, most damage is done when the energy of the radiation is dissipated in a small volume. The amount of damage inflicted by irradiation of protein or nucleic acid solutions

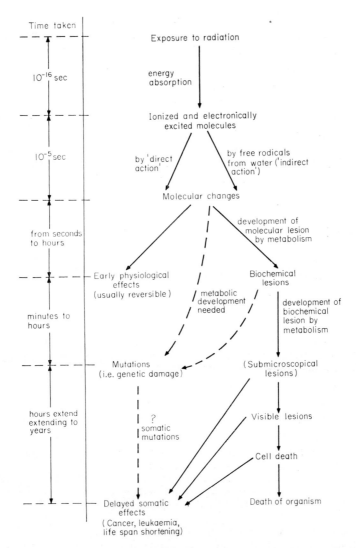

Figure 9.1. The effects of radiation of living organisms. From Bacq and Alexander, *Fundamentals of Radiobiology*, 2nd ed., Pergamon, London, 1961

increases when the ionizations produced by the radiation are dispersed as widely as possible. This is because each ionization is capable of activating one molecule and thus if the ionizations are well separated the probability of many molecules being affected will be higher than if all the ionizations occurred close together. This suggests that radiation damage *in vivo* is not a consequence of the destruction of individual molecules but is the result of damage to some subcellular structure which breaks down as a result of several ionizations occurring simultaneously in a small volume. This conclusion is consistent with the view that intracellular membranes are the sites of primary radiation damage.

It is clear that our understanding of the processes leading to overt radiation damage is rudimentary. Enough is clear, however, for the following picture to be drawn up (Figure 9.1). Radiation incident upon the cell causes changes at the molecular level which in their turn cause changes such as the release of hydrolases and the uncoupling of oxidative phosphorylation. These lesions lead to further lesions such as the breakdown of cell structure, the hydrolysis of polymers and the inhibition of syntheses. The pathological changes that are characteristic of radiation sickness are thus the products of a complex network of changes which develop over hours and days following exposure to ionizing radiations.

Chemical protection against ionizing radiation

The injection of various compounds into an animal before, but not after, it is exposed to ionizing radiation can afford some protection against the irradiation. Compounds bearing SH groups are the most effective and especially cysteine, its decarboxylation product cysteamine and the peptide glutathione. However, not all compounds bearing an SH group act as radiation protection agents *in vivo*. For activity *in vivo* compounds appear to require an SH group separated from a basic group by two or three methylene groups. The way in which these compounds exert their effects is not understood. It may be that they react with free radicals formed by the irradiation of water and so reduce the chances of some compound or structure of biochemical importance being damaged; or they may repair damaged molecules by hydrogen transfer, i.e.

$$AH + O\dot{H} \longrightarrow \dot{A} + H_2O$$
$$\dot{A} + X\text{–}SH \longrightarrow AH + X\text{–}\dot{S}$$

In contrast to radioprotective substances are drugs which increase the effectiveness of irradiation. One of these which has been studied extensively is Synkavit (2-methyl-1,4-naphthohydroquinone diphosphate) which is related to the lipid soluble vitamin K. Such compounds may prove to be useful therapeutically if they can be used to increase the radiosensitivity of tumours. Indeed some limited success has already been achieved in the treatment of inoperable bronchial carcinoma by using such compounds in conjunction with radiotherapy. Work to develop radiosensitizing drugs that are selectively concentrated by tumours is now in progress.

SECTION 10

The Biochemical Basis of Therapeutics

Although many metabolic pathways are common to widely divergent groups of organisms, it is important to realize that the metabolism of all organisms shows distinctive features. These characteristic features not only distinguish different species but also different tissues in the same organism. The use of drugs, to combat infections or to alter the balance of metabolism back to, or away from, the steady state accepted as normal depends upon the exploitation of metabolic differences between the parasite and the host or between one tissue and another. Two branches of therapeutics, chemotherapy and pharmacodynamics, are now recognized. The former term was coined by Paul Ehrlich who defined it as 'the use of drugs to injure an invading organism without injury to the host'. The second term, of more recent origin, describes the use of drugs to modify the metabolism of certain cells in the organism without affecting the remaining cells to any marked extent. Besides these two branches of therapeutics there is a third called replacement therapy; this is concerned with treating pathological conditions by providing the patient with substances, such as hormones, vitamins and trace elements, in which he may be deficient.

The following sections do not pretend to give an exhaustive review of the topics selected but are intended to underline some of the basic principles of drug action. First of all some aspects of chemotherapy will be considered because it was with the chemotherapeutic drugs that the earliest and most successful advances in treating diseases were made.

Antibacterial drugs

The theoretical foundations of chemotherapy were firmly laid by Paul Ehrlich at the end of the 19th century. He suggested that the most successful drugs would be found amongst compounds of low molecular weight which could combine with reactive groups in proteins and inhibit their normal reactions. This view has been completely vindicated and most drugs in use today have a molecular weight less than 500. Erhlich also drew attention to the fact that a chemotherapeutic agent should combine a high toxicity towards the parasite with a low toxicity towards the host. In other words, the toxicity must be selective.

The first really effective chemotherapeutic agents for use against bacteria were the *sulphonamides*, of which sulphanilamide is the parent compound.

$$SO_2NH_2$$

$$NH_2$$

sulphanilamide

The work of D. D. Woods, which was carried out in 1940, showed that the inhibition of bacterial growth by sulphanilamide could be overcome by adding *para*-aminobenzoic acid to the bacterial culture.

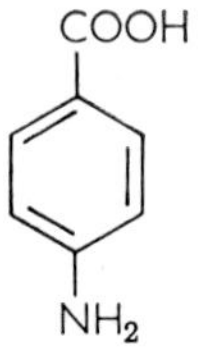

COOH

NH$_2$

para-aminobenzoic acid (PAB)

Later in 1940 PAB was shown to be a growth factor for *Clostridium aceto-butylicum*. Thus it appeared that the sulphonamides owed their bacteriostatic action to their structural similarity to PAB. In 1945 PAB was shown to be a component of folic acid (pteroylglutamic acid) and more recently

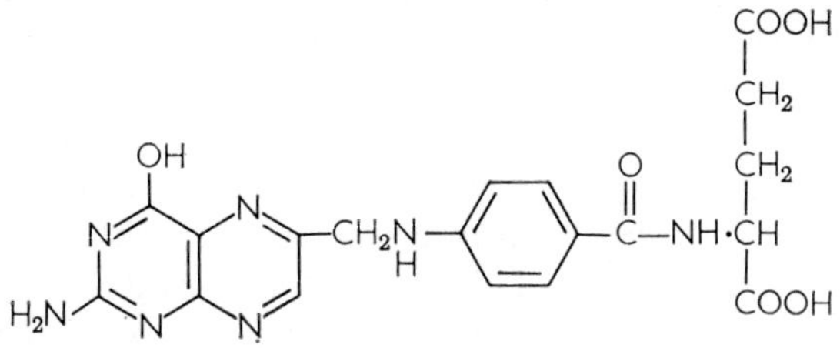

COOH
CH$_2$
CH$_2$
—C—NH·CH
COOH

OH
—CH$_2$N—
H
H$_2$N—

folic acid

tetrahydrofolic acid derivatives have been shown to be coenzymes involved in the transfer of units containing a single carbon atom (see p. 132). Thus the sulphonamides are chemotherapeutic agents because they prevent the biosynthesis of a coenzyme that is essential for the invading organism, by competing with PAB for a site on one of the enzymes responsible for synthesizing folic acid. The sulphonamides are not toxic to the host because the host relies on a supply of preformed folic acid in the diet. Thus the toxicity of sulphonamides is selective for those organisms which must convert PAB to folic acid for rapid growth.

The sulphonamides were synthetic products of organic chemistry but the second generation of antibacterial drugs to become available were natural products; the first of these was *penicillin*.

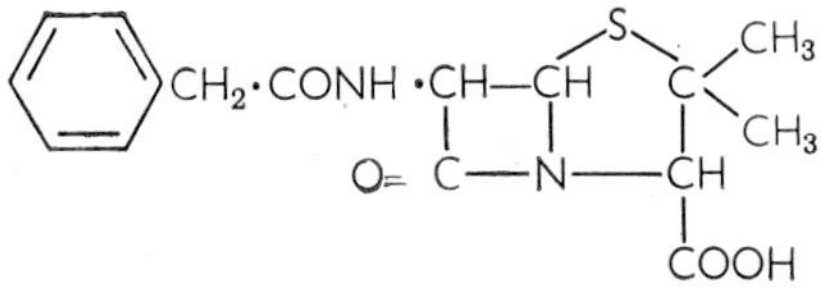

CH$_2$·CONH ·CH—CH
O= C—N——CH
COOH

penicillin G or benzyl penicillin

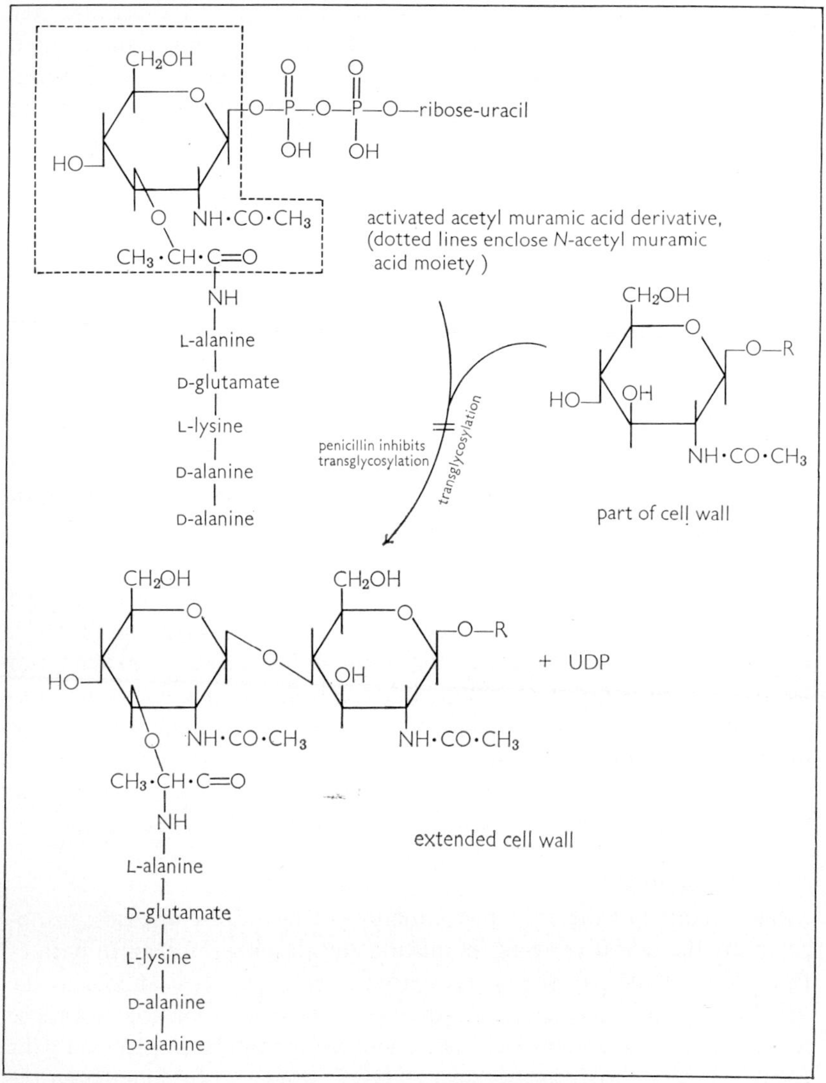

CH₂OH

O—P—O—P—O—ribose-uracil

OH   OH

HO

O   NH·CO·CH₃

CH₃·CH·C=O

NH

L-alanine

D-glutamate

L-lysine

D-alanine

D-alanine

activated acetyl muramic acid derivative,
(dotted lines enclose N-acetyl muramic
acid moiety)

CH₂OH

O—R

HO   OH

NH·CO·CH₃

part of cell wall

penicillin inhibits
transglycosylation

transglycosylation

CH₂OH

HO

O   NH·CO·CH₃

CH₃·CH·C=O

NH

L-alanine

D-glutamate

L-lysine

D-alanine

D-alanine

CH₂OH

OH

O—R

NH·CO·CH₃

+ UDP

extended cell wall

Figure 10.1. Action of penicillin on the synthesis of bacterial cell walls.

Penicillin was isolated from fungi of the *Penicillium* species and is highly toxic towards Gram positive bacteria but has a low toxicity to mammals; it is, therefore, a good chemotherapeutic agent. The high degree of selective toxicity exhibited by penicillin is explained by the biochemical action of the antibiotic. Gram positive bacteria develop an osmotic pressure of

13+

up to 30 atmospheres across their protoplast membranes and because they
have a very rigid cell wall they are able to withstand the pressure. When
the bacteria are growing and dividing, new cell walls must be synthesized
to protect the daughter cells. Penicillin inhibits this synthesis by preventing
the incorporation of a complex molecule, containing acetyl muramic acid
and five amino acids, into certain parts of the cell wall (Figure 10.1). In the
presence of penicillin the growing protoplast, encased in a defective and
weakened cell wall, eventually ruptures under the osmotic pressure that it
develops across its unprotected cell membrane. The action of penicillin is
summed up in Figure 10.1.

Since, in contrast to Gram positive bacteria, mammals do not synthesize cell walls, it can be seen that penicillin is a selectively toxic agent
because it takes advantage of a metabolic difference between the parasite
and host.

Some antibiotics are inhibitors of protein synthesis. Since this is a
process common to parasite and host, a successful antibiotic of this type
must show considerable selectivity.

Chloramphenicol (see p. 255) is an antibiotic whose utility is limited because
it is toxic to mammals at low doses. Thus, when chloramphenicol is used
in the treatment of bacterial infections (for example, in typhoid fever), it
can be administered for short periods only, if damage to the patient is to
be avoided. In contrast to chloramphenicol, the *tetracycline* antibiotics
and *streptomycin* are more satisfactory because they are more selective, the
mammal being able to tolerate high doses without danger. Thus even in
pathways that appear to be similar in the parasite and host there may be
subtle differences which can be exploited by chemotherapeutic agents.

Antimalarial drugs

Bacteria are not the only microorganisms which cause diseases; proto-
zoans are the causative agents in malaria and sleeping sickness. In both of
these diseases the parasite is transferred from an infected animal to the
new host by an insect vector, mosquitoes in the case of malaria and tsetse
flies in the case of sleeping sickness. These vectors can be controlled by the
use of selectively toxic agents such as DDT, which act by stimulating the

DDT

insect's nerve fibres to convulsion but are without effect on the mammalian nervous system.

A drug which has recently been introduced to control the parasite rather than its insect vector is *pyrimethamine,* which is a folic acid antagonist.

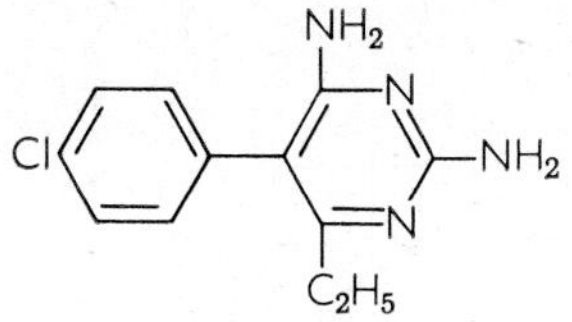

pyrimethamine

The lipophilic groups

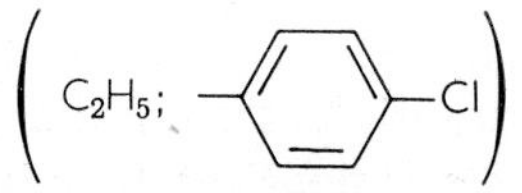

were introduced into the molecule to facilitate its uptake by erythrocytes. Inside the red cells the anti-folic acid actions of the drug interfere with nucleic acid synthesis by the parasite during gametocyte formation. The life cycle of the malarial parasite is thus broken, since no viable gametocytes are formed which can complete the sexual reproductive stage in the mosquito (see Figure 10.2). Pyrimethamine is therefore widely used as a prophylactic against malaria but is of little use in treating acute attacks of the disease. The selective toxicity of pyrimethamine lies in the fact that the parasite has to synthesize folic acid whilst the host does not.

Acute attacks of malaria can be treated with schizonticides such as *chloroquine* which are active against the parasite at all stages of the asexual cycle. Chloroquine is thought to be toxic because it combines with nucleic acids.

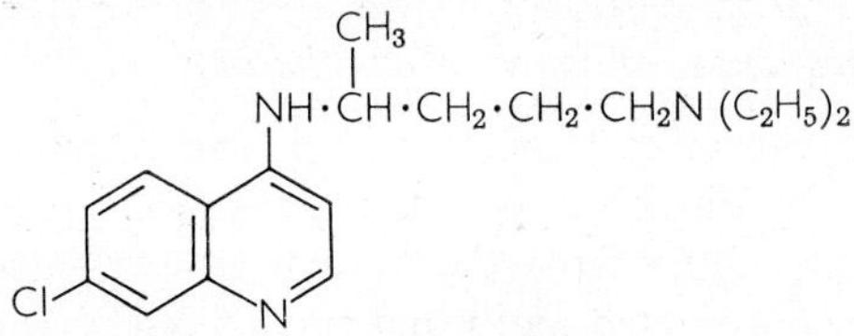

chloroquine

The single small dose of chloroquine needed to kill the parasites (about 600 mg) is not toxic to the host, but if given regularly in larger doses it can give rise to undesirable side effects. Perhaps chloroquine owes its selective toxicity against malarial parasites to the more rapid replication of nucleic acids in the parasite than in the host.

Antiviral drugs

This is a provocative heading since few antiviral drugs exist. At present the best known are the *thiosemicarbazones* such as Marboran which has

Marboran

proved to be outstandingly successful in preventing the development of smallpox although it is unable to cure established infections. Why is it that antiviral drugs are rare whilst there is a large range of antibacterial drugs? The bacterium is a self-sufficient organism which is able to carry out all its essential metabolism within its protoplast membrane. Fortunately the bacterial metabolism usually differs from that of its host so that drugs which are selectively toxic against the bacteria can be synthesized and used. Viruses on the other hand do not have a metabolism of their own; they merely take over the metabolism of the host cell and reprogramme it to their own ends by using the information encoded in their own DNA (or RNA). Thus in many respects the metabolism of the infected cells is basically the same as that of non-infected cells, consequently it is difficult to find drugs which can prevent viral replication without disturbing the metabolism of the host. One aspect of viral biochemistry that is unique is the enzymology of DNA penetration into the host cell and perhaps this could be exploited by drugs.

Biochemical consequences of cancer chemotherapy

In considering cancer chemotherapy we turn from chemotherapy as originally defined by Ehrlich to pharmacodynamics.

Cancerous tissues differ from the normal differentiated tissues of the body by their uncoordinated and rapid rate of cell division and by their relative loss of specialization. This loss of differentiation is often accompanied by changes in the pattern of enzymes which was characteristic of the non-malignant tissue of origin. However, the enzyme systems which are present are qualitatively the same as in normal tissues. Cancer therapy is therefore complicated by the necessity to find drugs which can selectively

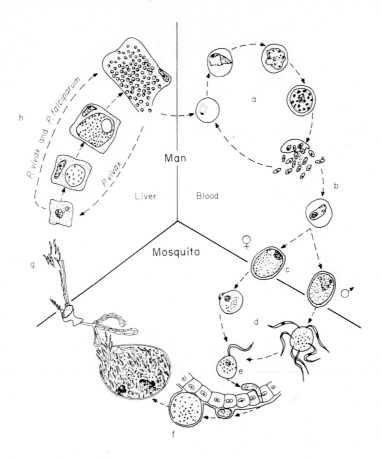

Figure 10.2. The life cycle of the malaria parasite

a	Erythrocytic cycle	e	Zygote
b	Segmenting schizont	f	Oocysts
c	Gametocytes	g	Sporozoites
d	Gametes	h	Exoerythrocytic stages

From Robson and Stacey, *Recent Advances in Pharmacology*, Churchill, London, 1962

inhibit the growth of neoplastic cells having a metabolism differing little in essence from that of most normal cells. The majority of the drugs that have been used to treat cancer have interfered either directly or indirectly with the replication of nucleic acids in the rapidly dividing cells. Examples of these compounds are the purine analogue *6-mercaptopurine*

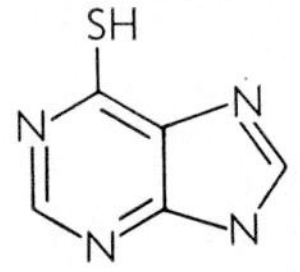

6-mercaptopurine

the pyrimidine analogue *5-fluorouracil*

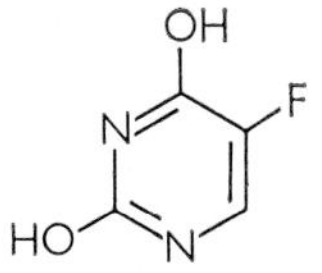

5-fluorouracil

and the folic acid antagonists *aminopterin* and *amethopterin*

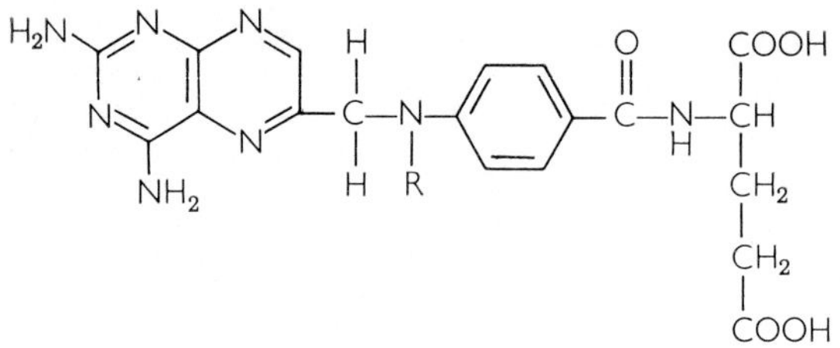

aminopterin R = H
amethopterin R = CH_3

Whilst these compounds can keep the neoplastic cells in check they also cause serious side effects because they are not selective and inhibit the division of rapidly dividing cells in other normal tissues, for example, in the intestinal mucosa and bone marrow. The anticancer drugs available at present have what Ehrlich termed a low chemotherapeutic index (i.e. the ratio minimal curative dose : maximal tolerated dose is low). They are, in other words, toxic but not selective.

Drugs affecting the central nervous system

One of the triumphs of pharmacodynamics in recent years has been the development of drugs which act selectively on the nervous system and are able to alleviate certain forms of mental disorders.

Amine oxidase inhibitors, for example, have proved to be beneficial in treating mental depression. Within the neurones of the central and sympathetic nervous systems physiologically active transmitter substances such as noradrenaline, adrenaline and 5-hydroxytryptamine can be oxidized by the mitochondrial enzyme monoamine oxidase. By inhibiting this enzyme with drugs, the levels of the amines in the neurones can be increased, and, in some manner which is not understood (but which must depend upon the increased availability of transmitter), this leads to an improvement in the condition of the depressed patient. In contrast, psychotic patients can be tranquillized by treatment with the alkaloid, *reserpine.* This drug depletes the central and sympathetic nervous systems of their stores of amines and consequently reduces the level of neuronal activity. One of the actions of reserpine is to prevent newly synthesized amines from being stored in special storage granules. Thus the unbound amines fall ready prey to the monoamine oxidase and are destroyed. Once the preexisting stores have been depleted (reserpine may also facilitate this process) the levels of amines will remain low as the stores cannot be replenished by newly synthesized amines.

Both reserpine and amine oxidase inhibitors act as useful pharmacodynamic agents because the processes with which they interfere are very largely confined to the nervous system, thus they cause little disturbance to the metabolism of other tissues which are not concerned with amine storage and metabolism. However, since monoamine oxidase is present in the liver where it destroys pressor amines absorbed from the diet (e.g. from cheese and bananas), it is necessary to exercise careful dietary control over patients treated with monoamine oxidase inhibitors.

Conclusion

It should be possible to design enzyme inhibitors which exhibit a high degree of specificity for a particular enzyme and which are of use therapeutically. At present this goal has not been achieved to any great extent although a few drugs have been developed in this way. For example, α-methyl tyrosine has been used as a specific inhibitor of tyrosine hydroxylase, one of the enzymes involved in the biosynthesis of catecholamines, and may prove to be useful in the treatment of some forms of hypertension. Inhibitors of xanthine oxidase have also been developed for use in the treatment of gout (see p. 146). However, up to the present time most of the useful drugs have been discovered by screening thousands of compounds for therapeutic properties. As the biochemists' understanding of enzyme specificities and metabolic control improves it ought to become possible to design drugs on a more scientific basis.

Index